PEDIGREE
HANDICAPPING

PEDIGREE
HANDICAPPING

by
Lauren Stich

DRF Press
NEW YORK

Published by
Daily Racing Form Press
100 Broadway, 7th Floor
New York, NY 10005

ISBN: 0-9726401-3-4
Library of Congress Control Number: 2004100500

Cover and jacket designed by Chris Donofry
Text design by Neuwirth and Associates

Printed in the United States of America

All entries, results, charts and related information provided by

COMPANY

821 Corporate Drive • Lexington, KY 40503-2794 Toll Free (800) 333-2211 or
(859) 224-2860; Fax (859) 224-2811 • Internet: www.equibase.com

The Thoroughbred Industry's Official Database for Racing Information

Contents

Acknowledgments

*T*HERE IS NO question that without the guidance and support of Steven Crist this manuscript would not have been possible. It was his suggestion that I write a book on pedigree handicapping, which had never been done before.

A great deal of gratitude to my colleagues at *Daily Racing Form*, including Dean Keppler, Mandy Minger, Sarah Feldman, Jennifer Lusk, Chris Donofry, and Tim O'Leary of O'Leary and Cosentino Communications. Special thanks to Robin Foster, whose expert copyediting refined the manuscript.

I am forever indebted to Leon Rasmussen and Rommy Faversham, whose mutual passion in breeding and warm friendship enhanced my knowledge of Thoroughbred pedigrees.

I am grateful to so many people for their encouragement and friendship over the years, including Tony Meola, who repeatedly urged me to write to Steven Crist when he was starting up *The Racing Times*; three men who championed my work from the start: Jeff Mende, the former racing editor for *The Staten Island Advance*, Harold Tannenbaum, formerly the head of the editorial department of

The Morning Telegraph, and Steve Haskin, the senior correspondent for *The Blood-Horse;* and to Fred Mancuso, Donald Johnson, Pat Grande, and Helen Schneider, who always pushed me to achieve my goals and who surely must be smiling in heaven.

This book could not have been written without the unwavering support of precious friends and family who have shared my dreams: Jim Schneider, whose loyal friendship and advice I cherish; Vincent (Cenza) Stoppia, my lifelong friend whose compassion, wisdom, and joie de vivre have truly enriched my life; my aunt, Dorothea Richter, who has stuck by me through the good times and bad; my brother, Don (who proves that full siblings, whether human or equine, are not necessarily alike); my late father, Paul, whose interest in racing was the catalyst for my career, and ultimately, my mother, Vicki, who is my mirror image. Her unconditional love and support have been the inspiration of my life.

Introduction

OKAY, I'LL ADMIT it: I am a pedigree geek. I was barely a teenager when I got involved with horse racing in 1964, watching a weekly television show on WOR-TV in New York on Saturday afternoons that spotlighted the big stakes of the weekend. In 1964, it was the only racing show on television and was hosted by Win Elliot, Sam Renick, and New York Racing Association announcer Fred "Cappy" Caposella. I was unwittingly introduced to racing by my father, who always had the racing show on to see the results of his bets. Little did he know that the seeds of his daughter's future were being planted.

And what a year to be introduced to racing! After watching Kelso, Gun Bow, Northern Dancer, Affectionately, Bold Lad, and Tosmah, I was hooked for life. The mid-60's were magical years in the history of racing. It was still the era of the great dynasties who bred to race, such as Belair Stud, Bohemia, Brookmeade, Cain Hoy, Calumet, Darby Dan, Elmendorf, Greentree, Harbor View, Hobeau, King Ranch, Meadow Farm, Powhatan, Rokeby, Tartan, George D. Widener, C. V. Whitney, and Wheatley, which was owned by Mrs. Henry Carnegie Phipps, the mother of Ogden Phipps, and grandmother of Ogden Mills Phipps.

In the fall of 1969, while still a freshman at the University of Hartford, I wrote letters to both Tommy Trotter, who was the racing secretary at NYRA, and to Bill Veeck, the colorful and controversial entrepreneur who was then president of Suffolk Downs, telling them about my passion for racing and inquiring about positions within their organizations. I received a form letter from Trotter, saying there were no openings at that time, while the letter from Veeck was exhilarating. It was actually written by Veeck's secretary, Bea Furlong (yes, that was her real name), who said he would like to schedule a meeting with me.

Unfortunately, when I arrived for my interview at Suffolk Downs, Ms. Furlong informed me that Veeck had been called away to an emergency meeting and our appointment had to be rescheduled for sometime in the near future. While that never materialized, there was another interview that was about to plot the course for my life.

I had been born and raised in West Hempstead, New York, and my family moved to Newton, Massachusetts, in 1965, but when my father came back from a business trip to New York City in January 1970, he told me that he arranged an interview with Fred Grossman, who was then editor-in-chief of *The Morning Telegraph* (the East Coast version of *Daily Racing Form*). After meeting with Grossman, my dream of making my passion my occupation was coming true, and my first day at *The Morning Telegraph* was March 16, 1970.

The best part of working at the "Telly" was the vast racing library. Discovering resources such as *The American Racing Manual* and the American Stud Book sparked my preoccupation with bloodlines. I pored over the voluminous amount of material at my disposal, especially studying the foundation mares that were the cornerstone of the great racing families.

In 1972, after I had been with the company for only two years,

The Morning Telegraph went on strike and was shut down. In effect, the paper just changed its name to *Daily Racing Form* and relocated to Hightstown, New Jersey, but moving across the Hudson River was not an option for me, as I was also pursuing a singing career. Since childhood, my two passions were always music and racing, racing and music. They took turns being the priority in my life.

I sang professionally with some of the girl groups of the 1960's—Arlene Smith & the Chantels ("Maybe"), Reparata and the Delrons ("Whenever a Teenager Cries"), the Shangri-Las ("Leader of the Pack")—and sang backup for Little Eva ("Loco-Motion") and Barbara Harris, lead singer of the Toys ("Lover's Concerto").

But in December 1990, I met with Steven Crist, who was starting up a new racing newspaper, *The Racing Times*, and it was finally time to turn all my attention to racing. Thus, my career in music ended and I joined *The Racing Times* as a copy editor and also wrote "Today's Maidens," a daily column that highlighted notable pedigrees in maiden races.

My passion for racing in general, and pedigrees in particular, morphed into pedigree handicapping. Using this knowledge and applying it to handicapping paid immediate dividends, and I never looked back.

While there are many handicapping tools for horseplayers, one of the most rewarding is pedigree handicapping. Even players who do not know much about pedigrees now realize that using them to handicap is an essential part of the game, whether in multirace exotics or in the ever-growing world of handicapping tournaments. Invariably, maiden special weight races and/or turf races are part of multiple wagers and, more and more, serious players are arming themselves with a fundamental knowledge of pedigrees.

But pedigree handicapping is a tool that can be used for more than just maiden races. Knowledge of pedigrees is crucial when horses are trying different distances or surfaces for the first time, and while this information can be used on a daily basis, it also has great merit as a handicapping tool on racing's big days, such as the Kentucky Derby and Breeders' Cup.

Information is key to horseplayers, and betting first-time starters is usually agony because there are no Beyer Speed Figures or other race data to look at. With little to go on except pedigree and trainer patterns, many players prefer skipping these races. But as this book will show, even a basic knowledge of pedigrees can open up a new world of betting opportunities. In particular, when it comes to maiden special weight races, pedigree is indeed everything. And turf racing is strictly about pedigrees.

Before horseplayers can use pedigree handicapping, they must first learn how to correctly read a pedigree, and although this may seem like basic "Pedigree Handicapping 101," reading a pedigree is universally misunderstood. Chapter 1, "How the Sire and Dam Influence a Runner," defines the essence of pedigree handicapping by clarifying the importance of the sire and dam and their specific effects on racing performance.

Chapter 2, "Betting the 2-Year-Olds," unlocks betting strategies for the unwritten but very real two seasons for juveniles. The first half of the year (April-August) belongs to the precocious 2-year-olds who are bred for speed and perfectly suited to distances from three to six furlongs. The second season for 2-year-olds starts in late August, when late-developing juveniles who are by stallions known for stamina start to emerge. And then there is the increased focus on grass racing for 2-year-olds as well, which presents a totally different approach. This chapter discusses how players can familiarize themselves with the traits of sire lines and will give them a crucial edge in how to bet juveniles according to their sires. The chapter concludes with a list of the three major sire lines for speed.

Chapter 3, "Betting the Freshman Stallions," uses two examples—the 2004 freshman sires and 2005 freshman sires—which demonstrate the importance of the characteristics of the sire and his tail-male sire line in determining what kind of racehorse this new stallion is likely to produce.

Chapter 4, "The Hidden Turf Factor," exposes the most profitable angle of pedigree handicapping and concludes with an extensive list of hidden turf sires.

Chapter 5, "Handicapping the Kentucky Derby by Pedigree," explains how to separate the contenders from the pretenders strictly by pedigree with an analysis of the Kentucky Derby from 1990 through 2004, with numerous examples of pedigree throwouts that burned money in the past.

Chapter 6, "Handicapping the Breeders' Cup by Pedigree," takes a look at past Breeders' Cup races, focusing on the two races for 2-year-olds, the Breeders' Cup Juvenile and the Juvenile Fillies, and how pedigree handicapping resulted in some big paydays.

Finally, Chapter 7, "Playing the Handicapping Tournaments by Pedigree," examines the application of pedigree handicapping as a powerful tool in winning major handicapping tournaments.

1

HOW THE SIRE AND DAM INFLUENCE A RUNNER

IT HAS LONG been my belief that the single most important thing about pedigree handicapping is understanding that although the sire and dam are equally significant factors in a pedigree, each plays a different role in determining how the racehorse will run.

I cannot emphasize enough the distinction between what the sire and his tail-male sire line (sire, sire's sire, sire's grandsire, etc.) bring to a pedigree, and what the dam and, most importantly, her tail-female family (dam, dam's dam, dam's granddam, etc.) bring to the pedigree.

The male parts of a pedigree (primarily the sire, and secondly, the damsire, or broodmare sire) determine the *distance* and *surface* where the runner will be most effective. The female parts of a pedigree (dam and her tail-female family) determine racing *class*.

When looking at a pedigree, the female family will determine the quality of the individual. Whether the horse has the right stuff to become a stakes winner or whether he is more likely to be a common horse is chiefly—more than 80 percent—the result of the quality of the tail-female line. The key to racing class runs through the dam and her tail-female family, going back generation after generation. If quality mares are bred to inferior stallions, this high class may be diluted for a generation or two, but is usually restored by breeding back to a superior stallion.

For general everyday pedigree handicapping, however, players should concern themselves primarily with the ***sire*** and the ***damsire***. That is because when analyzing a maiden race, the first thing to look at is the ***distance*** and ***surface*** of the race and how the sire/damsire of a runner fits that condition. Of course, class (dam and her family) is important, but most players do not have the time, inclination, or resources to research the dam's family, which can be laborious.

EXAMPLE 1

Analyzing a seven-furlong maiden special weight race

This is the kind of high-quality and competitive race that Gulfstream Park is known for during its premier winter meet. Below is a pedigree analysis of each filly's chances at this particular distance (seven furlongs) and surface (dirt).

Gulfstream Park

6

7 Furlongs (1:20) MAIDEN SPECIAL WEIGHT. Purse $32,000 FOR MAIDENS, FILLIES THREE YEARS OLD. Weight, 121 lbs. ⓕMd Sp Wt 32k 7 FURLONGS

1 Present Danger
Own: G Watts Humphrey Jr
Forest Green, White Diamonds, White
DAY P (—) 2003: (985 215 .22)

Dk. b or br f. 3 (Feb) KEESEP02 $60,000
Sire: Souvenir Copy (Mr. Prospector) $12,500
Dam: Stormy Gal (Storm Cat)
Br: Patchen Wilkes Farm LLC (Ky)
Tr: Oliver Victoria(4 0 0 1 .00) 2003:(82 14 .17)

121

	Life	0 M 0 0	$0	—	D.Fst	0 0 0 0	$0	—
	2004	0 M 0 0	$0	—	Wet(401)	0 0 0 0	$0	—
	2003	0 M 0 0	$0	—	Turf(282)	0 0 0 0	$0	—
	GP	0 0 0 0	$0	—	Dst(380)	0 0 0 0	$0	—

WORKS: Jan30 Pay 5f fst 1:05 B *10/13* ● Jan22 Pay 3f fst :37 Bg *1/5* ● Jan16 Pay 5f fst 1:04 B *1/4* Jan10 Pay 5f fst 1:05 B *14/20* Jan4 Pay 4f fst :51 B *4/22* Dec29 Pay 4f fst :51² B *18/38* Dec18 Pay 4f fst :52 B *18/23* Dec12 Pay 4f fst :51 B *10/26* Dec5 Pay 4f fst :50¹ B *4/15* Nov25 Pay 4f fst :52 B *5/10* Nov13 Pay 3f fst :38³ B *1/3*
TRAINER: 1stStart(11 .00 $0.00) Dirt(41 .10 $1.62) Sprint(12 .08 $3.08) MdnSpWt(32 .12 $2.67)

2 Joyful Chaos
Own: Lewis Schaffel
Black & White Blocks, Red Sleeves, Black
BRAVO J (112 10 16 21 .09) 2003: (590 128 .22)

Dk. b or br f. 3 (Feb) $80,000
Sire: Rahy (Blushing Groom*Fr) $80,000
Dam: Alya (Deputy Minister)
Br: Normandy Farm (Ky)
Tr: Clement Christophe(9 1 0 5 .11) 2003:(389 75 .19)

121

	Life	0 M 0 0	$0	—	D.Fst	0 0 0 0	$0	—
	2004	0 M 0 0	$0	—	Wet(381)	0 0 0 0	$0	—
	2003	0 M 0 0	$0	—	Turf(326)	0 0 0 0	$0	—
	GP	0 0 0 0	$0	—	Dst(365)	0 0 0 0	$0	—

WORKS: Jan30 Pay 4f fst :51³ B *15/22* Jan20 Pay 4f fst :50 Bg *2/14* Jan11 Pay 4f fst :51¹ B *8/23* Jan3 Pay 4f fst :51² B *11/27* Dec26 Pay 4f fst :53 B *12/13* Dec16 Pay 4f fst :51 Bg *4/12* ● Dec8 Pay 4f fst :51² B *1/7* Dec1 Pay 3f fst :39 B *3/3* Nov19 Pay 3f fst :40 B *7/7* Oct9 Bel 3f fst :36³ Hg *5/8* Oct2 Bel 4f fst :48⁴ Bg *13/36* Sep25 Bel 4f fst :50² B *47/72*
TRAINER: 1stStart(54 .09 $1.25) Dirt(116 .16 $1.23) Sprint(71 .15 $1.31) MdnSpWt(108 .13 $1.45)

3 My Time Now
Own: Phillips Racing Partnership
Blue White, Kelly Green Diamond Belt, Kelly
COA E M (77 5 10 7 .06) 2003: (1275 209 .16)

B. f. 3 (Feb)
Sire: Unbridled (Fappiano) $200,000
Dam: Darby Trail (Roberto)
Br: Phillips Racing Partnership (Ky)
Tr: Nafzger Carl A(24 2 4 2 .08) 2003:(285 31 .11)

Ⓛ 121

Life	1	M	0	1	$4,270	70	D.Fst	1	0	0	1	$4,270	70
2003	1	M	0	1	$4,270	70	Wet(382)	0	0	0	0	$0	–
2002	0	M	0	0	$0	–	Turf(310)	0	0	0	0	$0	–
GP	0	0	0	0	$0	–	Dst(328)	0	0	0	0	$0	–

2Nov03-3CD fst 6½f :22⁴ :46¹ 1:11²1:18 ⒻMd Sp Wt 41k 70 7 3 75¾ 65 34½ 33¾ D'Amico A J 122 38.70 77-16 AllElectric1221¾ GoldenCache122² MyTimeNow122⁷ 5-6w bid,no late gain 12
WORKS: Jan31 PmM 5f sly 1:03⁴ B *9/11* Jan25 PmM 5f fst 1:02¹ Bg *15/47* Jan20 PmM 5f fst 1:02³ B *11/21* Jan15 PmM 4f fst :49 B *10/39* Jan9 PmM 4f fst :52 B *20/21* Nov24 CD 4f gd :49⁴ B *11/21*
TRAINER: 61-180Days(28 .11 $0.88) 2ndStart(24 .12 $1.64) 1stLasix(19 .16 $2.07) Dirt(239 .11 $1.30) Sprint(187 .09 $1.43) MdnSpWt(122 .08 $0.77)

---

4 Pretty Jane
Own: Gary Redmond
Yellow Light Blue Yellow Cap
CRUZ M R (57 3 8 3 .05) 2003: (1579 262 .17)

Dk. b or br f. 3 (Feb)
Sire: Subordination (Mt. Livermore) $5,000
Dam: Girl in Velvet (Afleet)
Br: Ballycapple (Ky)
Tr: Caramori Eduardo(2 2 0 0 1.00) 2003:(69 8 .12)

121

Life	0	M	0	0	$0	–	D.Fst	0	0	0	0	$0	–
2004	0	M	0	0	$0	–	Wet(297)	0	0	0	0	$0	–
2003	0	M	0	0	$0	–	Turf(164)	0	0	0	0	$0	–
GP	0	0	0	0	$0	–	Dst(328)	0	0	0	0	$0	–

WORKS: Jan23 GP 5f fst 1:01 B *4/13* Jan18 GP 5f fst 1:03³ B *15/17* Jan9 GP 5f fst 1:02² B *7/14* ●Dec27 GP 4f fst :46³ H *1/41* Dec22 GP 4f fst :50 B *19/24* Dec9 TTC 4f fst :49² B *10/33* Nov22 TTC 4f fst :50 B *13/28* Nov1 TTC 3f fst :40³ B *15/17*
TRAINER: 1stStart(8 .12 $1.32) Dirt(66 .17 $1.72) Sprint(46 .22 $2.37) MdnSpWt(14 .07 $0.76)

---

5 Magical Illusion
Own: William L Clifton Jr
Green Burgundy, White Diamond Frame, White
PRADO E S (136 17 19 28 .12) 2003: (1478 259 .18)

Ch. f. 3 (May) KEESEP02 $110,000
Sire: Pulpit (A.P. Indy) $35,000
Dam: Voodoo Lily (Baldski)
Br: Joseph Allen (Ky)
Tr: Bond Harold James(1 0 1 0 .00) 2003:(196 46 .23)

Ⓛ 121

Life	0	M	0	0	$0	–	D.Fst	0	0	0	0	$0	–
2004	0	M	0	0	$0	–	Wet(352)	0	0	0	0	$0	–
2003	0	M	0	0	$0	–	Turf(279)	0	0	0	0	$0	–
GP	0	0	0	0	$0	–	Dst(361)	0	0	0	0	$0	–

WORKS: ●Jan27 PmM 6f fst 1:15³ Bg *1/4* Jan20 PmM 5f fst 1:02³ B *11/21* Jan13 PmM 4f fst :51 Bg *24/32* Jan4 PmM 5f fst 1:02³ B *33/50* Dec27 PmM 4f fst :48⁴ B *11/44* Dec20 PmM 4f fst :49 B *21/50*
TRAINER: 1stStart(33 .15 $2.35) 1stLasix(1 .00 $0.00) Dirt(141 .23 $2.13) Sprint(52 .29 $2.10) MdnSpWt(86 .26 $2.25)

---

6 Maren Approved
Own: Ziba F Graham
Black Light Blue, Green Sash, Green Sleeves
BOULANGER G (71 5 5 7 .07) 2003: (1254 183 .15)

Gr/ro. f. 3 (Feb)
Sire: With Approval (Caro*Ire) $7,500
Dam: Yellow Springs (Piker)
Br: Ziba F Graham (Ky)
Tr: Hennig Mark(21 4 7 0 .19) 2003:(503 73 .15)

121

Life	0	M	0	0	$0	–	D.Fst	0	0	0	0	$0	–
2004	0	M	0	0	$0	–	Wet(349)	0	0	0	0	$0	–
2003	0	M	0	0	$0	–	Turf(301)	0	0	0	0	$0	–
GP	0	0	0	0	$0	–	Dst(309)	0	0	0	0	$0	–

WORKS: Jan23 GP 4f fst :49 Bg *11/31* Jan16 GP 5f fst 1:02 B *7/17* Jan10 GP 4f fst :48 B *3/35* Dec18 GP 4f fst :51 B *15/20* ●Nov20 Tdn 5f fst 1:01³ B *1/5* Nov10 Tdn 5f fst 1:04³ Bg *3/5* Nov5 Tdn 4f fst :50¹ B *2/3* Oct29 Tdn 3f fst :38 B *8/15* ●Sep30 Tdn 5f fst 1:03¹ B *1/4* Sep20 Tdn 4f fst :50³ Bg *8/14* Sep13 Tdn 5f fst 1:04³ B *7/9* Sep6 Tdn 3f fst :37³ B *2/8*
TRAINER: 1stStart(65 .09 $2.16) Dirt(447 .16 $1.78) Sprint(215 .15 $1.88) MdnSpWt(213 .14 $1.94)

---

7 Platinum Heights
Own: Laura & Eugene Melnyk
Orange Navy Blue, Gold Chevrons, Navy Blue
VELAZQUEZ J R (112 29 24 10 .26) 2003: (1308 306 .23)

Ch. f. 3 (Apr) KEEJUL02 $2,800,000
Sire: Storm Cat (Storm Bird) $500,000
Dam: Amelia Bearhart (Bold Hour)
Br: Richard D Maynard (Ky)
Tr: Pletcher Todd A(42 13 9 2 .31) 2003:(826 199 .24)

Ⓛ 121

Life	0	M	0	0	$0	–	D.Fst	0	0	0	0	$0	–
2004	0	M	0	0	$0	–	Wet(379)	0	0	0	0	$0	–
2003	0	M	0	0	$0	–	Turf(319)	0	0	0	0	$0	–
GP	0	0	0	0	$0	–	Dst(406)	0	0	0	0	$0	–

WORKS: Feb2 PmM 5f fst 1:04⁴ B *18/22* Jan26 PmM 5f fst 1:01⁴ B *9/18* Jan19 PmM 5f fst 1:03² B *6/14* Jan11 PmM 5f fst 1:03² Bg *38/56* Jan4 PmM 5f fst 1:01 B *4/50* Dec28 PmM 4f fst :49² B *9/46* Nov23 Bel tr.t 5f fst 1:01⁴ B *19/63* Nov16 Bel tr.t 5f fst 1:01 B *7/52* Nov8 Bel tr.t 5f fst 1:03 B *30/47* Oct31 Bel 4f fst :50³ B *66/96* Oct24 Bel 4f fst :48⁴ B *10/27* Oct17 Bel 4f fst :50³ B *31/46*
TRAINER: 1stStart(130 .20 $1.47) 1stLasix(10 .40 $3.79) Dirt(682 .24 $1.69) Sprint(396 .27 $1.86) MdnSpWt(318 .24 $1.64)

DAILY RACING FORM Friday, Fe

---

8 Aimer
Own: Bentley L Smith
Pink Gold, Silver Diamond Belt, Gold Cap
BLANC B (28 2 2 3 .07) 2003: (349 41 .12)

Dk. b or br f. 3 (Feb) KEEJUL02 $150,000
Sire: Swain*Ire (Nashwan) $25,000
Dam: Vickey's Echo (Clever Trick)
Br: Arthur B Hancock III (Ky)
Tr: Nafzger Carl A(24 2 4 2 .08) 2003:(285 31 .11)

L 121

Life	1	M	0	0	$0	52	D.Fst	1	0	0	0	$0	52
2003	1	M	0	0	$0	52	Wet(267)	0	0	0	0	$0	–
2002	0	M	0	0	$0	–	Turf(370)	0	0	0	0	$0	–
GP	0	0	0	0	$0	–	Dst(292)	0	0	0	0	$0	–

9Nov03-1CD fst 6f :21² :46 :58⁴1:11³ ⒻMd Sp Wt 37k 52 1 10 10¹⁰ 11¹¹ 8⁶½ 7⁸½ Blanc B L122 66.30 72-20 *SltwterRunner*122²¾ LovePower122² *ProspectivSint*122½ Improved position 12
WORKS: Jan28 PmM 5f fst 1:02 B *10/20* Jan14 PmM 5f fst 1:01 B *3/20* Dec30 PmM 5f fst 1:02⁴ B *26/37* Dec24 PmM 5f fst 1:01³ B *7/33*
TRAINER: 61-180Days(28 .11 $0.88) 2ndStart(24 .12 $1.64) Dirt(239 .11 $1.30) Sprint(187 .09 $1.43) MdnSpWt(122 .08 $0.77)

---

9 Evasive
Own: Jay Em Ess Stable
Turqse Blue, Lime Green Ms, Lime Green Sleeves
BAILEY J D (53 8 12 8 .15) 2003: (776 206 .27)

B. f. 3 (Feb) FTKJUL02 $225,000
Sire: Elusive Quality (Gone West) $50,000
Dam: Stephanie's Road (Strawberry Road*Aus)
Br: Taylor Made Farm Inc & Brian Kahn (Ky)
Tr: Dutrow Richard E Jr(7 1 2 0 .14) 2003:(531 132 .25)

Ⓛ 121

Life	1	M	0	0	$0	26	D.Fst	1	0	0	0	$0	26
2003	1	M	0	0	$0	26	Wet(328)	0	0	0	0	$0	–
2002	0	M	0	0	$0	–	Turf(257)	0	0	0	0	$0	–
GP	0	0	0	0	$0	–	Dst(351)	0	0	0	0	$0	–

30Aug03-6Sar fst 6½f :21⁴ :45¹ 1:11¹1:18¹ ⒻMd Sp Wt 45k 26 12 1 4² 6⁴¾ 12²¹ 12²²½ Bailey J D 119 8.30 62-11 BojnglesCt119hd EndersSistr1194¾ *Ellionthmrch*1192¾ Chased 4 wide, tired 12
WORKS: Feb3 PmM 4f fst :48³ B *8/68* Jan28 PmM 5f fst 1:01³ B *5/20* Jan21 PmM 4f fst :50 B *22/31* Jan15 PmM 5f fst 1:03³ Bg *16/21* Jan8 PmM 5f fst 1:05 B *18/19* Jan2 PmM 5f fst 1:03³ B *15/16*
TRAINER: 61-180Days(68 .31 $2.70) 2ndStart(20 .30 $1.84) 1stLasix(29 .31 $1.98) Dirt(533 .26 $1.83) Sprint(349 .26 $1.73) MdnSpWt(68 .25 $1.70)

---

10 Stormy Season
Own: Overbrook Farm
Purple White, Green O On Blue Ball, Green Cap
COURT J K (31 3 4 3 .10) 2003: (1137 146 .13)

Dk. b or br f. 3 (Feb)
Sire: Storm Cat (Storm Bird) $500,000
Dam: Timely Broad (Broad Brush)
Br: Overbrook Farm (Ky)
Tr: Lukas D Wayne(7 1 1 0 .14) 2003:(663 71 .11)

L 121

Life	5	M	1	0	$6,980	61	D.Fst	4	0	1	0	$5,380	56
2004	1	M	0	0	$1,600	61	Wet(428)	0	0	0	0	$0	–
2003	4	M	1	0	$5,380	56	Turf(358)	1	0	0	0	$1,600	61
GP	0	0	0	0	$0	–	Dst(423)	1	0	0	0	$180	19

9Jan04-5GP fm *1$\frac{1}{16}$ Ⓣ :24⁴ :52 1:17¹1:48 ⒻMd Sp Wt 32k 61 4 2hd 1hd 1hd 1hd 4²½ Velasquez C L121 b 15.10 62-26 Desert Deed121nk Laville1211½ Crimson121¾ On rail, weakened 10
17Aug03-7EIP fst 7f :22 :45² 1:11²1:25¹ ⒻMd Sp Wt 24k 19 7 1 2½ 1hd 6¹⁰ 6²² Douglas R R L120 b 6.20 64-11 La Cerca1204½ Wateree1202½ Too Much Class120¾ Bobble start,faltered 8
24Jly03-5AP fst 5½f :22³ :46 :58⁴1:05² ⒻMd Sp Wt 30k 27 6 10 8²¾ 7⁹½ 9¹⁴ 9¹⁵½ Lang C T L118 b 18.20 72-13 Willow Cove118nk *Bad Kitty*118½ Wateree118² Gave way 10
4Jly03-4AP fst 5f :22² :46³ :59² ⒻMd Sp Wt 26k 4 6 5 4¹½ 5⁵½ 8¹¹ 8²⁰½ Lang C T L118 b 4.90 69-15 Zosima1184½ Speak Easy118no *Willow Cove*1181½ Came out 1/4 8
15Jun03-1AP fst 5f :22⁴ :46³ :59 ⒻMd Sp Wt 26k 56 3 3 3² 2½ 2⁴ 2⁸ Douglas R R 117 b *1.00 83-14 LadysRoom117⁸ StormySeason1171½ AtlanticAffir117¹ Second best, bled 8
WORKS: Jan24 GP 4f fst :49 B *14/44* Jan17 GP 3f fst :36¹ B *4/11* Jan4 GP 5f fst 1:01⁴ B *8/22* ●Dec27 GP 3f fst :36 Bg *1/12* Dec14 GP 4f fst :48² B *2/19* Dec1 CD 4f fst :51 B *13/16*
TRAINER: 2Off45-180(71 .06 $0.69) Turf/Dirt(40 .08 $1.74) Route/Sprint(69 .16 $2.35) Dirt(613 .11 $1.18) Sprint(432 .11 $1.11) MdnSpWt(298 .11 $1.08)

(handwritten annotations: "SP²", "HK²", "AUGUST DAYS IN REALITY")

11 Holy Kate
Gray
Own: Dorothy Alexander Matz
Forest Green, Pink Sash, Green Stripes
TRUJILLO E (25 3 1 2 .12) 2003: (376 46 .12)

Gr/ro. f. 3 (Apr) EASOCT02 $72,000
Sire: Holy Bull (Great Above) $15,000
Dam: Angel Kate (Mt. Livermore)
Br: Marion G Montanari (Fla)
Tr: Matz Michael R(12 1 2 0 .08) 2003: (187 25 .13)

121

Life	1 M 1 0	$6,400	38	D.Fst	0 0 0 0	$0 –
2003	1 M 1 0	$6,400	38	Wet(380)	1 0 1 0	$6,400 38
2002	0 M 0 0	$0	–	Turf(260)	0 0 0 0	$0 –
GP	0 0 0 0	$0	–	Dst(320)	0 0 0 0	$0 –

16Aug03–6Del gd 5f :22 :47 1:00³ ⑤Md 100000(100-80) 38 7 5 45½ 35½ 44½ 23½ Castillo O O 119 7.20 81– 17 SaucyBid117³½ HolyKte119ⁿᵏ TomorrowsNumber119³ 4 wide trip, got 2nd 7
WORKS: Jan28 PBD 3f gd :38 B 1/3 Jan12 PBD 5f gd 1:03 B 3/6 ●Jan3 PBD 5f gd 1:02¹ B 1/4 Dec16 PBD 3f fst :38 B 1/1
TRAINER: 61-180Days(29 .10 $3.67) 2ndStart(17 .12 $6.59) Dirt(106 .10 $1.97) Sprint(41 .05 $0.81) MdnSpWt(66 .12 $1.41)

12 Wickedly Wise
Lime
Own: Padua Stable
Green, Gold Diamond Belt, Gold Diamonds
DOUGLAS R R (127 16 12 7 .13) 2003: (1075 201 .19)

Gr/ro. f. 3 (Apr) FTKJUL02 $105,000
Sire: Tactical Cat (Storm Cat) $10,000
Dam: Winter Display (Cold Reception)
Br: Dr & Mrs A Leonard Pineau (Md)
Tr: Margolis Stephen R(19 3 1 2 .16) 2003: (94 16 .17)

L 121

Life	1 M 0 1	$3,200	53	D.Fst	1 0 0 1	$3,200 53
2004	1 M 0 1	$3,200	53	Wet(384*)	0 0 0 0	$0 –
2003	0 M 0 0	$0	–	Turf(333*)	0 0 0 0	$0 –
GP	1 0 0 1	$3,200	53	Dst(351*)	0 0 0 0	$0 –

4Jan04–5GP fst 6f :21⁴ :44⁴ :56⁴ 1:09¹ ⑤Md Sp Wt 32k 53 10 2 63½ 78 6¹¹ 31⁵½ Velasquez C L121 27.20 81– 10 MdcpEscpd121¹⁰ DnmWldct121⁵½ WckdlWs121¹¾ Toward outside,evenly 12
WORKS: ●Jan29 PmM 5f fst 1:01¹ B 1/16 Dec30 PmM 4f fst :48⁴ Hg 6/22 Dec2 CD 4f fst :49⁴ B 4/13 Nov23 CD 5f fst 1:02² B 24/40
TRAINER: 2ndStart(7 .00 $0.00) 31-60Days(29 .17 $4.03) Dirt(95 .13 $2.68) Sprint(82 .17 $2.80) MdnSpWt(14 .07 $0.41)

Also Eligible:

13 We've Got a Chance
Brown
Own: Kay Hale & Mr. T Stables
White, Light Blue & Yellow Stripes
BOULANGER G (71 5 5 7 .07) 2003: (1254 183 .15)

B. f. 3 (Feb) OBSFEB03 $57,000
Sire: American Chance (Cure the Blues) $7,500
Dam: Crysta (Pine Bluff)
Br: E W Thomas (Ky)
Tr: Hale Robert A(13 2 2 1 .15) 2003: (193 31 .16)

121

Life	1 M 0 0	$320	32	D.Fst	1 0 0 0	$320 32
2004	1 M 0 0	$320	32	Wet(345)	0 0 0 0	$0 –
2003	0 M 0 0	$0	–	Turf(264)	0 0 0 0	$0 –
GP	1 0 0 0	$320	32	Dst(330)	0 0 0 0	$0 –

4Jan04–5GP fst 6f :21⁴ :44⁴ :56⁴ 1:09¹ ⑤Md Sp Wt 32k 32 6 11 10⁶½ 10¹⁰ 81³ 82³½ Castro E 121 11.70 72– 10 MdcpEscpd121¹⁰ DnmWildct121⁵ WckdlyWs121¹¾ Steadied briefly early 12
WORKS: ●Dec30 Crc 3f fst :34⁴ H 1/13 Dec22 Crc 3f fst :37 Bg 5/16 Dec17 Crc 3f fst :35⁴ H 3/17 Nov28 Crc 3f fst :36⁴ B 8/14 Nov26 Crc 3f fst :37² B 15/27
TRAINER: 2ndStart(10 .30 $1.12) 31-60Days(36 .14 $1.99) Dirt(156 .14 $1.99) Sprint(124 .15 $2.10) MdnSpWt(20 .05 $0.24)

(handwritten: "SCR")

14 Peer
Maroon
Own: Cherry Valley Farm LLC
Cherry Red, Two Yellow Hoops, Yellow
BAILEY J D (53 8 12 8 .15) 2003: (776 206 .27)

Dk. b or br f. 3 (Mar) KEESEP02 $65,000
Sire: Pulpit (A.P. Indy) $35,000
Dam: Scope (Devil's Bag)
Br: Cherry Valley Farm LLC (Ky)
Tr: Mott William I(36 6 4 4 .17) 2003: (718 138 .19)

(handwritten: "UE, MR. P—HARB? FLG")

121

Life	0 M 0 0	$0	–	D.Fst	0 0 0 0	$0 –
2004	0 M 0 0	$0	–	Wet(372)	0 0 0 0	$0 –
2003	0 M 0 0	$0	–	Turf(274)	0 0 0 0	$0 –
GP	0 0 0 0	$0	–	Dst(370)	0 0 0 0	$0 –

WORKS: ●Jan24 Pay 4f fst :50¹ Bg 1/28 Jan17 Pay 5f fst 1:04² B 5/16 Jan10 Pay 4f fst :50 B 3/25 ●Jan3 Pay 5f fst 1:02⁴ B 1/8 Dec29 Pay 4f fst :52 B 23/38 Dec20 Pay 4f fst :50¹ Bg 3/27
Dec13 Pay 4f fst :51³ B 12/19 Dec6 Pay 3f fst :37³ B 2/10
TRAINER: 1stStart(90 .02 $0.22) Dirt(400 .18 $1.34) Sprint(215 .18 $1.51) MdnSpWt(254 .11 $1.19)

Present Danger: The first thing that catches the eye is sire Souvenir Copy, a young stallion whose name is synonymous with speed. One of 2002's best freshman sires, who had 17 2-year-old winners in his first crop, Souvenir Copy was a good 2-year-old himself, winning the Del Mar Futurity and Norfolk Stakes, and is by Mr. Prospector (speed). A check mark immediately goes next to Souvenir Copy as a speed influence. A check mark also goes next to Storm Cat as the damsire, since his presence adds more speed than stamina to the pedigree. If the pedigree has this kind of speed from both the sire and damsire, I label it SP^2 (speed x 2).

(If a player wants to know the class of the horse, the next step is to find out who the dam is. In this case, Stormy Gal comes from the female family of multiple stakes winner Gay Serenade, and other prominent runners produced by this family are Navesink, Imah, Ring Dancer, Cefis, and Run Smartly. So, this is a pedigree of speed *and* class, or SP^2/C).

Joyful Chaos: Rahy has had broad success as a sire of turf and dirt runners, and his fillies, in particular, have shown speed on dirt, including Serena's Song, Raw Gold, and Exotic Wood. The damsire is Deputy Minister, a champion at 2 and a world-class sire. While many of his runners have raced successfully at classic distances as late-maturing 3-year-olds and as older runners (Touch Gold, Awesome Again, Deputy Commander, Flag Down, etc.), Deputy Minister's presence in a pedigree indicates speed. Thus, this filly is bred for speed on the grass and figures to be a price because her trainer, Christophe Clement, has had better success with turf runners and has a low percentage with first-time starters on dirt. (The female family is high-class and has produced Carson City, General Meeting, Prides Profile, and Dixie Dot Com.) With Rahy, Deputy Minister, and Pleasant Colony up close in her pedigree, Joyful Chaos will get better with maturity and be best from seven furlongs to $1\frac{1}{8}$ miles on all surfaces, preferably on grass.

My Time Now: The late Unbridled was known for siring very big offspring, the majority of which have needed time to mature and have been best stretching out in distance. In addition, grass influence Roberto is the damsire of this filly, which makes this a pedigree heavily laced with stamina (or ST^2), with little speed. This is a strong pedigree for distances of more than one mile on dirt and turf. (My Time Now's dam, Darby Trail, is a full sister to Darby Creek Road and is closely related to Dynaformer.) She finished third in a $6\frac{1}{2}$-furlong maiden race at Churchill Downs in her only race at 2, indicating talent, and she should only get better at 3 and 4. Gets first-time Lasix and will probably need the race. Regardless of today's outcome, this is a filly with a future as the year progresses.

Pretty Jane: By Subordination, a multiple stakes winner on turf who had high speed (from his sire, Mt. Livermore). Gets more speed from damsire, Afleet. (The female family traces to foundation mares cultivated by Christiana Stables.) Wait for maiden race on turf, where her speed will be dangerous. T/SP^2 pedigree.

Magical Illusion: Gets an SP^2 rating, as well as HT^2 (hidden turf x 2). Her sire, Pulpit, is very capable of getting runners who win first time out (as he did), especially when they are out of mares by speed influences, such as Baldski. (Dam Voodoo Lily was a stakes winner and this filly is a half-sister to stakes-placed Shah Jehan.) Combining pedigree with high-profile connections (trainer H. James Bond and jockey Edgar Prado), this filly is a logical contender.

Maren Approved: By Canadian Horse of the Year and champion 3-year-old With Approval (a half-brother to Touch Gold), a multiple stakes winner on grass in the U.S. whose sire line is all turf (Caro). This filly is strictly bred for grass, or T^2.

Platinum Heights: The $2.8 million purchase price first grabs the attention, and is important as it denotes that her conformation obviously matched her star-studded pedigree. By Storm Cat (a speed influence and a stakes-winning 2-year-old), who is an excellent sire of first-time starters, this filly is out of a mare by Bold Hour, one of Bold Ruler's best runners. Bold Hour, who was from the same crop as Dr. Fager, Damascus, Successor, and In Reality, won the 1966 Hopeful and Futurity Stakes and is a source of speed. In addition, Platinum Heights is out of an exceptional broodmare, Amelia Bearhart, who produced stakes winners Chief Bearhart, Ruby Ransom, and Explosive Red. High speed top and bottom, with high class from female family (SP^2/C), in the hands of a winning trainer/jockey combination, Todd Pletcher and John Velazquez.

Aimer: By Swain, a champion older runner in England and Ireland who is best known in this country for Frankie Dettori's extremely wide ride in the 1998 Breeders' Cup Classic, in which Swain finished third behind Awesome Again and Silver Charm. While his runners do win on dirt, they are really bred for grass (e.g., American Oaks winner Dimitrova). This filly's damsire, Clever Trick, does add speed to the mix, but I can't wait to see Aimer on turf. The T/SP rating means the sire provides turf while the damsire imparts speed.

Evasive: Showed speed before tiring in wide Saratoga debut. This filly gets first-time Lasix and is by Elusive Quality, whose runners are known for their high speed on all surfaces. Trainer Richard Dutrow Jr. has been red-hot and this was Jerry Bailey's second call (behind Peer, an also-eligible who got into the race). A must-use in all exotics, and with the T^2 (Elusive Quality/Strawberry Road) cross, this filly should be on a "Horses to Watch" list on turf.

Stormy Season: Another Storm Cat, this filly has shown very little in five starts against inferior competition on dirt. An immediate toss.

Holy Kate: By Holy Bull out of a Mt. Livermore mare, this filly is bred for high speed (SP^2). (Her dam, Angel Kate, is a half-sister to the stakes-winning sprinter For Really.) For future reference, both Holy Bull (Great Above) and Mt. Livermore (Blushing Groom) are hidden turf sires, thus she also has an HT^2 rating.

Peer: Another filly by Pulpit, out of a Devil's Bag mare from a strong Claiborne/Cherry Valley Farm female family. Peer was an also-eligible who got into the race. Trained by Bill Mott and ridden by Bailey, this filly figured to be an underlay, and although bred for speed, she had to contend with a far-outside post and others with speed. Runners by Pulpit are showing a strong affinity for grass, and Devil's Bag has been a better sire of turf runners than dirt. Would not be surprising to see this filly do her best running on grass.

Considering her pedigree and high-profile connections, Platinum Heights offered value at nearly 4-1, and the second-time starter by Elusive Quality, Evasive, was very attractive at 8-1, providing a $2 exacta of $76.40. While I would not have selected Present Danger to win, she was certainly a candidate to finish in the money because of her speed. A creative trifecta ticket keying Platinum Heights and Evasive in the first and second spots, and Present Danger, Joyful Chaos, My Time Now, Magical Illusion, Holy Kate, and Peer in the third spot, would have cost $12. The $1 trifecta returned $520.80.

SIXTH RACE
Gulfstream
FEBRUARY 6, 2004

7 FURLONGS. (1.20) MAIDEN SPECIAL WEIGHT . Purse $32,000 FOR MAIDENS, FILLIES THREE YEARS OLD. Weight, 121 lbs.

Value of Race: $32,000 Winner $19,200; second $5,760; third $3,200; fourth $1,280; fifth $320; sixth $320; seventh $320; eighth $320; ninth $320; tenth $320; eleventh $320; twelfth $320. Mutuel Pool $332,752.00 Exacta Pool $287,587.00 Trifecta Pool $197,234.00 Superfecta Pool $53,835.00

Last Raced	Horse	M/Eqt.	A.	Wt	PP	St	1/4	1/2	Str	Fin	Jockey	Odds $1
	Platinum Heights	L	3	121	7	10	$7\frac{1}{2}$	3^1	$1\frac{1}{2}$	$12\frac{1}{2}$	Velazquez J R	3.80
30Aug03 6Sar12	Evasive	L	3	121	9	4	4^3	2^1	2^1	2^{nk}	Santos J A	8.30
	Present Danger	L	3	121	1	9	10^1	9^{hd}	5^{hd}	3^{nk}	Day P	29.20
	Joyful Chaos		3	121	2	11	1^2	10^{hd}	$7\frac{1}{2}$	$4\frac{1}{2}$	Bravo J	72.80
16Aug03 6Del2	Holy Kate		3	121	11	1	1^{hd}	7^1	6^{hd}	$5\frac{3}{4}$	Trujillo E	27.80
	Peer		3	121	12	2	3^{hd}	1^{hd}	3^1	6^{nk}	Bailey J D	3.40
	Pretty Jane	b	3	121	4	6	5^{hd}	$5\frac{1}{2}$	$42\frac{1}{2}$	7^4	Cruz M R	33.00
9Nov03 1CD7	Aimer	L	3	121	8	7	11^{hd}	12	8^1	$81\frac{3}{4}$	Blanc B	35.00
	Maren Approved		3	121	6	5	9^1	$111\frac{1}{2}$	12	9^{nk}	Boulanger G	56.00
2Nov03 3CD3	My Time Now	L f	3	121	3	8	8^{hd}	$81\frac{1}{2}$	$10\frac{1}{2}$	$101\frac{3}{4}$	Coa E M	3.00
9Jan04 5GP4	Stormy Season	L b	3	121	10	3	2^{hd}	4^{hd}	9^2	$112\frac{1}{4}$	Court J K	15.90
	Magical Illusion	L b	3	121	5	12	6^{hd}	6^1	$11\frac{1}{2}$	12	Prado E S	4.60

OFF AT 3:53 Start Good For All But MAGICAL ILLUSION. Won driving. Track fast.

TIME :22, :45, 1:10⁴, 1:24 (:22.12, :45.09, 1:10.85, 1:24.03)

$2 Mutuel Prices:

7 – PLATINUM HEIGHTS................ 9.60 5.20 4.40
9 – EVASIVE........................ 8.40 6.40
1 – PRESENT DANGER................ 12.40

$1 EXACTA 7–9 PAID $38.20 $1 TRIFECTA 7–9–1 PAID $520.80
$1 SUPERFECTA 7–9–1–2 PAID $13,458.70

Ch. f, (Apr), by Storm Cat – Amelia Bearhart , by Bold Hour . Trainer Pletcher Todd A. Bred by Richard D Maynard (Ky).

PLATINUM HEIGHTS advanced into contention three wide on the turn, rallied to gain a slim lead at the top of the stretch, then drew clear late under urging. EVASIVE vied for the lead along the inside, continued on well to deep stretch, then couldn't stay with the winner while just saving the place. PRESENT DANGER unhurried early, angled out leaving the turn and rallied to just miss the place. JOYFUL CHAOS outrun after breaking slowly, was knocked into MAREN APPROVED on the turn, fanned wide entering the stretch and finished willingly. HOLY KATE showed speed between horses, dropped back when caught in tight leaving backstretch, swung out for the stretch run and failed to threaten. PEER vied for the lead from the outside to the top of the stretch and weakened. PRETTY JANE tracked the pace along the inside to past the eighth pole and gave way. AIMER outrun early, was racing four wide when forced to steady in behind rivals on the turn, angled to the inside and failed to menace. MAREN APPROVED unhurried early, was not a factor after being bumped soundly by JOYFUL CHAOS on the turn. MY TIME NOW rated off the pace, angled out on the turn and knocked JOYFUL CHAOS into MAREN APPROVED, then steadied from tight quarters at the top of the stretch and tired. STORMY SEASON showed speed into the turn and faltered. MAGICAL ILLUSION broke poorly, then steadied in behind HOLY KATE leaving the backstretch, raced four wide on the turn and faded.

Owners– 1, Melnyk Eugene and Laura; 2, Jay Em Ess Stable; 3, Humphrey G Watts Jr; 4, Schaffel Lewis; 5, Matz Dorothy A; 6, Cherry Valley Farm LLC; 7, Gary Redmond; 8, Smith Bentley L; 9, Graham Ziba F; 10, Phillips Racing Partnership; 11, Overbrook Farm; 12, Clifton William L Jr

Trainers– 1, Pletcher Todd A; 2, Dutrow Richard E Jr; 3, Oliver Victoria; 4, Clement Christophe; 5, Matz Michael R; 6, Mott William I; 7, Caramori Eduardo; 8, Nafzger Carl A; 9, Hennig Mark; 10, Nafzger Carl A; 11, Lukas D Wayne; 12, Bond Harold James

Scratched– Wickedly Wise (04Jan04 5GP 3) , We've Got a Chance (04Jan04 5GP 8)

$1 Pick Three (1–5–7) Paid $14.70 ; Pick Three Pool $75,557 .

EXAMPLE 2
Analyzing a maiden special weight race on turf

BETTING OBSCURE BUT WELL-BRED TURF STALLIONS

Many stallions who achieved success in Europe over the grass but were relatively unknown in the U.S. have a limited number of starters in this country. One such sire is King of Kings, a son of Sadler's Wells out of a mare by champion turf miler Habitat.

King of Kings won 4 of 5 starts (including the Group 1 National Stakes and Group 2 Railway Stakes) at 2 in Ireland, and won the prestigious English 2000 Guineas at 3. He started off his stud career as a Southern Hemisphere stallion, and then was based at Ashford Stud in Kentucky. His first North American foals were 2-year-olds of 2002 and not surprisingly, they were ill-suited for dirt racing and showed poor form sprinting at 2 and 3. It did not take long for King of Kings to be sent back overseas.

Given a chance on grass, however, his runners sprang to life. Never was this more apparent than on January 24, 2004, in a maiden race for 3-year-old fillies on the grass at Fair Grounds.

5 **Fair Grounds** — Ⓕ**Md Sp Wt 28k** — TURF COURSE ABOUT 1 MILE (START / FINISH)

About 1 MILE **(Turf). (1:35⁴) MAIDEN SPECIAL WEIGHT. Purse $28,000 For Maidens, Fillies Three Years Old. Weight, 119 lbs. (Preference To Horses That Have Not Started For Less Than $25,000). (If deemed inadvisable by management to run this race over the turf course, it will be run on the main track at One Mile) (Rail at 15 feet).**

2 T

1 Beach Side (Red)
Own: William C Schaffrick
White, Green Braces, White 'Bs' On Green
LANERIE C J (194 27 27 28 .14) 2003: (1341 231 .17)

B. f. 3 (Apr)
Sire: Lit de Justice (El Gran Senor) $5,000
Dam: Meryl's Myth (Lion d'Or) 'SECRETARIAT
Br: William Schaffrick (Ky)
Tr: Kassen David C(18 1 0 3 .06) 2003:(114 12 .11)

L 119

Life	9	M	0	4	$9,570	60	D.Fst	5	0	0	2	$3,630 44
2004	1	M	0	0	$0	-	Wet(318)	0	0	0	0	$0 -
2003	8	M	0	4	$9,570	60	Turf(253)	4	0	0	2	$5,940 60
FGⓉ	2	0	0	1	$3,080	55	DstⓉ(296)	2	0	0	1	$3,080 55

3Jan04-7FG fm *1 1/16 Ⓣ:231 :474 1:132 1:451 ⒻMd Sp Wt 28k – 2 99¼ 98 64¼ - - Lanerie C J L119 b 15.00 - 14 Dynamia1194½ Sea Merge1191 Vagabond Saint119no Clipped heels, fell 12
6Dec03-5FG fm *1 Ⓣ:25 :494 1:161 1:403 ⒻMd Sp Wt 28k 55 1 65 55 54 53½ 34¼ Lanerie C J L119 b 4.00 77-21 Greygoosegal119nk Tomoka Bound1194 Beach Side119¾ Along for show 9
7Nov03-1CD fst 1 :231 :47 1:134 1:391 ⒻMd 50000(50-45) 37 7 1½ 12½ 2hd 44½ 618 Lanerie C J L122 b 5.50 53-29 TwilightGllop1223¾ MyCtsMeow1226¼ WildctLdy1221¾ Duck in bmp start 7
24Sep03-4AP fm 1 1/16 Ⓣ:23 :484 1:134 1:46 ⒻMd Sp Wt 26k 60 11 65¾ 47½ 1½ 11½ 32 Lanerie C J L119 b 6.80 77-14 Random Chance119½ Skip Poker1191½ Beach Side119¾ Couldn't last 12
5Sep03-7AP fm *1 Ⓣ:242 :50 1:152 1:411 ⒻMd Sp Wt 27k 48 8 109¾1010 41½ 21 73¼ Thornton T7 L112 b 33.40 70-21 GinghmndLc1192¼ *Shmkndwondrful*119nk FrcPrncss119nk Bore out stretch 10
23Aug03-4AP fst 6f :224 :463 :593 1:131 ⒻMd 50000(50-40) 40 3 3 31 54 45½ 78 Thornton T7 L111 b 18.90 70-15 *Notable Kindness*118nk Esthers Ball118¾ Western Hussy118¾ Weakened 10
24Jly03-1AP fst 5f :222 :461 :59 ⒻMd 25000(25-22.5) 44 2 1 2½ 31½ 34½ 37¼ Thornton T7 L111 b 12.90 84-13 Stormy Rosa1182¾ CottonuousPeaks1184½ BeachSide1113 No winning bid 8
3Jly03-1AP fst 5f :221 :453 1:002 ⒻMd 30000(30-25) 18 3 3 34 36½ 48 310 Thornton T10 L111 5.80 74-14 Brodnicki1184 Gritty Kitty1186 Beach Side1111½ Fractious in gate 6
15Jun03-1AP fst 5f :224 :463 :59 ⒻMd Sp Wt 26k 24 7 6 65½ 57 510 818¼ Thornton T10 107 11.20 73-14 Lady's Room1178 Stormy Season1171¼ Atlantic Affair1171 Gave way, bled 8

WORKS: Jan20 FG 4f fst :49 B *9/31* Jan13 FG 4f fst :501 B *10/18* Dec31 FG 4f fst :51 B *68/105* Dec24 FG 4f fst :494 B *25/77* Dec16 FG 4f fst :491 B *9/38* Dec3 FG 4f fst :52 B *27/31*
TRAINER: Turf(33 .03 $0.18) Routes(72 .10 $0.98) MdnSpWt(31 .10 $0.82)

T 57

2 True Blonde Beauty (White)
Own: V Devi & K K Jayaraman
Blue, White 'T' On Red Ball
LAVIOLETTE B S (24 2 1 4 .08) 2003: (853 89 .10)

Ch. f. 3 (Jan)
Sire: Proudest Romeo (Proud Truth) $2,500
Dam: Blonde Actress (Lyphard's Ridge)
Br: K K Jayaraman MD & V Devi Jayaraman MD (Fla)
Tr: Daly Patrick J(16 0 2 3 .00) 2003:(72 10 .14)

L 119

Life	2	M	0	1	$3,760	68	D.Fst	2	0	0	1	$3,760 68
2003	2	M	0	1	$3,760	68	Wet(316)	0	0	0	0	$0 -
2002	0	M	0	0	$0	-	Turf(203*)	0	0	0	0	$0 -
FGⓉ	0	0	0	0	$0	-	DstⓉ(383)	0	0	0	0	$0 -

12Sep03-3AP fst 1 :232 :463 1:113 1:383 ⒻMd Sp Wt 34k 68 2 54 31½ 41¼ 33½ 31¾ Douglas R R L119 *2.50 73-29 Journey Fever1191¾ Defuhr119hd True Blonde Beauty1196 No winning bid 8
17Aug03-7EIP fst 7f :22 :452 1:112 1:251 ⒻMd Sp Wt 24k 49 5 8 78½ 64¼ 55 47½ Bejarano R L120 12.20 78-11 La Cerca1204½ Wateree1202¼ Too Much Class120¾ Inside,no late gain 8

WORKS: Jan19 FG 4f fst :491 B *23/70* Jan13 FG 5f fst 1:04 B *18/25* Jan7 FG 5f fst 1:041 B *35/45* Dec31 FG 4f fst :484 B *10/105* Dec24 FG 4f fst :502 B *39/77* Dec17 FG 3f fst :362 B *8/26*
TRAINER: 61-180Days(5 .00 $0.00) 1stTurf(4 .25 $9.10) Dirt/Turf(7 .14 $5.20) Turf(17 .24 $3.07) Routes(32 .12 $1.94) MdnSpWt(21 .10 $1.00)

POOR SIRE DAM 1/2 QUIET AMERICAN

3 Pleasure Hunt (Blue)
Own: Emerald Pastures Corp Inc
Cream, Gold 'Ep' On Green Shamrock
PERRODIN E J (89 12 6 13 .13) 2003: (525 85 .16)

Ch. f. 3 (Apr) KEESEP02 $25,000
Sire: Coronado's Quest (Forty Niner) $50,000
Dam: Unbridled Delight (Unbridled) — DEMURE
Br: Overbrook Farm (Ky)
Tr: Romero Terry M(2 0 0 0 .00) 2003:(255 20 .08)

119

Life	3	M	0	0	$460	16	D.Fst	3	0	0	0	$460 16
2003	3	M	0	0	$460	16	Wet(344)	0	0	0	0	$0 -
2002	0	M	0	0	$0	-	Turf(301)	0	0	0	0	$0 -
FGⓉ	0	0	0	0	$0	-	DstⓉ(420)	0	0	0	0	$0 -

12Dec03-4DeD fst 5f :23 :472 1:004 ⒻMd Sp Wt 15k 14 6 4 43½ 64¼ 610 616½ Romero S P 119 b 19.60 67-20 Fluidly1195 Katestormedthebird119no Proud Abby1192¼ Finished evenly 9
Previously trained by Hayford Jennifer
25Jly03-8Crc fst 4½f :223 :464 :532 ⒻMd Sp Wt 28k 16 2 7 77 77¾ 812¼ Bain G W 118 b 24.20 80-13 Velma Kelly1184 Lau Mor's Glitter1181½ Harmony Light113½ Outrun 8
5Jly03-6Crc fst 6f :222 :461 :592 1:13 ⒻMd Sp Wt 28k -0 4 7 67½ 79½ 715 733½ Bain G W 118 b 30.80 46-14 Sweet Serenade1183½ Chantilly Light1137¾ Cleito118¾ Poor start 7

WORKS: Jan15 DeD 5f fst 1:04 B *6/9* Dec30 DeD 6f hy 1:182 B *1/1* Dec1 DeD 4f fst :481 B *3/9* Nov19 DeD 4f fst :502 Bg *3/23*
TRAINER: 2Off45-180(26 .08 $0.80) 1stTurf(5 .00 $0.00) Dirt/Turf(15 .00 $0.00) Sprint/Route(23 .17 $2.75) 2Sprints/Route(6 .00 $0.00) 31-60Days(53 .09 $1.81)

handwritten: 2 — NO CLASS / weak

4 Lively Number

Yellow — Own: Beth H Clifton & Mary Lester — Turquoise, Orange Sash, Orange Chevrons
PAVLOVIC G (1 0 0 0 .00) (—)

B. f. 3 (Apr)
Sire: Mt. Livermore (Blushing Groom*Fr) $35,000
Dam: Numeradora*Arg (Senor Pete)
Br: Beth H Clifton & Mary Lester (Ky)
Tr: Kessinger Burk Jr(7 0 0 2 .00) 2003:(15 1 .07)

L 119

	Life	3 M 0 0	$240 22	D.Fst	1 0 0 0	$60 22
	2004	1 M 0 0	$0 -	Wet(359)	1 0 0 0	$180 22
	2003	2 M 0 0	$240 22	Turf(279)	0 0 0 0	$0 -
	FG ⑦	1 0 0 0	$0 -	Dst⑦(339)	0 0 0 0	$0 -

3Jan04–7FG fm *1⅟₁₆ ⑦ :23¹ :47⁴ 1:13²1:45¹	⑤Md Sp Wt 28k	–0 5 10¹¹10¹²11²4 10²4 10⁴2⅟₄	Perrodin E J	L119	44.10	44– 14 Dynamia119⁴⅟₄ Sea Merge119¹ VagabondSaint119no			Avoided fallen jockey 12

Previously trained by Quinn Jerry

| 20ct03–4TP fst 1 | :22⁴ :46³ 1:12³1:39¹ | ⑤Md Sp Wt 25k | 22 11 6⁵⅟₂ 5⁵⅟₂ 5⁶⅟₂ 9¹7 10²³⅟₄ | Zuniga J E | L121 | 38.70 | 54– 17 Shorewalk Drive121⁸ ALuluOfaMenifee121¹⅟₂ RushNote121¹⅟₄ | '7 wide early 12 |
| 3Aug03–4EIP gd 6f | :22⁴ :47 1:00 1:13³ | ⑤Md Sp Wt 27k | 22 6 10 9⁶⅟₄ 11¹4 8¹3⅟₄ | Zuniga J E | L120 | 72.10 | 64– 18 In Rome120nd Josie G.120⅟₂ Hot Chipotle120¹⅟₄ | Not a factor 12 |

WORKS: Dec20 FG 4f fst :49 B 7/61 Nov22 VHT 3f fst :38¹ B 1/2 Nov10 VHT 3f fst :37¹ B 1/1 ●Oct31 VHT 3f fst :37² B 1/6
TRAINER: 2Off45-180(1 .00 $0.00) Turf(10 .00 $0.00) Routes(12 .00 $0.00) MdnSpWt(14 .07 $0.57)

handwritten: T2 but weak female family — STAR APPEAL

5 Madame Galore

Green — Own: William A Hamilton — Blue, Lime Sash
BOREL C H (161 21 19 18 .13) 2003: (1220 162 .13)

Ch. f. 3 (Mar)
Sire: Fantastic Fellow (Lear Fan) $777
Dam: Presence Galore (Deputy Minister)
Br: William Hamilton III (Ky)
Tr: Matthews Doug(9 1 0 0 .11) 2003:(81 9 .11)

handwritten: Blinkers ON — Ⓛ 119 — NO LEASING

	Life	1 M 0 0	$0 7	D.Fst	1 0 0 0	$0 7
	2003	1 M 0 0	$0 7	Wet(316)	0 0 0 0	$0 -
	2002	0 M 0 0	$0 -	Turf(316)	0 0 0 0	$0 -
	FG ⑦	0 0 0 0	$0 -	Dst⑦(313)	0 0 0 0	$0 -

| 27Dec03–6Haw fst 6f | :22¹ :46³ :59²1:13² | ⑤Md Sp Wt 37k | 7 7 8 10¹¹ 11²4 10²0 10²2⅟₂ | Campbell J M | 121 | 113.80 | 53– 21 Miss Denouncer116⅟₂ Proven Cat121⁴⅟₄ My Patriot Lady121nk | Never close 11 |

WORKS: Jan19 FG 5f fst 1:03¹ B 39/63 Jan10 FG 5f fst 1:04³ B 49/61 Dec20 Haw 5f fst 1:05⁴ B 20/27 Dec7 Haw 5f gd 1:04 Bg 17/30 Nov22 Haw 5f fst 1:05² B 39/49
TRAINER: 2ndStart(4 .00 $0.00) 1stBlink(2 .00 $0.00) Dirt/Turf(14 .00 $0.00) BlinkOn(3 .33 $1.67) Sprint/Route(7 .14 $1.29)

handwritten: T/S

6 Praire Katydid

Black — Own: Sara Margaret Hamilton — Red, Black And Gold Stars
ALBARADO R J (175 36 40 18 .21) 2003: (1123 185 .16)

Dk. b or br. f. 3 (Feb)
Sire: Deerhound (Danzig) $5,000
Dam: Anna* (Groovy)
Br: Sara H Hamilton (Ky)
Tr: Barnett Bobby C(38 7 4 5 .18) 2003:(350 45 .13)

L 119

	Life	3 M 1 0	$7,900 58	D.Fst	3 0 1 0	$7,900 58
	2004	1 M 0 0	$0 50	Wet(350)	0 0 0 0	$0 -
	2003	2 M 1 0	$7,900 58	Turf(263)	0 0 0 0	$0 -
	FG ⑦	0 0 0 0	$0 -	Dst⑦(314)	0 0 0 0	$0 -

2Jan04–10FG fst 6f	:22¹ :46¹ :58³1:12	⑤Md Sp Wt 28k	50 7 2 4² 41⅟₂ 6⁷ 7⁹⅟₄	Meche L J	L119	6.90	70– 21 Anna Em119nk Carolina Rose119¹ Night Heron119nk	Between foes, faded 10
16Oct03–9Kee fst 6f	:22 :45³ 1:13³1:18	⑤Md Sp Wt 50k	52 2 3 1⅟₂ 1⅟₂ 7⁴ 4¹0⅟₄	Sellers S J	L117	7.40	72– 17 Everheart117²⅟₄ SteadyCourse117⁶ ErickasEyes117²	Pace,inside,weakened 12
24Aug03–6EIP fst 5f	:22⁴ :46² :59	⑤Md Sp Wt 26k	58 4 3 1hd 2hd 2³ 2⁶⅟₄	Coa D	L120	16.40	88– 15 StormingWay120⁶⅟₄ PraireKtydid120⅟₂ Wetherwise120²⅟₂	Dueled,no match 12

WORKS: Jan26 FG 4f fst :49 B 9/31 Jan12 FG 5f fst 1:03 B 18/47 Dec29 FG 4f fst :49² B 9/23 Dec29 FG 3f fst :35⁴ B 1/12 Dec12 FG 3f fst :35 B 1/3 ●Dec6 FG 5f fst 1:01 B 10/56
TRAINER: 2Off45-180(30 .07 $0.73) 1stTurf(28 .11 $2.66) Dirt/Turf(45 .13 $3.74) Sprint/Route(56 .14 $1.89) Turf(88 .11 $2.28) Routes(217 .15 $2.17)

7 Gran Lady Jade

Orange — Own: Ernest Wampler — Lime, Purple 'W' In Diamond Frame
TERRY D M (76 2 3 10 .03) 2003: (76 6 .08)

Ch. f. 3 (Apr)
Sire: Jade Hunter (Mr. Prospector) $15,000
Dam: Gran Ole Flag (El Gran Senor)
Br: Pegasus Stud LLC & Ledgelands LLC (Ky)
Tr: Trivigno Michael(2 0 0 0 .00) 2003:(94 16 .17)

L 114⁵

	Life	3 M 0 0	$225 24	D.Fst	1 0 0 0	$125 1
	2003	3 M 0 0	$225 24	Wet(338)	1 0 0 0	$100 -
	2002	0 M 0 0	$0 -	Turf(299)	1 0 0 0	$0 24
	FG ⑦	0 0 0 0	$0 -	Dst⑦(356)	1 0 0 0	$0 24

20Nov03–5CD gd 1	⑦:24 :47⁴ 1:14 1:40	⑥Md Sp Wt 43k	24 3 7⁸⅟₂ 6⁹ 8¹3 10¹9 8²3⅟₂	Zuniga J E	L122	110.40	49– 25 Code Song121²⅟₂ High Speed Access122⁴ Baxter Hall21nk	Tired 10
30ct03–6Hoo my 6f	:23 :47⁴ 1:00¹1:14	⑥Md Sp Wt 10k	–0 2 7 7⁵⅟₂ 7¹⅟₄ 6¹4 6²4⅟₂	Morgan M R	B118	21.50	49– 21 Deceit118⁹ Take the Ship118⁴⅟₄ Malign118⁸	Saved ground,no avail 7
4Sep03–6TP fst 1	:23⁴ :46⁴ :58⁴	⑥Md Sp Wt 22k	1 5 5 6⁵⅟₂ 7¹³ 7¹9 7²4⅟₂	Coa D	121	17.60	65– 13 CharismaticAppel121³⅟₄ Dorell121⁷⅟₂ SunbemMusic121²⅟₄	4 wide, no factor 8

WORKS: Dec27 EvD 5f fst 1:19 B 2/2 Dec20 EvD 5f fst 1:05¹ B 17/24 Nov15 CDT 4f sly :49⁴ B 5/13
TRAINER: 61-180Days(11 .00 $0.00) Turf(8 .12 $1.72) Routes(34 .12 $0.72) MdnSpWt(38 .18 $2.77)

handwritten: T2

8 Richwood Royal

Pink — Own: Robert C Durr — White, Turquoise Sleeves
MARTINEZ J R JR (75 7 3 8 .09) 2003: (517 55 .11)

B. f. 3 (Jan)
Sire: Royal Academy (Nijinsky II) $20,000
Dam: Magic Feeling*Ire (Magical Wonder)
Br: R C Durr & George Budig (Ky)
Tr: Carroll David(8 1 1 1 .12) 2003:(132 35 .27)

L 119

	Life	2 M 0 0	$1,680 73	D.Fst	0 0 0 0	$0 -
	2004	1 M 0 0	$1,680 73	Wet(297)	0 0 0 0	$0 -
	2003	1 M 0 0	$0 19	Turf(284)	2 0 0 0	$1,680 73
	FG ⑦	0 0 0 0	$0 -	Dst⑦(299)	1 0 0 0	$0 19

| 3Jan04–7FG fm *1⅟₁₆ ⑦:23¹ :47⁴ 1:13²1:45¹ | ⑥Md Sp Wt 28k | 73 10¹¹14¹¹15 10¹0 6⁷⅟₂ 45⅟₄ | Martinez J R Jr | L119 | 19.10 | 81– 14 Dynamia119⁴⅟₄ Sea Merge119¹ Vagabond Saint119no | Late interest 12 |
| 20Nov03–5CD gd 1 | ⑦:24 :47⁴ 1:14 1:40 | ⑥Md Sp Wt 43k | 19 5 7⅟₂ 11²1 2²1 9¹9 10²5⅟₂ | Martinez J R Jr | L122 fb | 5.90 | 46– 25 Code Song121²⅟₂ High Speed Access122⁴ BaxterHall122nk | Chased,4w,tired 10 |

WORKS: Dec27 FG 4f fst :49⁴ B 21/70 Dec21 FG 5f fst 1:01² B 6/52 Dec8 FG 4f fst :49² B 12/54 Nov13 CD 3f fst :38³ B 9/12 Nov7 CD 5f fst 1:00³ Bg 20 Oct31 CD 5f fst 1:01² Bg 13/42
TRAINER: Turf(18 .28 $6.66) Routes(60 .28 $2.93) MdnSpWt(38 .18 $2.77)

handwritten: 2

9 Sasafras

Turqse — Own: Catherine A Dillon — Kelly Green, Kelly Green Shamrock On
MARTIN E M JR (190 32 30 26 .17) 2003: (1175 203 .17)

B. f. 3 (Apr)
Sire: Tomorrows Cat (Storm Cat) $7,500
Dam: Worldly Nell (World Appeal)
Br: Cynthia McKee (NY)
Tr: Badgett William Jr(26 3 3 6 .12) 2003:(133 22 .17)

L 119

	Life	3 M 0 0	$0 35	D.Fst	2 0 0 0	$0 21
	2003	3 M 0 0	$0 35	Wet(324)	1 0 0 0	$0 35
	2002	0 M 0 0	$0 -	Turf(325*)	0 0 0 0	$0 -
	FG ⑦	0 0 0 0	$0 -	Dst⑦(296)	0 0 0 0	$0 -

Previously trained by Sciacca Gary

18Oct03–1Bel gd 1 ⊗ :23² :47² 1:13²1:40	⑥Md Sp Wt 42k	35 1 7¹⅟₄ 6⁴ 8¹⅟₄ 8¹4⅟₄	Castellano J J	L119	20.20	52– 26 Leedle Dee119⁴⅟₂ Tough City Girl119no Cat's Roar114no	No response 12
25Sep03–8Bel fst 7f	:22⁵ :46 1:11¹1:24⁴	⑤Md Sp Wt 41k	21 3 3 5⁴⅟₂ 8⁹ 9¹4 7¹8	Espinoza J L	119	90.75	48– 21 So Sweet a Cat119⁵ High Peaks119³⅟₄ Art of Dance119¹⅟₂	Inside trip, tired 11
27Aug03–2Sar fst 5⅟₂f	:22 :46 1:11³1:18²	⑤Md Sp Wt 41k	17 2 11 9⁶⅟₂ 8¹0 9²0 9²3⅟₂	Bridgmohan S X	119	42.50	60– 16 HurrcnHnnh119⁸⅟₂ NursCulkn119²⅟₂ BoldJublton119⅟₂	Bumped backstretch 11

WORKS: 1stW/Tm(16 .25 $3.19) 61-180Days(27 .04 $0.77) Dirt/Turf(18 .28 $4.56) Turf(67 .21 $2.12) Routes(80 .16 $1.77)
(WORKS line partially:) Jan4 FG 4f fst 1:04 B 41/46 Dec17 Crc 4f fst :49³ Bg 23/42 Nov25 Crc 4f fst :50¹ Bg 28/58 Nov22 Crc 4f fst :49 B 60/85

handwritten: 2

10 Make My Heart Sing

Purple — Own: Christopher Ellis — Purple, Red Heart, Red Sleeves
LOVATO F JR (152 16 16 20 .11) 2003: (697 82 .12)

B. f. 3 (Apr)
Sire: King of Kings*Ire (Sadler's Wells) $5,612
Dam: Songlines (Diesis*GB)
Br: Liberation Farm & Oratis Thoroughbreds (Ky)
Tr: Gabriel Toni(2 0 0 0 .00) 2003:(29 5 .17)

handwritten: Roomy

119

	Life	0 M 0 0	$0 -	D.Fst	0 0 0 0	$0 -
	2004	0 M 0 0	$0 -	Wet(193)	0 0 0 0	$0 -
	2003	0 M 0 0	$0 -	Turf(281)	0 0 0 0	$0 -
	FG ⑦	0 0 0 0	$0 -	Dst⑦(240)	0 0 0 0	$0 -

WORKS: Jan13 FG 5f fst 1:03 B 2/2 Jan5 FG 5f fst 1:03 H 22/49 Dec29 FG TR 5f fst 1:02⁴ Hg 3/7 Dec19 FG 4f fst :51³ Bg 28/36 Oct7 VHT 3f fst :40² B 2/2
TRAINER: 1stStart(4 .00 $0.00) 1stTurf(3 .33 $1.53) Turf(5 .20 $0.92) Routes(13 .15 $0.83) MdnSpWt(7 .14 $0.66)

11 Cimarron Summer

Gray — Own: J David Richardson & Tom Carey — Maroon, Tan Sash, Tan Bars On Sleeves
MELANCON G (219 32 30 33 .15) 2003: (1409 247 .18)

B. f. 3 (May)
Sire: Repriced (Roberto) $5,000
Dam: Rose of Cimarron (Mi Cielo)
Br: Hiram C Polk MD & J David Richardson MD (Ky)
Tr: Kohnhorst Richard B(16 3 1 1 .19) 2003:(125 18 .14)

handwritten: Blinkers OFF — L 119

	Life	3 M 0 0	$103 45	D.Fst	1 0 0 0	$0 45
	2003	3 M 0 0	$103 45	Wet(323)	0 0 0 0	$0 -
	2002	0 M 0 0	$0 -	Turf(317)	2 0 0 0	$103 30
	FG ⑦	1 0 0 0	$0 27	Dst⑦(329)	1 0 0 0	$0 27

| 6Dec03–2FG fm *1 ⑦:24³ :50¹ 1:16⁴1:41² | ⑥Md Sp Wt 28k | 27 2 2⅟₂ 2¹ 2¹⅟₂ 7⅟₂ 6¹³ | Meche L J | L119 b | 21.30 | 64– 21 KeytotheCt119¹⅟₂ ALuluOfMenif119³ StormStrm119no | Stalked, weakened 9 |

Previously trained by Drury Thomas Jr

| 9Nov03–6CD fst 1 | :23⁴ :47⁴ 1:12²1:45 | ⑥Md Sp Wt 43k | 45 1 75 108⅟₂ 115 1119 10²4⅟₂ | Johnston J A | L122 b | 64.50 | 59– 18 Last Song122¹⅟₄ Jinny's Gold122²⅟₄ Amanuensis122nk | Ck 1st turn,tired 10 |

Previously trained by Mott William I

| 16Sep03–2KD fst 6f | :22⁴ :46² 1:14² | ⑥Md Sp Wt 24k | 30 4 7 10⁸⅟₂ 10¹7 9¹0 7¹4⅟₂ | Bejarano R | 121 | 10.90 | 62– 22 Storm Fleet121nk Deceit121²⅟₂ Laville121⁵ | Improved position 12 |

WORKS: Jan16 FG 5f fst 1:06 B 36/36 Jan8 FG 5f fst 1:04 B 17/28 Dec15 FG 4f fst :51¹ B 47/63 Nov29 FG 3f fst 1:05³ B 71/74
TRAINER: BlinkOff(3 .33 $4.13) 31-60Days(30 .23 $3.00) Turf(31 .13 $1.59) Routes(57 .12 $1.33) MdnSpWt(22 .09 $0.75)

12 Wood Not — Own: Estate of John Franks
Lime — Green, Orange 'Jf' On White Ball, Orange
LEBLANC K P (128 11 24 10 .09) 2003: (1030 154 .15)

B. f. 3 (May)
Sire: Kissin Kris (Kris S.) $7,500
Dam: Wood So (Baederwood)
Br: John Franks (Fla)
Tr: Wilson Shane(48 3 2 5 .06) 2003:(236 23 .10)

L 119

Life	7	M	2	1	$13,360	68	D.Fst	6	0	1	1	$8,160	68
2004	1	M	0	1	$1,320	68	Wet(341)	0	0	0	0	$0	-
2003	6	M	2	0	$12,040	56	Turf(228)	1	0	1	0	$5,200	56
FG(T)	0	0	0	0	$0	-	Dst(T)(332)	1	0	1	0	$5,200	56

Previously trained by McKeever Billy C Jr
9Jan04-10FG fst 1 :241 :49 1:153 1:413 (F)Md 30000(30-25) 68 5 3$1\frac{1}{2}$ 1$1\frac{1}{2}$ 11 2½ 32¾ Bourque C C L121 7.20 72-30 Search the Sky1212 Singit121¾ Wood Not121nk Weakened 9
21Dec03-7FG fst 1 1/16 :232 :471 1:13 1:46 (F)Md Sp Wt 28k 53 6 21 21½ 2½ 56 514 Bourque C C L119 39.40 66-18 Good Humor Gal119¾ *Song Track*1191¼ Explicitly1192 Stalked, tired 11
Previously trained by Brothers Frank L
14Nov03-6Haw fst 170 :24 :474 1:141 1:48 (F)Md Sp Wt 36k 41 10 67 58 42½ 64¾ 710½ Baird E T L120 4.40 50-35 Defuhr1202 *Wretched Excess*120½ Doing It Our Way1201¼ Tired 10
10Oct03-8Haw fm 1 (T) :224 :463 1:113 1:363 (F)Md Sp Wt 26k 56 8 54 42½ 21 1hd 2nk Baird E T L118 4.70 88-06 Sahmkindawonderful118nk Wood Not1181 *Restock*118¾ Caught late 11
12Sep03-3AP fst 1 :232 :463 1:113 1:383 (F)Md Sp Wt 34k 53 5 32 63¼ 64¼ 68½ 610 Baird E T 119 3.80 65-29 JourneyFever1191¾ Defuhr119hd **TrueBlondeButy**1196 Through early, bled 8
27Aug03-4AP fst 1 :241 :481 1:14 1:41 (F)Md Sp Wt 30k 56 3 51¼ 3½ 3nk 25 210½ Baird E T 118 6.10 52-34 Anapest11810½ Wood Not118½ Bennington11810 Second best 7
24Jly03-5AP fst 5½f :223 :46 :584 1:052 (F)Md Sp Wt 30k 55 9 2 61¾ 55 56½ 65¼ Baird E T 118 63.00 82-13 Willow Cove118nk *Bad Kitty*118½ Wateree1182 No factor 10
WORKS: Jan18 FG 5f my 1:02 B *5/14* Dec11 FG 5f fst 1:023 B *5/27* Nov30 FG 4f fst :493 B *24/72* Nov3 Haw 4f my :49 B *4/24* Oct27 Haw 4f fst :484 B *9/52*
TRAINER: 1stW/Trn(23 .09 $0.43) Dirt/Turf(27 .04 $1.01) Turf(73 .10 $1.47) Routes(159 .10 $1.27) MdnSpWt(24 .00 $0.00)

Beach Side: Beach Side is by Lit de Justice, a late-bloomer who became a champion at age 6 when he captured the Breeders' Cup Sprint. Lit de Justice was bred for turf but was inexplicably better on dirt. But his sire line (El Gran Senor-Northern Dancer) is known for turf, and it is not surprising that runners by Lit de Justice are performing well on grass. Beach Side's dam is by Lion d'Or, a son of Secretariat out of champion racemare Fanfreluche (Northern Dancer), and thus a full brother to champion Medaille d'Or and stakes winner D'Accord, and a half-brother to Canadian Horse of the Year L'Enjoleur and stakes winners La Voyageuse and Grand Luxe. Secretariat is a powerful turf influence, thus Beach Side's pedigree is T^2.

True Blonde Beauty: Plenty of turf and stamina in this pedigree. Although her sire, Proudest Romeo, was 0 for 2 on turf, he is a son of Proud Truth (Graustark-Ribot sire line), and her damsire, Lyphard's Ridge, adds more turf.

Pleasure Hunt: On paper, a classy pedigree, but only so-so for grass. Coronado's Quest is more than capable of getting winners on turf, but was deemed a disappointment at stud and was shipped to Japan. Dam is a half-sister to major stakes winner Quiet American, but it is noteworthy that this royally bred filly brought only $25,000 as a yearling, indicating something amiss physically.

Lively Number: By Mt. Livermore out of a mare by Senor Pete (Green Dancer), this filly has turf from both sides of her pedigree, but the class is very questionable.

Madame Galore: Another filly with many turf influences in her pedigree (Fantastic Fellow, Deputy Minister, and Star Appeal), but the female family is weak.

Praire Katydid: By underrated sire Deerhound (Danzig), a half-brother to Weekend Surprise, the dam of A.P. Indy, Summer Squall, and Honor Grades. Deerhound is the sire of champion 2-year-old filly Countess Diana, Sassy Hound, and Deer Run. Anytime you see Danzig in the sire line, the runner automatically moves up dramatically on turf and wet tracks. Praire Katydid's damsire, Groovy, was a champion sprinter, but surprisingly, his runners were superior on grass.

Gran Lady Jade: Jade Hunter started his career in Europe on grass and is a good, if not spectacular, turf sire. The damsire is turf influence El Gran Senor, and the fourth dam is a half-sister to Arts and Letters, but this filly has shown nothing in three lifetime races, which include a dull effort on turf.

Richwood Royal: By an outstanding turf stallion, Royal Academy (Nijinsky II), this filly is out of a mare by Magical Wonder, a half-brother to Mt. Livermore, by Storm Bird (Northern Dancer). Her pedigree, combined with a good effort in her last race behind the promising Michael Dickinson-trained filly Dynamia, points her out as the one to beat.

Sasafras: Since her sire, Tomorrows Cat, is by Storm Cat, she has a license to like turf, and damsire World Appeal (Valid Appeal) was a very good turf runner. She should show better speed on grass, but her female line is very poor. T^2.

Make My Heart Sing: This first-time starter is bred strictly for grass. By King of Kings (Sadler's Wells), a multiple Group 1 winner who was the 1998 3-year-old champion in Ireland, this filly is out of the stakes-winning turf mare Songlines, who is by another strong grass influence, Diesis. Plenty of class as well; Songlines is a half-sister to stakes-winning sprinter Binalong.

Cimarron Summer: By Repriced (a son of powerful turf influence Roberto), this filly is certainly bred for grass but has a very weak female family.

Wood Not: Sire Kissin Kris is a son of Kris S. (Roberto), and it is hardly surprising that he is getting a fair amount of winners on turf. Damsire Baederwood is a son of grass star Tentam (Intentionally), whose offspring were naturally gifted on that surface. Nothing notable, however, from the dam's family.

Richwood Royal, who had a T^2 pedigree (by Royal Academy out of a mare by Magical Wonder) and had finished a closing fourth in her last race at 15-1 on turf, was the logical favorite at 7-5. But catching my eye was the first-time starter, Make My Heart Sing, who also had a T^2 pedigree (King of Kings—Songlines, by Diesis). Not only was Make My Heart Sing bred for turf, she was also bred to handle the distance of about one mile in her debut. Her dam, Songlines, was a half-sister to top-class sprinter Binalong (Known Fact), and won the 1999 Susquehanna Handicap and finished third in the Queen Elizabeth II Challenge Cup Invitational, also on turf, at Keeneland.

American horseplayers were generally in the dark about King of Kings and dismissed Make My Heart Sing, but astute handicappers who realize pedigrees can make a difference, especially on turf, took heed, especially at 21-1. Unfortunately, Make My Heart Sing ran second behind Richwood Royal, but the exacta still returned a very healthy $79.20. Beach Side, who clipped heels and fell in her last start (where Richwood Royal finished fourth), finished a closing third at 9-2 and capped off a $1 trifecta of $243.70.

FIFTH RACE

Fair Grounds

JANUARY 24, 2004

ABOUT 1 MILE. (Turf) (1.35²) MAIDEN SPECIAL WEIGHT . Purse $28,000 For Maidens, Fillies Three Years Old. Weight, 119 lbs. (Preference To Horses That Have Not Started For Less Than $25,000). (If deemed inadvisable by management to run this race over the turf course, it will be run on the main track at One Mile) (Rail at 15 feet).

Value of Race: $28,000 Winner $16,800; second $5,600; third $3,080; fourth $1,680; fifth $840. Mutuel Pool $226,374.00 Exacta Pool $165,185.00 Quinella Pool $17,161.00 Trifecta Pool $133,916.00 Superfecta Pool $48,678.00

Last Raced	Horse	M/Eqt. A. Wt	PP	St	1/4	1/2	3/4	Str	Fin	Jockey	Odds $1
3Jan04 7FG4	Richwood Royal	L	3 119 8	11	9¹	8³½	8³	32½	12¾	Martinez J R Jr	1.40
	Make My Heart Sing	f	3 119 10	12	11	9²	9⁴	6²	21¼	Lovato F Jr	21.70
3Jan04 7FG11	Beach Side	L b	3 119 1	1	7³	7²	7hd	5½	3nk	Lanerie C J	4.80
9Jan04 10FG3	Wood Not	L	3 119 12	8	3½	3³	2½	1hd	4½	LeBlanc K P	4.70
2Jan04 10FG7	Praire Katydid	L	3 119 6	2	1½	1hd	1hd	2³	52¼	Albarado R J	7.00
12Sep03 3AP3	True Blonde Beauty	L	3 119 2	4	6²	5hd	5¹	4½	68½	Laviolette B S	6.40
27Dec03 6Haw10	Madame Galore	L b	3 119 5	5	2¹	2½	32½	82½	7nk	Borel C H	33.30
18Oct03 1Bel8	Sasafras	L	3 119 9	7	41½	4hd	4hd	72	8¾	Martin E M Jr	16.10
3Jan04 7FG10	Lively Number	L	3 119 4	3	5hd	61½	6½	9³	9⁹	Pavlovic G	130.30
12Dec03 4DeD6	Pleasure Hunt	b	3 119 3	6	102½	11	11	11	101½	Perrodin E J	61.60
20Nov03 5CD8	Gran Lady Jade	L	3 119 7	9	8½	10³	10⁸	10³	11	Nichols J E	132.00
6Dec03 2FG6	Cimarron Summer	L	3 119 11	10	—	—	—	—	—	Melancon G	30.40

OFF AT 2:23 Start Good . Won driving. Course firm.

TIME :24, :48², 1:14, 1:39⁴ (:24.05, :48.47, 1:14.08, 1:39.92)

$2 Mutuel Prices:

8 – RICHWOOD ROYAL	4.80	3.20	2.40
10 – MAKE MY HEART SING		12.40	7.00
1 – BEACH SIDE			3.20

$2 EXACTA 8–10 PAID $79.20 $2 QUINELLA 8–10 PAID $54.80
$2 TRIFECTA 8–10–1 PAID $487.40 $2 SUPERFECTA 8–10–1–12 PAID $2,147.40

Ch. f, (Jan), by Royal Academy – Magic Feeling–Ire , by Magical Wonder . Trainer Carroll David. Bred by R C Durr & George Budig (Ky).

RICHWOOD ROYAL reserved early, advanced off the rail, circled foes for the drive, drifted in when getting by the leaders and cleared late. MAKE MY HEART SING well back early, advanced entering the second turn, swung out for the drive and closed gamely for second. BEACH SIDE unhurried along the inside, advanced around the second turn, steadied behind foes entering the drive, angled out and closed willingly. WOOD NOT forwardly placed three wide, moved up to prompt PRAIRE KATYDID around the second turn, gained the edge a furlong out and then faltered late. PRAIRE KATYDID set a pressured pace and weakened inside the final sixteenth. TRUE BLONDE BEAUTY never far back, had no final kick. MADAME GALORE between until before the second turn, gave way. SASAFRAS forwardly placed, weakened. LIVELY NUMBER was outrun. PLEASURE HUNT was always back. GRAN LADY JADE showed little. CIMARRON SUMMER broke down entering the first turn and was vanned off.

Owners– 1, Durr Robert C; 2, Elia Christopher; 3, Schaffrick William C; 4, Franks Farms; 5, Hamilton Sara M; 6, Jayaraman Kalarikkal K and Vilasini D; 7, Hamilton William A; 8, Dillon Catherine A; 9, Clifton Beth H and Lester Mary; 10, Emerald Pastures Corp Inc; 11, Wampler Ernest; 12, Richardson J David and Carey Tom

Trainers– 1, Carroll David; 2, Gabriel Toni; 3, Kassen David C; 4, Wilson Shane; 5, Barnett Bobby C; 6, Daly Patrick J; 7, Matthews Doug; 8, Badgett William Jr; 9, Kessinger Burk Jr; 10, Romero Terry M; 11, Trivigno Michael; 12, Kohnhorst Richard B

$2 Pick Three (3–2–8) Paid $56.00 ; Pick Three Pool $10,351 .
$2 Pick Four (8–3–2–8) Paid $319.20 ; Pick Four Pool $14,260 .

EXAMPLE 3

Betting maiden special weight races

Another example of how the sire and dam affect the running style and class of a young horse was demonstrated in a six-furlong maiden race for 3-year-old fillies on dirt at Ellis Park on July 18, 2004. Below is a pre-race pedigree analysis:

Lovers Bend: By Arch (Kris S.) out of a Deputy Minister mare, she figured to benefit from a move to the turf after three dull starts on dirt and improved slightly on that surface in her last start. Dubious move back to dirt. Toss.

6

Ellis Park *6 Furlongs* (1:09) ⒻMd Sp Wt 25k Purse $25,000 (include $8,000 KTDF – KY TB Devt Fund) For Maidens, Fillies And Mares Three Years Old And Upward. Three Year Olds, 117 lbs.; Older, 123 lbs.

6 FURLONGS

1 Lovers Bend
Own: Ducharme Stables
Red Green, Cream 'D' On Maroon Ball, Green
PRESCOTT R (58 4 8 8 .07) 2004: (941 134 .14)
B. f. 3 (May) KEENOV01 $40,000
Sire: Arch (Kris S.) $5,000
Dam: Love From the Air (Deputy Minister)
Br: Silver Springs Stud Farm Inc & Mrs J Costelloe (Ky)
Tr: Pate David E(5 0 0 1 .00) 2004:(55 7 .13)
L 117

Life	4	M	0	0	$1,560	49	D.Fst	2	0	0	0	$1,230 49
2004	4	M	0	0	$1,560	49	Wet(418)	1	0	0	0	$160 16
2003	0	M	0	0	$0	-	Turf(319)	1	0	0	0	$170 49
EIP	0	0	0	0	$0	-	Dst(340)	2	0	0	0	$1,230 49

8Jly04-5EIP gd 5½f Ⓣ :221 :472 1:001 1:07 3↑ⒻMd Sp Wt 25k 49 9 6 42½ 51½ 64½ 66 Prescott R L117 44.60 61-33 Blush117nk Granita1171½ Sistine's Hope117nk 4-5w,tired 10
6May04-10CD fst 6f :213 :452 :58 1:113 3↑ⒻMd 30000(30-25) 9 5 12 1215 1219 1220 1222 McKee J L116 10.00 61-18 ChampgneNow1141¾ WouldYouBeMine1231 Tolu1111½ Dwelt start,outrun 12
14Apr04-6Kee fst 6f :214 :451 :581 1:123 ⒻMd Sp Wt 49k 40 2 7 710 511 49½ 510½ Shepherd J5 L114 b 70.60 67-14 *Wildcard Cat*1191¾ Royalty Gal1194½ Two Hearts1191 Drift in bmp start 8
1Apr04-8TP my 6½f :224 :462 1:114 1:182 ⒻMd Sp Wt 32k 16 11 2 95½ 86½ 714 719 Herrell J C L122 b 32.20 69-11 Decidedlydiffernt122¾ Asfstsshcnnow1221 *SkyHirss*122¾ 5 wide late turn 11
WORKS: Jly1 EIP 4f fst :50 Bg 2/16 Jun25 Kee 5f fst 1:03 B 6/6 Jun12 Kee 4f fst :49 B 11/32 ●Jun5 Kee 4f fst :473 Hg 1/35 May28 Kee 4f gd :491 Bg 2/5 May13 Kee 4f fst :494 Bg 10/18
TRAINER: 2Off45-180(11 .18 $2.22) Turf/Dirt(10 .30 $2.06) Dirt(117 .13 $1.58) Sprint(88 .12 $1.12) MdnSpWt(51 .12 $1.61)

2 Crafty Closure
Own: Bennett Bell Williams
White Lime, Lime Cap
ZUNIGA J E (33 0 5 3 .00) 2004: (639 92 .14)
Ch. f. 3 (Jan)
Sire: Crafty Friend (Crafty Prospector) $7,500
Dam: Atlantis (Time for a Change)
Br: John R Williams & Bennett B Williams (Ky)
Tr: Bell John A IV(—) 2004:(41 3 .07)
L 117

Life	1	M	0	0	$217	6	D.Fst	1	0	0	0	$217 6
2004	1	M	0	0	$217	6	Wet(284)	0	0	0	0	$0 -
2003	0	M	0	0	$0	-	Turf(234*)	0	0	0	0	$0 -
EIP	0	0	0	0	$0	-	Dst(307)	1	0	0	0	$217 6

4May04-6Mnr fst 6f :221 :463 :593 1:132 3↑ⒻMd Sp Wt 21k 6 6 8 710 717 815 720½ Parker D L LB115 5.50 52-23 Exit Laughing1213½ Fly Amery Fly1132½ Olivia's Dollar1212½ Offered little 8
WORKS: Jly8 TTC 3f fst :382 B 6/7 May29 TTC 4f fst :523 B 27/28 Apr29 TTC 3f fst :39 B 7/8
TRAINER: 61-180Days(7 .14 $5.57) 2ndStart(4 .00 $0.00) Dirt(130 .12 $2.12) Sprint(69 .10 $2.26) MdnSpWt(18 .22 $3.23)

3 La Tache
Own: Mike G Rutherford
Blue Blue, Orange Star, Blue Bars On Orange
GUIDRY M (6 2 0 3 .33) 2004: (526 74 .14)
Ch. f. 3 (Feb)
Sire: Hennessy (Storm Cat) $35,000
Dam: Copano Bay (Seattle Slew)
Br: Mike G Rutherford Sr (Ky)
Tr: Brothers Frank L(—) 2004:(54 11 .20)
L 117

Life	1	M	0	0	$0	51	D.Fst	1	0	0	0	$0 51
2004	1	M	0	0	$0	51	Wet(361)	0	0	0	0	$0 -
2003	0	M	0	0	$0	-	Turf(329)	0	0	0	0	$0 -
EIP	0	0	0	0	$0	-	Dst(343)	1	0	0	0	$0 51

19Jun04-10CD fst 6f :212 :453 :572 1:094 3↑ⒻMd Sp Wt 45k 51 11 11 810 710 610 615¾ Martinez W 116 15.50 76-11 *Gilded Gold*1163½ Don't Tell Ashlie1167¾ Toot's Lil Chic116¾ No rally 12
WORKS: Jly15 CD 3f fst :361 B 2/12 Jly9 CD 4f fst :503 B 35/40 Jly1 CD 4f fst :474 B 5/30 Jun13 CD 5f gd 1:02 Bg 6/15 Jun6 CD 5f fst 1:004 B 14/30 ●May30 CD 5f sly 1:001 B 1/14
TRAINER: 2ndStart(31 .06 $1.00) 1stLasix(20 .20 $2.40) Dirt(154 .16 $2.24) Sprint(85 .16 $2.99) MdnSpWt(84 .13 $2.44)

4 Trulips
Own: Coffeepot Stables
Yellow Maroon And White Blocks, White Band On
CASTANON J L (31 5 2 6 .16) 2004: (652 87 .13)
Ch. f. 3 (Mar) KEEAPR03 $70,000
Sire: Elusive Quality (Gone West) $41,294
Dam: Lip Sing (Clever Trick)
Br: Dr & Mrs A Leonard Pineau (Md)
Tr: O'Callaghan Niall M(—) 2004:(97 11 .11)
L 117

Life	2	M	0	0	$870	21	D.Fst	0	0	0	0	$0 -
2004	2	M	0	0	$870	21	Wet(326)	2	0	0	0	$870 21
2003	0	M	0	0	$0	-	Turf(283)	0	0	0	0	$0 -
EIP	0	0	0	0	$0	-	Dst(423)	1	0	0	0	$145 13

Previously trained by Huffman Pat
18Jan04-5TP my 5½f :233 :474 1:003 1:072 ⒻMd Sp Wt 25k 21 1 8 68½ 610 412 410¾ Herrell J C L122 8.60 70-19 Royal Banker1228 Missing Jackie1222 Hurricane Natalie122¾ No threat 8
3Jan04-7TP my 6f :221 :461 :59 1:121 ⒻMd Sp Wt 24k 13 3 12 118½ 1111 1018 920¼ Chavez C R L122 f 39.20 64-17 PlumlakeLady122½ *CleverMaid*1222 *TheWrongFce*1223¾ Shuffled back start 12
WORKS: Jly16 CD 4f fst :491 B 19/52 Apr18 CD 5f fst 1:02 B 18/43
TRAINER: 1stW/Trn(19 .00 $0.00) +180Days(25 .00 $0.00) Dirt(242 .12 $1.65) Sprint(115 .12 $2.11) MdnSpWt(75 .12 $2.77)

5 Freedom Fries
Own: B Wayne Hughes
Green Purple And Orange Quarters, Orange
BLANC B (5 0 4 0 .00) 2004: (295 32 .11)
Ch. f. 3 (Feb) KEESEP02 $300,000
Sire: French Deputy (Deputy Minister) $28,906
Dam: Affirmative Choice (Affirmed)
Br: Frederick J Seitz (Ont-C)
Tr: McGee Paul J(—) 2004:(132 24 .18)
L 117

Life	3	M	1	0	$7,200	73	D.Fst	1	0	1	0	$7,200 73
2004	3	M	1	0	$7,200	73	Wet(371)	1	0	0	0	$0 60
2003	0	M	0	0	$0	-	Turf(321)	1	0	0	0	$0 49
EIP	0	0	0	0	$0	-	Dst(385)	1	0	1	0	$7,200 73

12Jun04-12CD yl 1 Ⓣ :243 :492 1:15 1:401 3↑ⒻMd Sp Wt 38k 49 2 11 1011 11 913 89¼ 810½ Borel C H L116 9.50 57-25 Moonlight Cruise1161½ *What to Wear*1113 Thin Air1161 Passed tired foes 11
14May04-10CD sly 1 :223 :453 1:111 1:384 3↑ⒻMd Sp Wt 44k 60 2 10 12 1010 1015 815 712¼ Butler D P L116 8.00 64-24 *Too Much Class*1164¾ Moon Dolly1171¼ Two Hearts116¾ Improved position 12
24Apr04-5CD fst 6f :214 :46 :582 1:113 3↑ⒻMd Sp Wt 42k 73 9 12 1114 1011 68 22½ Butler D P L115 90.10 80-16 MossRose1152½ FreedomFries1153¾ ShsEnough1151½ Near inside,gaining 12
WORKS: Jly12 CD 5f fst 1:021 B 10/20 Jly5 CD 5f fst 1:05 B 17/17 Jun28 CD 4f fst :511 B 35/39 Jun10 CD 3f fst :37 B 8/18 Jun3 CD 5f fst 1:04 B 11/14 May27 CD 5f gd 1:021 B 8/14
TRAINER: Turf/Dirt(25 .12 $1.12) Route/Sprint(43 .12 $0.57) 31-60Days(136 .16 $1.44) Dirt(372 .16 $1.52) Sprint(268 .16 $1.47) MdnSpWt(84 .08 $0.97)

6 Present
Own: Jo L Williams
Black Light Blue, Grey Chevron, Grey Cap
BUTLER D P (26 3 2 6 .12) 2004: (330 29 .09)
B. f. 3 (Feb)
Sire: Subordination (Mt. Livermore) $5,000
Dam: Coronation Bay (Eskimo)
Br: Jo Williams (Ky)
Tr: Vance David R(5 1 0 0 .20) 2004:(152 19 .12)
L 117

Life	4	M	0	0	$0	61	D.Fst	1	0	0	0	$0 36
2004	4	M	0	0	$0	61	Wet(344)	2	0	0	0	$0 61
2003	0	M	0	0	$0	-	Turf(231)	1	0	0	0	$0 24
EIP	0	0	0	0	$0	-	Dst(318)	1	0	0	0	$0 61

5Jun04-2CD fst 1 1/16 :24 :483 1:14 1:452 3↑ⒻMd Sp Wt 46k 36 5 66 43 63½ 714 723¼ Johnston J A L116 b 80.60 58-16 *Teenage Temper*1168¼ Struttin'1233½ Mazel Tov1162 Moved inside,tired 8
19May04-10CD yl 1 1/16 Ⓣ :242 :491 1:142 1:453 3↑ⒻMd Sp Wt 46k 24 2 33½ 32 78½ 820 824¾ Shepherd J5 L111 b 64.20 51-24 Hold a Moonbeam1161 Erhu1163¼ Aimer116¾ Tired,far turn 10
30Apr04-11CD my 1 1/16 :234 :48 1:14 1:461 3↑ⒻMd Sp Wt 45k 20 6 11 14 11 15 1017 927 835¾ Shepherd J5 L110 b 43.40 41-17 TwoMIHII123no *SusnsAngl*1152 MoonlghtCrs1158 Slow start,bmp,squeeze 11
28Mar04-10OP sly 6f :214 :454 :582 1:11 ⒻMd Sp Wt 32k 61 3 5 69 76½ 68 66½ Berry M C L117 62.10 78-15 Riverbrook1173½ Right Mix117nk Destiny Bay1171¼ Little impact 9
WORKS: Jly9 CD 4f fst :50 B 30/40 Jun2 CD 4f fst :481 B 11/51 Apr28 CD 4f fst :524 B 33/33 Apr21 CD 5f fst 1:012 B 4/15
TRAINER: Route/Sprint(40 .12 $0.66) 31-60Days(83 .17 $1.78) Dirt(390 .14 $1.52) Sprint(210 .11 $1.28) MdnSpWt(102 .07 $0.65)

7 Miss Magnolia
Own: North Wales Farm LLC
Orange Green, Tan Blocks, White Sleeves, Green
MARTINEZ J R JR (29 5 2 4 .17) 2004: (307 27 .09)
Dk. b or br f. 3 (Mar) KEEAPR03 $55,000
Sire: Forestry (Storm Cat) $50,000
Dam: Bangled (Alysheba)
Br: Brylynn Farm Inc (Fla)
Tr: Byrne Patrick B(1 1 0 0 1.00) 2004:(60 11 .18)
L 117

Life	1	M	0	0	$0	40	D.Fst	1	0	0	0	$0 40
2004	1	M	0	0	$0	40	Wet(345)	0	0	0	0	$0 -
2003	0	M	0	0	$0	-	Turf(322)	0	0	0	0	$0 -
EIP	0	0	0	0	$0	-	Dst(419)	0	0	0	0	$0 -

26Jun04-2CD fst 7f :223 :454 1:12 1:244 3↑ⒻMd Sp Wt 45k 40 1 5 1hd 1hd 87½ 915 Peck B D L116 b 14.10 63-15 FvortGrl1162½ HonourblAsst116nk Dputymyormrgrt1161 Dueled,gave way 10
WORKS: Jun18 CD 4f fst :481 Bg 5/26 May28 CD 5f fst 1:012 Bg 9/20 May19 CD 4f fst :493 B 26/46 May8 CD 3f fst :352 Bg 2/13
TRAINER: 2ndStart(19 .37 $1.78) Dirt(131 .25 $1.47) Sprint(72 .26 $1.53) MdnSpWt(55 .27 $1.73)

8 Red Blaze
Own: Windmill Manor Farm
Pink Red, Black Chevrons, Black And Gold
DEJARANO R (49 19 11 5 .39) 2004: (1053 204 .25)
B. f. 3 (Apr) KEESEP02 $80,000
Sire: Red Ransom (Roberto) $49,553
Dam: [illegible] (Royal Academy)
Br: Robert E Sangster & Ben Sangster (Ky)
Tr: Werner Ronny(3 2 1 0 .67) 2004:(146 27 .18)
Ⓛ 117

Life	0	M	0	0	$0	-	D.Fst	0	0	0	0	$0 -
2004	0	M	0	0	$0	-	Wet(318)	0	0	0	0	$0 -
2003	0	M	0	0	$0	-	Turf(322)	0	0	0	0	$0 -
EIP	0	0	0	0	$0	-	Dst(310)	0	0	0	0	$0 -

WORKS: Jly11 CD 5f fst 1:04 B 10/10 Jun30 CDT 5f fst 1:011 B 2/4 Jun24 CD 6f fst 1:15 B 1/2 Jun16 CD 5f fst 1:011 Bg 3/22 Jun2 Kee 5f gd 1:024 B 7/8
TRAINER: 1stStart(65 .15 $1.70) 1stLasix(7 .29 $3.11) Dirt(343 .22 $1.73) Sprint(304 .21 $1.73) MdnSpWt(118 .18 $1.43)

9 Perspicacity
Own: C Steven Duncker
Turquoise Pink, Black Blocks On Sleeves, Pink Cap
JOHNSON J M (12 2 1 2 .17) 2004: (439 36 .08)

B. f. 3 (Mar) KEESEP02 $170,000
Sire: Carson City (Mr. Prospector) $35,000
Dam: Not So Careless (Desert Wine)
Br: Ray Stark (Ky)
Tr: Huffman William G(3 0 0 2 .00) 2004:(63 8 .13)

L 117

Life	1	M	0	0	$0	36	D.Fst	0	0	0	0	$0	-
2004	1	M	0	0	$0	36	Wet(401)	1	0	0	0	$0	36
2003	0	M	0	0	$0	-	Turf(243)	0	0	0	0	$0	-
EIP	0	0	0	0	$0	-	Dst(386)	0	0	0	0	$0	-

12Jun04-4CD sly 6½f :223 :463 1:13 1:194 3↑ Ⓕ Md Sp Wt 44k 36 2 10 44 88¼ 810 914¾ Melancon L L116 15.40 58- 17 Private Joke1163¾ *Speedy Sunrise*1162¼ Two Punch Gal1163 Inside,tired 12
WORKS: Jly18 CD 3f fst :37 B *2/5* Jly9 CD 4f fst :492 B *25/40* Jun29 CD 4f fst :491 B *28/46* Jun9 CD 4f fst :482 B *12/57* Jun3 CD 4f fst :493 Bg *18/34* May18 CD 5f fst 1:031 B *18/24*
TRAINER: 2ndStart(11 .00 $0.00) 31-60Days(50 .16 $3.12) Dirt(157 .13 $2.14) Sprint(80 .14 $2.99) MdnSpWt(41 .07 $0.84)

10 Send for an Angel
Own: Oratis Thoroughbreds
Purple Black, Red Heart, Black Cap
MCKEE J (41 9 8 3 .22) 2004: (803 113 .14)

Dk. b or br f. 3 (May)
Sire: Southern Halo (Halo) $21,050
Dam: Schematic (Upper Nile)
Br: Liberation Farm & Oratis Thoroughbreds (Ky)
Tr: Bradley William(8 0 0 0 .00) 2004:(122 13 .11)

L 117

Life	4	M	1	1	$8,075	71	D.Fst	4	0	1	1	$8,075	71
2004	2	M	1	1	$7,200	71	Wet(394)	0	0	0	0	$0	-
2003	2	M	0	0	$875	35	Turf(302)	0	0	0	0	$0	-
EIP	0	0	0	0	$0	-	Dst(371)	1	0	0	1	$2,400	62

25Jun04-6CD fst 6½f :223 :454 1:11 1:174 3↑ Ⓕ Md 50000(50-40) 71 2 10 65¼ 65½ 34 22 Velasquez C L116 b 13.60 80- 16 Myfvoritepssion1162 SendfornAngl1165½ JssisChnc1162 5-6w bid,2ndbest 10
3Jun04-4CD fst 6f :22 :462 :582 1:11 3↑ Ⓕ Md 50000(50-40) 62 5 7 72¾ 66½ 46 36½ Velasquez C L116 b 28.60 79- 14 ILovthOrgn1161½ *Myfvoritpssion*1165 SndfornAngl1163½ No final response 10
10Oct03-2TP fst 6½f :231 :464 1:13 1:20 Ⓕ Md Sp Wt 25k 35 8 6 93½ 85¼ 79½ 78½ Thompson T J L121 17.50 68- 17 U Got theTouch121½ LaLunadeOro1212 SophiasHumor1141¼ 4-5 wide turn 10
4Sep03-6TP fst 5f :232 :464 :584 Ⓕ Md Sp Wt 22k 35 2 7 78¼ 611 511 413½ McKee J L121 6.00 76- 13 ChrismticAppl1213½ *Dorl*f1217¾ SunbmMusic1212¼ Unseated rider pst prd 8
WORKS: ●Jly15 EIP 4f fst :493 B *1/21* Jly9 EIP 4f fst :502 B *10/26* Jun19 CDT 4f gd :493 B *11/24* ●Jun12 CDT 3f fst :352 B *1/13* May31 CDT 3f gd :361 B *2/2* May25 CDT 5f fst 1:031 B *7/11*
TRAINER: Dirt(278 .10 $1.89) Sprint(207 .10 $1.59) MdnSpWt(55 .05 $0.98)

Crafty Closure: By Crafty Friend out of a Time for a Change mare, this filly has an SP^2 pedigree (speed from both sides of her pedigree). That being said, she started her career at Mountaineer Park vs. inferior fillies, and ran poorly. Toss.

La Tache: By Hennessy, out of a full sister to stakes winner Lakeway. This filly also showed little in her debut, but in this instance that race should be dismissed. Gets Lasix today after showing two very sharp works since last race, the red-hot Mark Guidry takes the call, and the pedigree screams class. Her second dam is a full sister to Saratoga Six and the third dam is a full sister to Bold Forbes. Top play at possible price due to last race.

Trulips: While she is bred for high speed (SP^2 pedigree with Elusive Quality and Clever Trick), she has shown nothing in two starts against lesser at Turfway Park in January. Toss.

Freedom Fries: A pricey ($300,000) Keeneland September yearling purchase, she finished a fast-closing second in a six-furlong Churchill debut in April, then threw in two clunkers. Although her last effort on grass was dull, it came over a yielding turf course and her T^2 pedigree suggests she should remain on grass (by hidden turf sire French Deputy out of an Affirmed mare). Consider for minor award only.

Present: By Subordination out of a mare by Eskimo (Northern Dancer), this filly has poor dirt form and showed speed but tired in her only try on a yielding grass course. She also has a strong T^2 pedigree and is a toss on dirt.

Miss Magnolia: Showed good speed in her debut before stopping in a seven-furlong maiden race at Churchill. Her trainer has a gaudy win percentage (37 percent) with runners making their second start, and most importantly, she has a speed/class pedigree. By Forestry, one of the best young speed sires, she's a half-sister to stakes winner Anklet. Expect a much improved effort today.

Red Blaze: Some Red Ransom offspring win on dirt, but their specialty is turf and this filly gets a double dose of grass from her dam-sire, Royal Academy (T^2 pedigree). The biggest pluses are her trainer, Ronny Werner, who is exceptional with young runners, and her jockey, emerging superstar Rafael Bejarano. Wait for maiden race on grass, and longer distance.

Perspicacity: Bred to be especially fast and has a classy female family. By the highly successful sprint sire Carson City, she's a half-sister to turf stakes winners Subordination and Domination. In addition, her dam is a half-sister to major group winner Cacoethes, and stakes winners Fabulous Notion and Margaret Booth. Showed nothing in sloppy-track debut at 15-1 and could turn it around today.

Send for an Angel: Has shown little against open company and her last two starts at the $50,000 maiden claiming level suggest she's a notch below these.

SIXTH RACE

Ellis Park

JULY 18, 2004

6 FURLONGS. (1.09) MAIDEN SPECIAL WEIGHT . Purse $25,000 (includes $8,000 KTDF – KY TB Devt Fund) FOR MAIDENS, FILLIES AND MARES THREE YEARS OLD AND UPWARD. Three Year Olds, 117 lbs.; Older, 123 lbs.

Value of Race: $23,800 Winner $15,570; second $5,000; third $1,700; fourth $850; fifth $170; sixth $170; seventh $170; eighth $170. Mutuel Pool $112,772.00 Exacta Pool $94,657.00 Trifecta Pool $86,815.00 Superfecta Pool $28,872.00

Last Raced	Horse	M/Eqt.	A.	Wt	PP	St	1/4	1/2	Str	Fin	Jockey	Odds $1
19Jun04 10CD6	La Tache	L	3	117	3	3	1½	1hd	11½	13½	Guidry M	4.20
	Red Blaze	L	3	117	8	4	31½	33	21	23½	Bejarano R	1.70
26Jun04 2CD9	Miss Magnolia	L b	3	117	7	1	21	2hd	34	32	Martinez J R Jr	7.30
12Jun04 12CD8	Freedom Fries	L	3	117	5	8	10	84	42	41¾	Blanc B	4.00
25Jun04 6CD2	Send for an Angel	L b	3	117	10	2	53	54	54	5½	McKee J	3.10
18Jan04 5TP4	Trulips	L	3	117	4	5	4hd	41½	62½	65½	Castanon J L	45.00
12Jun04 4CD9	Perspicacity	L	3	117	9	9	82	72	7½	74½	Johnson J M	21.20
8Jly04 5EIP6	Lovers Bend	L	3	117	1	10	64	62½	84	8¾	Prescott R	59.60
5Jun04 2CD7	Present	L b	3	117	6	6	9½	94	98	912½	Butler D P	70.60
4May04 6Mnr7	Crafty Closure	L	3	117	2	7	7½	10	10	10	Zuniga J E	95.40

OFF AT 3:07 Start Good . Won driving. Track fast.

TIME :23, :463, :583, 1:112 (:23.02, :46.60, :58.78, 1:11.40)

$2 Mutuel Prices:

3 – LA TACHE	10.40	4.60	4.00
8 – RED BLAZE		3.40	3.00
7 – MISS MAGNOLIA			6.00

$2 EXACTA 3–8 PAID $49.80 $2 TRIFECTA 3–8–7 PAID $201.40

$2 SUPERFECTA 3–8–7–5 PAID $608.60

Ch. f, (Feb), by Hennessy – Copano Bay , by Seattle Slew . Trainer Brothers Frank L. Bred by Mike G Rutherford Sr (Ky).

LA TACHE gained a narrow lead inside early, battled with MISS MAGNOLIA and RED BLAZE, put them away leaving the turn and drove clear. RED BLAZE forced the pace three abreast to the stretch and couldn't keep pace as second best. MISS MAGNOLIA battled for the lead from between foes to the lane and weakened. FREEDOM FRIES, jostled about when in tight just after the start, was outrun for a half, came out six wide for the drive and offered a mild gain. SEND FOR AN ANGEL, within easy striking distance five wide, failed to rally. TRULIPS came out bumping with FREEDOM FRIESS early, raced in contention to the stretch and tired. PERSPICACITY was outrun. LOVERS BEND was through after a half. PRESENT never was prominent. CRAFTY CLOSURE was done early.

Owners– 1, Rutherford Mike G; 2, Windmill Manor Farm; 3, North Wales Farm LLC; 4, Hughes B Wayne; 5, Oratis Thoroughbreds; 6, Coffeepot Stables; 7, Duncker C Steven; 8, Ducharme Stables; 9, Williams Jo L; 10, Williams Bennett B

Trainers– 1, Brothers Frank L; 2, Werner Ronny; 3, Byrne Patrick B; 4, McGee Paul J; 5, Bradley William; 6, O'Callaghan Niall M; 7, Huffman William G; 8, Pate David E; 9, Vance David R; 10, Bell John A IV

$1 Pick Three (3–3–3) Paid $75.40 : Pick Three Pool $13.736 .

As the chart shows, first-time starter Red Blaze was made the 8-5 favorite, and while she ran a good race, she was second best behind my top selection, La Tache, who drew off easily to win by 3½ lengths, paying $10.40. While I expected Red Blaze to be a force when she tries turf, the tote action indicated she was well-meant, and could have been used in the exotics. Miss Magnolia, my second choice, dueled with La Tache early and finished third at 7-1. The $2 exacta paid $49.80 and the $2 trifecta returned $201.40. While the exacta and trifecta were feasible, the key to the race remained La Tache, and a substantial win bet at 4-1 was a gift in itself.

HOW CLASS IN THE DAM TRANSLATES INTO BETTING OPPORTUNITIES

The most intricate aspect of pedigree handicapping requires knowledge of female families. This is the kind of information that can yield staggering results, and below are four towering examples of how knowing class in the dam can produce a major score.

Hula Queen

Trainer Luis Seglin claimed Hula Queen (Irish River—Yafill, by Nureyev) for $25,000 in late 1997 after several lackluster performances on the dirt. Although she won that day, Hula Queen was impeccably bred for grass on both sides (T^2 pedigree), and Seglin wisely placed her in an open allowance race on the surface she was bred for. The filly responded with a super effort, just getting nosed at the wire at 104-1.

In September 1999, Hula Queen rewarded Seglin's prescience by winning Santa Anita's opening-day feature, the Sen. Ken Maddy Handicap, by $3\frac{1}{2}$ authoritative lengths at nearly 15-1, and became the latest stakes winner for her extraordinary female family. With her pedigree—and stakes victory—5-year-old Hula Queen turned out to be a great claim by Seglin, as she is easily worth $500,000 as a broodmare prospect.

Hula Queen's sire, the late Irish River, was a champion at 2 and 3 in France, where he won 10 of 12 starts with one third. His name has been synonymous with class on grass since his first foals graced the track in 1983. Irish River was by far the most successful son of Riverman (Never Bend) at stud. Although his runners have won on dirt, they have been far superior on grass. Irish River's champions include Paradise Creek, Hatoof, and Brief Truce. His son Exit to Nowhere, a Group 1-winning half-brother to Machiavellian (Mr. Prospector), is a leading sire in France. Another son, With the Flow, a Group 3 winner in France, won the Belmont Breeders' Cup over Comic Strip (Red Ransom) at 17-1.

Irish River has also been an extraordinary broodmare sire. His daughters include Albertine, the dam of Breeders' Cup Classic winner Arcangues; Ballinderry, the dam of Sanglamore; Irish Valley, the dam of Alhaarth; Litani River, the dam of The Editor; Or Vision, the dam of the full siblings Saffron Walden and Insight; Primevere, the dam of champion Priolo; and Seven Springs, the dam of champion Distant View.

It is Hula Queen's female family, however, that makes her valuable as a future broodmare. Her fifth dam, Lady Be Good (Better Self—Past Eight, by Eight Thirty), is one of racing's "blue hens," a broodmare whose influence has had a profound effect over multiple generations.

Lady Be Good produced 13 foals, including four stakes winners: Discipline (Princequillo), Full of Hope (Bold Ruler), Disciplinarian (Bold Ruler), and In Hot Pursuit (Bold Ruler). Discipline played second fiddle to stablemate Queen Empress (Bold Ruler), the 1964 champion 2-year-old filly, but Discipline was a better broodmare, producing stakes winner Duty Dance (Nijinsky II), Sorority winner Squander (Buckpasser), and Fiddlesticks (Northern Dancer). Fiddlesticks was the dam of stakes winner Vivano (Island Whirl) and While Rome Burns (Overskate); the latter produced stakes winner Burning Roma. Party Manners (Private Account), All Gone (Fappiano), Lost Opportunity (Mr. Prospector), Mining (Mr. Prospector), and Goodbye Halo (Halo) all trace to Lady Be Good. Her daughter Uncommitted (Buckpasser) was not a stakes winner but produced the successful stallion Wavering Monarch (Majestic Light).

Bred to 1964 2-year-old champion and 1966 Metropolitan Handicap winner Bold Lad (Bold Ruler), Lady Be Good produced her most important foal, Bold Example. Stakes-placed in the Polly Drummond and Blue Hen Stakes at 2, Bold Example became a prized broodmare, producing two stakes winners, Highest Regard (Gallant Romeo) and French Charmer (Le Fabuleux). How influential was

Bold Example? Five different daughters produced Grade 1 or Group 1 stakes winners.

In 1989, three of Bold Example's daughters—French Charmer, Past Example, and Highest Regard—produced two champions and a major stakes winner. French Charmer produced Zilzal (Nureyev), Horse of the Year and champion 3-year-old in England; Past Example (Buckpasser) produced Polish Precedent (Danzig), champion 3-year-old in France; and Highest Regard produced Awe Inspiring (Slew o' Gold), winner of the Flamingo Stakes and the American Derby, and third to Sunday Silence and Easy Goer in the Kentucky Derby. To have three daughters produce three outstanding individuals in three different countries in the same year is extraordinary, and it was an incredible injustice that Bold Example was not named Broodmare of the Year.

Even Bold Example's unraced daughters produced stakes winners. Perfect Example (Far North) produced Culture Vulture (Timeless Moment), champion 2-year-old filly in France and champion older mare in England and Italy. Gallant Youth (Youth) produced Sharp Youth (Sharpen Up), a stakes winner in France.

In addition to Awe Inspiring, Highest Regard also produced Recognizable (Seattle Slew), winner of the Distaff Handicap. Past Example also produced stakes winner Jasmina (Forli) and Zienelle, a full sister to Polish Precedent, who is the granddam of Intikhab (Red Ransom). Besides Zilzal, French Charmer also produced stakes winner Charmante (Alydar) and Taras Charmer (Majestic Light), the dam of stakes winner Naughty Notions (Relaunch). Taras Charmer is the dam of Yafill (Nureyev), the unraced dam of Hula Queen.

Although Lady Be Good is found in Hula Queen's fifth generation (tail-female), her considerable influence is still felt through successive generations of female descendants.

This is what is known as class in the dam, and this in-depth information, combined with the powerful grass influence of Irish River as the sire, made Hula Queen a tremendous pedigree play on grass.

Hula Queen
Own: Firmamento Corp

B. m. 5 (May)
Sire: Irish River*Fr (Riverman) $25,000
Dam: Yafill (Nureyev)
Br: Gainsborough Farm Inc. (Ky)
Tr: Seglin Luis E(0 0 0 0 .00) 2004:(16 1 .06)

Life	15	5	3	1	$217,520	100	D.Fst	3	0	0	0	$4,500 64
1999	6	3	1	1	$161,620	100	Wet(333)	2	1	0	0	$8,400 69
1998	4	1	2	0	$43,000	92	Turf(330)	10	4	3	1	$204,620 100
	0	0	0	0	$0	-	Dst(0)	0	0	0	0	$0 -

29Sep99- 8SA	fm	*6½f	Ⓣ	:21^{2}	:43^{3}	1:07	1:13	3↑ⒻSKMaddyH-G3	100	8	7	$10^{6\frac{1}{2}}$	6^{6}	$6^{4\frac{1}{4}}$	$1^{3\frac{1}{2}}$	Solis A	LB116	14.80	92- 08	Hula Queen116$^{3\frac{1}{2}}$ *Desert Lady*121$^{\frac{3}{4}}$ Ecudienne117^{nk}	Far wide into lane	11
5Jly99- 8Hol	fm	5½f	Ⓣ	:21^{4}	:43^{4}	:55^{3}	1:01^{3}	3↑ⒻGreatLdyMH76k	84	9	4	2^{hd}	$2^{\frac{1}{2}}$	3^{3}	$7^{6\frac{1}{2}}$	Garcia M S	LB118	8.60	89- 05	Royal Shyness117^{2} Iza Bon Bon117^{1} Chichim117^{no}	4wd early,dueled,wknd	9
31May99- 1Hol	fm	5½f	Ⓣ	:22^{1}	:44^{2}	:56^{2}	1:02^{4}	3↑ⒻAlw 57960N$Y	97	5	1	$2^{\frac{1}{2}}$	$2^{\frac{1}{2}}$	$2^{\frac{1}{2}}$	1^{hd}	Garcia M S	LB118	*1.60	90- 10	HulaQueen118^{hd} *NijinskysPassion*116$^{\frac{1}{2}}$ Heptthlon116^{hd}	Dueled, led, gamely	5
18Apr99- 4SA	fm	*6½f	Ⓣ	:22^{1}	:44^{3}	1:07^{2}	1:13^{2}	4↑ⒻLsCngasH-G3	98	5	3	$1^{1\frac{1}{2}}$	1^{2}	$1^{\frac{1}{2}}$	2^{hd}	Garcia M S	LB112	13.40	90- 10	*DesertLady*118^{hd} *HulaQueen*112^{2} BellaChiarr115^{nk}	Bumped late,worn down	7
27Mar99- 2SA	gd	*6½f	Ⓣ	:22	:44^{2}	1:07^{3}	1:14	4↑ⒻAlw 54000N$Y	98	6	3	1^{1}	$1^{1\frac{1}{2}}$	1^{hd}	$1^{1\frac{1}{4}}$	Garcia M S	LB118	6.90	87- 13	HulQueen118$^{1\frac{1}{4}}$ *CornflowerFields*118$^{\frac{1}{2}}$ SweetNtli118^{no}	Off rail,held gamely	7
28Feb99- 8SA	fm	*6½f	Ⓣ	:22	:44	1:07	1:13	4↑ⒻOC 80k/N$Y -N	95	3	1	1^{1}	$1^{2\frac{1}{2}}$	1^{4}	3^{2}	Solis A	LB118	9.20	90- 09	Bella Chiarra117^{2} Sweet Natalie118^{hd} *Hula Queen*118$^{\frac{1}{2}}$	Early ft., tirdon rail	9
19Jly98- 7Hol	fm	5½f	Ⓣ	:22	:44^{2}	:56^{4}	1:03	3↑ⒻAlw 46000N$Y	75	6	3	$1^{\frac{1}{2}}$	$2^{\frac{1}{2}}$	$2^{2\frac{1}{2}}$	6^{6}	Davila Y B	LB119	7.30	81- 12	TempestCat116^{nk} SweetMazrine116^{1} BccrtQueen116$^{2\frac{1}{2}}$	Dueled, weakened	10
19Jun98- 5Hol	fm	5½f	Ⓣ	:21^{2}	:43^{4}	:55^{4}	1:02^{2}	3↑ⒻAlw 43680N$Y	85	5	4	3^{2}	$3^{1\frac{1}{2}}$	$3^{\frac{1}{2}}$	1no	Davila Y B	LB118	*2.10	90- 08	Hula Queen118^{no} Sugar 'n Oats118$^{3\frac{1}{2}}$ Charming Gal122^{nk}	Clear 1/16, held	9
3Jun98- 6Hol	fm	5½f	Ⓣ	:21^{1}	:43^{3}	:55^{3}	1:02^{1}	3↑ⒻAlw 47544N$Y	86	1	4	$2^{1\frac{1}{2}}$	2^{1}	2^{hd}	2^{1}	Davila Y B	LB118	4.30	90- 09	MadmeMrtini122^{1} *HulQueen*118no FncyStockings120^{hd}	Dueled, just failed	7
22Jan98- 7SA	fm	*6½f	Ⓣ	:21^{3}	:43^{3}	1:07^{1}	1:13^{4}	4↑ⒻAlw 52640N$Y	92	8	1	1^{1}	$1^{2\frac{1}{2}}$	$1^{2\frac{1}{2}}$	2no	Davila Y B	LB115	104.30	88- 12	SovietNights116^{no} HulQuen115$^{2\frac{1}{2}}$ GoodnightIrn110^{2}	Clear lead, just faild	9
27Nov97- 5Hol	wf	5½f	⊗	:21^{4}	:44^{2}	:56	1:02	3↑ⒻAlw 33924N$Y	64	8	2	$2^{\frac{1}{2}}$	3^{3}	$3^{4\frac{1}{2}}$	6^{11}	Gomez G K	LB116 b	31.00	92- 08	NughtynHughty118^{4} RedHeddDoll118^{1} GmdLFmm117^{2}	Speed, hard used	8
14Nov97- 8Hol	wf	6f		:22^{4}	:45^{4}	:58^{2}	1:12	3↑ⒻMd c-(25-22.5)	69	7	2	1^{3}	1^{5}	1^{3}	1^{1}	Garcia J A	LB120 b	3.80	79- 20	Hula Queen120^{1} Ronnie's Delight120^{2} December Bride118$^{1\frac{1}{2}}$	Ridden out	11
Claimed from 6 C Stable LLC for $25,000, Polanco Marcelo Trainer 1997(as of 11/14): (-)																						
22Oct97- 3SA	fst	6f		:21^{3}	:45	:58	1:12	3↑ⒻMd 25000(25-22.5)	57	11	1	1^{hd}	$1^{\frac{1}{2}}$	3^{1}	5^{3}	Gonzalez J C^{5}	LB115 b	*2.00	75- 18	HecsLilAngel118^{1} MrlenesQueen120^{no} Armnce120$^{\frac{3}{4}}$	Short lead, weakened	11
18Apr97- 4SA	fst	6f		:21^{4}	:44^{4}	:57^{3}	1:10^{4}	ⒻMd c-(32-28)	60	9	3	1^{3}	1^{4}	2^{1}	$4^{6\frac{3}{4}}$	Sanchez K A	LB117 b	3.00	77- 11	*TomorrowsSunshine*117$^{1\frac{3}{4}}$ CoxsDiblo117$^{\frac{1}{2}}$ NskrsLockt117$^{4\frac{1}{2}}$	Ran off to lead	9
Claimed from Al Maktoum Sheik Maktoum bin Rashid for $32,000, MacDonald Brad Trainer 1997(as of 4/18): (-)																						
27Jly96- 6Dmr	fst	6f		:21^{3}	:44^{3}	:57	1:09^{4}	ⒻMd Sp Wt 37k	64	3	6	$5^{1\frac{3}{4}}$	$4^{2\frac{1}{2}}$	$4^{5\frac{1}{2}}$	$4^{8\frac{1}{4}}$	Blanc B	LB118 b	5.00	82- 10	QueenofMoney118$^{1\frac{1}{4}}$ *CriticlFctor*118^{5} DerestPlc118^{2}	Lacked late response	11

Nanogram

When Nanogram (Quiet American—Nannetta, by Falstaff) roared home first in a maiden special weight event for fillies at 6 ½ furlongs on Santa Anita's downhill turf course in March 2000, she lit up the tote board at $152. When a racehorse wins at 75-1 it is noteworthy in itself, but what made this victory so exceptional is the fact that Nanogram was the product of a carefully planned mating, combining turf ability (Quiet American) and a high-class female family.

Her dam, Nannetta, scored her biggest victory in the 1994 California Cup Distaff at the same distance and racecourse. Her sire, Quiet American, blossomed at age 4 when he won the San Diego Handicap (defeating Bayakoa). He finished second in the Charles H. Strub Stakes (to Flying Continental) and in the Woodward (to Dispersal). In a questionable decision by the Breeders' Cup selection committee, Quiet American did not make the cut for the 1990 Breeders' Cup Classic. His scintillating victory in the NYRA Mile, where he ran the fastest mile of the year (1:32⅘), only fueled the controversy regarding his exclusion from the Breeders' Cup Classic.

Quiet American got off to a quick start at stud, siring Cara Rafaela, one of the best juvenile fillies of her generation. From the same crop came Hidden Lake, who matured late and became a champion older mare, winning three Grade 1 races, the Hempstead Handicap, Beldame Stakes, and Go for Wand Stakes.

Quiet American's stock rose considerably when Real Quiet emerged as the 1998 3-year-old champion, winning the Kentucky Derby and Preakness Stakes. Real Quiet went on to capture the Hollywood Gold Cup and Pimlico Special and is now at stud.

Nanogram was bred by Esprit de Corps, which was headed by the late Leon Rasmussen and noted pedigree scholar Rommy Faversham. Rasmussen had a 50-year career at *Daily Racing Form*, contributing his "Bloodlines" column for 37 of them. Faversham has written numerous articles for *Owner-Breeder*, *Thoroughbred Times*, *Australian Bloodhorse Review*, and *Daily Racing Form*, and along with Rasmussen, he co-authored the definitive book on female-family inbreeding, *Inbreeding to Superior Females* (Australian Bloodhorse Review, Sydney, 1999).

Nanogram

Own: Faversham Jerome, Millard, Lee and Ra

B. m. 6 (Mar)
Sire: Quiet American (Fappiano) $35,000
Dam: Nannetta (Falstaff)
Br: Esprit de Corps Stable & Millard & Rasmussen (Ky)
Tr: Vienna Darrell(0 0 0 0 .00) 2004:(122 15 .12)

Life 25 2 7 4 $189,672 96	D.Fst 3 0 1 0 $9,200 66	
2003 6 0 2 2 $38,860 93	Wet(368) 0 0 0 0 $0 –	
2002 4 0 1 1 $23,432 96	Turf(278) 22 2 6 4 $180,472 96	
0 0 0 0 $0 –	Dst(0) 0 0 0 0 $0 –	

(Detailed past-performance race lines follow)

Star Queen

As noted in my chapter in *Bet with the Best* (DRF Press, 2001), one of the most sensational betting coups based solely on pedigree occurred on May 25, 2000, when Star Queen, a spectacularly bred filly by Kingmambo out of the Seattle Slew mare Starboard Tack, won a maiden special weight race and paid $101.20.

A one-mile maiden race for fillies and mares, 3-year-olds and up, featured a full field of 12 with no apparent standouts, but pedigree handicapping yielded an intriguing possibility in Star Queen.

Star Queen began her career in France, finishing second on a soft turf course in August 1999. Almost nine months later, she returned in a six-furlong dirt race and finished last after being bumped at the start. It was basically a non-effort.

Star Queen opened at 20-1 and her odds kept rising. But her pedigree could not be overlooked. For starters, she was by the world-class stallion Kingmambo, predominantly a grass sire, but whose runners win often on dirt (led by Belmont Stakes winner Lemon Drop Kid). Star Queen had an imposing female family to boost her attraction. She was a half-sister to Derby Trial winner Patience Game (Woodman), and pedigree-wise, nothing in this field of underachieving maiden fillies was in the same league. At post time, her odds had skyrocketed to 49-1. Star Queen was always in good position behind the early pacesetters and took the lead around the far turn. She drew off in the stretch to win by $10^{3}/_{4}$ lengths. My modest $20 win bet at the Fiesta Hotel in Las Vegas returned a nifty $1,012.

With just a two-week rest, Star Queen came back in a turf race at $1^{1}/_{8}$ miles. Well-placed throughout, she finished an even third, beaten three lengths, this time at even money. Obviously, her connections held her in high esteem, for they sent her to Hollywood Park to contest the Princess Stakes. After a slow, awkward start, she finished fourth, a half-length behind 1999 Breeders' Cup Juvenile Fillies winner Cash Run, at 7-1. Returned to Kentucky, Star Queen easily won a grass allowance at $1^{1}/_{16}$ miles at 1-2. Obviously, the time to jump on Star Queen was when she was 49-1, as she never offered anything close to that value again!

2 Star Queen

Own: Highland Farms Inc
KUNTZWEILER G (95 6 13 10 .06) 2000:(513 58 .11)

B. f. 3 (Feb)
Sire: Kingmambo (Mr. Prospector) $45,000
Dam: Starboard Tack (Seattle Slew)
Br: Ross Valley Farm (Md)
Tr: Salmen Peter W Jr(24 1 2 1 .04) 2000:(97 11 .11)

L 116⁵

	Life	3 1 1 0	$25,412	D.Fst	2 1 0 0	$19,530	95
	2000	2 1 0 0	$19,530	Wet	0 0 0 0	$0	—
	1999	1 M 1 0	$5,882	Turf	1 0 1 0	$5,882	—
	CD ①	0 0 0 0	$0	Dist①	0 0 0 0	$0	—

25May00–6CD fst 1   :22⁴ :46 1:10⁴ 1:35 3↑ⒻMd Sp Wt 34k   95 8 5 53¼ 2² 12½ 110¾ Kuntzweiler G⁵   L 107   49.60 95–05 Star Queen107¹⁰ For Haymarket114½ Jayla122¹   Drew off,hand urging 12
30Apr00– 3CD fst 6f   :21¹ :45 :57³ 1:10¹ 3↑ⒻMd Sp Wt 33k   –0 2 11 9⁹ 11¹⁷ 11²¹ 11³⁵½ Hebert T J   L 112 b   16.30 59–10 Kldouny113¹¾ AmricnSlw114¹¾ Kristi'sSunshin1125¾ Bumped start,outrun 11
 Previously trained by Andre Fabre
8Aug99♦ Deauville(Fr)   sf *1 ①RH   ⒻPrix des Marettes-EBF   2⁴ Peslier O   126 *1.20   Wind Silence126⁴ Star Queen126²¾ Queen of the Park126¹⁵   4
                                          Mdn (FT)29400   Trailed to 2f out,gained 2nd 100y out.Time not taken
WORKS: Jun3 CDT 4f fst :49 B 4/15 May22 CDT 3f fst :37² Bg4/7 May16 CDT 5f fst 1:02 B 2/8 May9 CDT 5f fst 1:02³ B 1/3 Apr26 Kee 3f fst :36³ B 5/25 Apr19 Kee 6f gd 1:15³ B 1/2

Offlee Wild

During the 2003 Daily Racing Form/NTRA National Handicapping Championship, one of the races that looked like a tasty pedigree play was Offlee Wild in the Holy Bull Stakes. At the time, Offlee Wild had raced just three times at age 2, with one win and one second. But I loved the idea of him going 1¹⁄₁₆ miles.

Offlee Wild was by the successful sire Wild Again, but I was immediately drawn to him because of his dam, Alvear. A modest winner of two races in nine starts, Alvear is a full sister to stakes winner White Bridle (Seattle Slew), and more notably, a half-sister to Dynaformer. The high quality of Offlee Wild's Darby Dan female family, which produced grass champion Sunshine Forever, Kentucky Derby winner Monarchos, and stakes runners Brian's Time, Memories of Silver, Ryafan, and Darby Creek Road, was all I needed to know. Offlee Wild won the Holy Bull Stakes at 27-1 and looked like a bona fide Triple Crown aspirant. But physical problems hindered his talent and he finished 12th in the Derby behind Funny Cide, whom he had soundly beaten in the Holy Bull. Nagging problems followed Offlee Wild throughout his 3-year-old year, but he finally returned to that once-promising form as a 4-year-old under a new trainer, Richard Dutrow Jr., in an allowance race on May 14, 2004, defeating 3-year-olds Shaniko and Mustanfar. He proved that race was no fluke when he came right back to win his next start, the Massachusetts Handicap, over Funny Cide, and joined the list of better older runners.

By a popular sire who is now 24 years old, Offlee Wild is from a female family known for producing stallions, and will be an attractive stallion after his racing days are over, especially if he can add more stakes to his resume.

Offlee Wild
Own: Azalea Stables LLC

Dk. b or b. c. 4 (Apr) KEESEP01 $325,000
Sire: Wild Again (Icecapade) $50,000
Dam: Alvear (Seattle Slew)
Br: Dorothy A. Matz (Ky)
Tr: Dutrow R E Jr(0 0 0 0 .00) 2004:(372 95 .26)

Life	14	4	2	2	$523,825	110	D.Fst	14	4	2	2	$523,825 110
2004	4	2	1	0	$335,640	110	Wet(384)	0	0	0	0	$0 -
2003	7	1	0	2	$152,400	99	Turf(303)	0	0	0	0	$0 -
	0	0	0	0	$0	-	Dst(0)	0	0	0	0	$0 -

19Jun04-10Suf	fst	1⅛	:48^3 1:12^2 1:36^3 1:49	3↑ MassH-G2	**110**	1	3^1	4^2	3$^{1\frac{1}{2}}$	1^{hd}	1^{hd}	Prado E S	LB113	3.20	98-10	OffleWild113^{hd} FunnyCid117^{hd} ThLdysGroom116$^{1\frac{1}{2}}$	3wd bid 1/4,strong drv	9
14May04-7Bel	fst	1 1/16	:23^1 :45^4 1:10^1 1:41^2	3↑ Alw 48000N2x	**100**	6	5^4	5$^{6\frac{1}{2}}$	2^{hd}	1$^{1\frac{1}{2}}$	1$^{4\frac{1}{2}}$	Castellano J J	L121	2.55	93-20	*Offlee Wild*121$^{4\frac{1}{2}}$ Shaniko117$^{\frac{1}{2}}$ Mustanfar114$^{7\frac{1}{2}}$	3 wide move, clear	7
Previously trained by Smith Thomas V																		
13Mar04-13GP	fst	1 1/16	:24 :48^1 1:12 1:43^1	3↑ SkipAwyH-G3	**85**	8	8$^{6\frac{1}{4}}$	9$^{7\frac{1}{2}}$	8$^{4\frac{3}{4}}$	7$^{6\frac{1}{4}}$	8$^{11\frac{1}{2}}$	Guidry M	L114	12.70	81-15	Newfoundland116$^{\frac{1}{2}}$ SupahBlitz114$^{2\frac{1}{4}}$ BowmansBnd117$^{4\frac{1}{4}}$	3 wide, no factor	10
9Feb04-5GP	fst	1 1/16	:22^3 :45^2 1:10^3 1:43^4	4↑ Alw 36000N2x	**90**	1	5^{11}	5^{16}	4$^{4\frac{1}{2}}$	1^1	2^{hd}	Guidry M	L118	*1.40	90-21	CollateralDamage118^{hd} OffleeWild118^5 IndyDncer118^1	Drifted str, failed	8
17Oct03-8Kee	fst	1 1/16	:23^1 :46^3 1:11^2 1:45^1	3↑ Alw 54000N2x	**89**	3	8$^{7\frac{3}{4}}$	7$^{8\frac{1}{2}}$	6$^{4\frac{3}{4}}$	1^1	3^{nk}	Borel C H	L116	*1.20	81-22	PerfectCut118^{hd} CollateralDamge116^{hd} OffleeWild116$^{4\frac{3}{4}}$	Exch bmps 1/4p	11
4Oct03-9Hoo	fst	1 1/16	:22^3 :46^2 1:10^3 1:43^2	IndnaDby-G3	**88**	5	4^3	5^4	5$^{3\frac{1}{2}}$	7^8	7$^{8\frac{3}{4}}$	Borel C H	LB124	11.20	83-29	Excessiveplesur124^1 GrndHombr124$^{1\frac{1}{4}}$ *Wndo*124$^{1\frac{1}{4}}$	Inside,stalked,weaken	8
13Sep03-13TP	fst	6f	:21^2 :44^1 :56^3 1:09^2	KyCpSpnt-G3	**89**	8	2	7^6	8$^{9\frac{3}{4}}$	10$^{9\frac{1}{4}}$	9$^{9\frac{1}{2}}$	Court J K	L116	6.70	86-17	*Cajun Beat*122$^{\frac{3}{4}}$ *Clock Stopper*116$^{3\frac{1}{2}}$ Champali122$^{2\frac{1}{2}}$	Faded	11
3May03-10CD	fst	1¼	:46^1 1:10^2 1:35^3 2:01	KyDerby-G1	**92**	6	11^9	9$^{5\frac{1}{2}}$	6^4	9$^{6\frac{1}{2}}$	12$^{11\frac{1}{2}}$	Albarado R J	L126	29.90	83-06	*FunnyCide*126$^{1\frac{3}{4}}$ *EmpireMaker*126^{hd} PeceRules126^{hd}	Bmp repeatedly start	16
12Apr03-9Kee	fst	1⅛	:47 1:11^1 1:37^4 1:51^3	BlueGras-G1	**91**	3	4$^{2\frac{1}{2}}$	4^3	3$^{2\frac{1}{2}}$	3^4	3^8	Day P	L123	5.80	74-30	Peace Rules123$^{3\frac{1}{2}}$ Brancusi123$^{4\frac{1}{2}}$ Offlee Wild123$^{10\frac{1}{2}}$	Exch bmps 1st turn	9
15Feb03-11GP	fst	1 1/16	:23^3 :46^3 1:10^4 1:43^1	FntnOYth-G1	**93**	8	4$^{2\frac{1}{4}}$	5$^{4\frac{1}{2}}$	5$^{2\frac{1}{2}}$	4^6	4$^{7\frac{1}{2}}$	Guidry M	L120	3.80	85-13	Trust N Luck122$^{5\frac{1}{4}}$ Supah Blitz120$^{2\frac{1}{4}}$ MidwayCat116^{hd}	4 wide, no response	8
18Jan03-10GP	fst	1 1/16	:23^2 :47^1 1:11^2 1:43	HolyBull-G3	**99**	9	3^1	3^1	3^3	2$^{\frac{1}{2}}$	1^{hd}	Guidry M	L116	27.40	94-10	Offlee Wild116^{hd} Powerful Touch116^3 Bham118$^{2\frac{1}{2}}$	3 wide, prevailed	13
17Nov02-8CD	fst	6½f	:22^3 :46 1:10^3 1:17^1	Alw 36870N1x	**87**	2	4	2^1	2$^{\frac{1}{2}}$	2$^{1\frac{1}{2}}$	2$^{3\frac{1}{4}}$	Court J K	L122	3.40	82-15	*Rojo Toro*120$^{3\frac{1}{4}}$ *Offlee Wild*122^1 Broke Again118$^{4\frac{1}{2}}$	Pressed,no match	8
27Oct02-2CD	fst	6f	:21^2 :45^1 :57^4 1:11	Md Sp Wt 37k	**90**	7	3	3^2	3$^{1\frac{1}{2}}$	1^1	1^5	Court J K	L120	3.70	83-14	OffleeWild120^5 Outofthebnk120^{nk} *PremierRocket*120$^{6\frac{1}{2}}$	Drew off,hand urg	12
6Oct02-5Kee	fst	*7f	:22^3 :46 1:12 1:29^3	Md Sp Wt 47k	**51**	7	7	2^{hd}	1^{hd}	2^2	4$^{5\frac{3}{4}}$	Lopez J	L119 b	9.00	70-20	FlyingJzz119$^{1\frac{1}{4}}$ TenFortyEsy119$^{3\frac{1}{2}}$ IndinExprss119^1	Dueled,led,weakened	11

2

BETTING THE
2-YEAR-OLDS

BETTING 2-YEAR-OLD RACES, and first-time starters in particular, presents the biggest challenge to horseplayers because there is little to go on except for pedigree and trainer patterns. The upside, of course, is that because of the unknown factor, these races can also present great betting opportunities.

Pedigree plays its most important role in 2-year-old racing. In addition to analyzing how first-time starters will fare at various distances, the trickiest element in betting 2-year-olds is the addition of freshman sires.

Freshman sires are those stallions whose first crops of runners are 2-year-olds. Since these sires have never had any offspring to race, there is usually mass confusion as to how their babies will be most effective. Will they be precocious, win-early types with speed, or will they be slow to develop their best form and be better as they mature at age 3 and older, and stretch out in distance? To further complicate analysis, who are the freshman stallions who should be superior sires of grass runners?

In a word, the answer to all of these questions is pedigree. This chapter will unlock the mystery of playing 2-year-olds and is followed by a chapter dealing with betting the offspring of freshman sires.

In 2-year-old handicapping, the year is divided into two distinct seasons. The first half of the year belongs to runners with high speed, those who are bred to be at their best from three to six furlongs. While I am personally opposed to racing 2-year-olds in two- and three-furlong sprints in March and April (they are still growing, and pushing them to such extremes increases the likelihood of injury), the early $4^1/_2$- and five-furlong races for juveniles in April at Keeneland and in May at Belmont are usually showcases for early-maturing runners by brilliant (speed) influences.

Things begin to change in August as races for 2-year-olds start to increase in distance. That, plus the fact that these young runners can develop quickly toward the end of their juvenile year, has the potential to create attractive betting opportunities for the savvy pedigree handicapper.

HANDICAPPING FOR SPEED

The sire and his tail-male sire line is the best barometer of gauging speed in a horse's pedigree. The best sources of speed are those stallions from the sire lines of Raise a Native (especially Mr. Prospector), In Reality, and Bold Ruler (with the notable exceptions of Secretariat and grandson Foolish Pleasure, who are strong sources of stamina on dirt and turf).

Betting offspring from these sire lines is the key to winning 2-year-old races at distances up to six furlongs.

Raise a Native

Raise a Native may have been the best member of his crop, which is saying something, since the 1961 foal crop included Northern Dancer. Raise a Native never had the chance to fulfill the promise he showed in winning all four of his starts at age 2 because he bowed a tendon training for the Sapling Stakes, forcing his retirement in July of his juvenile year. After he won his debut in a three-furlong straightaway sprint at Hialeah in March, he set a new Aqueduct track record of 57⁴/₅ for five furlongs, then equaled his own track record running the same time in the Juvenile Stakes. In what was to be his final start, the Great American Stakes, he established yet another Aqueduct track record of 1:02 ³/₅ for 5¹/₂ furlongs. Veteran horsemen and distinguished journalists of that era, such as the late Charles Hatton, executive columnist for *Daily Racing Form*, were awed by his great speed.

In the 1964 *American Racing Manual*, where Hatton reviewed the 2-year-olds of the previous year, he wrote of Raise a Native:

". . . All his races were alike. He would be off in front and simply smother his rivals with speed up to 5¹/₂ furlongs, the longest distance he was asked to travel. Nobody ever got exactly to know how fast Raise a Native could run. It was never to be imagined any of those he met could cope with him. . . . Indeed, no horse ever got his head in front of Raise a Native once the off bell was sounded."

But the greatness that was forecast in his all too brief career was realized at stud. Raise a Native was by far Native Dancer's best son at stud, and his magic blood can be found today in almost every pedigree around the world. But Raise a Native cannot be categorized as just a speed sire, and it is important to know which branch of the Raise a Native line is most likely to produce precocious runners and which branch is most likely to produce horses with staying power.

Raise a Native's most influential sons at stud were Alydar, Exclusive Native, Majestic Prince, and, of course, Mr. Prospector. While 1978 Triple Crown runner-up Alydar and multiple stakes winner Exclusive Native sired many runners with speed, the majority of offspring by these sires were most comfortable at classic distances (1¹/₄ miles and beyond). Alydar's best runners were Easy Goer, Alysheba, Criminal Type, and Turkoman. Exclusive Native's best runners were Affirmed, Genuine Risk, and Our Native.

Majestic Prince, a flashy chestnut like Raise a Native, was undefeated when he won the 1969 Kentucky Derby and Preakness over Arts and Letters, and finished second to that rival in the Belmont Stakes, which turned out to be his last race. Majestic Prince was a success at stud and his runners were most effective at middle distances.

Mr. Prospector was in a class by himself. While Northern Dancer, nine years older than Mr. Prospector, stamped his greatness as a stallion by siring one top-class runner after another in Europe—such as Nijinsky II, The Minstrel, El Gran Senor, Nureyev, Lyphard, and Storm Bird—Mr. Prospector's forte was speed on dirt. But Mr. Prospector cannot be pigeonholed into a single category. His prepotence as a sire had no boundaries. His offspring won sprinting, yet many were able to negotiate classic distances. They were also exceptional on wet tracks and, as documented by his many European champions, were equally effective on grass.

As a racehorse, Mr. Prospector emulated Raise a Native's blinding speed, and while he was expected to be a decent sire of sprinter/miler types when he went to stud in Florida, nobody was prepared for the super stallion he was to become.

An example of having some knowledge of a sire line (such as Mr. Prospector's) and applying it to freshman sires occurred on July 12, 2004, at Ellis Park.

Whether it is in an open maiden race, a race restricted to statebreds, or a maiden claiming event, 2-year-olds by Cape Canaveral (a 2004 freshman sire) should never be overlooked in sprints. A son of Mr. Prospector who showed flashes of brilliance in a career cut short by injuries, Cape Canaveral is a full brother to 2-year-old champion filly Golden Attraction, and a half-brother to young sire Cape Town (Seeking the Gold). Miss Rocket Jag, a 2-year-old filly by Cape Canaveral making her first start, showed speed and just lasted to win a five-furlong $15,000 maiden claiming race by a neck, at 27-1. Getting more speed from her damsire, Mountain Cat, she had an SP^2 pedigree (speed from both her sire and damsire), and paid $56.20.

The vast majority of Mr. Prospector's sons are sources of speed and are listed below. Some of them, such as Fappiano, Gulch, Kingmambo, Machiavellian, Miswaki, Seeking the Gold, and Woodman, are noted with an asterisk, indicating that while some of their sons are speed influences, these stallions are sources of stamina. T = turf ability, and HT = hidden turf.

MR. PROSPECTOR sire line

AFLEET
      A FLEETS DANCER
      LEFT BANKER
      MR. SHAWKLIT
      NORTHERN AFLEET
      RIZZI
            RICHLY BLENDED
ALDEBARAN
ALLEN'S PROSPECT
BANKBOOK
BARKERVILLE
BIG MUKORA
CANVAS
CAPE CANAVERAL
CARSON CITY
      BOONE'S MILL
      CITY STREET
      CITY ZIP
      CUVEE
      FIVE STAR DAY
      FLYING CHEVRON
      GOOD AND TOUGH
      LEELANAU
      LORD CARSON
      ORMSBY
CAT'S CAREER

CLAIM

CLASSY PROSPECTOR

CLOUD HOPPING

CONQUISTADOR CIELO

    IRISH CONQUEST

    MARQUETRY

        ARTAX

        MAX'S PAL

    MATTER OF HONOR

    MI CIELO

    PERUVIAN

    NORQUESTOR

    STATELY CIELO

    TRULUCK

    WAGON LIMIT

CRAFTY PROSPECTOR

    CRAFTY C.T.

    CRAFTY DUDE

    CRAFTY FRIEND

    GOLDMINERS GOLD

    LIBERTY GOLD

    PROSPECT BAY

    PROSPECTORS GAMBLE

    ROBYN DANCER

        ABAJO

DANCE BRIGHTLY

DEMIDOFF

DIAMOND

DISTANT VIEW (T)

    DECARCHY (T)

    EXPLICIT (T)

DISTINCTIVE PRO

DOUBLE NEGATIVE

E DUBAI

EXCELLENT SECRET

FALTAAT (HT)

FAMILY CALLING

*FAPPIANO

      A. P JET

      ALL GONE

      CAHILL ROAD

      COMET SHINE

      *CRYPTOCLEARANCE (HT)

            MILLENIUM WIND (HT)

            RIDE THE RAILS (HT)

      *DEFENSIVE PLAY (HT)

      PENTELICUS

      PHONE ORDER

            SMOKIN MEL

      PICCOLINO

      *PRESS CARD (HT)

      *QUIET AMERICAN (HT)

            *REAL QUIET (HT)

      ROY

      RUBIANO (HT)

      SEFAPIANO

      *SIGNAL TAP (T)

      *UNBRIDLED

            GRINDSTONE

                OMMADON

            MALABAR GOLD (HT)

            NO ARMISTICE

            *RED BULLET (HT)

            UNBRIDLED JET

            UNBRIDLED'S SONG (HT)

                SONGANDAPRAYER

                UNBRIDLED TIME

            UNTUTTABLE (HT)

FASHION FIND
*FAST GOLD
      SENOR SPEEDY
*FORTY NINER
      BANKER'S GOLD
      CARTWRIGHT
      CORONADO'S QUEST
      *DISTORTED HUMOR
      END SWEEP
            PRECISE END
            TRIPPI
      FLIGHT FORTY NINE
      FORTY WON
      GOLD CASE
      GOLD FEVER
      JULES
            PEACE RULES (HT)
      MARKED TREE
      MERCER MILL
      QUAKER RIDGE
      *RICH MAN'S GOLD
            *LIDO PALACE
      ROAR
      ROYAL MERLOT
      SUNDAY BREAK
      TACTICAL ADVANTAGE
      TWINING
      WEST ACRE
*FUSAICHI PEGASUS (HT)
GEIGER COUNTER
      FREESPOOL
GOLD ALERT
GOLD REGENT
GOLD STAGE

PROSPECTOR'S HALO

GOLD TOKEN

GOLDWATER

GONE WEST (HT)

AUTHENTICATE (HT)

CAME HOME (HT)

CHANGEINTHEWEATHER (HT)

CIVILISATION (HT)

COMMENDABLE (HT)

DANCE MASTER (HT)

DOUBLE HONOR (HT)

ELUSIVE QUALITY (HT)

GONE FOR REAL (HT)

GONE HOLLYWOOD (HT)

GRAND SLAM (HT)

MR. GREELEY (HT)

EL CORREDOR (HT)

WHYWHYWHY (HT)

MUQTARIB (T)

PEMBROKE (HT)

PERFORMING MAGIC (HT)

PROUD CITIZEN (HT)

RODEO (HT)

SUPREMO (HT)

TRAJECTORY (HT)

WAY WEST (HT)

WEST BY WEST (HT)

WESTERN BORDERS (HT)

WESTERN EXPRESSION (HT)

WESTERN FAME (HT)

WINNING BID (HT)

ZAFONIC (T)

GREATNESS

GREAT PROSPECTOR

GRUB

*GULCH (HT)

    COOL CAT (HT)

    GOLDEN GEAR (HT)

    *KIPLING (HT)

    *RAGE (HT)

    *THUNDER GULCH (HT)

        *HOLIDAY THUNDER (HT)

        *INVISIBLE INK (HT)

        *POINT GIVEN (HT)

HERE WE COME

*HUSSONET

*JADE HUNTER (HT)

    *HALORY HUNTER (HT)

KAN D'ORO

KAYRAWAN

*KINGMAMBO (T)

    *DUBAI DESTINATION (T)

    *KING CUGAT (T)

    *KING'S BEST (T)

    *LEMON DROP KID (HT)

    *MULDOON (T)

    *PARADE GROUND (T)

    *UNCLE ABBIE (HT)

LINE IN THE SAND

LION CAVERN (T)

*MACHIAVELLIAN (T)

    *STREET CRY (HT)

MANCINI

MAN FROM ELDORADO

MANLOVE

MIESQUE'S SON (T)

    WHIPPER (T)

*MISWAKI (T)

BIONIC PROSPECT

*BLACK TIE AFFAIR (HT)

    FORMAL GOLD (HT)

DILIGENCE (HT)

HURRICANE STATE

MOJAVE MOON

MR HENRYSEE

NAEVUS

NATIVE PROSPECTOR

    ALOHA PROSPECTOR

NORTHERN PROSPECT

    FORTUNATE PROSPECT

        LIGHTNING AL

        SUAVE PROSPECT

NOT FOR LOVE

NUMEROUS (HT)

OUR EMBLEM

PAYNES BAY (HT)

PIN STRIPE (HT)

PIONEERING

POLISH PRO (HT)

POWER OF MIND

    POWER BY FAR

PROSPECTOR'S MUSIC

PROSPER FAGER

PROUD AND TRUE

RARE PERFORMER (HT)

    RARE BRICK

    FENTER

REGAL SEARCH

    COUNT THE TIME

*RHYTHM (HT)

SAHM (T)

*SEEKING THE GOLD (HT)

CAPE TOWN

GOLD MARKET

HUNTING HARD

MUTAKDDIM

PETIONVILLE

SEEKING DAYLIGHT

SEEK SMARTLY

SHAH JEHAN

SILVER GHOST

SILVER MUSIC

SOUVENIR COPY

STRATEGIC MISSION (T)

STUTZ BLACKHAWK

TANK'S PROSPECT

TANK

TANK'S NUMBER

TEXAS CITY

TREASURE COVE

TWO PUNCH (HT)

FISTFITE

K.O. PUNCH

PONCHE

*SMOKE GLACKEN (HT)

TWO SMART

UNREAL ZEAL

*WOODMAN (T)

*FRUITION (T)

*HANSEL (HT)

*JOHANN SEBASTIAN (T)

*TIMBER COUNTRY (HT)

*HECTOR PROTECTOR (T)

HOLZMEISTER (HT)

IN REALITY sire line

In Reality has single-handedly been the savior of the Man o' War sire line. Stallions descending from this sire line have transmitted high speed to their offspring over the last five decades. As the following list shows, In Reality's most influential sons have been Relaunch and Valid Appeal, and their sons and grandsons continue this line's legacy of speed. Note: *All* runners from this sire line are notoriously gifted on both **wet** tracks and on **grass**.

AMERICAN STANDARD

BELIEVE IT

     AL MAMOON

     BELIEVE THE QUEEN

          SPICY MONARCH

     COST CONSCIOUS

     GARTHORN

          NEAR THE LIMIT

     REALITY ROAD

BIG SAL

DIGNITAS

JUDGE SMELLS

     JUDGE TC

KNOWN FACT

     BINALONG

KYLE'S OUR MAN

PROPER REALITY

     SLICE OF REALITY

REAL COURAGE

RELAUNCH

     BRIGHT LAUNCH

     CANAVERAL

     CAPTAIN COUNTDOWN

CEE'S TIZZY

      TIZNOW

CONSCIENCE CLEAR

HONOUR AND GLORY

      PUT IT BACK

LAUNCHING

SKYWALKER

      BERTRANDO

            OFFICER

SLEW GIN FIZZ

STAR OF THE CROP

WAQUOIT

SMILE

      SMILIN SINGIN SAM

TAYLOR'S FALLS

      DAZZLING FALLS

TENTAM

      COOL VICTOR

VALID APPEAL

      KIPPER KELLY

          KELLY KIP

      LITTLEEXPECTATIONS

      MISTER JOLIE

      PROUD APPEAL

          APPEALING GUY

      SUCCESSFUL APPEAL

      VALID EXPECTATIONS

      VALID WAGER

      WORLD APPEAL

          THE VID

BOLD RULER sire line

The foal crop of 1954, which included Bold Ruler, Round Table, Gallant Man, and the ill-fated Gen. Duke, who may have been best of all, is generally regarded as the greatest of all time. Bold Ruler became the dominant sire of his era, leading the general sires list for seven straight years (1963 through 1969) and again in 1973, due to the heroics of his best offspring, Secretariat. The name Bold Ruler is unquestionably associated with speed. His runners were precocious, win-early types and he had an amazing run of champion 2-year-olds in the 1960's. He was the sire of both the champion juvenile colt (Bold Lad) and filly (Queen Empress) in 1964; the champion juvenile colt (Successor) in 1966; once again sired both the champion juvenile colt (Vitriolic) and filly (Queen of the Stage) in 1967; and of course, sired the champion juvenile colt and Horse of the Year (Secretariat) in 1972.

Bold Ruler was bred to many mares by Princequillo and his sons, most notably Round Table, and this mating "nick" was the most successful cross during the 1960's. Despite Princequillo's strong stamina influence, Bold Ruler's offspring usually demonstrated more speed than staying power. That is, until Secretariat came along.

Secretariat and Foolish Pleasure (a son of Bold Ruler's son What a Pleasure), some sons of Seattle Slew, and to a minor extent, Dewan, were exceptions to the Bold Ruler sire line. Offspring descending from these branches of the Bold Ruler sire line were not limited to being just speed influences and were very effective going a route as well as being exceptional turf influences. An asterisk indicates a source of stamina; T = turf ability, and HT = hidden turf.

BLADE

      DEE LANCE

*BOLD BIDDER

      CANNONADE (T)

         CANNON BAR

         CAVEAT (T)

AWAD (T)

CEFIS (T)

OPS SMILE (T)

SPECTACULAR BID (HT)

LENS (T)

BOLD LAD (HT)

ON TO GLORY

SIRLAD (T)

BOLDNESIAN

BOLD REASONING

*SEATTLE SLEW

*A.P. INDY

A. P. FIVE HUNDRED

*ALMOSTASHAR

*APTITUDE (HT)

*CROMWELL (T)

*CROWD PLEASER (T)

*FLATTER

*FULL MANDATE

GENERAL ROYAL

*GOLDEN MISSILE

*INDY FILM

*INDY MOOD

*JUMP START

*JUST TYPICAL

MALIBU MOON

*MINESHAFT

OLD TRIESTE (HT)

*PULPIT (HT)

*ESSENCE OF DUBAI (HT)

*SKY MESA (HT)

*ROCK SLIDE

*STEPHEN GOT EVEN

SWING LORD

AVENUE OF FLAGS

BOULDER DAM

CAPOTE

    ACCEPTABLE

    BOSTON HARBOR

    CAPOTE'S PROSPECT

    FERRARA

    HOLLYCOMBE

    MATTY G

        MAYAKOVSKY

CAYELI

CHIEF SEATTLE

COMPELLING SOUND

CORSLEW

CYRANO

DIGRESSION

DONERAILE COURT

DOUBLE D. SLEW

DR. CATON

EASTOVER COURT

EVENT OF THE YEAR

FAST PLAY

GENERAL MEETING

GOLD LEGEND

HARRY THE HAT

HICKMAN CREEK

HOUSTON

HUBBLE

KING OF THE HUNT

LEGION FIELD

MANASTASH RIDGE

METFIELD

NELSON

OCALA SLEW

SANDLOT STAR

*SCORPION

SEATTLE SLEET

       SIX BELOW

*SEATTLE SONG (T)

       *WHADJATHINK (T)

*SEPTIEME CIEL (T)

       GUIDED WAY (T)

SLEWDLEDO

*SLEW CITY SLEW

       CITY BY NIGHT

       EVANSVILLE SLEW

*SLEW O' GOLD

       *SLEW THE SLEWOR

       *THIRTY SIX RED

SLEWPY (T)

       GRAY SLEWPY

SLEWTHEBRIDE (T)

       SLEW THE SURGEON (T)

*SLEW THE COUP (T)

*SLEW THE KNIGHT (T)

*SLEWVESCENT (T)

STATELY SLEW

TURKEY SHOOT

VINDICATION

WESTERN TRICK

WILLIAMSTOWN

SUPER CONCORDE (T)

       CONCORDE BOUND (T)

       CONCORDE'S TUNE (T)

BOLD RUCKUS

       BEAU GENIUS

       BOLD EXECUTIVE

       APALACHIAN CHIEF

BOLD N' FLASHY

DEMALOOT DEMASHOOT

HIGHLAND RUCKUS

KIRIDASHI

ROWDY RUCKUS

CHIEFTAIN

FIT TO FIGHT

BLARE OF TRUMPETS

KEY CONTENDER

CORNISH PRINCE

ZUPPARDO'S PRINCE

DEWAN (HT)

GLITTERMAN (T)

TEXAS GLITTER

IRISH CASTLE

BOLD FORBES

AIR FORBES WON

BADGE

MERCEDES WON

BUSH WON

IRISH TOWER

IRISH OPEN

PLUM BOLD

ANOTHER REEF

RAJA BABA

IS IT TRUE

YES IT'S TRUE

NEPAL

RAJA'S REVENGE

ROYAL PENNANT

WELL DECORATED

FORMAL DINNER

NOTEBOOK

BOOKLET

DELAWARE TOWNSHIP

FAPPIE'S NOTEBOOK

WELL NOTED

PULVERIZING

*SECRETARIAT (T)

*ACADEMY AWARD (T)

D'ACCORD (T)

MONTREAL RED (T)

EXECUTIVE ORDER (T)

GENERAL ASSEMBLY (T)

*PRESIDIUM (T)

*MIGHTY FORUM (T)

MEDAILLE D'OR (T)

TOUR D'OR

PANCHO VILLA (T)

*RISEN STAR (T)

*TINNERS WAY (T)

WHAT A PLEASURE

*FOOLISH PLEASURE (T)

FOLIGNO (T)

*KIRI'S CLOWN (T)

MARFA (T)

FARMA WAY (T)

COBRA KING (T)

*MILITRON (T)

*MAUDLIN (T)

*MECKE (T)

NATIVE FACTOR

HONEST PLEASURE

BETTING 2-YEAR-OLDS ON TURF

It used to be if you had a 2-year-old bred for turf, you had no choice but to race him on dirt, since grass racing for juveniles was a rarity in the U.S. Thankfully, this is changing due to the popularity of grass racing and the fact that more Thoroughbreds have some grass in their pedigrees than ever before.

While most of the sire lines known for their turf prowess are also geared more toward late-developing, stamina-oriented runners (such as the Roberto line, which includes his sons Brian's Time, Dynaformer, Kris S., Red Ransom, Lear Fan, and Silver Hawk), there are many grass sires who also impart a good deal of speed to their offspring. Cozzene, Diesis, Holy Bull, and a plethora of young stallions from the Northern Dancer sire line (such as Hennessy, Tale of the Cat, Bianconi, Bernstein, Spinning World, etc.) and the Gone West sire line (such as Grand Slam, Elusive Quality, Mr. Greeley, Zafonic, Tamayaz, etc.) are having success with many of their 2-year-olds who are now able to compete on grass.

On July 16, 2004, Winsomemoneyhoney, a 2-year-old colt by 1997 Breeders' Cup Mile winner Spinning World (Nureyev), won his career debut in a 5½-furlong maiden race on turf at Ellis Park at 8-1. Winsomemoneyhoney gets speed from his damsire, Afleet (Mr. Prospector), thus his pedigree reads: Turf/Speed. Applying knowledge of turf pedigrees, pedigree handicappers had a solid play in Winsomemoneyhoney, who was an overlay, returning $19.80.

For further information on grass sire lines, see Chapter 4, "The Hidden Turf Factor."

3

BETTING THE
FRESHMAN STALLIONS

*T*HE MOST PERPLEXING element for horseplayers is betting horses by freshman stallions—that is, sires whose first crop of runners are 2-year-olds. Since these stallions have never had any offspring to race, many players are at a loss as to what to expect from them. To help handicappers get a handle on first-crop sires, I started writing an annual series for *Daily Racing Form* on how to play the offspring of freshman stallions, beginning with the freshman sires of 1999.

Pedigree handicapping is at its most powerful when it is the sole source of handicapping information, and the only way to understand how to play the offspring of freshman stallions is through pedigree analysis. Without some knowledge of pedigrees, horseplayers are betting blind—the worst way to play racehorses.

To assist serious horseplayers, the pedigrees of the 2004 and 2005 freshman sires are analyzed on the following pages.

This analysis is timeless, and will continue to aid players when offspring of these stallions turn 3 and 4. It will identify whether they will be precocious, win-early types who will be at their best at age 2, be better as they mature and stretch out in distance at ages 3 and 4, and which sires should be closely followed when their offspring perform on wet tracks and try turf.

Judy Wagner's victory in a handicapping tournament at River Downs in July 2004 (see Chapter 7, "Playing the Handicapping Tournaments by Pedigree") is a prime example. Wagner had cut out an analysis I wrote on the 2001 freshman sires, and used a 3-year-old filly by Sandpit who was 35-1 to win the $25,000 first prize and also qualified for a berth in the 2005 *Daily Racing Form*/NTRA National Handicapping Championship.

2004 FRESHMAN SIRES

(Note: RF is a symbol for the Rasmussen Factor, a significant pedigree pattern that refers to inbreeding to a superior female within five generations—through different individuals. HT = hidden turf; HT^2 = hidden turf x 2; SP = speed; SP^2 = speed x 2; T = turf; T^2 = turf x 2. Stallions' ages are current as of 2004.)

ADCAT (Storm Cat—Adorable Micol, by Riverman). Florida. Just as every son of Mr. Prospector became an automatic stallion in the '90s, the same thing is now happening with sons of Storm Cat, even if they never raced. Adcat, however, did race, and like so many sons of the versatile Storm Cat (especially if out of mares by strong turf influences), he found a home on turf, registering stakes victories in the New Hampshire Sweepstakes and Mohawk Handicap. Adcat's dam was a stakes winner in France and his third dam is Tempted, a champion bred by Christiana Stable. Expect his runners, out of mares with speed-oriented pedigrees, to perform quite well as 2-year-olds on all surfaces. A T^2 pedigree, as Riverman adds a powerful grass influence.

Adcat
Own: Gallagher's Stud Kimmel, Caesar and S

Ch. h. 9 (Mar)
Sire: Storm Cat (Storm Bird) $500,000
Dam: Adorable Micol (Riverman)
Br: Gallagher's Stud (NY)
Tr: Hennig Mark A(0 0 0 0 .00) 2004:(321 46 .14)

Life	28	5	5	3	$435,597	100	D.Fst	3	0	0	0	$3,880 50
2000	10	1	2	2	$168,546	100	Wet(382)	1	0	0	0	$0 72
1999	10	2	2	1	$203,046	99	Turf(351)	24	5	5	3	$431,717 100
	0	0	0	0	$0	-	Dst(0)	0	0	0	0	$0 -

9Dec00-11Crc	yl	1⅛	(T)	:484 1:123 1:364 1:483	3↑ TropTrfH-G3	85	9	1010	108¼	118	88¼	86¾	Santos J A	L115 b	4.70	79-11	Stokosky114¾ [DH]Special Coach114 [DH]Band Is Passing1191	No factor	11
11Nov00-9Lrl	fm	1½	(T)	:504 1:154 2:053 2:29	3↑ LrlTrfCp-G3	98	7	86¼	810	75½	51¾	2nk	Pino M G	L119 b	*2.30	91-10	Dynamic Trick119nk Adcat119½ Antitrust117nk	Rallied between horses	9
21Oct00-8Bel	fm	1⅛	[T]	:482 1:121 1:363 1:482	3↑ [S]MohawkH150k	93	5	109	108¼	94¼	5¾	1nk	Smith M E	L119 b	5.00	86-13	Adcat119nk Pebo's Guy116no Doctor Cat116½	5 wide move, prevailed	11
30Sep00-8Bel	gd	1⅛	[T]	:49 1:131 1:38 1:504	3↑ [S]ATColeH86k	85	6	104¾	104½	104¾	96¼	94	Bailey J D	L120 b	*1.70	70-25	Currency Arbitrage1161 Pebo's Guy116nk Doctor Cat116½	No response	12
Previously trained by McAnally Ronald																			
9Aug00-7Dmr	fm	1⅜	(T)	:494 1:144 1:383 2:151	3↑ [R]EscondidoH80k	90	8	98¼	107¼	96¾	45	34	Nakatani C S	LB116 b	*2.70	88-14	Alvo Certo1151 Perssonet1153 Adcat1162½	3wd into lane,3rd best	10
25Jun00-9Hol	fm	1¼	(T)	:463 1:102 1:351 1:584+	3↑ [R]JMurryMemH78k	89	4	712	712	51¾	77¾	38½	Solis A	LB116 b	2.90	93 -	*Bienamado*1217 Casino King1171½ Adcat116½	Blocked 1/4-1/8	8
21May00-8Hol	fm	1 1/16	(T)	:241 :481 1:111 1:403	3↑ InglewdH-G3	100	1	86	86	84	63½	42	Solis A	LB115 b	10.90	88-14	Montemiro1131¼ Bonapartiste118nk Takarian118½	Waited 1/4,rallied	8
29Apr00-7GG	fm	1	(T)	:243 :474 1:104 1:352	3↑ SnFrnBCH-G2	98	5	107¾	107½	85	75	44	Alvarado F T	LB115 b	13.30	90-06	Ladies Din120hd Fighting Falcon1163 Self Feeder1161	Fanned 6w 2nd turn	10
23Mar00-7SA	fm	1⅛	(T)	:473 1:113 1:344 1:461	4↑ Alw 74000N$Y	98	1	55	55½	52½	43	21	Flores D R	LB120 b	10.10	97-05	Star Performance1161 Adcat120½ Self Feeder122no	Broke out,inside rally	6
13Feb00-3BM	sly	1 1/16	⊗	:232 :463 1:101 1:432	4↑ TanfornH-G3	72	5	77½	75	710	714	714¼	Alvarado F T	LB115 b	9.10	68-21	HighTechFriend1151¼ *Wegotohaveharte*110nk BolchinsPrize1132	No factor	7
Previously trained by Hennig Mark																			
23Oct99-8Bel	sf	1⅛	[T]	:492 1:15 1:412 1:542	3↑ [S]MohawkH150k	96	7	118¾	1110	115½	42	2no	Smith M E	L119 b	3.55	56-46	Top C Jim112no Adcat1191¼ Draw Shot120¾	Inside move, missed	11
25Sep99-8Bel	fm	1⅛	[T]	:482 1:123 1:37 1:491	3↑ BelBCH-G2	85	5	910	911	99¼	910	88¾	Chavez J F	L113 b	10.80	73-24	With the Flow114½ Comic Strip1181 Wised Up112¾	Came wide, no punch	9
23Aug99-8Sar	fm	1⅛	(T)	:464 1:101 1:342 1:463	3↑ [S]WestPointH87k	94	7	107¾	119½	107	51¼	3¾	Smith M E	L120 b	4.00	96-03	Plato's Love117nk *Draw Shot*120½ Adcat120½	4 wide both turns	12
31Jly99-10Mth	fm	1⅜	(T)	:494 1:16 1:40 2:16	3↑ UntdNtnH-G1	79	2	68	54½	64½	610	613¼	Wilson R	L114 b	16.30	91-10	Yagli1241½ Supreme Sound1131 Amerique1152	Outrun	6
19Jun99-10Rkm	fm	*1⅛	(T)	1:461	3↑ NHSweepH-G3	99	2	66½	66½	67¼	52½	1hd	Hampshire J F Jr	LB113 b	9.00	104-05	Adcat113hd Hurrahy113¾ Hibernian Rhapsody113¾	Rallied 3w 2nd,up late	8
16May99-8Bel	fm	1⅛	[T]	:464 1:093 1:342 1:463	3↑ [S]KingstonH57k	95	6	45	610	47½	3nk	2no	Smith M E	L115 b	5.00	95-05	Pebo's Guy121no *Adcat*115¾ Blues Event115¾	Game finish on rail	11
17Apr99-5Aqu	fm	1 1/16	(T)	:234 :48 1:123 1:442	3↑ [S]Alw 45000N2x	90	3	510	59	55½	3½	1½	Smith M E	L119 b	4.00	89-11	Adcat119½ White Blaze119nk Senor ChopChop1213¾	Came wide, prevailed	8
10Mar99-11GP	fm	*1⅛	(T)	:512 1:152 1:394 1:512	4↑ Alw 34000N2x	84	7	62¾	63½	41½	44	53	Santos J A	L119 b	*3.10	76-20	FlorescentHlo1192¼ FindthFcts119nk *FstivBiddr*119nk	Couldn't sustain bid	9
19Feb99-10GP	fm	*1⅛	(T)	:483 1:121 1:373 1:493	4↑ Alw 34000N2x	89	4	32½	36	33	1hd	42½	Sellers S J	L119 b	3.10	85-10	Greenlander119nk *Bogatyr*1192¼ FlorescentHlo119hd	3 wide, led, weakened	10
10Jan99-10GP	yl	*1⅜	(T)	:493 1:161 1:412 2:203	3↑ MDiarmdH-G3	87	5	511	510	46½	54½	510¼	Sellers S J	L113 b	5.60	56-34	Panama City1144¼ The Kaiser1132½ Notoriety111nk	Showed little	5
14Nov98-9Lrl	fm	1¼	(T)	:494 1:144 1:401 2:031	JapanRacng57k	93	8	65¾	76¾	75¼	61	13	Verge M E	L117 b	12.00	77-23	[D]Adcat1173 *La Reine's Terms*1172¼ Karra Kul117¾	Came 6w,struck foe,drg	11
Disqualified and placed second																			
12Sep98-1Bel	fm	1⅛	[T]	:474 1:121 1:371 1:492	3↑ [S]Alw 41000N1x	85	4	75¼	73¼	54½	1hd	14	Nakatani C S	L116 b	4.90	81-12	Adcat1164 York Harbor116hd Senor Bundle114½	Split rivals, driving	12
17Aug98-9Sar	fm	1 1/16	[T]	:233 :48 1:124 1:424	3↑ [S]Alw 38000N1x	57	5	53	54	63¼	76¾	412¾	Gryder A T	L116 b	*1.55	80-05	Plato's Love1095 Caro's Bid1207 How Goes120¾	No response	10
12Jly98-1Bel	fm	1⅛	[T]	:48 1:122 1:364 1:483	3↑ [S]Md Sp Wt 36k	78	1	510	52	53¾	11	14	Gryder A T	L115 b	*1.80	85-15	Adcat1154 Blazing Saddle1102½ *Jokers Frangrance*115½	Hand ride	9
Previously trained by Kimmel John C																			
29Mar98-11Hia	fm	1⅛	(T)	1:492	Md Sp Wt 14k	67	12	2hd	21	2hd	31½	64¼	Migliore R	L122 b	12.90	79-11	GoldnMissil1222¼ *OriginlSin*122¾ ClosthBook122nk	Pressed pace, gave way	12
16Feb98-7GP	fst	1 1/16		:242 :481 1:124 1:463	Md Sp Wt 28k	41	10	55	54	56½	612	623	Davis R G	L120 b	21.30	51-29	LongPoint1202 PuppetMster1201¾ *AFltsDncr*1207¼	Middle of pack outside	11
10Dec97-6Aqu	fst	170	[•]	:24 :49 1:153 1:464	[S]Md Sp Wt 31k	34	4	32	3nk	1hd	33	411½	Migliore R	119	*1.90	52-31	Iron Cop1142½ Thunder Search1193½ Crossofthepassion1145½	Drifted	10
21Nov97-3Aqu	fst	6f		:222 :462 :591 1:122	[S]Md Sp Wt 29k	50	1	12	52¾	41¼	32½	46½	Migliore R	119	*.65	70-21	Farm Saver119hd Lauren's Lad1194 LuckyScruffy1142½	Off slowly,greenly	12

ALJABR (Storm Cat—Sierra Madre, by Baillamont). Kentucky. Aljabr has the distinction of being a Group 1 winner at 2, 3, and 4, and his best distance was one mile. His high-quality book of mares included winners and the dams of winners of the Epsom Derby, Irish 1000 Guineas, Breeders' Cup Juvenile Fillies, Yorkshire Oaks, etc., so his runners will be strongly bred for grass. While they will ultimately perform best on grass, it would be no surprise to see some of Aljabr's offspring win on dirt because of Storm Cat's brilliant (speed) influence.

Aljabr
Own: Godolphin

Gr/ro. h. 8 (Feb)
Sire: Storm Cat (Storm Bird) $500,000
Dam: Sierra Madre*Fr (Baillamont)
Br: Shadwell Farm, Inc. (Ky)
Tr: Saeedbinsuroor(0 0 0 0 .00) 2004:(0 0 .00)

Life	9	5	1	0	$593,796	-	D.Fst	0	0	0	0	$0 -
2000	3	1	0	0	$140,906	-	Wet(327)	0	0	0	0	$0 -
1999	3	1	1	0	$334,137	-	Turf(323)	9	5	1	0	$593,796 -
	0	0	0	0	$0	-	Dst(0)	0	0	0	0	$0 -

2Aug00♦Goodwood (GB)	gd	1	(T) RH 1:383	3↑ Sussex Stakes-G1 Stk 410800	54¾	Hills R	133	5.50	*Giant's Causeway*126¾ Dansili1331½ *Medicean*1261¼ *Led, ridden over 2f out, headed over 1f out, soon weakened*	10
20Jun00♦Ascot (GB)	gd	1	(T) Str 1:393	3↑ Queen Anne Stakes-G2 Stk 182200	44	Hills R	133	*2.25	Kalanisi128½ Dansili131no *Swallow Flight*1283¼ *Chased leader, led 2f out, ridden, headed 1f out, soon beaten*	11
20May00♦Newbury (GB)	gd	1	(T) Str 1:373	4↑ Lockinge Stakes-G1 Stk 201000	12	Dettori L	126	*.60	Aljabr1262 *Trans Island*126no Indian Lodge126½ *Led throughout,tacked over to stands side after 1f,driving*	7
5Sep99♦Longchamp (Fr)	gd	*1	(T) RH 1:351	3↑ Prix du Moulin de Longchamp-G1 Stk 247600	43½	Dettori L	123	1.60	*Sendawar*1231½ Gold Away128hd *Dansili*1232 *Tracked in 4th,led briefly 2f out,soon wknd.Fly To The Stars 8th*	9
28Jly99♦Goodwood (GB)	gd	1	(T) RH 1:353	3↑ Sussex Stakes-G1 Stk 399300	11	Dettori L	125	*1.10	Aljabr1251 Docksider1335 Almushtarak133¾ *Led throughout,met challenge 2f out,ridden out.New course record*	8
15Jun99♦Ascot (GB)	gd	1	(T) RH 1:394	St James's Palace Stakes-G1 Stk 430400	21¼	Dettori L	126	3.30	*Sendawar*1261¼ *Aljabr*1265 Gold Academy1261 *Tracked in 3rd,dueled or led 5f to 1f out,gave ground grudgingly*	11
19Sep98♦Longchamp (Fr) Timeform rating: 121	sf	*7f	(T) RH 1:24	Prix de la Salamandre-G1 Stk 119600	1½	Dettori L	126	1.50	Aljabr126½ Stravinsky1261 *Kingsalsa*1264 *Led throughout,met challenge,ridden out*	6
29Jly98♦Goodwood (GB) Timeform rating: 109+	gd	7f	(T) RH 1:29	Lanson Champagne Vintage Stks-G3 Stk 69800	13	Dettori L	123	*.65	*Aljabr*1233 *Raise a Grand*1231¼ Gold Academy1233 *Led virtually throughout,angled over to rail,easily clear 1f out*	7
4Jly98♦Sandown Park (GB) Timeform rating: 94+	gd	7f	(T) Str 1:294	EBF Paddock Maiden Stakes Maiden 11100	14	Dettori L	126	*1.00	*Aljabr*1264 Lots of Magic1264 Pulau Tioman1261¼ *Led throughout,drew clear over 1f out,kept to task*	10

ANEES (Unbridled—Ivory Idol, by Alydar. Died, 2002). Like most offspring by Unbridled, Anees developed later in his 2-year-old season than his contemporaries, but he put it all together when it counted in the 1999 Breeders' Cup Juvenile. He was bred to run all day, but his career was compromised by unsoundness at 3 and he died prematurely before his first runners ever raced. While you would expect all sons of Unbridled to emulate their sire and be better sires of 3-year-olds as their runners mature and stretch out in distance, many sons of Unbridled have been speed influences, such as Unbridled's Song and Grindstone. Although offspring by Anees may have more speed than expected, they should still be more effective as they mature as 3- and 4-year-olds, from six furlongs to 1¼ miles.

Anees
Own: The Thoroughbred Corporation

Sire: Unbridled (Fappiano) $200,000
Dam: Ivory Idol (Alydar)
Br: Farfellow Farms, Ltd. (Ky)
Tr: Hassinger A L Jr(0 0 0 0 .00) 2004:(0 0 .00)

Life	7	2	0	2	$699,200	102	D.Fst	7	2	0	2	$699,200	102
2000	3	0	0	1	$90,000	99	Wet(414)	0	0	0	0	$0	-
1999	4	2	0	1	$609,200	102	Turf(286)	0	0	0	0	$0	-
	0	0	0	0	$0	-	Dst(0)	0	0	0	0	$0	-

6May00-8CD	fst	1¼	:454 1:094 1:353 2:01	KyDerby-G1	**77**	1	1611158	115½	119	1320½	Nakatani C S	L126 b	17.10	84 -	FusichiPegsus1261½ Aptitude1264 Impechmnt126½	Awkward,swerve start	19
8Apr00-5SA	fst	1⅛	:471 1:112 1:362 1:49	SADerby-G1	**99**	3	68	69½	68	54	46	Nakatani C S	LB120 b	4.20	84-16	The Deputy1201 War Chant1202 Captain Steve1203	Improved position	6
19Mar00-7SA	fst	1 1/16	:23 :454 1:101 1:423	SnFelipe-G2	**99**	1	65½	57	44½	43½	33¾	Bailey J D	LB119 b	3.90	86-14	*Fusaichi Pegasus*116¾ *The Deputy*1223 Anees119hd	Saved grd, up for show	7
6Nov99-8GP	fst	1 1/16	:221 :46 1:101 1:421	BCJuven-G1	**102**	9	1411148	87¾	41¾	12½	Stevens G L	L122 b	30.30	96 -	Anees1222½ Chief Seattle122¾ High Yield1222¼	Bumped start,drifted	14
10Oct99-7SA	fst	1	:221 :454 1:094 1:353	Norfolk-G2	**95**	2	67½	68½	39½	35	35	Stevens G L	LB118 b	9.50	88-15	Dixie Union118½ Forest Camp1184½ *Anees*1189½	Inside move,bested rst	6
3Sep99-3Dmr	fst	1	:224 :47 1:12 1:373	Md Sp Wt 48k	**82**	5	45	44	41¾	1hd	12	Stevens G L	LB118 b	4.90	84-09	Anees1182 Silver Axe1182½ Gilty Moment1181½	4 wide bid, driving	8
21Aug99-5Dmr	fst	5½f	:22 :452 :574 1:042	Md Sp Wt 46k	**48**	9	6	918	919	814	613	Desormeaux K J	LB118	7.70	78-14	*Tavasco*1183½ Brave Slew118nk *Valiant Vision*118¾	Lugged out start	9

BADGE (Air Forbes Won—Revenge Time, by Raja's Revenge). New York. Badge is a perfect addition to stand in New York, and his first crop of statebred foals should win often and early. Although his pedigree is top-heavy with speed, Badge was able to win the one-mile Gotham Stakes and also finished a surprisingly game third behind Charismatic and Menifee in the Preakness Stakes at 1³⁄₁₆ miles.

Badge
Own: Southbelle Stable

Ch. h. 8 (Mar)
Sire: Air Forbes Won (Bold Forbes) $2,500
Dam: Revenge Time (Raja's Revenge)
Br: Michael Anchel (Ky)
Tr: Aquilino Joseph(0 0 0 0 .00) 2004:(92 14 .15)

Life	12	5	0	4	$380,630	113	D.Fst	11	4	0	4	$356,630	113
2000	2	0	0	1	$22,000	113	Wet(336)	1	1	0	0	$24,000	77
1999	7	4	0	2	$330,370	104	Turf(302)	0	0	0	0	$0	-
	0	0	0	0	$0	-	Dst(0)	0	0	0	0	$0	-

21Feb00-9Lrl	fst	7f	:23 :46 1:10 1:22	3↑ GenGrgeH-G2	**113**	1	7	85	74½	53¼	3½	Luzzi M J	L117	3.90	96-17	AffirmedSuccess121½ YoungAtHert114no Bdg1174¾	Between foes,clolsed	9
22Jan00-9Aqu	fst	1 1/16 ⊡	:234 :474 1:12 1:442	3↑ AquH-G3	**95**	3	53½	31½	31½	53½	65½	Luzzi M J	L122	*.85	81-23	SkyApprovl115½ PrntlPrssur115½ PhonthKing114nk	Close at flanks,flatnd	8
2Dec99-8Aqu	fst	170 ⊡	:24 :473 1:114 1:403	3↑ Alw 60000N$MY	**100**	2	43	44½	31½	3nk	12¼	Luzzi M J	L120	*1.35	95-15	Bdge1202¼ PhonethKing1151 SophistictdMn115nk	Urged 4wd,edged clear	7
15May99-10Pim	fst	1 3/16	:451 1:101 1:351 1:551	Preaknss-G1	**104**	4	127½118	95¼	54¼	31½	Luzzi M J	L126	58.00	87-09	Charismatic1261½ Menifee126hd *Badge*1262½	Traffc 3-1/2,bid btwn	13
10Apr99-10Aqu	fst	1⅛	:464 1:103 1:351 1:473	WoodMem-G2	**97**	1	31½	3½	2hd	31½	43¾	Bridgmohan S X	L123	*2.00	94-09	Adonis1232 Best of Luck1231¾ *Cliquot*123no	3 wide move, stayed on	11
21Mar99-9Aqu	fst	1	:221 :443 1:092 1:343	Gotham-G3	**104**	4	105¾	73¾	32½	11½	17½	Bridgmohan S X	L120	11.80	95-15	Badge1207½ *Apremont*120¾ Robin Goodfellow1136	Split rivals,drew off	11
27Feb99-8Aqu	fst	6f ⊡	:223 :452 :572 1:101	BestTurn65k	**92**	6	5	54½	42½	43	11½	Bridgmohan S X	L115	2.30	91-11	*Badge*1151½ Robin Goodfellow115nk Royal Ruby115¾	4 wide move, driving	7
28Jan99-3Aqu	fst	170 ⊡	:223 :462 1:113 1:412	Alw 43650N$Y	**91**	4	35½	32	31	32½	33	Bridgmohan S X	L117	2.25	88-21	*Noteasybeingreen*1172¾ KarlysHrley114nk *Bdge*11726	Outfinished for place	4
10Jan99-7Aqu	my	6f ⊡	:231 :47 :591 1:114	Alw 40000N1X	**77**	3	3	45½	3½	14	17¾	Leon F	L121	*1.15	83-14	Badge1217¾ Peak's Sweep109½ Ordained1165	Mild drive	7
13Dec98-5Aqu	fst	6f ⊡	:232 :471 :592 1:113	Md Sp Wt 38k	**86**	10	9	94¾	42	1hd	1½	Leon F	L119	*2.40	84-17	*Badge*119½ Sailor's Warning1199¾ Oros1191¾	Brk slw,check turn	11
12Nov98-6Aqu	fst	1⅛	:482 1:134 1:40 1:531	Md Sp Wt 39k	**68**	3	44½	43½	31½	34½	35	Leon F	L119	7.00	65-24	*LegalStreet*1193¾ MchinetoTower1191¼ *Bdge*1197¾	Awkward start, gamely	6
5Nov98-2Aqu	fst	1	:234 :474 1:133 1:384	Md Sp Wt 39k	**58**	6	92¾	92½	85¼	59	58¼	Leon F	L118	11.30	67-21	Why So Quiet118½ *Cloud Club*1186¾ *Stellar Brush*118½	Lost whip stretch	9

BEHRENS (Pleasant Colony—Hot Novel, by Mari's Book). Kentucky. Unraced at 2, Behrens was a stakes winner at 3, but really developed into one of the leading older runners at 5, when he won four major stakes (the Oaklawn, Gulfstream Park, Massachusetts, and Suburban Handicaps) and also placed in four major stakes (the Jockey Club Gold Cup and the Whitney, Donn, and Broward Handicaps) from nine starts. He returned at 6 to score a repeat victory in the Gulfstream Park Handicap and placed second in the Dubai World Cup, the Woodward Stakes, and the Suburban Handicap, and third in the Whitney and Donn Handicaps. As a son of Pleasant Colony, he should sire runners who will not reach their best until age 3 and beyond, when they stretch out on dirt and turf. Behrens has an HIT^2 pedigree, as both Pleasant Colony and Mari's Book (by Maribeau, a son of Ribot) are strong turf influences.

Behrens
Own: Rudlein Stable and Clifton Jr., Willi

B. h. 10 (Feb)
Sire: Pleasant Colony (His Majesty)
Dam: Hot Novel (Mari's Book)
Br: Joanne H. Nor (Ky)
Tr: Bond H. J(0 0 0 0 .00) 2004:(125 25 .20)

Life	27	9	8	3	$4,563,500	118	D.Fst	22	8	7	2	$3,794,000	118
2000	7	1	3	2	$1,764,500	113	Wet(388)	5	1	1	1	$769,500	117
1999	9	4	4	0	$1,735,000	117	Turf(329)	0	0	0	0	$0	-
	0	0	0	0	$0	-	Dst(0)	0	0	0	0	$0	-

14Oct00-10Bel	fst	1¼	:464 1:101 1:342 1:591	3↑ JkyClbGC-G1	96	5	41½	51¾	65	612	615½	Bailey J D	L126 b	3.10	82- 09	AlberttheGret1226 Gnder1263 VisionndVerse126no	Ducked in start, bump	7
16Sep00- 8Bel	fst	1⅛	:461 1:104 1:364 1:502	3↑ Woodward-G1	105	1	2hd	1hd	2hd	2hd	2hd	Bailey J D	L126 b	3.15	79- 14	Lemon Drop Kid126hd Behrens126¾ Gander1263¾	Fought it out gamely	5
6Aug00- 9Sar	gd	1⅛	:463 1:101 1:35 1:481	3↑ WhitneyH-G1	108	2	41½	42½	51½	34	36¼	Bailey J D	L122 b	2.20	94 -	*Lemon Drop Kid*1232 Cat Thief1174¼ Behrens1221½	Clipped heels, stumble	6
4Jly00- 9Bel	fst	1¼	:463 1:094 1:341 1:584	3↑ SuburbnH-G2	113	1	31½	31½	4nk	22½	22½	Chavez J F	L122 b	1.40	97- 13	*Lemon Drop Kid*1222½ Behrens1224¼ Lager1131	Speed inside, gamely	6
Previously trained by Bond Harold James																		
25Mar00♦Nad Al Sheba (UAE)	ft	*1¼	LH 1:592	4↑ Dubai World Cup-G1							26	Chavez J F	126 b	-		*Dubai Millennium*1266 Behrens1265½ Public Purse126hd		13
Timeform rating: 130				Stk 6000000													*Chased in 7th,2nd 4f out,no chance with winner.Puerto Madero 4th*	
Previously trained by Bond Harold James																		
26Feb00-10GP	fst	1¼	:473 1:113 1:36 2:013	3↑ GPH-G1	111	3	21½	21½	1½	12½	15	Chavez J F	L120 b	*.30	89- 14	Behrens1205 Adonis1151 With Anticipation1138	Drew clear, driving	6
5Feb00-10GP	fst	1⅛	:464 1:104 1:354 1:482	3↑ DonnH-G1	111	3	64½	84½	73¾	33½	35¼	Chavez J F	L121 b	*2.40	90- 18	StephenGotEven115¾ GoldenMissile1141½ *Behrens*1214	Steadied first turn	10
6Nov99-10GP	fst	1¼	:453 1:094 1:341 1:592	3↑ BCClasic-G1	104	2	108¾	85¾	88	87¾	79½	Chavez J F	L126 b	*2.30	104 -	Cat Thief1221¼ Budroyale126hd Golden Missile1262	Steadied 1st turn,dull	14
10Oct99- 6Bel	sly	1¼	:462 1:101 1:352 2:012	3↑ JkyClbGC-G1	112	1	65	64	42	33½	23¼	Chavez J F	L126 b	*.85	84- 23	River Keen1263¼ Behrens126hd Almutawakel1264¼	Hustled, stayed gamely	8
1Aug99- 9Sar	fst	1⅛	:47 1:104 1:36 1:483	3↑ WhitneyH-G1	116	6	65	63	2hd	1hd	2no	Chavez J F	L123 b	1.35	93- 07	Victory Gallop123no Behrens12312 Catienus1133	5 wide move 2nd turn	8
5Jly99- 8Bel	fst	1¼	:464 1:104 1:353 2:01	3↑ SuburbnH-G2	110	5	31	2hd	11	12½	12¾	Chavez J F	L121 b	*.30	89- 15	Behrens1212¾ Catienus1134¼ SocialCharter1137½	When asked,shown whip	8
29May99-13Suf	fst	1⅛	:472 1:11 1:36 1:49	3↑ MassH-G2	117	3	31	31	2½	2½	1½	Chavez J F	LB118 b	.90	91- 16	*Behrens*118½ *Running Stag*1132¾ *Real Quiet*1214½	4 path turns, driving	6
3Apr99-11OP	sly	1⅛	:461 1:094 1:352 1:473	4↑ OaklawnH-G1	117	2	32½	31½	22½	1½	12½	Chavez J F	L116 b	*1.50	99- 10	*Behrens*1162½ *Littlebitlively*1121¾ Precocity1195¼	Outside bid, riddn out	7
27Feb99-10GP	fst	1¼	:481 1:122 1:364 2:014	3↑ GPH-G1	111	6	22	2hd	1hd	11½	12½	Chavez J F	L114 b	*1.40	102- 14	*Behrens*1142½ Archers Bay1142 Sir Bear1183¼	Edged away, driving	8
30Jan99-10GP	fst	1⅛	:463 1:102 1:353 1:481	3↑ DonnH-G1	110	9	74½	74¼	43½	41	22¾	Chavez J F	L113 b	9.60	93- 14	PuertoMadero1202¾ *Behrens*1132½ SilverChrm126nk	Broke inward, rallied	12
9Jan99-10GP	fst	1$\frac{1}{16}$	:241 :472 1:111 1:433	3↑ BrowardH-G3	108	3	2hd	2hd	1hd	2hd	2¾	Chavez J F	L113 b	5.30	88- 11	Sir Bear119¾ Behrens1132¼ Hanarsaan1103	Gamely, edged late	8
13Jun98- 8Bel	my	1⅛	:452 1:09 1:332 1:463	3↑ BrooklnH-G2	91	9	86	63½	67	98¾	910¾	Chavez J F	L115 f	5.00	86- 11	Subordination1141¼ Sir Bear1181 Mr. Sinatra114½	Wide trip,empty	11
Previously trained by Bond Harold James																		
28Mar98♦Nad Al Sheba (UAE)	ft	*1¼	LH 2:041	4↑ Dubai World Cup-G1							517½	Bailey J	126 b	-		Silver Charm126no Swain1262½ Loup Sauvage126no		9
Timeform rating: 100				Stk 4000000													*Led to over 2f out,weakened.Malek 4th,Borgia 8th.No betting*	
Previously trained by Bond Harold James																		
28Feb98-10GP	fst	1¼	:463 1:101 1:351 2:031	3↑ GPH-G1	108	6	11	1hd	21½	22	34	Chavez J F	L114 fb	5.70	91- 16	*Skip Away*1272¼ Unruled1121¾ Behrens1141¼	Bore in start, tired	6
7Feb98-10GP	fst	1⅛	:463 1:104 1:362 1:50	3↑ DonnH-G1	80	8	85½	85¾	77½	913	718	Smith M E	L116 f	3.60	69- 24	*Skip Away*1262¾ Unruled112½ Sir Bear113nk	Bumped start	10
8Nov97- 8Hol	fst	1¼	:461 1:093 1:334 1:59	3↑ BCClassc-G1	83	8	61¾	77	715	717	724¾	Bailey J D	L122 f	3.50	77- 06	*SkpAwy*1266 DptyCommndr122¾ ⒹWhskyWsdom1263	5 wide backstretch	9
20Sep97- 8Med	fst	1⅛	:46 1:092 1:341 1:463	PegasusH-G2	118	1	2½	2½	1½	13	15¾	Bailey J D	L117 f	4.50	106- 06	Behrens1175¾ Anet1202½ Frisk Me Now1198	Much the best stretch	4
23Aug97- 9Sar	fst	1¼	:471 1:111 1:364 2:04	Travers-G1	110	2	42¾	42½	31	2hd	2no	Bailey J D	L126 f	2.45	88- 21	*Deputy Commander*126no *Behrens*1267 Awesome Again1200	Gamely,missed	8
3Aug97- 8Sar	sly	1⅛	:47 1:114 1:374 1:51	JimDandy-G2	99	6	66	54	33	42	44¾	Bailey J D	121 f	*2.10	76 25	AwesomeAgin1163 Glitmn1141 AffirmdSuccss114¾	Steadied deep stretch	9
5Jly97- 9Del	fst	1$\frac{1}{16}$	:232 :454 1:10 1:421	Dwyer-G2	104	6	51¼	52¼	3nk	2hd	11¼	Bailey J D	117 f	1.95	88- 11	Behrens1171¼ Glitman1147 Banker's Gold1223½	4w move turn,driving	6
24May97- 3Bel	fst	1$\frac{1}{16}$	:221 :452 1:101 1:414	3↑ Alw 38000N1x	96	5	44½	42	1hd	13½	13	Bailey J D	112 f	*.60	90- 17	*Behrens*1123 StandingOnEdge1123 GallantPelham1144	4w move,kept busy	9
18Jan97-11GP	fst	1$\frac{1}{16}$	:232 :471 1:124 1:451	Md Sp Wt 27k	84	9	33	32½	11½	13½	14¾	Bailey J D	120	*1.50	81- 18	*Behrens*1204¾ Tiberio1202¼ N X S Ice1205	Ridden out	11

BERNSTEIN (Storm Cat—La Affirmed, by Affirmed). Kentucky. Possessing a red-hot pedigree and standing for $7,500, Bernstein may be the big sleeper of this freshman group of sires. A group winner at 2 and 3 in Ireland, Bernstein is a full brother to stakes winners Caress (the dam of Sky Mesa) and Country Cat, and a half-brother to stakes winner Della Francesca and the unraced Emmaus (dam of Wiseman's Ferry). Bernstein's dam is a half-sister to champion 2-year-old filly Outstandingly, and most significantly, his third dam is a half-sister to Buckpasser. Bernstein had quality speed on grass, and his 2-year-olds, especially if out of mares by speed influences (Crafty Prospector, Valid Appeal, Hold Your Peace, Phone Trick, etc.), will offer great value on dirt as well as grass because he is unfamiliar to most horseplayers in this country. Speed, and especially grass, are the keywords here. (T^2)

Bernstein
Own: Tabor Michael, Magnier, Sue and Moran

B. h. 7 (Mar)
Sire: Storm Cat (Storm Bird) $500,000
Dam: La Affirmed (Affirmed)
Br: Brushwood Stable (Ky)
Tr: O'Brien Aidan P(0 0 0 0 .00) 2004:(0 0 .00)

Life	8	4	0	0	$173,120	91	D.Fst	0	0	0	0	$0	–
2000	5	2	0	0	$116,870	91	Wet(386)	0	0	0	0	$0	–
1999	3	2	0	0	$56,250	–	Turf(357)	8	4	0	0	$173,120	91
	0	0	0	0	$0	–	Dst(0)	0	0	0	0	$0	–

5Nov00–9CD	fm 1⅛ Ⓣ :48 1:12^2 1:36^1 1:48	3↑ RivrCtyH-G3	**91** 7 3$^{1\frac{1}{2}}$ 3^3 2^1 4$^{3\frac{1}{2}}$	5$^{7\frac{1}{4}}$	Kinane M J	L115	10.70	89–09	*Brahms*112½ Vergennes115$^{1\frac{3}{4}}$ Super Quercus116$^{2\frac{1}{4}}$	Tracked 4w,empty	9
Previously trained by O'Brien Aidan P											
1Oct00♦Cork (Ire) Timeform rating: 115	sf 7f Ⓣ RH 1:30	3↑ Concorde Stakes-G3 Stk 56000		1^{hd}	Heffernan J A	124	5.00		Bernstein124^{hd} *Cobourg Lodge*126$^{2\frac{1}{2}}$ Conormara124$^{2\frac{1}{2}}$	*Pressed pace,dueled over 1f out,gamely prevailed*	11
24Aug00♦York (GB) Timeform rating: 96	gd 5f Ⓣ Str :57^4	2↑ Nunthorpe Stakes-G1 Stk 259400		11$^{10\frac{3}{4}}$	Kinane M J	133 b	6.00		Nuclear Debate135$^{1\frac{1}{4}}$ Bertolini135$^{1\frac{1}{2}}$ *Pipalong*132^{hd}	*Always outrun*	13
12Aug00♦Ascot (GB) Timeform rating: 111	gd 6f Ⓣ Str 1:14^4	Shergar Cup Sprint Alw 150100		1^{hd}	Kinane M J	124	5.00		Bernstein124^{hd} Auenklang130^{nk} Vita Spericolata119^5	*Pressed pace,dueled 1f out,led final strides*	9
6May00♦Newmarket (GB)	gd 1 Ⓣ Str 1:37^3	2000 Guineas Stakes-G1 Stk 458300		26$^{40\frac{1}{2}}$	Peslier O	126	16.00		King's Best126$^{3\frac{1}{2}}$ Giant's Causeway126$^{1\frac{1}{2}}$ Barathea Guest126^2	*Tracked leaders to 2-1/2f out,weakened quickly*	27
19Sep99♦Curragh (Ire) Timeform rating: 95	sf 1 Ⓣ Str 1:46^1	National Stakes-G1 Stk 264600		5$^{3\frac{3}{4}}$	Kinane M J	126	*.35		Sinndar126^{hd} Murawwi126^1 Jammaal126^{hd}	*Rank setting pressured pace,clear 1-1/2f out,headed 100y out,wknd*	8
27Jun99♦Curragh (Ire) Timeform rating: 114	gd 6f Ⓣ Str 1:13	Railway Stakes-G3 Stk 62900		1$^{4\frac{1}{2}}$	Kinane M J	125	*.25		Bernstein125$^{4\frac{1}{2}}$ *Desert Sky*119^3 Appalachia119^{15}	*Soon led,drew clear in hand over 1f out,easily*	4
23May99♦Curragh (Ire) Timeform rating: 101	gd 6f Ⓣ Str 1:13^2	Beverly Smyth EBF Maiden Maiden 13400		1$^{5\frac{1}{2}}$	Kinane M J	128	*.30		*Bernstein*128$^{5\frac{1}{2}}$ Still Going On128$^{4\frac{1}{2}}$ *King of Russia*128^1	*Led virtually throughout,surged clear over 1f out,handily*	6

BEST OF LUCK (Broad Brush—Crowned, by Chief's Crown). Kentucky. By a top-class runner and from a renowned female family cultivated by George D. Widener, Best of Luck won the Peter Pan Stakes and finished second in the Wood Memorial and Withers Stakes, and the Discovery Handicap. His 2-year-olds should develop late in the season and be much more effective at distances over six furlongs. Because of the Broad Brush/Chief's Crown cross, he is a "hidden turf" sire and his runners will be tremendous overlays on grass. (HT^2)

Best of Luck
Own: Bohemia Stable

B. h. 8 (Mar)
Sire: Broad Brush (Ack Ack) $100,000
Dam: Crowned (Chief's Crown)
Br: Mrs. Richard C. DuPont (Md)
Tr: Jerkens H. A(0 0 0 0 .00) 2004:(267 55 .21)

	Life	23	4	7	3	$616,790	109		D.Fst	20	3	7	3	$508,790	109
	2000	5	0	1	1	$103,240	109		Wet(404)	2	1	0	0	$108,000	107
	1999	15	4	4	1	$493,860	108		Turf(318)	1	0	0	0	$0	51
		0	0	0	0	$0	–		Dst(0)	0	0	0	0	$0	–

Burbank
Own: Burbank Stables

Dk. b or b. h. 11 (Mar)
Sire: Wild Again (Icecapade) $50,000
Dam: Cagey Exuberance (Exuberant)
Br: Dr. L. D. Burbank (Ky)
Tr: Von Hemel Donnie K(0 0 0 0 .00) 2004:(270 47 .17)

	Life	46	14	12	7	$746,126	106		D.Fst	13	2	3	3	$79,586	100
	2000	9	1	1	2	$64,100	100		Wet(346)	2	0	1	0	$12,000	96
	1999	9	4	1	2	$204,000	99		Turf(277)	31	12	8	4	$654,540	106
		0	0	0	0	$0	–		Dst(0)	0	0	0	0	$0	–

Placed 8th through disqualification

55

BURBANK (Wild Again—Cagey Exuberance, by Exuberant). Oklahoma. Burbank was unraced at 2, but was a throwback to yesteryear's Thoroughbred, making 46 starts from ages 3 to 7 (see previous page). Standing in Oklahoma, he could prove to be a useful stallion in the Southwest, including Texas, Louisiana, and Arkansas. A winner of seven stakes, he placed in 13 other added-money events, all but two of them on turf. His dam was a major sprinter/miler and Burbank's 2-year-olds should be very effective on all surfaces.

CAPE CANAVERAL (Mr. Prospector—Seaside Attraction, by Seattle Slew). Kentucky. By one of the world's great stallions and a noted sire of sires, stakes winner Cape Canaveral is out of a Kentucky Oaks winner, Seaside Attraction, also the dam of stakes winners Cape Town, Red Carnival, and Cape Canaveral's full sister, champion 2-year-old filly Golden Attraction. His high speed reflected his brilliant pedigree and Cape Canaveral's juveniles will be off to a flying start in the early-season baby sprints. (SP^2)

Cape Canaveral
Own: Overbrook Farm

Dk. b or b. h. 8 (Feb)
Sire: Mr. Prospector (Raise a Native)
Dam: Seaside Attraction (Seattle Slew)
Br: Overbrook Farm (Ky)
Tr: Lukas D. W(5 1 1 0 .20) 2004:(427 48 .11)

Life	4	3	0	1	$128,640	111	D.Fst	4	3	0	1	$128,640	111
2000	1	1	0	0	$32,400	111	Wet(419)	0	0	0	0	$0	-
1999	2	1	0	1	$69,240	100	Turf(348)	0	0	0	0	$0	-
	0	0	0	0	$0	-	Dst(381)	0	0	0	0	$0	-

15Jan00–1SA	fst	7f	:22^2	:44^2	1:08^3	1:21^1	4↑OC 62k/N2X-N	111	2	1	2½	1½	1^2	1^3	Day P	LB117 b	*1.40	99–09	Cape Canaveral117^3 Sing Because118^{hd} Haflinger1172½	Steady handling	6
26Dec99–7SA	fst	6½f	:22^1	:45	1:09	1:15^2	3↑OC 62k/N3L-N	91	5	2	1½	1^{hd}	2^1	3^5	Day P	LB117	*1.10	86–08	LakeWilliam1192½ Haflinger1172½ *CapeCanaveral*1171½	Inside duel,held 3rd	8
9Jan99–7SA	fst	6f	:21^2	:44^2	:56^2	1:09	SMiguel-G3	100	2	2	1^{hd}	11½	11½	1^1	Flores D R	LB118 b	*.20	95–11	Cape Canaveral118^1 Aristotle1147½ Actin Time116^{18}	Speed,held gamely	4
26Dec98–6SA	fst	6½f	:21^1	:43^3	1:09	1:15^3	Md Sp Wt 47k	97	1	4	12½	13½	1^4	12½	Flores D R	LB119 b	5.40	91–08	*CapeCanaveral*1192½ Snowdoubtboutit119^2 *FindersGold*119^6	Inside, driving	9

CAT THIEF (Storm Cat—Train Robbery, by Alydar). Kentucky. While Cat Thief won only three stakes in his 30 career starts (but placed in 14 others), the one that will be remembered is his upset victory in the 1999 Breeders' Cup Classic. Cat Thief won his maiden race at Saratoga as a juvenile, and he also captured the Lane's End Breeders' Futurity. He was bred to an above-average book of mares, and his runners should be especially good as 3-year-olds, at middle distances. But since Cat Thief did win at 2, they should also have enough speed to be competitive as juveniles, most likely in the fall, when they should start catching up to their more precocious contemporaries. Since he is a son of Storm Cat, his runners should also be followed if they appear on grass. (HT)

Cat Thief
Own: Overbrook Farm

Ch. h. 8 (Jan)
Sire: Storm Cat (Storm Bird) $500,000
Dam: Train Robbery (Alydar)
Br: Overbrook Farm (Ky)
Tr: Lukas D. W(0 0 0 0 .00) 2004:(359 40 .11)

Life	30	4	9	8	$3,951,012	118	
2000	10	0	3	2	$496,900	115	
1999	13	2	3	5	$3,020,500	118	
	0	0	0	0	$0	-	
D.Fst	25	4	7	7	$3,480,012	118	
Wet(419)	5	0	2	1	$471,000	115	
Turf(345)	0	0	0	0	$0	-	
Dst(0)	0	0	0	0	$0	-	

4Nov00-10CD	fst	1¼	:472 1:12 1:36 2:003	3↑ BCClasic-G1	102	3	94 103½ 106¾ 76½ 79½	Day P	L126	11.50	97 -	Tiznow122nk GiantsCauseway1223¼ CptinSteve122hd	Bump,steady 1st turn	13
16Sep00-10TP	fst	1⅛	:462 1:104 1:362 1:494	3↑ KyCpClH-G2	87	2	44 41½ 32 58½ 617¾	Day P	L118 b	2.90	68- 23	CaptainSteve115¾ GoldenMissile1214½ ErlyPioneer1202½	3 wide, gave way	6
6Aug00- 9Sar	gd	1⅛	:463 1:101 1:35 1:481	3↑ WhitneyH-G1	115	6	21 2½ 1½ 21½ 22	Chavez J F	L117 b	9.40	98 -	Lemon Drop Kid1232 Cat Thief1174¼ Behrens1221½	With pace, stayed on	6
9Jly00- 5Hol	fst	1¼	:462 1:10 1:344 2:012	3↑ HolGldCp-G1	106	1	43½ 66½ 66 75 53¾	Day P	LB124 b	5.40	84- 12	EarlyPioneer1241 GeneralChllenge1241½ Dvid1241¼	Saved ground to lane	9
17Jun00- 8CD	sly	1⅛	:473 1:122 1:37 1:492	3↑ SFosterH-G2	108	4	21 22 21½ 22½ 34¾	Sellers S J	L117 b	6.10	84- 16	Golden Missile1182¾ EctonPark1142 CatThief117nk	Pull even,weaken late	6
13May00-10Pim	fst	1 3/16	:472 1:111 1:361 1:543	3↑ PimSpclH-G1	98	5	1hd 1hd 1hd 2hd 510¾	Day P	L118 b	4.50	81- 18	GoldenMissile1162 PlesntBrz111no LmonDropKid1204	Brk thru gt,rail,wknd	8
8Apr00-11OP	fst	1⅛	:454 1:10 1:352 1:48	4↑ OaklawnH-G1	112	5	31 32 1½ 31½ 32	Espinoza V	L118 b	3.40	96- 18	K One King1131¾ Almutawakel117nk Cat Thief1184¼	4w 1st turn, brushed	6
4Mar00- 5SA	gd	1¼	:472 1:12 1:363 2:012	4↑ SAH-G1	104	3	1½ 1hd 1hd 32½ 68¾	Day P	LB120 b	2.20	85- 13	GenerlChlleng1211¼ Budroyl1221 PurtoMdro1181½	Inside duel, weakened	8
6Feb00- 7SA	fst	1⅛	:46 1:101 1:353 1:483	4↑ SnAntnoH-G2	106	5	53½ 56 53¾ 43 21¼	Day P	LB120 b	*1.70	91- 17	Budroyale1211¼ Cat Thief1201½ Elaborate116½	Wide into lane,rallied	5
15Jan00- 8SA	fst	1 1/16	:223 :462 1:101 1:414	SnFndoBC-G2	102	3	31½ 42 31½ 41¼ 21½	Day P	LB122 b	*1.50	92- 06	SaintsHonor1171½ CatThief122hd MrBroadBlade1181	Bumped,bit tight 3/8	7
26Dec99- 6SA	fst	7f	:221 :441 1:084 1:22	Malibu-G1	101	7	2 42½ 43½ 42½ 3nk	Day P	LB123 b	*1.90	95- 08	Love That Red119nk StraightMan118hd CatThief123½	4 wide turn,willingly	7
6Nov99-10GP	fst	1¼	:453 1:094 1:341 1:592	3↑ BCClasic-G1	118	6	2½ 2hd 1hd 1hd 11¼	Day P	L122 b	19.60	114 -	Cat Thief1221¼ Budroyale126hd Golden Missile1262	Drift,brsh,drv.,gamely	14
25Sep99-10TP	fst	1⅛	:47 1:113 1:372 1:502	3↑ KyCpClH-G2	107	1	1hd 1hd 2hd 31½ 3½	Day P	L117 b	*1.80	82- 24	Da Devil112½ Social Charter115hd Cat Thief1174	Coming again	8
28Aug99- 9Sar	fst	1¼	:481 1:122 1:364 2:02	Travers-G1	92	4	1hd 1hd 3½ 55 712¼	Smith M E	L126 b	4.60	86- 13	LemonDropKid126¾ VisionndVerse1261¾ Menife1261¾	Speed inside, tired	8
8Aug99-11Mth	gd	1⅛	:461 1:094 1:35 1:48	HsklInvH-G1	109	7	31½ 31 3½ 2hd 2½	Smith M E	L123 b	2.60	95- 07	Menifee124½ Cat Thief123½ Forestry118½	Bobbled brk, gamely	7
18Jly99- 6Hol	fst	1⅛	:47 1:11 1:351 1:474	Swaps-G1	107	4	2hd 1hd 1½ 2hd 1hd	Day P	LB120 b	2.80	87- 13	CatThief120hd GeneralChallenge12211 WalkThtWlk1178	Very game rail lane	4
29May99- 9Bel	fst	1	:222 :443 1:09 1:342	3↑ MtropltH-G1	05	1	2½ 2½ 3½ 54¾ 615½	Bailey J D	L112 b	2.85	76- 22	Sir Bear1171¾ Crafty Friend114¾ Liberty Gold1142¼	Bumped start, inside	8
15May99-10Pim	fst	1 3/16	:451 1:101 1:351 1:551	Preaknss-G1	90	3	2hd 1hd 2hd 23 710¾	Smith M E	L126 b	5.20	78- 09	Charismatic1261½ Menifee126hd Badge1262½	Disputed 2wd, weakened	13
1May99- 8CD	fst	1¼	:474 1:122 1:372 2:031	KyDerby-G1	107	10	2½ 2hd 1hd 1½ 31	Smith M E	L126 b	7.40	88- 14	Charismatic126nk Menifee126¾ Cat Thief1261¼	Stalked, led, gamely	19
10Apr99- 9Kee	fst	1⅛	:47 1:104 1:36 1:483	BlueGras-G1	105	6	31½ 31 1hd 2hd 21¼	Smith M E	L123 b	5.90	91- 19	Menifee1231¼ Cat Thief123½ Vicar1232½	3 wide, bid, gamely	8
13Mar99-12GP	fst	1⅛	:481 1:123 1:374 1:504	FlaDerby-G1	101	2	2hd 1hd 1½ 2hd 3½	Day P	L122 b	*1.80	82- 19	Vicar122no Wondertross122½ Cat Thief1221¾	Dueled game, weakened	10
20Feb99- 6GP	fst	1 1/16	:233 :472 1:123 1:453	FntnOYth-G1	97	7	2hd 2½ 2hd 2hd 2nk	Day P	L119 b	*3.10	79- 29	Vicar114nk Cat Thief119¾ Certain1172¼	Gamely, 2nd best	10
31Jan99- 8GP	fst	7f	:213 :433 1:081 1:221	Hutchesn-G2	93	7	5 76 57½ 35 33½	Day P	L119 b	2.10	85- 15	Bet Me Best122hd Texas Glitter1193½ Cat Thief1196	3 wide trn,mild rally	7
7Nov98- 4CD	fst	1 1/16	:231 :463 1:113 1:44	BCJuven-G1	95	7	65 68 42½ 22 3¾	Day P	L122 b	3.20e	90- 07	Answer Lively122hd Aly's Alley122¾ Cat Thief1225½	Checked first turn	13
18Oct98- 8Kee	fst	1 1/16	:223 :454 1:111 1:44	BrdrsFut-G2	97	7	56 59½ 43 31 1nk	Day P	L121 b	6.80	88- 20	Cat Thief121nk Answer Lively1213½ Yes It'sTrue1214½	Bid between, driving	8
11Sep98- 3Bel	fst	6f	:222 :463 :581 1:102	Alw 40000N2L	80	3	2 1hd 1hd 3½ 22	Sellers S J	L117 b	*.75	87- 13	SuccessfulAppl1172 CtThif117nk ExildGroom1138½	Pace,came again for2nd	5
21Aug98- 4Sar	fst	7f	:224 :46 1:102 1:23	Alw 37000N2L	90	5	3 11½ 11 1hd 23	Bailey J D	L116 b	3.15	87- 13	Menifee1163 Cat Thief11610½ Lemon Drop Kid1164½	Set pace, 2nd best	5
1Aug98- 6Sar	fst	6f	:222 :46 :581 1:11	Md Sp Wt 35k	85	3	7 1½ 1½ 13 16	Bailey J D	L116 b	4.40	86- 12	Cat Thief1166 Conserve1162 Walkonby116no	Speed inside, driving	10
1Jly98- 7ElP	fst	5f	:23 :47 :592	Md Sp Wt 23k	63	2	6 64½ 64½ 33 21¼	Woods C R Jr	L120	*2.00	92- 15	ColorofSmoke1201¼ CtThif1202¾ MoonOvrProspct1204½	4wide bid,2nd best	12
22Apr98- 2Kee	my	4½f	:223 :464 :532	Md Sp Wt 40k	–	7	10 85¾ 66 66	Bailey J D	118	*1.70	83- 13	Discrimintion118nk Memento1183½ WesternShow1181	Passed tiring rivals	12

CATIENUS (Storm Cat—Diamond City, by Mr. Prospector). New York. A winner at 2 and 3 in England, Catienus won one of three starts in the U.S. at age 4. He became a stakes winner at 5, but was never better than when he finished second in the Suburban behind Behrens and second in the Saratoga Breeders' Cup Handicap behind Running Stag. His third dam, Cathy Honey, was one of 1970's best 3-year-old fillies, winning the Acorn Stakes and finishing second in the Mother Goose and Coaching Club American Oaks. Cathy Honey produced Aloma, the dam of 1982 Preakness Stakes winner Aloma's Ruler. With speed on both sides of his pedigree (SP^2), his runners should have good speed and be effective at 2.

Catienus
Own: Ramsey Kenneth L. and Sarah K

Dk. b or b. h. 10 (May)
Sire: Storm Cat (Storm Bird) $500,000
Dam: Diamond City (Mr. Prospector)
Br: Darley Stud Management, Inc. (Ky)
Tr: Simon Charles(0 0 0 0 .00) 2004:(151 25 .17)

Life	22	5	5	2	$370,386	115	D.Fst	12	2	5	1	$337,840	115
2000	3	0	2	0	$71,800	105	Wet(432)	1	0	0	0	$0	103
1999	8	1	3	1	$248,040	115	Turf(364)	9	3	0	1	$32,546	84
	0	0	0	0	$0	-	Dst(0)	0	0	0	0	$0	-

7Oct00-9Haw	fst 1¼	:484 1:124 1:374 2:03	3↑ HawGldCH-G3	97 4 53½ 42 32 44 66½	St Julien M	L114	7.30e	80-25	Dust OntheBottle1121 GuidedTour113nk GoldenMissile1213½	Bid, faltered	8
27Aug00-8Sar	fst 1¼	:49 1:124 1:37 2:02	3↑ SarBCH-G2	105 6 41½ 42 31 32 22¾	Day P	L114	3.85	92-05	Pleasant Breeze1162¾ Catienus1142¼ Gander114½	Game finish outside	7
4Aug00-6Sar	fst 1⅛	:453 1:092 1:35 1:481	3↑ Alw 59000c	105 3 511 513 59½ 35½ 24¾	St Julien M	L119	9.00	95-11	*Pleasant Breeze*1214¾ Catienus119½ DeputyDiamond1198¾	Rallied for place	5
Previously trained by Schosberg Richard											
6Nov99-10GP	fst 1¼	:453 1:094 1:341 1:592	3↑ BCClasic-G1	85 1 1312129 1314 1317 1321¾	Prado E S	L126	86.50	92 -	Cat Thief1221¼ Budroyale126hd Golden Missile1262	Outrun	14
10Oct99-6Bel	sly 1¼	:462 1:101 1:352 2:012	3↑ JkyClbGC-G1	103 5 711 77 62¾ 66½ 69½	Prado E S	L126 f	23.20e	77-23	River Keen1263½ Behrens126hd Almutawakel1264½	4 wide run second turn	8
29Aug99-8Sar	fst 1¼	:474 1:114 1:362 2:01	3↑ SarBCH-G2	115 2 85¼ 74¾ 52 33½ 2½	Bailey J D	L115	4.10	102-16	Running Stag122½ Catienus115½ Golden Missile1158½	Game finish outside	8
1Aug99-9Sar	fst 1⅛	:47 1:104 1:36 1:483	3↑ WhitneyH-G1	96 3 811 710 78¼ 56¾ 312	Davis R G	L113	39.25	81-07	Victory Gallop123no Behrens12312 Catienus1133	Mild rally outside	8
5Jly99-8Bel	fst 1¼	:464 1:104 1:353 2:01	3↑ SuburbnH-G2	106 6 711 79¾ 44 33 22¾	Davis R G	L113	41.50	86-15	Behrens1212¾ Catienus1134¼ Social Charter1137½	Courageously outside	8
31May99-7Del	fst 1$\frac{1}{16}$	:23 :461 1:111 1:441	3↑ CStaatsMem55k	95 1 77¾ 66 51½ 3½ 11½	McCarthy M J	L114	2.50	86-16	Catienus1141½ *Tappat*1161½ Big Rut1133	Boxed, found room	7
25Apr99-6Aqu	fst 1⅛	:484 1:131 1:374 1:501	4↑ Clm c-(60-50)	95 4 54½ 54½ 52½ 3nk 2½	Migliore R	L114	8.70	84-13	Buck Strider115½ *Catienus*1141 Fortress Strong1131½	4 wide move, gamely	6
Claimed from Al Maktoum Sheikh Mohammed for $50,000, Clement Christophe Trainer 1999(as of 4/25): (-)											
23Mar99-10Hia	fst 1$\frac{1}{16}$	:232 :471 1:113 1:432	4↑ OC 150k/N4X-N	60 3 44½ 44½ 58½ 513 420	Davis R G	L115	*1.70	74-11	UnitedStates115¾ *EgleCounty*1157¼ Streeterville11512	Saved grnd, outrun	5
17Jun98-8Mth	fst 1$\frac{1}{16}$ ⊗	:231 :462 1:111 1:424	3↑ Alw 30000N3X	103 5 44½ 46 42½ 2½ 11½	McCauley W H	L119	*1.40	87-19	Catienus1191½ *Mi Narrow*1199¼ Show Off1211¼	Drew clear late	7
13May98-7Bel	fst 1⅛	:454 1:092 1:342 1:474	3↑ Alw 42000N3X	90 6 64½ 73¼ 75¼ 66¾ 68¼	Bailey J D	L116	12.10	83-16	Ordway116nk Las VegasErnie120½ Dan'sPromise1164	Betwn rivals,no rally	8
25Apr98-8CD	fm 1 Ⓣ	:24 :473 1:114 1:352	3↑ Alw 52360N$Y	84 5 44 43½ 43 44½ 45¼	Bailey J D	L116	4.80	86-08	OpticNerve1163 Smoke1202¼ PrmirKrischif120hd	Stalked pace, weakened	10
Previously trained by Michael Stoute											
4Sep97♦York (GB)	sf 1⅛ Ⓣ LH	1:594	3↑ Strensall Stakes (Listed) Stk 46700	628½	Darley K	122	*1.20		Winter Romance128½ Weet-A-Minute1285 Balalaika1283½	*Led to approaching 2f out,gave way.Acharne 4th*	6
16Aug97♦Curragh (Ire)	yl 1¼ Ⓣ RH	2:044	3↑ Royal Whip Stakes-G3 Stk 43900	4¾	Weaver J	119	8.00		King Alex127no Rayouni119½ *Oscar Schindler*136nk	*Led to 1f out,dueled briefly,gave ground grudgingly*	7
11Jly97♦Chester (GB)	gd 1$\frac{5}{16}$ Ⓣ LH	2:091	3↑ Farndon Conditions Stakes Alw 24500	44	Darley K	123	*2.25		Bright Water1282 Maralinga1322 Premier Bay117no	*Tracked leader,weakened over 1f out*	6
17May97♦Thirsk (GB)	sf 1 Ⓣ RH	1:441	Dishforth Conditions Stakes Alw 21900	11¾	Darley K	132	3.00		Catienus1321¾ *Intikhab*1326 Premier Bay1272½	*Led throughout,roused over 2f out,ridden out*	4
8Nov96♦Doncaster (GB)	sf 1 Ⓣ Str	1:432	Co-Operative Bank Conditions S Alw 13200	1hd	Darley K	127	2.50		*Catienus*127hd Sunbeam Dance1276 Kaiser Kache123½	*Led for 2f,led again hlfwy,dueled final furlong,gamely prevailed*	6
16Oct96♦Haydock (GB)	hy 7½f Ⓣ LH	1:362	EBF Hawthorn Maiden Stks(Div1) Maiden 7800	18	Darley K	126	*2.00		*Catienus*1268 Outflanker1263½ Right Wing126hd	*Led throughout,ridden clear final furlong*	10
20Sep96♦Ayr (GB)	gd 7f Ⓣ LH	1:273	- Alw 11100	31½	Darley K	124	*1.35		What Happened Was116½ Halowing1251 *Catienus*1242	*Tracked in 3rd,ridden without reponse over 2f out,evenly late*	6
6Sep96♦Kempton (GB)	gd 7f Ⓣ RH	1:261	Chertsey Lock Conditions Stks Alw 12500	54¼	Hughes R	122	33.00		Falak122hd Captain Collins122nk Mukaddar1273½	*Rated in 5th,lacked rally*	10

CHIEF SEATTLE (Seattle Slew—Skatingonthinice, by Icecapade). Kentucky. Chief Seattle only raced at 2, but was brilliant in his short career, winning a maiden race at Saratoga by 9¾ lengths and finishing second in both the Breeders' Cup Juvenile and Champagne Stakes. Chief Seattle has all the tools to be a top sire of 2-year-olds: His pedigree is rife with speed influences and he showed that brilliance as a racehorse. (SP^2)

Chief Seattle
Own: Betz William J. and Needham, Philip D

Dk. b or b. h. 7 (Apr)
Sire: Seattle Slew (Bold Reasoning) $300,000
Dam: Skatingonthinice (Icecapade)
Br: Atwood Richards, Incorporated (Ky)
Tr: Kimmel John C(0 0 0 0 .00) 2004:(161 22 .14)

Life	4	1	2	0	$327,000	98	D.Fst	4	1	2	0	$327,000	98
1999	4	1	2	0	$327,000	98	Wet(355)	0	0	0	0	$0	-
1998	0	M	0	0	$0	-	Turf(320)	0	0	0	0	$0	-
	0	0	0	0	$0	-	Dst(0)	0	0	0	0	$0	-

6Nov99-8GP	fst 1$\frac{1}{16}$	:221 :46 1:101 1:421	BCJuven-G1	98 1 33 42 22 1hd 22½	Prado E S	L122	4.40	93 -	Anees1222½ Chief Seattle122¾ High Yield1222¼	3wide bid,led,2nd best	14
9Oct99-8Bel	fst 1$\frac{1}{16}$	:234 :462 1:104 1:433	Champagn-G1	87 5 1hd 1½ 1½ 11½ 22½	Prado E S	L122	2.45	76-23	*GreenwoodLke*1222½ ChiefSettle1224 HighYild1226¾	Set pace,clear,gamely	7
19Sep99-6Bel	fst 1	:232 :454 1:103 1:36	Futurity-G1	97 3 52¼ 42 61¼ 32 41¼	Prado E S	122	3.60	83-22	*Bevo*122nk *GreenwoodLake*122nk MoreThnRedy122¾	Stumbled start,steady	8
25Aug99-5Sar	fst 5½f	:213 :451 :571 1:033	Md Sp Wt 40k	93 1 3 1½ 11 14½ 19¾	Prado E S	117	5.60	100-11	ChiefSettl1179¾ KingsMssngr117½ GmorningGovnor117¾	Wrapped up late	9

CHULLO (Equalize—Que Ilusion, by Cipayo). California. While he may not be a familiar name in this country, Chullo was an exceptional racehorse in Argentina, where he was the 1997 Horse of the Year and champion 3-year-old. He was a Group 1 winner from one mile to about 1½ miles. His sire, Equalize, is a grandson of Northern Dancer, and was a major-league grass horse, winning the United Nations, Red Smith, and Canadian Turf Handicaps. While his California-bred offspring will win on dirt, they should really blossom into solid runners at 3, especially on turf. (T^2)

Chullo (Arg)
Own: Bunge Hernan, J. Cirilo and Montagna,

Dk. b or b. h. 10 (Aug)
Sire: Equalize (Northern Jove)
Dam: Que Ilusion (Cipayo*Arg)
Br: San Pablo (Arg)
Tr: Mandella Richard E(0 0 0 0 .00) 2004:(94 13 .14)

Life	11	6	1	1	$556,139	105	D.Fst	2	1	0	1	$106,619	-
2000	2	0	1	0	$42,210	105	Wet(309)	1	0	1	0	$40,000	105
1999	1	0	0	0	$0	99	Turf(248)	8	5	0	0	$409,520	99
	0	0	0	0	$0	-	Dst(0)	0	0	0	0	$0	-

21May00-8Hol	fm	1 1/16 Ⓣ	:241 :481 1:111 1:403	3↑ InglewdH-G3	99	4 21 42½ 32 41½ 52¼	Nakatani C S	LB118	2.50	88-14	Montemiro1131¼ Bonapartiste118nk Takarian118½	Lame after,vanned off	8
5Mar00-5SA	sly	1 ⊗	:233 :462 1:10 1:363	4↑ ArcadiaH-G3	105	5 21 31 21 22½ 2½	Nakatani C S	LB117 f	*1.40	87-20	*Commitisize*112½ Chullo1174 Sultry Substitute1143½	Came back on late	6
13Jun99-9Hol	fm	1 Ⓣ	:231 :46 1:084 1:324	3↑ ShoeBCM-G2	99	5 32½ 32½ 74¼ 63¼ 64½	McCarron C J	LB124	3.60	94-09	Silic124no Ladies Din124½ Hawksley Hill124nk	Pulled,weakened	8
Previously trained by Eduardo Martinez Dehoz													
14Mar98 ♦ San Isidro (Arg)	fm	*1¼ Ⓣ LH	1:572	3↑ GP Asoc Latinoamericano JCs-G1 Stk 270000		710½	Conti O F	123	*.90		Jimwaki1½ Sidon1233 Gabarito½	Tracked in 5th,weakened 2f out.Quari Bravo 4th,Mash One 6th	13
13Dec97 ♦ San Isidro (Arg)	gd	*1½ Ⓣ LH	2:32	3↑ Gran Premio Carlos Pellegrini-G1 Stk 284000		14½	Conti O	119	*1.00		Chullo1194½ Quari Bravo119nk Bueno Bob1191½	Tracked in 4th,led 2f out,handily.Mario Eterno 4th,Jimwaki 5th	13
8Nov97 ♦ Hipodromo (Arg)	ft	*1 9/16 LH	2:313	Gran Premio Nacional(Arg Drby)-G1 Stk 136000		14	Conti O	126	*1.00		*Chullo*1264 *Lazy Lode*126½ Intempestivo126½	Close up,led 2f out,going away.Mario Eterno 4th,De Un Suspiro 5th	10
11Oct97 ♦ San Isidro (Arg)	fm	*1¼ Ⓣ LH	1:59	Gran Premio Jockey Club-G1 Stk 142200		12½	Conti O	123	*.65		*Chullo*1232½ De Un Suspiro1231½ Intempestivo1231½	Well placed in 3rd,led 1f out,ridden out.Lazy Lode 5th	11
7Sep97 ♦ Hipodromo (Arg)	ft	*1 LH	1:342	Polla de Potrillos(Arg2000Gns)-G1 Stk 81700		3nk	Conti O	123	*.65		*Golfer*123nk Enrulao123no *Chullo*1239	Tracked leaders,bid 1f out,failed	6
9Aug97 ♦ San Isidro (Arg)	fm	*1 Ⓣ LH	1:33	San Isidro 2000 Guineas-G1 Stk 71100		14½	Conti O	123	*.85		Chullo1234½ Handsome Halo1236 Mr. Grillo1231½	Well placed in 3rd,led 2f out,drew clear.Mario Eterno 4th	12
5Jly97 ♦ San Isidro (Arg)	fm	*1 Ⓣ LH	1:33	Gran Criterium-G1 Stk 64000		16	Conti O	123	3.15		*Chullo*1236 Bat Marsico123no Mario Eterno1231	Led after 3f,handily.Nineth Sprout 4th	17
9May97 ♦ San Isidro (Arg)	fm	*7½f Ⓣ LH	1:292	Cl JB Zubiaurre(Lst-1st-timrs) Stk 17100		16	Conti O	121	*1.70		*Chullo*1216 Naviero Hei1211½ Knighthood121nk	Tracked leaders,led 2f out,quickly clear.Carlacho 4th	17

CLASSIC CAT (Mountain Cat—Sahsie, by Forli). Florida. Stakes-placed at 2, Classic Cat won three stakes at 3—the Lexington, Ohio Derby, and Remington Park Derby. He was also second in the Super Derby behind Arch, and finished third in the Preakness to Real Quiet and Victory Gallop. Classic Cat has a balanced pedigree with speed from his grandsire, Storm Cat, and stamina from the male influences in his female family, including Forli. (HT^2)

Classic Cat
Own: Garber Gary M

Ch. h. 9 (Mar)
Sire: Mountain Cat (Storm Cat) $4,608
Dam: Sahsie (Forli)
Br: Vintage Meadow Stable (Ky)
Tr: Baffert Bob(0 0 0 0 .00) 2004:(371 70 .19)

Life	20	6	3	5	$1,221,300	112	D.Fst	16	4	2	5	$883,000	106
2000	3	0	0	2	$24,300	100	Wet(301)	4	2	1	0	$338,300	112
1999	4	2	0	0	$132,420	112	Turf(262)	0	0	0	0	$0	-
	0	0	0	0	$0	-	Dst(0)	0	0	0	0	$0	-

16Jun00-9CD	fst	1 1/16	:234 :471 1:12 1:432	3↑ Alw 54970c	88	5 2½ 21½ 1hd 34 39¼	St Julien M	L118 b	*.80	84-18	Relic Reward1183¾ Glacial1235½ Classic Cat1182¼	Pressed,led,weakened	6
13May00-8Hol	fst	1 1/16	:232 :462 1:102 1:414	3↑ MrvnLRyH-G2	100	7 43½ 47½ 46 55 47	Nakatani C S	LB119	3.50	84-17	Out of Mind116½ Early Pioneer1164½ *Skimming*1112	3wd,angled in,no rally	7
16Apr00-8SA	fst	1	:223 :461 1:103 1:352	4↑ OC 100k/c -N	99	4 44½ 54½ 31½ 1hd 32	Espinoza V	LB118	*1.70	92-06	*OutofMind*1181 DancingAfleet1181 ClassicCt1187	3wd move,led,outkicked	6
25Sep99-10TP	fst	1⅛	:47 1:113 1:372 1:502	3↑ KyCpClH-G2	76	5 53½ 53½ 75¼ 715 719¾	Flores D R	L122 b	2.20	63-24	Da Devil112½ *Social Charter*115hd *Cat Thief*1174	Inside final 3 furs	8
22Aug99-7EmD	fst	1	:23 :453 1:10 1:343	3↑ LgaMileH-G3	76	2 67¾ 76¾ 64¼ 810 815¾	Baze R A	LB123	*.80	77-18	*Budroyale*119½ *Mike K*1174¼ Kid Katabatic1161½	Dull effort, trailed	8
11Apr99-7SA	wf	1⅛	:463 1:10 1:344 1:473	4↑ SnBrdnoH-G2	112	2 42½ 31 3½ 1½ 13½	Stevens G L	LB122	*.40	97-14	Classic Cat1223½ *Budroyale*1198 Klinsman11515	3wd,strong hand ride	4
12Mar99-7SA	fst	1 1/16	:231 :464 1:101 1:412	4↑ TokyoCityH74k	106	6 65½ 52½ 3nk 1hd 11¼	Stevens G L	LB120	*.80	96-04	*Classic Cat*1201¼ Budroyale1204 Sea of Secrets1175	Drifted in 1/8,gamely	6
Previously trained by Cross David C Jr													
27Sep98-9LaD	fst	1¼	:47 1:103 1:354 2:012	SuperDby-G1	99	1 48½ 46 43¼ 22½ 23	Sellers S J	L126	*.90	91-13	*Arch*1263 *Classic Cat*1261 Sir Tiff1261½	Strong move, 2nd best	7
30Aug98-8RP	fst	1⅛	:47 1:11 1:353 1:48	RpDerby300k	100	1 54 63¼ 22 1hd 1¾	Sellers S J	LB124	*.30	105-07	Classic Cat124¾ *Leave a Legacy*121½ Sir Tiff1175½	Bmp st,up in fnl strds	8
19Jly98-11Tdn	fst	1⅛	:47 1:11 1:37 1:494	OhioDrby-G2	100	8 73¼ 63¼ 42 2hd 1no	Sellers S J	LB122	*2.10	90-13	*Classic Cat*122no One BoldStroke1185 HotWells1183¾	Long drive prevailed	10
6Jun98-9Bel	fst	1½	:483 1:132 2:29	Belmont-G1	88	5 119¼ 1010 1013 816 818	Velazquez J R	L126	10.40	81-09	VictoryGallop126no RealQuiet1266 *ThomasJo*1261¼	Roused 2nd turn empty	11
16May98-10Pim	fst	1 3/16	:462 1:11 1:354 1:543	Preaknss-G1	106	3 64 58 62¾ 32½ 33	Albarado R J	L126	12.30	89-13	Real Quiet1262¼ *Victory Gallop*126¾ Classic Cat1263¾	Rail,angld 3w,fin well	10
19Apr98-8Kee	my	1 1/16	:232 :463 1:104 1:424	Lexingtn-G2	108	1 66 65½ 52¼ 32 1hd	Albarado R J	L114	9.50	94-18	Classic Cat114hd Voyamerican1144 *Grand Slam*1231½	Angled out driving	8
4Apr98-5SA	fst	1⅛	:46 1:094 1:342 1:47	SADerby-G1	83	5 55 67½ 55 59½ 516¾	Alvarado F T	LB120	25.80	84-05	Indian Charlie1202¼ *Real Quiet*1207 Artax1206	Hit gate, no rally	7
13Mar98-7SA	fst	1	:224 :462 1:102 1:35	Alw 51520N$Y	103	5 43½ 53½ 52½ 44 34½	Delahoussaye E	LB116 b	10.20	91-14	*Indian Charlie*1152½ Quake1172 Classic Cat1161¾	Passed tiring rivals	5
18Jan98-7GG	sly	1 1/16	:222 :461 1:104 1:431	GGDerby200k	69	6 55 75¾ 75¾ 710 716½	Alvarado F T	LB120	13.10	69-19	Clover Hunter1206½ Mantles Star1201½ Allen's Oop1204	3w trip, empty	8
20Dec97-7GG	fst	1 1/16	:233 :463 1:113 1:413	SmplyMjstH63k	87	4 43½ 33 31½ 33½ 24½	Alvarado F T	LB115	5.00	90-11	DixieDotCom1164½ ClssicCt115¾ ATouchofGrey1133½	Stlkd 3w, no match	5
15Nov97-9BM	sly	1	:24 :481 1:124 1:363	CalJuv-G3	83	4 54½ 44½ 42 32½ 25½	Stevens G L	LB115	*1.10	80-19	KingSlewie1155½ ClassicCat115hd Champ'sStar1151	4w trip, bid, no match	6
26Oct97-6SA	fst	7f	:231 :46 1:104 1:23	Md Sp Wt 33k	83	2 3 42 41½ 1½ 16	Stevens G L	LB120	*2.30	89-14	Classic Cat1206 Crypt de Chine1201½ *Artax*120no	Strong rally,rddn out	8
5Oct97-6SA	fst	6f	:213 :442 :563 1:091	Md Sp Wt 33k	76	3 8 44 32 33 33¾	Nakatani C S	LB120	3.20	88-07	MyfavoritePlace1201¼ RedFlgRising1202½ *ClssicCt*120½	Steady rally inside	11

COMMENDABLE (Gone West—Bought Twice, by In Reality). Kentucky. With a pedigree top-heavy with brilliant influences (Gone West, In Reality, and Dr. Fager), Commendable was the unlikely winner of one of the strangest renewals of the Belmont Stakes in 2000. A flashy chestnut, he finished second in the Super Derby to Tiznow and third in the Travers Stakes behind Unshaded and Albert the Great. Make no mistake, however, about this horse's potential as a stallion. His appeal stems not only from the natural speed inherited from Gone West and In Reality, but the unusually high class of his female family. His dam is a half-sister to five stakes winners, most notably Fappiano, and stakes winners Honour and Glory, Quiet American, and Ogygian also come from this prolific family. Commendable will be attractive to breeders worldwide because of the tremendous versatility in his pedigree. Gone West and In Reality were major stakes winners on dirt, and became influential stallions, siring stakes winners on dirt, and especially on wet tracks and grass. Commendable will certainly sire a large number of winners on dirt, but because he was ideally bred for turf, Commendable is another hidden turf sire. His runners will be overlooked on that surface, providing spectacular betting opportunities, at least until the public catches on. (HT^2)

Commendable
Own: Lewis Robert B. and Beverly J

Ch. h. 7 (Apr)
Sire: Gone West (Mr. Prospector) $150,000
Dam: Bought Twice (In Reality)
Br: Edward J. Kelly Jr., Gregory W. Kelly & Michael M. Kel (Ky)
Tr: Lukas D. W(0 0 0 0 .00) 2004:(359 40 .11)

Life	12	2	1	1	$907,470	105	D.Fst	10	2	1	1	$894,470	105
2000	10	1	1	1	$864,870	105	Wet(338)	2	0	0	0	$13,000	101
1999	2	1	0	0	$42,600	87	Turf(310)	0	0	0	0	$0	-
	0	0	0	0	$0	-	Dst(0)	0	0	0	0	$0	-

30Sep00- 6LaD	fst	1¼	:47^{1}	1:10^{2}	1:35^{1}	1:59^{4}	SpDbyXXI-G1	105	1	2½	2^{hd}	2^{1}	2^{3}	2^{6}	Day P	L124 b	2.20	97- 05	*Tiznow*124^{6} Commendable124^{1} Mass Market124^{9}	Dueled, ducked out 1/8	6
26Aug00- 9Sar	fst	1¼	:48^{2}	1:12^{3}	1:37^{3}	2:02^{2}	Travers-G1	99	3	1½	3^{nk}	3^{1}	3^{3}	$3^{6½}$	Day P	L126 b	9.20	86- 07	*Unshded*126^{hd} AlbertthGrt$126^{6½}$ Commndbl$126^{2¾}$	Argued pace, weakened	9
6Aug00-11Mth	fst	1⅛	:47^{2}	1:11	1:36^{3}	1:50	HsklInvH-G1	83	7	5^{2}	$3^{1½}$	$3^{1½}$	$7^{7½}$	8^{17}	Day P	L122 b	4.50e	69- 16	DixieUnion$117^{¾}$ *CptinSteve*118^{hd} MilwukeeBrew117^{2}	Traffic 1st turn,tired	9
9Jly00- 8Bel	fst	1 1/16	:24	:46^{3}	1:10^{2}	1:42^{3}	Dwyer-G2	99	2	2½	$2^{1½}$	4^{3}	$4^{3½}$	$4^{5¼}$	Blanc B	L123 b	9.70	79- 22	AlberttheGret115^{3} MoreThnRdy$119^{1¾}$ *RdBullt*$123^{½}$	Bumped start, steadied	4
10Jun00- 9Bel	fst	1½	:49^{1}	1:14^{1}	2:05	2:31	Belmont-G1	101	3	2½	2^{hd}	$1^{1½}$	$1^{2½}$	$1^{1½}$	Day P	L126 b	18.80	84- 19	Commendable$126^{1½}$ *Aptitude*126^{1} Unshaded126^{6}	Vigorous hand ride	11
6May00- 8CD	fst	1¼	:45^{4}	1:09^{4}	1:35^{3}	2:01	KyDerby-G1	69	12	$9^{4¾}$	$13^{7½}$	16^{8}	17^{13}	17^{26}	Prado E S	L126 b	6.20e	79 -	FusaichiPegsus$126^{1½}$ Aptitude126^{4} Impechment$126^{½}$	Wide, trip, gave way	19
22Apr00- 9Kee	fst	1 1/16	:22^{2}	:45^{4}	1:10^{3}	1:43^{3}	Lexingtn-G2	93	4	4^{4}	4^{2}	$4^{1¼}$	$6^{3¼}$	$4^{3¼}$	Day P	L116 b	*2.30	84- 15	Unshaded116^{3} Globalize120^{hd} HarlanTrveler116^{no}	No room briefly strtch	8
19Mar00- 7SA	fst	1 1/16	:23	:45^{4}	1:10^{1}	1:42^{3}	SnFelipe-G2	99	3	1^{1}	1^{2}	1^{2}	3^{2}	$4^{3¾}$	Antley C W	LB118 b	7.90	86- 14	*Fusaichi Pegasus*$116^{¾}$ *The Deputy*122^{3} Anees119^{hd}	Speed, rated, tired	7
4Mar00- 9SA	gd	1	:23^{1}	:46^{1}	1:10	1:36^{2}	SnRafael-G2	101	5	$4^{3½}$	$4^{3½}$	$4^{3½}$	$4^{3¼}$	4^{1}	Day P	LB115	5.20	88- 13	War Chant$116^{½}$ Archer City Slew118^{nk} Cocky115^{nk}	Late bid outside	6
12Feb00- 3SA	my	6f	:21^{2}	:44^{3}	:56^{4}	1:09^{4}	Alw 57500n1x	85	1	6	4^{4}	4^{4}	$3^{4½}$	$5^{4½}$	Day P	LB119	2.70	85- 13	Echo Eddie121^{1} Here's Zealous119^{2} Star Maker$117^{1½}$	Bit slow into stride	6
8Sep99- 8Dmr	fst	7f	:22^{2}	:44^{4}	1:09	1:21^{3}	DmrFut-G2	87	4	3	$4^{1½}$	$5^{2¾}$	$4^{6½}$	$4^{8¾}$	Stevens G L	LB116	5.60	86- 09	ForestCamp$116^{5½}$ *DixieUnion*121^{2} *CaptainSteve*$115^{1¼}$	Angled in, no late bid	5
14Aug99- 6Dmr	fst	6½f	:22	:45	1:10^{3}	1:17^{2}	Md Sp Wt 46k	81	11	2	3^{4}	2^{hd}	$1^{2½}$	1^{4}	Antley C W	LB118	*1.30	84- 13	Commendable118^{4} Silver Axe118^{nk} Ronton118^{no}	3 wide bid, handily	11

CROWD PLEASER (A.P. Indy—Creaking Board, by Night Shift). Maryland. Followers of trainer Jonathan Sheppard will undoubtedly remember the exploits of Crowd Pleaser, who developed into a stakes winner on turf after beginning his career on dirt. At 3, he won the Saranac Handicap, Virginia Derby, and Calder Derby, all on grass. Crowd Pleaser is by A.P. Indy, who gets runners on all surfaces, and is out of a mare by Night Shift, a strong turf influence who just happens to be a full brother to champion racemare and broodmare Fanfreluche. The key to Crowd Pleaser's runners: distance and turf. (T^2)

Crowd Pleaser
Own: Augustin Stable

Dk. b or b. h. 9 (Feb)
Sire: A.P. Indy (Seattle Slew) $300,000
Dam: Creaking Board*GB (Night Shift)
Br: George Strawbridge Jr. (Pa)
Tr: Sheppard Jonathan E(0 0 0 0 .00) 2004:(237 36 .15)

Life	24	9	1	3	$605,150	102	D.Fst	6	1	0	1	$32,080	87
2000	4	1	1	1	$118,019	102	Wet(416)	2	2	0	0	$33,450	71
1999	6	1	0	1	$51,780	90	Turf(306)	16	6	1	2	$539,620	102
	0	0	0	0	$0	-	Dsl(0)	0	0	0	0	$0	-

22Oct00-8Kee	yl	1⅝	(T)	1:412 2:313 2:44	3↑	Sycamore74k	101	3	21	2hd	2½	1hd	1no	Borel C H	L118 b	2.40	73-21	CrowdPlsr118no DxsCrown1222½ KmLovsBucky114½	Pressed pace,gamely	7
23Sep00-14KD	fm	1½	(T)	:481 1:144 2:024 2:273	3↑	KyCupTurfH300k	102	8	32	21	22½	21½	2hd	Borel C H	L113 b	17.00	100-03	DownthAisl117hd *CrowdPlsr*1131½ RoylStrnd1151	Stalk,drw even,outgamd	8
3Sep00-7Del	fm	1⅛	(T)	:474 1:112 1:361 1:484	3↑	SussexH100k	95	6	611	613	79½	77	32¼	Umana J L	L114 b	8.00	94-07	PrivteSlip117½ JohnnyDollr1141¾ CrowdPleser1141	Stumbled, gaining 7w	8
30Jly00-5Del	fst	1		:233 :464 1:12 1:38	3↑	OC 80k/N$MY-N	75	2	57½	59	511	59	48¼	Martin C W	L116 b	3.90	81-20	GoldStrDputy1161¼ MontnDrmin1161½ GllntGrrick1165½	Failed to menace	5
30Oct99-8Aqu	fm	1⅛	(T)	:494 1:131 1:37 1:49	3↑	KnkrbkrH-G2	90	5	52½	52½	53	65¾	54¼	Samyn J L	L115 b	13.40	94-08	ChargedAffires114hd *ComicStrip*1191 NtsBigPrty1131	Rated, no response	7
15Oct99-7Med	yl	1⅜	(T)	:491 1:15 1:404 2:192	3↑	MedEndurnc60k	90	8	813	810	63½	43½	32½	Samyn J L	L126 b	*1.40	60-27	Mi Narrow126½ A Little Luck1262 Crowd Pleaser126no	Finished well	8
25Sep99-8Bel	fm	1⅛	[T]	:482 1:123 1:37 1:491	3↑	BelBCH-G2	85	2	72¼	72¾	75¼	89½	98¾	Samyn J L	L116 b	12.80	73-24	With the Flow114½ Comic Strip1181 Wised Up112¾	Bumped second turn	9
2Sep99-6Sar	fst	1⅛		:47 1:11 1:36 1:483	3↑	Alw 57000c	71	5	59½	514	514	511	416	Samyn J L	L119 b	7.70	77-07	*Hanarsaan*117½ Social Charter1227 Prory1148½	Bobbled start, inside	5
1Aug99-6WO	gd	1⅜	(T)	:51 1:154 1:413 2:182	3↑	HngKngJC-G2	88	1	42¼	21½	2hd	43	45	Samyn J L	L121 b	*1.30	70-25	Crown Attorney117hd Incitatus1172 Desert Waves1193	Middle move	7
13Jly99-7Del	fm	1⅛	(T)	:491 1:134 1:381 1:50	3↑	OC 75k/N1M-N	90	2	62½	63	64¾	31½	1nk	Samyn J L	L116 b	*1.00	90-10	Crowd Pleaser116nk Hardy's Halo1191¾ Spindletop116nk	Ran down leader	8
29Nov98-8Hol	yl	1⅛	(T)	:484 1:13 1:363 1:492		ETHolDby-G1	82	8	44	44½	53	710	812	Samyn J L	L122 b	5.00	64-32	Vergennes1221¾ *Dixie Dot Com*1221¾ Lone Bid122½	Close up, weakened	10
31Oct98-8Crc	fm	1⅛	(T)	:483 1:114 1:353 1:473		CrcDerby200k	102	5	74½	63¼	41½	1hd	12¼	Samyn J L	L122 b	*1.20	86-16	Crowd Pleaser1222¼ Stay Sound1221¾ *TheKaiser*117no	Best under pressure	10
3Oct98-11Cnl	fm	1¼	(T)	:49 1:134 1:364 2:001		VrgniaDrby250k	99	6	51¾	41	2hd	13	13	Samyn J L	L117 b	*1.40	- -	*CrowdPleaser*1173 DistntMirge1152 *ErrntEscort*115hd	In tight 1st,4w,drivng	10
5Sep98-8Sar	fm	1 3/16	(T)	:471 1:11 1:351 1:532		SarancH-G3	98	7	44	44	63¾	1hd	14	Samyn J L	L115 b	28.75	94-07	*CrowdPleser*1154 *PrdeGround*1221¾ RformrRlly115¾	Wide move, drew clear	7
7Aug98-7Sar	fm	1⅜	[T]	:492 1:15 1:401 2:173	3↑	Alw 42000N3x	89	2	53	42½	41½	4¾	1¾	Bailey J D	L113 b	2.95	72-27	*CrowdPleaser*113¾ RussianRuler1174 IrishSilence1211¼	Angled out, in time	5
26Jly98-6Del	fm	1⅛	(T)	:49 1:13 1:382 1:503		KentBC201k	87	4	107	108½	86	64½	44¾	Umana J L	L115 b	19.50	82-16	Keene Dancer1173 Red Reef1151 Danielle's Gray117¾	In tight, taken u. trn	11
5Jly98-9Del	fst	1⅛		:474 1:122 1:382 1:504	3↑	Alw 28300N2x	87	4	55½	56½	64½	5½	1no	Umana J L	L109 b	2.30	86-08	CrowdPlesr109no BdnsFlsh1162¼ TrimAccount116¾	Crcled field,prevailed	6
17Jun98-6Del	fst	1 1/16		:24 :474 1:122 1:434		Alw 28300N3L	86	3	66	67	56	45½	34¼	McCarthy M J	L116 b	3.00	90-06	EasternDaydream1191½ MtLurel1162¾ *CrowdPleser*1163¾	Angled in, rallied	6
25Apr98-8Hia	fm	1 1/16	(T)	1:42		Davie27k	69	11	89½	87	96¾	89¼	79	Elliott S	117 b	*1.70	74-17	Dr. Gigolo1143¾ Midnight Coyote113½ Adeli113½	Wide trip	11
13Mar98-7GP	fm	*1 1/16	(T)	:24 :484 1:13 1:433		ParadseCrk51k	86	4	53½	65½	53½	54¾	42¾	McCarthy M J	117 b	3.70	80-19	*Chilito*1191½ East of Easy122no Silver Launch1191¼	Lacked late response	6
Run in divisions																				
30Nov97-8Aqu	fst	1⅛		:50 1:141 1:392 1:521		Remsen-G2	66	6	75¼	74¾	712	615	515½	Krone J A	115 b	11.80	59-22	CorondosQst1225 HloryHntr1154 BrklynNck115no	Taken up back stretch	7
15Nov97-8Pha	my	1 1/16		:232 :482 1:14 1:47		ValleyForg32k	71	7	911	84	41½	41½	11½	Umana J L	117 b	*1.40	78-24	CrowdPleser1171½ Poolmn1171½ *GlidingDrgon*122nk	Squeezed str, blocked	9
25Oct97-3Del	sly	1 1/16		:241 :484 1:14 1:472		Md Sp Wt 23k	63	6	21½	32½	11½	12	14	Umana J L	118 b	5.60	76-16	*Crowd Pleaser*1184 Twice as Big1183½ Entrapment1187¾	Driving	6
5Oct97-1Del	fst	6f		:213 :451 :58 1:112		Md Sp Wt 23k	36	1	7	816	818	712	712¾	Rice D S	119	3.20	72-13	*SouthernBostonion*1191½ FlamingBridle1192¾ TmoksTlking1191½	No threat	9

DANCE MASTER (Gone West—Nijinsky's Lover, by Nijinsky II). Florida. Gone West is fast becoming a sire of sires with such outstanding sons as Grand Slam and Elusive Quality, and because Dance Master showed precocious speed at 2, winning the Bashford Manor Stakes, his runners should also be very quick at 2. His third dam is a half-sister to 1969 2-year-old champion Silent Screen. Speed on top and a strong T^2 pedigree.

Dance Master
Own: Padua Stables

Ch. h. 7 (Apr)
Sire: Gone West (Mr. Prospector) $150,000
Dam: Nijinsky's Lover (Nijinsky II)
Br: Gilman Investment Co (Fla)
Tr: Lukas D. W(0 0 0 0 .00) 2004:(359 40 .11)

Life	19	4	2	1	$196,455	101	D.Fst	14	3 1 1 $165,855 101
2000	10	2	2	0	$59,529	101	Wet(345)	3	1 0 0 $22,050 88
1999	9	2	0	1	$136,926	92	Turf(350)	2	0 1 0 $8,550 81
	0	0	0	0	$0	-	Dst(0)	0	0 0 0 $0 -

23Sep00-15TP	sly	6½f	:223 :452 1:104 1:171	3↑ Marfa75k	88	3	1	2hd	1hd	2½	56	King E L Jr	L113	6.80	83-18	*SeofTrnquility*1142½ WouldntWAll1161½ VictorAvnu114½	3 path, weakened	6
14Sep00-9TP	fst	6f	:221 :453 :573 1:102	3↑ Alw 27230N$Y	101	5	1	21½	2hd	11½	11	Borel C H	L113 f	*.90	89-22	DanceMaster1131 LakeHamilton1163½ PicsLegend113hd	3 wide, held sway	6
26Aug00-8Mth	fst	6f	:213 :442 :563 1:094	3↑ OC 35k/N3X-N	92	5	1	2hd	1hd	11½	2½	King E L Jr	L114	3.80	91-13	Driver118½ *Dance Master*1144¾ Humberto1181¼	Overcome final strides	6
12Aug00-6Mth	sly	5f	⊗ :213 :45 :58	3↑ OC 35k/N3X-N	87	2	1	2½	1½	13	15¾	King E L Jr	L113	2.40	90-15	Dance Master1135¾ *Mad River*120nk D'part1142¼	Drew off,steady urging	6
5Aug00-10Mth	fst	6f	:214 :451 :574 1:104	SmokeGlakn45k	56	2	2	11½	2½	54½	515¼	Velez J A Jr	L117	9.10	72-10	Energized1142¼ DontTllthKids1193 *PolishMissil*115½	Set early pace, faded	6
9Jly00-9Mth	fm	5f	Ⓣ :204 :431 :552	AndrsnFwlr45k	81	9	2	2hd	1hd	2½	22½	King E L Jr	L113	8.80	96-01	D'part1132½ Dance Master113½ Skyrunner113no	Pressed,led,no match	10
7Apr00-8Kee	fm	1	Ⓣ :224 :46 1:103 1:35	Transylvna113k	43	4	2½	21	75	915	924¼	Peck B D	L116	22.20	73-09	Field Cat1161½ Lendell Ray1162 Go Lib Go1231½	Pressed pace, tired	9
25Mar00-8SA	fst	6½f	:222 :45 1:093 1:16	SanPedro81k	83	1	1	32½	3nk	31½	48	Espinoza V	LB119	18.00	80-12	SweptOvrbord1195½ Fortifir1191 GibsonCounty1191½	Rail trip, weakened	5
27Feb00-7SA	wf	6½f	⊗ :21 :433 1:094 1:163	Baldwin-G3	56	7	3	33	43½	711	815½	Antley C W	LB122	12.00	69-16	Fortfr1141½ PrformngMgc116hd JoopyDpy117nk	Swung 5wd lane,gve way	8
5Jan00-9GP	fst	6f	:221 :452 :574 1:103	SpectBid-G3	74	5	2	2hd	1hd	2hd	43	Bailey J D	L119	9.70	83-20	B L's Appeal114hd AmericanBullet1142½ TourtheHive112½	Vied, weakened	8
28Nov99-8Aqu	fst	6f	:214 :452 :581 1:112	Huntington85k	51	8	1	3½	21	43	712¼	Prado E S	L122	4.00	69-21	Twilight Time1221 *Never Wink*1171½ *Lord of Time*117nk	Forced pace, tired	10
5Nov99-6GP	fst	6f	:222 :45 :572 1:101	GildedTime100k	84	3	5	2hd	1hd	1hd	33	Bailey J D	L117	5.00	88-07	Outrigger115½ *BLsAppeal*1132½ DanceMaster117¾	Dueled,inside,weakened	12
15Oct99-6Kee	fst	6f	:212 :442 :562 1:082	FtSprings64k	70	9	1	32	3½	42	79	Day P	L121	*1.30e	91-02	ChrliesBeu1191½ LcGrnd1175½ *TemperedAppl*117nk	Stalked pace,weakened	10
18Aug99-9Sar	fst	6½f	:214 :45 1:104 1:173	SarSpcl-G2	29	1	4	1½	2hd	56½	524¼	Bailey J D	L122	2.90	62-15	*Bevo*1172½ Afternoon Affair1141 Settlement1148	Vied inside, tired	6
29Jly99-9Sar	fst	6f	:221 :45 :564 1:093	Sanford-G2	66	5	1	1hd	1hd	27	415¼	Bailey J D	L119	3.10	78-09	More Than Ready1229¾ Mighty1143 Bulling1142½	Set pace, tired	5
26Jun99-10CD	fst	6f	:212 :45 :57 1:101	BshfdMnr-G2	92	1	2	11	11½	16	13	Peck B D	L115	3.20	92-09	Dance Master1153 Sky Dweller1154¾ *Snuck In*115hd	Drifted out start,drvg	8
5Jun99-1Bel	fst	5½f	:224 :461 :581 1:044	Md Sp Wt 40k	89	8	4	1½	1½	13½	14	Bailey J D	L116	*1.05	91-10	*DanceMaster*1164 *Settlement*117½ BrodwyBrney111¾	Pace, clear, kept busy	10
16May99-1CD	fst	5f	:221 :451 :573	Md Sp Wt 37k	83	2	1	11	1hd	1½	21	Day P	L118	*.60	99-07	Sky Dweller1181 [D]*DanceMaster*1183 *SnuckIn*1182	Bumped start,outgamed	9
Disqualified and placed 9th																		
18Apr99-1Kee	fst	4½f	:22 :452 :513	Md Sp Wt 43k	–	7	4	2hd		2hd	42¼	Bailey J D	118	*1.40	96-02	Ultimate Warrior118¾ Scouting Report118hd Gadir1181½	Dueled, tired	10

DAVID (Mt. Livermore—Fateful Beauty, by Turkoman). New York. One of the best New York-breds of recent years, David won the Bertram F. Bongard Stakes at 2, the New York Derby at 3, and then stepped out of statebred company to finish second in the San Bernardino Handicap and third in the Massachusetts Handicap and Grade 1 Hollywood Gold Cup. David's runners should be best from six furlongs to 1 1/16 miles on dirt, and he is another hidden turf sire because he has some strong turf influences up close in his pedigree, most notably Blushing Groom, Turkoman, and Codex. His second dam is a half-sister to champion sprinter Gold Beauty, the dam of Dayjur and Maplejinsky. (HT^2)

David
Own: Schwartz Barry K

Ch. h. 8 (Mar)
Sire: Mt. Livermore (Blushing Groom*Fr) $35,000
Dam: Fateful Beauty (Turkoman)
Br: Stonewall Farm (NY)
Tr: Hushion Michael E(0 0 0 0 .00) 2004:(201 34 .17)

Life	14	5	3	2	$403,920	114	D.Fst	11	5 3 2 $394,920 114
2000	4	0	1	2	$201,830	113	Wet(365)	2	0 0 0 $9,000 99
1999	7	3	1	0	$141,930	114	Turf(273)	1	0 0 0 $0 51
	0	0	0	0	$0	-	Dst(0)	0	0 0 0 $0 -

6Aug00-9Sar	gd	1⅛	:463 1:101 1:35 1:481	3↑ WhitneyH-G1	76	4	11	1½	3½	611	625	Gryder A T	L114 f	16.50	75 -	*Lemon Drop Kid*1232 Cat Thief1174¼ Behrens1221½	Vied inside, tired	6
9Jly00-5Hol	fst	1¼	:462 1:10 1:344 2:012	3↑ HolGldCp-G1	108	2	11½	11	1½	3½	32½	Gryder A T	LB124 f	11.40	85-12	Early Pioneer1241 General Challenge1241½ David1241¼	Inside,wkened late	9
3Jun00-13Suf	fst	1⅛	:462 1:103 1:361 1:492	3↑ MassH-G2	113	6	1½	1½	11	2hd	32½	Gryder A T	LB113 f	5.10	86-17	Running Stag1161¼ Out of Mind1161¼ David113¾	Rail 2nd, weakened	8
9Apr00-8SA	fst	1⅛	:474 1:111 1:36 1:49	4↑ SnBrdnoH-G2	112	2	11½	11½	11½	11	2hd	Gryder A T	LB113 f	5.30	90-18	EarlyPioneer113hd David1132½ GenerlChllenge1232	Fought back,game try	5
18Dec99-7Aqu	fst	1⅛	⊡ :471 1:113 1:361 1:483	3↑ Alw 48000N3X	114	4	11½	1½	11½	13½	15½	Gryder A T	L114 f	2.25	98-13	Dvid1145½ CrryMyColors11412½ TickleMRd119nk	Drew away when roused	10
18Aug99-8Sar	fm	1⅛	Ⓣ :462 1:102 1:344 1:462	Alw 50000C	51	8	11½	1hd	2hd	77	921¼	Gryder A T	L122 f	3.85	77-07	MonrchsMz1155½ GoldFrmthWst1171 Rhythmn1191½	Dueled inside, tired	9
31Jly99-8FL	fst	1 1/16	:234 :472 1:12 1:452	[S]MINYDerby100k	94	3	11	11	12½	18	16¼	Gryder A T	L113 f	*.80	88-29	David1136¼ Hearts At Risk115½ Flora'spersonalboy1171¼	Drew off	7
26Jun99-7Bel	fst	7f	:223 :453 1:102 1:232	[S]MikeLee85k	88	11	5	21½	21	2½	2¾	Gryder A T	L117 f	*.55	84-13	Hearts At Risk119¾ *David*117½ Brocco's Magick115¾	Vied 4 wide, gamely	12
23May99-8Bel	my	1⅛	:451 1:09 1:344 1:474	PeterPan-G2	99	1	1½	11½	11	1hd	44½	Gryder A T	L113 f	10.50	87-27	BstofLuck1131 TrsrIslnd1141½ *LmonDropKd*1202	Gave ground grudgingly	9
10Apr99-10Aqu	fst	1⅛	:464 1:103 1:351 1:473	WoodMem-G2	87	7	2hd	2hd	1hd	53½	89¼	Gryder A T	L123 f	9.20	89-09	Adonis1232 Best of Luck1231¾ *Cliquot*123no	Vied outside, tired	11
19Mar99-9Aqu	fst	1	:24 :472 1:113 1:36	3↑ [S]Alw 45000N2X	100	1	2hd	1½	12½	16	18½	Bravo J	L110 f	*.95	88-21	David1108½ *Emilys Dad*1191 Gander1107¾	On his own courage	9
4Oct98-8Bel	fst	7f	:231 :463 1:111 1:24	[S]BFBongard53k	90	5	2	1hd	1½	11½	13½	Gryder A T	L117 f	*1.50	82-18	*David*1173½ Ewer All Wet11714 Hearts At Risk1222½	Speed,clear,driving	6
21Aug98-1Sar	fst	6f	:223 :463 :59 1:114	[S]Md Sp Wt 35k	75	6	2	1hd	11½	11	12	Gryder A T	L116 f	*.70	82-13	*David*1162 *Hearts AtRisk*1169¾ TwentyThreeRed1166	Speed in hand, driving	9
3Aug98-3Sar	fst	5½f	:221 :454 :574 1:042	[S]Md Sp Wt 35k	63	8	6	32	21	22½	26½	Gryder A T	116 f	14.10	89-10	Silk Broker1166½ *David*1162 Doomsday Defense1111	Game finish outside	12

DIXIE UNION (Dixieland Band—She's Tops, by Capote). Kentucky. Dixie Union is poised to be a major stallion. He is by one of Northern Dancer's best sons at stud, and his third dam is a half-sister to Fall Aspen, 1994 Broodmare of the Year and dam of a remarkable nine high-quality stakes winners. Dixie Union was a classy juvenile, winning the Norfolk and Best Pal Stakes and Hollywood Juvenile Championship. At 3, he won the Malibu Stakes and carried his speed 1⅛ miles to win the Haskell Invitational Handicap. Dixie Union should be among 2004's top five freshman sires, and his offspring will be characterized by speed. (SP^2)

Dixie Union
Own: Diamond A Racing Corporation and Sark

Dk. b or b. h. 7 (Mar)
Sire: Dixieland Band (Northern Dancer) $50,000
Dam: She's Tops (Capote)
Br: Herman Sarkowsky (Ky)
Tr: Mandella Richard E(0 0 0 0 .00) 2004:(94 13 .14)

Life	12	7	3	0	$1,233,190	112	D.Fst	12	7	3	0	$1,233,190	112
2000	6	3	2	0	$863,170	112	Wet(383)	0	0	0	0	$0	-
1999	6	4	1	0	$370,020	104	Turf(296)	0	0	0	0	$0	-
Aik Ⓣ	0	0	0	0	$0	-	DstⓉ(360)	0	0	0	0	$0	-

26Dec00-6SA	fst	7f	:221 :442 1:083 1:213	Malibu-G1	**104**	3	2	3½	3nk	2½	11	Solis A	LB121	1.60	97-09	Dixie Union1211 *Caller One*119½ Wooden Phone1161	3 wide bid, gamely	6
26Aug00-9Sar	fst	1¼	:482 1:123 1:373 2:022	Travers-G1	**95**	7	31	2hd	41¼	43	49¼	Solis A	L126	*2.55	84-07	*Unshaded*126hd Albert the Great1266½ Commendable1262¾	In tight early	9
6Aug00-11Mth	fst	1⅛	:472 1:11 1:363 1:50	HsklInvH-G1	**111**	8	62¼	63	53½	42	1¾	Solis A	L117	4.70	86-16	DixieUnion117¾ *CptinSteve*118hd MilwukeeBrw1172	Checked 1st turn,drvg	9
1Jly00-8Hol	fst	1 1/16	:231 :46 1:101 1:421	AffirmdH-G3	**103**	5	31	21	2½	1hd	2nk	Solis A	LB122	*.80	89-18	Tiznow111nk *Dixie Union*1222 Millencolin1172	3wd,led,outgamed	6
29May00-9Hol	fst	7f	:221 :441 1:08 1:21	LBrreraMem99k	**112**	3	2	32	22½	24	22	Pincay L Jr	LB122	*1.10	92-13	*Caller One*1222 Dixie Union1222 *Swept Overboard*1225	Stalked,2nd best	4
7May00-9Hol	fst	6½f	:221 :45 1:09 1:151	Alw 62700NC	**107**	5	1	32	1hd	12	11½	Solis A	LB122	1.90	95-16	DixieUnion1221½ SweptOverbord1224½ ElgntFllow1224	Bid rail,led,gamely	5
6Nov99-8GP	fst	1 1/16	:221 :46 1:101 1:421	BCJuven-G1	**85**	12	95¼	73¼	77¼	76¾	59½	Solis A	L122	4.40	86 -	Anees1222½ Chief Seattle122¾ High Yield1222¼	Failed to rally	14
10Oct99-7SA	fst	1	:221 :454 1:094 1:353	Norfolk-G2	**104**	6	43	21	21½	21	1½	Solis A	LB118	4.20	93-15	Dixie Union118½ Forest Camp1184½ *Anees*1189½	Gamely wore down foe	6
8Sep99-8Dmr	fst	7f	:222 :444 1:09 1:213	DmrFut-G2	**94**	2	2	2hd	3½	23½	25½	Solis A	LB121	*.80	89-09	ForestCamp1165½ *DixieUnion*1212 *CptinSteve*1151¼	Dueled,no match,2d bst	5
18Aug99-7Dmr	fst	6½f	:22 :443 1:094 1:162	BestPal-G3	**97**	1	4	2½	21	2½	1½	Solis A	B121	*1.40	89-13	Dixie Union121½ *Exchange Rate*1175½ CaptainSteve1174½	Game on rail lane	5
18Jly99-5Hol	fst	6f	:213 :443 :57 1:094	HolJuvCh-G3	**88**	2	5	2hd	1hd	2hd	11¼	Solis A	B117	*.70	88-11	*DixieUnion*1171¼ ExchangeRate1173½ *HighYield*1156½	Dueled,game rail lane	5
13Jun99-5Hol	fst	5f	:212 :443 :563	Md Sp Wt 42k	**99**	3	5	2½	22	21½	11½	Solis A	B118	*2.40	100-12	*DixieUnion*1181½ *CallerOne*1187½ FourwayAction1184½	Wore down rival late	8

Down the Aisle
Own: Deters Charles H

Gr/ro. h. 11 (Apr)
Sire: Runaway Groom (Blushing Groom*Fr) $15,000
Dam: That's My Hon (L'Enjoleur)
Br: Charles H. Deters (Ky)
Tr: Mott William I(0 0 0 0 .00) 2004:(414 83 .20)

Life	21	9	5	5	$1,007,988	107	D.Fst	2	0	1	1	$33,700	103
2000	6	3	0	2	$505,500	103	Wet(378)	2	1	0	1	$20,043	89
1999	3	2	0	1	$88,433	97	Turf(285)	17	8	4	3	$954,245	107
	0	0	0	0	$0	-	Dst(0)	0	0	0	0	$0	-

4Nov00-9CD	fm	1½ Ⓣ	:501 1:151 2:033 2:264	3↑BCTurf-G1	**93**	12	117½	127	1310	1312	129¾	Day P	L126 f	9.10	99 -	Kalanisi126½ Quiet Resolve126no John's Call126hd	No factor	13
23Sep00-14KD	fm	1½ Ⓣ	:481 1:144 2:024 2:273	3↑KyCupTurfH300k	**102**	5	810	85½	74¾	42½	1hd	Albarado R J	L117	*2.80	100-03	DowntheAisle117hd *CrowdPleser*1131½ RoylStrnd1151	7wide trip,hard drive	8
1Jly00-9Mth	fm	1⅜ Ⓣ	:484 1:142 1:38 2:133	3↑UntdNtnH-G1	**102**	7	58½	58	53	31½	1¾	Davis R G	L114	2.50	112-02	*Down the Aisle*114¾ Aly's Alley1111¼ Honor Glide116½	Outside,steady finish	7
11Jun00-8Bel	fst	1⅛	:47 1:114 1:371 1:494	3↑BroklynH-G2	**103**	5	55	79	711	65¾	37¼	Bailey J D	L112	17.10	75-29	*LemonDropKid*1207¼ Lager114hd *DowntheAisle*112hd	Altered course stretch	7
22Apr00-9GP	fm	1⅜ Ⓣ	:49 1:141 1:38 2:132	3↑HiaTfCpH-G2	**96**	11	86¼	84¼	51¾	31½	31½	Castellano J J	L115	3.00	84-15	MonkeyPuzzle1141¼ HonorGlide117nk DowntheAisl115½	In tight 1/16 pole	12
25Mar00-9GP	fm	1⅛ Ⓣ	:494 1:132 1:374 1:492	3↑BgnvllaH-G3	**100**	7	63½	74½	83½	52¼	1½	Castellano J J	L113	3.30	85-18	Down the Aisle113½ Mi Narrow113½ Honor Glide1181¼	Circled field	11
13Jun99-8WO	fm	1⅛ Ⓣ	:47 1:104 1:341 1:462	3↑KngEdBCH-G2	**92**	3	4¾	41¾	3½	31½	32¼	Castillo H Jr	L115	*.95	96-07	Desert Waves1101 *CrownAttorney*1161¼ *DowntheAisle*115nk	Finished evenly	7
13May99-7CD	fm	1⅛ Ⓣ	:492 1:133 1:381 1:502	3↑Alw 56300c	**97**	2	43	32½	31½	3½	1¾	Day P	L123	*.70	84-15	DownthAisl123¾ MidwyMgstrt1231¼ Doublthbtwc1184	4 wide, hand urging	6
18Feb99-5GP	fm	*1⅛ Ⓣ	:503 1:132 1:384 1:511	4↑Alw 38000N4X	**97**	6	32	31½	51¾	31	1nk	Bailey J D	L117	*.90	80-23	*Down the Aisle*117nk El Mirasol1191¼ Draw Again1171	All out, prevailed	8
19Oct97-8WO	fm	1½ Ⓣ	:504 1:144 2:043 2:29	3↑CanIntnl-G1	**107**	5	56¾	63¼	21½	23	22¼	Day P	L126	3.95	81-11	*Chief Bearhart*1262¼ *Down the Aisle*1263¼ *Romanov*1198½	3 wide, 2nd best	6
31Aug97-7WO	fm	1½ Ⓣ	:523 1:18 2:06 2:302	3↑NiagrBC-G3	**102**	8	69½	78¾	86¾	54	2½	Day P	L115	*1.35	75-17	DesertWaves117½ DowntheAisle115¾ CrownAttorney1172	Closed willingly	9
8Aug97-9Sar	fm	1½ [T]	:463 1:113 2:011 2:243	3↑Alw 43000N3X	**104**	5	89¾	86	61¾	22½	12	Day P	L115	*.95	102 -	Down the Aisle1152 *South Salem*11510 Silvange115¾	Going away late	11
4Jly97-6AP	fm	1½ Ⓣ	:51 1:154 2:292	3↑StrStBCH-G3	**101**	8	31	21	1hd	41¼	42¼	Day P	L111	3.10	97-11	Lakeshore Road114hd *Chief Bearhart*1191¾ *Awad*119½	Weakened, inside	9
8Jun97-9CD	yl	1⅜ Ⓣ	:514 1:18 1:43 2:192	3↑LouisvillH109k	**100**	1	11	1½	2½	1hd	2no	Day P	L111	*1.10	80-20	Chorwon113no DowntheAisle1111¾ SnkeEyes1161¾	Slow pace outfinished	5
3May97-7CD	fm	1⅛ Ⓣ	:492 1:131 1:371 1:491	3↑TurfClsc-G1	**101**	3	22	2hd	21	22	32¼	Day P	L114	7.60	85-14	AlwaysaClassic1201¼ Lbeeb1181 DowntheAisle114½	Drew even, weakened	8
19Apr97-7Kee	fm	1 1/16 Ⓣ	:222 :462 1:104 1:42	4↑Alw 43000c	**96**	8	715	711	77¾	55¼	2nk	Day P	L118	*1.80	93-11	Middleberg112nk Down the Aisle118nk Sealaunch1152	Bid widest, gaining	8
8Feb97-8GP	fm	1⅜ Ⓣ	:483 1:142 1:383 2:141	4↑Alw 32000N2X	**92**	9	1hd	1hd	2hd	13	14½	Day P	L122	*1.20	85-12	Down the Aisle1224½ Exaltado1192¾ SovereignRullah1221	Vied, ridden out	11
8Jan97-5GP	fm	*1⅛ Ⓣ	:491 1:14 1:384 1:50	4↑Alw 29000N1X	**88**	6	2hd	2hd	2hd	1½	12¼	Day P	L119	*2.00	86-13	*Down the Aisle*1192¼ Togher1193½ Cheerful Earful119nk	Drew off driving	10
2Mar96-11GP	gd	1 1/16	:231 :474 1:131 1:444	Md Sp Wt 28k	**89**	5	88¾	95¾	84¼	23	11¼	Day P	122	3.40	- -	*Down the Aisle*1221¼ *Left Banker*12211½ Orient1223	Driving, bled	11
14Nov95-6CD	my	7f	:23 :472 1:132 1:262	Md Sp Wt 30k	**74**	4	10	1013	108¾	47	34½	Day P	119	*1.10	- -	GarconRouge1194¼ GoingFr119hd *DowntheAisle*119nk	Late rally, some gain	12
19Oct95-3Kee	fst	7f	:223 :461 1:114 1:244	Md Sp Wt 31k	**73**	3	11	110¼	910	40	22½	Day P	119	4.10	- -	*Storm Creek*1192½ Down the Aisle1194 Bombardier1194	4 wide, closed fast	12

DOWN THE AISLE (Runaway Groom—That's My Hon, by L'Enjoleur). Kentucky. Easily one of the most underrated stallions, Canadian champion and Travers Stakes winner Runaway Groom's stakes winners include Cherokee Run, Wekiva Springs, Najran, Groomstick, The Groom Is Red, and Down the Aisle. Down the Aisle's runners should develop slowly, be better at distances over seven furlongs, and be superior on grass, like their sire.

FIVE STAR DAY (Carson City—Reggie V, by Vanlandingham). Kentucky. Five Star Day was one of Carson City's fastest sons, winning the Vanderbilt Handicap in 1:08.57 and the Phoenix Breeders' Cup in 1:07.90. Because of this speed, Five Star Day has the potential to be an explosive sire of 2-year-olds, and his runners should be best from five to seven furlongs. (SP^2)

Five Star Day
Own: Columbine Stable and Kitchwa Stables

Ch. h. 8 (Feb)
Sire: Carson City (Mr. Prospector) $35,000
Dam: Reggie V (Vanlandingham)
Br: Robert P. McGovern (Ky)
Tr: Greely C. B(0 0 0 0 .00) 2004:(90 6 .07)

Life	16	6	5	0	$575,365	116	D.Fst	15	6	5	0	$575,365 116
2001	3	1	1	0	$130,000	111	Wet(402)	0	0	0	0	$0 -
2000	4	1	1	0	$180,245	116	Turf(255)	1	0	0	0	$0 62
	0	0	0	0	$0	-	Dst(0)	0	0	0	0	$0 -

27Oct01-6Bel	fst	6f		:222	:443	:561	1:082	3↑ PnskBCSp-G1	106	9	6	4¾	41½	53½	85	Gomez G K	L126	48.50	91-03	Squirtle Squirt124½ Xtra Heat121nk Caller One126nk	Chased 4 wide, tired	14
5Aug01-9Sar	fst	6f		:214	:443	:562	1:082	3↑ AGVndbtH-G2	111	1	3	11½	1hd	12½	11½	Gomez G K	L117	8.20	102-05	FiveStarDay1171½ *DelawareTownship*1162 Bonpw1172½	Pace, clear, driving	7
26May01-8BM	fst	6f		:214	:44	:56	1:083	3↑ SaratogaH61k	84	7	7	33	34½	35½	27½	Gomez G K	LB122	1.90	90-10	*FlomsProspctor*1147½ *FivStrDy*122nk ElDordoShootr1221	Broke in a tangle	7
24Nov00-9Hol	fm	5½f	Ⓣ	:22	:434	:553	1:013	3↑ HolTrExH-G3	62	4	7	21	43½	710	715¼	Gomez G K	LB120	7.20	83-04	*ElCielo*122nk *TexsGlitter*117½ FullMoonMdness1213	Drifted wide,gave way	7
4Nov00-6CD	fst	6f		:204	:432	:551	1:073	3↑ BCSprnt-G1	62	5	8	42½	65¾	1418	1419¾	Gomez G K	L126	13.30	87 -	*KonGold*126½ HonestLdy123½ BetOnSunshine1262	Bmp foe start,gave way	14
14Oct00-6Kee	fst	6f		:213	:444	:561	1:074	3↑ PhoenxBC-G3	116	3	1	1½	11	11½	14	Gomez G K	L119	1.80	101-10	FiveStarDay1194 Istintj1191¼ BetOnSunshine1237	Widen,strong handling	6
28Aug00-7Dmr	fst	6f		:213	:443	:572	1:10	3↑ Alw 63700N$Y	94	1	4	1½	1½	2hd	25½	Solis A	LB122 f	*.70	84-16	Old Topper1165½ *FiveStarDay*1222 TreasureHunt1161½	Inside duel,2nd best	4
26Dec99-6SA	fst	7f		:221	:441	1:084	1:22	Malibu-G1	100	3	1	1hd	12	2hd	4¾	Solis A	LB119	5.80	94-08	LoveThatRed119nk StraightMn118hd CtThief123½	Cleared,fought gamely	7
5Dec99-7Hol	fst	6f		:222	:451	:572	1:094	3↑ VOUndrwd-G3	109	2	3	16	14	12½	1½	Solis A	LB120	*.80	88-20	Five Star Day120½ YourHalo122¾ SonofaPistol1221	Inside, held on gamely	5
5Nov99-5GP	fst	6f		:214	:443	:562	1:091	ThirtySlws100k	106	1	6	1½	1hd	13	13¾	Stevens G L	L115	*1.30	96-07	*Five Star Day*1153¾ Silver Season1222½ *Abajo*1155½	Off rail, ridden out	7
25Sep99-8TP	fst	6f		:212	:444	:564	1:092	KyCpSpnt-G2	103	3	5	11	1hd	22½	26	Solis A	L114	*.60	88-20	SuccessfulAppl1226 *FivStrDy*1142 AmricnSpirit118½	Pace, 3 path, 2nd best	6
28Aug99-7Sar	fst	7f		:213	:432	1:073	1:21	KngsBshp-G1	113	4	12	12	1½	2hd	21½	Solis A	L115	9.60	98-09	Forestry1241½ FiveStrDy1153¾ *SuccessfulAppel*124½	Off slowly, bumped st.	12
30Jly99-5Dmr	fst	6f		:213	:434	:554	1:083	3↑ Alw 51500N1x	108	2	4	1½	14½	16	14	Gomez G K	LB117	6.30	97-10	Five Star Day1174 House Special1175½ B J's Dream119¾	Inside, ridden out	10
5Jly99-1Hol	fst	6f		:214	:443	:563	1:092	3↑ Md Sp Wt 41k	94	3	5	2½	21	21½	11	Gomez G K	LB116	*.70	90-13	*FiveStrDy*1161 WestofthePcos1172¾ TllAmricn1163½	Pulled,wore down foe	6
13Jun99-3Hol	fst	6f		:212	:441	:562	1:09	3↑ Md Sp Wt 41k	94	1	5	11	12	11½	21¾	Gomez G K	LB115	3.70	90-12	Very Caerleon1221¾ *Five Star Day*1154½ King of Tap1202	Bled from mouth	9
6Mar99-4SA	fst	6f		:212	:442	:57	1:101	Md Sp Wt 45k	48	8	10	3nk	3½	87¼	1015¼	Black C A	LB120	5.30	74-05	KingoftheHunt120½ BestofTim1201 Frspool120¾	Squeezed start, bumped	11

FUSAICHI PEGASUS (Mr. Prospector—Angel Fever, by Danzig). Kentucky. The only son of Mr. Prospector to win the Kentucky Derby, Fusaichi Pegasus is one of the stars of this year's freshman sires. Bred to the crème de la crème of broodmares, he should sire foals of the highest quality who will develop into major 3-year-olds. Because they are grandsons of Mr. Prospector, however, they should start to show their talent at 2, especially later in the year. His dam, Angel Fever, is a full sister to Pine Bluff and a half-sister to Demons Begone, and the immortal Ruffian comes from this exceptional female family. His runners should be played on all surfaces, fast and wet tracks, as well as on grass.

Fusaichi Pegasus
Own: Sekiguchi Fusao, Haruya, Katsumi, Har

B. h. 7 (Apr)
Sire: Mr. Prospector (Raise a Native)
Dam: Angel Fever (Danzig)
Br: Arthur B. Hancock III & Stonerside Ltd. (Ky)
Tr: Drysdale Neil D(0 0 0 0 .00) 2004:(99 20 .20)

Life	9	6	2	0	$1,994,400	115	D.Fst	7 5 1 0	$1,344,400 115
2000	8	6	1	0	$1,987,800	115	Wet(445)	2 1 1 0	$650,000 111
1999	1	M	1	0	$6,600	95	Turf(383)	0 0 0 0	$0 -
Aik ⓣ	0	0	0	0	$0	-	Dstⓣ(447)	0 0 0 0	$0 -

4Nov00-10CD	fst	1¼	:472 1:12 1:36 2:003	3↑ BCClasic-G1	105	8	72¾	83	86¼	66	67½	Desormeaux K J	L122	*1.20	99 -	*Tiznow*122nk GiantsCauseway1223¼ *CaptinSteve*122hd	7-8 wide trip,no rally	13
23Sep00-8Bel	fst	1	:223 :441 1:081 1:34	JeromeH-G2	115	1	52¾	52½	3nk	1hd	1¾	Desormeaux K J	L124 f	*1.20	95-05	FusichiPegsus124¾ *ElCorredor*1173¾ *AlberttheGrt*1208½	Vigorous hand ride	6
20May00-10Pim	gd	1 3/16	:463 1:111 1:37 1:56	Preaknss-G1	103	7	65	55	52	31½	23¾	Desormeaux K J	L126 f	*.30	81-11	RedBullt1263¾ *FusichiPgsus*126hd Impchmnt126nk	Pinched break,5wd trip	8
6May00-8CD	fst	1¼	:454 1:094 1:353 2:01	KyDerby-G1	108	15	138¾	116½	62¼	1hd	11½	Desormeaux K J	L126 f	*2.30	105 -	FusichiPegsus1261½ Aptitude1264 Impchmnt126½	Angle 7wide,hand urged	19
15Apr00-9Aqu	wf	1⅛	:464 1:102 1:352 1:474	WoodMem-G2	111	5	53½	3½	32	1½	14¼	Desormeaux K J	L123 f	*.90	98-10	*Fusaichi Pegasus*1234¼ *Red Bullet*1231½ Aptitude123nk	Vigorous hand ride	12
19Mar00-7SA	fst	1 1/16	:23 :454 1:101 1:423	SnFelipe-G2	106	5	21	22	22	11	1¾	Desormeaux K J	LB116 f	*1.30	90-14	*Fusaichi Pegasus*116¾ *The Deputy*1223 Anees119hd	Stalked, led, held	7
19Feb00-3SA	fst	1 1/16	:231 :46 1:103 1:423	Alw 54000N1x	103	3	21	32	2½	12	13½	Desormeaux K J	LB117 f	*1.20	90-20	*Fusaichi Pegasus*1173½ Tribunal1193 Toqueville1174	Bid,clear,ridden out	7
2Jan00-1SA	fst	6f	:22 :454 :58 1:104	Md Sp Wt 45k	95	6	2	21½	3½	1hd	12	Desormeaux K J	B120 f	*.20	85-18	FschPgss1202 SpcyStff12011 LghtofthWoods1205½	3wd bid,mild hand ride	6
11Dec99-6Hol	fst	6½f	:224 :452 1:101 1:163	Md Sp Wt 33k	95	1	8	52½	2hd	1hd	2nk	Espinoza V	B120 f	3.30	88-20	DvidCopprfild120nk *FusichiPgsus*1205 Forboding1201	Inside,led,outgamed	10

GIANT'S CAUSEWAY (Storm Cat—Mariah's Storm, by Rahy). Kentucky. A champion at 3 in England and Ireland, Giant's Causeway will always be remembered for his tenacity and stirring neck loss to Tiznow in the 2000 Breeders' Cup Classic—his only dirt start. The combination of his outstanding race record, high-profile pedigree, and extraordinary physical appearance make Giant's Causeway one of this year's glamour freshman sires and his runners should win on all surfaces, but be especially proficient on turf. Like Fusaichi Pegasus, he was bred to an exceptional book of mares and has been given every opportunity to succeed at stud. (T^2)

Giant's Causeway
Own: Tabor Michael and Magnier, Mrs. John

Ch. h. 7 (Feb)
Sire: Storm Cat (Storm Bird) $500,000
Dam: Mariah's Storm (Rahy)
Br: Orpendale & Michael Tabor (Ky)
Tr: O'Brien Aidan P(0 0 0 0 .00) 2004:(0 0 .00)

Life	13	9	4	0	$3,078,989	116	D.Fst	1 0 1 0	$954,000 116
2000	10	6	4	0	$2,964,727	116	Wet(411)	0 0 0 0	$0 -
1999	3	3	0	0	$114,262	-	Turf(360)	12 9 3 0	$2,124,989 -
	0	0	0	0	$0	-	Dst(0)	0 0 0 0	$0 -

4Nov00-10CD	fst	1¼	:472 1:12 1:36 2:003	3↑ BCClasic-G1	116	13	31	31	31½	2hd	2nk	Kinane M J	L122	7.60	107 -	*Tiznow*122nk GiantsCusewy1223¼ *CptinSteve*122hd	5w,drew even,outfinshd	13

Previously trained by O'Brien Aidan P

23Sep00♦Ascot (GB)	Timeform rating: 129	yl	1	ⓣ RH 1:412	3↑ Queen Elizabeth II Stakes-G1 Stk 503000	2½	Kinane M J	123	*1.10	*Observatory*123½ Giant's Causeway1233½ *Best of The Bests*123¾ *Trckd in 3rd,led ovr 2f out,headed 100y out,gamely.IndianLodge7th*	12
9Sep00♦Leopardstwn (Ire)	Timeform rating: 124	gd	1¼	ⓣ LH 2:03	3↑ Irish Champion Stakes-G1 Stk 859800	1½	Kinane M J	123	*.70	Giant's Causeway123½ Greek Dance1301 Best of The Bests1232 *Trckd entrymate in 2nd,led over 1f out,held well.IndianDanehill4t*	7
22Aug00♦York (GB)	Timeform rating: 130	gd	1 5/16	ⓣ LH 2:09	3↑ Juddmonte International Stakes-G1 Stk 667600	1hd	Kinane M J	123	*.90	*Giant's Causeway*123hd *Kalanisi*1317 *Lear Spear*131½ *Tracked leader,led ovr 2-1/2f out,headed 2f out,led again on line*	6
2Aug00♦Goodwood (GB)	Timeform rating: 126	gd	1	ⓣ RH 1:383	3↑ Sussex Stakes-G1 Stk 410800	1¾	Kinane M J	126	*3.00	*Giant's Causeway*126¾ Dansili1331½ *Medicean*1261¼ *Trckd ldr,2nd again 3f out,led 1-1/2f out,dueled 1f out,led late*	10
8Jly00♦Sandown Park (GB)	Timeform rating: 128	gd	1¼	ⓣ RH 2:051	3↑ Eclipse Stakes-G1 Stk 544800	1hd	Duffield G	122	8.00	*Giant's Causeway*122hd Kalanisi1332½ Shiva1301½ *Tracked in 3rd,2nd 3f out,led 1-1/2f out,headed 120y out,led line*	8
20Jun00♦Ascot (GB)	Timeform rating: 120	gd	1	ⓣ RH 1:423	St James's Palace Stakes-G1 Stk 410000	1hd	Kinane M J	126	*3.50	*Giant's Causeway*126hd Valentino126¾ Medicean126½ *Tracked leader,led 2f out,held gamely.Bachir 6th,China Visit 10th*	11
27May00♦Curragh (Ire)	Timeform rating: 117	yl	1	ⓣ Str 1:394	Irish 2000 Guineas-G1 Stk 236600	2nk	Kinane M J	126	*.90	Bachir126nk *Giant's Causeway*126¾ Cape Town126¾ *Tracked in 2nd or 3rd,bid 1f out,held by winner.Barathea Guest4th*	8
6May00♦Newmarket (GB)	Timeform rating: 121	gd	1	ⓣ Str 1:373	2000 Guineas Stakes-G1 Stk 458300	23½	Kinane M J	126	*3.50	King's Best1263½ Giant's Causeway1261½ Barathea Guest1262 *Close up,pressed pace 3f out,led 1-1/2f,drftd lft,headed 100y out*	27
9Apr00♦Curragh (Ire)	Timeform rating: 117	yl	7f	ⓣ Str 1:30	3↑ Gladness Stakes-G3 Stk 42400	1¾	Kinane M J	126	*.70	Giant's Causeway126¾ Tarry Flynn1361 *Namid*1331 *Tracked leaders,angled out over 2f out,led 1f out,driving*	11
18Sep99♦Longchamp (Fr)	Timeform rating: 119p	sf	*7f	ⓣ RH 1:224	Prix de la Salamandre-G1 Stk 108000	12	Kinane M J	126	*1.00	*Giant's Causeway*1262 *Race Leader*1262 *Bachir*1261 *Led throughout,drew clear 3f out,ridden out*	5
29Aug99♦Curragh (Ire)	Timeform rating: 109	yl	7f	ⓣ Str 1:25	Futurity Stakes-G3 Stk 67500	12½	Kinane M J	124	*.20	*Giant's Causeway*1242½ Brahms124¾ Polish Panache1244 *Tracked leader,led over 1-1/2f out,drew clear*	4
21Jly99♦Naas (Ire)	Timeform rating: 101	gd	6f	ⓣ Str 1:113	Yeomanstown/Morristown EBF Mdn Maiden 10000	17	Kinane M J	128	*.30	*Giant's Causeway*1287 Soorah1232 Rainbow Style128nk *Tracked leader,led 2-1/2f out,clear over 1f out,going away*	9

GOLDEN MISSILE (A.P. Indy—Santa Catalina, by Cure the Blues). Kentucky. Like many runners by A.P. Indy (such as Mineshaft), Golden Missile got better with age. A stakes winner at 3, 4, and 5, he blossomed into one of the best older runners of his generation as a 5-year-old, winning the Pimlico Special and Stephen Foster Handicap. He also finished second in the Donn, Kentucky Cup Classic, and Westchester Handicap and third in the Hawthorne Gold Cup. While his runners should also be most effective stretching out at age 3 and older, some may mature at 2 if out of mares by speed influences, such as stallions from the Mr. Prospector, In Reality, and Nasrullah sire lines.

Golden Missile
Own: Stronach Stables

Ch. h. 9 (Mar)
Sire: A.P. Indy (Seattle Slew) $300,000
Dam: Santa Catalina (Cure the Blues)
Br: W. Bruce Lunsford (Ky)
Tr: Orseno Joseph F(0 0 0 0 .00) 2004:(210 24 .11)

Life	25	7	7	4	$2,194,510	119	D.Fst	17	3	5	4	$1,561,470	119
2000	10	2	3	1	$1,261,700	119	Wet(416)	3	2	0	0	$572,700	116
1999	9	2	2	2	$838,240	116	Turf(291)	5	2	2	0	$60,340	95
	0	0	0	0	$0	-	Dst(0)	0	0	0	0	$0	-

25Nov00-8Aqu	fst	1	:23 :454 1:10 1:343	3↑CigarMiH-G1	86	3	99¾	910	94½	88½	813¾	Smith M E	L119 b	10.10	81-17	*ElCorredor*1161¾ *PpingTom*111nk *AffirmdSuccss*1203½	Hustled, 5 wide, tired	11
4Nov00-10CD	fst	1¼	:472 1:12 1:36 2:003	3↑BCClasic-G1	79	2	83	93½	118¾	1314	1325	Bailey J D	L126 b	13.20	82 -	*Tiznow*122nk Giant'sCauseway1223¼ *CaptainSteve*122hd	Drift out bmp start	13
7Oct00-9Haw	fst	1¼	:484 1:124 1:374 2:03	3↑HawGldCH-G3	105	1	22	1½	1½	1½	31¼	Desormeaux K J	L121 fb	*.50	86-25	DustOntheBottle1121 GuidedTour113nk GoldenMissile1213½	Couldn't last	8
16Sep00-10TP	fst	1⅛	:462 1:104 1:362 1:494	3↑KyCpClH-G2	115	1	32½	3½	1hd	2½	2¾	Desormeaux K J	L121 b	*1.40	85-23	CaptainSteve115¾ GoldenMissile1214½ ErlyPioneer1202½	Bid, held gamely	6
6Aug00-9Sar	gd	1⅛	:463 1:101 1:35 1:481	3↑WhitneyH-G1	96	3	31	31	2½	55½	513	Desormeaux K J	L121 b	2.30	87 -	*Lemon Drop Kid*1232 Cat Thief1174¼ Behrens1221½	Vied 3 wide, tired	6
17Jun00-8CD	sly	1⅛	:473 1:122 1:37 1:492	3↑SFosterH-G2	116	5	11	12	11½	12½	12¾	Desormeaux K J	L118 b	2.50	89-16	GoldenMissile1182¾ EctonPark1142 CatThief117nk	Mild hand urging,clear	6
13May00-10Pim	fst	1 3/16	:472 1:111 1:361 1:543	3↑PimSpclH-G1	115	6	51¼	31	2hd	1hd	12	Desormeaux K J	L116 b	4.70	92-18	*GoldenMissile*1162 PlsntBrz111no *LmonDropKid*1204	Unruly,3-4wd trip,drvg	8
8Apr00-8Aqu	fst	1	:23 :452 1:081 1:341	3↑WschstrH-G3	103	7	33	43	44½	37½	23¾	Gryder A T	L116 b	*1.15	93-17	*YnkVictor*1153¾ *GoldnMissl*1162 WtchmnsWrnng113no	Rated 3 wide, rallied	7
5Mar00-8FG	fst	1⅛	:472 1:112 1:361 1:484	4↑NwOrlnsH-G3	103	5	64¾	66	76	64½	55¼	Prado E S	L114 b	*.90	91-16	Allen's Oop1121 *Take Note of Me*1161 Ecton Park1172	5w middle move	8
5Feb00-10GP	fst	1⅛	:464 1:104 1:354 1:482	3↑DonnH-G1	119	6	53	52½	3½	21	2¾	Prado E S	L114 b	3.80	94-18	StephenGotEven115¾ GoldenMissile1144½ *Behrns*1214	Five wide, 2nd best	10
6Nov99-10GP	fst	1¼	:453 1:094 1:341 1:592	3↑BCClasic-G1	116	4	65½	52	3½	2hd	31¼	Desormeaux K J	L126 b	75.30	113 -	Cat Thief1221¼ Budroyale126hd Golden Missile1262	5wide bid,weaken late	14
9Oct99-10Haw	fst	1¼	:47 1:111 1:36 2:01	3↑HawGldCH-G3	105	5	43½	42	31½	2hd	2no	St Julien M	L115 b	*.80	97-02	Supreme Sound112no Golden Missile1152 Beboppin Baby1136	Just missed	8
29Aug99-8Sar	fst	1¼	:474 1:114 1:362 2:01	3↑SarBCH-G2	115	4	52½	52¾	41	22	31	Day P	L115 b	6.00	102-16	RunningStg122½ Ctienus115½ GoldenMissile1158½	Stumbled start, gamely	8
8Aug99-9Mth	gd	1 1/16	:234 :47 1:111 1:413	3↑SkipAway80k	109	1	43	34	2½	1hd	17¼	Day P	L122 b	*1.10	93-07	Golden Missile1227¼ Super Marfalous1131 Tappat1174¾	Kept to task late	6
5Jly99-8Bel	fst	1¼	:464 1:104 1:353 2:01	3↑SuburbnH-G2	88	3	2½	31½	54¼	48½	414½	Smith M E	L114 b	9.80	74-15	Behrens1212¾ Catienus1134¼ Social Charter1137½	Chased pace, tired	8
12Jun99-8Bel	fst	1⅛	:461 1:10 1:34 1:461	3↑BroklynH-G2	96	3	53¼	33	3nk	46	412¾	Smith M E	L114 b	3.70	87-08	RunningStg1177¼ DeputyDimond1132¼ SirBr1193¼	Wide move turn, faded	8
14May99-8Bel	fm	1 Ⓣ	:23 :452 1:084 1:332	4↑Alw 54000c	94	3	2½	2hd	11	1hd	21¼	Smith M E	L118 b	2.05	90-13	LiteApprovl1141¼ GoldenMissil118nk StkScm1162¾	Speed outside, gamely	9
Previously trained by Byrne Patrick B																		
20Mar99-10Hia	fst	1⅛	:472 1:111 1:352 1:473	3↑WidenerH-G3	109	6	21	21	2½	2hd	1½	Day P	L109 b	2.90	99-01	Golden Missile109½ Early Warning1132¼ *Sir Bear*1182	4 wide, prevailed	7
27Feb99-9GP	fm	1 1/16 Ⓣ	:233 :48 1:111 1:41	4↑Alw 36000N3x	89	11	114	114½	74½	62¾	42¾	Day P	L117 b	*2.00	91-11	Tekken1171¼ DivideandConquer119½ FlshofJoy1171	Angled out, willingly	12
2Aug98-9EIP	fm	1⅛ Ⓣ	:49 1:124 1:372 1:491	Cumberland50k	95	4	87¾	75¾	74	11½	15	Borel C H	L113 b	*.90	77-22	GoldenMissile1135 NorthcoteRod112¾ Eightis110nk	6wide stretch,driving	8
13Jun98-7CD	fst	1	:232 :461 1:102 1:353	Hcp 100000	97	1	42½	2hd	3nk	33½	35	Day P	L112 b	1.80	90-07	Shot of Gold1193½ Souvenir Copy1221½ *Golden Missile*112¾	Bid, weakened	7
24May98-7CD	fst	1 ⊗	:224 :453 1:10 1:344	3↑Alw 50340N1x	99	2	43½	44½	44½	12	18½	Day P	L111 b	*.80	99-13	GoldenMissile1118½ NwEdg111no HrvysPoint1231¾	Drew clear, ridden out	5
23Apr98-4Kee	gd	1⅛ Ⓣ	:48 1:13 1:374 1:494	Alw 46000N2L	75	4	4nk	63¼	54	52¼	22	Sellers S J	L117 b	*1.80	78-17	Magest1192 *GoldenMissile*117¾ WveringFreddie114nk	Gaining, up for place	10
29Mar98-11Hia	fm	1⅛ Ⓣ	1:492	Md Sp Wt 14k	76	3	73¼	73¾	61½	1½	12¼	Bravo J	L122 b	*1.40	83-11	GoldenMissil1222¼ *OriginlSin*122¾ ClosthBook122nk	Slippd thru,ridden out	12
Previously trained by Vella Daniel J																		
16Jly97-6WO	fst	6f	:224 :46 :583 1:114	Md Sp Wt 20k	61	5	3	2hd	1hd	21	22¾	Kabel T K	120	*.60	81-16	Patriot Love1152¾ *Golden Missile*1202½ Itpaystobelate1151½	Weakened	5

GREENWOOD LAKE (Meadowlake—Au Printemps, by Dancing Champ). Kentucky. As expected from a son of high-speed influence Meadowlake, Greenwood Lake was a good 2-year-old, winning the Champagne and Remsen Stakes. An injury forced his early retirement, and he should be an excellent sire of 2-year-olds. Of particular interest is his very classy female family. Greenwood Lake is a half-brother to Canadian champion Charlie Barley and Breeders' Cup Juvenile winner Success Express, a leading sire in Australia. With Meadowlake (Hold Your Peace) and Dancing Champ (Nijinsky II) up close in his pedigree, Greenwood Lake is another hidden turf sire and his runners will offer tremendous value when they show up on grass. (HT^2)

Greenwood Lake
Own: Conway Delores, Cornacchia, Joseph P.

B. h. 7 (Apr)
Sire: Meadowlake (Hold Your Peace) $20,000
Dam: Au Printemps (Dancing Champ)
Br: Dave Bowman, et al. (Ky)
Tr: Zito Nicholas P(0 0 0 0 .00) 2004:(281 45 .16)

Life	7	3	1	1	$430,620	99	D.Fst	5	1	1	1	$286,620	99
2000	2	0	0	0	$12,000	90	Wet(366)	2	2	0	0	$144,000	91
1999	5	3	1	1	$418,620	99	Turf(224)	0	0	0	0	$0	-
	0	0	0	0	$0	-	Dst(0)	0	0	0	0	$0	-

19Feb00-10GP	fst	1 1/16	:231 :46 1:0941:422	FntnOYth-G1	90	3 11241130 1022 710 46	Nakatani C S	L122	3.90	90- 10	High Yield1173¼ *Hal'sHope*1172½ EliteMercedes117nk	Angled out, willingly	11
15Jan00-10GP	fst	1 1/16	:232 :473 1:1231:442	HolyBull-G3	80	1 11231117 1010 612 611½	Samyn J L	L122	*1.30	74- 21	Hal's Hope1125¼ Personal First1171¾ Megacles1131½	Slow st, 6 wide far tn	11
27Nov99-7Aqu	my	1⅛	:48 1:124 1:3741:503	Remsen-G2	91	1 811 810 77¾ 63½ 1hd	Samyn J L	L122	*1.05	83- 11	GreenwoodLke122hd *UnFinoVino*113nk PolishMiner1131	Wide trip, up late	8
9Oct99-8Bel	fst	1 1/16	:234 :462 1:1041:433	Champagn-G1	91	1 713 716 710 34½ 12½	Samyn J L	L122	6.80	79- 23	*GreenwoodLke*1222½ ChiefSettl1224 HighYild1226¾	Steady 4 wide advance	7
19Sep99-6Bel	fst	1	:232 :454 1:1031:36	Futurity-G1	99	4 810 89½ 72¼ 42¼ 2nk	Samyn J L	L122	30.25	84- 22	*Bevo*122nk *GreenwoodLake*122nk MoreThnRedy122¾	Circled widest,gamely	8
1Sep99-3Sar	fst	6½f	:222 :46 1:1031:171	Alw 42000N1x	77	3 7 710 76¼ 45 33	Prado E S	L118	3.40	85- 13	Entepreneur116¾ UncleAbbie1182¼ GrenwoodLk1181¾	Going well rail late	7
14Aug99-5Sar	my	7f	:22 :454 1:1231:254	Md Sp Wt 40k	81	3 9 1013 88 41 12	Prado E S	117	8.80e	76- 21	GrnwoodLk1172 MndrinMrsh1171½ SintJosph1172¾	Bumped start,driving	10

HIGH YIELD (Storm Cat—Scoop the Gold, by Forty Niner). Kentucky/Australia. Storm Cat has proven to be a sire of sires, and he still has an untold number of young sons with a huge potential at stud, including High Yield. High Yield won the Hopeful Stakes and placed in four other major stakes at 2, and won the Blue Grass and Fountain of Youth Stakes at 3. His stakes-winning dam is a half-sister to Forest Flower, a champion filly at 2 in England and champion at 3 in Ireland. Standing at Ashford Stud, High Yield was bred to quality mares and his runners should have good speed and win early at 2. Like the majority of sons of Storm Cat, High Yield is another hidden turf sire. (HT)

High Yield
Own: Lewis Robert B. and Beverly, Magnier,

Ch. h. 7 (Mar)
Sire: Storm Cat (Storm Bird) $500,000
Dam: Scoop the Gold (Forty Niner)
Br: Brushwood Stable (Pa)
Tr: Lukas D. W(0 0 0 0 .00) 2004:(350 40 .11)

Life	14	4	4	3	$1,170,196	106	D.Fst	13	4	4	3	$1,170,196	106
2000	6	2	2	0	$748,960	106	Wet(406)	1	0	0	0	$0	95
1999	8	2	2	3	$421,236	97	Turf(321)	0	0	0	0	$0	-
	0	0	0	0	$0	-	Dst(0)	0	0	0	0	$0	-

20May00-10Pim	gd	1 3/16	:463 1:111 1:37 1:56	Preaknss-G1	95	5 2½ 1½ 2hd 21 78¾	Day P	L126 b	7.30	76- 11	RdBullt1263¾ *FusichiPgsus*126hd Impchmnt126nk	Dueled 3-path,weakened	8
6May00-8CD	fst	1¼	:4541:094 1:3532:01	KyDerby-G1	72	17 53 52½ 105 1513 1524	Day P	L126 b	6.20e	81 -	FusichiPegsus1261½ Aptitude1264 Impechmnt126½	Bumpd start,wide,tire	19
15Apr00-9Kee	fst	1⅛	:46 1:094 1:3521:483	BlueGras-G1	106	4 1½ 1hd 1½ 1hd 1hd	Day P	L123 b	*1.90	92- 19	HighYield123hd MoreThnRedy1233 Wheelwy123½	Brushed repeatdly,drvg	8
11Mar00-12GP	fst	1⅛	:47 1:104 1:3731:512	FlaDerby-G1	102	1 2½ 2hd 2½ 2hd 2hd	Day P	L122 b	*1.00	80- 23	Hal's Hope122hd *High Yield*12210 Tahkodha Hills1222	Angled out, 2nd best	10
19Feb00-10GP	fst	1 1/16	:231 :46 1:0941:422	FntnOYth-G1	101	4 11 11½ 1hd 11 13¼	Day P	L117 b	*2.40	96- 10	HighYield1173¼ *Hal'sHope*1172½ EliteMercedes117nk	Rail, strong hand ride	11
30Jan00-7SA	fst	1 1/16	:23 :46 1:1041:43	StCtlina-G2	101	5 2hd 2hd 2hd 2hd 21	Nakatani C S	LB117 b	3.10	87- 19	The Deputy1151 *High Yield*1175½ Captain Steve1233½	Dueled, second best	6
18Dec99-9Hol	fst	1 1/16	:224 :46 1:1031:431	HolFut-G1	94	5 47 56 1hd 21½ 24	Nakatani C S	LB121	3.90	80- 25	Captain Steve1214 High Yield12111 Cosine1213½	Bid 3wd,led,outkickd	6
27Nov99-11CD	fst	1 1/16	:24 :473 1:1141:43	B&WKyJC-G2	87	11 52½ 52½ 21 33 610¼	Bailey J D	L119	*1.40	85- 22	*Captain Steve*1225¾ Mighty122nk *Personal First*1192	Jolted start,tired	12
6Nov99-8GP	fst	1 1/16	:221 :46 1:1011:421	BCJuven-G1	96	2 64½ 52½ 42½ 2hd 33¼	Bailey J D	L122	6.80	93 -	Anees1222½ Chief Seattle122¾ High Yield1222¼	4wide bid,empty late	14
9Oct99-8Bel	fst	1 1/16	:234 :462 1:1041:433	Champagn-G1	80	4 3nk 31 2½ 21½ 36½	Bailey J D	L122	2.65	72- 23	*GreenwoodLake*1222½ ChiefSettle1224 HighYield1226¾	Speed 3 wide, faded	7
4Sep99-5Sar	fst	7f	:221 :45 1:0941:224	Hopeful-G1	97	2 5 42½ 32 11½ 15	Bailey J D	L122	*1.85	91- 13	HighYield1225 Settlement1223 *ExcitingStory*1224¼	3 wide move,ridden out	9
7Aug99-6Sar	fst	6f	:22 :453 :5741:103	Md Sp Wt 40k	89	7 2 1½ 1½ 18 18¾	Bailey J D	L117	*.55e	88- 13	*HighYield*1178¾ PolishMiner1172 HighestPris1171¼	Sped to front,drew off	10
18Jly99-5Hol	fst	6f	:213 :443 :57 1:094	HolJuvCh-G3	76	4 3 43 41¾ 31½ 34¾	McCarron C J	LB115	6.10	83- 11	*DixieUnion*1171¼ ExchangeRte1173½ *HighYield*1156½	4wd into lane,held 3rd	5
3Jly99-6Hol	fst	5½f	:214 :444 :5631:03	Md Sp Wt 41k	80	7 3 41½ 21 22 23½	McCarron C J	LB118	2.80	91- 10	*Caller One*1183½ High Yield1183½ Hollywood Bull1182	3 wide, second best	8

IMPEACHMENT (Deputy Minister—Misconduct, by Criminal Type). Florida. Impeachment finished third in the 2000 Kentucky Derby behind Fusaichi Pegasus and Aptitude, and while he was not a stakes winner, he also finished second in the Tampa Bay Derby and third in the Preakness and Arkansas Derby. By Deputy Minister, a world-class sire who was a Horse of the Year in Canada as well as a U.S. champion at 2, Impeachment is out of a half-sister to champion sprinter Gold Beauty, the dam of Dayjur and Maplejinsky. Impeachment could follow in the footsteps of Open Forum, another unheralded son of Deputy Minister who was a top freshman sire in 2001. Because he has much more stamina than Open Forum, however, Impeachment's runners should win at middle distances and most likely be best as they mature at 3.

Impeachment
Own: Dogwood Stable

B. h. 7 (Apr)
Sire: Deputy Minister (Vice Regent) $100,000
Dam: Misconduct (Criminal Type)
Br: Courtlandt Farm (Ky)
Tr: Pletcher Todd A(0 0 0 0 .00) 2004:(570 146 .26)

Life	11	1	1	3	$350,450	103	D.Fst	10	1	1	2	$250,450	100
2000	10	0	1	3	$339,950	103	Wet(335)	1	0	0	1	$100,000	103
1999	1	1	0	0	$10,500	84	Turf(238)	0	0	0	0	$0	-
	0	0	0	0	$0	-	Dst(0)	0	0	0	0	$0	-

26Aug00-9Sar	fst	1¼	:482	1:123	1:373	2:022	Travers-G1	95	8	915	916	910	79	59½	Migliore R	L126	17.60	83-07	*Unshaded*126hd AlberttheGret1266½ Commendble1262¾	Wide, no response	9
6Aug00-11Mth	fst	1⅛	:472	1:11	1:363	1:50	HsklInvH-G1	97	6	98¼	86¼	85¼	65½	68¼	Perret C	L116	4.50e	78-16	DixieUnion117¾ *CptinSteve*118hd MilwukeeBrew1172	Outside, no solid bid	9
10Jun00-9Bel	fst	1½	:491	1:141	2:05	2:31	Belmont-G1	87	8	1010	78¾	74¾	59	511¾	Perret C	L126	6.40	72-19	Commendable1261½ *Aptitude*1261 Unshaded1266	3 wide, no late bid	11
20May00-10Pim	gd	1³⁄₁₆	:463	1:111	1:37	1:56	Preaknss-G1	103	3	813	817	87¾	63	33¾	Perret C	L126	19.10	81-11	RedBullt1263¾ *FusichiPgsus*126hd Impchmnt126nk	Broke slow,angled wide	8
6May00-8CD	fst	1¼	:454	1:094	1:353	2:01	KyDerby-G1	100	14	1922	1712	136	75¼	35½	Perret C	L126	6.20e	99 -	Fusaichi Pegasus1261½ Aptitude1264 Impeachment126½	Rallied, rail	19
15Apr00-9OP	fst	1⅛	:464	1:113	1:363	1:49	ArkDerby-G2	98	7	1417	1316	107¾	56	33¾	Perret C	L118	34.80	89-16	Graeme Hall1183¾ Snuck In122hd Impeachment1181¼	Last away, 5-w rally	14
19Mar00-11Tam	fst	1¹⁄₁₆	:24	:474	1:123	1:434	TampaByDby150k	90	8	1010	87½	64¼	33	22½	Velazquez J R	L116	21.60	99-04	Wheelaway1162½ Impeachment116nk Perfect Cat1162¾	4 wide 2nd turn	10
4Mar00-10Tam	fst	1¹⁄₁₆	:24	:48	1:123	1:444	SamFDavis35k	77	10	1020	1022	1017	76¾	46¼	Houghton T D	L113	7.20	91-05	Go Lib Go122nk Kombat Kat1174 Cool N Crafty1172	Far back, closed gap	10
29Jan00-10GP	fst	1¹⁄₁₆	:242	:49	1:124	1:433	Alw 32000N1x	80	6	86	53	56¼	48	49¼	Bailey J D	L119	2.40e	81-14	PolishMiner119hd WywrdWys119no *RollinWithNoln*1199	Passed tired rivals	8
15Jan00-7GP	fst	1¹⁄₁₆	:233	:473	1:123	1:462	Alw 32000N1x	73	5	56	57	43½	43½	44½	Velazquez J R	L119	*.70	71-21	Rupert Herd119¾ Malagot1221¾ Eli Lilliput1192	3 wide, no response	7
26Dec99-6Crc	fst	7f	:223	:46	1:111	1:241	Md Sp Wt 17k	84	4	10	1013	88¼	34½	1¾	Velazquez J R	L120	2.50	88-10	Impeachment120¾ Firefighter Rob1202¾ *Skip a Grade*1207	Poor st, up late	10

INDY FILM (A.P. Indy—Foresta, by Alydar). California. While he never won a race in 10 starts, Indy Film ran third behind runner-up Aptitude at 1¹⁄₁₆ miles in only his second start. Indy Film is a half-brother to the dam of Victory U.S.A., and his foals should develop late and will be better stretching out as 3-year-olds. A.P. Indy has also proven to be an effective sire of grass runners, and Indy Film's dam was one of Alydar's few runners to excel on turf. (HT^2)

Indy Film
Own: Krikorian George

Dk. b or b. h. 7 (Feb)
Sire: A.P. Indy (Seattle Slew) $300,000
Dam: Foresta (Alydar)
Br: River Bend Farm, Inc. (Ky)
Tr: Hofmans David E(0 0 0 0 .00) 2004:(66 11 .17)

Life	10	M	1	3	$32,420	88	D.Fst	3	0	0	1	$6,900	80
2000	7	M	1	2	$23,720	83	Wet(429)	2	0	1	1	$15,040	83
1999	3	M	0	1	$8,700	88	Turf(308)	5	0	0	1	$10,480	88
	0	0	0	0	$0	-	Dst(0)	0	0	0	0	$0	-

12Jly00-6Hol	fst	1¹⁄₁₆		:231	:461	1:11	1:451	3↑ Md Sp Wt 45k	–	4	613	-	-	-	-	Desormeaux K J	LB117	5.30	- 32	Alyaxy116½ Dinnerathepalms11714 *Airiasaffair*11613	Spill,impeded,eased	7
3Jun00-4Hol	fm	*1³⁄₁₆	Ⓣ	:471	1:111	1:351	1:533	3↑ Md Sp Wt 45k	79	9	63¾	53	62¼	84	63½	Valdivia J Jr	LB115	6.80	- -	GentleGint115½ *MonsignorCsle*1151½ SilvrPct115nk	Chased 3wd,outkicked	10
21Apr00-3GG	fst	1¹⁄₁₆		:222	:453	1:094	1:42	Md Sp Wt 32k	80	7	89¾	88¼	54	32	34	Baze R A	LB118	*.80	88-09	Kolob1182 Tuckaway Boy1182 Indy Film1187	Hsitated, lunged start	8
25Mar00-9SA	fm	1⅛	Ⓣ	:492	1:141	1:384	1:511	Md Sp Wt 49k	76	11	116½	96¾	94¾	74¼	41½	Valdivia J Jr	LB122	3.40	71-22	Lunar Cat122½ Timber Yield122no Brave World1221	5 wide into lane	11
4Mar00-2SA	gd	1¹⁄₁₆		:223	:463	1:12	1:443	Md Sp Wt 47k	83	7	55	34	31	1hd	32½	Nakatani C S	LB122 b	4.40	77-13	*Ronton*1222 *Oration*122½ Indy Film1222	3wd bid,led,outkicked	9
11Feb00-1SA	my	1	⊗	:232	:462	1:111	1:374	Md Sp Wt 47k	69	1	1hd	2hd	1hd	1hd	21½	Delahoussaye E	LB121 b	*.90	80-15	L. A. Bull1211½ IndyFilm121nk Livingonthestrand1211	Inside duel,held 2nd	6
16Jan00-8SA	fm	1	Ⓣ	:23	:462	1:111	1:362	Md Sp Wt 47k	82	11	104¾	53¾	2hd	31	51¼	Delahoussaye E	LB120 b	2.80	76-23	Calamari120hd Senor Billy120½ Pizza N Beer120nk	Wide trip,willingly	12
1Dec99-2Hol	fst	1¹⁄₁₆		:241	:482	1:132	1:45	Md Sp Wt 36k	71	3	63¼	64¼	45	46½	413	Delahoussaye E	LB120	1.50	62-27	*BosqRdondo*1201½ ColdwtrCnyon1209½ ShrpLkngDd1202	Pulled,no threat	7
14Nov99-4Hol	fm	1¹⁄₁₆	Ⓣ	:232	:464	1:111	1:422	Md Sp Wt 35k	88	6	54½	67	55½	42¼	31½	Flores D R	LB120	*2.30	79-19	Jekyll and Hyde120½ *Aptitude*1201 Indy Film1203	Saved ground,willingly	10
21Oct99-8SA	fm	1	Ⓣ	:224	:462	1:111	1:362	Md Sp Wt 40k	81	9	99¾	88½	64½	63¼	4½	Flores D R	LB120	8.10	77-22	LongTrmInvstor120hd UndrSurvlInc120no CpotSun120nk	Off slow,late bid	9

INTIDAB (Phone Trick—Alqwani, by Mr. Prospector). New York. While he sported an American dirt pedigree, Intidab was raced intermittently on turf and dirt with mixed results until he came to the U.S. at age 6. Intidab ran to his high-speed pedigree winning the A Phenomenon Handicap over subsequent sprint champion Artax, and also won the Eillo Stakes. He added the True North Handicap at age 7, and his New York-bred foals should have abundant speed and be precocious juveniles. (SP^2)

Intidab
Own: Shadwell Stable

Dk. b or b. h. 11 (Mar)
Sire: Phone Trick (Clever Trick) $25,000
Dam: Alqwani (Mr. Prospector)
Br: Shadwell Farm, Inc. (Ky)
Tr: McLaughlin Kiaran P(0 0 0 0 .00) 2004:(278 53 .19)

Life	36	7	12	5	$531,221	120	D.Fst	20	5	7	2	$467,614 120
2000	5	1	3	0	$208,800	112	Wet(395)	1	0	1	0	$9,200 107
1999	13	3	4	2	$264,065	120	Turf(275)	15	2	4	3	$54,407 75
	0	0	0	0	$0	-	Dst(0)	0	0	0	0	$0 -

30Aug00-9Sar	fst	6½f	:213 :441 1:0821:15	3↑ForegoH-G2	112	2	9	85¾	63	62	21	Bailey J D	L118 b	4.20	98-07	ShdowCster1131 Intidb118no SuccessfulAppl119nk	Angled 4 wide, willing	10
9Aug00-9Sar	fst	6f	:213 :443 :5631:091	3↑AGVndbtH-G2	112	7	5	56	42½	1hd	1hd	Davis R G	L117 b	3.30	99-13	[D]Intdb117hd SuccssflAppl1183½ ChsnWmmn1122	Came in stretch, bump	8
Disqualified and placed second																		
15Jly00-9Lrl	fst	6f	:22 :442 :56 1:074	3↑DeFrncsM-G1	105	3	4	44	45½	44	42¼	Davis R G	L119 b	2.30	101-10	Richter Scale1231¾ Just CallMeCarl119nk Falkenburg114nk	Eased out 3/16	4
10Jun00-8Bel	fst	6f	:224 :46 :58 1:101	3↑TruNrthH-G2	109	7	5	62¾	41¼	1hd	11	Davis R G	L117 b	2.30	07-13	Intidab1171 BrutallyFrank1191¾ OrodeMexico1131	Altered course stretch	7
12May00-8Bel	fst	6½f	:222 :451 1:0921:154	3↑Alw 54000N1Y	101	3	5	55½	53¼	2½	21	Davis R G	L123 b	1.95	92-13	Bevo1161 *Intidab*1232¼ *Laredo*1165¾	Game finish outside	5
7Nov99-1GP	fst	6f	:22 :442 :5631:084	3↑[R]Eillo75k	102	1	7	65½	65	33	11	Davis R G	L119 b	*.80	98-04	Intidab1191 Salty Glance115½ Mayor Steve1157¾	Slow start, up late	7
16Oct99-9Bel	fst	6f	:221 :443 :5541:073	3↑FrstHlsH-G2	102	7	7	73¾	74¼	56¼	38	Davis R G	L116 b	4.90	95-11	*Artax*1206½ Good and Tough1181½ *Intidab*116nk	3 wide, no punch	7
25Sep99-9Bel	fst	7f	:221 :443 1:0831:213	3↑Vosburgh-G1	102	3	4	53¼	54¾	56	44	Davis R G	L126 b	15.60	90-09	*Artax*1263½ Stormin Fever126hd *Mountain Top*126½	4 wide, good finish	6
6Sep99-9Sar	fst	7f	:221 :441 1:0811:211	3↑ForegoH-G2	85	6	6	83¾	87¾	78¾	713¾	Davis R G	L116 b	6.80	85-12	CrftyFrind119nk AffirmdSuccss1191¼ SirBr1192¼	Came wide, no response	9
11Aug99-9Sar	fst	6f	:224 :452 :57 1:09	3↑APhenomH-G2	120	7	2	31	3nk	1hd	11½	Davis R G	L113 b	10.40	96-12	Intidab1131½ Artax1172¾ Yes It's True117½	Speed 3 wide, driving	7
14Jly99-3Bel	fst	6f	:224 :453 :5711:091	3↑Alw 48000N4X	102	4	5	42½	41	31½	2nk	Velazquez J R	L118 b	*.55	95-15	Gray Raider116nk *Intidab*1181 Adverse116¾	4 wide, game finish	5
5Jly99-3Bel	fst	6f	:224 :442 :5621:082	3↑Alw 46000N3X	107	5	5	53½	4¾	1hd	13	Velazquez J R	L119 b	*1.60	99-13	Intidab1193 Not So Wacky114nk Mr. Buffum1183	4 wide move, hand ride	5
16Jun99-8Bel	fm	1 Ⓣ	:231 :461 1:0911:33	3↑Alw 47000N3X	75	5	31	21½	3½	75¼	811¾	Velazquez J R	L119 b	6.50	81-12	Scgnelli119no ForbiddenApple1233¼ BluesEvent119½	Chased 3 wide, tired	9
19May99-8Bel	sly	6½f	:222 :451 1:09 1:152	3↑Alw 46000N3X	107	9	6	41	2hd	1½	2½	Bravo J	L118 b	14.50	94-07	Master O Foxhounds122½ Intidab1186¾ Iron Will1223	3 wide move, gamely	10
2May99-8Aqu	fst	7f	:223 :444 1:08 1:20	3↑CarterH-G1	75	4	7	52½	63½	99¼	921¼	Bravo J	L114 b	53.75	81-11	Artx1143¼ AffirmedSuccss1192½ WstrnBordrs1132½	4 wide between rivals	9

Previously trained by Sateesh Seemar

28Mar99♦Nad Al Sheba (UAE) Timeform rating: 107	ft	*6f	Str 1:094	4↑	Nad Al Sheba Sprint (Listed) Stk 95300	21	Hind G	121 b	-	Ramp and Rave1211 Intidab1213 Abreeze122½	*Raced alone in center,dueled hfwy,led 1f out,headed late.Kahal7th*	9
19Feb99♦Jebel Ali (UAE) Timeform rating: 93	ft	*6f	Str 1:104	4↑	Jebel Ali Sprint (Prestige) Stk 27200	35¼	Hills R	121 b	-	Abreeze1215 Persuasivo Fitz125nk Intidab121no	*Pressed pace,weakened 1f out.Pearl d'Azur 4th.No betting*	5
29Jan99♦Abu Dhabi (UAE) Timeform rating: 107	ft	*7f	Ⓣ RH 1:221	4↑	President's Cup (Listed) Stk 49000	22¾	Birrer G	121 b	-	Susu1182¾ Intidab121½ *Kahal*1213¼	*Tracked in 4th,led 1-1/2f out,headed 170y out.No betting*	8
31Dec98♦Nad Al Sheba (UAE) Timeform rating: 83	ft	*7f	LH 1:243	3↑	Faraj Butti Al Muhairbi Race Alw 19100	47¾	Hills R	121 b	-	*Pearl d'Azur*121nk *Susu*1184½ Earl of March1213	*Close up in 4th,always one-paced.No betting*	7
3Dec98♦Abu Dhabi (UAE) Timeform rating: 105	gd	*1	Ⓣ RH 1:354	3↑	National Day Cup (Listed) Stk 27200	32½	Hills R	121	-	Murheb1211 River Usk1221½ Intidab12112	*Tracked pacesetting winner,outfinished.No betting*	4
24Apr98♦Abu Dhabi (UAE) Timeform rating: 83	gd	*6f	Ⓣ Str 1:092	3↑	Handicap Hcp 16300	69	Scriven S	136	-	*Cornish Snow*1192 Angaar112nk Night Bell1121¼	*Tracked in 3rd on rail,weakened 1f out.No betting*	8
1Mar98♦Nad Al Sheba (UAE) Timeform rating: 94	ft	*1	Ⓣ LH 1:381	3↑	Concord Mile Handicap Hcp 16300	57½	Hills R	137	-	*Mashhaer*1222 *Maftool*1231 Viva Nureyev1233¼	*Rated at rear,close 5th 3f out,one-paced late.No betting*	10
30Jan98♦Abu Dhabi (UAE) Timeform rating: 107	gd	*7f	Ⓣ RH 1:22	3↑	President's Cup (Prestige) Stk 49000	21½	Hills R	128	-	Diffident1291½ Intidab1282 *Indian Rocket*1284	*Close up in 3rd,no room 2f out,angled out,fnshd well.No betting*	7
28Dec97♦Nad Al Sheba (UAE)	ft	*1	LH 1:422	3↑	Allowance Race Alw 16300	21	Hind G	119	-	*Wathik*1191 Intidab1191 Airport1192¼	*Tracked leader,led 2f to 100y out,second best.No betting*	5
4Dec97♦Abu Dhabi (UAE)	gd	*1	Ⓣ RH 1:344	3↑	National Day Cup (Listed) Stk 27200	21½	Hills R	125	-	*Diffident*1251½ Intidab1252½ *Wathik*125nk	*Rated in 4th,angled out 1-1/2f out,finished well.No betting*	7
7Nov97♦Abu Dhabi (UAE)	fm	*1	Ⓣ RH 1:351	3↑	Allowance Race Alw 12300	1¾	J Arias	119	-	Intidab119¾ Airport1195¼ Select Few11914	*Well placed in 3rd,led 1-1/2f out,ridden out.No betting*	5
10Apr97♦Abu Dhabi (UAE)	fm	*7f	Ⓣ RH 1:222	3↑	ADNOC-FOD Gold Medal Trophy Hp Hcp 15000	511	Clarke M	131	-	Yoush131½ Cornish Snow1252¾ Rafferty's Rules1231¾	*Tracked in 3rd,weakened final furlong.No betting*	6
23Mar97♦Abu Dhabi (UAE)	gd	*7f	Ⓣ RH 1:23	3↑	FAMCO Trophy Handicap Hcp 15000	32¾	Hills R	129	-	*Vilayet*1311½ Benevento1151¼ Intidab129nk	*Tracked in 3rd,dueled 3f out,close 3rd 2f out,faded.No betting*	5
9Feb97♦Nad Al Sheba (UAE)	ft	*7f	LH 1:252	3↑	Chopard Handicap Hcp 16300	22¼	Hills R	127	-	Insiyabi1252¼ Intidab127nk Showgi136hd	*Rated in last,bid 2f out,dueled 1-1/2f out,faded 1f out*	5
16Jan97♦Nad Al Sheba (UAE)	ft	*7f	LH 1:24	3↑	Shadwell Farm Inc Handicap Hcp 12300	11¼	Hills R	114	-	Intidab1141¼ Wisam114nk Cornish Snow1187	*Rated at rear,4th 2-1/2f out,led 1f out,driving.No betting*	7
27Dec96♦Jebel Ali (UAE)	ft	*6f	Str 1:133	3↑	Fujairah Natl Constrc Sprint H Hcp 15000	51½	M Clarke	131	-	Laafee127no Wisam121hd Bin Nashwan118nk	*Veered left start,soon close up,outfinished.No betting*	7

Previously trained by John Gosden

22Aug96♦York (GB)	gd	1	Ⓣ LH 1:344	3↑	Bradford & Bingley Rated Hcp Hcp 68600	1615¾	Carson W	119	*5.50	*Concer Un*1221 North Song118no Moments of Fortune125½	*Mid-pack,wknd 3f out.Beauchamp Jazz(125)7th,New Century(125) 17th*	18
10Aug96♦Haydock (GB)	gd	1	Ⓣ LH 1:433	3↑	Harvey Jones Rated Handicap Hcp 13900	2no	Eddery P	119	*2.25	Elmi Elmak118no Intidab1196 Options Open1293	*Soon led,met challenge over 1f out,dueled,just failed*	9
26Jly96♦Thirsk (GB)	fm	7f	Ⓣ LH		Hutton Wandesley Maiden Stakes Maiden 9200	12	unknown jockey	126	*.00	Intidab1262 Classic Form1211¼ Balinsky1168	*Pressed pace,led over 2f out,willingly*	6
30Aug95♦York (GB)	gd	7f	Ⓣ LH 1:252		Knightsbridge Gin Maiden Stks Maiden 13500	3½	Dettori L	126	10.00	Red Robbo126no Sasuru126½ *Intidab*1261¾	*Chased in 5th,finished well.Astor Place 4th,Albaha 6th*	9
17Jun95♦York (GB)	gd	6f	Ⓣ Str		Leonard Sainer EBF Maiden Stks Maiden 10200	43¼	unknown jockey	126	-	Kahir Almaydan1262 House of Riches1261¼ Desert Bell126no	*Slowly away,soon tracking in 3rd,drifted left & faded over 1f out*	4

IRISH CONQUEST (Conquistador Cielo—Irish Colors, by Hoist the Flag). New York. Irish Conquest finished third in the Illinois Derby and Lafayette Stakes at 3, but did not became a stakes winner until age 5, when he captured the seven-furlong Deputy Minister Handicap. Most sons of Conquistador Cielo have speed (e.g., Marquetry, Wagon Limit, Lexicon), so expect Irish Conquest's 2-year-olds to have speed also, and be especially good on wet tracks.

Irish Conquest
Own: Fantasy Lane Stable

B. h. 11 (Feb)
Sire: Conquistador Cielo (Mr. Prospector) $15,000
Dam: Irish Colors (Hoist the Flag)
Br: William Floyd (Ky)
Tr: Seewald Alan S(0 0 0 0 .00) 2004:(110 17 .15)

Life	41	7	4	9	$362,635	110	D.Fst	37	7	4	8	$358,345	110
2000	12	3	1	3	$62,500	98	Wet(344)	4	0	0	1	$4,290	86
1999	9	0	0	3	$22,400	89	Turf(299)	0	0	0	0	$0	-
Aik Ⓣ	0	0	0	0	$0	-	DstⓉ(376)	0	0	0	0	$0	-

5Oct00-5Med	fst	6f	:221 :45 :5721:102	3↑ Clm 7500(7.5-6.5)	57	7	6	63¾	52¾	64½	56¼	Tejeira J E	L119 fb	*1.40	81-14	The Chess King1191¼ Lost Pleasure1161 Big Dave1193½	Raced widest	8
14Sep00-5Med	fst	6f	:214 :45 :5741:114	3↑ Clm 10000(10-9)	63	3	5	43¼	55½	33½	41½	Tejeira J E	L119 fb	*.60	78-22	RftbyNght116½ WvrngFrdd116nk Nndznpnstrps116¾	Steadied between 1/2	6
1Sep00-5Mth	fst	6f	:222 :45 :5711:10	3↑ Clm 22000(22-18)	66	6	5	53¼	43¾	46	410¼	Tejeira J E	L122 fb	2.40	81-17	FullRetil1164¼ WhirlsFlme1166 LunchLeroux111no	Never far back, no bid	6
20Aug00-5Mth	fst	6f	:214 :452 :5741:103	3↑ Clm 25000(25-20)	87	6	1	55	32	2½	1no	Tejeira J E	L119 fb	*2.20	88-17	Irish Conquest119no Paco's Friend1161½ *Nork*117½	Outside bid, prevailed	6
12Jly00-5Mth	fst	6f	:214 :451 :5811:111	3↑ Clm 25000(25-20)	82	2	5	44¼	32	2hd	1nk	Tejeira J E	L116 fb	*1.90	85-16	*IrishConquest*116nk BriellLnding1113¾ PcosFrind116½	Bid, eased out, drvg	7
29Jun00-5Mth	fst	6f	:221 :45 :5721:10	3↑ Clm 25000(25-20)	76	3	4	65½	55½	54	45¼	Tejeira J E	L116 fb	*1.70	86-13	Full Retail116½ Report On Rain1161¼ Fly to Houston1193½	No solid bid	6
7Apr00-7GP	fst	7f	:224 :453 1:1021:232	4↑ Clm 35000(35-30)	87	6	5	31	21½	2hd	31	Pitty C D	L116 b	*.60	82-22	*Derivative*119½ *United States*116½ IrishConquest1164¾	Drew even weakened	8
12Mar00-6GP	fst	7f	:23 :461 1:1121:24	4↑ Clm 45000(50-45)	80	5	3	64	64	55	34½	Nunez E O	L117 b	3.20	75-20	Madok1173½ Miners Gamble1171 Irish Conquest117nk	Lacked room turn	7
26Feb00-6GP	fst	6½f	:22 :443 1:10 1:163	4↑ Clm 40000(40-35)	87	11	1	65¾	64	3½	41½	Sellers S J	L119 b	*2.10	93-14	Wildfarel117¾ Glitter Lad115hd Miners Gamble117¾	5 wide, bid, hung	11
6Feb00-6GP	fst	6½f	:222 :451 1:0941:161	4↑ Clm 50000(50-45)	98	6	4	44	32	31½	1¾	Sellers S J	L117 b	3.00	97-15	Irish Conquest117¾ *Sun Fighter*1171 He BeIrish117hd	Bumped st, prevailed	7
19Jan00-3GP	fst	7f	:223 :453 1:1041:24	4↑ Clm c-(50-45)	88	4	2	3½	2hd	2½	21	Sellers S J	L117 b	*.90	79-20	FortunteStrek1171 *IrishConquest*1173½ *Wildfrel*1173½	Vied 3 wide, 2nd best	5
Claimed from Buckram Oak Farm for $50,000, Moubarak Mohammed Trainer 1999: (-)																		
3Jan00-8GP	fst	6½f	:221 :45 1:0941:162	4↑ Clm 62500(62.5-57.5)	98	3	6	31	21	22	31¾	Coa E M	L117 b	6.10	94-16	KlbinsGold117½ FstDeprtur1151¼ IrishConqust1171¼	Lacked late response	9
19Dec99-11Crc	fst	7f	:222 :452 1:1021:233	3↑ KenyNoeJrH100k	86	6	2	52¾	65	77½	78	Prado E S	L113 b	9.10e	83-15	Thrillin Discovery112nk *Mountain Top*115hd Stormy Do1133½	Outrun	7
7Nov99-8GP	fst	7f	:221 :444 1:0841:212	3↑ DancngSpre100k	89	4	1	41¼	52¼	44	36	Coa E M	L115 b	17.20	87-04	MountinTop1153½ MyJeffsMombo1152½ IrishConqust115¾	Best of others	7
22Oct99-9Crc	fst	6f	:22 :453 :5811:112	3↑ Alw 35000NC	82	2	7	51¾	51½	63	42	Velasquez C	L115 fb	6.40	89-15	FstDprtur115no *BtthSights*1151¾ SofTrnquility114nk	Lacked late response	7
30Sep99-9Crc	fst	6f	:213 :443 :5721:104	3↑ OC 50k/N4x -N	82	5	4	23	22	33½	35	Leon F	L117 fb	5.20	89-14	SltyGlnce1191¼ FvoritFightr1173¾ IrishConqust1175½	Bmpd st, weakened	6
29Aug99-3Crc	fst	6½f	:223 :46 1:1031:171	3↑ Alw 35000NC	88	1	4	41¾	42	34	34½	Nunez E O	L112 fb	9.60	90-15	ThrillinDscovry119½ StormyDo1194 IrshConqust1129½	Rail trip, weakened	5
31Jly99-4Crc	fst	6f	:222 :46 :5821:111	3↑ Alw 32000NC	83	4	2	41¼	32	45½	46½	Nunez E O	L115 f	11.90	85-14	*ThrillinDiscovery*119½ FvoritFightr1173½ MyorStv1082½	Chased pace, tired	7
8Jly99-3Crc	fst	6f	:214 :443 :5711:104	3↑ Alw 26000N4x	75	1	6	32	56	45	45¼	Coa E M	L117 f	2.00	89-14	FvoriteFightr117hd MyorStv1121½ ImImprssd1193¾	Saved grnd, no threat	6
20Jun99-10Crc	sly	7f	:22 :444 1:1011:232	3↑ ThtsOurBkH33k	86	4	3	52½	43	56¼	69¼	Nunez E O	L114 f	7.40e	83-14	*ThrillinDiscovry*1162 StormyDo1163¼ BornMighty1131	Saved grnd, faltered	10
23May99-7Crc	fst	6f	:22 :45 :5741:11	3↑ Alw 30000NC	72	3	5	42	52¼	67	613	Douglas R R	L115	9.70	80-11	Stormy Do1152¼ *Thrillin Discovery*1192¾ Salty Glance1102	Bumped start	8
20Jun98-12Crc	fst	6f	:213 :451 :58 1:112	3↑ MiamiBchH300k	83	4	4	41	64	108¾	1011½	Coa E M	L115	5.20	79-22	Heckofarlph1151 ThunderBreeze1133 NicholsDs1152	Brief foot, fast pace	13
11Apr98-8Kee	fst	7f	:213 :44 1:0811:202	3↑ CmwlthBC-G2	98	1	4	74	75½	45½	48	Coa E M	L114	6.00	95-09	*Distorted Humor*1192 El Amante1143 Partner's Hero1213	Mild late bid	8
13Mar98-10GP	fst	7f	:224 :451 1:0911:22	3↑ GPBCSprH-G3	110	1	1	31½	41¼	31½	2½	Coa E M	L114	4.80e	89-16	*Rare Rock*117½ Irish Conquest1141 FriscoView118nk	Boxed, closed gamely	7
16Feb98-9Lrl	fst	7f	:224 :461 1:1031:23	3↑ GenGrgeH-G2	89	7	1	32	31	75¾	810	Coa E M	L114	4.80	84-16	RoylHven1222 PurplPssion1161¾ WirMCollct1171	4wd 1/2,3wd turn,wkned	9
18Jan98-10GP	fst	7f	:221 :444 1:0921:222	3↑ DepMinstrH100k	106	2	4	2½	21	1hd	11¼	Coa E M	L113	11.40	88-17	IrishConquest1131¼ FriskMNow119no OrodMxico1141¼	Pressed fast pace	10
26Dec97-10Crc	fst	7f	:222 :454 1:1131:253	3↑ KenyNoeJrH100k	97	11	2	31½	42½	21½	2¾	Coa E M	L113	11.80	80-24	Heckofrlph116¾ *IrishConqust*1131¼ OrodMxico1131	Stalked fast pace,hung	11
4May97-8Aqu	gd	7f	:221 :45 1:0931:224	3↑ CarterH-G1	76	4	3	63½	88¼	911	913¾	Santos J A	114	9.00e	79-07	*Lngfuhr*122nk StlwrtMmbr1133 WstrnWintr1121½	Roused trn,no response	9
13Apr97-8Kee	fst	7f	:222 :45 1:10 1:222	3↑ CmwlthBC-G2	98	3	3	41½	32	43½	44¼	Sellers S J	113	4.60e	89-15	VictorCooly114nk WstrnWintr1123½ ApplingSkir121½	Chased pace evenly	7
12Mar97-9GP	fst	7f	:22 :443 1:09 1:22	4↑ Alw 32000N3L	100	8	1	2hd	2hd	1hd	1nk	Sellers S J	117	2.30	94-16	IrshConqust117nk FndthTrsr1199¾ HrrcnHlmr117nk	Vied fast pace,prevail	11
15Feb97-8GP	fst	6f	:213 :441 :5711:102	4↑ Alw 31000N2x	84	9	4	42¼	42½	3nk	2no	Sellers S J	119	*2.50	88-12	MngoSmsh119no *IrishConquest*119no PickDnce1191	Stalk pace,just missed	12
21Aug96-8Sar	gd	7f	:214 :442 1:0911:221	3↑ Alw 39000N2x	67	5	3	82	52¼	68½	619	Castillo H Jr	114 f	8.00	76-15	Gold Token1157 *Robb*1124 Crowns Runner1132	Wide turn,no rally	8
31Jly96-6Sar	sly	7f	:222 :444 1:09 1:22	Alw 39000N2x	65	4	2	2½	35½	310	319	Krone J A	117 fb	3.50	77-10	Delay of Game11414 Robb1175 Irish Conquest117no	Speed between,tired	7
6Jly96-9Bel	fst	1 1/16	:232 :47 1:1041:412	Dwyer-G2	72	3	11½	1hd	32	411	420¾	Krone J A	112 fb	11.20	71-08	*Victory Speech*1175½ Gold Fever1197½ Robb1177¾	Pace for a half,tired	6
23Jun96-14Tdn	fst	1⅛	:4611:104 1:3531:474	OhioDrby-G2	37	3	63¾	75	97½	1025	1043½	Velasquez C	B116 f	15.80	59-08	*Skip Away*1223½ *Victory Speech*1189¼ Clash by Night118nk	Fractious in gate	10
11May96-7Spt	fst	1⅛	:47 1:111 1:3621:483	IllDerby-G2	96	3	32	42½	43	47½	37½	Ramos W S	114 f	6.50e	- -	NturlSelection1144 *ElAmnte*1243½ IrishConqust114½	Drifted, stretch tired	13
27Apr96-9CD	fst	1	:231 :461 1:11 1:364	DerbyTrl-G3	85	5	41½	62	73¾	56	57¼	Sellers S J	114 f	3.20e	- -	*VlidExpcttons*1194½ GrtSouthrn1141¼ *StormCrk*1171	Dropped back mild bid	10
10Apr96-8Kee	fst	7f	:221 :442 1:09 1:214	Lafayett-G3	99	1	6	52	42½	32½	3hd	Krone J A	112 f	10.40	- -	WrMCollct112no *ApplngSkr*121no IrshConqst112hd	Closd fast outfinished	9
16Mar96-7GP	fst	7f	:214 :441 1:0911:23	Alw 29000N1x	87	1	9	52	53¼	21½	1no	Sellers S J	120 f	2.90e	- -	Irish Conquest120no Valid Victor1172¼ *Gameel*1203½	Rallied, just up	9
24Feb96-4GP	fst	7f	:222 :452 1:1011:233	Md Sp Wt 25k	85	9	1	43	31½	2hd	11½	Sellers S J	120 f	20.80	- -	*Irish Conquest*1201½ *Handel*120hd Exasperating1204¼	Stalked fast pace	10
9Sep95-6Crc	fst	6f	:22 :461 :5921:131	Md Sp Wt 15k	40	6	7	78¼	64½	68	512½	Castillo H Jr	117 f	3.30	- -	ValidRomeo1174¼ Primasea1171¼ RecycledCode1175¼	Passed tiring rivals	7

JOE WHO (Jolly Quick—Jour du Soleil, by Big Lark). Louisiana. A champion miler at age 3 and 4 in Brazil, Joe Who was imported to the U.S. at 5, winning two stakes and setting a new one-mile record of 1:33⅖ on the Del Mar turf. He also won the Grade 1 Eddie Read Handicap and the Firecracker Breeders' Cup Handicap at age 6.

His offspring should have speed and be versatile winning on all surfaces, but should have a preference for turf.

Joe Who (Brz)
Own: Helzer James E

Ch. h. 11 (Sep)
Sire: Jolly Quick (Caduto*Brz)
Dam: Jour du Soleil (Big Lark*Brz)
Br: Haras Interlagos Ltda (Brz)
Tr: Baffert Bob(0 0 0 0 .00) 2004:(371 70 .19)

Life	38	14	2	0	$751,043	108	D.Fst	5	0	0	0	$8,811	92
2000	3	0	0	0	$7,400	92	Wet(210)	2	0	0	0	$512	-
1999	10	3	2	0	$446,110	108	Turf(336)	31	14	2	0	$741,720	108
	0	0	0	0	$0	-	Dst(0)	0	0	0	0	$0	-

3Jly00-9CD	fm	1 1/16	(T) :243 :483 1:121 1:42	3↑ Alw 64665c	92	2	2hd 1hd 1hd 31 43¼	Albarado R J	L117	4.50	91-03	Chorwon117nk MidwayMagistrte1221½ RoylStrnd1171½	Dueled,weakened	6
17Jun00-7CD	yl	1 1/16	(T) :244 :50 1:142 1:46	3↑ Alw 51420c	84	3	21½ 22 23½ 35 45	Sellers S J	L120	*1.20	69-22	Thesaurus1201¼ Phil the Grip1201¼ Air Rocket1162½	Stalked, faded	5
28May00-9CD	fst	1	⊗ :222 :443 1:092 1:351	3↑ Alw 58070c	88	4	34½ 38½ 37 35½ 48	Albarado R J	L120	3.10	86-10	Alisios1232½ Chorwon1201½ Dyhim Diamond1164	Bobbled start,empty	6
21Nov99-9CD	fm	1⅛	(T) :474 1:123 1:374 1:503	3↑ RivrCtyH-G3	95	5	54½ 65¾ 53½ 42½ 64¼	Borel C H	L118	3.00	79-22	ComicStrip1191½ KetsndYets112½ AboriginlApx114hd	Inside,flattened out	10
5Nov99-9GP	gd	*1⅛	(T) :494 1:142 1:39 1:503	3↑ Fraise250k	96	6	63¾ 74¾ 42 75¼ 44½	Albarado R J	L122	3.70	78-20	Bouccaneer1133 ShmrockCity1151½ ShrpAppel122hd	Bumped start,empty	11
9Oct99-7Kee	yl	1	(T) :241 :482 1:132 1:374	3↑ KeeTurfM-G2	–	9	106¾ 96¼ - - -	Antley C W	L126	*2.60	- 22	Kirkwall126nk Delay of Game1264½ Ladies Din1261½	Clipped heels, fell	10
28Aug99-8Sar	sf	1 1/16	(T) :231 :463 1:11 1:413	3↑ 4strdavH-G3	99	11	96½ 105½ 104½ 84 44	Antley C W	L119	4.10	84-12	ComicStrip1152½ DividendConquer1141 Bomfim113½	Game finish outside	11
1Aug99-4Dmr	fm	1⅛	(T) :501 1:14 1:371 1:483	3↑ EdReadH-G1	108	10	2½ 2hd 2hd 22 1nk	Antley C W	LB116	6.70	92-10	Joe Who116nk Ladies Din119½ Bouccaneer1151½	Came back gamely	10
27Jun99-12CD	yl	1	(T) :231 :47 1:113 1:363	3↑ FrckrBCH-G3	107	7	96¾ 96¾ 62¾ 41½ 1nk	Albarado R J	L113	12.90	86-19	*Joe Who*113nk *Middlesex Drive*116hd Wild Event1212¾	4 wide run 2nd turn	9
6Jun99-7CD	fm	1	(T) :243 :482 1:122 1:362	3↑ Alw 50845c	97	5	21½ 32 21½ 21 21½	Albarado R J	L123	*.80	85-10	Richter Scale1161½ *Joe Who*123hd Rod and Staff1231¾	Rail bid, 2nd best	6
16May99-9CD	fm	1 1/16	(T) :24 :474 1:112 1:413	3↑ Alw 53305c	106	2	31 3½ 31½ 21½ 1¾	Albarado R J	L118	3.90	96-12	Joe Who118¾ Buff1234½ Northcote Road1201	Steadied 7/16 pole	6
18Feb99-7SA	fm	1	(T) :233 :472 1:112 1:353	4↑ Alw 70000N$MY	95	6	44½ 45½ 65 66½ 64	Ramsammy E	LB122	8.50	77-19	Majorien118no Shellbacks1182 Night Player118¾	Lacked late response	8
29Jan99-7SA	fm	1	(T) :243 :491 1:133 1:374	4↑ Alw 65325N$MY	98	5	11 21 21½ 21½ 2¾	McCarron C J	LB118	2.80	69-31	*Lord Smith*116¾ Joe Who118¾ Martiniquais1187	Willingly	5
20Dec98-7Hol	fst	1⅛	:474 1:112 1:361 1:482	3↑ NtvDivrH-G3	92	3	43 42½ 45 46½ 412¼	Flores D R	LB117	10.60	72-16	*PuertoMadero*1212½ *MusicIGmbler*1171¼ RiverKeen1148½	Off rail, weakened	5
28Nov98-8Hol	gd	1⅛	(T) :48 1:122 1:371 1:502	3↑ CitatonH-G2	98	4	31 21½ 31 43 44¼	Ramsammy E	LB115	17.30	67-27	Military1182½ Mr Lightfoot117½ Worldly Ways1141¼	Stalked,outfinished	8
18Oct98-7SA	fm	1	(T) :251 :493 1:132 1:363	3↑ OakTrBCH-G3	101	3	21 21 41¼ 42 42¼	Ramsammy E	LB119	3.30	74-28	HwksleyHill123nk MrLightfoot1191¾ Mgelln119nk	Stalked pace,outkicked	5
9Sep98-3Dmr	fm	1	(T) :241 :483 1:121 1:35	3↑ LiveDreamH76k	104	4	1½ 1hd 11 12 13	Ramsammy E	LB115	*1.00	94-06	Joe Who1153 *Brave Act*116½ El Angelo1151½	Inside, kicked clear	6
30Jly98-7Dmr	fm	1	(T) :223 :464 1:10 1:332	3↑ [R]WickerrH71k	104	10	21 21 32½ 21½ 12	Ramsammy E	LB113	33.40	102 -	*Joe Who*1132 *Expelled*1171½ *Manzoni*117¾	Stalked, gamely	10
23May98-9Hol	fm	1	(T) :234 :472 1:11 1:342	3↑ FastnessH72k	88	6	42½ 41¾ 42½ 74 88	Flores D R	LB116	13.30	83-17	Vetheuil113nk Via Lombardia1183 Fllck1182½	Steadied 1/16	9
18Apr98-5SA	fm	*6½f	(T) :221 :441 1:071 1:124	4↑ SnSmeonH-G3	96	8	1 21 3½ 31 43	Flores D R	LB113	13.10	90-07	*Labeeb*1202¼ Surachai118½ Captain Collins115nk	Weakened late stretch	11
7Mar98-4SA	fm	1	(T) :224 :46 1:10 1:344	4↑ ArcadiaH-G2	86	2	34½ 46 56 77¼ 79	Alvarado F T	LB113	18.10	76-18	*Hawksley Hill*1151½ Via Lombardia1172¾ A Magicman120nk	3 wide, tired	10
20Feb98-6SA	fst	1	:231 :471 1:111 1:36	4↑ Alw 63120N$MY	61	4	56 69¼ 611 720 623½	Stevens G L	LB121	4.10	67-09	Trafalger1208 Pacificbounty1203½ Funontherun120½	Settled, no factor	8
31Aug97♦Gavea (Brz)	fm	*1	(T) LH 1:333	3↑ GP Jose Crlos de Figueiredo-G3-G3 Stk 30800			16¼	M Fontoura	129	.90		Joe Who1296¼ Fast Goer1291¼ Oak's Printed132nk	*Led from start to finish, very easily*	8
3Aug97♦Gavea (Brz)	fm	*1	(T) LH 1:331	3↑ GP Presidente da Republica-G1-G1 Stk 62200			112	M Fontoura	128	2.20		*Joe Who*12812 Gentle King121nk Thessalie128½	*Led from start to finish, very easily*	20
6Jly97♦Ciudad Jardim (Brz)	fm	*1	(T) LH 1:342	4↑ GP Henrique de Toledo Lara-G3-G3 Stk 37500			14½	M Fontoura	130	1.10		*Joe Who*1304½ Calcareo130½ Salteno1301	*Led from start to finish, very easily*	9
4May97♦Ciudad Jardim (Brz)	fm	*1	(T) LH 1:33	3↑ GP Presidente da Republica-G1-G1 Stk 73800			12¼	M Fontoura	128	1.40		*Joe Who*1282¼ Tadzio1323 Leoncavallo1323¾	*Led from the start to finish, very easily*	10
5Apr97♦Ciudad Jardim (Brz)	fm	*1	(T) LH 1:324	3↑ GP Jose Cerquinho Assumpcao-G3-G3 Stk 37500			16	M Fontoura	126	2.50		*Joe Who*1266 Rai da Toca1321½ Tadzio1324		8
23Feb97♦Gavea (Brz)	fm	*1	(T) LH 1:34	GP Estado do Rio de Janeiro-G1-G1 Stk 53400			129½	M Fontoura	123	13.30		Fettuccine1231 Oferecido123nk *Job Di Caroline*123nk		21
6Jan97♦Ciudad Jardim (Brz)	fm	*7½f	(T) LH 1:273	Allowance Race Alw 6600			16½	Souza N	117	2.80		Joe Who1176½ *Dolero*1231 Sami Slew1231½		7
28Nov96♦Ciudad Jardim (Brz)	fm	*6½f	(T) 1:161	Allowance Race Alw 7400			16½	Souza N	117	2.80		*Joe Who*1176½ Dolero1231 Sami Slew1231½		13
14Nov96♦Ciudad Jardim (Brz)	fm	*6½f	(T) LH 1:163	Claiming Race Cl 4000			16	Fontoura M	123	2.70		*Joe Who*1236 Juruna do Porto123½ Red Bull1284½		12
11Oct96♦Ciudad Jardim (Brz)	sly	*7f	LH 1:264	Claiming Race Cl 6600			814	Fontoura M	121	2.20		Red Bull1194½ Xancer Xino123¾ European Art1231¼		9
6Jly96♦Ciudad Jardim (Brz)	ft	*1	1:373	- Alw 7600			719¾	Fontoura M	117	62.80		*Tenpins*1176 Kalf1173 Abbey Road1175		10
2Jun96♦Ciudad Jardim (Brz)	fm	*7f	(T) LH 1:234	Premio Fervent Lover-Alw Alw 8100			920	Fontoura M	121	11.70		*Jato Bianco*1217 Call Min1211½ Tacamahac1216½		10
5May96♦Ciudad Jardim (Brz)	fm	*5f	(T) :561	- Alw 8300			44½	Fontoura M	121	3.60		Easy Light1214 Operator121nk Easy World121nk		7
13Apr96♦Ciudad Jardim (Brz)	fm	*5f	(T) :57	- Maiden 8400			12	Fontoura M	121	3.10		Joe Who1212 Ericus121nk Continental121¾		12
9Mar96♦Ciudad Jardim (Brz)	my	*5½f	1:08	- Maiden 8500			44½	Fontoura M	121	3.60		Dr. Edward121½ Copy Clare1211¾ Decollor1212¼		8
11Feb96♦Ciudad Jardim (Brz)	ft	*5½f	1:061	- Maiden 8400			421½	Fontoura M	121	5.00		Aracai1216 Zslew1219 Exclusive Bold1216½		11

KELLY KIP (Kipper Kelly—Marianne Theresa, by John's Gold). New York. Kelly Kip was so fast at 2, he must have reminded Hall of Fame trainer Allen Jerkens of his good stakes horses Handsome Boy and Blessing Angelica. In fact, Kelly Kip's fourth dam, Lullah, was unraced but is a full sister to Handsome Boy and Blessing Angelica. Kelly Kip won the Sanford, Tremont, and Huntington

Stakes at 2, the Forest Hills Handicap at 3, and was at his best at 4, capturing five stakes, including the Frank J. De Francis Memorial Dash, A Phenomenon Handicap, and Bold Ruler Handicap, in which he set a new track record of 1:07.61 for six furlongs at Aqueduct. (He lowered that mark to 1:07.54 in the 1999 Bold Ruler.) With this kind of high speed (from the Valid Appeal-In Reality sire line), Kelly Kip should be a superior sire of 2-year-olds and his offspring should especially prosper in New York-bred races. (SP2)

Kelly Kip
Own: Hobeau Farm

Dk. b or b. h. 10 (Apr)
Sire: Kipper Kelly (Valid Appeal) $2,000
Dam: Marianne Theresa (John's Gold)
Br: Hobeau Farm, Ltd (Fla)
Tr: Jerkens H. A(0 0 0 0 .00) 2004:(267 55 .21)

Life	31	15	3	4	$1,157,142	121	D.Fst	27	12	2	4	$1,032,042	121
2000	5	1	1	1	$75,460	112	Wet(343)	4	3	1	0	$125,100	120
1999	2	2	0	0	$90,840	120	Turf(203)	0	0	0	0	$0	–
Aik Ⓣ	0	0	0	0	$0	–	DstⓉ(275)	0	0	0	0	$0	–

14Oct00-7Bel	fst	6f	:213 :442 :561 1:082	3↑ FrstHlsH-G2	73	2	1	52¾	62¾	77½	614¼	Rojas R I	118	5.20	82-10	DelawreTownship1141½ Bevo1144 VlintHlory1132¾	Chased between rivals	7
15Apr00-7Aqu	gd	6f	:212 :44 :56 1:083	3↑ BoldRlrH-G3	112	2	5	1hd	11	1hd	2hd	Samyn J L	121	*.95	94-12	*Brutally Frank*115hd Kelly Kip1214½ Kashatreya1151¾	Fought it out gamely	7
10Mar00-10GP	fst	7f	:221 :444 1:094 1:231	3↑ GPBCSprH-G2	100	2	3	52	43	34½	35	Samyn J L	120	6.60	79-22	*RichterScale*1181 FortyOneCarats1164 KellyKip120½	Bobbled st, weakened	10
3Feb00-9GP	fst	5f	:213 :443 :571	4↑ Alw 45000NC	92	7	2	41¾	2½	21½	1½	Smith M E	115	*.40	97-15	Kelly Kip115½ Mayor Steve1153½ Alligator Bay1151	Fully extended	7
16Jan00-10GP	fst	6f	:221 :45 :572 1:104	3↑ HalndalH-G3	92	2	2	2hd	1hd	2hd	41½	Samyn J L	123	*.60	83-16	MountinTop115nk Lifeiswhirl112¾ SilverSeson115½	Dueled rail, weakened	6
10Apr99-7Aqu	fst	6f	:213 :433 :551 1:072	3↑ BoldRlrH-G3	120	4	1	1hd	1½	11½	12½	Samyn J L	123	*.45	101-07	Kelly Kip1232½ *Artax*1156¾ Brushed On115nk	Sharp pace, ridden out	5
5Mar99-3GP	fst	6f	:222 :45 :57 1:093	4↑ Alw 44000N$Y	108	2	1	2hd	12½	12½	12¾	Samyn J L	119	*.40	94-18	*Kelly Kip*1192¾ Cache In1191¼ Stormy Do1154	Vigorous hand ride	5
26Sep98-9Bel	fst	7f	:224 :451 1:09 1:214	3↑ Vosburgh-G1	102	5	1	1½	1hd	32	57½	Samyn J L	126	4.60	85-14	AffirmedSuccess1261½ StorminFvr1265 TlofthCt1261	Set pressured pace	7
12Aug98-9Sar	fst	6f	:223 :451 :571 1:093	3↑ APhenomH-G2	113	2	2	1½	1hd	14½	13	Samyn J L	122	*1.05	93-18	Kelly Kip1223 Trafalger1142½ Receiver1132¼	Dictated pace, driving	7
18Jly98-10Lrl	fst	6f	:222 :45 :564 1:082	3↑ DeFrncsM-G2	119	4	3	21	1½	1hd	11¾	Samyn J L	121	*1.20	100-12	*Kelly Kip*1211¾ *Affirmed Success*1146¾ Partner's Hero1141½	Driving	6
20Jun98-8FL	fst	6f	:212 :433 1:081	3↑ FLBC-G3	115	4	1	2hd	1½	12½	12	Samyn J L	119	*1.10	103-13	*KellyKip*1192 AffirmedSuccess1151 *LucynPrinc*1132¾	Vied for lead, driving	6
6Jun98-5Bel	fst	6f	:222 :45 :563 1:084	3↑ TruNrthH-G2	111	7	3	2½	1hd	2½	32	Samyn J L	122	*1.50	95-11	Richter Scale1191¼ Trafalger114¾ *Kelly Kip*1222	Spd outside,wknd	8
30May98-11Suf	fst	6f	:22 :45 :564 1:084	3↑ SufBCH196k	108	3	1	1hd	11½	11	13¾	Samyn J L	B119	*.60	99-09	Kelly Kip1193¾ Wire Me Collect114½ Trafalger114hd	Well handled, driving	5
3May98-8Aqu	fst	7f	:222 :442 1:082 1:21	3↑ CarterH-G1	111	4	3	3½	1hd	4nk	42	Samyn J L	120	3.00	97-12	*WildRush*117nk BnkersGold114nk WestrnBordrs1151½	Speed,gamely inside	10
11Apr98-7Aqu	fst	6f	:22 :443 :554 1:073	3↑ BoldRlrH-G3	121	2	3	32	11½	14	16	Samyn J L	117	*1.65	101-05	KellyKip1176 *SayFloridaSandy*1111¾ *JohnnyLegit*114½	3 wide move,drew off	8
13Mar98-10GP	fst	7f	:224 :451 1:091 1:22	3↑ GPBCSprH-G3	107	6	5	41¾	31	41¾	41¾	Samyn J L	115	14.70	88-16	*Rare Rock*117½ Irish Conquest1141 Frisco View118nk	Stalked fast pace	7
11Feb98-10GP	fst	6f	:214 :44 :56 1:083	3↑ HallndaleH75k	92	1	6	42	43	64¼	67½	Samyn J L	118	*1.70	91-15	*Rare Rock*1161¼ Heckofaralph1152 Banjo114½	Good position, tired	8
23Jan98-9GP	fst	6f	:214 :441 :562 1:093	4↑ Alw 50000N$Y	106	2	6	51¼	5¾	1½	11	Samyn J L	122	3.30	94-16	Kelly Kip1221 Appealing Skier119½ Star Trace1171½	Fast pace, ridden out	8
3Jan98-3GP	fst	5½f	:214 :442 1:022	4↑ Alw 44000N$Y	95	4	1	1hd	1hd	31½	45¼	Samyn J L	119	*1.00	110-12	*RareRock*119nk WesternFame1154 AppelingSkier1171	Fast pace, lost whip	6
27Nov97-9Aqu	fst	6f	:224 :462 :581 1:103	3↑ FallHwtH-G2	102	3	6	1hd	11	21½	33½	Samyn J L	135	2.30	82-20	*Royal Haven*1361½ *King Roller*1292 Kelly Kip1354	Set pace,weakened	7
19Oct97-7Bel	fst	6f	:223 :451 :563 1:084	3↑ FrstHlsH-G2	111	8	2	3½	1½	12	11½	Samyn J L	111	13.50	97-11	Kelly Kip1111½ Crafty Friend1173 *Royal Haven*119no	Took over after a 1/2	11
5Oct97-6Bel	fst	6f	:222 :452 :572 1:094	3↑ Alw 46000	96	1	5	2hd	1½	1½	22	Samyn J L	119	*.75	90-16	King Roller1192 *Kelly Kip*119¾ Star Trace1153	Spd on rail,gamely	6
27Sep97-9Bel	fst	7f	:224 :451 1:093 1:22	3↑ Vosburgh-G1	90	1	3	3nk	1½	62¾	910½	Samyn J L	122	10.40	80-13	Victor Cooley1261½ Score aBirdie126nk *TaleoftheCat*122½	Tired after a half	12
23Aug97-4Sar	gd	6½f	:221 :442 1:081 1:144	3↑ Alw 45000N1Y	120	2	1	1hd	2hd	11½	13½	Samyn J L	116	*.55	103-05	Kelly Kip1163½ Reality Road1205½ Algar1164	Rapid pace,kept busy	5
1Aug97-8Sar	fst	6f	:213 :444 :572 1:102	ScreenKing82k	99	5	4	1½	11	1½	31½	Samyn J L	122	2.30	87-19	Oro de Mexico117½ Trafalger1221 *Kelly Kip*1221½	Stmbld strt,strong pce	7
5Jan97-10GP	fst	6f	:212 :432 :562 1:094	SpectBid-G3	84	9	1	5½	1½	2½	23¾	Samyn J L	119	*.60	87-11	Confide1143¾ Kelly Kip1191½ Crown Ambassador117¾	Vied lead,fast pace	9
27Nov96-8Aqu	fst	6f	:222 :462 :591 1:123	Huntington54k	92	2	3	1hd	1hd	1½	12	Samyn J L	122	*1.35	80-25	Kelly Kip1222 *Confide*1173½ Oro Bandito114¾	Set pressured pace	6
31Aug96-8Sar	fst	7f	:213 :441 1:093 1:233	Hopeful-G1	36	1	6	1hd	21	710	726¼	Samyn J L	122	*.80	62-12	Smoke Glacken1229 *Ordway*1222 Gun Fight122¾	Speed on rail,tired	8
26Jly96-7Sar	my	6f	:213 :45 :571 1:101	Sanford-G3	107	6	1	11½	11½	14	110½	Samyn J L	118	*1.40	90-12	KllyKip11810½ *BostonHrbor*118nk *SyFloridSndy*1154½	Set strong pace,drvng	8
5Jly96-8Bel	fst	5½f	:22 :454 :58 1:043	Tremont-G3	94	3	3	1½	1½	12½	14½	Samyn J L	114	*1.55	96-12	*Kelly Kip*1144½ Say FloridaSandy1142¾ Leestown114nk	Drew off,ridden out	7
21Jun96-2Bel	sly	5f	:221 :442 :553	Md 35000(40-35)	104	4	3	1½	1½	12	16½	Samyn J L	114	3.65	108-02	*KllyKip*1146½ HomOnthRdg11712 BuffloHuntr1171½	Strong pace,hand ride	8

KING OF THE HUNT (Seattle Slew—Alydar's Promise, by Alydar). California. A full brother to successful California-based stallion General Meeting, King of the Hunt was a winner of one race in three lifetime starts. In that maiden victory he defeated future stakes winners Five Star Day and Freespool, but because he is not as famous as his more illustrious brother, his runners should provide good value in statebred sprints.

King of the Hunt
Own: Golden Eagle Farm

B. h. 8 (Apr)
Sire: Seattle Slew (Bold Reasoning) $300,000
Dam: Alydar's Promise (Alydar)
Br: Mr. & Mrs. John C. Mabee (Ky)
Tr: Canani Julio C(0 0 0 0 .00) 2004:(133 28 .21)

Life	3 1 0 0	$29,080	87	D.Fst	2 1 0 0	$28,080	87
2000	1 0 0 0	$1,000	65	Wet(384)	1 0 0 0	$1,000	65
1999	2 1 0 0	$28,080	87	Turf(323)	0 0 0 0	$0	–
	0 0 0 0	$0	–	Dst⑪(391)	0 0 0 0	$0	–

13Feb00–3SA	wf 6½f	:21⁴ :44 1:08²1:14⁴	4↑ Alw 50750n1x	65 6 4 5⁵ 69½ 51⁴ 51⁹	Gomez G K	LB119	4.60 75– 13 Norcielo117² Freedom Crest117⁴ Diamant119⁸	Angled in 1/4,no rally 6
Previously trained by Mandella Richard							
3Apr99–4SA	fst 1¹⁄₁₆	:22³ :46 1:10⁴1:43	Alw 54000n1x	55 3 34½ 3⁸ 47½ 51² 526½	Nakatani C S	LB118	*.40e 62– 13 Finder's Gold120⁴ Red Eye118ⁿᵏ Caledonian Colours118⁸	Gave way 6
6Mar99–4SA	fst 6f	:21² :44² :57 1:10¹	Md Sp Wt 45k	87 5 4 2ʰᵈ 2ʰᵈ 2ʰᵈ 1½	Nakatani C S	LB120	3.00 89– 05 KingoftheHunt120½ BestofTime120¹ Freespool120¾	Led 1/16,cleared,held 11

KING'S BEST (Kingmambo—Allegretta, by Lombard). Ireland. With King's Best standing in Ireland, it will be rare to see any of his off-spring in the U.S., but runners from the first crops of European-based Fasliyev and Cape Cross were spotted in this country in 2003. King's Best's most important victory was England's 2000 Guineas, in which he defeated the mighty Giant's Causeway. King's Best is a half-brother to Urban Sea, a champion older female in France who defeated males in the Prix de l'Arc de Triomphe. Urban Sea became a special broodmare, producing champions Galileo, Urban Ocean, and Black Sam Bellamy, and group-placed Melikah. King's Best's runners are strictly bred for grass and should be much better stretching out to classic distances at age 3. (T^2)

King's Best
Own: Mr Saeed Suhail

B. h. 7 (Jan)
Sire: Kingmambo (Mr. Prospector) $225,000
Dam: Allegretta*GB (Lombard)
Br: M3 Elevage (Ky)
Tr: Sir M Stoute(0 0 0 0 .00) 2004:(0 0 .00)

Life	6 3 1 0	$324,199	–	D.Fst	0 0 0 0	$0	–
2000	3 1 1 0	$277,984	–	Wet(325)	0 0 0 0	$0	–
1999	3 2 0 0	$46,215	–	Turf(281)	6 3 1 0	$324,199	–
	0 0 0 0	$0	–	Dst(428)	0 0 0 0	$0	–

2Jly00	Curragh (Ire)	gd 1½ ① RH 2:33⁴	Irish Derby-G1 Stk 1030500	–	Eddery P	126	4.50	Sinndar126⁹ Glyndebourne126½ Ciro126½	11
								Held up towards rar, pulled before half, lame
6May00	Newmarket (GB)	gd 1 ① Str 1:37³	2000 Guineas Stakes-G1 Stk 458300	13½	Fallon K	126	6.50	King's Best126¾ Giant's Causeway126¼ Barathea Guest126²	27
								Headway & hampered 2f & 1f out, rallied to lead final f, ran on
20Apr00	Newmarket (GB)	yl 1 ① Str 1:41	Craven Stakes-G3 Stk 55300	2½	Fallon K	121	3.50	Umistim121½ Kings Best121² Ekraar121½	9
								Led & quickened 2f out, headed in final f
16Oct99	Newmarket (GB)	gd 7f ① Str 1:26⁴	Dewhurst Stakes-G1 Stk 334000	55¾	Fallon K	126	2.75	Distant Music126¹ Brahms126² Zentsov Street126²¹	5
								Pulled hard, held up, headway 1f out, ridden 1f out, no gain
17Aug99	York (GB)	gd 7f ① LH 1:23	Acomb Stakes (Listed) Stk 56300	1²	Stevens G	125	*.55	King's Best125² Shamrock City122ⁿᵏ Race Leader125¹	5
								Made all, shaken up over 1f out, ran on well
6Aug99	Newmarket (GB)	gd 7f ① 1:28	- Maiden 11200	1²	Stevens G	126	*1.50	King's Best126² Jalad126³½ Alasan126ʰᵈ	8
								Set steady pace, rallied over 2f out, quickened clear final f

LEMON DROP KID (Kingmambo—Charming Lassie, by Seattle Slew). Kentucky. Lemon Drop Kid competed at the highest level, winning Grade 1 races at age 2 (Futurity Stakes), 3 (Belmont, Travers Stakes), and 4 (Whitney Handicap and Woodward Stakes). He was bred to be at his best stretching out in distance, so his offspring should develop as late-maturing 2-year-olds and be even more formidable at 3 and older. By Kingmambo, Lemon Drop Kid is a good example of the hidden turf sire. Because he achieved success on dirt, horseplayers will tend to dismiss his runners when they appear on turf, causing attractive overlays. Lemon Drop Kid's dam is a half-sister to the 1992 Broodmare of the Year, Weekend Surprise, dam of A.P. Indy, Summer Squall, and Honor Grades. The combination of stamina and class in his female family suggests that his runners will be best suited to classic distances, especially on grass. (HT)

Lemon Drop Kid
Own: Vance Jeanne G

B. h. 8 (May)
Sire: Kingmambo (Mr. Prospector) $225,000
Dam: Charming Lassie (Seattle Slew)
Br: W. S. Farish & W. S. Kilroy (Ky)
Tr: Schulhofer Flint S(0 0 0 0 .00) 2004:(0 0 .00)

Life	24	10	3	3	$3,245,370	118	D.Fst	18	9	1	2	$2,366,870	117
2000	9	5	0	1	$1,673,900	118	Wet(350)	6	1	2	1	$878,500	118
1999	9	3	1	1	$1,349,400	111	Turf(345)	0	0	0	0	$0	-
	0	0	0	0	$0	-	Dst(386)	1	1	0	0	$90,000	92

4Nov00-10CD	fst	1¼	:472 1:12 1:36 2:003	3↑BCClasic-G1	108	6	41¼	41¼	43	54	55¼	Prado E S	L126 b	6.20	102 -	*Tiznow*122nk Giant's Causeway1223¼ *Captain Steve*122hd	Empty in drive	13
14Oct00-10Bel	fst	1¼	:464 1:101 1:342 1:591	3↑JkyClbGC-G1	105	4	63¼	63¾	54½	48½	59½	Prado E S	L126 b	*.95	88- 09	AlberttheGret1226 Gnder1263 VisionndVers126no	Bumped start, steadied	7
16Sep00-8Bel	fst	1⅛	:461 1:104 1:364 1:502	3↑Woodward-G1	105	5	51¾	3½	1hd	1hd	1hd	Prado E S	L126 b	*.70	79- 14	Lemon Drop Kid126hd Behrens126¾ Gander1263¾	4 wide, resolutely	5
6Aug00-9Sar	gd	1⅛	:463 1:101 1:35 1:481	3↑WhitneyH-G1	118	1	51¾	52½	41	11½	12	Prado E S	L123 b	*2.05	100 -	*Lemon Drop Kid*1232 Cat Thief1174¼ Behrens1221½	4 wide move, driving	6
4Jly00-9Bel	fst	1¼	:463 1:094 1:341 1:584	3↑SuburbnH-G2	117	2	21	21	1hd	12½	12½	Prado E S	L122 b	*.80	100- 13	*Lemon Drop Kid*1222½ Behrens1224¼ Lager1131	Speed outside, driving	6
11Jun00-8Bel	fst	1⅛	:47 1:114 1:371 1:494	3↑BroklynH-G2	115	4	3½	31	2hd	12½	17¼	Prado E S	L120 b	2.10	82- 29	*Lemon Drop Kid*1207¼ Lager114hd *Down theAisle*112hd	Speed 3 wide, driving	7
13May00-10Pim	fst	1 3/16	:472 1:111 1:361 1:543	3↑PimSpclH-G1	112	4	61¾	62¾	52¼	4¾	32	Prado E S	L120	4.10	90- 18	*GoldenMissile*1162 PlesntBreeze111no *LmonDropKid*1204	3wd trip, willingly	8
15Apr00-3Aqu	fst	1⅛	:463 1:102 1:353 1:491	4↑Alw 60000c	98	5	44	44½	21½	1½	11½	♦Santos J A	L122	*.65	91- 10	DH LmonDrpKd122 DH EndfthRd1131½ GldStrDpty11616¼	4 wide first turn	5
18Mar00-10GP	sly	1⅛	:474 1:12 1:373 1:513	3↑WidenerH-G3	105	3	32½	31	3½	12	12	Santos J A	L119	*.60	79- 21	D *LemonDropKid*1192 BlazingSword112hd WithAnticipation1112½	Duckd in	4
Disqualified and placed 4th																		
6Nov99-10GP	fst	1¼	:453 1:094 1:341 1:592	3↑BCClasic-G1	111	11	98¼	95¾	64½	53¼	64½	Santos J A	L122	6.30	109 -	CatThief1221¼ Budroyle126hd GoldenMissile1262	Swerve in start,bumped	14
10Oct99-6Bel	sly	1¼	:462 1:101 1:352 2:012	3↑JkyClbGC-G1	103	7	54½	52½	52½	56	59¼	Santos J A	L121	5.30	78- 23	River Keen1263¼ Behrens126hd Almutawakel1264¼	Inside run second turn	8
28Aug99-9Sar	fst	1¼	:481 1:122 1:364 2:02	Travers-G1	110	6	31	3½	2hd	1hd	1¾	Santos J A	L126	3.65	98- 13	LemonDropKid126¾ VisionndVerse1261¾ Menif1261¾	Close 3w, hard drive	8
8Aug99-8Sar	sly	1⅛	:474 1:12 1:364 1:492	JimDandy-G2	103	5	5¾	41	42¼	22½	25¼	Santos J A	L124	3.25	84- 18	EctonPrk1165¼ *LmonDropKid*1242 BdgrGold1141¾	Came wide, game finish	7
5Jun99-9Bel	fst	1½	:473 1:12 2:014 2:274	Belmont-G1	109	6	83¾	84¾	41¼	1½	1hd	Santos J A	L126	29.75	105- 06	LmonDropKid126hd VisonndVrs1261½ Chrsmtc1264¾	Swung wide 1/4pl,drv	12
23May99-8Bel	my	1⅛	:451 1:09 1:344 1:474	PeterPan-G2	103	6	41½	43	42	3½	32½	Santos J A	L120	3.60	89- 27	BestofLuck1131 TrsurIslnd1141½ *LmonDropKid*1202	Tight quarters stretch	9
1May99-8CD	fst	1¼	:474 1:122 1:372 2:031	KyDerby-G1	100	19	167	178¼	158¼	1510	95½	Santos J A	L126	11.60e	83- 14	*Charismatic*126nk Menifee126¾ Cat Thief1261¼	No threat,8wide,drive	19
10Apr99-9Kee	fst	1⅛	:47 1:104 1:36 1:483	BlueGras-G1	97	5	62¾	62¾	52¼	63¾	55¾	Velazquez J R	L123	4.30	86- 19	Menifee1231¼ Cat Thief123½ Vicar1232½	In close 7/16 pole	8
27Feb99-3GP	fst	1 1/16	:234 :474 1:121 1:443	Alw 34000N2X	98	2	32	31½	2hd	11½	13½	Velazquez J R	L119	*.80	84- 14	LmonDropKid1193½ Cryptodiplomcy1194 *Alnnn*119¾	Jumped tracks 1/16 pl	6
7Nov98-4CD	fst	1 1/16	:231 :463 1:113 1:44	BCJuven-G1	86	2	89	79½	63¼	64	56½	Velazquez J R	122	3.70	84- 07	Answer Lively122hd Aly's Alley122¾ Cat Thief1225½	No late bid	13
10Oct98-9Bel	sly	1 1/16	:222 :451 1:10 1:424	Champagn-G1	88	3	43½	33	43	2½	22¾	Velazquez J R	122	2.55	82- 14	ThGroomIsRd1222¾ LmnDrpKd1222 WkndMny122½	Wide move, game fin	7
20Sep98-9Bel	fst	1	:24 :473 1:121 1:372	Futurity-G1	92	5	41	31	21	22	1½	Velazquez J R	122	6.40	77- 26	LemonDropKid122½ YesItsTrue1229 MedivilHro1225	Speed 3w, along late	5
21Aug98-4Sar	fst	7f	:224 :46 1:102 1:23	Alw 37000N2L	68	4	2	51¾	31½	34½	313½	Santos J A	116	2.75	76- 13	*Menifee*1163 Cat Thief11610½ *Lemon Drop Kid*1164½	Wide trip, lugged in	5
1Aug98-3Sar	fst	6f	:223 :461 :582 1:104	Md Sp Wt 35k	88	2	5	31	2hd	2½	1nk	Santos J A	116	*1.00	87- 12	Lemon Drop Kid116nk Arrested1169 Kipling116nk	3 wide move, driving	10
12Jly98-2Bel	fst	5½f	:224 :454 :574 1:041	Md Sp Wt 35k	89	9	7	42½	3½	21	2no	Santos J A	115	3.25	94- 10	Treasure Island115no *Lemon Drop Kid*1151¾ Arrested1151	Gamely,outside	9

LION HEARTED (Storm Cat—Cadillacing, by Alydar). Maryland. The Maryland breeding program has been successful standing stallions bred and raced by the Phipps family, such as Polish Numbers, Not For Love, and Diamond. Lion Hearted, a half-brother to stakes winners Strolling Along and Cat Cay, is the latest Phipps-bred sire to come to Maryland. He was twice stakes-placed (Riva Ridge and Amsterdam Stakes), and his foals should be heard from in statebred races, while showing high speed. By the world's most popular stallion, Lion Hearted is out of stakes winner Cadillacing, a full sister to Easy Goer who, unlike her brother, preferred distances up to seven furlongs. (SP^2)

Lion Hearted
Own: Phipps Ogden

Dk. b or b. h. 8 (Mar)
Sire: Storm Cat (Storm Bird) $500,000
Dam: Cadillacing (Alydar)
Br: Phipps Stable (Ky)
Tr: McGaughey III Claude R(5 0 3 1 .00) 2004:(196 31 .16)

Life	18	4	6	3	$191,630	107	D.Fst	14	2	6	2	$141,390	107
2000	3	1	0	1	$33,370	101	Wet(417)	4	2	0	1	$50,240	94
1999	12	2	6	1	$129,000	107	Turf(346)	0	0	0	0	$0	-
	0	0	0	0	$0	-	Dst(407)	0	0	0	0	$0	-

4Nov00-4Aqu	fst	7f	:222 :45 1:091 1:214	3↑ SportPgH-G3	98	5	3	41¾	31	52¼	64½	Bridgmohan S X	L113	5.40	86-12	*Stalwart Member*1171 *Istintaj*1172½ Mister Tricky112¾	3 wide trip, tired	6
18Oct00-3Bel	fst	6f	:224 :452 :573 1:101	3↑ Alw 47000N3x	101	3	2	31	2½	1½	13¼	Velazquez J R	L119	*1.10	87-19	Lion Hearted1193¼ Runspastum117nk Too Costly1193½	3 wide, ridden out	5
10Sep00-8Bel	fst	7f	:224 :454 1:094 1:223	3↑ Alw 47000N3x	89	7	1	2½	2½	22½	36¾	Bailey J D	L119	3.45	83-18	Big E E1205½ Mint1191¼ *Lion Hearted*1192¼	Pressed pace, tired	7
25Nov99-3Aqu	sly	7f	:232 :48 1:121 1:241	3↑ Alw 45000N2x	94	2	3	31½	31	3½	1¾	•Velazquez J R	L119	*1.85	81-18	DH LionHertd119 DH GrkTycoon115¾ SilkySwp1152½	Game duel,stayed on	5
21Oct99-4Bel	my	7f	:23 :461 1:104 1:233	3↑ Alw 43000N1x	82	6	1	52¼	4¾	2hd	1¾	Velazquez J R	L114	*.40	84-15	*Lion Hearted*114¾ Boodles1181¼ Mercy Be1144¼	4 wide, ridden out	6
8Oct99-7Bel	fst	6f	:22 :451 :564 1:09	3↑ Alw 43000N1x	107	3	2	43	3½	2hd	21	Velazquez J R	L114	*.70	95-12	Falkenburg1171 *Lion Hearted*1146¼ Flying Kris1163	Clear chance on rail	9
28Aug99-7Sar	fst	7f	:213 :432 1:073 1:21	KngsBshp-G1	81	12	2	66¾	79¼	812	1015¾	Velazquez J R	L114	18.50	84-09	Forestry1241½ Five Star Day1153¾ *Successful Appeal*124½	No response	12
6Aug99-8Sar	fst	6f	:221 :451 :573 1:101	Amstrdam-G3	99	1	4	72½	41¾	2½	21¼	Smith M E	L114	5.70	89-15	SuccessfulAppel1221¼ LionHertd114¾ SilvrSson1191½	Game finish outside	9
4Jly99-4Bel	fst	7f	:231 :461 1:10 1:22	3↑ Alw 44000N2x	92	3	2	4¾	41	2hd	21¼	Smith M E	L114	*.50	91-08	*Mountain Top*1191¼ Lion Hearted1144¼ SenseofDuty114½	Clear path on rail	7
5Jun99-6Bel	fst	7f	:224 :45 1:092 1:221	RivaRidg-G2	101	2	6	42	5¾	51½	21	Smith M E	L114	24.25	90-10	*YesIt'sTrue*1231 LionHearted114nk *SilverSeason*1131¼	Caught in traffic 3/16	8
16May99-7Bel	fst	7f	:222 :452 1:101 1:23	3↑ Alw 42000N1x	91	1	4	3½	4¾	2hd	2hd	Bravo J	L113	6.20	87-19	KngsCrown113hd LnHrtd113nk WstrnExprssn1133	Through on rail,gamely	11
10Apr99-8Aqu	fst	6f	:213 :442 :562 1:084	3↑ Alw 42000N2L	85	1	5	2hd	31	41¼	75	Gryder A T	L114	*2.55	89-07	Spirited Child110½ *Bought inDixie*112hd RegalValor1133¾	Vied inside, faded	10
26Feb99-10GP	fst	6f	:214 :443 :564 1:10	Ⓡ Eillo54k	74	6	3	51¾	43	47	49	Bailey J D	L115	3.30	83-19	Lifeisawhirl1154½ Late Carson1173½ Silk Broker1151	4 wide turn, no rally	7
13Feb99-9GP	fst	6f	:221 :454 :58 1:104	Alw 32000N1x	91	9	1	32½	2hd	1½	2½	Bailey J D	L119	*1.10	87-16	Alannan119½ Lion Hearted1195 Search for Luv1194¼	Gamely, edged late	9
16Jan99-3GP	sly	6f	:213 :442 :564 1:103	Alw 32000N2L	84	3	3	21½	21	22	33¾	Bailey J D	L120	*1.60	85-20	SeptemberDesert1173¼ *MrUnitdStts*120½ LionHrtd1201½	3 wide, weakened	7
28Nov98-9Aqu	fst	6f	:222 :46 :582 1:104	Md Sp Wt 38k	81	6	2	1½	1hd	12	15	Desormeaux K J	L119	*1.55	85-16	LionHearted1195 *SargentStreet*119hd Driggs1191¾	When roused, kept busy	10
10Oct98-5Bel	sly	6f	:213 :45 :574 1:112	Md Sp Wt 38k	51	4	2	31	21	25	49½	Bailey J D	118	*.95	74-11	Ordained1132 Secret Greeting1185 *Why So Quiet*1182½	Speed outside, tired	8
19Sep98-1Bel	fst	6f	:221 :46 :582 1:111	Md Sp Wt 38k	72	4	2	2hd	4¾	43	35¼	Day P	117	*1.80	80-19	*Millions*1175 Iron Prince117nk Lion Hearted117no	Lugged in, gamely	11

LITTLEBITLIVELY (Lively One—Littlebitapleasure, by I'ma Hell Raiser). Florida. Littlebitlively is one of three stakes winners from his multiple-stakes-winning dam, who also produced Built for Pleasure and Herat's Pleasure. Littlebitlively's sire, Lively One, produced champion 2-year-old Answer Lively, but Lively One's runners were predominantly late-maturing types and Littlebitlively's offspring should also be late-maturing juveniles.

Littlebitlively
Own: Franks John

Dk. b or b. h. 10 (Mar)
Sire: Lively One (Halo) $13,118
Dam: Littlebitapleasure (I'ma Hell Raiser)
Br: John Franks (Fla)
Tr: Barnett Bobby C(0 0 0 0 .00) 2004:(298 36 .12)

Life	33	10	9	5	$1,303,343	113	D.Fst	28	9	7	4	$853,577	113
1999	12	4	4	2	$868,303	113	Wet(313)	4	1	1	1	$439,766	113
1998	11	2	4	1	$370,210	113	Turf(242)	1	0	1	0	$10,000	83
	0	0	0	0	$0	-	Dst(318)	4	3	0	0	$376,672	113

27Dec99-9FG	fst	1 1/16	:243 :484 1:131 1:433	3↑ LouisianaH75k	101	7	31	32	31	2hd	3nk	Borel C H	L122	*.70	93-22	NeonShdow113nk TkeNotofM120hd Littlbitlivly1226¼	3-w bid, lacked kick	7
26Nov99-11CD	gd	1⅛	:473 1:12 1:373 1:504	3↑ ClarkH-G2	105	5	66½	65½	53¼	2hd	1no	Borel C H	L118	*2.20	89-10	Littlebitlively118no PlesntBreeze1123¾ NitDrmr114¾	Graze rail 1/2 pl,game	12
31Oct99-9CD	fst	7½f	:224 :454 1:101 1:284	3↑ AckAckH-G3	111	5	7	41	32½	21	1½	Borel C H	L119	*2.60	102-12	*Littlebitlively*119½ *Run Johnny*1174 TacticalCat117no	Angled 4-wide,driving	11
15Oct99-7Kee	fst	6f	:213 :443 :561 1:08	3↑ Alw 56850N$Y	102	3	4	32½	33	31	2no	Borel C H	L118 b	*1.40	102-02	LeveLegcy118no *Littlebitlively*1181¾ QustMstr116no	Inside,bid,outfinished	6
4Jly99-10Mth	fst	1⅛	:461 1:101 1:354 1:49	3↑ PIselinH-G2	104	2	2hd	1½	2hd	2½	42¾	Gonzalez C V	L118 b	*1.30	88-13	Frisk Me Now117¾ Call Me Mr. Vain1101½ *BlackCash*112½	Dueled, tired late	6
12Jun99-9CD	fst	1⅛	:464 1:11 1:352 1:471	3↑ SFosterH-G2	108	2	1hd	1hd	1hd	31½	35¾	Borel C H	L115 b	3.30e	101-03	*Victory Gallop*1205 *Nite Dreamer*110¾ Littlebitlively1152¾	Dueled, weakened	7
31May99-8LS	fst	1 1/16	:234 :47 1:10 1:431	3↑ LSParkH303k	108	1	41¼	1hd	1hd	1½	2no	Gonzalez C V	L118 b	*1.00	88-30	MochExprss116no Littlbitlivly118¾ NitDrmr1135¼	Hopped out,just missed	7
18Apr99-7LS	fst	1	:24 :471 1:111 1:353	3↑ TexsMile-G3	110	4	11	12	2½	1½	1nk	Gonzalez C V	L116 b	2.70	94-15	Littlebitlively116nk *Real Quiet*1161¾ Allen's Oop1134¾	Game finish	8
3Apr99-11OP	sly	1⅛	:461 1:094 1:352 1:473	4↑ OaklawnH-G1	113	3	1½	1½	12½	2½	22½	Gonzalez C V	L112 b	2.60e	96-10	*Behrens*1162½ *Littlebitlively*1121¾ Precocity1195¼	Quick splits, stubborn	7
19Mar99-9OP	fst	1 1/16	:233 :471 1:114 1:433	4↑ Alw 35000N$Y	99	4	33½	2½	2hd	1hd	1¾	Gonzalez C V	L114	*.30	86-22	Littlebitlively114¾ *FortMetfield*1181¼ BattleMountin1142½	Stalked, all out	6
20Feb99-9OP	fst	1 1/16	:233 :48 1:124 1:431	4↑ EssexH-G3	103	2	42	3nk	2hd	2hd	2nk	Gonzalez C V	L115	*1.10	88-17	BrushWithPride116nk *Littlebitlivly*1152¾ TrtMDoc1143	Forward, stubborn	7
30Jan99-10GP	fst	1⅛	:463 1:102 1:353 1:481	3↑ DonnH-G1	93	5	1½	1½	1hd	31	813	Migliore R	L113	29.60	83-14	Puerto Madero1202¾ *Behrens*1132½ Silver Charm126nk	Set pace rail, tired	12
28Dec98-9FG	gd	1 1/16	:241 :48 1:124 1:433	3↑ LouisianaH48k	85	1	21½	21½	22	45½	413	Gonzalez C V	L117	*.60	80-21	*TkNotfM*1143 CmOnGtHppy1174½ CrmsnClssc1135½	Stalked, flattened out	4
27Nov98-11CD	fst	1⅛	:472 1:112 1:361 1:49	3↑ ClarkH-G2	113	6	42¼	31	41¾	1½	2hd	Borel C H	L113	37.80	99-14	*SilverChrm*124hd Littlebitlively1131 WildRush117½	Brushed rail, outgamed	8
1Nov98-8CD	fst	7½f	:222 :452 1:101 1:293	3↑ AckAckH-G3	75	3	5	42	42½	66½	613½	Day P	L116	4.20	83-13	Distorted Humor1201¾ Crafty Friend113nk *Chindi*113nk	Inside, tired	6
16May98-7Pim	fst	1⅛	:461 1:103 1:36 1:483	3↑ WDSchaferH105k	106	5	58	32	32½	1hd	2no	Gonzalez C V	L118	3.70	97-13	Acceptable118no Littlebitlively118½ *Testafly*1143¼	Ratd 3w,bid,led,hung	8
19Apr98-6LS	fst	1	:24 :47 1:111 1:37	3↑ TexasMile250k	113	2	31½	1½	2hd	1½	1nk	Gonzalez C V	L118	6.70	87-32	Littlebitlively118nk *Anet*1167¼ Scott's Scoundrel1182¼	Prevailed, all out	5
8Apr98-9OP	fst	1 1/16	:233 :473 1:114 1:422	3↑ 5thSeasnBC100k	106	7	33	31	3½	1hd	2hd	Gonzalez C V	L117	4.50	96-15	*Acceptable*117hd *Littlebitlively*1173 Brush With Pride1241	Outfinished	8
14Mar98-9OP	fst	1 1/16	:232 :473 1:123 1:432	4↑ RazrbakH-G3	105	5	21	21	2hd	1½	2nk	Pettinger D R	L112	4.60	91-14	BrushWithPride115nk Littlebitlively1121½ KrigeorjsGold1152	Outfinished	7
1Mar98-9FG	fst	6f	:22 :452 :571 1:094	4↑ TaylrSpclH75k	102	3	5	5¾	2hd	3½	3nk	Gonzalez C V	L112	4.40	95-12	GoldnOrintl112no FindthTrsur116nk Littlbitlivly112no	Dueled, good effort	7
16Feb98-9Lrl	fst	7f	:224 :461 1:103 1:23	3↑ GenGrgeH-G2	101	8	2	66	75¼	44	44¾	Reynolds L C	L113	63.50	89-16	RoylHven1222 PurplPssion1161¾ WirMCollct1171	3wd 3-1/2,mv bw,willng	9
17Jan98-10FG	fst	6f	:221 :452 :571 1:094	4↑ ColPowerH48k	102	4	2	41½	41½	1hd	1no	Gonzalez C V	L110	4.90	95-12	Littlebitlively110no *GoldenOrintl*111½ *YouKnowHowItIs*1131	Dueled, gamely	4
2Jan98-9FG	fst	6f	:213 :441 :571 1:101	4↑ Alw 32000N$Y	83	7	7	64	75	75	75¾	Gonzalez C V	L117	4.40	87-13	Galileo117no *Phantom On Tour*117no Crowns Runner1171	No rally	8
Previously trained by Convento Mario																		
1Dec97-8FG	fst	6f	:22 :453 :573 1:10	3↑ Alw 28000N4L	97	3	5	77¾	54¼	12	14	Gonzalez C V	L115	*2.10	94-15	Littlebitlively1154 Bush Won117nk DH Handel117	Drew clear, driving	9
Previously trained by Barnett Bobby C																		
8Nov97-8LaD	fst	1 1/16	:241 :473 1:112 1:423	3↑ Alliance25k	93	7	1½	1½	1hd	34½	36¼	Trosclair A J	L112	4.70	91-20	ScottsScoundrl1231¼ *KingndHrt*1125 *Littlbitlivly*1122½	Set pace, weakened	9
24Oct97-9LaD	gd	7f	:224 :453 1:101 1:234	3↑ Alw 21000N$Y	91	5	4	3nk	1½	21	32½	Lanerie C J	L113	8.30	86-21	*Galileo*1161½ Takeawakatlove1161 Littlebitlively113nk	Dueled, weakened	10
4Sep97-4LaD	fst	1 1/16	:24 :471 1:113 1:441	3↑ Alw 19000c	84	3	55½	55¾	31½	12	12	Gonzalez C V	L112	2.30	89-13	Littlebitlively1122 Val de Iano1141 Cameron Park112½	Drew clear, driving	11
27Jly97-8LaD	fm	*1 1/16 Ⓣ	:233 :481 1:122 1:423	BossrCityH50k	83	3	2½	2½	1hd	2hd	22½	Gonzalez C V	L113	8.30	93-11	Oscar Magic1132½ *Littlebitlively*113nk Royalty Case1171	Dueled, held place	6
13Jly97-9LaD	fst	170	:243 :483 1:132 1:414	3↑ Alw 16000N2L	81	4	21½	2½	1hd	13½	16	Trosclair A J	L115	*1.00	90-17	Littlebitlively1156 Yukon Due It115½ Drillsite11210	Drew off, driving	6
15Jun97-8LS	fst	1 1/16	:231 :464 1:11 1:434	3↑ Alw 22000N1x	65	1	51¾	4nk	21	49	615	Ardoin R D	L114	2.90	- -	PerfectDputy1156 Bcktt1161¾ Lookouthrigo1166¼	Saved ground, no rally	11
23May97-4LS	fst	1 1/16	:232 :473 1:123 1:441	3↑ Md Sp Wt 19k	92	7	21	2hd	11	12	12¼	Pettinger D R	L114	6.80	- -	Littlebitlively1142¼ *YukonDuIt*1145¼ WolfFctor1149	Well placed, drew off	8
19Apr97-4LS	fst	6f	:223 :462 :59 1:111	3↑ Md Sp Wt 19k	55	12	11	84¼	31½	42	55	Gonzalez C V	L114	4.90	- -	DemandNote1143 BallyinOrbit114nk StylishDn1161¾	Dueled, flattened out	14
5Apr97-6OP	fst	6f	:213 :451 :581 1:113	Md Sp Wt 22k	53	5	7	72¼	64¾	812	914	Perner E C	L119	9.00	69-17	Ice Tizzy1191½ Mr. Pickled Gap1191 Lucky Spurs1195	Inside, weakened	12

LUHUK (Forty Niner—Royal Stance, by Dr. Fager). Kentucky. While Luhuk's first crop of U.S-breds are 2, he has actually had five crops to race in Argentina, with six Grade 1 horses in his first crop. He is the sire of the stakes-winning sprinter Avanzado, and it is rare these days to see the immortal speed influence Dr. Fager up close in a pedigree. With so much brilliance in his pedigree, expect Luhuk's 2-year-olds to be quite precocious and surprise at square prices. (SP^{2})

Luhuk
Own: Sh Rashid Bin Hamdan Al Maktoum

Ch. h. 13 (Feb)
Sire: Forty Niner (Mr. Prospector) $31,482
Dam: Royal Stance (Dr. Fager)
Br: E. A. Cox Jr. (Ky)
Tr: P. Rudkin(0 0 0 0 .00) 2004:(0 0 .00)

Life	18	6	2	1	$107,105	-	D.Fst	7	3	1	0	$33,359	-
1996	4	2	0	0	$20,424	-	Wet(341)	1	0	0	0	$0	-
1995	4	1	1	0	$12,935	-	Turf(265)	10	3	1	1	$73,746	-
	0	0	0	0	$0	-	Dst(352)	0	0	0	0	$0	-

14Apr96	Nad Al Sheba (UAE)	ft	*1¼	LH 2:05	3+ Handicap Hcp 16300	1^{4}	P Brette	126	-	Luhuk126^{4} Zama114$^{2\frac{3}{4}}$ Charillus114^{no}	6
10Mar96	Nad Al Sheba (UAE)	hy	*1¼	LH 2:08^{2}	4+ Maktoum Al Maktoum Chlng(Lstd) Stk 54500	-	Hills R	125	-	Tamayaz123^{5} Cezanne125^{10} Esbooain125^{4} *Tracked leader,weakened,stumbled and fell 150y out.No betting*	6
25Feb96	Nad Al Sheba (UAE)	ft	*1½	LH 2:30^{3}	4+ Maktoum Al Maktoum Chlng(Lstd) Stk 40900	$4^{17\frac{1}{4}}$	Hills R	127	-	Larrocha120^{8} Learmont127^{nk} Cayumanque127^{9} *Tracked leader on rail,weakened 2f out.No betting*	10
25Jan96	Nad Al Sheba (UAE)	ft	*1¼	LH 2:05^{4}	4+ Allowance Race Alw 16300	1	Hills R	126	-	Luhuk126 Cayumanque126 Zama119 *Rated in 4th,led 2f out,ridden clear.Linney Head 4th.No betting*	4
31Mar95	Jebel Ali (UAE)	ft	*1¼	RH 2:02^{4}	3+ - Hcp 13600	$2^{1\frac{1}{2}}$	Hills R	123	-	Najm Almaydaan112$^{1\frac{1}{2}}$ *Luhuk*123^{hd} Learmont114$^{2\frac{1}{4}}$ *Tracked in 3rd,bid 3f out,one-paced late,just held 2nd.No betting*	5
5Mar95	Nad Al Sheba (UAE)	ft	*1¼	LH 2:06^{1}	3+ Handicap (Class 2) Hcp 13600	5^{14}	Hills R	130	-	Rehlat Farah129^{5} Royal Fandango127^{no} Ijlal116^{1} *Tracked in 4th,faded through last quarter.No betting*	8
9Feb95	Nad Al Sheba (UAE)	ft	*1¼	LH 2:04^{1}	3+ Maktoum Al Maktoum Chlng-Rnd 2 Alw 13600	$4^{10\frac{3}{4}}$	Hills R	126	-	*Halling*126^{4} Rainbow Heights126$^{\frac{3}{4}}$ *Dover Straits*126^{6} *Towards rear,close 5th 3f out,one-paced last quarter.No betting*	9
8Jan95	Nad Al Sheba (UAE)	ft	*1¼	LH 2:04^{3}	3+ Allowance Race Alw 16300	1^{1}	Hills R	127	-	Luhuk127^{1} Rainbow Heights123^{2} Grafin127^{8} *Handily palced in last,rallied to lead 1f out,driving.No betting*	4
Previously trained by John Dunlop											
30Sep94	Goodwood (GB)	gd	1¼ Ⓣ	RH 2:09^{1}	3+ ROA Foundation Stakes (Listed) Stk 36500	$1^{2\frac{1}{2}}$	unknown jockey	123	-	*Luhuk*123$^{2\frac{1}{2}}$ *Zilzal Zamaan*120$^{\frac{3}{4}}$ Young Buster129$^{1\frac{1}{2}}$ *Rated in 4th,roused to lead over 2f out,drew clear in hand*	6
9Sep94	Doncaster (GB)	gd	1½ Ⓣ	LH 2:30^{4}	Troy Stakes (Listed) Stk 26900	$7^{7\frac{1}{4}}$	Carson W	128	*3.30	Estimraar123^{nk} Tatami123^{nk} Florid123^{nk} *Rated in 5th,drifted left 2f out,weakened*	8
16Aug94	York (GB)	gd	1½ Ⓣ	LH 2:28^{1}	Great Voltigeur Stakes-G2 Stk 131700	4^{2}	Carson W	121	5.50	Sacrament121^{nk} Ionio121$^{1\frac{1}{4}}$ Broadway Flyer121$^{\frac{1}{2}}$ *Tracked in 4th,pushed along & lacked room 2-1/2f out,fnshd well*	7
6Aug94	Haydock (GB)	gd	1$\frac{5}{16}$ Ⓣ	LH 2:09^{2}	3+ Rose of Lancaster Stakes-G3 Stk 55600	3^{8}	Carson W	119	4.00	Urgent Request129^{5} *Cezanne*129^{3} Luhuk119^{2} *Midpack on rail,no room & shuffled back to last 4f out,fnshd well*	12
16Jly94	Newbury (GB)	gd	1¼ Ⓣ	LH 2:05^{1}	3+ Arlngtn Int Racecourse S(Lstd) Stk 27300	$1^{2\frac{1}{2}}$	unknown jockey	118	-	Luhuk118$^{2\frac{1}{2}}$ Young Buster134^{4} Shintillo128^{4} *Tracked in 3rd,led 2-1/2f out,drew clear over 1f out,ridden out*	6
5Jly94	Newmarket (GB)	gd	1½ Ⓣ	RH 2:27^{2}	3+ Princess of Wales's Stakes-G2 Stk 98000	$4^{6\frac{1}{4}}$	unknown jockey	113	-	Wagon Master126^{hd} Bobzao129^{6} Prince of Andros126^{no}	12
14Jun94	Ascot (GB)	gd	1¼ Ⓣ	RH 2:05	3+ Prince of Wales's Stakes-G2 Stk 170200	5^{3}	Quinn T R	116	20.00	Muhtarram133^{nk} *Ezzoud*133no Chatoyant129^{2}	11
16Apr94	Newbury (GB)	yl	7f Ⓣ	1:30^{4}	Greenham Stakes-G3 Stk 50400	2^{8}	Carson W	126	16.00	Turtle Island126^{8} Luhuk126^{hd} Cool Jazz126$^{\frac{3}{4}}$	8
16Oct93	Newmarket (GB)	gd	7f Ⓣ	1:28^{2}	- Alw 21300	$6^{6\frac{1}{2}}$	unknown jockey	124	-	Indhar124^{1} Suplizi126$^{\frac{1}{2}}$ *Masnad*124^{2}	9
15Sep93	Sandown Park (GB)	sf	7f Ⓣ	1:34^{2}	- Maiden 9600	$1^{\frac{3}{4}}$	unknown jockey	126	-	Luhuk126$^{\frac{3}{4}}$ William Tell126$^{1\frac{1}{2}}$ Rory Creek126^{hd}	13

MAGIC CAT (Storm Cat—With a Twist, by Fappiano). Texas. There seems to be a never-ending supply of Storm Cat sons entering stud, and since most are out of blue-blooded broodmares, they will get a chance to become stallions, even if they did not have stellar careers or were unraced. Such is the case with Magic Cat, who won only once in 11 starts. His dam, however, was a popular stakes winner in New York, and this female line produced Majestic Prince. Bred for speed, his Texas-bred foals should do well at 2. (SP)

Magic Cat
Own: Scharbauer Dorothy

Ch. h. 9 (Apr)
Sire: Storm Cat (Storm Bird) $500,000
Dam: With a Twist (Fappiano)
Br: Riverbend Farm (Ky)
Tr: Barnett Bobby C(0 0 0 0 .00) 2004:(298 36 .12)

Life	11	1	1	2	$26,325	90	D.Fst	8	1	1	1	$23,025	90
2000	2	0	0	1	$5,800	87	Wet(418)	3	0	0	1	$3,300	87
1999	3	1	0	1	$10,245	87	Turf(331)	0	0	0	0	$0	-
	0	0	0	0	$0	-	Dst(399)	2	0	0	2	$7,300	87

6Feb00-8OP fst 1 :23 :462 1:1111:373 4↑Crabapple40k 87 3 916 915 810 55½ 35¾ Pettinger D R L113 29.30 85-17 Temperence Time1134½ Jim'smrtee1131¼ Magic Cat1131 Broke in air 9
8Jan00-10FG fst 1 1/16 :242 :484 1:1331:45 4↑Alw 30000N1x 83 1 75½ 63½ 53 32 44¾ Perret C L117 *2.30 81-14 Regal Dom1173½ Nedlog1171 Penwest119nk 4w 2nd turn, weakened 11
18Dec99-5FG sly 140 :234 :48 1:1331:414 3↑Alw 30000N1x 87 2 55 43 75½ 55½ 34½ Gonzalez C V L117 13.00 78-27 Talkmeister1143 *Regal Dom*1141½ Magic Cat117½ Rail trip, mild close 8
Previously trained by Dodwell Edward
16Oct99-10LaD fst 6f :23 :463 :5831:12 3↑Md Sp Wt 15k 67 11 7 41½ 31 22 13 Gonzalez C V L121 f 4.00 84-14 [DH]GambleSoup118 [DH]MagicCat1213 *DevilBound*1181 Bid, came again late 11
25Sep99-10LaD fst 6½f :232 :463 1:1041:171 3↑Md Sp Wt 15k 57 7 10 85¾ 67½ 66¾ 410¾ Meche L J L122 fb 2.40 77-16 *Freehold*1185 Devil Bound1185½ Blue Twisted Steel118nk Five wide turn 10
Previously trained by Lukas D Wayne
19Apr98-7SA fst 6f :214 :451 :5741:102 Md Sp Wt 38k 81 2 7 1hd 12 1hd 42¾ Gonzalez J C5 LB115 b 14.30 85-13 KimoKrogfoss1201¼ *PradosCpote*1201 CommncheCode120½ Brushed early 11
26Mar98-5SA gd 6f :214 :451 :5741:104 3↑Md Sp Wt 39k 51 7 3 63¾ 75¾ 710 616 Flores D R LB114 b 2.00 70-13 *Saint Jim*1233 *Another Star*1234½ Weather1232 Never a factor 8
1Mar98-6SA fst 1 1/16 :223 :46 1:1021:431 Md Sp Wt 40k 63 3 31½ 31 32 513 821 Flores D R B117 b *1.50 66-13 *Shot of Gold*11710 *Smile Again*1173½ Lucky Sandman117hd Used up, inside 12
31Jan98-9SA fst 1 1/16 :224 :464 1:1111:432 Md Sp Wt 40k 90 10 21 11½ 11½ 2hd 22 Flores D R B117 b 10.30 84-12 Quake1172 Magic Cat1174½ Nationalore1171 Ducked out start 11
11Jan98-3SA wf 6½f :213 :443 1:1011:164 Md Sp Wt 37k 69 3 3 1½ 11 21½ 24½ Flores D R B118 b 2.20 80-11 Tahoe Prospector1184½ [D]MagicCat1185½ ScoreEarly1182½ Headed, faded 5
Disqualified and placed 5th
28Dec97-6SA fst 6½f :22 :444 1:0911:152 Md Sp Wt 38k 39 1 10 1020 1023 924 926 Stevens G L B118 2.50 67-12 *Liquid Gold*1189 Gadilimi1181 *Tahoe Prospector*1182 Greenly, far back 10

MALIBU WESLEY (Storm Cat—La Spia, by Capote). New York. Like Magic Cat, Malibu Wesley did not accomplish much on the track, but New York breeders have a golden opportunity to breed to a son of Storm Cat from a significant female family for the bargain price of $1,500. His dam, La Spia, won the Del Mar Debutante and finished second in the 1991 Breeders' Cup Juvenile Fillies. Malibu Wesley's fourth dam is In the Clouds, a full sister to stakes winner Sunrise Flight (the damsire of Pleasant Colony), one of five stakes winners from multiple champion and Broodmare of the Year Misty Morn (who also produced champion 2-year-olds Bold Lad and Successor). Malibu Wesley's 2-year-olds are bred to win early, and because he is not that familiar to horseplayers, his runners should provide value.

Malibu Wesley
Own: Franks John

Dk. b or b. h. 9 (Mar)
Sire: Storm Cat (Storm Bird) $500,000
Dam: La Spia (Capote)
Br: Calumet Farm (Ky)
Tr: Irwin Ralph R(0 0 0 0 .00) 2004:(90 9 .10)

Life	21	2	2	1	$91,080	95	D.Fst	17	2	2	1	$90,380	95
2000	11	1	0	1	$40,760	85	Wet(409)	1	0	0	0	$0	18
1999	6	1	1	0	$42,360	95	Turf(334)	3	0	0	0	$700	79
	0	0	0	0	$0	-	Dst(389)	1	0	0	0	$1,170	75

5Nov00-8LaD my 6½f :223 :452 1:1121:184 3↑IslndWhrlH25k 18 2 8 87½ 811 810 833½ Melancon G L114 13.30 48-27 *Donapaw*1161½ *Shinnecock*1114 Right Code1143 Trailed 8
Previously trained by Bell David R
27Sep00-5WO fst 7f :214 :441 1:0921:222 3↑OC 62k/N2x-N 78 2 9 83½ 83¼ 73¾ 85¾ Poznansky N E L116 56.90 88-14 SeismicReport1181¼ AGenuineHonour1192¼ Taos116½ Saved ground, tired 11
10Sep00-3WO fst 7f :221 :443 1:0841:21 3↑OC 62k/N2x-N 74 7 3 61 42 58 59¼ Walls M K L117 18.60 92-05 Van Patten1224¾ Mr. Spike112nk Silver Saint1162½ Lacked late response 8
27Aug00-10WO fst 7f :221 :453 1:1141:251 3↑OC 62k/N2x-N 65 11 6 74 32 42 53¼ McKnight J L116 28.10 77-20 Mr. Bagdad1151 Paco El Prado118½ Taos116½ Stumbled start 11
6Aug00-9WO fm 7f Ⓣ:22 :444 1:0841:212 3↑OC 62k/N2x-N 65 9 6 52¼ 73¼ 1212 1212½ Somsanith N L116 18.45 85-04 *Van Patten*116¾ Hoptuit Bud116nk [DH]*Academic*113 Failed to respond 13
7Jly00-8WO fst 7f :222 :453 1:1041:242 3↑OC 62k/N2x-N 74 7 5 31 31½ 33 66¾ Kabel T K L116 6.10 77-22 Deputy Call119no Regal Sahib1161 Taos116nk Failed to respond 8
24Jun00-7WO fst 6½f :22 :45 1:1011:164 3↑OC 62k/N2x-N 77 6 1 75 74¼ 46½ 37½ Kabel T K L116 29.70 81-16 Hopeful Moment1197¼ Taos116nk Malibu Wesley116nk Late rally 4 wide 8
10Jun00-4WO fst 6f :22 :442 :5631:092 3↑OC 62k/N2x-N 63 1 6 31½ 33 57½ 514½ Kabel T K L119 4.50 78-09 DougsLegcy1164½ Tos116¾ EndSweepsAdvnce1162¼ Saved ground, faded 6
14May00-8WO fst 1 1/16 :233 :463 1:1121:453 4↑EclipseH-G2 51 1 31 34½ 44½ 814 1032¼ Kabel T K L117 26.60 47-31 Black Cash1193 *The Fed*1123¼ Catahoula Parish115hd Faded stretch 10
23Apr00-7WO fst 7f :221 :452 1:1121:25 4↑Alw 45320N1x 85 11 6 73¾ 41¼ 2½ 11¼ Kabel T K L118 2.95 81-21 MlibuWesly1181¼ AccountblBoy1183¼ *DputyCll*1181¼ Bid 4 wide trn, drvng 12
1Apr00-7WO fst 5f :214 :45 :58 4↑Alw 45320N1x 66 9 9 87¼ 64½ 45½ 65¼ Kabel T K L118 5.45 86-11 Doug's Legacy1182½ Deputy Call1181 Kind of Golden118¾ Bore out start 9
Previously trained by Flint Bernard S
17Jly99-7EIP fst 1 :24 :471 1:1241:401 3↑Alw 23400N1x 75 5 32 32½ 3nk 22½ 46½ Torres F C L112 *1.60 69-27 Johnbill1155½ PrimeVintage112no DixiesCrown1121 Stalked, flattened out 6
Previously trained by Barnett Bobby C
4Jly99-8LaD fm 1 1/16 Ⓣ:243 :481 1:1211:43 3↑IndpndcBCH100k 75 5 42½ 40 44½ 67 610½ LeBlanc K P L113 4.30e 80-15 Burbank1161¼ *Beaufort*110hd Esperero1134 Finished early 6
13Jun99-6CD fst 1 1/16 :241 :481 1:12 1:434 3↑Alw 43800N1x 90 3 41½ 41½ 42 42 43¼ Albarado R J L120 *2.10 88-09 ParkRoyal1121½ *CoastofMne*116¾ ColorMeQuickly1161 Pocketed 2nd turn 10
28May99-8CD fst 1 1/16 :232 :464 1:1131:444 3↑Alw 43800N1x 88 7 56 55 41½ 2½ 21½ Albarado R J L120 f *2.00 84-18 Alisios1131½ MlibuWesley1202¾ WoodyBeGood1131¾ 3 path, no match late 9
Previously trained by Ellis Ronald W
13Feb99-6SA fst 1 1/16 :231 :462 1:1031:432 4↑Alw 54000N$Y 90 4 41½ 31 2½ 1hd 42 McCarron C J LB117 4.80 84-15 Atwood118½ Lucky Sandman117nk *DancingAfleet*1171¼ Bid,led,outfinished 11
17Jan99-4SA fst 7f :23 :46 1:10 1:223 4↑Md Sp Wt 45k 95 9 6 41¾ 31½ 21½ 1½ McCarron C J LB121 *2.20 92-08 MlbuWsly121½ DynmcDd1215½ FrnchChoppr1211¼ Stalked,wore down foe 9
11Dec98-6Hol fst 1 1/16 :232 :473 1:1231:434 3↑Md Sp Wt 33k 84 5 21 2hd 2hd 11 1hd Smith A E7 LB112 2.10 81-19 [D]*MalibuWesley*112hd SkyHwk1195 RockHound1193 Drifted out,bmpd lane 5
Disqualified and placed second
6Nov98-3SA fm 1 Ⓣ:242 :50 1:1421:384 3↑Md Sp Wt 39k 79 8 85½ 95¾ 94½ 74¼ 53¼ Black C A LB120 6.90 62-35 Sky Champion1202 *Golden Isle*120hd To the West1221 6 wide into lane 10
10Oct98-6SA fst 6½f :214 :444 1:0921:153 3↑Md Sp Wt 33k 81 5 5 2hd 2hd 31½ 58 Solis A LB120 23.40 83-11 Zeriab1201½ Kona Wind120hd *Margeds Ditto*1202½ Dueled between foes 12
6Sep98-9Dmr fst 6f :214 :442 :5631:094 3↑Md Sp Wt 37k 72 8 9 1113 1013 78½ 88 Douglas R R LB118 17.70 82-12 *Gold Press*118no *Zeriab*1184½ To the West1221 Saved ground 12

MILLIONS (Dehere—Liturgism, by Native Charger). New York. Millions was a good 2-year-old, winning the Laurel Futurity and finishing second in the Remsen Stakes. He failed to develop at 3, but has the potential to do well at stud, particularly as a New York-based stallion. His sire, Dehere was a champion at 2, but like so many U.S.-based horses, was undervalued as a stallion and exported to Japan before his runners started winning stakes races. His offspring should also do well at 2, and because of his Northern Dancer sire line, he is another hidden turf sire whose runners should return big dividends on grass. (HT)

Millions
Own: Akindale Farm

Gr/ro. h. 8 (May)
Sire: Dehere (Deputy Minister) $37,165
Dam: Liturgism (Native Charger)
Br: Silver Springs Stud Farm & Mrs. J. Costelloe (Ky)
Tr: Zito Nicholas P(8 1 1 0 .12) 2004:(329 53 .16)

Life	14	3	2	1	$213,022	103	D.Fst	13	3	1	1	$206,182	98
2000	3	0	1	0	$8,472	103	Wet(376)	1	0	1	0	$6,840	103
1999	6	0	0	1	$36,750	98	Turf(300)	0	0	0	0	$0	-
	0	0	0	0	$0	-	Dst(336)	0	0	0	0	$0	-

7Apr00-7Kee	fst	6½f	:221	:45	1:094	1:161	4↑Alw 63520N3x	**87**	2	8	85¾	78	76½	55¼	Chavez J F	L115	3.20	88-10	Chief Howcome118¾ Kutsa1182½ Slick Report115½	Improved position	9
11Mar00-11GP	fst	1 1/16	:234	:47	1:111	1:444	3↑CrmFrchH-G3	**95**	1	31½	33	43	74¾	66½	Nakatani C S	L116	4.40	77-23	DncingGuy1201 *YnkeeVictor*113hd *MidwyMgistrte*1172½	Stdy 1st turn, tired	8
9Feb00-5GP	gd	7f	:23	:461	1:111	1:234	4↑Alw 36000N3x	**103**	3	7	31½	31½	33	21½	Castellano J J	L117	4.10	79-26	Mac's Rule1191½ Millions1171¼ Hangin in There1172¼	Slow st, up for 2nd	7
Previously trained by Blusiewicz Leon J																					
24Jly99-10Tdn	fst	1⅛	:461	1:103	1:363	1:491	OhioDrby-G2	–	12	51¼	31	53	1318	-	Lumpkins J	L116	9.30	- 12	*Stellar Brush*119nk *Ecton Park*116¾ *Valhol*1142¾	Stalked 6w,stopped,ezd	13
11Jly99-8Bel	fst	1 1/16	:23	:444	1:082	1:41	Dwyer-G2	**98**	1	32	37	35	33½	43¼	Santos J A	L119	5.60	89-10	Forestry1222¼ DonerileCourt119½ *SuccessfulAppel*122½	Drifted out stretch	6
5Jun99-6Bel	fst	7f	:224	:45	1:092	1:221	RivaRidg-G2	**98**	8	1	63¾	63¾	62½	42½	Santos J A	L118	16.30	88-10	*YesItsTrue*1231 LionHearted114nk *SilverSeson*1131¼	Came wide,good finish	8
2May99-7Del	fst	1 1/16	:23	:471	1:124	1:433	FLaBellMem75k	**81**	5	21½	21	3½	46¼	512	Prado E S	L119 b	*.90	77-20	Smart Guy1227½ Memory Tap116nk Lyracist1193¾	Rated, faltered	6
17Apr99-10Pim	fst	1⅛	:463	1:111	1:37	1:50	FdrcoTesio163k	**91**	6	31	21	21	2hd	32¼	Prado E S	L122 b	*2.20	91-18	*Talk's Cheap*1151½ Stellar Brush117¾ Millions122¾	3wd trip,duel,stbbrnly	10
27Mar99-10Lrl	fst	1⅛	:461	1:114	1:38	1:502	PrivatTrms55k	**75**	2	44	45½	31	55½	713½	Prado E S	L122	*.30	73-24	HrrysHlo115hd SevenPipers1156½ LedEmHom115no	Drifted wd.1/4,fll bck	9
28Nov98-7Aqu	fst	1⅛	:462	1:103	1:362	1:494	Remsen-G2	**94**	7	33½	33	2½	3nk	2nk	Prado E S	L122	2.90	87-14	Comonmom113nk Millions122½ *Wondrtross*113hd	3w move,bumped,gamely	9
31Oct98-9Lrl	fst	1⅛	:491	1:141	1:39	1:512	LrlFut-G3	**84**	5	2½	2hd	2hd	1½	13¾	Prado E S	L122	*.20	81-25	Millions1223¾ RaireStandrd122nk MoreBetter1224½	Dueled 2-wide, driving	6
17Oct98-7Del	fst	1 1/16	:23	:464	1:121	1:454	FirstState75k	**83**	5	22½	31½	31	2hd	14¾	Krone J A	L115	*.90	84-18	*Millions*1154¾ *Lyracist*115½ Imaginary Sword1174	Won in handy fashion	6
19Sep98-1Bel	fst	6f	:221	:46	:582	1:111	Md Sp Wt 38k	**85**	8	7	51¾	3½	11½	15	Prado E S	L117	3.20	85-19	*Millions*1175 Iron Prince117nk Lion Hearted117no	5 wide turn, driving	11
24Aug98-6Sar	fst	7f	:222	:452	1:103	1:233	Md Sp Wt 35k	**71**	5	10	31½	3½	53	67½	Velazquez J R	L116	19.00	79-14	MedievilHero116¾ Arrstd1162½ WinningConnction1164	Chased pace, tired	12

MORE THAN READY (Southern Halo—Woodman's Girl, by Woodman). Kentucky. This is a freshman sire that should have a major impact with his first crop. Very precocious at 2, he won the WHAS-11 Stakes in early May, and then added the Sanford, Tremont, and Flash Stakes, while finishing third in the Futurity. A sprinter/miler, he won the Grade 1 King's Bishop and the Hutcheson Stakes (in a dead heat) at 3, and his class enabled him to finish second in the longer Blue Grass Stakes, Dwyer Stakes, and Louisiana Derby. He should be among this year's top five freshman sires. (SP)

More Than Ready
Own: Scatuorchio James T

Dk. b or b. h. 7 (Apr)
Sire: Southern Halo (Halo) $21,050
Dam: Woodman's Girl (Woodman)
Br: Woodlynn Farm, Inc. (Ky)
Tr: Pletcher Todd A(0 0 0 0 .00) 2004:(684 174 .25)

Life	17	7	4	1	$1,026,229	110	D.Fst	17	7	4	1	$1,026,229	110
2000	10	2	4	0	$716,000	110	Wet(402)	0	0	0	0	$0	-
1999	7	5	0	1	$310,229	105	Turf(300)	0	0	0	0	$0	-
Aik Ⓣ	0	0	0	0	$0	-	DstⓉ(361)	0	0	0	0	$0	-

25Nov00-8Aqu	fst	1	:23 :454 1:10 1:343	3↑ CigarMiH-G1	102	2	87¼	89¼	74¼	62½	45½	Day P	L119	3.10	89-17	*ElCorredor*1161¾ *PeepingTom*111nk *AffirmedSuccss*1203½	4 wide, good finish	11
4Nov00-6CD	fst	6f	:204 :432 :551 1:073	3↑ BCSprnt-G1	105	11	11	99	87¼	76½	53½	Day P	L124	5.00	103 -	*KonGold*126½ HonestLdy123½ BetOnSunshin1262	8w lane,bump foe,empty	14
23Sep00-9Bel	fst	7f	:221 :443 1:083 1:213	3↑ Vosburgh-G1	110	2	9	94	84¼	33½	2½	Day P	L123	*1.75	94-13	Trippi123½ More ThanReady1232¼ *OneWayLove*1261	Bumped start, gamely	10
26Aug00-8Sar	fst	7f	:214 :441 1:092 1:222	KngsBshp-G1	103	4	4	64¼	63¾	1hd	11½	Day P	L124	*1.30	93-09	MoreThnRedy1241½ VlintHlory1143¾ Millncolin121nk	5 wide move, driving	6
6Aug00-11Mth	fst	1⅛	:472 1:11 1:363 1:50	HsklInvH-G1	106	2	21	42	41½	3½	42¾	Migliore R	L119 b	3.20	83-16	DixieUnion117¾ *CptinSteve*118hd MilwukeeBrew1172	Steadied early, tight	9
9Jly00-8Bel	fst	1 1/16	:24 :463 1:102 1:423	Dwyer-G2	103	3	42	42	22	2½	23	Velazquez J R	L119	1.90	81-22	AlberttheGret1153 MoreThnRdy1191¾ *RdBullt*123½	Bumped start, between	4
6May00-8CD	fst	1¼	:454 1:094 1:353 2:01	KyDerby-G1	99	9	32	32	41¼	2hd	46	Velazquez J R	L126	11.30	99 -	FusichiPegsus1261½ Aptitude1264 Impechmnt126½	Rail bid 1/4,emptylate	19
15Apr00-9Kee	fst	1⅛	:46 1:094 1:352 1:483	BlueGras-G1	106	7	31½	31½	32	2hd	2hd	Velazquez J R	L123	4.80	92-19	HighYield123hd MoreThanReady1233 Wheelwy123½	Lean in brushed,hung	8
12Mar00-9FG	fst	1 1/16	:23 :461 1:11 1:431	LaDerby-G2	102	4	1½	1½	1½	13	22	Velazquez J R	L122	5.00	93-13	Mighty1222 MoreThanReady122½ CaptinSteve122hd	Led, clear, saved 2nd	10
29Jan00-9GP	fst	7f	:222 :45 1:09 1:213	Hutchesn-G2	102	1	5	1hd	1½	11	18¼	♦Velazquez J R	L122	*.90	92-13	DH MorThnRdy122 DH *SummrNot*1138¼ AmricnBullt1141	Pressured, lasted	8
9Oct99-8Bel	fst	1 1/16	:234 :462 1:104 1:433	Champagn-G1	67	2	51¾	2½	3½	47	513¾	Velazquez J R	L122	*1.45	65-23	*Greenwood Lake*1222½ Chief Seattle1224 High Yield1226¾	Tired after 3/4s	7
19Sep99-6Bel	fst	1	:232 :454 1:103 1:36	Futurity-G1	98	6	3½	3½	2hd	2hd	3½	Velazquez J R	L122	*.40	83-22	*Bevo*122nk *Greenwood Lake*122nk More ThanReady122¾	Bumpd upr stretch	8
29Jly99-9Sar	fst	6f	:221 :45 :564 1:093	Sanford-G2	105	4	2	2hd	2hd	17	19¾	Velazquez J R	L122	*.35	93-09	More Than Ready1229¾ Mighty1143 Bulling1142¼	Sudden move,ridden out	5
4Jly99-6Bel	fst	5½f	:222 :451 :562 1:022	Tremont-G3	105	3	2	1½	11½	12½	14¼	Velazquez J R	119	*.50	103-08	*MoreThnRedy*1194¼ AftrnoonAffir1155¾ KingKoknd1152¼	Wrapped up late	6
4Jun99-8Bel	fst	5f	:214 :444	:57 Flash82k	102	4	3	1½	1hd	1hd	1hd	Velazquez J R	119	*.65	93-15	*MoreThanReady*119hd DiblosAddition1155¾ *Bevo*115½	Determined,prevailed	6
1May99-3CD	fst	5f	:22 :453	:574 WHAS-11120k	90	9	9	73¼	53	11½	14¼	Velazquez J R	117	3.70	99-08	*MoreThnRedy*1174¼ HouseBurnr117½ AdmirlPrry1172¼	5-wide, hand urging	12
11Apr99-2Kee	fst	4½f	:222 :453	:514 Md Sp Wt 42k	–	1	2	1½		13	17½	Velazquez J R	118	3.10	97-09	*MoreThanReady*1187½ NoLimitSoldier1181 BocaBaby118¾	Bumped, driving	8

MUQTARIB (Gone West—Shicklah, by The Minstrel). California. A Group 2 winner at 2 in England on turf, Muqtarib is by Gone West, one of the world's best sources of speed (on all surfaces). What makes Muqtarib so attractive as a stallion is that when he is bred to mares who have either Habitat or Northfields in their pedigree, it will create exquisite female-family inbreeding (Rasmussen Factor) to the superior broodmare Little Hut. While his California-bred foals may win on dirt, they should show their best on grass because of the Gone West/The Minstrel cross. (T^2)

Muqtarib
Own: Marinos Jane E. and Alex A

B. h. 8 (Apr)
Sire: Gone West (Mr. Prospector) $150,000
Dam: Shicklah (The Minstrel)
Br: Shadwell Farm, Inc. (Ky)
Tr: Moschera Gasper S(0 0 0 0 .00) 2004:(0 0 .00)

Life	15	3	3	2	$140,164	97	D.Fst	8	1	2	1	$80,570	90
2000	10	1	2	2	$87,520	97	Wet(328)	1	0	0	1	$4,070	80
1999	2	0	0	0	$0	-	Turf(324)	6	2	1	0	$55,524	97
Aik Ⓣ	0	0	0	0	$0	-	DstⓉ(372)	0	0	0	0	$0	-

22Oct00-5Bel	fst	6f	:221 :451 :564 1:091	3↑ Clm 75000(75-65)	58	6	6	66½	67	614	616¼	Prado E S	L119	7.90	76-11	Full Retail1215 McRyanne1172½ The Third Dan1192	Outrun	6
5Oct00-6Bel	gd	6f	:231 :462 :574 1:10	3↑ Clm c-(50-40)	80	5	4	33	2hd	31½	32¾	Bailey J D	L119	*.75	85-12	McRyanne1141¾ Flashing Tammany1191 Muqtarib1192	Vied 3 wide, tired	5
Claimed from Shadwell Stable for $50,000, McLaughlin Kiaran P Trainer 2000(as of 10/5): (-)																		
30Aug00-8Sar	fm	1 1/16 Ⓣ	:233 :464 1:11 1:403	3↑ Alw 48000N3X	97	7	57	55¼	52½	22	42	Bailey J D	L119	3.80	91-13	GulfStorm1171 WitforthSword121¾ DoctorCt119nk	3 wide move, even late	8
16Jly00-6Bel	fst	6f	:23 :461 :574 1:102	3↑ Alw 47000N3X	88	4	4	42	41¼	31½	31¼	Bailey J D	L123	2.70	85-13	Chasin'Wimmin119no TexasGlitter1191¼ Muqtarib123¾	Game finish on rail	6
28Jun00-8Bel	fst	7f	:233 :462 1:10 1:222	3↑ Alw 45590N3X	88	3	2	2½	2½	25½	28¾	Bailey J D	L123	2.30	82-16	*Left Bank*1178¾ Muqtarib123½ Momsmercedes1193¼	Prompted, held place	4
25May00-7Bel	fst	6½f	:224 :462 1:103 1:17	3↑ Alw 45000N2X	90	1	3	31	31	1hd	1nk	Velazquez J R	L120	*1.30	87-18	Muqtarib120nk Bulling1096 Storm'n Eddy120½	Clear trip inside	7
26Apr00-8Aqu	fst	6f	:222 :46 :58 1:10	3↑ Alw 45000N2X	88	3	7	34½	31½	31	22¾	Velazquez J R	L121	4.10	84-15	Bold Pic1212¾ *Muqtarib*1211½ Suntee1211	3 wide move, gamely	7
25Mar00 Nad Al Sheba (UAE)	ft	*6f	Str 1:08	4↑ Dubai Golden Shaheen (Listed) Stk 1000000							58¾	Velazquez J R	126	-		Big Jag1264 Bertolini126no *Bet Me Best*126nk	*Outrun early,prgrss ovr 1f out,nearest at finish.Ramp and Rave4th*	14
5Mar00 Nad Al Sheba (UAE)	ft	*6f	1:091	4↑ - Alw 19100							710½	Ahern E	119	-		Ramp and Rave1212¼ Holy Pole1191 Munjiz1195	*Outpaced halfway, no impression from 1.5f out*	11
18Feb00 Jebel Ali (UAE)	ft	*5f	Str :561	4↑ Jebel Ali Sprint (Prestige) Stk 95300							35	Ahem E	121	-		Hattab1215 Levelled121no Muqtarib1211¼	*Outrun early,up for 3rd.DQ'd,placed last.Ramp and Rave 5th*	8
Disqualified and placed 8th Previously trained by Dunlop John																		
6Nov99 Doncaster (GB) Timeform rating: 95	sf	6f Ⓣ	Str 1:182	3↑ Wentworth Stakes (Listed) Stk 39300							108½	Hills R	123	6.00		*Pipalong*118no *Two Clubs*1183 Qilin119½	*Towards rear,passed tired ones.Cretan Gift 8th*	20
15Oct99 Newmarket (GB) Timeform rating: 109+	gd	6f Ⓣ	Str 1:133	3↑ Bentinck Stakes (Listed) Stk 44300							92¾	Reid J	123	20.00		Gaelic Storm1241¼ *Pipalong*118½ Delegate124hd	*Rated towards rear,finished well w/o threatening.Rambling Bear5th*	20
30Jly98 Goodwood (GB) Timeform rating: 108	gd	6f Ⓣ	Str 1:142	Richmond Stakes-G2 Stk 69600							12	Hills R	123	4.50		Muqtarib1232 Sarson123nk Rosselli1268	*Close up in 3rd,led 1-1/2f out,ridden out*	4
26Jun98 Goodwood (GB) Timeform rating: 85+	gd	6f Ⓣ	Str 1:131	EBF Superior Novice Stakes Alw 12200							23	Hills R	130	*.15		El Tango1263 *Muqtarib*1303 Dillionaire12814	*Rated in last,2nd over 2f out,lacked finishing bid*	4
5Jun98 Goodwood (GB) Timeform rating: 80+	gd	6f Ⓣ	Str 1:112	EBF Hitachi Seiki Maiden Stks Maiden 12000							1nk	Hills R	126	5.00		Muqtarib126nk Compton Admiral1261¼ Pilot's Harbour126½	*Rated twrds rear,bid over 1f out,in tight but led 150y out,gamely*	8

OLD TOPPER (Gilded Time—Shy Trick, by Phone Trick). California. By a champion 2-year-old out of a top-class sprinter known for getting sprinters, Old Topper was naturally good at 2, winning the Best Pal Stakes and placing in the Del Mar Futurity and Hollywood Juvenile Championship Stakes. His runners will also be best sprinting and be win-early types. (SP^2)

Old Topper
Own: Hunter Barbara

Ch. h. 9 (Mar)
Sire: Gilded Time (Timeless Moment) $17,500
Dam: Shy Trick (Phone Trick)
Br: Frances B. Jelks (Ky)
Tr: Threewitt Noble(0 0 0 0 .00) 2004:(9 0 .00)

Life	25	7	6	4	$655,861	108	D.Fst	22	6	6	3	$588,145	108
2000	7	1	2	2	$136,246	108	Wet(372)	2	1	0	1	$67,716	103
1999	2	1	0	1	$80,160	101	Turf(254)	1	0	0	0	$0	44
Aik Ⓣ	0	0	0	0	$0	-	DstⓉ(361)	0	0	0	0	$0	-

28Aug00-7Dmr	fst	6f	:213 :443 :572 1:10	3↑ Alw 63700N$Y	108	4	2	47½	45	41½	15½	Delahoussaye E	LB116	2.70	90-16	Old Topper1165½ *FiveStarDay*1222 TreasureHunt1161½	Hopped strt,handily	4
3Jun00-3Hol	fst	6f	:214 :443 :564 1:09	3↑ LsAnglsH-G3	82	3	5	511	59½	68	69¼	Pincay L Jr	LB117	3.00	83-10	Highland Gold1151¼ Mellow Fellow113no Your Halo114½	Broke in,no rally	6
10May00-5Hol	fst	6½f	:22 :441 1:081 1:144	3↑ OC 150k/N$Y-N	106	3	5	32½	45½	35	21	Delahoussaye E	LB116	2.70	96-12	Lexicon1221 Old Topper1161½ Your Halo117hd	Chased,inside rally	6
8Apr00-3SA	fst	6½f	:221 :441 1:081 1:143	4↑ PtrGrBCH-G2	108	4	3	35	36½	36	24½	Delahoussaye E	LB116	6.90	90-14	*Kona Gold*1224½ Old Topper1162 Your Halo116½	Rail rally for 2nd	4
4Mar00-4SA	gd	7f	:232 :462 1:10 1:22	4↑ SnCrlosH-G2	103	2	4	52¼	41½	53	32½	Delahoussaye E	LB116	5.00	92-10	Son of a Pistol117no *Kona Gold*1222½ Old Topper116no	Rail,waited bit 1/4	6
29Jan00-8SA	fst	6f	:214 :441 :561 1:082	4↑ PlsVrdsH-G2	97	4	2	2½	33	43½	45¾	Delahoussaye E	LB116	10.50	91-12	Kona Gold1212 *Big Jag*1213 Freespool115¾	Pressed pace, weakened	5
2Jan00-8SA	fst	5½f	:214 :442 :563 1:031	4↑ ElConejoH107k	100	2	6	33	23½	23	32	Delahoussaye E	LB116	4.50	90-18	Freespool1141½ Mellow Fellow115½ Old Topper1163	Awkward start,rail	6
12Feb99-6SA	fst	1	:233 :47 1:102 1:352	4↑ Alw 72100N$MY	101	3	11	1hd	2hd	1hd	13	Pincay L Jr	LB117	4.00	94-15	OldTopper1173 ProfoundSecrt122nk Budroyl122hd	Came back, drew clear	7
16Jan99-7SA	fst	1 1/16	:231 :47 1:104 1:41	SnFndoBC-G2	98	2	31	31	4nk	43	39	Pincay L Jr	LB118	34.90	89-16	DixieDotCom1164½ *EventoftheYr*1224½ *OldToppr*118½	Rail trip,game for 3rd	8
26Dec98-8SA	fst	7f	:23 :452 1:09 1:212	Malibu-G1	98	10	5	96¾	95½	76½	64	Solis A	LB117	9.30	94-08	Run Man Run1151½ Artax1192 Event of the Year121nk	5 wide into stretch	10
17Oct98-5SA	fst	6f	:212 :44 :56 1:082	3↑ AnTtlBCH-G3	82	5	7	51¾	74¼	85¾	88¾	Ramsammy E	LB117	8.30	89-09	Gold Land117¾ A. P. Assay116¾ Swiss Yodeler114no	5 wide, weakened	8
12Sep98-9BM	fst	6f	:221 :442 :561 1:082	3↑ BMBCSprntH200k	94	3	3	77½	77¾	65¼	53¼	Baze R A	LB117	2.30	94-12	*Musf*116nk DH ThBrkngShrk116 DH *MrDobldown*1161½	Lacked late response	7
15Aug98-4Dmr	fst	7f	:222 :442 1:084 1:212	3↑ POBrienH-G3	108	3	5	2hd	2hd	2hd	12	Delahoussaye E	LB116	10.50	93-09	OldTopper1162 SonofaPistol123hd UncagedFury1152	Gamely inched clear	5
19Jly98-8Hol	fst	1⅛	:46 1:092 1:341 1:47	Swaps-G2	90	3	53½	59½	510	49	315½	Pincay L Jr	LB117	6.90	75-09	*Old Trieste*11812 Grand Slam1203½ *Old Topper*1176½	Pulled bit early	6
21Jun98-7Hol	fst	1 1/16	:231 :461 1:092 1:414	AffirmdH-G3	97	1	43	45½	410	27	24½	Pincay L Jr	LB117	2.30	86-09	*Old Trieste*1184½ Old Topper1177 Kraal116½	Second best	4
25May98-7Hol	fst	7f	:222 :444 1:093 1:214	HarryHensn70k	98	4	6	88	89¼	41¾	11	Pincay L Jr	LB120	*1.00	93-11	OldTopper1201 ChmpsStr120¾ FullMoonMdnss1165	Far back, circled foes	8
10May98-7Hol	fm	1	Ⓣ :233 :463 1:101 1:334	WilRgrsH-G3	44	2	44½	45	68	817	823¾	Pincay L Jr	LB117	5.80	70-07	*Magical*1143 *Commitisize*119no Son's Corona114½	No response	8
29Mar98-7SA	gd	6½f	:221 :453 1:104 1:17	SanPedro80k	93	3	4	53½	53½	2hd	13½	Pincay L Jr	LB119	4.00	84-17	Old Topper1193½ Son's Corona1163 Search Me1152	Strong stretch run	6
19Oct97-7SA	fst	1	:221 :452 1:094 1:36	Norfolk-G2	75	6	69½	69½	69	67½	713¼	Solis A	LB118	2.30	77-10	SouvenirCopy1181¾ OldTrieste1184 DoublHonor1183½	No rally,dull effort	7
10Sep97-8Dmr	fst	7f	:22 :444 1:093 1:23	DmrFut-G2	91	6	5	88½	75½	65½	2no	Solis A	LB119	*1.40	85-18	*Souvenir Copy*115no Old Topper119nk Commitisize115½	Closed rush 5-wide	8
20Aug97-7Dmr	fst	6½f	:221 :444 1:10 1:162	BestPal-G3	92	2	6	61¾	21	21	11	Solis A	LB117	*2.30	89-13	OldToppr1171 KingofthWld1173 *SouvnrCopy*1171¼	Wore down rival,drivng	8
20Jly97-9Hol	fst	6f	:214 :441 :564 1:094	HolJuvCh-G3	81	4	9	98¾	85½	54½	22	Solis A	LB117	3.60	88-06	KOPunch1202 *OldTopper*1171¼ Mjorbigtimsht1202½	Angled out,closd rush	9
28Jun97-6Hol	fst	5f	:22 :451 :571	Md Sp Wt 34k	87	4	1	1½	11	12½	15½	Solis A	LB118	*.70	98-11	OldTopper1185½ RussetMantle1183½ KingCaspin118½	Drew off, much best	10
1Jun97-7Hol	fst	5f	:214 :451 :574	Md Sp Wt 34k	75	8	3	53	55½	44½	2no	Solis A	LB118	3.30	95-13	Double Honor118no *Old Topper*1184½ Arosa1181	Late surge,just missed	9
15May97-4Hol	fst	4½f	:223 :46 :521	Md Sp Wt 34k	50	7	7	76		87	45	Solis A	L118	6.10	86-11	ShingenSpeed1182 *Calculted*1182¾ SwissEcho118nk	Closed willingly insde	9

PRECISE END (End Sweep—Precisely, by Summing). New York. A son of the strong speed influence End Sweep, Precise End won the Display Stakes and placed in the Cowdin Stakes at 2. He won the Bay Shore and finished second in the Withers. His foals will be win-early types and will be best from five to seven furlongs. Some could get 1 1/16 miles under ideal circumstances. (SP)

Precise End
Own: Mangurian H T Jr

Dk. b or b. h. 7 (Apr)
Sire: End Sweep (Forty Niner) $34,980
Dam: Precisely (Summing)
Br: Harry T. Mangurian Jr. (Fla)
Tr: Casse Mark E(0 0 0 0 .00) 2004:(208 31 .15)

Life	9	4	1	4	$225,941	99	D.Fst	7	3	1	3	$143,595	90
2000	2	1	1	0	$96,000	99	Wet(338)	1	1	0	0	$66,000	99
1999	7	3	0	4	$129,941	89	Turf(267)	1	0	0	1	$16,346	79
Aik Ⓣ	0	0	0	0	$0	-	DstⓉ(354)	0	0	0	0	$0	-

6May00-9Aqu	fst	1	:214 :434 1:08 1:353	Withers-G3	90	3	1½	11½	13	12½	21½	Husbands P	L123 b	*2.90	88-15	Big E E1161½ Precise End1231¾ Port Herman1162½	Strong pace, gamely	8
15Apr00-8Aqu	gd	7f	:22 :441 1:084 1:221	BayShore-G3	99	7	3	1½	12½	17	15¼	Chavez J F	L116 b	6.30	89-12	PrcsEnd1165¼ Turnofthcntry1142¼ PortHrmn114hd	Soon clear, ridden out	7
14Nov99-8WO	fst	1 1/16	:231 :472 1:121 1:471	Display81k	84	4	14	12	11	14	11	Husbands P	L115 b	*1.55	68-37	*PrecisEnd*1151 Grillhous1153½ PrimTimTlkin11320	Driving,led throughout	5
16Oct99-6Bel	fst	6½f	:222 :443 1:101 1:17	Cowdin-G2	70	1	4	12½	13	2hd	33	Chavez J F	L122 b	3.25	84-11	TwilightTime1222 *SkyDweller*1221 *PrecisEnd*122no	Jumped shadows, inside	4
26Sep99-1WO	fst	7f	:221 :452 1:102 1:25	Alw 36700N2L	70	1	3	1hd	16	112	17½	Husbands P	L122 b	*.30	81-13	Precise End1227½ Donald's Tomorrow1194½ Samsula Slew1224½	Easily	5
11Sep99-8WO	fm	1	Ⓣ :231 :463 1:11 1:352	Summer-G2	79	2	11½	11½	11	2hd	33¾	Husbands P	L122 b	9.75	83-13	*FourOntheFloor*1221¾ KingCugt1222 *PrcisEnd*1221¾	Weakened late stretch	7
17Jly99-8WO	fst	6f	:214 :444 :573 1:114	Colin82k	63	3	4	1hd	1hd	22	35	Husbands P	L117 b	*.75e	77-16	Vorticity1191 Irish Opinion1154 Precise End11714½	Weakened	5
4Jly99-3WO	fst	5f	:213 :443 :572	Md Sp Wt 31k	89	1	3	14	18	19	17½	Husbands P	L120 b	*.35	96-13	Precise End1207½ Irish Opinion12013 Clovelly1152½	Easily, much the best	5
30May99-7WO	fst	4½f	:221 :45 :512	Md Sp Wt 28k	59	5	7	45		34	34¼	Husbands P	120	2.95	91-05	Knight Teaser1153½ *When You Believe*115¾ *Precise End*1202	Off slowly	7

RIVER KEEN (Keen—Immediate Impact, by Caerleon). New York. From the sire line of strong turf influence Sharpen Up (sire of Diesis) and out of a mare by Caerleon (Nijinsky II), River Keen was expected to be a grass runner, but found success on dirt. He had his best year at 7, winning the Jockey Club Gold Cup, Woodward Stakes, and Bel Air Handicap. While his runners should also win on dirt, they are still bred for turf. His sire, Keen, is a full brother to world-class turf stallions Diesis and Kris. (T^2)

River Keen (Ire)
Own: Reynolds Hugo

Ch. h. 12 (Mar)
Sire: Keen*GB (Sharpen Up*GB) $2,675
Dam: Immediate Impact*Ire (Caerleon)
Br: Ballylinch Stud (Ire)
Tr: Baffert Bob(0 0 0 0 .00) 2004:(434 80 .18)

Life	42	11	5	5	$1,642,385	117	D.Fst	24	9	5	3	$1,020,275	117
2000	5	0	0	1	$23,000	100	Wet(283)	3	1	0	0	$600,000	117
1999	10	3	4	1	$1,303,880	117	Turf(258)	15	1	0	2	$22,110	90
Aik Ⓣ	0	0	0	0	$0	-	DstⓉ(263)	0	0	0	0	$0	-

15Oct00–7SA fst 1⅛ :47 1:104 1:35 1:471 3↑GdwdBCH-G2 **100** 1 54 53½ 62¾ 68½ 611½ Desormeaux K J LB118 20.30 87–13 *Tiznow*116½ Captain Steve1171½ Euchre1154 Rail, 4wd 1/4, outrun 7
23Sep00–3BM fm *1⅛ Ⓣ :484 1:131 1:374 1:47 3↑BayMedH-G3 **90** 2 1½ 11 1½ 2hd 55¾ Carr D LB118 4.90 85–15 DevineWind1141 IrishPrize1152½ DeployVntur1171½ Set pace, dug in,tired 6
26Aug00–8Dmr fst 1¼ :452 1:094 1:35 2:011 3↑PacifcCl-G1 **86** 1 44 41½ 55 711 721¼ Espinoza V LB124 14.70 74–14 Skimming1242 *Tiznow*1171¼ Ecton Park124½ 3wd bid,gave way 7
6Aug00–8Dmr fst 1 1/16 :223 :454 1:093 1:41 3↑SnDiegoH-G3 **79** 7 76½ 65¼ 45½ 58½ 719¼ Espinoza V LB122 *1.40 79–02 *Skimming*1128 PrimeTimber1161½ NationalSaint1173½ 4wd,3wd,empty lane 7
15Jly00–8Hol fst 1 1/16 :233 :47 1:104 1:413 3↑BelAirH-G2 **100** 5 64 61¾ 41¼ 2½ 33¾ Espinoza V LB122 *1.30 88–08 Euchre1141¼ SultrySubstitute1142½ RiverKeen1222 Stmbld strt,4wd move 7
6Nov99–10GP fst 1¼ :453 1:094 1:341 1:592 3↑BCClasic-G1 **95** 3 75½ 64½ 76½ 1110 1115 Antley C W L126 6.50 99 – Cat Thief1221¼ Budroyale126hd Golden Missile1262 Inside, tired 14
10Oct99–6Bel sly 1¼ :462 1:101 1:352 2:012 3↑JkyClbGC-G1 **117** 4 2½ 1½ 1½ 11½ 13¼ Antley C W L126 12.00 87–23 River Keen1263¼ Behrens126hd Almutawakel1264¼ Speed outside, driving 8
18Sep99–9Bel fst 1⅛ :454 1:094 1:342 1:464 3↑Woodward-G1 **117** 3 41¼ 21½ 3½ 1hd 1no Antley C W L126 5.50 97–14 *RiverKeen*126no Almutwkel1261½ StephnGotEvn121nk Determinedly inside 7
29Aug99–5Dmr fst 1¼ :464 1:11 1:35 2:002 3↑PacifcCl-G1 **115** 6 74 64¾ 33 22 23 Antley C W LB124 7.00 94–11 GenerlChllenge1173 *RiverKen*1242¼ BrtrTown1242 Swung out, second best 8
7Aug99–4Dmr fst 1 1/16 :23 :461 1:094 1:403 3↑SnDiegoH-G3 **107** 1 46 45½ 45 23 26 Antley C W LB116 5.20 95 – Mazel Trick1176 River Keen1162 Tibado11610 Saved ground to 1/4 4
10Jly99–8Hol fst 1 1/16 :232 :462 1:101 1:403 3↑BelAirH-G2 **113** 6 53½ 62¾ 2hd 1hd 1nk Antley C W LB115 7.10 97–08 River Keen115nk Barter Town1135½ Quake1162½ 5 wide move,gamely 7
4Jun99–2Hol fst 1 1/16 :233 :463 1:103 1:423 3↑OC 80k/N3X **102** 5 42½ 41¾ 31 21½ 2¾ Ramsammy E LB116 1.90 86–20 Refried Dreams118¾ *River Keen*1165 *Bold Words*1162½ 3 wide,slow late gain 5
1May99–3Hol fst 1 1/16 :233 :463 1:101 1:42 3↑MrvnLRyH-G2 **91** 6 54½ 56¼ 54¼ 45 611¼ Baze R A LB115 9.50 79–20 Budroyale1188 Moore's Flat107nk Wild Wonder1202 4 wide 7-1/2,no rally 6
2Apr99–7SA fst 1 :223 :454 1:101 1:36 4↑OC 100k/N3X **105** 3 43½ 43 32½ 1hd 2½ Stevens G L LB118 1.50 90–19 SmileAgain122½ RiverKeen1183½ *BusyLittleBever*1185 Bid, led, outfinished 5
3Mar99–6SA fst 1 :223 :454 1:10 1:354 4↑OC 100k/N$Y **97** 4 31 21 1hd 21½ 35 Stevens G L LB118 *1.50 87–19 Klinsman120½ Bold Words1184½ River Keen1181¼ Bid,led rail,weakened 5
20Dec98–7Hol fst 1⅛ :474 1:112 1:361 1:482 3↑NtvDivrH-G3 **106** 2 32½ 31 21½ 2½ 33¾ Gomez G K LB114 2.50 80–16 *Puerto Madero*1212½ *Musical Gambler*1171¼ River Keen1148½ Steadied 7-1/2 5
4Dec98–7Hol fst 1 1/16 ⊗ :24 :464 1:103 1:42 3↑OC c-100k/N$Y **110** 5 3½ 11 11½ 12½ 14 Gomez G K LB116 *.80 90–24 River Keen1164 Saratoga Seven1207 Indiahoma1201 Outside, ridden out 5
Claimed from Gamel, Roncelli Family Trust, Sigband, et al for $100,000, Hess R B Jr Trainer 1998(as of 12/4): (-)
6Nov98–7SA fst 1 :222 :454 1:093 1:352 3↑ⓇSkywalkerH71k **98** 1 31½ 31½ 2½ 21 21 Gomez G K LB116 3.90 93–06 MusiclGmbler1181 *RiverKeen*11610 StlwrtTsu116hd Stalked,bid,outgamed 7
11Jly98–7Hol fst 1 1/16 :224 :454 1:093 1:413 3↑BelAirH-G2 **65** 4 55 43½ 33 512 523 Espinoza V LB115 6.70 69–14 *Free House*1247 *Wild Wonder*1214½ Albaha11410 Slow,awkward start 5
3Jun98–7Hol fst 1 1/16 :232 :47 1:11 1:411 3↑OC 80k/N$Y **106** 4 42½ 31 1hd 11½ 12½ Espinoza V LB116 5.20 94–14 River Keen1162½ YoungAtHeart1166½ Kukulcan1163½ 3 wide, middle move 7
11Apr98–7SA wf 1⅛ :453 1:093 1:351 1:482 4↑SnBrdnoH-G2 **81** 5 76¼ 64¾ 33 711 716 Espinoza V LB115 11.50 78–11 Budroyale1125 Don't Blame Rio114½ Bagshot116½ Good position, tired 10
10Jan98–7SA wf 1 1/16 :233 :472 1:104 1:414 4↑SnPsqalH-G2 **79** 3 41½ 3½ 63¾ 810 713½ Desormeaux K J LB116 3.60 80–10 Hal's Pal1133 *Malek*1161 Flick1161 Rushed, tired 9
9Aug97–5Dmr fst 1¼ :47 1:113 1:352 2:002 3↑PacClasc-G1 **84** 3 32½ 31½ 46 512 525 Desormeaux K J LB124 5.80 70–05 Gentlemen1242¾ Siphon1244 Crafty Friend1242¼ Contended,eased late 5
1Jun97–9Hol fst 1⅛ :47 1:103 1:343 1:471 3↑Calfrnin-G2 **112** 3 52¼ 31 2½ 2hd 11 Desormeaux K J LB117 7.50 90–16 River Keen1171 Hesabull1182 Benchmark1183½ Bid 1/8, driving 6
Previously trained by Robert Armstrong
29Mar97 Haydock (GB) sf 1½ Ⓣ LH 2:421 4↑ Daihatsu Handicap Hcp 13200 856¾ Carter G 136 *2.25 Sugar Mill1251¾ Eskimo Nel1155 Midyan Blue1183 9 *Tracked leader,weakened 4f out,tailed off*
17Mar97 Southwell (GB) ft 1½ LH 2:414 4↑ Gleneagles Handicap (dirt) Hcp 15000 18 Carter G 140 5.50 River Keen1408 Calder King1072 Greenspan11812 8 *Led throughout,roused clear 2f out,easily*
26Oct96 Doncaster (GB) gd 1½ Ⓣ LH 2:35 3↑ - Hcp 30600 65 Hills R 131 10.00 Henry Island121no Wild Rita1233½ Sugar Mill1241 19 *Mid-pack on rail,lacked room over 2f out,mild late gain*
11Oct96 Ascot (GB) gd 1½ Ⓣ RH 2:36 3↑ Tankerville Handicap Hcp 18700 510½ Hills M 134 *7.00 Shadow Leader1262 Polydamas134nk Dance So Suite1391¼ 15 *Led to 1f out,weakened*
6Apr96 Kempton (GB) gd 2 Ⓣ RH 3:343 4↑ Queen's Prize Handicap Hcp 20300 1643 Woods W 137 12.00 Wannaplantatree1151¼ Witney-de-Bergerac112hd *Upper Mount Clair*1123½ 18 *Mid-pack,weakeneing when bumped over 2f out*
6Mar96 Wolverhampton (GB) ft 1½ LH 2:44 4↑ Hurricane Handicap (dirt) Hcp 12500 1hd Woods W 140 5.50 River Keen140hd Northern Union138¾ Calder King1136 11 *Rated towards rear,progress 4f out,led 100y out,held well*
2Dec95 Wolverhampton (GB) ft 1½ LH 2:36 Plyvine Catering Hcp (dirt) Hcp 24600 110 Price R 118 8.00 *River Keen*11810 Sea Victor1146 Far Ahead1142 12 *Rated in 6th,cruised to lead over 3f out,quickly clear*
8Nov95 Lingfield (GB) ft 1¼ LH 2:041 3↑ Thames Handicap (dirt) Hcp 9200 11 Woods W 129 10.00 *River Keen*1291 South Eastern Fred1395 *Dance So Suite*1176 11 *Rated in 5th,long drive to lead 2f out,drifted left,ridden out*
17Oct95 Chepstow (GB) sf 1½ Ⓣ LH 2:49 Pasture Handicap Hcp 10000 1771¼ Carson W 129 b 10.00 *Snow Princess*1182 Fabillion1134 Shift Again1194 18 *Chased in 8th,weakened over 3f out,distanced*
6Oct95 Ascot (GB) sf 1½ Ⓣ RH 2:402 3↑ Tankerville Handicap Hcp 18000 55¾ Price R 123 b 33.00 Indigo Time1263 Lucayan Sunshine1261¾ Reimei1211 15 *Progress into 6th 3-1/2f out,one-paced through stretch*
13Sep95 Yarmouth (GB) gd 1¼ Ⓣ LH 2:072 3↑ - Hcp 16600 1431¼ Price R 132 33.00 *Quandary*1403 Domappel113no Myfontaine1222 17 *Never a factor.Placed 14th via DQ*
Placed 13th through disqualification
27Jly95 Goodwood (GB) fm 1⅛ Ⓣ RH 1:524 3↑ Drawing Room Handicap Hcp 20000 1118 Hills R 131 b 6.00 Vena1321 *Conspicuous*1181½ Raise the Stakes130no 11 *Lead after 2f,soon clear,headed 2f out,weakened quickly*
21Jly95 Ascot (GB) gd 1¼ Ⓣ RH 2:091 Balmoral Handicap Hcp 21600 1nk Carson W 118 b 14.00 River Keen118nk *Polydamas*1254 Major Change1312 11 *Led throughout,ridden 1f out,held gamely*
17Jun95 Sandown Park (GB) gd 1⅛ Ⓣ RH 1:56 North-South Challenge Series H Hcp 17700 62¾ Quinn J 121 b 11.00 Rokeby Bowl125nk Jalfrezi126½ Elpidos1141¼ 10 *Rated towards rear,mild bid 2f out,one-paced late*
5May95 Newmarket (GB) gd 7f Ⓣ Str 1:241 March Handicap Hcp 36800 920 Price R 113 12.00 Royal Rebuke1183 Lipizzaner126¾ Pelleman1131½ 9 *Tracked in 3rd,weakened 2f out.Mister Fire Eyes (122) 7th*
6Apr95 Leicester (GB) gd 1 Ⓣ Str 1:412 Bescaby Maiden Stakes Maiden 9900 47 Price R 126 6.50 Daunt1262½ Viyapari1262½ *Al Safeer*1262 12 *Tracked leaders,ridden without response 2f out*
1Oct94 Goodwood (GB) gd 7f Ⓣ RH 1:281 The News Maiden Auction Stakes Maiden 19900 32¾ Price R 124 *1.75 Judge Advocate112nk Blomberg1242½ River Keen1243 11 *Rated in mid-pack,mild gain 3f out,no late response*
14Sep94 Sandown Park (GB) yl 7f Ⓣ RH 1:34 EBF Innings Opener Maiden Stks Maiden 9600 31½ Price R 126 33.00 *Wijara*1261 Chattaroy126½ River Keen1261½ 13 *Mid-pack,progress to lead 1-1/2f out,headed 150y out*

ROYAL ANTHEM (Theatrical—In Neon, by Ack Ack). Kentucky. As expected from a son of the late-maturing grass sire Theatrical (Nureyev), Royal Anthem was unraced at 2, but developed into a multiple stakes winner at 3 on turf, winning the King Edward VII Stakes and Canadian International Stakes. A high-class racehorse, he also finished third to Swain and High-Rise in the prestigious King George VI and Queen Elizabeth Diamond Stakes (ahead of Daylami). At age 4, he captured the Juddmonte International Stakes and finished second to Daylami in both the Coronation Cup and Breeders' Cup Turf. He is out of 1998 Broodmare of the Year In Neon, and is a half-brother to stakes winners Sharp Cat and Star Recruit. Bred to go long on turf, his runners will be at a disadvantage sprinting at age 2 on dirt, but they should assert themselves at 3 on grass.

Royal Anthem
Own: The Thoroughbred Corporation

B. h. 9 (Apr)
Sire: Theatrical*Ire (Nureyev) $75,000
Dam: In Neon (Ack Ack)
Br: John Franks (Ky)
Tr: Mott William I(0 0 0 0 .00) 2004:(480 93 .19)

Life	12	6	3	1	$1,876,876	113	D.Fst	0	0	0	0	$0	-
2000	1	1	0	0	$120,000	110	Wet(318)	0	0	0	0	$0	-
1999	5	1	3	0	$872,175	113	Turf(356)	12	6	3	1	$1,876,876	113
Aik Ⓣ	0	0	0	0	$0	-	DstⓉ(325)	0	0	0	0	$0	-

12Feb00-10GP	fm	1⅜ Ⓣ	:471 1:123 1:362 2:111	3↑ GPBCH-G1	110	6	46	46	3½	11½	13	Bailey J D	L121	*.40	97- 14	RoyalAnthem1213 Thesaurus1123¾ BandIsPassing1161¼	3 wide, ridden out	7
6Nov99- 9GP	gd	1½ Ⓣ	:47 1:103 2:243	3↑ BCTurf-G1	113	2	34	33	21	3nk	22½	Stevens G L	126	8.70	91- 09	Daylami1262½ *Royal Anthem*1262 Buck's Boy1261¼	Outfinished,gained 2nd	14
Previously trained by Cecil Henry																		
11Sep99 Leopardstwn (Ire)	sf	1¼ Ⓣ LH	2:082	3↑ Irish Champion Stakes-G1							513½	Stevens G	130	*1.35		Daylami1309 Dazzling Park1202½ Dream Well130½		7
Timeform rating: 110				Stk 889100													*Set pressured pace,headed over 1-1/2f out,weakened.Sunshine St4th*	
Previously trained by Cecil Henry																		
17Aug99 York (GB)	gd	1 5/16 Ⓣ LH	2:064	3↑ Juddmonte International Stakes-G1							18	Stevens G	131	*3.00		Royal Anthem1318 Greek Dance1311¾ Chester House131no		12
Timeform rating: 138				Stk 593400													*Close up,led 5f out,drew clear 1-1/2f out,handily.Almutawakel 7th*	
Previously trained by Cecil Henry																		
18Jun99 Ascot (GB)	fm	1½ Ⓣ RH	2:283	4↑ Hardwicke Stakes-G2							23	Fallon K	126	*1.20		Fruits of Love1243 *Royal Anthem*1261½ Sea Wave124hd		8
Timeform rating: 124				Stk 215500													*5th early,3rd 5f out,bid 2-1/2f out,led 2f to 1f out,one-paced*	
Previously trained by Cecil Henry																		
4Jun99 Epsom (GB)	yl	1½ Ⓣ LH	2:401	4↑ Coronation Cup-G1							2¾	Fallon K	126	*2.00		*Daylami*126¾ Royal Anthem126½ Dream Well1261		7
Timeform rating: 124				Stk 324000													*Rank trckng leader,led 3f out,headed 100y out.SilverPatriarch 4th*	
Previously trained by Cecil Henry																		
7Nov98- 9CD	fm	1½ Ⓣ	:491 1:134 2:033 2:283	3↑ BCTurf-G1	82	7	55	64½	66½	814	715¾	Stevens G L	122	*2.70	76- 09	*Buck's Boy*1261¼ Yagli1261¾ Dushyantor126no	No late bid	13
18Oct98- 6WO	fm	1½ Ⓣ	:521 1:161 2:043 2:293	3↑ CanIntnl-G1	110	8	1½	1½	1hd	12	12	Stevens G L	119	1.75	84- 17	RoyalAnthem1192 ChiefBearhrt126½ *PrdeGround*1193	Driving,well handled	8
25Jly98 Ascot (GB)	gd	1½ Ⓣ RH	2:293	3↑ King George VI & Queen Eliz St-G1							32½	Fallon K	121	3.50		*Swain*1331 High-Rise1211½ *Royal Anthem*121½		8
Timeform rating: 127				Stk 995700													*Tracked leader,led ovr 2f out,headed 1-1/2f out,faded.Daylami 4th*	
19Jun98 Ascot (GB)	yl	1½ Ⓣ RH	2:342	King Edward VII Stakes-G2							12	Fallon K	120	*2.25		Royal Anthem1202 Kilimanjaro1202½ Scorned1204		10
Timeform rating: 119+				Stk 209000													*Tracked leader,led 1-1/2f out,ridden clear.Central Park 4th*	
6Jun98 Newmarket (GB)	gd	1¼ Ⓣ RH	2:021	Fairway Stakes (Listed)							12½	Fallon K	124	*.40		*Royal Anthem*1242½ Kilimanjaro1248 Sensory12413		5
Timeform rating: 120				Stk 30900													*Rated in 4th,led 1-1/2f out,drew clear.New July Course record*	
16May98 Newbury (GB)	gd	1¼ Ⓣ LH	2:08	Hatherden Maiden Stakes							13	Ryan W	126	4.50		*Royal Anthem*1263 Generous Rosi126¾ *Cyber World*1263½		16
Timeform rating: 100+				Maiden 9800													*Progress after a half,led over 1f out,ridden clear*	

RUNNING STAG (Cozzene—Fruhlingstag, by Orsini II). Florida. The globe-trotting Running Stag finished third the Woodward Stakes at 4, and was best at 5, winning the Brooklyn and Saratoga Breeders' Cup Handicaps. He also finished second in the Massachusetts Handicap and Hong Kong Cup (on turf). Although his runners should be versatile and win on all surfaces like Cozzene, they will ultimately prove best on grass.

Running Stag

Own: Cohen Richard J

B. h. 10 (Jun)
Sire: Cozzene (Caro*Ire) $60,000
Dam: Fruhlingstag*Fr (Orsini II)
Br: Juddmonte Farms (Ky)
Tr: Mitchell Philip(0 0 0 0 .00) 2004:(0 0 .00)

Life	40	7	11	2	$1,663,227	118	D.Fst	18	6	5	1	$1,127,490	118
2000	7	2	1	0	$524,975	117	Wet(321)	2	0	0	0	$105,000	105
1999	9	2	4	0	$837,782	118	Turf(310)	20	1	6	1	$430,737	97
Aik Ⓣ	0	0	0	0	$0	-	DstⓉ(324)	0	0	0	0	$0	-

19Aug00-9AP yl 1¼ Ⓣ :473 1:114 1:371 2:011 3↑ ArlMilln-G1 97 6 25 23 2½ 21 66 Sellers S J L126 10.90 95-04 Chester House1263¼ Manndar126½ Mula Gula1261 Stalked, tired late 7
6Aug00-9Sar gd 1⅛ :463 1:101 1:35 1:481 3↑ WhitneyH-G1 105 5 63¾ 63 63 45 47¾ Sellers S J L120 10.40 92 - *Lemon Drop Kid*1232 Cat Thief1174¼ Behrens1221½ Steadied first turn 6
11Jun00-8Bel fst 1⅛ :47 1:114 1:371 1:494 3↑ BroklynH-G2 102 6 1hd 2½ 1hd 22½ 67¾ Sellers S J L121 *1.45 74-29 *LemonDropKid*1207¼ Lger114hd *DowntheAisle*112hd Between foes, gave way 7
3Jun00-13Suf fst 1⅛ :462 1:103 1:361 1:492 3↑ MassH-G2 117 8 41½ 31½ 21 1hd 11¼ Velazquez J R LB116 *1.60 89-17 Running Stag1161¼ Out of Mind1161¼ David113¾ Wide 1st, driving 8
24May00-8Bel fst 1⅛ :451 1:091 1:343 1:48 4↑ Alw 59000N$Y 107 2 33½ 32 21 1½ 11½ Sellers S J L123 *1.60 91-16 *RunningStg*1231½ ErlyWrning1173½ WldImgnton1143¼ With something left 6
Previously trained by Mitchell Philip
25Mar00 Nad Al Sheba (UAE) ft *1¼ LH 1:592 4↑ Dubai World Cup-G1 717¾ Sellers S J 126 - *Dubai Millennium*1266 Behrens1265½ Public Purse126hd 13
Timeform rating: 109 Stk 6000000 *Tracked in 4th,3rd 3f out,weakened 1-1/2f out.Puerto Madero 4th*
Previously trained by Mitchell Philip
12Mar00 Nad Al Sheba (UAE) ft *7½f LH 1:29 4↑ Al Futtaim Trophy 21¼ Ryan W 121 - Blue Snake1191¼ Running Stag121no Jila1191¾ 5
Timeform rating: 107 Alw 19100 *Wide in 4th,dueled 170y out,headed 50y out.No betting*
Previously trained by Mitchell Philip
12Dec99 Sha Tin (HK) gd *1¼ Ⓣ RH 2:012 3↑ Hong Kong Cup-G1 23¾ Sellers S 126 25.00 Jim and Tonic1263¾ Running Stag1261½ Lear Spear1261¼ 12
Timeform rating: 117 Stk 1286000 *Tracked leader,led briefly over 1f out,second best.Kabool 4th*
Previously trained by Mitchell Philip
16Nov99 Lingfield (GB) ft 1¼ LH 2:043 3↑ Ind Prchsng Asso Cndtn S(dirt) 2nk Eddery P 126 *.30 Brilliant Red126nk Running Stag1261¼ Pas de Memoires1311¼ 11
Timeform rating: 97+ Alw 25600 *Rated in 7th,close 3rd 3f out,led 1f out,caught near line*
Previously trained by Mitchell Philip
18Sep99-9Bel fst 1⅛ :454 1:094 1:342 1:464 3↑ Woodward-G1 114 6 72½ 62¾ 41 3nk 41¾ Sellers S J L126 *.95 95-14 *RiverKeen*126no Almutwkel1261½ StephnGotEvn121nk Rated, 4 wide move 7
29Aug99-8Sar fst 1¼ :474 1:114 1:362 2:01 3↑ SarBCH-G2 116 7 31 3½ 1hd 12 1½ Sellers S J L122 *1.00 103-16 RunningStag122½ Ctienus115½ GoldenMissile1158½ Stalked 3 wide,driving 8
Previously trained by Mitchell Philip
3Jly99 Sandown Park (GB) gd 1¼ Ⓣ RH 2:062 3↑ Eclipse Stakes-G1 54¾ Cochrane R 133 9.00 Compton Admiral122nk Xaar133½ *Fantastic Light*1221½ 8
Timeform rating: 115 Stk 465100 *Tracked leader,weakened over 1f out.Insatiable 6th,Croco Rouge7th*
Previously trained by Mitchell Philip
12Jun99-8Bel fst 1⅛ :461 1:10 1:34 1:461 3↑ BroklynH-G2 118 6 63¾ 64¼ 52¼ 13 17¼ Sellers S J L117 3.95 100-08 RunningStag1177¼ DeputyDiamond1132¼ SirBear1193¼ Quick 5 wide burst 8
29May99-13Suf fst 1⅛ :472 1:11 1:36 1:49 3↑ MassH-G2 116 1 1½ 11 1½ 1½ 2½ Sellers S J LB113 8.20 90-16 *Behrens*118½ *Running Stag*1132¾ *Real Quiet*1214½ Off rail, faltered 6
Previously trained by Mitchell Philip
8May99 Goodwood (GB) gd 1⅛ Ⓣ RH 2:074 4↑ Shergar Cup Classic 2½ Cochrane R 124 10.00 Handsome Ridge124½ Running Stag1242 Border Arrow1242½ 10
Timeform rating: 120 Alw 163100 *Rated in 7th,bid over 1f out,held by winner.Happy Valentine 4th*
Previously trained by Mitchell Philip
28Mar99 Nad Al Sheba (UAE) ft *1¼ LH 2:003 4↑ Dubai World Cup-G1 714½ Cochrane R 126 b - Almutawakel126¾ Malek126¾ *Victory Gallop*1261½ 8
Timeform rating: 100 Stk 5000000 *Rank at rear,wide 6th 3f out,never threatened.Silver Charm 6th*
Previously trained by Mitchell Philip
27Nov98-11CD fst 1⅛ :472 1:112 1:361 1:49 3↑ ClarkH-G2 110 8 53¾ 41½ 51¾ 42 41½ Velazquez J R L116 13.20 97-14 *Silver Charm*124hd Littlebitlively1131 Wild Rush117½ Lacked room 3/16s 8
7Nov98-10CD fst 1¼ :473 1:12 1:371 2:02 3↑ BCClasic-G1 107 7 62¾ 73¾ 63¼ 74¼ 76¼ Velazquez J R L126 104.70 89-07 Awesome Again126¾ *Silver Charm*126nk Swain126no Steadied early 10
10Oct98-10Bel sly 1¼ :462 1:093 1:341 2:003 3↑ JkyClbGC-G1 94 1 58½ 37½ 37 46½ 414¼ Cochrane R 126 f 19.80 77-14 Wagon Limit1265½ Gentlemen1264¾ Skip Away1264 Rail run second turn 6
19Sep98-9Bel fst 1⅛ :452 1:09 1:341 1:474 3↑ Woodward-G1 106 1 52¾ 52 52¾ 34½ 37¾ Cochrane R 126 48.50 83-18 Skip Away1261¾ Gentlemen1266 Running Stag1269 Determinedly on rail 5
16Aug98 Deauville (Fr) yl *1¼ Ⓣ RH 2:052 4↑ Prix Gontaut-Biron-G3 13 Cochrane R 123 28.30 Running Stag1233 Garuda1231½ Lord of Men121½ 11
Timeform rating: 119 Stk 60300 *Rated at rear,rail bid to lead ovr 1f out,ridden clear.Sasuru 5th*
18Jun98 Longchamp (Fr) sf *1¼ Ⓣ RH 2:032 4↑ La Coupe-G3 34½ Day N 123 14.00 *Public Purse*1232 Farasan1232½ *Running Stag*1231½ 11
Timeform rating: 103 Stk 60500 *Rated in 7th,steady progress,5th 2-1/2f out,gained 3rd 100y out*
6Jun98 Epsom (GB) gd 1½ Ⓣ LH 2:333 4↑ Vodafone International Rated H 918¾ Cochrane R 133 20.00 Hajr119no Sabadilla1261½ Tough Leader1192 15
Timeform rating: 87 Hcp 70800 *Never a factor*
26Apr98 Cologne (Ger) sf *1½ Ⓣ RH 2:361 4↑ Gerling-Preis-G2 65¼ Swinburn W R 126 24.10 Ferrari1262 Asolo126½ Ungaro1301 10
Timeform rating: 105 Stk 69800 *Rated in 7th,lacked room 2f out,outfinished*
5Apr98 Gelsenkirchen (Ger) hy *1¼ Ⓣ RH 2:154 4↑ GP Gelsenkirchner-Wirtschaft-G3 58½ Cochrane R 126 6.80 Eden Rock1284 Sambakoenig126½ Orsuno1212 10
Timeform rating: 95 Stk 55200 *Trailed to 3f out,some late progress.Ferrari 4th*
21Mar98 Lingfield (GB) ft 1¼ LH 2:054 3↑ Winter Derby (dirt) 13½ Cochrane R 132 4.50 Running Stag1323½ Refuse to Lose1327 Fayik132½ 14
Timeform rating: 118 Alw 90500 *Rated towards rear,long drive to lead over 1f out,ridden clear*
6Dec97 Wolverhampton (GB) ft 1 3/16 LH 2:003 3↑ Wulfrun Stakes (Listed) 2½ Clark A 123 4.50 Farmost125½ *Running Stag*1237 Puzzlement123hd 7
Stk 89900 *Settled in 6th,bid 2f out,drifted left,2nd best.Centre Stalls 7th*
25Nov97 Lingfield (GB) ft 1¼ LH 2:032 3↑ Faucets Conditions Stks (dirt) 2nk Clark A 127 *.80 Unconditional Love121nk Running Stag12713 Acharne1262½ 6
Alw 8800 *Tracked in 4th,bid 2f out,dueled 1f out,outgamed*
24Sep97 Goodwood (GB) gd 1¼ Ⓣ RH 2:092 3↑ ROA Foundation Stakes (Listed) 41¼ Clark A 120 4.50 *Danish Rhapsody*126½ Proper Blue126no Sandstone120¾ 5
Stk 43600 *Tracked in 3rd,2nd and drifted left over 1f out,outfinished*
8Sep97 Longchamp (Fr) sf *1⅜ Ⓣ RH 2:152 Prix du Lion d'Angers (Listed) 25 Clark A 120 35.00 *Majorien*1285 Running Stag120no Kaizen1201 7
Stk 43500 *Rated in 6th,prevailed in duel for 2nd.Tavildaran 5th,Rate Cut6th*
Sep97 Saint-Cloud (Fr) yl *1 Ⓣ RH 1:403 Prix Ridgway (Listed) 44 Clark A 128 4.50 Such Charisma1283 Stingy128½ Blue Sky128½ 7
Stk 42500 *Tracked in 3rd,dueled briefly 2f out,gradually weakened*
Aug97 Goodwood (GB) gd 1 Ⓣ RH 1:37 Conditions Stakes 43 Eddery P 124 10.00 Cape Cross1242½ Dragonada123nk Kenmist119nk 6
Alw 37800 *Rated in 5th,mild bid over 1f out,one-paced late*
7Jun97 Ascot (GB) gd 1 Ⓣ RH 1:39 St James's Palace Stakes-G1 714 Fallon K 126 66.00 Starborough1261 Air Express1264 Daylami126½ 8
Stk 373400 *Tracked in 3rd,weakened 2f out.Desert King 4th*
0May97 Goodwood (GB) gd 1¼ Ⓣ RH 2:123 Predominate Stakes (Listed) 22½ Fallon K 120 12.00 *Grapeshot*1232½ Running Stag1201 Shii-Take1201¼ 6
Stk 57700 *Tracked in 4th,progress halfway,chased winner home last quarter*
7Apr97 Newmarket (GB) gd 1 Ⓣ Str 1:38 Craven Stakes-G3 52¾ Fallon K 121 33.00 Desert Story124¾ *Grapeshot*121hd Cape Cross1211½ 8
Stk 54800 *Squeezed back start,rated in last,mild late gain.Air Express 4th*
9Mar97 Kempton (GB) gd 1¼ Ⓣ RH 2:07 Stanmore Conditions Stakes 21¾ Clark A 125 3.00 *Palio Sky*1221¾ Running Stag1259 Drive Assured1221 5
Alw 12800 *Rank in 4th,ridden into lead 2f out,headed 1f out*
7Feb97 Lingfield (GB) ft 1¼ LH 2:073 Atlanta Maiden Stakes (dirt) 17 Clark A 126 *1.40 Running Stag1267 Around Fore Alliss1262 Solar Dawn1218 6
Maiden 8400 *Rated in 4th,led over 2f out,quickly clear*
Previously trained by Maurice Zilber
0Sep96 Maisons Laffitte (Fr) gd *7½f Ⓣ Str 1:320 Prix Aethelstan-EBF 2½ Vion V 118 17.00 With Fire123½ *Running Stag*118¾ Alekos1181½ 9
Alw 27100 *Led to 1f out,dueled,gave ground grudgingly*
6Sep96 Saint-Cloud (Fr) gd *1 Ⓣ LH 1:413 Prix Hauban-EBF 11 Guignard G 123 b 3.75e Catfriend123nk Babalover123hd Point Proven1231 16
Alw 27200 *Never a factor*
3Aug96 Deauville (Fr) gd *1 Ⓣ RH 1:48 Prix des Roches Noires-EBF 67 Guignard G 121 2.25 Peintre Celebre1212 New Frontier121no Safarid1211½ 6
Alw 35300 *Pressed pace,led 3f out,weakened 1-1/2f out*

SILIC (Sillery—Balletomane, by Sadler's Wells). Kentucky. From the Blushing Groom sire line and out of a mare by Sadler's Wells, Silic was strictly bred for grass and blossomed into a top turf miler at age 4, when he won three stakes races culminating with the Breeders' Cup Mile. His runners should have little impact at 2, especially if they are raced on dirt, but will show dramatic improvement as older runners on grass. (T^2)

Silic (Fr)
Own: Lanni J. Terrence, Poslosky, Ken, Sch

B. h. 9 (May)
Sire: Sillery (Blushing Groom*Fr) $7,185
Dam: Balletomane*Ire (Sadler's Wells)
Br: M. Armenio Simoes de Almeida (Fr)
Tr: Canani Julio C(0 0 0 0 .00) 2004:(133 28 .21)

Life	15	8	2	0	$1,422,299	110	D.Fst	0	0	0	0	$0 -
2000	1	1	0	0	$304,800	110	Wet(241)	0	0	0	0	$0 -
1999	5	3	0	0	$999,700	110	Turf(308)	15	8	2	0	$1,422,299 110
Aik Ⓣ	0	0	0	0	$0	-	DstⓉ(315)	1	0	1	0	$5,861 -

18Jun00-8Hol fm 1 Ⓣ:23³ :46⁴ 1:09⁴ 1:33¹ 3↑ShoeBCM-G1 **110** 2 3 2½ 5 2½ 4² 1 1½ 1½ Nakatani C S LB124 *.70e 97-13 Silic124½ *Ladies Din*1241½ Sharan124² Bid,cleared,held 11
6Nov99-5GP gd 1 Ⓣ:22⁴ :47 1:10⁴ 1:34¹ 3↑BCMile-G1 **110** 12 10 6¼ 10³ 5½ 2hd 1nk Nakatani C S L126 7.20 - - *Silic*126nk Tuzla123hd *Docksider*126no 4 wide rally, lasted 14
16Oct99-5SA fm 1 Ⓣ:23³ :46⁴ 1:10 1:33³ 3↑OkTrBCMI-G3 **109** 7 6 4¼ 6 5¼ 6 3¼ 3 1½ 1¹ Nakatani C S LB121 2.20 91-13 *Silic*121¹ *Bouccaneer*119¹ Brave Act119 2½ Swng out,closed gamely 7
19Sep99-10WO fm 1 Ⓣ:22³ :45 1:08⁴ 1:33 3↑AttoMile-G1 **104** 3 8⁴ 5 3¼ 5 2¾ 6 1¾ 5² Nakatani C S L121 5.30 97-10 ⒹHwksleyHill117hd QuietResolv117nk RobnGin119nk Finished well inside 15
13Jun99-9Hol fm 1 Ⓣ:23¹ :46 1:08⁴ 1:32⁴ 3↑ShoeBCM-G2 **109** 2 7⁶ 7 4½ 5 2¾ 1hd 1no Nakatani C S LB124 4.10e 99-09 Silic124no Ladies Din124½ Hawksley Hill124nk Rail trip, gamely 8
25Apr99-8GG fm 1 Ⓣ:23² :47 1:11 1:35² 3↑SnFrnBCH-G2 **102** 4 9⁸ 9 7½ 9⁴ 7 1¾ 4¾ Nakatani C S LB116 8.20 93-09 *Tuzla*112hd *Poteen*116nk Rob 'n Gin117½ Shftd out twice strtch 10
11Nov98-5Hol fm 1 Ⓣ:24 :47 1:10⁴ 1:35 ⓇItsgrktome44k **82** 6 4³ 3¹ 2¹ 5 2½ 6 4¼ Stevens G L LB122 *1.00 84-09 Bodygurd122 1¾ MoonlghtMtng117nk ByStrtBlus122no Stalked,took up 1/8 8
Placed 5th through disqualification Previously trained by Pascal Bary
4Oct98 Longchamp (Fr) sf *1 Ⓣ RH 1:41¹ 3↑ Prix du Rond-Point-G2 Stk 123100 4 5½ Guillot S 123 5.00 Fly to the Stars127 2½ Gold Away123³ *Decorated Hero*127hd 7
Timeform rating: 111 *Rated in 6th,some late progress.Ramooz 7th*
7Jun98 Chantilly (Fr) sf *1 Ⓣ RH 1:40¹ Prix de la Jonchere-G3 Stk 61200 1 1½ Guillot S 123 *1.70 Silic123 1½ Bouccaneer123¾ Nobelist123 1½ 6
Timeform rating: 113 *Rated in last,rallied to lead 100y out,handily.Esperero 4th*
13May98 Chantilly (Fr) gd *1 Ⓣ RH 1:40¹ Prix de Pontarme (Listed) Stk 43600 1hd Guillot S 128 *1.00 *Silic*128hd Nobelist128no Esperero128 2½ 6
Timeform rating: 104 *Rated in last,wide bid 1-1/2f out,dueled 150y out,prevailed*
30Apr98 Longchamp (Fr) hy *7f Ⓣ RH 1:29 Prix de Tivoli Alw 33200 1 2½ Guillot S 123 *.40 *Silic*123 2½ Bright Prospect120³ *Enjoleur*123⁴ 5
Timeform rating: 101+ *Tracked leader,led 2-1/2f out,drew clear,held well*
9Apr98 Maisons-Laffitte (Fr) hy *7f Ⓣ Str 1:34 Prix Djebel (Listed) Stk 42500 2² Guillot S 128 4.00 Ippon128² *Silic*128³ Roi Gironde128hd 5
Timeform rating: 102 *Tracked slow pace in 3rd,took 2nd 1f out.Hayil 5th*
4Oct97 Longchamp (Fr) gd *1⅛ Ⓣ RH 1:50² Prix de Conde-G3 Stk 61700 4² Guillot S 128 *1.50 Thief of Hearts128¹ *Special Quest*128½ Daymarti128½
Tracked leader,brief bid 2f out,outfinished.Quel Senor 5th
7Sep97 Longchamp (Fr) gd *1 Ⓣ RH 1:41⁴ Prix des Aigles-EBF Alw 29700 1⁵ Guillot S 126 2.10 Silic126⁵ Dolfikar126½ *Stifelio*126½
Tracked leader,led over 1f out,drew clear
16Aug97 Deauville (Fr) sf *6½f Ⓣ Str 1:20¹ Prix de Tancarville-EBF Maiden 29300 2¹ Guillot S 128 2.00 Fantastic Quest128¹ *Silic*128⁵ Naholy128 2½
Tracked in 3rd,bid with winner,always held

SIX BELOW (Seattle Sleet—Sixy Minister, by Deputy Minister). California. Unraced at 2 and 3, Six Below won two of his three lifetime starts, and finished third in the San Pasqual Handicap behind Dixie Dot Com and Budroyale in his final start. He is from the Seattle Slew sire line and the female family that produced the high-class French star Gyr; his 2-year-olds should have above-average speed in Cal-bred races. (SP^2)

Six Below
Own: McCaffery Trudy and Toffan, John A

Ch. h. 9 (Mar)
Sire: Seattle Sleet (Seattle Slew) $2,500
Dam: Sixy Minister (Deputy Minister)
Br: John Toffan & Trudy McCaffery (Ky)
Tr: Gonzalez J. P(0 0 0 0 .00) 2004:(39 2 .05)

Life	3	2	0	1	$66,000	111	D.Fst	3	2	0	1	$66,000 111
2000	1	0	0	1	$24,000	111	Wet(337)	0	0	0	0	$0
1999	2	2	0	0	$42,000	106	Turf(273)	0	0	0	0	$0
	0	0	0	0	$0	-	DstⓉ(345)	0	0	0	0	$0

16Jan00-7SA fst 1 1/16 :23 :46 1:09² 1:40⁴ 4↑SnPsqalH-G2 **111** 1 1½ 1¹ 1 1½ 2½ 3³ Flores D R LB116 2.20 96-10 Dixie Dot Com118 1½ *Budroyale*122 1½ Six Below116nk Speed,rail,held 3rd
10Dec99-7Hol fst 1 1/16 :23¹ :46¹ 1:10² 1:42² 3↑OC 40k/n1x-N **106** 4 1½ 1 1½ 1⁶ 1¹⁰ 1¹³ Flores D R LB118 *.50 88-19 Six Below118¹³ *Moonlight Charger*118¹ Saint Wynn116 1½ Drew off, in hand
13Nov99-6Hol fst 6½f :22² :44³ 1:09 1:15¹ 3↑Md Sp Wt 33k **102** 5 4 2½ 1 2½ 1 2½ 1 3½ Flores D R B122 *1.50 95-14 *Six Below*122 3½ Brigade120³ Right Attitude120² 4 wide to turn,driving

SLEW GIN FIZZ (Relaunch—Slew Princess, by Seattle Slew). Florida. Slew Gin Fizz is not exactly a freshman sire since he has had five crops to race in Argentina and Chile, but he is included in this list since his first crop of North American-bred horses are 2. Bred in Kentucky, Slew Gin Fizz was an unqualified success at stud in South America, siring at least 11 stakes winners, and his emergence as a stallion, combined with his American pedigree, brought him back to the U.S. He has an SP^2 pedigree and because he is by Relaunch (In Reality), his runners are sure to excel on wet tracks and also be dangerous on turf. Most notably, he has the chance to become an important stallion. His second dam is a half-sister to Mr. Prospector, so be especially aware if he is bred to mares who have Mr. Prospector in their pedigree. This will create the coveted Rasmussen Factor to stakes winner Gold Digger, the dam of Mr. Prospector. This pedigree pattern is usually a strong indicator of quality in a Thoroughbred.

Slew Gin Fizz
wn: Hudson River Farms

Gr/ro. h. 13 (Mar)
Sire: Relaunch (In Reality)
Dam: Slew Princess (Seattle Slew)
Br: Lee Pokoik & Lion's Farm (Ky)
Tr: Kelly Thomas J(0 0 0 0 .00) 2004:(0 0 .00)

Life	12	4	2	2	$210,994	102	D.Fst	10	4	2	2	$209,704	102
1994	7	3	0	1	$113,088	102	Wet(405)	2	0	0	0	$1,290	59
1993	5	1	2	1	$97,906	91	Turf(328)	0	0	0	0	$0	-
	0	0	0	0	$0	-	Dst(T)(396)	0	0	0	0	$0	-

)Aug94-9Sar	fst	7f	:22 :443 1:091 1:214	KngsBshp-G2	**48**	2	5	53	74½	79¼	728¼	Santos J A	122	7.00	- -	Chimes Band1174½ End Sweep122¾ *Halo's Image*117½	No response	7
Jly94-8Sar	fst	1⅛	:472 1:113 1:363 1:493	JimDandy-G2	**78**	4	1hd	21	43	49½	418	Bailey J D	120	5.00	- -	Unaccounted For1121 Tabasco Cat1265 Ulises11412	Spd, faded	5
7Jly94-8Bel	fst	6f	:222 :453 :572 1:094	3↑ Alw 32000N3x	**102**	5	3	3½	2½	1½	13	Santos J A	111	*.50	- -	SlewGinFizz1113 ScarletRge111nk DiggingIn1176¼	Stalked 3w, ridden out	6
Jun94-6Bel	fst	7f	:22 :441 1:08 1:201	RivaRidg-G3	**93**	2	6	11	1½	32	36½	Santos J A	122 b	4.70	- -	You and I122 2¾ *End Sweep*1143¾ *Slew Gin Fizz*1221¼	Dueled, wknd str	9
Previously trained by Kelly Larry																		
8May94-8AP	fst	1	:222 :443 1:094 1:364	Sheridan-G3	**90**	8	1½	1½	1½	1½	2½	Meier R	113 b	*2.90	- -	[D]*Dynamic Asset*115½ Slew Gin Fizz1133 No Terms1142¼	Dueled, inside	9
Placed first through disqualification																		
3May94-9AP	fst	6f	:22 :45 :572 1:10	Alw 18500N2L	**93**	1	7	11	11	14	17	Fires E	116 b	*.60	- -	*Slew Gin Fizz*1167 *Fully Motivated*1222½ Travel Claim116½	Led throughout	7
Previously trained by Kelly Thomas J																		
5Apr94-6Kee	sly	6f	:223 :463 1:121	Alw 25320N2L	**59**	2	8	2hd	68½	511	411¼	Bailey J D	L121	*.50	- -	Exhilarator121nk Sultan's Treat1185 OhioBlues1156	Off slow rushed, used	8
3Sep93-6Bel	sly	7f	:222 :453 1:101 1:231	Futurity-G1	**–0**	5	6	51¾	43½	618	650	Bailey J D	122	5.30	- -	*Holy Bull*122½ *Dehere*1225 Prenup1228	Bore in start, stopped	6
3Aug93-8Sar	fst	6½f	:222 :453 1:092 1:154	Hopeful-G1	**91**	7	7	5¾	51¾	31½	22½	Bailey J D	122	5.30	- -	Dehere1222½ Slew Gin Fizz1222 Whitney Tower1221¼	Hit gate, rallied	7
Jly93-9Sar	fst	6f	:214 :45 :572 1:094	SarSpcl-G2	**88**	4	8	41½	5¾	2½	2nk	Samyn J L	117	7.00	- -	*Dehere*117nk Slew Gin Fizz1172 Whitney Tower1175¾	Split foes, outfnshd	9
5Jly93-9Bel	fst	5½f	:211 :444 :574 1:043	TremntBC-G3	**66**	1	7	57	57	54	33½	Samyn J L	115 f	4.40	- -	Distinct Reality1152 Gusto Z1151½ Slew Gin Fizz1153½	Late rally, inside	7
3Jun93-3Bel	fst	5½f	:222 :461 :584 1:051	Md Sp Wt 23k	**72**	1	6	52	31½	21	1¾	Samyn J L	118	2.10	- -	SlewGinFizz118¾ SultnofJv1183½ PeceNegotitions1182	Split foes, driving	8

STEPHEN GOT EVEN (A.P. Indy—Immerse, by Cox's Ridge). Kentucky. Second in his only race at 2, Stephen Got Even matured slowly and won the Gallery Furniture.com Stakes and also finished third in the Woodward Stakes. He won the Donn Handicap in his only race at 4 before an injury shortened his career. His pedigree is loaded with middle-distance influences, and like the majority of A.P. Indy's offspring, Stephen Got Even's foals should also be slow to develop at 2 and be best beyond one mile at age 3. His third dam, Avum, is a half-sister to 2-year-old champion Lord Avie.

Stephen Got Even
Own: Hilbert Tomisue and Stephen C

B. h. 8 (May)
Sire: A.P. Indy (Seattle Slew) $300,000
Dam: Immerse (Cox's Ridge)
Br: William S. Farish & W. S. Kilroy (Ky)
Tr: Zito Nicholas P(0 0 0 0 .00) 2004:(329 53 .16)

Life	11	5	1	1	$1,019,200	120	D.Fst	10 5 1 1	$959,200 120
2000	1	1	0	0	$300,000	120	Wet(410)	1 0 0 0	$60,000 106
1999	9	4	0	1	$711,600	114	Turf(294)	0 0 0 0	$0 -
Aik Ⓣ	0	0	0	0	$0	-	DstⓉ(359)	0 0 0 0	$0 -

5Feb00-10GP	fst	1⅛	:464 1:104 1:354 1:482	3↑ DonnH-G1	**120**	1	21	2½	2hd	11	1¾	Sellers S J	L115	3.30	95- 18	Stephen Got Even115¾ Golden Missile1144½ *Behrens*1214	Dug in gamely
10Oct99-6Bel	sly	1¼	:462 1:101 1:352 2:012	3↑ JkyClbGC-G1	**106**	8	42	31	32	45½	47½	Velazquez J R	L121	7.00	79- 23	River Keen1263¼ Behrens126hd Almutawakel1264¼	Chased 4 wide, tired
18Sep99-9Bel	fst	1⅛	:454 1:094 1:342 1:464	3↑ Woodward-G1	**114**	4	31	52¾	51½	42¾	31½	Stevens G L	L121	4.10	95- 14	*RiverKeen*126no Almutwkel1261½ StephnGotEvn121nk	Game finish outside
1Sep99-6Sar	fst	1⅛	:481 1:123 1:364 1:492	3↑ Alw 49000N4X	**104**	1	1½	1hd	1½	13	14¼	Velazquez J R	L115	*.65	89- 11	StephenGotEven1154¼ Talavera1162 CraftyMn1187¾	Speed, clear, driving
5Jun99-9Bel	fst	1½	:473 1:12 2:014 2:274	Belmont-G1	**101**	11	3½	31	2hd	42	56¾	Sellers S J	L126	9.30	98- 06	LmonDropKid126hd VisionndVrs1261½ Chrsmtc1264¾	Four wide trip, tired
15May99-10Pim	fst	1 3/16	:451 1:101 1:351 1:551	Preaknss-G1	**101**	11	96	97¼	105¾	75¾	44	Stevens G L	L126	11.00	85- 09	Charismatic1261½ Menifee126hd *Badge*1262½	5wd to str,altrd crse
1May99-8CD	fst	1¼	:474 1:122 1:372 2:031	KyDerby-G1	**95**	4	42½	84¼	127½	1410	148¾	McCarron C J	L126	5.10	80- 14	*Charismatic*126nk Menifee126¾ Cat Thief1261¼	Steadied bump,1st turn
27Mar99-5TP	fst	1⅛	:49 1:13 1:37 1:49	GalFurnC-G2	**104**	8	52	31	3½	1½	12½	Sellers S J	L121	7.00	90- 15	StphnGotEvn1212½ KOnKing1215 EpicHonor1212½	6w most of way, drving
27Feb99-11GP	fst	1 1/16	:232 :472 1:122 1:442	Alw 32000N1X	**94**	6	31½	31	2hd	12½	12	Bailey J D	L122	*1.70	85- 14	*StphnGotEvn*1222 FrstAmrcn1195¾ BostonPrty1221¼	Ducked in str,driving
30Jan99-12GP	fst	1 1/16	:234 :482 1:131 1:444	Md Sp Wt 30k	**90**	6	62¼	31	2hd	1hd	11½	Bailey J D	L120	*1.50	83- 14	*StephenGotEven*1201½ SilverSeason1201 *DramCritic*1202¼	All out, prevailed
28Nov98-2Aqu	fst	6f	:223 :461 :58 1:101	Md Sp Wt 38k	**80**	7	5	72¼	41½	33	23¾	Bailey J D	L119	3.70	84- 16	SilverSenstion1193¾ *StephenGotEven*1193 *CoolCt*1192¾	3w trip, game finish

STRAIGHT MAN (Saint Ballado—Brilliant Melody, by Cornish Prince). Florida. With speed from both sides of his pedigree, Straight Man finished second in the Malibu Stakes and finally became a stakes winner at age 4 when he won the Winnercom Handicap. His sales yearlings brought much higher prices than his moderate $6,000 stud fee, and his runners are bred to do very well sprinting at age 2 but will be hard-pressed to be as brilliant beyond 1 1/16 miles. (SP^2)

Straight Man
Own: Schettine William C

B. h. 8 (Mar)
Sire: Saint Ballado (Halo) $125,000
Dam: Brilliant Melody (Cornish Prince)
Br: Casey Seaman (Fla)
Tr: Baffert Bob(0 0 0 0 .00) 2004:(434 80 .18)

Life	15	5	2	1	$333,304	109	D.Fst	15 5 2 1	$333,304
2000	7	3	0	0	$175,324	106	Wet(354)	0 0 0 0	$0
1999	8	2	2	1	$157,980	109	Turf(282)	0 0 0 0	$0
	0	0	0	0	$0	-	DstⓉ(341)	0 0 0 0	$0

10Dec00-8Hol	fst	6f	:214 :442 :563 1:09	3↑ VOUndrwd-G3	**87**	6	1	1½	2½	32	48	Flores D R	LB120	2.40	84- 14	Men's Exclusive1163 Love All theWay1171 Lexicon1224	Dueled, weakened
24Nov00-10CD	fst	6f	:213 :451 :57 1:092	3↑ Alw 49820N$Y	**106**	6	2	1hd	11	11	1¾	Sellers S J	L118	*1.70	98- 12	StrightMn118¾ *UltimteWrrior*119¾ ClliendJke114no	Drft out bmp start,drv
29May00-9Bel	fst	1	:23 :452 1:10 1:343	3↑ MtropltH-G1	**70**	6	11	2hd	71¾	813	823¾	Chavez J F	L115	19.80	68- 19	Yankee Victor1174¾ *Honest Lady*112¾ *Sir Bear*117¾	Tired inside turn
6May00-4CD	fst	7f	:214 :434 1:081 1:212	4↑ WnrcomH-G2	**103**	3	1	1½	1½	1½	1hd	Chavez J F	L112	4.60	98- 01	StraightMan112hd MulGul1143¼ PtienceGme114hd	Duel,long drive,gamely
31Mar00-7SA	fst	7f	:223 :452 1:091 1:213	4↑ Alw 57000N2X	**103**	2	1	11½	11	12½	11½	Flores D R	LB118	*1.90	97- 14	*StrightMn*1181½ OutstndingHro118nk PtincGm1183½	Rail,strong hand ride
5Feb00-3SA	fst	6f	:211 :44 :563 1:094	4↑ OC 62k/N2X-N	**89**	3	1	2hd	2hd	21	54½	Nakatani C S	LB117	1.10	85- 14	LoveAlltheWy1181¼ LtsGoSurfing120¾ ThToyMn1181½	Dueled, weakened
15Jan00-8SA	fst	1 1/16	:223 :462 1:101 1:414	SnFndoBC-G2	**98**	1	11	11	1½	1hd	63¾	Flores D R	LB116	7.50	90- 06	SaintsHonor1171½ CatThief122hd MrBroadBlade1181	Speed,4wd 3/8,wknd
26Dec99-6SA	fst	7f	:221 :441 1:084 1:22	Malibu-G1	**101**	4	5	3½	32½	31	2nk	Valenzuela P A	LB118	17.60	95- 08	LoveThatRed119nk StraightMan118hd CtThief123½	Bid again 3wd,gamely
4Dec99-8Hol	fst	7f	:222 :451 1:101 1:23	3↑ OC 62k/N2X-N	**94**	2	3	11	11½	1hd	2½	Flores D R	LB116	*1.00	86- 17	*Spinelessjellyfish*117½ StraightMn116½ Windstrike1172	Game inside in lane
6Jun99-6CD	fst	6f	:21 :441 :563 1:093	3↑ Alw 37800N2X	**90**	3	1	1hd	1hd	2hd	42¼	Albarado R J	L113	*.70	93- 07	TodaysTomorrow112nk HisWord119no VlidPennnt1132	Dueled, weakened
15May99-6Pim	fst	1 1/16	:224 :46 1:104 1:431	SirBarton100k	**68**	8	1hd	2½	22½	109¼	1116	Stevens G L	L117	*1.60	74- 09	*LeadEmHome*1171¼ RaireStndrd1152 *StellrBrush*115¾	3wd,pressd 6fur,tired
24Apr99-9CD	fst	1	:23 :461 1:112 1:374	DerbyTrl-G3	**96**	3	11	11	1hd	32½	35	Flores D R	L116	2.60	76- 24	PtienceGme1162¼ PrimeDirctiv1222¾ StrightMn116½	Off inside, tired late
27Mar99-5TP	fst	1⅛	:49 1:13 1:37 1:49	GalFurnC-G2	**87**	1	11	1½	1hd	35½	410	Flores D R	L121	*2.00	80- 15	StphnGotEvn1212½ KOnKng1215 EpcHonor1212½	Bumpd, bobbld, 3-4path
6Mar99-1SA	fst	1 1/16	:234 :472 1:11 1:421	Alw 54000N$Y	**106**	1	11	1½	1½	1hd	1½	Stevens G L	LB117	*.50	92- 11	StraightMn117½ LethlInstrument1172 SintsHonor1197	Clear past 1/8,held
14Feb99-6SA	fst	6f	:214 :443 :562 1:084	Md Sp Wt 46k	**109**	10	1	3½	2hd	1½	14	Stevens G L	LB120	*.40e	96- 09	*Straight Man*1204 Patience Game1203½ Macward120¾	Confident handling

SUCCESSFUL APPEAL (Valid Appeal—Successful Dancer, by Fortunate Prospect). Florida. This is a stallion born to be a major sire of fast 2-year-olds. Valid Appeal (In Reality) had phenomenal success as a sire of precocious and quick horses, and two of his sons, Valid Expectations and Valid Wager, are also successful 2-year-old and sprint sires. Successful Appeal was a sprinter/miler who won the

Cowdin, Withers, Kentucky Cup Sprint, and Amsterdam Stakes, and the A.G. Vanderbilt Handicap (via disqualification). His Florida-bred runners will be best from three to seven furlongs, and some may be able to stretch out to win at 1 1/16 miles. (SP^2)

Successful Appeal
Own: Starview Stable and Jones Jr., John T

Dk. b or b. h. 8 (Mar)
Sire: Valid Appeal (In Reality)
Dam: Successful Dancer (Fortunate Prospect)
Br: Harry T. Mangurian, Jr. (Fla)
Tr: Kimmel John C(0 0 0 0 .00) 2004:(188 23 .12)

Life	22	8	2	4	$654,681	119	D.Fst	20	8	2	3	$632,681 119
2000	5	2	0	1	$189,500	112	Wet(372)	2	0	0	1	$22,000 88
1999	11	3	0	3	$316,601	119	Turf(246)	0	0	0	0	$0 -
	0	0	0	0	$0	-	Dst(T)(354)	0	0	0	0	$0 -

4Nov00-6CD	fst	6f	:204 :432 :551 1:073	3↑BCSprnt-G1	97	9	4	85	76¾	86¾	76¼	Prado E S	L126 f	25.80	101 -	*KonaGold*126½ HonestLady123½ BetOnSunshine1262	Bobbled start,no rally	14
23Sep00-9Bel	fst	7f	:221 :443 1:083 1:213	3↑Vosburgh-G1	99	5	3	31	41¼	54½	55¼	Prado E S	L126 f	3.05	90- 13	Trippi123½ More Than Ready123¼ *One Way Love*1261	Chased 4 wide, tired	10
30Aug00-9Sar	fst	6½f	:213 :441 1:082 1:15	3↑ForegoH-G2	111	7	4	53½	41½	51½	31	Prado E S	L119 f	2.85	98- 07	ShdowCster1131 Intidb118no SuccessfulAppl119nk	Chased 3 wide, willing	10
9Aug00-9Sar	fst	6f	:213 :443 :563 1:091	3↑AGVndbtH-G2	112	6	3	34½	32	2hd	2hd	Prado E S	L118 f	*1.60	99- 13	[D]Intidb117hd SuccessfulAppel1183½ ChsinWimmin1122	Bumpd str, game	8
Placed first through disqualification																		
30Jun00-8Bel	fst	6f	:231 :461 :573 1:092	3↑Alw 55000N$Y	104	4	2	2hd	2hd	1hd	1½	Prado E S	L123 f	*1.50	91- 13	*SuccessfulAppeal*123½ OrodeMexico1161¾ Vicr1163¾	Speed outside, driving	6
6Nov99-6GP	fst	6f	:22 :44 :554 1:074	3↑BCSprint-G1	114	6	6	31½	31	43	53¾	Prado E S	L124 f	16.40	99 -	Artax126½ *Kona Gold*126¾ Big Jag126½	Weakened, stretch	14
25Sep99-8TP	fst	6f	:212 :444 :564 1:092	KyCpSpnt-G2	119	6	2	33	2hd	12½	16	Prado E S	L122 f	3.20	94- 20	SuccessfulAppel1226 *FiveStrDy*1142 AmricnSpirit118½	5 wide, bid, driving	6
28Aug99-7Sar	fst	7f	:213 :432 1:073 1:21	KngsBshp-G1	104	7	5	55¼	37½	35	35¼	Prado E S	L124 f	8.40	95- 09	Forestry1241½ FiveStarDay1153¾ *SuccessfulAppel*124½	Game finish outside	12
6Aug99-8Sar	fst	6f	:221 :451 :573 1:101	Amstrdam-G3	102	9	7	3½	31½	1½	11¼	Prado E S	L122 f	4.00	90- 15	SuccessfulAppel1221¼ LionHrtd114¾ SilvrSson1191½	3w, strong hand ride	9
11Jly99-8Bel	fst	1 1/16	:23 :444 1:082 1:41	Dwyer-G2	99	2	52½	47½	45¼	43½	32¾	Migliore R	L122 f	8.10	89- 10	Forestry1222¼ DonerileCourt119½ *SuccssfulAppl*122½	Game between rivals	6
13Jun99-7Del	wf	1 1/16	:23 :462 1:111 1:423	LRichards200k	86	5	45	44½	44	37	310¼	Espinoza J L	L122 f	5.40	84- 19	StellrBrush1141¼ SmrtGuy1159 SuccessfulAppl1222½	Failed to sustain bid	8
23May99-8Bel	my	1⅛	:451 1:09 1:344 1:474	PeterPan-G2	88	9	31	32½	31½	61¾	711½	Migliore R	L120 f	8.50	80- 27	BstofLuck1131 TrsurIslnd1141½ *LmonDropKd*1202	Speed 3 wide, weakened	9
1May99-9Aqu	fst	1	:233 :463 1:101 1:35	Withers-G2	96	5	2hd	2hd	1½	12½	1½	Espinoza J L	L120 f	4.60	93- 08	SuccessfulAppl120½ *BstofLuck*1164¼ TrsurIslnd116½	Speed outside,driving	8
18Apr99-8Kee	fst	1 1/16	:231 :464 1:103 1:41	Lexingtn-G2	92	6	95¾	116	75¼	53¾	58¾	Migliore R	L115	4.00	94- 07	*Charismatic*1152½ Yankee Victor115¾ Finder's Gold1152	Drifted 4w 1st turn	12
21Mar99-9Aqu	fst	1	:221 :443 1:092 1:343	Gotham-G3	64	7	54	51¼	107½	99¼	721¼	Migliore R	L120	2.05	74- 15	Badge1207½ *Apremont*120¾ Robin Goodfellow1136	Taken up sharply turn	11
20Feb99-6GP	fst	1 1/16	:233 :472 1:123 1:453	FntnOYth-G1	91	6	76¼	74½	62¼	53¼	53¾	Migliore R	117	5.40	75- 29	*Vicar*114nk Cat Thief119¾ Certain1172¼	Checked in tight early	10
28Nov98-7Aqu	fst	1⅛	:462 1:103 1:362 1:494	Remsen-G2	93	9	55½	46	42½	1hd	4¾	Migliore R	119	3.45	86- 14	Comonmom113nk Millions122½ *Wondrtross*113hd	3wmove,bumped, gamely	9
8Nov98-9Aqu	fst	1	:24 :473 1:12 1:36	Nashua-G3	96	8	3½	32	2½	22	2¾	Velazquez J R	122	*1.45	88- 17	DonrlCourt115¾ SccssflAppl1226¼ ExldGroom113nk	Speed 3 wide, gamely	8
17Oct98-7Bel	fst	6½f	:222 :452 1:102 1:17	Cowdin-G2	93	3	3	1hd	1hd	1½	11¼	Migliore R	122	1.60	87- 15	SuccssflAppl1221¼ Notsybngrn1224 ExldGroom122nk	Pace on rail,driving	5
11Sep98-3Bel	fst	6f	:222 :463 :581 1:102	Alw 40000N2L	85	5	5	2hd	2hd	1½	12	Migliore R	117	1.70	89- 13	*SuccessfulAppel*1172 *CtThief*117nk ExiledGroom1138½	Pressed pace,driving	5
19Aug98-6Sar	fst	5½f	:222 :462 :583 1:05	Md Sp Wt 35k	88	4	6	65¼	51¾	13	16	Migliore R	116	*1.50	93- 16	*SuccessfulAppel*1166 *Hctor*1166½ ChssursTrsor1163	5 wide move,ridden out	7
6Aug98-3Sar	fst	5½f	:221 :454 :583 1:054	Md 75000	78	8	9	1hd	2hd	2hd	21½	Migliore R	116	3.20	87- 10	FortLRoc1161½ *SuccssfulAppl*1166 CrpntrsHlo1161	Off slow, gamely insde	11

SWEETSOUTHERNSAINT (Saint Ballado—Sweetsoutherncross, by Tri Jet). Florida. Yet another speedy son of Saint Ballado, Sweetsouthernsaint was undefeated in three starts at 2, including a victory in the What a Pleasure Stakes. Injured in his only start at 3 in the Holy Bull Stakes, he still finished third behind Cape Town and Comic Strip. With high speed from Saint Ballado and damsire Tri Jet (sire of Copelan), Sweetsouthernsaint should get fast 2-year-olds. Expect Sweetsouthernsaint to be among Florida's leading freshman sires. (SP^2)

Sweetsouthernsaint
Own: Plumley Harold J

Ch. h. 9 (Feb)
Sire: Saint Ballado (Halo) $125,000
Dam: Sweetsoutherncross (Tri Jet)
Br: Joanne W. Wilson (Fla)
Tr: Picou James E(0 0 0 0 .00) 2004:(28 2 .07)

Life	6	4	0	1	$131,400	99	D.Fst	4	3	0	1	$102,600 99
1999	2	1	0	0	$28,800	97	Wet(373)	1	0	0	0	$0 79
1998	1	0	0	1	$11,000	98	Turf(293)	1	1	0	0	$28,800 97
Aik(T)	0	0	0	0	$0	-	Dst(T)(339)	0	0	0	0	$0 -

3Oct99-8Bel	fm	1	(T):231 :462 1:10 1:342	3↑Alw 48000N3x	97	8	51½	53¾	32½	34	1hd	Chavez J F	L116	7.70	86- 15	Sweetsouthrnsint116hd Alwl1161 SidEnough1161	Game outside,last jump	0
Previously trained by Clardullo Richard Jr																		
6Sep99-10Crc	sly	1 1/16	:232 :472 1:122 1:443	3↑SpndABuckH100k	79	9	97¼	97½	98¼	711	816¼	Jurado E M	L113	7.90	77- 14	Best of the Rest1149½ *Dancing Guy*1131½ High Security114½	Dull effort	10
Previously trained by Azpurua Leo Jr																		
17Jan98-10GP	fst	1 1/16	:234 :483 1:124 1:44	HolyBull-G3	98	5	65	72½	73¼	4¾	31½	Day P	119	*1.00	85- 20	CpTown119½ *ComicStrp*1141 Swtsouthrnsnt1191½	Bumped,rallied between	7
13Dec97-10Crc	fst	1 1/16	:242 :493 1:143 1:471	WhtAPlsr-G3	99	1	83½	61¾	32	1hd	14½	Toribio A R	115	*.40	80- 28	Sweetsouthrnsint1154½ RoguishPrinc1132¾ Rportr1151	Circled,ridden out	9
27Nov97-11Crc	fst	1 1/16	:242 :483 1:13 1:461	Alw 23500N1x	99	2	74¼	54	21½	11	15	Toribio A R	120	*.40	85- 21	*Sweetsouthernsaint*1205 OutamywySir1177¼ Brookins1171¾	Much the best	8
27Oct97-9Crc	fst	1	:24 :48 1:143 1:41	Md Sp Wt 22k	94	5	55½	37	32½	12	18	Toribio A R	117	3.30	82- 24	*Sweetsouthernsaint*1178 *NashOK*1179¼ Ferlico1174¾	Much the best, handily	8

THE DEPUTY (Petardia—Manfath, by Last Tycoon). Kentucky. As a young 3-year-old, The Deputy was the darling of California, capturing the Santa Anita Derby, Santa Catalina Stakes, and Hill Rise Handicap, but was never a factor in the Kentucky Derby, which turned out to be his final race. From the sire line of the speedy Jaipur, he descends from a high-quality female line that produced Blushing Groom, Alwuhush, Husband, Simply Majestic, and Tejano Run. He should impart speed to his offspring and they should perform well on all surfaces from seven furlongs to 1⅛ miles, particularly grass. (T^2)

The Deputy (Ire)
Own: Team Valor Stables LLC and Barber Gar
Dk. b or b. h. 7 (Mar)
Sire: Petardia*GB (Petong) $3,000
Dam: Manfath*Ire (Last Tycoon*Ire)
Br: John McEnery (Ire)
Tr: Sahadi Jenine(0 0 0 0 .00) 2004:(87 14 .16)

Life	10	4	2	3	$817,270	109	D.Fst	4	2	1	0	$714,380	109
2000	5	3	1	0	$760,010	109	Wet(248)	0	0	0	0	$0	-
1999	5	1	1	3	$57,260	-	Turf(199)	6	2	1	3	$102,890	99
Aik Ⓣ	0	0	0	0	$0	-	DstⓉ(193)	0	0	0	0	$0	-

6May00-8CD fst 1¼ :454 1:094 1:353 2:01 KyDerby-G1 73 10 126¼ 147½ 179½ 1613 1423¼ McCarron C J L126 4.60 82 - Fusaichi Pegasus1261½ Aptitude1264 Impeachment126½ Wide trip, no bid 19
8Apr00-5SA fst 1⅛ :471 1:112 1:362 1:49 SADerby-G1 109 5 42½ 31½ 31½ 1½ 11 McCarron C J LB120 2.40 90-16 The Deputy1201 War Chant1202 Captain Steve1203 3wd bid,led,gamely 6
19Mar00-7SA fst 1$\frac{1}{16}$:23 :454 1:101 1:423 SnFelipe-G2 105 2 44½ 46½ 33 21 2¾ McCarron C J LB122 2.30 89-14 *Fusaichi Pegasus116¾ The Deputy1223* Anees119hd Loomed 1/4, game try 7
30Jan00-7SA fst 1$\frac{1}{16}$:23 :46 1:104 1:43 StCtlina-G2 103 3 1hd 1hd 1hd 1hd 11 McCarron C J LB115 4.90 88-19 The Deputy1151 *High Yield1175½* Captain Steve1233½ Rail,steady handling 6
2Jan00-3SA fm 1 Ⓣ :223 :464 1:112 1:361 HillRiseH76k 99 2 55½ 54 32 21 11 McCarron C J LB117 2.70 78-23 *ThDputy1171 PromontoryGold11710* PurlyCozzn120no Off slow,rail bid lane 6
Previously trained by John Hills
8Sep99 Doncaster (GB) gd 6f Ⓣ Str 1:133 St Leger Yearling Stakes 3hd Weaver J 123 7.00 Sheer Hamas123no Blue Bolivar123no *The Deputy123hd* 21
Timeform rating: 101 Alw 505600 *Squeezed back,behind after 1f,bid 2-1/2f out,drftd lft,fnshd fast*
3Sep99 Epsom (GB) gd 7f Ⓣ LH 1:221 Median Auction Maiden Stakes 12½ Cochrane R 126 2.50 The Deputy1262½ Muntej12612 Mush123¾ 12
Timeform rating: 95 Maiden 9000 *Tracked in 3rd,roused to lead over 1f out,ridden clear*
21Aug99 Chester (GB) yl 7f Ⓣ LH 1:311 EBF Grey Friars Maiden Stakes 31¾ Hills M 126 *1.35 Rainbow Melody1211¼ Bhutan Prince126½ *The Deputy1261* 6
Timeform rating: 76 Maiden 9100 *Rated in 4th,outside bid 2-1/2f out,outfinished*
31Jly99 Newmarket (GB) gd 6f Ⓣ Str 1:124 EBF Express Racing Week Mdn St 21¾ Hills M 126 5.50 Mastermind1261¾ The Deputy126¾ *Winning Venture126hd* 9
Timeform rating: 84 Maiden 11100 *Tracked leaders,outpaced 2f out,finished well,up for 2nd*
16Jly99 Newbury (GB) gd 6f Ⓣ Str 1:141 EBF Ecchinswell Maiden Stakes 31½ Hills M 120 14.00 *Elaflaak126¾* Starlyte Girl116¾ The Deputy1202 6
Timeform rating: 82 Alw 12200 *Rated in 5th on rail,outpaced halfway,angled out,finished well*

TIGER RIDGE (Storm Cat—Weekend Surprise, by Secretariat). Florida. Unraced at 2 and 3, Tiger Ridge was winless in five starts at 4, but as a son of Storm Cat and half-brother to A.P. Indy, Honor Grades, and three-quarter brother to Summer Squall, he automatically gets a chance at stud. His sales yearlings sold quite well and his Florida-bred runners should show speed at 2. (HT^2)

Tiger Ridge
Own: Farish William S. and Kilroy, Mrs. W.
Dk. b or b. h. 8 (Feb)
Sire: Storm Cat (Storm Bird) $500,000
Dam: Weekend Surprise (Secretariat)
Br: William S. Farish & William S. Kilroy (Ky)
Tr: Howard Neil J(0 0 0 0 .00) 2004:(105 25 .24)

Life	5	M	1	1	$11,950	71	D.Fst	3	0	0	1	$5,050	71
2000	5	M	1	1	$11,950	71	Wet(383)	2	0	1	0	$6,900	69
1999	0	M	0	0	$0	-	Turf(360)	0	0	0	0	$0	-
	0	0	0	0	$0	-	Dst(0)	0	0	0	0	$0	-

20Jun00-3Del fst 170 :234 :48 1:131 1:434 3↑ Md Sp Wt 30k 71 7 73½ 73¾ 61 42 41¾ Bartram B E L122 *1.50 80-20 DReasontoHail115no MilesAhead115¾ *VinniesPic1151* Middle move, outfin 7
Placed third through disqualification
20May00-5Del sly 170 :231 :48 1:13 1:433 3↑ Md Sp Wt 31k 67 4 55 56 58 43½ 55½ Bartram B E 122 *1.40 77-21 Imperioso1221 CrossExmintion114¾ WhispringPin1142 Failed to respond 9
18Apr00-3Del sly 1$\frac{1}{16}$:223 :472 1:133 1:473 3↑ Md Sp Wt 30k 69 1 511 510 56 45½ 24¾ Bartram B E 122 *1.50 64-29 IronPrince1224¾ TigerRidge122¾ MisterMatthew122hd Outside, up for 2nd 5
Previously trained by McGaughey III Claude R
1Apr00-3Aqu fst 1 :232 :47 1:114 1:373 3↑ Md Sp Wt 42k 64 6 52 62½ 63¼ 73¼ 66 Bailey J D 122 *1.15 74-19 Knock Again1141¼ Silent West114½ Red Ace122hd Inside, no response 7
8Mar00-4GP fst 6f :22 :452 :574 1:112 Md Sp Wt 35k 56 7 2 611 511 410 49¾ Bailey J D 122 2.50 72-20 Just a Miner1221¼ Lush1222 *Concielo1226½* Failed to menace 8

TRULUCK (Conquistador Cielo—Michelle Mon Amour, by Best Turn). Texas. Having miler speed, stakes winner Truluck is a half-brother to multiple stakes winner Posen, and his third dam is the 1966 champion 3-year-old filly, Lady Pitt, whose descendants include Blitey, Dancing Spree, and Heavenly Prize. His runners should be best from six furlongs to 1⅛ miles in restricted statebred races, especially over sloppy surfaces.

Truluck
Own: Stoneside Stable LLC

B. h. 9 (Feb)
Sire: Conquistador Cielo (Mr. Prospector) $15,000
Dam: Michelle Mon Amour (Best Turn)
Br: Arthur B. Hancock III, Robert C. McNair & Janice McNai (Ky)
Tr: Walden W. E(0 0 0 0 .00) 2004:(113 20 .18)

Life	25	5	5	3	$411,655	109		
2000	7	0	1	0	$20,875	90		
1999	10	2	2	1	$239,010	109		
	0	0	0	0	$0	-		
D.Fst	20	5	3	3	$384,230	108		
Wet(344)	3	0	2	0	$27,425	109		
Turf(244)	2	0	0	0	$0	75		
Dst(0)	0	0	0	0	$0	-		

4Sep00-6Tdn	sly	1⅛		:471 1:122 1:381 1:511	3↑ HIOFmBCH-G3	79	5	52¼	67	64	57½	413¾	Johnson J M	L115 b	6.00	71-21	Guided Tour1165¼ Sleight1141½ Desert Demon1147	Failed to menace	6
6Aug00-8Sar	gd	1 1/16	Ⓣ	:234 :482 1:124 1:433	4↑ Alw 59000c	75	2	75¼	61¼	86¼	79	714	St Julien M	L118 b	75.50	64-22	AffirmedSuccss122nk DlyofGm1203¾ ForignLnd118no	Inside, no response	9
4Jly00-8Mnr	gd	1	⊗	:231 :46 1:091 1:334	3↑ IndepDayH38k	76	6	67	55½	46	49	28¾	Deegan J C	LB120 b	*1.80	99 -	Find the Mine1148¾ Truluck1202½ BoyGenius1182¾	1/4p move, second best	9
16Jun00-9CD	fst	1 1/16		:234 :471 1:12 1:432	3↑ Alw 54970c	84	2	66½	65½	54½	57	411½	Melancon L	L118 b	10.30	81-18	Relic Reward1183¾ Glacial1235½ Classic Cat1182½	Not a threat	6
13May00-7Spt	fst	1 1/16		:241 :482 1:123 1:45	3↑ Alw 49600c	88	4	32½	32	31½	54	66½	Coa E M	L116 b	1.70	86-15	Chicago Six122½ Muchacho Fino1163½ *Dust On the Bottle*116½	Tired	7
12Apr00-9OP	fst	1 1/16		:232 :47 1:111 1:424	3↑ 5thSnBC-G3	80	5	55	54½	46½	715	714¾	Doocy T T	L114 b	2.80	75-23	Mr Ross1152¾ Relic Reward114¾ Crimson Classic1143¾	Never involved	7
18Mar00-9TP	fst	1⅛		:481 1:123 1:374 1:503	4↑ TejanoRun43k	90	2	64½	53½	43	43½	43¼	D'Amico A J	L111 b	1.90	79-24	Irish Silence113hd La War113nk Glacial1193	Inside, lacked bid	9
31Oct99-9CD	fst	7½f		:224 :454 1:101 1:284	3↑ AckAckH-G3	82	7	9	103½	108¼	911	914½	Albarado R J	L114 b	4.70	87-12	*Littlebitlively*119½ *Run Johnny*1174 Tactical Cat117no	No factor, dull trip	11
25Sep99-10TP	fst	1⅛		:47 1:113 1:372 1:502	3↑ KyCpClH-G2	100	8	65½	64¼	41¾	44	44½	Albarado R J	L115 b	2.00e	78-24	Da Devil112½ *Social Charter*115hd *Cat Thief*1174	5 wide move, tired	8
28Aug99-9Mth	fst	1		:232 :454 1:094 1:35	3↑ SlvtrMlH-G3	104	2	52½	42½	31	1½	12¾	Bravo J	L115 b	1.40e	99-08	Truluck1152¾ Rock and Roll1194 Siftaway1144½	Wide bid, drew clear	6
11Aug99-8Sar	fst	1⅛		:47 1:111 1:37 1:503	4↑ Alw 49000N4X	89	3	3½	32½	35	33½	36	Sellers S J	L122 b	*1.40	77-18	Tejano Couture1143½ Crafty Man1192½ *Truluck*1221	Speed outside, empty	7
31May99-8LS	fst	1 1/16		:234 :47 1:10 1:431	3↑ LSParkH303k	97	5	63¾	53¼	56½	55½	46	Melancon L	L114 b	3.10	82-30	Mocha Express116no Littlebitlively118¾ Nite Dreamer1135¼	No factor	7
5May99-9CD	gd	1 1/16		:24 :474 1:121 1:434	3↑ Alw 53305c	109	5	53¼	41¾	1½	1½	2nk	Melancon L	L123 b	*.80	91-17	*Relic Reward*120nk Truluck1239 Shed SomeLight1183¾	Bid,led, outfinished	7
7Apr99-9OP	fst	1 1/16		:232 :47 1:111 1:421	3↑ 5thSnBC-G3	108	7	42½	31½	31	32	1¾	Melancon L	L114 b	3.10	93-23	Truluck114¾ Slide to the Left114nk *Rock and Roll*1143½	In time outside	8
27Feb99-10GP	fst	1¼		:481 1:122 1:364 2:014	3↑ GPH-G1	99	2	12	1hd	2hd	42	58¼	Day P	L111 b	33.40	94-14	*Behrens*1142½ Archers Bay1142 Sir Bear1183¼	Inside, gave way	8
30Jan99-10GP	fst	1⅛		:463 1:102 1:353 1:481	3↑ DonnH-G1	97	3	87½	88¼	88¼	76	610¾	Smith M E	L113 b	76.80	85-14	Puerto Madero1202¾ *Behrens*1132½ Silver Charm126nk	Drifted stretch	12
14Jan99-8GP	fst	1 1/16		:243 :474 1:113 1:433	4↑ Alw 44000c	100	1	63¾	64¾	54	34½	24½	Sellers S J	L115 b	*.90	84-26	Early Warning1194½ Truluck1151 *Dancing Guy*1151	Between, up for 2nd	7
28Nov98-4CD	fst	1 1/16		:234 :471 1:12 1:431	3↑ Alw 46200N2X	99	3	63¾	62¾	42½	1hd	14	Sellers S J	L113 b	*.80e	95-05	Truluck1134 WitchersCreek1131 BattleRoyle1157¾	Stumbled start,driving	7
19Nov98-6CD	fst	1 1/16		:234 :474 1:121 1:43	3↑ Alw 44880N2X	104	6	55	42	31	11½	22	Sellers S J	L113 b	3.80	94-15	Mr Dixie1132 *Truluck*1135 Dixielander1185½	Bid, led, outfinished	7
12Sep98-5Bel	fm	1 1/16	Ⓣ	:232 :461 1:10 1:401	3↑ Alw 43000N2X	70	5	87	99¼	96¼	911	611½	McCarron C J	L115	5.30	79-08	StrConnection1203 *Scgnelli*117½ PondPrkRd118no	Wide move,nothing left	12
29Mar98-11TP	fst	1⅛		:451 1:092 1:342 1:47	JimBeam-G2	101	8	85¾	77	67	48½	38	Day P	L121	12.50	94-07	Event of the Year1215 Yarrow Brae1213 Truluck1214	Unhurried, late bid	10
14Mar98-2GP	fst	1⅛		:482 1:132 1:383 1:513	Alw 33000N1X	88	2	33½	21	21½	22½	11	Day P	L117	*1.30	79-15	Truluck1171 Vergennes12011 *Flaming Bridle*1172½	Stalked pace, up late	8
14Feb98-5GP	fst	7f		:222 :452 1:102 1:231	Alw 31000N2L	87	1	8	72¾	64½	47	37	Day P	120	7.10	77-19	Diamond Studs1205½ Jess M1201½ *Truluck*1203	Mild rally inside	10
8Nov97-5CD	fst	7f		:23 :464 1:133 1:271	Md Sp Wt 36k	68	11	3	88	912	36	1nk	Perret C	L121	*1.50	72-20	Truluck121nk General Aviation1211 Benelli121½	Wore down rivals	12
11Oct97-3Kee	fst	7f		:222 :454 1:104 1:234	Md Sp Wt 36k	87	4	3	3½	2½	2½	2nk	Albarado R J	L118	6.50	86-14	Silver Launch118nk *Truluck*1181 Western City11811	Dueled, outfinished	10

UNBRIDLED JET (Unbridled—Easy Summer, by Easy Goer). Maryland. Stakes-placed Unbridled Jet is best remembered for his troubled trip in the 1999 Haskell Invitational Handicap. He appeared to be headed to victory but checked sharply at the eighth pole and finished fourth behind Menifee, Cat Thief, and Forestry in an amazing effort. Although he is out of an unraced dam, his second dam, Summer Mood, was a champion sprinter in Canada and is a half-sister to million-dollar earner Present Value. With Unbridled and Easy Goer up close in his pedigree, expect his foals to be late developers and to be effective at 3 at distances over one mile.

Unbridled Jet
Own: Double H Stable

Dk. b or b. h. 8 (Apr)
Sire: Unbridled (Fappiano) $200,000
Dam: Easy Summer (Easy Goer)
Br: Harold Harrison (Ky)
Tr: Mott William I(0 0 0 0 .00) 2004:(414 83 .20)

Life	13	3	2	0	$255,364	109
2000	1	1	0	0	$20,400	102
1999	7	1	2	0	$199,204	109
	0	0	0	0	$0	-
D.Fst	11	3	2	0	$190,864	109
Wet(413)	2	0	0	0	$64,500	108
Turf(286)	0	0	0	0	$0	-
Dst(0)	0	0	0	0	$0	-

9Jan00-6GP	fst	1 1/16	:232 :464 1:114 1:434	4↑ Alw 34000N2X	102	7	76¾	54½	1½	14	112¼	Bailey J D	L119	*.30	89-20	Unbridled Jet11912¼ Bold Advantage119¾ *Little Lee*1222½	Ridden out	8
9Oct99-8Med	fst	1⅛	:46 1:09 1:331 1:452	PegasusH-G2	109	1	66¼	63½	51½	22	2no	Bailey J D	L116	*1.60	103	FortyOneCarats120no *UnbridledJet*1105¼ *TiksChep*1180½	Game duel to wire	6
8Aug99-9Sar	fst	1¼	:481 1:124 1:364 2:02	Travers-G1	89	7	62¼	61¾	5¾	89½	814	Bailey J D	L126	5.30	84-13	Lemon Drop Kid126¾ Vision and Verse1261¾ Menifee1261¾	Wide trip, tired	8
8Aug99-11Mth	gd	1⅛	:461 1:094 1:35 1:48	HsklInvH-G1	108	5	54½	53	42	42¾	41½	Castillo H Jr	L114	20.10	94-07	Menifee124½ Cat Thief123½ *Forestry*118½	Blocked taken up 1/8pl	7
7Jly99-10Mth	fst	1 1/16	:231 :461 1:10 1:423	LngBrnchBC100k	100	1	52½	31	1hd	2hd	2hd	Castillo H Jr	L114	*1.40	88-21	Ghost Story112hd Unbridled Jet1141¼ *Clever Gem*114no	Game effort	6
4Jun99-8Bel	fst	1 1/16	:23 :454 1:094 1:421	3↑ Alw 45000N2X	90	5	62	22	2½	31	44¾	Bailey J D	L116	*.60	81-24	*Crafty Man*1191¼ Qumran1141¾ King's Crown1141¾	Speed 3 wide,weakened	8
3May99-8Bel	my	1⅛	:451 1:09 1:344 1:474	PeterPan-G2	99	7	51½	63½	52	41	55	Bailey J D	L118	3.75	87-27	BestofLuck1131 TresurIslnd1141½ *LmonDropKid*1202	Bobbled start, 4 wide	9
4Apr99-6Kee	fst	1 1/16	:224 :462 1:11 1:414	Alw 51000N1X	99	4	45	45	3nk	11½	15	Bailey J D	L117	*.90	99-06	Unbridled Jet1175 Quaker Ridge1195½ Camino Cielo1178	Ridden out	6
8Nov98-9Aqu	fst	1	:24 :473 1:12 1:36	Nashua-G3	83	2	52½	53	42	45½	47¼	Gryder A T	L115	16.40	82-17	DonrlCourt115¾ SccssflAppl1226¼ ExldGroom113nk	4w move, nothing left	8
5Sep98-3Bel	fst	1	:234 :473 1:124 1:381	Alw 41000N2L	78	4	42	41¾	3½	3½	42½	Bailey J D	L119	1.60	70-33	*The Groom Is Red*119no Holmdel1191½ Glockenspiel1141	3 wide, stayed well	5
Previously trained by Rice Clyde D																		
2Aug98-9Mth	fst	6f	:212 :442 :564 1:10	Sapling-G3	69	1	6	55½	57	48	48	Wilson R	L122	11.70	84-05	Yes It's True1227¼ *Erlton*122¾ Herofthegame122no	Mild bid 4 wide	7
8Aug98-5Mth	fst	5½f	:221 :453 :581 1:044	Md Sp Wt 24k	66	5	4	42¼	33	1hd	1nk	Beckner D V	L118	*1.10	96-08	Unbridled Jet118nk Native Sailor1185 Sweep Well1181¼	Prevailed	9
5Jly98-1Mth	fst	5½f	:221 :454 :582 1:05	Md Sp Wt 24k	37	1	12	65½	67¾	712	813¾	Beckner D V	L118 b	*1.30	81-10	*TwoPunchSonny*118hd [D]*ImginrySword*1181 NghtCllr1184	Unprepared start	12
Placed 7th through disqualification																		

UNTUTTABLE (Unbridled—Tutta, by In Reality). Florida. While his sire was a source of stamina, Untuttable also has more speed influences in his pedigree, particularly because he is inbred to In Reality (4 x 2) and Gold Digger (4 x 3), the dam of Mr. Prospector. In fact, Untuttable's second dam, Gold Mine, is a full sister to Mr. Prospector. Untuttable's runners should have speed on dirt and turf and just may be able to stretch that speed from seven furlongs to 1 ¼ miles.

Untuttable
Own: Evans Edward P

Ch. h. 8 (Mar)
Sire: Unbridled (Fappiano) $200,000
Dam: Tutta (In Reality)
Br: Edward P. Evans (Va)
Tr: Hennig Mark A(0 0 0 0 .00) 2004:(321 46 .14)

Life	5	1	1	1	$32,230	82	D.Fst	2	0	0	0	$600	55
1999	5	1	1	1	$32,230	82	Wet(372)	0	0	0	0	$0	–
1998	0	M	0	0	$0	–	Turf(285)	3	1	1	1	$31,630	82
	0	0	0	0	$0	–	Dst(0)	0	0	0	0	$0	–

10Jun99-9Bel	fm	1¼	Ⓣ :494 1:143 1:384 2:021	3↑ Md Sp Wt 41k	82	1 52¼ 52½ 5¾ 2hd 12	Bravo J	L114 b	*.80	80-20	Untuttable1142 Regal Dynasty114hd Koutoubia122½	With something left 7
12May99-5Bel	fm	1	Ⓣ :221 :442 1:094 1:341	3↑ Md Sp Wt 41k	80	2 64¼ 73¾ 54 55½ 31¾	Bravo J	L114 b	6.10	85-12	*Green Fee*114¾ *Restless Fury*1141 *Untuttable*1141¼	Steadied turn, gamely 12
4Apr99-11Hia	fm	1⅛	Ⓣ 1:474	Md Sp Wt 14k	76	11 62½ 57 33 36½ 26	Castellano J J	L122 b	13.10	85-08	TmpttionBound1226 Untuttbl122nk Stokosky1229¼	Gained 2nd, no match 11
6Mar99-7GP	fst	1 1/16	:232 :473 1:132 1:463	Md Sp Wt 30k	45	1 88 84¾ 57 612 920¼	Santos J A	L122 b	39.60	54-21	*Torrid Sand*1223¾ Steel City1221 Salty Sea1223¼	Hopped st,chckd 1st tn 12
15Feb99-7GP	fst	1 1/16	:234 :473 1:124 1:452	Md Sp Wt 30k	55	4 22½ 24 33 710 916¼	Santos J A	L122 b	20.70	64-22	UpndAwy1221½ RCIndyGo1221¼ HrrngtnSnd1222½	Chased pace, gave way 12

VICAR (Wild Again—Escrow Agent, by El Gran Senor). Kentucky. Stakes-placed at 2, Vicar won the Florida Derby and Fountain of Youth Stakes and placed in the Jerome Handicap, Blue Grass, and Phoenix Breeders' Cup Stakes at 3. His 2-year-olds should mature late and be best in the fall stretching out to 1 1/16 miles.

Vicar
Own: Tafel James B

Dk. b or b. h. 8 (Feb)
Sire: Wild Again (Icecapade) $50,000
Dam: Escrow Agent (El Gran Senor)
Br: John W. Meriwether & Richard F. Leahy (Ky)
Tr: Mott William I(0 0 0 0 .00) 2004:(414 83 .20)

Life	17	4	2	3	$835,142	104	D.Fst	15	4	2	3	$823,142	104
2000	3	0	0	1	$11,486	98	Wet(360)	2	0	0	0	$12,000	93
1999	11	2	1	2	$725,900	104	Turf(311)	0	0	0	0	$0	–
	0	0	0	0	$0	–	Dst(0)	0	0	0	0	$0	–

22Jly00-9Mth	fst	1	:24 :474 1:121 1:371	3↑ SalvtrMH-G3	87	1 33½ 31 32 42½ 510¼	Ferrer J C	L115 f	1.80	78-12	LvIttoBzr1201¼ *DlwrTownship*1125 PrimDirctiv1141¾	4-wide 1/4,weakened 5
30Jun00-8Bel	fst	6f	:231 :461 :573 1:092	3↑ Alw 55000N$Y	98	1 3 41¾ 41¼ 32½ 32¼	Bailey J D	L116 f	2.05	89-13	*Successful Appeal*123½ Oro de Mexico1161¾ Vicar1163¾	Good finish outside 6
30Apr00-7GP	fst	7f	:224 :46 1:102 1:224	3↑ MiamiBeach36k	67	1 6 54½ 31 46 515½	Castellano J J	L114 f	*.80	70-25	Excellent Luck1141¾ Stormy Do114½ Certain11412¼	Stumbled st, rushed 6
Previously trained by Nafzger Carl A												
6Nov99-6GP	fst	6f	:22 :44 :554 1:074	3↑ BCSprint-G1	93	10 3 74½ 106 1011 1111½	Day P	L124 f	16.20	91 -	Artax126½ *Kona Gold*1262¾ Big Jag126½	Tired near stretch 14
16Oct99-8Kee	fst	6f	:22 :45 :562 1:082	3↑ PhoenixBC269k	101	1 5 61¾ 42 41¼ 3nk	Day P	L121 f	*1.60	100-05	*Richter Scale*117nk *Bet On Sunshine*117hd Vicar121nk	5wide bid, hung 6
18Sep99-7Bel	fst	1	:232 :464 1:114 1:353	JeromeH-G2	100	4 21 2½ 3nk 2hd 2hd	Day P	L120 f	*1.20	86-14	*Doneraile Court*117hd Vicar1202¼ Badger Gold115hd	Lost whip midstretch 7
28Aug99-7Sar	fst	7f	:213 :432 1:073 1:21	KngsBshp-G1	103	8 6 119½ 99¾ 59 45¾	Day P	L124 f	7.40	94-09	Forestry1241½ Five StarDay1153¾ *SuccessfulAppeal*124½	4 wide, good finish 12
8Aug99-8Sar	sly	1⅛	:474 1:12 1:364 1:492	JimDandy-G2	91	7 2hd 2hd 1hd 44 513	Albarado R J	L124 f	4.00	76-18	Ecton Park1165¼ *Lemon Drop Kid*1242 Badger Gold1141¾	With pace, tired 7
15May99-10Pim	fst	1 3/16	:451 1:101 1:351 1:551	Preaknss-G1	74	13 1hd 3½ 3½ 913 1020¾	Albarado R J	L126 f	24.00	68-09	Charismatic1261½ Menifee126hd *Badge*1262½	3wd trip,pressed,tired 13
1May99-8CD	fst	1¼	:474 1:122 1:372 2:031	KyDerby-G1	80	17 94½145¾ 117½ 1711 1819	Sellers S J	L126 f	8.20	70-14	*Charismatic*126nk Menifee126¾ Cat Thief1261¼	6wide trip, no threat 19
10Apr99-9Kee	fst	1⅛	:47 1:104 1:36 1:483	BlueGras-G1	104	2 1hd 2hd 3½ 1hd 31¾	Sellers S J	L123 f	2.80	90-19	Menifee1231¼ Cat Thief123½ Vicar1232½	Came again, gamely 8
13Mar99-12GP	fst	1⅛	:481 1:123 1:374 1:504	FlaDerby-G1	102	5 63¼ 41¼ 31½ 1hd 1no	Sellers S J	L122 f	4.60	83-19	Vicar122no Wondertross122½ Cat Thief1221¾	Stalked wide, gamely 10
20Feb99-6GP	fst	1 1/16	:233 :472 1:123 1:453	FntnOYth-G1	97	3 1hd 1½ 1hd 1hd 1nk	Sellers S J	L114 f	4.60	79-29	*Vicar*114nk Cat Thief119¾ Certain1172¼	Hard drive,drifted 10
16Jan99-10GP	gd	1 1/16	:242 :481 1:122 1:451	HolyBull-G3	93	2 31½ 41¾ 32 33½ 54¼	Sellers S J	L114 f	*1.20	77-23	GrtsnHrdTost1141¾ DonrlCort119no MontnRng1191¾	Bmpd st, stdy 1st trn 7
28Nov98-11CD	fst	1 1/16	:234 :482 1:13 1:44	B&WKyJC-G2	98	6 31½ 2hd 2hd 2½ 21¾	Albarado R J	L113 f	6.10	89-05	*Exploit*1221¾ Vicar1136 *Grits'n Hard Toast*1131¼	Inside, weakened late 1
4Nov98-4CD	fst	1	:224 :47 1:124 1:38	Alw 43400N1X	90	3 63½ 43½ 42 2hd 11¼	Bailey J D	121 f	*1.10	83-21	Vicar1211¼ *Karly's Harley*115½ Merkaban1181½	4 wide turn 1
14Oct98-4Kee	fst	7f	:221 :451 1:102 1:232	Md Sp Wt 38k	81	12 6 73¼ 44½ 21 11½	Peck B D	120 f	10.90e	88-13	*Vicar*1201½ Vivious1201 Iron Prince1205	5wide trip, driving 1

WAR CHANT (Danzig—Hollywood Wildcat, by Kris S.). Kentucky. With a lofty stud fee of $60,000 and bred to a quality book of mares,

War Chant is considered by many to be among this year's most promising first-crop sires. A winner of his only start at 2, War Chant won the San Rafael Stakes but really developed into a formidable turf miler at the end of his sophomore year, winning the Oak Tree Breeders' Cup Mile Stakes and Breeders' Cup Mile. While his offspring should win on dirt, sons of Danzig at stud have prospered primarily as grass sires, such as Chief's Crown, Danehill, Anabaa, and Polish Precedent. (T^2)

War Chant
Own: Cowan Marjorie and Irving M

Dk. b or b. h. 7 (May)
Sire: Danzig (Northern Dancer) $200,000
Dam: Hollywood Wildcat (Kris S.)
Br: Marjorie Cowan & Irving Cowan (Ky)
Tr: Drysdale Neil D(0 0 0 0 .00) 2004:(99 20 .20)

Life	7	5	1	0	$1,130,600	108	D.Fst	4	2	1	0	$252,200	107
2000	6	4	1	0	$1,110,800	108	Wet(437)	1	1	0	0	$120,000	103
1999	1	1	0	0	$19,800	91	Turf(415)	2	2	0	0	$758,400	108
	0	0	0	0	$0	-	Dst(0)	0	0	0	0	$0	-

4Nov00-5CD	fm	1	Ⓣ :234 :474 1:112 1:343	3↑ BCMile-G1	108	11 12 7 12 7½ 9 6¼ 9 5¼ 1nk	Stevens G L	L123	*3.50	102 -	War Chant123nk North East Bound126no Dansili126no	6 wide turn, up late 14
14Oct00-9SA	fm	1	Ⓣ :23 :461 1:10 1:333	3↑ OkTrBCMI-G2	107	6 65 54 41 2hd 1 1¼	Stevens G L	LB117	3.00	91- 17	*War Chant*117 1¼ *Road to Slew*119 2 Sharan119 2½	3wd 1/4,led, edgd away 8
6May00-8CD	fst	1¼	:454 1:094 1:353 2:01	KyDerby-G1	86	8 10 5¼ 12 7 14 7½ 10 7 9 14½	Bailey J D	L126 b	9.90	90 -	Fusaichi Pegasus126 1½ Aptitude126 4 Impeachment126½	Tired, 2nd turn 19
8Apr00 5SA	fst	1⅛	:471 1:112 1:362 1:49	SADerby-G1	107	4 21 2½ 2½ 2½ 21	Bailey J D	LB120	*2.30	89- 16	The Deputy120 1 War Chant120 2 Captain Steve120 3	Bid,led,game inside 6
4Mar00-9SA	gd	1	:231 :461 1:10 1:362	SnRafael-G2	103	1 2 1½ 1½ 1hd 1hd 1½	Desormeaux K J	LB116	*.50	89- 13	War Chant116½ Archer City Slew118nk Cocky115nk	Inside trip, gamely 6
16Jan00-2SA	fst	1 1/16	:232 :471 1:111 1:42	Alw 54000N1x	104	2 1½ 1hd 1½ 1 1½ 15	Desormeaux K J	LB117	*.60	93- 10	*War Chant*117 5 *Reba's Gold*118 8 Smooth116 1	Inside, ridden out 8
28Nov99-8Hol	fst	6f	:223 :46 :581 1:103	Md Sp Wt 33k	91	9 1 4¾ 3½ 11 12	Bailey J D	B120	*1.10	84- 18	*War Chant*120 2 Ladir120 1½ Strollin120 1	4 wide,stdy handling 9

WESTERN EXPRESSION (Gone West—Tricky Game, by Majestic Light). New York. Second in the Carter Handicap, Western Expression is a half-brother to multiple turf stakes winner King Cugat. His runners should have good speed at 2 on all surfaces, but with the Gone West/Majestic Light cross, they are particularly well-suited for grass. His dam, Tricky Game, is a full sister to stakes winner Stacked Pack, and a half-sister to Seeking the Gold and Fast Play. (SP/HT^2)

Western Expression
Own: Flying Zee Stable

Dk. b or b. h. 8 (Apr)
Sire: Gone West (Mr. Prospector) $150,000
Dam: Tricky Game (Majestic Light)
Br: Dinwiddie Farm (Ky)
Tr: Martin Jose(0 0 0 0 .00) 2004:(0 0 .00)

Life	16	3	2	3	$140,114	107	D.Fst	15	3	2	3	$140,114	107
2000	11	2	1	2	$108,574	107	Wet(327)	0	0	0	0	$0	-
1999	5	1	1	1	$31,540	95	Turf(317)	1	0	0	0	$0	94
	0	0	0	0	$0	-	Dst(0)	0	0	0	0	$0	-

25Nov00-8Aqu	fst	1	:23 :454 1:10 1:343	3↑ CigarMiH-G1	83	5 10 10 10 10 11 7 10 10 9 15¼	Arroyo N Jr	L112	122.50	80- 17	*ElCorredor*116 1¾ *PeepingTom*111nk *AffirmedSuccss*120 3½	Wide, no response 11
4Nov00-4Aqu	fst	7f	:222 :45 1:091 1:214	3↑ SportPgH-G3	98	6 2 1hd 1hd 3 1½ 5 4½	Gryder A T	L114 b	4.80	86- 12	*Stalwart Member*117 1 *Istintaj*117 2½ Mister Tricky112¾	Speed outside, tired 6
Previously trained by Serpe Philip M												
27Sep00-8Bel	fst	6f	:224 :452 :571 1:093	3↑ Alw 47000N3x	85	5 3 2½ 22 25 37	Prado E S	L119 f	1.55	83- 17	Enteprnur120 5¾ Ordind119 1¼ WstrnExprssion119nk	Chased outside, tired 5
26Aug00-6Sar	fst	6f	:222 :45 :571 1:101	3↑ Alw 47000N3x	95	2 4 21 2hd 1hd 3nk	Prado E S	L121 f	*3.00	94- 09	*Enteprnur*117nk SunCt117hd WstrnExprssion121nk	Between rivals, gamely 9
9Aug00-9Sar	fst	6f	:213 :443 :563 1:091	3↑ AGVndbtH-G2	96	5 4 7 10 76 7 3¼ 56	Chavez J F	L112 f	8.60	93- 13	[D]Intidb117hd SuccssfulAppl118 3½ ChsinWimmin112 2	Wide move, no rally 8
4Jly00-8Bel	gd	1	Ⓣ :232 :462 1:093 1:34	3↑ PokerH-G3	94	10 35 3 3½ 32 4 3½ 8 6¼	Bridgmohan S X	L112 f	23.10	82- 12	*Affirmed Success*117 1¾ Rabi114½ Weatherbird113 1¾	Chased outside, tired 10
29May00-9Bel	fst	1	:23 :452 1:10 1:343	3↑ MtropltH-G1	72	1 5 1¾ 43 5 1½ 7 10 7 22¾	Prado E S	L113 f	25.25	69- 19	Yankee Victor117 4¾ *Honest Lady*112¾ *Sir Bear*117¾	Speed inside, empty 8
7May00-8Aqu	fst	7f	:222 :45 1:09 1:213	3↑ CarterH-G1	107	6 4 42 31 1hd 2hd	Prado E S	L113 f	21.70	92 18	BrtllFrnk116hd WstrnEprssn113½ *AffrmdSccss*122 1½	Speed 3 wide, gamely 7
8Apr00-8Aqu	fst	1	:23 :452 1:081 1:341	3↑ WschstrH-G3	99	6 2½ 21 2½ 2 2½ 4 5¾	Prado E S	L113	4.30	91- 17	*YnkVictor*115 3¾ *GoldnMss*116 2 WtchmnsWrnng113no	Tried winner 1/4 pole 7
4Mar00-4GP	fst	7f	:24 :472 1:122 1:242	4↑ Alw 40000N3L	97	4 3 2½ 1 1½ 12 1 4¾	Bailey J D	L119	*.40	78- 27	WstrnExprssion119 4¾ JolisIntntion117hd CllndJk117 8¼	Off rail, ridden out 5
29Jan00-1GP	fst	6f	:223 :451 :571 1:092	4↑ Alw 32000N2L	96	4 4 1½ 1½ 13 14	Bailey J D	L122	*.60	92- 13	*WesternExpression*122 4 *Suntee*119½ Actspectations122hd	Inside, ridden out 8
Previously trained by Donk David												
20Jun99-5Bel	fst	1 1/16	:224 :453 1:091 1:413	3↑ Alw 43000N1x	74	3 3 1½ 2½ 21 4 3½ 6 11¼	Bailey J D	L112	*.85	78- 16	PleasntBreeze119¾ *GhostStory*115 6½ WetherCll111nk	Between rivals, tired 7
5Jun99-11Bel	fst	1	:224 :452 1:093 1:354	Alw 43000N2L	95	4 1½ 11 1hd 1½ 2¾	Bailey J D	L114 b	4.90	84- 06	Qumrn114¾ WestrnExprssion114 3½ AlpinMicky114½	Dug in gamely on rail 12
16May99-7Bel	fst	7f	:222 :452 1:101 1:23	3↑ Alw 42000N1x	90	10 6 5 1¼ 5 1¼ 1hd 3nk	Bailey J D	L113 b	5.10	87- 19	KingsCrown113hd LionHrtd113nk WstrnExprsson113 3	Split rivals, gamely 11
6Mar99-10GP	fst	7f	:22 :443 1:103 1:234	Alw 32000N1x	39	5 4 42 43 8 11 8 24	Bailey J D	122 b	*1.10	57- 20	*Yankee Victor*119 3 *Hector*119 4½ *Birdshot*119nk	Bmpd hard st, 5 wide 9
13Feb99-7GP	fst	6f	:221 :454 :582 1:112	Md Sp Wt 30k	85	2 9 3 1½ 2hd 1 2½ 1 3¾	Bailey J D	122 b	*1.60	85- 16	WstrnEprssn122 3¾ LksGdtM122 1¼ Inllprbblty122 1½	Hopped st, drew clear 10

WISED UP (Dixieland Band—Wising Up, by Smarten). Florida. A proven stakes performer on the turf, Wised Up won the Fort Marcy Handicap. His dam is also a half-sister to turf stakes winner Foresta. The majority of Dixieland Band's offspring have speed (Dixie Union, Citidancer, Dixie Brass, Dixieland Heat), and Wised Up was bred to Florida-based mares from brilliant sire lines (In Reality, Mr. Prospector, Copelan), so expect his 2-year-olds to have speed on all surfaces. (SP^2)

Wised Up
Own: Ewald Wayne R

B. h. 9 (Apr)
Sire: Dixieland Band (Northern Dancer) $50,000
Dam: Wising Up (Smarten)
Br: Fares Farms, Inc. (Ky)
Tr: DeStasio Richard A(0 0 0 0 .00) 2004:(70 2 .03)

Life	19	4	2	7	$233,537	105	D.Fst	8	2	1	3	$54,180	85
2000	1	0	0	1	$12,408	105	Wet(366)	1	0	1	0	$5,250	76
1999	11	3	0	3	$189,539	102	Turf(317)	10	2	0	4	$174,107	105
	0	0	0	0	$0	-	Dst(0)	0	0	0	0	$0	-

6May00-8Aqu fm	1 1/16	Ⓣ	:232 :473 1:103 1:404	3↑ FtMarcyH-G3	105	5	44	41	31½	21½	31½	Espinoza J L	L114	18.60	103-01	Spindrift1151½ Middlesex Drive118hd Wised Up1141¾	Inside move, gamely	9
30Oct99-8Aqu fm	1⅛	Ⓣ	:494 1:131 1:37 1:49	3↑ KnkrbkrH-G2	89	6	2½	2½	2½	53¼	64¾	Espinoza J L	L114	6.30	93-08	ChrgedAffirs114hd *ComicStrip*1191 NtsBigPrty1131	Between rivals, empty	7
16Oct99-8Bel gd	1	Ⓣ	:232 :46 1:101 1:352	3↑ KelsoH-G2	99	6	54¼	64¼	54¼	45¼	35	Espinoza J L	L113	13.30	76-24	MddlsxDrv1171½ DvdndConqr1143½ WsdUp1131½	Wide move, game finish	10
25Sep99-8Bel fm	1⅛	[T]	:482 1:123 1:37 1:491	3↑ BelBCH-G2	101	8	51½	52	52¾	41	31½	Espinoza J L	L112	42.50	80-24	With the Flow114½ Comic Strip1181 Wised Up112¾	Rated 3 wide, gamely	9
12Aug99-3Sar fm	1⅛	Ⓣ	:47 1:102 1:34 1:46	4↑ Alw 49000n4x	95	3	42	41¾	41¾	42¾	53¾	Espinoza J L	L122 r	10.70	96-05	StrConncton117½ DvdndCnqr1172 KtsndYts1171¼	Saved ground,no punch	7
30Jly99-8Sar fm	1⅛	Ⓣ	:47 1:104 1:343 1:462	3↑ BBaruchH-G2	75	3	45	44½	61¾	88¼	813¼	Luzzi M J	L113 r	11.50	85-02	Middlesex Drive117nk Tangazi114½ *Comic Strip*116hd	Between rivals, tired	8
3Jly99-7Bel fm	1	Ⓣ	:231 :452 1:084 1:324	3↑ PokerH-G3	102	6	56½	56½	45	34	32¾	Luzzi M J	L115 r	11.50	91-13	Rob 'n Gin1182 *Bomfim*115¾ Wised Up1153	Game finish on rail	8
5Jun99-7Bel fm	1¼	[T]	:464 1:111 1:344 1:582	3↑ ManhttnH-G1	83	2	56	52	84¾	85¼	911½	Luzzi M J	L113	17.90	87-04	*Yagli*1222½ Federal Trial116nk Middlesex Drive1162	Tired after 3/4s	10
8May99-8Aqu sf	1 1/16	Ⓣ	:241 :49 1:132 1:45	3↑ FtMarcyH-G3	100	4	66	65	53½	3½	1hd	Luzzi M J	L112	31.50	86-14	Wised Up112hd *N B Forrest*116nk La-Faah1141¼	Rough trip,got there	11
24Apr99-7Aqu gd	1 1/16	Ⓣ	:224 :463 1:121 1:441	3↑ Alw 45000n2x	94	1	56½	49½	52½	2hd	11½	Luzzi M J	L119	9.50	90-10	*Wised Up*1191½ Sheikh Rattle121no Ay Rouge119¾	Split rivals, driving	10
3Apr99-7Aqu fst	7f		:224 :453 1:091 1:214	3↑ Alw 44000n2x	85	5	6	41¾	4¾	37	411½	Douglas R R	L120	3.70	81-15	BlackCash11810¾ KaneKati120nk QuietYnkee120½	Speed 4 wide,weakened	8
17Mar99-7Aqu fst	6f		:222 :451 :573 1:10	4↑ Alw 42000n2L	80	3	4	4¾	41½	2½	14¼	Douglas R R	L116	3.20	88-14	WisdUp1164¼ DvilsRnsom1162¼ ThundrPunch121½	Bumped soundly start	8
Previously trained by Motion H Graham																		
26Aug98-2Sar fst	7f		:224 :454 1:104 1:24	Clm 35000(35-30)	79	5	3	31	3½	1hd	21	Davis R G	L117 f	6.00	84-17	*Euroclydon*1171 *WisedUp*1171¼ MissionryMonk1172	3w, gamely, vanned off	6
25Jly98-9Lrl fst	1 1/16		:231 :464 1:13 1:45	3↑ Alw 27000n1x	61	3	713	615	67	59½	410½	Verge M E	L114	*1.80	75-16	Pentakato1174½ Sportin' Tricks113no Veater1176	Wide, lugged in	8
2Jly98-8Lrl fst	1 1/16		:24 :473 1:121 1:443	Alw 27000n1x	70	5	21	21½	21	4nk	32¼	Verge M E	L115	2.50	86-12	Prospects Copper1152 Craic115nk Wised Up115½	Promptd pace,held well	6
24May98-6Pim fst	6f		:231 :47 :592 1:122	Alw 25000n1x	73	1	3	1hd	1hd	3½	3¾	Verge M E	L120	*.90	82-15	BltimorGry117¾ GmsProspct120no WisdUp1206¼	Bmpd,dueled ins,gamely	6
10May98-6Pim sly	6f		:23 :462 :593 1:122	3↑ Alw 25000n1x	76	5	5	35½	35½	3½	2½	Verge M E	L114	2.70	82-15	Sticktothbordr117½ WisdUp1144 TkEvryChnc1101	Hustld 4w,bid 1/8,hung	7
19Apr98-5Pim fst	6f		:233 :471 :594 1:122	3↑ Md Sp Wt 20k	71	8	1	1hd	1hd	1½	13½	Verge M E	114	3.90	83-19	Wised Up1143½ Polish Star122¾ *Furaha*1222	Dueled 2w, drove clear	10
28Mar98-5Lrl fst	6f		:23 :464 :591 1:12	Md Sp Wt 20k	64	2	5	54	43	43	34¼	Verge M E	120	5.90	78-20	SkeetsCshdvnce1203 ThreMilDriv1201¼ *WisdUp*1202	Move btw 5/16,willing	7

YANKEE VICTOR (Saint Ballado—Highest Carol, by Caro). Kentucky. Saint Ballado is a high-speed influence, and his runners have been strong milers, such as Metropolitan Handicap winner Yankee Victor. From the female family that produced Jolie's Halo and Mister Jolie, expect Yankee Victor to be an excellent sire of 2-year-olds that will be most effective from six furlongs to 1 1/16 miles on all surfaces. (HT^2)

YES IT'S TRUE (Is It True—Clever Monique, by Clever Trick). Florida. From a sire line known for high speed (Is It True-Raja Baba-Bold Ruler), Yes It's True was naturally quick at 2, winning the Sapling, Hollywood Juvenile Championship, Kentucky Breeders' Cup, and WHAS-11 Stakes. A leading sprinter at 3, he captured the Frank J. De Francis Memorial Dash, Maryland Breeders' Cup Handicap, and Riva Ridge, Lafayette, Swale, and

Jersey Shore Breeders' Cup Stakes. His Florida-bred 2-year-olds should get off to a fast start winning from three furlongs to $1^1/_{16}$ miles. (SP^2)

Yankee Victor
Own: Binn Moreton, Enllomar Stable, et al

Dk. b or b. r. 8 (Feb)
Sire: Saint Ballado (Halo) $125,000
Dam: Highest Carol (Caro*Ire)
Br: R. G. Lundock DVM (Fla)
Tr: Morales Carlos J(0 0 0 0 .00) 2004:(40 4 .10)

Life	19	8	3	1	$833,806	116	D.Fst	17	8	3	1	$823,006	116
2000	7	4	1	0	$588,450	116	Wet(353)	2	0	0	0	$10,800	96
1999	9	3	1	1	$208,786	104	Turf(296)	0	0	0	0	$0	-
	0	0	0	0	$0	-	Dst(0)	0	0	0	0	$0	-

25Jun00-8AP	fst	1	:233 :462 1:102 1:344	3↑HanshinH-G3	105	4	12	14	11	14	13¾	Castillo H Jr	L122 b	*.10	95-16	[D]Yankee Victor122¾ Bright Valour1142¼ *Desert Demon*1132¼	Ridden out	5
Disqualified and placed 5th																		
29May00-9Bel	fst	1	:23 :452 1:10 1:343	3↑MtropltH-G1	115	8	21	1hd	1½	13½	14¾	Castillo H Jr	L117 b	4.30	92-19	Yankee Victor1174¾ *Honest Lady*112¾ *Sir Bear*117¾	When roused, driving	8
6May00-3Aqu	fst	1	:224 :45 1:082 1:332	4↑Alw 57000N2Y	116	1	1hd	1½	11½	15	14¾	Castillo H Jr	L123 b	*.40	101-15	*Yankee Victor*1234¾ Conflict1231¼ Deputy Diamond10815¾	As rider pleased	5
8Apr00-8Aqu	fst	1	:23 :452 1:081 1:341	3↑WschstrH-G3	110	3	1½	11	1½	12½	13¾	Castillo H Jr	L115 b	7.00	97-17	*YnkVictor*1153¾ *GoldnMissil*1162 WtchmnsWrnng113no	Pace, clear, driving	7
11Mar00-11GP	fst	1$\frac{1}{16}$	:234 :47 1:111 1:444	3↑CrmFrchH-G3	104	8	1½	1½	1hd	1hd	21	Prado E S	L113 b	6.30	83-23	DncingGuy1201 *YnkeeVictor*113hd *MidwyMgistrt*1172½	Pressured, held well	8
5Feb00-8GP	fst	1$\frac{1}{16}$	:232 :482 1:123 1:442	4↑Alw 38000N4X	100	5	11½	1½	11	13	13	Prado E S	L117 b	2.20	86-18	Yankee Victor1173 Adonis1171¾ Certain1171¾	Bmpd st, edged clear	8
9Jan00-9GP	fst	7f	:214 :434 1:084 1:222	4↑Alw 45000N$Y	82	6	4	3½	31½	24	68½	Chavez J F	L115 b	*1.10	79-15	Call Me Mr. Vain1151½ Powerful Goer1191¼ Limestone1153½	3 wide, tired	10
11Dec99-8Aqu	fst	1$\frac{3}{16}$ [•]	:471 1:111 1:354 1:55	3↑QeensCoH-G3	102	6	11½	11	1½	2hd	32	Castillo H Jr	L114 b	3.70	95-12	*EarlyWarning*1162 *DocMartin*112hd YankeeVictor114hd	Set pace, weakened	7
27Nov99-8Aqu	my	1	:222 :443 1:084 1:34	3↑CigarMiH-G1	96	4	1½	11½	21	35	56¾	Dominguez R A	L113 b	47.50	91-11	*Affirmed Success*1185 Adonis115¾ Honorifico1131	Set pace rail, tired	9
1Nov99-7Del	fst	1⅛	:48 1:114 1:363 1:491	Hcp 40000	99	3	1½	11	12	14	11	Dominguez R A	L119 b	*1.10	94-17	Yankee Victor1191 Lyracist1162¾ Test Pilot112½	Won in handy fashion	7
9Oct99-3Bel	fst	7f	:233 :463 1:102 1:224	3↑Alw 47000N3X	98	4	3	2½	2hd	2½	41¾	Velazquez J R	L114 b	*.90	86-11	*Pooska Hill*117hd *Adonis*114½ *Driver*1171¼	With pace, outfinished	6
13Jun99-7Del	wf	1$\frac{1}{16}$	:23 :462 1:111 1:423	LRichards200k	72	4	22½	33½	23	712	818½	Santos J A	L115	*.70	75-19	StellarBrush1141¼ SmartGuy1159 SuccessfulAppel1222½	Chased, faltered	8
8May99-8Haw	fst	1⅛	:463 1:102 1:353 1:482	IllDerby-G2	99	9	1½	1½	1½	11	42½	Sellers S J	L117 b	*2.30	111-07	VisionndVerse1141¼ PrimeDirctiv117hd Pinff1221¼	Weakened late stretch	10
18Apr99-8Kee	fst	1$\frac{1}{16}$	:231 :464 1:103 1:41	Lexingtn-G2	104	9	21	2½	1hd	1hd	22½	Sellers S J	L115 b	5.00	100-07	*Charismatic*1152½ Yankee Victor115¾ Finder's Gold1152	Pressed, gamely	12
27Mar99 10TP	fst	1$\frac{1}{16}$	:232 :473 1:12 1:424	Rushaway61k	99	2	43½	31½	2hd	1hd	11	Sellers S J	L112 b	*1.60	89-15	YnkeeVictor1121 BlckMercury1124 Prshing1151½	Bumped, 4 wide, drivng	6
6Mar99-10GP	fst	7f	:22 :443 1:103 1:234	Alw 32000N1X	90	1	7	31½	31½	2hd	13	Velazquez J R	L119 b	2.60	81-20	*Yankee Victor*1193 *Hector*1194½ *Birdshot*119nk	Angled out,drew clear	9
17Oct98-12Crc	fst	1$\frac{1}{16}$	:23 :471 1:123 1:47	[R]FSNReality408k	66	14	95½	32	21½	24	511½	Coa E M	L120 b	*1.60	69-21	TenPoundTest1202¾ *Comeonmom*1201½ GradeOne1205	Wide 1st turn, tired	16
6Sep98-6Sar	fst	7f	:222 :46 1:11 1:233	Md Sp Wt 35k	89	3	7	1½	1hd	11	13	Chavez J F	L117 b	10.20	87-14	YnkeeVictor1173 DonrilCourt1175¾ GonFishin1173½	Clear, something left	12
8Aug98-9Crc	fst	5½f	:222 :462 :592 1:062	Md Sp Wt 25k	64	7	3	21½	2½	22½	22	Castellano J J	L116 b	22.10	90-15	PressType1162 *YnkeeVictor*116hd FortyOneCrts1165½	Bumped st, 2nd best	10

Yes It's True
Own: Padua Stables

B. h. 8 (Mar)
Sire: Is It True (Raja Baba) $8,500
Dam: Clever Monique (Clever Trick)
Br: George Waggoner Stables Inc. (Ky)
Tr: Lukas D. W(0 0 0 0 .00) 2004:(427 48 .11)

Life	22	11	2	3	$1,080,700	118	D.Fst	20	10	2	3	$1,055,624	118
2000	2	0	0	0	$0	70	Wet(370)	2	1	0	0	$25,076	42
1999	11	6	0	2	$616,580	118	Turf(303)	0	0	0	0	$0	-
Aik(T)	0	0	0	0	$0	-	Dst(T)(360)	0	0	0	0	$0	-

20May00-9Pim	gd	6f	:231 :461 :582 1:104	3↑MdBCH-G3	42	5	7	4¾	43	716	723	Desormeaux K J	L117	2.30	69-13	DrMx113no MoonOverProspect114nk Crucibl1131¾	Bobbled start, stopped	7
6May00-4CD	fst	7f	:214 :434 1:081 1:212	4↑WnrcomH-G2	70	1	5	31	64	78½	714¾	Bailey J D	L117	7.80	83-01	Straight Man112hd Mula Gula1143¼ Patience Game114hd	Inside, gave way	7
16Oct99-8Kee	fst	6f	:22 :45 :562 1:082	3↑PhoenixBC269k	50	3	1	3nk	53½	67¼	619½	Antley C W	L121	2.10	80-05	*Richter Scale*117nk *Bet OnSunshine*117hd Vicar121nk	Dueled, gave way badly	6
28Aug99-7Sar	fst	7f	:213 :432 1:073 1:21	KngsBshp-G1	41	2	8	32	48½	1224	1233½	Bailey J D	L124	2.80	66-09	Forestry1241½ FiveStarDay1153¾ *SuccessfulAppel*124½	Chased, tired badly	12
11Aug99-9Sar	fst	6f	:224 :452 :57 1:09	3↑APhenomH-G2	109	5	1	2½	2hd	3½	34¼	Bailey J D	L117	*.75	92-12	Intidab1131½ Artax1172¾ Yes It's True117½	Between foes,weakened	7
17Jly99-9Lrl	fst	6f	:22 :444 :563 1:083	3↑DeFrncsM-G1	106	6	2	32½	31	2hd	1¾	Bailey J D	L114	*.70	99-06	YesIt'sTrue114¾ GoodandTough1233 *StormPunch*114½	3-wide turn, driving	6
19Jun99-9Mth	fst	6f	:212 :433 :554 1:082	JerShrBC-G3	106	3	1	1hd	2hd	12	17	Bailey J D	L122	*.20	100-09	*Yes It'sTrue*1227 Erlton1224¼ FlyingGriffoni1124¼	Impressive performance	4
5Jun99-6Bel	fst	7f	:224 :45 1:092 1:221	RivaRidg-G2	103	4	3	2½	1hd	1½	11	Bailey J D	L123	*.75	91-10	*YesItsTrue*1231 LionHearted114nk *SilverSeson*1131¼	Dug in gamely,driving	8
15May99-7Pim	fst	6f	:231 :453 :571 1:091	3↑MdBCH-G3	118	2	4	1hd	1hd	13	14¾	Bailey J D	L113	*1.20	99-06	*YesItsTrue*1134¾ TheTrdersEcho109½ PurplePssion114¾	Rail, pace, driving	8
24Apr99-9CD	fst	1	:23 :461 1:112 1:374	DerbyTrl-G3	95	9	31	21	2hd	22½	45½	Bailey J D	L122	*1.90	75-24	PtienceGme1162¼ PrimDirctiv1222¾ StrightMn116½	Bobbled slightly,tired	9
7Apr99-0Kee	fst	7f	:221 :442 1:091 1:22	Lafayett-G3	104	2	1	1hd	1hd	13½	15	Bailey J D	L123	*.20	92-10	Yes It's True1235 Trickey Crew1181½ FortLaRoca1156½	Dueled, ridden out	5
13Mar99-5GP	fst	7f	:22 :44 1:083 1:221	Swale-G3	103	1	3	2hd	2hd	1hd	1hd	Bailey J D	L122	3.70	89-12	*YesItsTrue*122hd TexsGlitter1175½ LuckyRoberto1191	Dueled, bumped late	5
6Feb99-5SA	fst	7f	:222 :45 1:092 1:22	SnVicnte-G2	88	2	1	1½	2hd	31½	37¼	Stevens G L	LB123	1.70	88-09	Exploit123nk Aristotle1167 *Yes It's True*123	Dueled, weakened	3
7Nov98-4CD	fst	1$\frac{1}{16}$	:231 :463 1:113 1:44	BCJuven-G1	67	3	1hd	1½	1hd	99½	1117½	Stevens G L	L122	10.10e	73-07	Answer Lively122hd Aly's Alley122¾ Cat Thief1225½	Dueled, gave way	13
18Oct98-8Kee	fst	1$\frac{1}{16}$	:223 :454 1:111 1:44	BrdrsFut-G2	91	2	32	36	33	21	33¾	Sellers S J	L121	*.90	84-20	Cat Thief121nk *Answer Lively*1213½ Yes It's True1214½	3 wide, bid, tired	8
20Sep98-9Bel	fst	1	:24 :473 1:121 1:372	Futurity-G1	91	3	1½	1hd	11	12	2½	Sellers S J	L122	*.20	76-26	LemonDropKid122½ YesItsTrue1229 MedievilHro1225	Pace, clear, gamely	5
22Aug98-9Mth	fst	6f	:212 :442 :564 1:10	Sapling-G3	90	2	2	1hd	1hd	12½	17¼	Sellers S J	L122	*.30	92-05	Yes It's True1227¼ *Erlton*122¾ Heroofthegame122no	Much the best stretch	7
19Jly98-6Hol	fst	6f	:213 :441 :563 1:092	HolJuvCh-G3	97	1	4	1½	11½	12	16	Bailey J D	LB120	*.60	90-13	*YesItsTrue*1206 OReyFntsm117hd *WorldlyMnnr*117½	Rail,vigorous handling	7
27Jun98-9CD	fst	6f	:213 :444 :572 1:103	BshfdMnr-G3	81	1	2	1hd	2hd	2½	21¾	Day P	121	*.20e	88-10	*Time Bandit*1151¾ *Yes It's True*1211¼ *Haus of Dehere*115nk	Dueled, 2nd best	8
25May98-9CD	fst	5½f	:221 :453 :572 1:033	KyBC138k	97	4	1	11	1hd	12	11¼	Sellers S J	121	*.20e	101-12	Yes It's True1211¼ *Tactical Cat*1154 *Alannan*1152½	Led throughout	8
2May98-3CD	fst	5f	:22 :45 :573	WHAS-11120k	88	2	2	1½	11	11	1no	Day P	117	*.40e	100-03	*Yes It's True*117no Tactical Cat1174 Alannan117nk	Headed, equalld record	9
17Apr98-3Kee	gd	4½f	:22 :452 :514	Md Sp Wt 38k	–	6	2	14½		16	15	Bailey J D	118	1.80	97-09	*YesItsTrue*1185 *DytimeRobbery*1185 SrtogSummr1183½	Drew clear, handily	9

2005 FRESHMAN SIRES

ADIOS MY FRIEND (Maria's Mon—Adios, by Devil's Bag). New York. A winner of four of 17 starts, he is by a champion 2-year-old and sire of Monarchos. His dam is a half-sister to stakes winners Secret Hello, Silent Account, Hadif, and By Your Leave. Since

Maria's Mon is by Wavering Monarch, and damsire Devil's Bag is a turf influence, Adios My Friend is an HT^2 sire.

Adios My Friend
Own: Englander Richard A

Gr/ro. h. 6 (Jan)
Sire: Maria's Mon (Wavering Monarch) $35,000
Dam: Adios (Devil's Bag)
Br: Mill Ridge Farm, Ltd. (Ky)
Tr: Lake Scott A(0 0 0 0 .00) 2004:(1198 261 .22)

Life	17	4	2	2	$79,814	84	D.Fst	13	4	1	2	$73,654 84
2002	1	0	0	0	$600	58	Wet(358)	4	0	1	0	$6,160 82
2001	15	4	2	1	$76,694	84	Turf(296)	0	0	0	0	$0 -
Aik ⓣ	0	0	0	0	$0	-	Dstⓣ(315)	0	0	0	0	$0 -

25Jan02-7CT my 7f :233 :471 1:131 1:273 4↑ Alw 20000N2X 58 3 1 31 23 412 513¼ Kravets J L115 3.50 70-25 Wager Due120no *Josh's Apple*1164¾ Avellino1174¾ Failed to respond 9
26Dec01-10Pha fst 7f :221 :451 1:103 1:241 Clm 25000(25-20) 52 7 2 53¼ 42½ 108¼ 1012¼ Flores J L L120 *1.20 70-17 Northern Castle1201 *Panther Pond*1201½ Kenny K118no Tired 11
8Dec01-7CT sly 7f :23 :463 1:12 1:254 3↑ Alw 21500N2X 82 1 1 2½ 23 23 22¾ Dunkelberger T L L119 *.80 90-16 Westerly1162¾ AdiosMyFriend119¾ JoshsApple1161¾ No match,held place 8
25Nov01-7Pha fst 6f :213 :441 :57 1:11 3↑ Alw 20000N1X 84 2 5 1hd 1hd 11½ 11½ Flores J L L117 *.70e 84-21 AdiosMyFriend1171½ WowMan119no Beckelmn1191¼ Off rail, steady drive 9
10Nov01-10Pha fst 6½f :223 :454 1:104 1:171 3↑ Alw 20000N1X 81 3 3 2½ 1½ 2hd 32½ Flores J L L117 3.70 83-19 CountrySBest1172½ FstLin117no *AdiosMyFrind*1173 Dueled rail, weakened 10
23Oct01-10Pha fst 6½f :22 :443 1:102 1:173 3↑ Clm 15000(15-13)N3L 74 5 1 51¾ 42½ 12 13¾ Flores J L L117 2.50 84-19 Adios My Friend1173¾ All Faithful1204¼ Beau Dashes120¾ Drew out 11
5Oct01-2Pim fst 1 1/16 :231 :46 1:102 1:45 3↑ Clm 25000(25-20)N3L 71 2 1hd 2hd 22½ 25½ 57 Johnston M T L119 *1.70 81-17 ClssicInvestment117½ *KrnlK*1194¼ Howydoinhon115no Vied rail, weakened 7
25Sep01-4Del sly 1 1/16 ⊗ :233 :473 1:113 1:442 3↑ Alw 25000s 66 3 21½ 21 21 34 49¾ Johnston M T L119 1.50 75-16 *Excuse My French*1164 Old Black Coyote1193 Obill1192¾ Tired after 3/4 5
7Sep01-3Pim fst 1 1/16 :244 :501 1:151 1:461 Clm 25000(25-20) 70 2 11½ 1½ 1½ 12 15½ Johnston M T L117 *.90 82-16 AdiosMyFriend1175½ GlideOnIn1191½ *ProspctLovr*1177½ Rail, pace, handily 5
19Aug01-3Pim fst 1 1/16 :231 :471 1:123 1:453 3↑ Clm 20000(25-20)N2L 72 2 44 34 2½ 2½ 22½ Johnston M T L118 *1.70 82-18 ChmpgnTony1242½ *AdosMyFrnd*1188 PolshOtlw1221 Inside bid, weakened 8
Previously trained by Schosberg Richard
22Jly01-8Pha fst 170 :231 :464 1:113 1:431 3↑ Alw 20000N1X 61 4 33 2hd 21 35 410 Flores J L L115 2.60 74-17 Photonic1191½ Loophole1145½ Majic Lite1193 Weakened 7
30Jun01-5Bel fst 1⅛ :461 1:104 1:36 1:481 3↑ Alw 44000N1X 55 4 1½ 2hd 2hd 612 723¼ Velazquez J R L116 5.50 66-10 *Ahpo Here*121nk Pure Prize1162¼ Equinox1166¾ Between rivals, tired 8
15Jun01-5Bel fst 7f :22 :443 1:09 1:214 3↑ Alw 43000N2L 56 8 1 34½ 35 411 421¾ Bailey J D L116 3.20 72-08 Not Wild11617¾ Source1162¼ Cobra Celtic1161¾ 3 wide, drifted str 8
25Feb01-9Lrl fst 1 1/16 :244 :494 1:142 1:462 Herat55k 76 4 21 2hd 2hd 36 413½ Dunkelberger T L L115 6.70 63-31 Mrcino1179¼ Unccountedle1154 *DissidentShh*115nk Vied btw,brf lead,wknd 6
10Feb01-5Aqu fst 1 1/16 ⊡ :231 :48 1:131 1:452 Md Sp Wt 42k 82 7 1hd 1½ 1½ 15 18 Arroyo N Jr L120 7.20 79-21 AdiosMyFrind1208 ChrmngMchl1203½ SpclSnt1202¼ Vied outside, driving 9
24Jan01-9Aqu sly 6f ⊡ :222 :451 :571 1:094 Md Sp Wt 41k 35 2 9 73¼ 710 714 716¼ Gryder A T L120 7.00 80-11 Stake Runner1205¾ Special Saint1201 *Greased Bullet*120½ Had no rally 10
17May00-8Hol fst 4½f :223 :462 :524 Md c-(40-35) 51 5 9 65¾ 46 35½ Rodriguez A C LB118 3.50 85-16 BenedictA.Kite1183½ MyKing'sStar1132 AdiosMyFriend1181½ Bit tight 3/8 10
Claimed from Herbert Michael W. for $40,000, Treece Charles S Trainer 2000(as of 5/17): (-)

ALBERT THE GREAT (Go for Gin—Bright Feather, by Fappiano). Kentucky. Far and away the best runner by Kentucky Derby winner Go for Gin, Albert the Great got better with age and his offspring should also be most effective at 3 and 4. Keep in mind that Go for Gin is a strong HT^2 sire, and runners by Albert the Great could offer good value on grass.

Albert the Great
Own: Farmer Tracy

B. h. 7 (May)
Sire: Go for Gin (Cormorant) $7,500
Dam: Bright Feather (Fappiano)
Br: Albert Clay (Ky)
Tr: Zito Nicholas P(0 0 0 0 .00) 2004:(329 53 .16)

Life	22	8	6	4	$3,012,490	119	D.Fst	21	8	6	4	$3,012,490 11
2001	9	3	4	1	$1,740,000	119	Wet(373)	1	0	0	0	$0 7
2000	13	5	2	3	$1,272,490	119	Turf(312)	0	0	0	0	$0 -
Aik ⓣ	0	0	0	0	$0	-	Dstⓣ(353)	0	0	0	0	$0 -

27Oct01-10Bel fst 1¼ :47 1:111 1:354 2:003 3↑ BCClasic-G1 114 9 2½ 11 11 2½ 31¾ Chavez J F L126 13.00 89-12 Tiznow126no *Sakhee*1261¾ Albert the Great1262¾ 4 wide bid, willingly 1
6Oct01-10Bel fst 1¼ :462 1:102 1:36 2:012 3↑ JkyClbGC-G1 94 6 42½ 2½ 32 410 419¾ Stevens G L L126 *1.20 67-21 Aptitude12610 Generous Rosi126¾ Country Be Gold1269 Wide move, tired
8Sep01-9Bel fst 1⅛ :463 1:101 1:343 1:472 3↑ Woodward-G1 111 4 1½ 1½ 1½ 1½ 21 Chavez J F L126 *1.30 92-14 Lido Palace1261 Albert the Great126½ Tiznow1268¼ Set pace, gamely
28Jly01-6Sar fst 1⅛ :463 1:101 1:344 1:474 3↑ WhitneyH-G1 111 7 42½ 32½ 2½ 2½ 22 Chavez J F L124 *.80 100 - *Lido Palace*1152 Albert the Great124nk Gander113nk 3 wide trip, gamely
1Jly01-8Bel fst 1¼ :463 1:102 1:35 2:001 3↑ SuburbnH-G2 119 2 1½ 1½ 11½ 11½ 12¼ Chavez J F L123 *1.00 93-07 Albert the Great1232¼ *Lido Palace*115hd Include1227 Pace off rail, driving
10Jun01-7Bel fst 1⅛ :462 1:10 1:342 1:472 3↑ BroklynH-G2 114 1 11 1½ 1½ 12½ 13¼ Chavez J F L122 *.30 93-12 *Albert the Great*1223¼ Perfect Cat1153 *Top Official*113½ Off rail, ridden out
12May01-10Pim fst 1 3/16 :47 1:112 1:363 1:553 3↑ PimSpclH-G1 117 3 2hd 21½ 2½ 11½ 2nk Chavez J F L121 *.60 93-25 *Include*114nk *AlberttheGreat*1213¾ PlesntBreeze1148 Brk in,2wd,clear,game
24Mar01-10Hia fst 1⅛ :463 1:094 1:34 1:452 3↑ WidenerH-G3 107 3 21½ 21½ 2½ 11 15¾ Chavez J F L120 *.05 110 - Albert the Great1205¾ USoBad112½ HighSecurity111½ Drew off,ridden out
3Feb01-11GP fst 1⅛ :464 1:11 1:36 1:484 3↑ DonnH-G1 114 1 66½ 67½ 42 21 21¼ Chavez J F L119 2.00 92-13 *Captain Steve*1201¼ *Albert the Great*11910½ Gander1151½ Bid, no late gain
4Nov00-10CD fst 1¼ :472 1:12 1:36 2:003 3↑ BCClasic-G1 111 5 2hd 1hd 2hd 3½ 43½ Chavez J F L122 9.00 103 - *Tiznow*122nk GiantsCauseway1223¼ *CaptinSteve*122hd Bump,checked start
14Oct00-10Bel fst 1¼ :464 1:101 1:342 1:591 3↑ JkyClbGC-G1 119 1 2hd 1hd 1½ 15 16 Chavez J F L122 5.50 98-09 AlberttheGreat1226 Gnder1263 VisionndVerse126no Speed inside, driving
23Sep00-8Bel fst 1 :223 :441 1:081 1:34 JeromeH-G2 106 2 1½ 1½ 1hd 2hd 34½ Chavez J F L120 4.20 90-05 FusichiPegsus124¾ *ElCorredor*1173¾ *AlberttheGret*1208½ Speed inside, tired
26Aug00-9Sar fst 1¼ :482 1:123 1:373 2:022 Travers-G1 109 9 2½ 1hd 1hd 1½ 2hd Chavez J F L126 7.90 93-07 *Unshded*126hd AlberttheGret1266½ Commndbl1262¾ Gamely on rail stretch
5Aug00-8Sar fst 1⅛ :46 1:103 1:354 1:484 JimDandy-G2 59 7 1½ 1½ 1hd 710 728½ Migliore R L120 b 2.50 68-09 Graeme Hall1201¾ Curule1142¼ *Unshaded*1205½ Set pressured pace
9Jly00-8Bel fst 1 1/16 :24 :463 1:102 1:423 Dwyer-G2 108 4 1½ 11½ 12 1½ 13 Migliore R L115 b 7.00 84-22 AlberttheGret1153 MoreThnRedy1191¾ *RedBullet*123½ Pace, clear, driving
9Jun00-3Bel fst 1⅛ :462 1:104 1:363 1:502 3↑ Alw 46000N2X 99 4 11½ 11½ 12½ 14½ 13¾ Migliore R L116 b *.55 79-21 *AlberttheGret*1163¾ CtsAtHome1143¾ TouchSilvr121hd Pace, clear, driving
12May00-3Bel fst 1⅛ :461 1:103 1:353 1:474 3↑ Alw 44000N1X 106 1 1½ 11½ 11½ 1½ 12¼ Migliore R L115 b *.90 92-24 *AlberttheGret*1152¼ PrfctCt11312¾ KnockAgin1156½ Controlled pace, drive
22Apr00-2Kee fst 1⅛ :453 1:101 1:37 1:50 Md Sp Wt 51k 101 9 11 11 13 17 110 Migliore R L118 b 5.50e 85-15 *AlberttheGret*11810 *IncSlew*1181½ TheComebckCts1181½ Gathered up, wire
8Apr00-5Kee gd 1 1/16 :233 :464 1:111 1:444 Md Sp Wt 46k 71 10 54 55 54 78½ 79¾ Sellers S J L118 *2.20 71-23 *Strike Smartly*118nk Special Terms1182½ Corrian1181 Tired
26Feb00-12GP fst 1 1/16 :233 :474 1:13 1:454 Md Sp Wt 34k 76 6 63¾ 74½ 65½ 35½ 22¾ Sellers S J L122 *1.10 76-14 Jeblar Sez Who1222¾ Albert theGreat1221¼ *Pete'sSake*1226¾ Rallied on rail
12Feb00-7GP fst 7f :221 :452 1:104 1:234 Md Sp Wt 30k 77 10 5 64¾ 41½ 21 31¼ Sellers S J L122 2.80 80-15 *Fajardo*122no *Trajectory*1221¼ Albert the Great1221 3 wide, outfinished
22Jan00-1GP fst 7f :224 :46 1:113 1:25 Md Sp Wt 30k 73 6 5 41 31½ 3nk 31 Sellers S J 122 5.00 74-19 SkipGrde122nk Littlebithome122¾ AlberttheGret122½ Slow st, outfinished

APTITUDE (A.P. Indy—Dokki, by Northern Dancer). Kentucky. Second behind Fusaichi Pegasus in the Kentucky Derby and second in the Belmont Stakes to Commendable, Aptitude was a good 3-year-old, but like most A.P. Indy offspring, blossomed as a 4-year-old, culminating with an eye-opening 10-length victory in the 2001 Jockey Club Gold Cup. He also was placed first in the Hollywood Gold Cup and won the Saratoga Breeders' Cup Handicap that year, and his runners should ultimately prove best at 3 and 4, when they have more opportunities to race beyond one mile. Standing at Juddmonte Farms, he was bred to some very classy broodmares and his offspring would be ideally suited to classic distances, such as the Kentucky Derby.

Aptitude
Own: Juddmonte Farms Inc

Dk. b or b. h. 7 (Mar)
Sire: A.P. Indy (Seattle Slew) $300,000
Dam: Dokki (Northern Dancer)
Br: Juddmonte Farms (Ky)
Tr: Frankel Robert J(0 0 0 0 .00) 2004:(288 83 .29)

Life	15	5	4	2	$1,965,410	123	D.Fst	12	5	3	1	$1,875,910 123
2001	6	3	0	1	$1,410,000	123	Wet(397)	1	0	0	1	$82,500 101
2000	7	2	3	1	$548,410	106	Turf(363)	2	0	1	0	$7,000 90
	0	0	0	0	$0	-	Dst(0)	0	0	0	0	$0 -

27Oct01-10Bel	fst	1¼	:47 1:111 1:354 2:003	3↑BCClasic-G1	102	12	74½	73¼	74¼	86¾	89¾	Bailey J D	L126 fb	*2.35	81-12	Tiznow126no *Sakhee*1261¾ Albert the Great1262¾	Very wide trip 13
6Oct01-10Bel	fst	1¼	:462 1:102 1:36 2:012	3↑JkyClbGC-G1	123	2	53½	32	12	18	110	Bailey J D	L126 fb	1.40	87-21	Aptitude12610 GnrousRosi126¾ CountryBGold1269	3 wide move, hand ride 7
19Aug01-9Sar	fst	1¼	:481 1:12 1:363 2:012	3↑SarBCH-G2	116	4	63½	52¾	1½	11½	14¼	Bailey J D	L122 fb	*1.00	98-08	*Aptitude*1224¼ Perfect Cat1151 A Fleets Dancer1151	Quick 4 wide move 7
1Jly01-5Hol	fst	1¼	:463 1:104 1:36 2:013	3↑HolGldCp-G1	107	2	55	53½	42½	42	21½	Pincay L Jr	LB124 b	1.60e	88-10	[D]Futural1241½ *Aptitude*1243 *Skimming*1241	Came out,bested rest 5
Placed first through disqualification																	
10Jun01-4Hol	fst	1⅛	:463 1:102 1:352 1:48	3↑Calfrnin-G2	103	2	66	76½	76	46½	35	Bailey J D	LB116	*.60e	87-13	Skimming1161 Futural1204 *Aptitude*1162	4w into lane,best rest 8
Previously trained by Frankel Robert																	
24Mar01♦Nad Al Sheba (UAE)	fst	*1¼	LH 2:002	4↑Dubai World Cup-G1 Stk 6000000							66	Stevens G L	126	-e		Captain Steve1263 *To the Victory*121½ Hightori126no *Wide towards rear,mild progress 2f out.Best Of The Bests 8th*	12
Timeform rating: 117																	
Previously trained by Frankel Robert																	
24Nov00-11CD	fst	1⅛	:472 1:113 1:361 1:483	3↑ClarkH-G2	91	4	55½	56	64½	89¼	814¾	Espinoza V	L115	*1.50	78-14	Surfside1134 *Guided Tour*1141¼ Maysville Slew1131¾	Bmp,in tght strt,tired 9
29Oct00-5CD	fst	1¼	:474 1:13 1:383 2:031	3↑Alw 43690N1X	101	5	510	57½	35½	23	12¾	Espinoza V	L111	*.10	94-19	Aptitude1112¾ SoldiersFortune1139¾ I'mHowlin1131¼	5w,lug in 1/8 pl,drvg 7
10Jun00-9Bel	fst	1½	:491 1:141 2:05 2:31	Belmont-G1	99	5	1111	1010	64½	32½	21½	Solis A	L126	*1.75	82-19	Commendable1261½ *Aptitude*1261 Unshaded1266	Brk slw, check early 11
6May00-8CD	fst	1¼	:454 1:094 1:353 2:01	KyDerby-G1	106	2	149¼	106¼	83½	4¾	21½	Solis A	L126	11.80	103 -	FusaichiPegasus1261½ Aptitude1264 Impechment126½	Bid 3/16s, 2nd best 19
15Apr00-9Aqu	wf	1⅛	:464 1:102 1:352 1:474	WoodMem-G2	101	4	109	87	88¾	66¼	35¾	Blanc B	L123 f	5.80	92-10	*Fusaichi Pegasus*1234¼ *Red Bullet*1231½ Aptitude123nk	Going well outside 12
19Mar00-9Aqu	fst	1	:224 :453 1:093 1:341	Gotham-G3	99	2	95¼	92½	72¾	61	2½	Blanc B	L113	8.80	96-11	Red Bullet113½ Aptitude1134 *PerformingMagic*114¾	Altered course stretch 9
1Jan00-9SA	fst	1 1/16	:231 :47 1:113 1:443	Md Sp Wt 47k	89	4	77	67	65½	33	1½	Blanc B	LB120	3.20	80-17	Aptitude120½ *Tribunal*1203 Hoover Tower1207	Bumped 7/8,rallied 9
14Nov99-4Hol	fm	1 1/16	Ⓣ :232 :464 1:111 1:422	Md Sp Wt 35k	90	5	44	46	45	52¾	2½	Blanc B	LB120	4.20	80-19	Jekyll and Hyde120½ *Aptitude*1201 Indy Film1203	4wd into lane,rallied 10
21Oct99-8SA	fm	1	Ⓣ :224 :462 1:111 1:362	Md Sp Wt 40k	78	1	89½	78½	77½	75¼	62	Blanc B	LB120	12.20	75-22	LongTrmInvstor120hd UndrSurvllnc120no CpotSn120nk	Steadied past 3/8 9

ARAMUS (Storm Bird—Nymphea, by General Assembly). Kentucky. Bred along the same sire/damsire cross as Storm Cat and Summer Squall. A winner of just a maiden race from four starts, it is unlikely Aramus was bred to major broodmares and the quality of his runners will be suspect. They will be best on turf. (T^2)

Aramus
Own: Golden Gate Stud

B. h. 6 (Jan)
Sire: Storm Bird (Northern Dancer)
Dam: Nymphea (General Assembly)
Br: Henri Mastey & Golden Gate Stud (Ky)
Tr: Amoss Thomas M(0 0 0 0 .00) 2004:(297 87 .29)

Life	4	1	0	0	$16,910	78	D.Fst	2	0	0	0	$1,040 56
2001	3	1	0	0	$16,910	78	Wet(306)	1	1	0	0	$15,000 78
2000	1	M	0	0	$0	40	Turf(290)	1	0	0	0	$870 69
	0	0	0	0	$0	-	Dst(0)	0	0	0	0	$0 -

17Mar01-10P	fst	1 1/16	:234 :483 1:142 1:45	Alw 26000N1X	56	5	22	21½	21½	511	517½	Albarado R J	L121 f	5.80	61-23	Gail's Drive1185 Quadrophonic Sound1214¾ Early1162½	Forward, gave way 5
17Feb01-2OP	gd	1	:232 :481 1:141 1:41	Md Sp Wt 25k	78	2	11½	1hd	1½	14	16¾	Borel C H	L119 f	7.50	74-28	Aramus1196¾ Pinncale Springs119nk Gold de Duz1193¾	Vied, drew out 8
22Jan01-2FG	fm	*1	Ⓣ :232 :483 1:151 1:401	Md Sp Wt 29k	69	9	87¼	75¾	63¼	54½	56	St Julien M	L119	19.80	78-13	Oisin1191½ *Khatef*1191½ *Arctic Boy*1191	Back early, no threat 11
17Sep00-4AP	fst	6f	:221 :46 :591 1:123	Md Sp Wt 28k	40	3	4	97¾	1013	911	911¾	Meche L J	L121	5.70	71-14	Te Deum1213½ Me and Thee121nk Storm Mist121no	Outrun 12

AUSTIN POWERS (Sadler's Wells—Guess Again, by Stradavinsky). Kentucky. Why this horse is standing in this country and not Europe is a mystery. By the world's greatest turf sire, whose offspring especially thrive at distances over 1¼ miles, he is a half-brother to Eva Luna, a champion 2-year-old filly in Ireland. His runners are strictly bred for grass and will be most effective racing at distances over one mile at 3 and 4. (T^2)

Austin Powers (Ire)
Own: Nielson Bjorn

B. h. 8 (Apr)
Sire: Sadler's Wells (Northern Dancer)
Dam: Guess Again*Ger (Stradavinsky*Ire)
Br: David Shubotham (Ire)
Tr: Sheppard Jonathan E(0 0 0 0 .00) 2004:(237 36 .15)

Life	4	1	0	1	$12,500	-	D.Fst	0	0	0	0	$0 -
2000	3	1	0	1	$12,500	-	Wet(253)	0	0	0	0	$0 -
1999	1	M	0	0	$0	-	Turf(311)	1	0	0	0	$0 -
	0	0	0	0	$0	-	Dst(0)	0	0	0	0	$0 -

29May00-4Fai gd *2¼	Hurdles	4:39	3↑ Md Sp Wt 15k	– 5 3³ 2¹ 2³ 2½ 1³¼	Kingsley A Jr	L144	*1.80	- - AustinPowers144³¼ *PerfectMatch*155¹¹ ColdCt144²¹	Stalked pace, driving 10
15Apr00-2Ath fm *2	Hurdles	3:53¹	4↑ Md Sp Wt 24k	– 2 31½ 21½ 2¹ 3¹ 3⁵½	O'Flynn Fennela⁵	L139	-	- - Shahrahere154⁵½ Not Bad154ʰᵈ *Austin Powers*139⁷¼	Good effort 6
4Mar00-5Tam fm *2 1/16	Hurdles	3:43⁴	4↑ Md Sp Wt 25k	– 7 7¹¹ 7⁸½ 6⁸½ 5¹² 5²⁰¼	O'Flynn Fennela⁵	L138	3.60	- - Red Classic154⁴¾ Banjo Man154³¾ Hall of Angels138⁵½	Raced greenly 7
Previously trained by Jeremy Noseda									
8Jly99♦Newmarket (GB) gd 1¼ Ⓣ RH 2:02¹	Greene King Maiden Stakes Maiden 12400			6³⁹¾	Fallon K	126	4.00	Dane121²½ *El Mobasherr*126²½ Surveillance126¹¾	6 Soon pushed along,trailed final half,tailed off

AUSTINPOWER (Sunday Silence—Eishin Austin, by Seattle Slew). Kentucky. A powerhouse of a pedigree. Austinpower raced only twice with two thirds, but what makes him so attractive is that he is a rare son of Sunday Silence to stand in the U.S., and his dam is a half-sister to Canadian Horse of the Year Glorious Song (dam of Rahy and Singspiel), 2-year-old champion Devil's Bag, and prominent stakes winner and sire Saint Ballado. Austinpower is very closely related to this trio as they are by Halo, and Austinpower is by Halo's son Sunday Silence. Expect his offspring to have tactical speed, be best at 3 and 4, and have a strong preference for grass. (T^2)

Austinpower (Jpn)
Own: Silky Green Inc

Dk. b or b. h. 6 (Apr)
Sire: Sunday Silence (Halo) $218,625
Dam: Eishin Austin (Seattle Slew)
Br: Eishin Bokujo (Jpn)
Tr: Mott William I(0 0 0 0 .00) 2004:(414 83 .20)

Life	2	M	0	2	$5,110	79	D.Fst	0	0	0	0	$0	-
2001	2	M	0	2	$5,110	79	Wet(324)	0	0	0	0	$0	-
2000	0	M	0	0	$0	-	Turf(317)	2	0	0	2	$5,110	79
	0	0	0	0	$0	-	Dst(0)	0	0	0	0	$0	-

22Mar01-9Hia fm 1 3/16 Ⓣ	1:57¹	3↑ Md Sp Wt 17k	79 11 3² 3¹ 3ⁿᵏ 1¹½ 3¹¾	Smith M E	L114	*1.90	70-24 DeputysLegcy114¾ *AlmostHom*115¹ Austinpowr114½	3 wide, gave way late 12
27Jan01-11GP fm *1⅛ Ⓣ :51¹ 1:16 1:40⁴	1:52¹	Md Sp Wt 31k	68 7 6⁴¼ 6³½ 5³¼ 3⁴ 3⁷¼	Bailey J D	122	4.80	70-14 CellrsMerlot122² *PrfctStrngr*122⁵¼ Austinpowr122½	Checked into far turn 10

BESTYOUCANBE (Danzig—Sky Beauty, by Blushing Groom). Venezuela. Sporting a classy pedigree, Bestyoucanbe was a disappointment, winning just once in nine starts. As a result, he was exported to Venezuela, but if any of his runners show up here, they will be better suited to grass. (T^2)

Bestyoucanbe
Own: Jayeff B Stables

Dk. b or b. h. 7 (May)
Sire: Danzig (Northern Dancer) $200,000
Dam: Sky Beauty (Blushing Groom*Fr)
Br: Georgia E. Hofmann (Ky)
Tr: Goldberg Alan E(0 0 0 0 .00) 2004:(119 19 .16)

Life	9	1	0	1	$26,410	70	D.Fst	8	1	0	1	$25,180	70
2001	6	1	0	1	$22,720	70	Wet(466)	1	0	0	0	$1,230	32
2000	3	M	0	0	$3,690	63	Turf(418)	0	0	0	0	$0	-
	0	0	0	0	$0	-	Dst(0)	0	0	0	0	$0	-

27Sep01-6Med fst	1 1/16		:224 :462 1:104 1:442	3↑ Clm 25000(25-20)N2L	60	1	714	714	712	610	517¼	Carrero V5	L117 f	4.60	62-19	[D][DH]Mendham111 [DH]*Profit*1225 *Strike Twice*1153¾	Dwelt,no factor	7
19Aug01-3Pim fst	1 1/16		:231 :471 1:123 1:453	3↑ Clm 25000(25-20)N2L	56	5	56	76	65½	510	411½	Douglas F G	L124 f	2.70	73-18	ChmpgneTony1242½ *AdiosMyFrind*1188 PolishOutlw1221	3wd 3/8, no threat	8
5Aug01-6Del fst	1		:23 :47 1:131 1:403	3↑ Alw 32900N2L	65	6	713	79	65¾	62½	34	Rose J5	L117 f	6.80	72-26	Friar Wolf1223¼ Smokie118¾ Bestyoucanbe117nk	Up for third	8
7Apr01-6Del fst	1 1/16		:23 :461 1:104 1:443	4↑ Alw 33500N1X	70	3	87½	78½	57½	59	410½	Velez J A Jr	L118	11.80	73-17	Pleasantly Rich1185 Go Code1181½ Stride On Over1184	Failed to menace	10
22Mar01-6Lrl fst	6f		:23 :47 :594 1:122	4↑ Md Sp Wt 26k	54	1	5	62¾	65¼	51¾	1hd	Dominguez R A	L122	4.80	77-20	Bestyoucnbe122hd HersthPln1221 UnbridldFury1221	Urgd rail,bid bw,held	7
11Jan01-4Aqu fst	6f	[•]	:224 :453 :571 1:094	4↑ Md Sp Wt 41k	59	5	4	77¾	711	719	515½	Lopez C C	L121 b	15.10	80-10	Mr. Kuck121½ *Mister Blues*1212¾ *Rogues Road*1214½	Had no rally	7
27Dec00-4Aqu fst	6f	[•]	:232 :463 :582 1:104	3↑ Md Sp Wt 41k	63	10	2	83¼	54	512	49¼	Lopez C C	L121 b	16.90	79-17	TwignBerries121¾ PrimCustomr1212¾ RogusRod1215¾	Wide, no response	10
9Dec00-5Aqu fst	6f	[•]	:232 :473 :592 1:113	3↑ Md Sp Wt 41k	56	8	2	55	85¼	89½	610½	Espinoza J L	L121	5.00	73-15	EglesRewrd121nk PrimeCustomr1212¼ MistrBlus121no	No factor after 1/4	8
15Nov00-3Aqu gd	7f		:223 :461 1:113 1:243	3↑ Md Sp Wt 41k	32	6	5	611	68½	616	515½	Duarte J C Jr5	114	3.30	61-17	Left n' Right121nk *Eagles Reward*119nk Infantry11911¾	Greenly inside	6

BIENAMADO (Bien Bien—Nakterjal, by Vitiges). California. By a strong influence of stamina and turf, Bienamado ran right to his pedigree, and his offspring will be best suited to European racing. His statebred runners should not be much of a force as juveniles, but they will blossom into long-distance turf runners. Most interesting about his pedigree is that his second dam, Kilavea (Hawaai), is a half-sister to Nureyev. (T^2)

Bienamado
Own: McCaffery Trudy, Toffan, John and San

Ch. h. 8 (Mar)
Sire: Bien Bien (Manila) $4,479
Dam: Nakterjal*GB (Vitiges)
Br: John Toffan & Trudy McCaffery (Ky)
Tr: Gonzalez J. P(0 0 0 0 .00) 2004:(37 1 .03)

Life	16	8	3	0	$1,261,089	111	D.Fst	1	0	0	0	$0	96
2001	5	3	0	0	$540,000	111	Wet(206)	0	0	0	0	$0	-
2000	4	3	0	0	$537,070	108	Turf(245)	15	8	3	0	$1,261,089	111
	0	0	0	0	$0	-	Dst(0)	0	0	0	0	$0	-

18Aug01-8AP yl	1¼ (T)	:482 1:124 1:374 2:023	3↑ ArlMilln-G1	73	10	41½	41½	43	710	720½	McCarron C J	L126	*1.50	72-11	Silvano1263 *Hap*1266 Redattore1264	4 wide, tired	12
10Jun01-9Hol fm	1¼ (T)	:482 1:122 1:36 1:591	3↑ CWhtghmH-G1	111	8	23	22½	2½	11½	11½	McCarron C J	LB124	*.50	98-15	Bienamado1241½ *Senure*117no Timboroa116hd	Stalked,bid,led,dvng	9
14Apr01-9SA fm	*1¾ (T)	1:093 1:351 2:261 2:424	4↑ SnJnCpoH-G1	108	9	34	32½	21	2½	1½	McCarron C J	LB122	*.80	115-02	*Bienamado*122½ Persianlux1143½ *Blueprint*1167	Bid,led past 1/8,game	11
3Mar01-9SA fst	1¼	:462 1:103 1:354 2:012	4↑ SAH-G1	96	12	911	99¾	109¼	910	914¼	Solis A	LB119	6.10	82-10	Tiznow1225 Wooden Phone1171½ Tribunal1162	Bmpd,stumbld bad early	12
20Jan01-8SA fm	1¼ (T)	:503 1:153 1:393 2:023	4↑ SnMarcos-G2	107	3	11	1½	1hd	1½	11½	McCarron C J	LB122	*.40	81-19	Bienamado1221½ *Kerrygold*116¾ Northern Quest1221½	Wide early,game rail	7
2Dec00-8Hol fm	1½ (T)	:491 1:131 2:011 2:254	3↑ HolTrfCp-G1	108	5	34	21½	2½	12	13	McCarron C J	LB126	*1.00	90-08	*Bienamado*1263 Northern Quest126½ *Lazy Lode*1265	Clear,steady handling	8
19Aug00-9AP yl	1¼ (T)	:473 1:114 1:371 2:011	3↑ ArlMilln-G1	100	5	58	54½	41	42	44¾	Desormeaux K J	L126	*2.90	96-04	Chester House1263¼ Manndar126½ Mula Gula1261	Wide, bid, tired	7
23Jly00-3Hol fm	1½ (T)	:474 1:122 2:003 2:25	3↑ SunsetH-G2	105	1	27	2½	1hd	11	11½	McCarron C J	LB122	*.20e	94-10	Bienmdo1221½ DeployVntur1151½ SinglEmpir1205½	Led 1/4,game rail lane	5
25Jun00-9Hol fm	1¼ (T)	:463 1:102 1:351 1:584+	3↑ [R]JMurryMemH78k	108	7	37	310	1hd	13	17	McCarron C J	LB121	*1.70	102 -	*Bienamado*1217 Casino King1171½ Adcat116½	3wd move,ridden out	8
Previously trained by Foster George																	
17Oct99-8WO gd	1½ (T)	:491 1:14 2:052 2:321	3↑ CanIntnl-G1	98	7	86½	57½	47	45	54	McCarron C J	119	4.20	68-31	Thornfield1261 Fruits of Love1261 Courteous1261	Mild bid 4 wide	9
Previously trained by Peter Chapple-Hyam																	

12Sep99♦Longchamp (Fr)	gd *1½ (T) RH 2:324	Prix Niel-G2	2hd	Hughes R	128	10.40	*Montjeu*128hd Bienamado1282 *First Magnitude*1283	4	Led after 4f,drifted left & right stretch,headed near line
Timeform rating: 119		Stk 107500							
17Aug99♦York (GB)	gd 1½ (T) LH 2:29	Great Voltigeur Stakes-G2	21¼	Hughes R	121	5.50	*Fantastic Light*1211¼ Bienamado1211¼ Glamis1211	7	Trailed,close 7th 4f out,2nd 2f out,held by winner.Mutafaweq 4th
Timeform rating: 119		Stk 160400							
6Jly99♦Newmarket (GB)	gd 1½ (T) RH 2:251 3↑	Princess of Wales's Stakes-G2	58½	Quinn T	115	14.00	Craigsteel1281 Arctic Owl1311¼ Silver Rhapsody125nk	8	Rated in 5th,3rd 2f out,weakened 1-1/2f out.Sea Wave 4th,Capri7th
Timeform rating: 106+		Stk 86300							
31Oct98♦Saint-Cloud (Fr)	hy *1¼ (T) LH 2:212	Criterium de Saint-Cloud-G1	26	Hughes R	126	*.70	Spadoun1266 Bienamado1263 *Cupid*1261½	6	Tracked clear leaders in 3rd,bid 2f out,no chance with winner
Timeform rating: 103		Stk 122600							
Oct98♦Longchamp (Fr)	sf *1⅛ (T) RH 1:59	Prix de Conde-G3	13	Hughes R	128	*1.90	Bienamado1283 Persianlux1281½ Franky Furbo1282	5	Tracked in 3rd,rallied between horses to lead 1f out,drew clear
Timeform rating: 111+		Stk 65900							
Sep98♦Haydock (GB)	gd 1 (T) LH 1:414	Stanley Racing Conditions Stks	14	↓Reid J	119	2.00	Mixsterthetrixster1244 *Bienamado*1194 Crown of Trees124	3	Tracked in 3rd,raced greenly,rallied to share lead on line
Timeform rating: 99+		Alw 18700							

BLACK MINNALOUSHE (Storm Cat—Coral Dance, by Green Dancer). Kentucky. Another young sire who should be standing in Europe. Undefeated at 2 (on grass), he was a champion at 3 in Ireland. He is a half-brother to Pennekamp, a champion 2-year-old in France, as well as Nasr El Arab, who won the Charles H. Strub Stakes. While his runners should have good speed, they will be bred strictly for grass. (T^2)

Black Minnaloushe
Own: Tabor Michael and Magnier, Mrs. John

B. h. 6 (Feb)
Sire: Storm Cat (Storm Bird) $500,000
Dam: Coral Dance*Fr (Green Dancer)
Br: John R. Gaines Thoroughbreds & William Condren (Ky)
Tr: O'Brien Aidan P(0 0 0 0 .00) 2004:(0 0 .00)

Life	11	4	1	1	$490,945	102	D.Fst	1	0	0	0	$0	102
2001	9	2	1	1	$454,741	102	Wet(380)	0	0	0	0	$0	-
2000	2	2	0	0	$36,204	-	Turf(350)	10	4	1	1	$490,945	-
	0	0	0	0	$0	-	Dst(0)	0	0	0	0	$0	-

27Oct01-10Bel fst 1¼ :47 1:111 1:3542:003 3↑ BCClasic-G1 102 3 105¼ 115¼ 107¾ 97¼ 1010¼ Murtagh J P L122 51.00 81- 12 Tiznow126no *Sakhee*1261¾ Albert the Great1262¾ Steadied far turn 13
Previously trained by O'Brien Aidan P
21Aug01♦York (GB) gd 1 5/16 Ⓣ LH 2:081 3↑ Juddmonte International Stakes-G1 Stk 653500 49¼ Kinane M J 123 3.50 *Sakhee*1317 *Grandera*1231 Medicean1311½ 8
Timeform rating: 116 *6th on rail,brief bid 3f out,one-paced from 1-1/2f out*
1Aug01♦Goodwood (GB) gd 1 Ⓣ RH 1:37 3↑ Sussex Stakes-G1 Stk 394500 33½ Kinane M J 126 *3.00 Noverre1262 *No Excuse Needed*1261½ Black Minnaloushe126¾ 10
Timeform rating: 118 *Wide in 5th,bid 1-1/2f out,one-paced late.Bach 7th,Ameerat 8th*
7Jly01♦Sandown Park (GB) gd 1¼ Ⓣ RH 2:043 3↑ Eclipse Stakes-G1 Stk 486600 51 Kinane M J 122 2.50 Medicean133½ Grandera122nk Bach133hd 8
Timeform rating: 118+ *Trailed to 4f out,bid 2f out,lost 4th on line.Tobougg 4th*
19Jun01♦Ascot (GB) gd 1 Ⓣ RH 1:411 St James's Palace Stakes-G1 Stk 378200 1nk Murtagh J 126 8.00 Black Minnaloushe126nk *Noverre*126hd Olden Times126½ 11
Timeform rating: 121+ *Angled to rail early,pulled out 1f out,led near line.Vahorimix 4t*
26May01♦Curragh (Ire) yl 1 Ⓣ Str 1:412 Irish 2000 Guineas-G1 Stk 245900 12 Murtagh J P 126 20.00 *Black Minnaloushe*1262 *Mozart*126¾ Minardi1263½ 12
Timeform rating: 122 *Rated in 7th,3rd 1-1/2f out,rail bid to lead 50y out,handily*
13May01♦Longchamp (Fr) gd *1 Ⓣ RH 1:352 Poule d'Essai de Poulains-G1 Stk 233800 74½ Spencer J P 128 7.40e Noverre128hd Vahorimix128hd Clearing1281½ 12
Timeform rating: 108 *Towards rear,mild late gain.Placed 6th via DQ.Okawango placed 4th*
Placed 6th through disqualification
7May01♦Curragh (Ire) gd 7f Ⓣ Str 1:261 Tetrarch Stakes-G3 Stk 79100 52 O'Donoghue C 123 7.00 Modigliani123hd Scarlet Velvet120no Mozart1231½ 5
Timeform rating: 103+ *Dwelt,trailed,finished well but never threatened*
21Apr01♦Curragh (Ire) sf 7f Ⓣ Str 1:422 Loughbrown Stakes (Listed) Stk 45900 22 Kinane M J 130 *.50 Lethal Agenda1262 Black Minnaloushe1301½ Princess Nutley1234½ 4
Timeform rating: 104+ *Rank tracking pacesetting winner,second best*
17Sep00♦Curragh (Ire) yl 6f Ⓣ Str 1:162 Blenheim Stakes (Listed) Stk 43400 1¾ Kinane M J 123 *1.00 Black Minnaloushe123¾ Imperial Dancer126nk Saying Grace1202 8
Timeform rating: 104 *Tracked in 4th,led 1-1/2f out,driving*
7Aug00♦Cork (Ire) gd 6f Ⓣ Str 1:114 Foxhound EBF Maiden Maiden 11500 14 Kinane M J 128 *.65 *Black Minnaloushe*1284 La Stellina1233 Solar At'em1282 6
Timeform rating: 100 *Tracked leader,led 2f out,drew clear*

BRAHMS (Danzig—Queena, by Mr. Prospector). Kentucky. Like most sons of Danzig, Brahms was best on grass and inherited speed from both his sire and champion dam, Queena. His runners should win early on all surfaces, but eventually prove best on turf. (T^2)

Brahms
Own: Van Meter T F II

Dk. b or b. h. 7 (Mar)
Sire: Danzig (Northern Dancer) $200,000
Dam: Queena (Mr. Prospector)
Br: Emory A. Hamilton (Ky)
Tr: Walden W. E(0 0 0 0 .00) 2004:(113 20 .18)

Life	17	5	4	4	$843,050	112	D.Fst	2	0	0	1	$83,100	112
2001	7	0	1	3	$248,335	112	Wet(451)	0	0	0	0	$0	-
2000	4	4	0	0	$483,462	107	Turf(412)	15	5	4	3	$759,950	107
	0	0	0	0	$0	-	Dst(0)	0	0	0	0	$0	-

27Oct01-5Bel fm 1 Ⓣ :223 :452 1:0831:32 3↑ BCMile-G1 104 10 97½ 96 105¾ 117 64½ Solis A L126 b 12.40 93 - Val Royal1261¾ Forbidden Apple126¾ Bach1261½ 7 wide, even finish 12
7Oct01-6Kee fm 1 Ⓣ :234 :472 1:12 1:354 3↑ KeeTurfM-G2 105 1 53¾ 53½ 42½ 54 42½ Stevens G L L126 b 3.40 87- 15 Hap1261½ Where's Taylor126hd Aly's Alley126¾ Lack room 5/16s 9
9Sep01-8WO fm 1 Ⓣ :23 :453 1:0921:323 3↑ AttoMile-G1 103 11 83¾ 104¼ 113½ 63½ 62¼ Day P L117 3.45 100 - NumerousTims117no AffirmdSuccss119no QuitRsolv121¾ Mild rally 5 wide 14
16Jun01-11CD fst 1⅛ :4641:103 1:3511:473 3↑ SFosterH-G2 112 4 34 47 43 45 33¼ Day P L114 7.60 95- 09 *Guided Tour*113½ Captain Steve1232¾ Brahms1141¼ Inside late,no bid 8
28May01-8Hol fm 1 Ⓣ :231 :453 1:0911:333 3↑ ShoeBCM-G1 106 8 79 716 75½ 74¼ 3½ Nakatani C S LB124 *1.30 95- 11 *IrishPrize*124nk TouchoftheBlues124nk Brhms1241½ Blocked upper stretch 9
5May01-7CD fm 1⅛ Ⓣ :4741:113 1:3611:483 3↑ TurfClsc-G1 105 6 51½ 53 55 41¾ 31½ Day P L123 b 2.30 91- 08 White Heart116nk King Cugat1201¼ Brahms123hd 6w,ck,in tight wire 8
13Apr01-8Kee fm 1 Ⓣ :232 :462 1:1021:342 4↑ MakrsMrk-G2 107 1 35 34 42½ 31 2nk Day P L123 b *1.50 96- 03 NorthEstBound120nk Brhms1231¼ *StrtgcMsson*116no Forced out late,hung 8
26Nov00-8Hol fm 1⅛ Ⓣ :48 1:114 1:3431:463 ETHolDby-G1 104 5 51¼ 62¼ 61½ 52¾ 2hd Day P LB122 b *1.70 95- 09 Ⓓ Designed for Luck122hd Brahms122½ David Copperfield1221 Rallied 4w 12
Placed first through disqualification
5Nov00-9CD fm 1⅛ Ⓣ :48 1:122 1:3611:48 3↑ RivrCtyH-G3 107 3 42½ 44 72¼ 2½ 1½ Day P L112 b 2.40 96- 09 *Brahms*112½ Vergennes1151¾ Super Quercus1162¼ Rallied inside,driving 9
14Oct00-8Kee fm 1 Ⓣ :232 :463 1:1011:341 SeattleSlw74k 103 1 55½ 54¾ 44 22½ 12 Melancon L L118 b *2.00 101- 05 *Brahms*1182 Final Row1182¼ *Gulf Storm*1182½ Angled 4 wide, clear 8
2Sep00-10Sar gd 1 Ⓣ :242 :482 1:1321:373 3↑ Alw 44000N1x 93 6 63¾ 72¾ 71¾ 61¾ 11½ Day P L117 b *1.50 80- 20 *Brahms*1171½ *Quiet Quest*117nk River Bed117nk Altered course stretch 10
Previously trained by O'Brien Aidan P
6Nov99-8GP fst 1 1/16 :221 :46 1:1011:421 BCJuven-G1 81 14 116½ 125½ 1417 98¾ 711¾ Peslier O L122 b 55.30 84 - Anees1222¼ Chief Seattle122¾ High Yield1222¼ Wide trip, no threat 14
16Oct99♦Newmarket (GB) gd 7f Ⓣ Str 1:264 Dewhurst Stakes-G1 Stk 334000 21 Peslier O 126 b 14.00 Distant Music1261 Brahms1262 Zentsov Street1262½ 5
Timeform rating: 115 *Tracked in 3rd,bid over 1f out,finished well.King's Best 5th*
30Sep99♦Newmarket (GB) yl 6f Ⓣ Str 1:124 Middle Park Stakes-G1 Stk 197700 31½ Kinane M J 123 b 9.00 Primo Valentino123nk Fath1231¼ Brahms1232½ 6
Timeform rating: 113 *Tracked leader,bid with winner,outfinished.Warm Heart 4th*
29Aug99♦Curragh (Ire) yl 7f Ⓣ Str 1:25 Futurity Stakes-G3 Stk 67500 22½ Heffernan J A 124 b 14.00 *Giant's Causeway*1242½ Brahms124¾ Polish Panache1244 4
Timeform rating: 109 *Tracked in 3rd,finished well to take 2nd near line*
4Aug99♦Fairyhouse (Ire) gd 6f Ⓣ Str 1:144 EBF Maiden Maiden 8200 11½ Kinane M J 128 b *.40 Brahms1281½ Jamieson1283 Contact128nk
Timeform rating: 85 *Tracked leader,led over 1f out,drifted right,ridden ou*
3Jly99♦Leopardstwn (Ire) gd 6f Ⓣ Str 1:131 Glenalua EBF Maiden Maiden 9700 2no Kinane M J 128 *.25 Miss Bidder123no *Brahms*1282½ Lake Victoria1231½
Timeform rating: 79+ *Close up in 3rd,led 1-1/2f out,dueled 1f out,drifted right,faile*

BROKEN VOW (Unbridled—Wedding Vow, by Nijinsky II). Kentucky. While runners by Unbridled were renowned for their stamina, a curious pattern is developing for his sons as stallions. Although many of his sons (such as Empire Maker and Red Bullet) are too young to have foals of racing age, his older sons Unbridled's Song and Grindstone sire precocious runners who have shown good speed at 2. Broken Vow, however, inherited more stamina (from damsire Nijinsky II) than those two examples, and I expect his offspring to be better at 3, stretching out over one mile.

Broken Vow
Own: Pin Oak Stable LLC

B. h. 7 (May)
Sire: Unbridled (Fappiano) $200,000
Dam: Wedding Vow (Nijinsky II)
Br: Pin Oak Stud, Inc. (Ky)
Tr: Motion H. G(0 0 0 0 .00) 2004:(247 49 .20)

Life	14	9	2	2	$725,296	116	D.Fst	11	7	2	1	$590,696 116
2001	10	5	2	2	$611,596	116	Wet(379)	3	2	0	1	$134,600 116
2000	4	4	0	0	$113,700	100	Turf(326)	0	0	0	0	$0 –
	0	0	0	0	$0	–	Dst(0)	0	0	0	0	$0 –

27Oct01-4Kee fst	1⅛	:473 1:111 1:364 1:50	3↑ Fayette-G3	105	8	32½	2½	2hd	13½	2½	Dominguez R A	L123 b	*.80	84- 15	Connected119½ BrokenVow1232¾ Outofthbox122nk	Dfficlt gate,no mishap	9
28Sep01-8Med fst	1⅛	:483 1:114 1:352 1:47	3↑ MedCupH-G2	104	5	21½	2½	21	1hd	2hd	Dominguez R A	L120 b	1.20	92- 09	Gander114hd Broken Vow120nk Include12115	Duel btween,outfinishd	5
26Aug01-10Mth fst	1⅛	:473 1:11 1:362 1:492	3↑ PIselinH-G2	108	5	2½	2hd	1hd	13½	12	Dominguez R A	L119 b	*.70	89- 19	BrokenVow1192 FirstLieutenant1157 SirBear117¾	Moved clear,steady drv	5
21Jly01-4Del fst	1$\frac{1}{16}$	:242 :49 1:131 1:45	3↑ RRMCarpMem97k	104	2	21½	21½	2hd	1hd	11	Dominguez R A	L123 b	*.40	82- 20	*Broken Vow*1231 *Jarf*1202 Connected1202½	Bid,driving,edged away	4
30Jun01-8Mth fst	1$\frac{1}{16}$	:233 :47 1:102 1:421	3↑ SkipAway75k	115	3	32	2hd	1½	13	15¾	Dominguez R A	L119 b	*.50	97- 12	*Broken Vow*1195¾ Rize1152½ Mercaldo1143½	Moderate pressure	6
2Jun01-13Suf sly	1⅛	:464 1:104 1:37 1:483	3↑ MassH-G2	108	4	31	1hd	2½	33	35½	Prado E S	LB116 b	*1.00	87- 10	Include1184 Sir Bear1171½ *Broken Vow*11613¼	3path, tired	7
27Apr01-9Kee fst	1⅛	:471 1:113 1:362 1:482	4↑ BenAli-G3	116	2	1½	1½	1½	12½	14¾	Prado E S	L116 b	*.50	93- 19	Broken Vow1164¾ *Perfect Cat*1163 Jadada116no	Riddn out,in hand late	5
3Mar01-10GP fst	1¼	:461 1:104 1:363 2:024	3↑ GPH-G1	107	2	52¼	42	32½	22	32	Prado E S	L114 b	*1.70	81- 24	Sir Bear116½ Pleasant Breeze1151½ *Broken Vow*1146	No late gain	9
5Feb01-8GP gd	170	:233 :47 1:111 1:404	4↑ OC 100k/N4X-N	116	4	12	12	12½	13	14¾	Prado E S	L118 b	4.30	97- 25	Broken Vow1184¾ Duckhorn1224 Vision and Verse1187½	Clear throughout	7
7Jan01-9GP fst	7f	:222 :443 1:092 1:224	4↑ OC 100k/N4X-N	81	7	6	62	54½	57½	76	Prado E S	L118 b	3.60	86- 16	FntsticFinish118hd FppisNotbook1181½ SlvrJt1221¾	Checked backstretch	11
20May00-6Pim gd	1$\frac{1}{16}$	:231 :464 1:114 1:431	SirBarton100k	100	8	42½	41½	1hd	12½	1¾	Sellers S J	L115 b	3.30	91- 11	BrokenVow115¾ *Grundlefoot*115½ InnrHrbour1153¾	Unruly,4wd trip,drivng	8
24Apr00-7Del fst	170	:224 :463 1:113 1:421	Alw 34900N2X	88	4	63	53	32	2½	13	Prado E S	L120 b	*.80	90- 17	*BrokenVow*1203 CoolSweep1171¼ MgiclMdness1172¼	Bobbled, tried to lug	8
1Apr00-6GP fst	1$\frac{1}{16}$	:231 :463 1:11 1:434	3↑ OC 150k/N1X-N	84	1	32½	22½	1½	2hd	1½	Prado E S	113 b	*.40	89- 11	*Broken Vow*113½ Spiritofspain1196¼ *Dan's Report*1191¾	Gamely, prevailed	6
26Feb00-7GP fst	7f	:223 :452 1:102 1:232	Md Sp Wt 34k	85	1	6	1hd	11½	12	12¾	Prado E S	122 b	13.20	83- 14	*Broken Vow*1222¾ Rover1225¼ Grey's Majesty122nk	Pressured, edged clear	10

BUSH WON (Mercedes Won—Toes Forward, by Your Alibhai). Arkansas. A half-brother to Kissin Kris (Kris S.), Bush Won is by a speed influence, and his Arkansas-bred foals should do well as sprinter/milers at 2 and 3.

Bush Won
Own: Williams Jo and Bush

Dk. b or b. h. 11 (Jan)
Sire: Mercedes Won (Air Forbes Won) $1,850
Dam: Toes Forward (Your Alibhai)
Br: Farnsworth Farms (Fla)
Tr: Azpurua L J Jr(0 0 0 0 .00) 2004:(0 0 .00)

Life	31	4	5	5	$106,803	93	D.Fst	17	2	3	2	$57,8
1999	4	0	0	1	$5,135	87	Wet(311)	6	1	2	1	$26,0
1998	8	1	0	2	$21,750	93	Turf(289)	8	1	0	2	$22,9
	0	0	0	0	$0	–	Dst(0)	0	0	0	0	$

13Sep99-4Crc gd	1$\frac{1}{16}$ ⊗	:24 :482 1:132 1:463	3↑ Clm 40000(40-35)	85	1	58½	57½	55½	52½	42¼	Bain G W	L117	9.40	81- 19	*Lord Bates*119hd Matt's Bubble115nk *Streeterville*1152	Failed to me
30Jly99-6Crc fm	1$\frac{1}{16}$ Ⓣ	:214 :452 1:091 1:391	3↑ Alw 23000N4X	83	2	614	614	59½	57½	47¼	Castellano J J	L117	10.40	94- 07	Spendable1171 Up Front117½ *Wertz*1145¾	Bobbled after s
5Jly99-5Crc fst	1$\frac{1}{16}$ ⊗	:233 :481 1:131 1:462	3↑ Alw 26000N4X	79	6	712	77¾	85	76¾	79	Velasquez C	L117	11.80	75- 24	Lord Bates1171½ Streeterville1171¼ Matt's Bubble1191	No fa
11Jun99-6Crc sly	1	:243 :482 1:13 1:394	3↑ OC 50k/N3X	87	1	68½	610	66	56	35¾	Douglas R R	L117 f	13.80	82- 25	Streeterville1171 *Lord Bates*1174¾ Bush Won117nk	Passed tired ri
Previously trained by Young Troy																
1Oct98-9LaD fm	*1$\frac{1}{16}$ Ⓣ	:244 :482 1:113 1:412	3↑ Alw 21000N$Y	81	2	711	818	810	78	74¾	Melancon G	L115 f	21.40	92- 07	Golden Ile118½ Eskimo Gigolo118nk *Fuddy*1181	No speed, no
6Sep98-8LaD fm	1$\frac{1}{16}$ Ⓣ	:233 :472 1:11 1:414	3↑ SportCityH50k	60	7	716	712	710	615	716¾	Lovelace A K	L112	24.80	80- 08	Illusive Ghost1142½ Milligan1131 Marastani114hd	Outmat
20Aug98-9LaD fm	1 Ⓣ	:253 :50 1:134 1:381	3↑ Alw 22000N2Y	79	5	55	58½	64¾	64¾	32½	Perrodin E J	L115	10.30	81- 19	Red Shadow1151½ Marastani1151 Bush Won115½	Mild
23Jly98-9LaD fm	1 Ⓣ	:233 :464 1:103 1:351	3↑ Alw 23000N$Y	79	5	613	617	612	511	39	Perrodin E J	L119	6.00	90- 07	Capote's Prospect1167 *Little Guy*1162 Bush Won1193	Late
12Jly98-9LS fm	1⅛ Ⓣ	:482 1:111 1:344 1:462	3↑ Alw 50000N$Y	75	6	57½	74¾	83¾	89¼	810½	Doocy T T	L116	18.00	89- 05	*SpecilMomnts*1221 RuggdBuggr1172¼ ColonilPowr116½	Wide trip, sto
29Apr98-5LS fm	1$\frac{1}{16}$ Ⓣ	:224 :461 1:103 1:411	3↑ Alw 28280N3X	93	7	911	910	85½	22	11	Martin E M Jr	L116	25.50	94- 09	Bush Won1161 Colonial Power1161½ Blinknumissit1161½	Fully exter
23Mar98-10FG fm	*1 Ⓣ	:234 :472 1:121 1:371	4↑ Alw 40000N3X	63	1	1022	1024	1017	915	715¼	Melancon G	L117	61.20	84- 04	*He's a Tough Cat*1198½ Howell's Poet1171½ Claim Santiago117½	No
15Jan98-9FG sly	140	:234 :472 1:124 1:41	4↑ Alw 30800N3X	68	3	88¼	86¼	88½	710	714	Ardoin R D	L117	16.40	73- 21	*EskimoGigolo*1171 MidwyMgistrte1192 JustAbout1171	No speed, no th
19Dec97-9FG fst	140	:241 :48 1:13 1:404	3↑ Alw 28000N3X	77	5	79½	68	66½	43	75½	Melancon G	L117	7.10	83- 19	Kitwe1191 Conquest1172 Dubai Dust117no	Failed to res
1Dec97-8FG fst	6f	:22 :453 :573 1:10	3↑ Alw 28000N4L	87	1	9	914	99¾	54½	24	Melancon G	L117	5.00	90- 15	Littlebitlively1154 Bush Won117nk DH Handel117	Best stride
Previously trained by Bohannan Thomas																
9Nov97-7CD fst	6½f	:23 :462 1:112 1:18	3↑ Alw 48300N$Y	81	6	8	89¾	85¼	79½	56	Borel C H	L116	11.00	82- 11	Special Guy1141 *Cliffty Falls*1191 Chant Away1163	Far back no s
22Oct97-8Kee fst	7f	:221 :45 1:094 1:224	3↑ Alw 45044N$Y	68	5	8	811	717	611	614	Borel C H	114	22.20	77- 14	Shakka Con1142½ Viv1142½ Chant Away1146	Far back ou
10Aug97-6RP fst	7f	:213 :433 1:073 1:21	3↑ SilBulCenH75k	90	4	5	516	514	510	44	Stevens G L	LB116	4.50	93- 07	HighlandIce1181½ *RunJohnny*1142½ DggettsCrossing114no	Rallied to
5Jly97-8LS gd	6f	:222 :451 :574 1:102	3↑ Alw 24240N2X	82	8	5	813	78½	54½	11¾	Doocy T T	L116	2.00	- -	Bush Won1161¾ *Duke Arlington*116½ Knox City1101¾	Late rush dr
6Jun97-6LS fst	1$\frac{1}{16}$	:242 :474 1:123 1:433	3↑ Alw 27810N1Y	79	10	73¼	63¾	42¼	44½	68¾	Lanerie C J	L119 b	*1.80	- -	*Hollie's Chief*114½ Vast Joy1145 Exclusive Zone114¾	4-wide backstr
30Apr97-8LS fst	1$\frac{1}{16}$	:233 :47 1:113 1:432	3↑ Alw 24000N3L	90	9	68½	69½	63½	4¾	3hd	St Julien M	119 b	*1.50	- -	TimberAck119no TollBoothWilli111hd BushWon119nk	Closed well, ga
3Apr97-9OP fst	1	:231 :462 1:111 1:371	4↑ Alw 27000N$Y	92	6	510	512	58½	35½	22½	Albarado R J	112	2.30	90- 19	PowrofOpinion1132½ BushWon1126½ BlusDncr1183½	Gaining, second
21Mar97-10OP fst	6f	:212 :45 :572 1:094	4↑ Alw 27000N2X	80	1	10	1010	90½	07¼	30½	Melancon L	116	2.60	86 16	CharlioChn1194 Ourconsoltion1112½ BushWon116nk	Angled out, willi
21Feb97-10OP gd	6f	:22 :462 :591 1:12	4↑ Alw 27000N2X	88	3	8	912	95¾	63¼	2nk	Melancon L	118	6.60	81- 23	NevrIsNvr116nk BushWon1163½ Ourconsoltion1121	Far back, just mi
19Nov96-7CD fst	6½f	:222 :453 1:112 1:181	3↑ Alw 35460N2X	85	6	6	611	715	510	54½	McCauley W H	116	6.10	82- 18	Crowns Runner113½ *Receiver*1122 Rare Coin114½	No speed, never
17Oct96-6Kee fst	6½f	:222 :453 1:11 1:173	3↑ Alw 33980N2L	88	2	9	85¾	64½	11	15	McCauley W H	113	8.30	87- 20	BushWon1135 TrackGoer1162 SpectacularMx116½	Drew clear, ridder
Previously trained by Azpurua Leo Jr																
28Jly96-9Crc fst	1$\frac{1}{16}$	:242 :483 1:134 1:474	3↑ Alw 15500N2L	70	8	107	119¼	108¼	67½	56¾	Nunez E O	L112	*2.30	73- 25	TurbulentGold1141¼ AmericnVenture1125 Nhru115nk	No speed, belat
13Jly96-4Crc fst	7f	:231 :47 1:13 1:26	Alw 16600N2L	70	4	8	64½	74	52¼	21½	Nunez E O	L122	2.60	78- 14	Slortrafickeeprite1191½ BushWon1222½ *Cield'Or*119½	Late rally,up to p
22Jun96-8Crc fst	7f	:23 :46 1:112 1:244	3↑ Alw 15000N2L	68	3	6	83¼	64¾	67	54¼	Toribio A R	L115	*2.10	82- 09	SrMchlsSon1122¼ SrchforGrn112¾ StormOtFront115¾	Passed tiring r
9Jun96-10Crc fst	7f	:224 :461 1:114 1:253	3↑ Md Sp Wt 17k	76	5	5	74	55	31	11¾	Toribio A R	L115	2.40	82- 14	BushWon1151¾ TunerAlaKing1153½ GallntLddie1151½	Rallied late str
11May96-6Hia gd	6f	:222 :46 :584 1:12	3↑ Md Sp Wt 15k	72	5	3	85¼	64	34	24¾	Toribio A R	113	*1.50	- -	Dennyandchris1134¾ *Bush Won*1131½ Luke the Great1226	Up for p
Previously trained by Bohannan Thomas																
15Oct95-5Kee fst	6½f	:22 :45 1:102 1:171	Md Sp Wt 26k	58	6	10	119½	911	510	511½	Gryder A T	120	19.90	- -	Sunny Forest1201½ Basic1204 Saratoga Squall1205	Bumped hard far

CERTAIN (Out of Place—Kristie's World, by Beau Genius). Arkansas. While a winner of just two stakes, Certain was arguably the best runner by Out of Place, a speed influence. His most important victory came in the Arkansas Derby, when he was placed first via disqualification, and he was also third in the Fountain of Youth behind Vicar and Cat Thief. Most importantly, Certain was an RF (Rasmussen Factor), as he was inbred 5 x 5 to the influential matron Exclusive. The RF has proven to be a consideration in determining racing class, and Certain's runners should have good speed. (SP^2)

Certain
Own: Williams Jo L

Ch. h. 8 (May)
Sire: Out of Place (Cox's Ridge) $10,000
Dam: Kristie's World (Beau Genius)
Br: Clarkie Leverette (Fla)
Tr: Brennan Terry J(0 0 0 0 .00) 2004:(67 13 .19)

Life	22	5	3	6	$527,142	102	D.Fst	17	4	2	5	$492,112	102
2001	3	0	0	1	$4,400	97	Wet(374)	4	1	1	1	$34,760	97
2000	9	0	1	4	$30,182	102	Turf(263)	1	0	0	0	$270	84
	0	0	0	0	$0	-	Dst(0)	0	0	0	0	$0	-

17May01-8CD	fst	1 1/16	:234	:464	1:104	1:42	3↑ Alw 55220c	91	3	42	41½	42½	65	67¼	Day P	L116 f	9.70	93-11	Unshaded1231¼ Da Devil1161¼ *Neon Shadow*123no	Inside,tired	6
14Apr01-8OP	sly	1	:233	:471	1:121	1:374	4↑ Alw 35000N$Y	71	7	76¼	76	62¾	57½	58¾	Borel C H	L114	*2.00	81-16	I Dancer1141¾ *L. A. Spider Legs*115nk CollegeDean1182¼	Dull effort outside	8
30Mar01-10OP	gd	1	:233	:473	1:123	1:381	4↑ Alw 30000N$Y	97	1	1½	11	1hd	2½	32¼	Thompson T J	L118 b	3.90	86-27	Dirty Mike113½ U. S. Jets1191¾ Certain1181	Pace, weakened	8
Previously trained by Jacobs Jeff																					
17Nov00-9CD	fst	7½f	:223	:451	1:093	1:284	3↑ Alw 52675N$Y	95	5	1	56	56	33½	43¾	Borel C H	L116 fb	2.60	96-08	LbrtyGold1162½ FghtforMldy1141¼ WoldntWAll116hd	5w,bid,flattened out	7
5Nov00-8CD	fst	6½f	:22	:443	1:09	1:152	3↑ Alw 52030N$Y	89	1	8	74¾	86¾	34½	32½	Borel C H	L118 fb	4.40	97-08	*Proven Cure*1142½ Subrogate114hd Certain1181¼	7w bid 1/8 pl	8
Previously trained by Azpurua Leo Jr																					
11Aug00-4Crc	fm	1 Ⓣ	:224	:463	1:102	1:344	3↑ Alw 27000N$MY	84	5	55	52¾	42½	56	55½	Rivera J A II	L115 fb	4.70	88-06	High Security115¾ Brassy Fred1172¾ FestiveBidder1151½	3 wide, no threat	7
22Jly00-7Crc	fst	6½f	:221	:451	1:103	1:171	3↑ OC 62k/N4X-N	81	4	4	52¾	54¼	36	39¾	Castellano J J	L117 fb	*1.20	85-09	Jolie's Intention1227 Orvald1122¾ Certain1173	4 wide, passed tired	6
19Jun00-8Crc	fst	1 1/16	:242	:49	1:133	1:46	3↑ SuavPrsptH35k	88	7	62¾	62¼	42	86	76¼	Coa E M	L114	*1.10	85-21	*Blazing Sword*1141 Reporter113½ *Lord Bates*113¾	5 wide move, faltered	9
29May00-11Crc	fst	1 1/16	:243	:49	1:131	1:461	3↑ MemDayH75k	102	5	32	21	21	22½	43¼	Castellano J J	L114 b	3.00	87-16	DncingGuy121nk Reportr1113 GroomstickStocks111hd	Stalked, weakened	9
30Apr00-7GP	fst	7f	:224	:46	1:102	1:224	3↑ MiamiBeach36k	96	4	2	21½	2½	2hd	32¼	Douglas R R	L114 fb	2.80	84-25	Excellent Luck1141¾ Stormy Do114½ Certain11412¼	Bid, not good enough	6
24Feb00-9GP	fst	1 1/16	:234	:472	1:114	1:432	4↑ Alw 42000N4X	94	3	44½	41½	52¼	34	23¾	Chavez J F	L117 f	1.80	87-20	*K One King*1173¾ Certain117½ *Well Noted*1174½	Angled out, gained 2nd	7
5Feb00-8GP	fst	1 1/16	:232	:482	1:123	1:442	4↑ Alw 38000N4X	92	6	33	31	31	23	34¾	Chavez J F	L117 f	3.30	81-18	Yankee Victor1173 Adonis1171¾ Certain1171¾	Jostled st, weakened	8
8May99-8Haw	fst	1⅛	:463	1:102	1:353	1:482	IllDerby-G2	86	4	74	87	85¼	106	1010¼	Desormeaux K J	L124 f	2.70	104-07	VisionndVerse1141¼ PrimeDirective117hd Pineff1221¼	Dull effort, outrun	10
10Apr99-10OP	fst	1⅛	:46	1:101	1:36	1:491	ArkDerby-G2	94	6	64	63½	42½	24	24½	Desormeaux K J	L122 f	2.90	86-16	[D]Valhol1184½ Certain1222 Torrid Sand1181	Good move 3-w,no match	7
Placed first through disqualification																					
13Mar99-12GP	fst	1⅛	:481	1:123	1:374	1:504	FlaDerby-G1	98	3	32	2hd	2½	3nk	42¼	Desormeaux K J	L122 f	6.50	81-19	Vicar122no Wondertross122½ Cat Thief1221¾	Forced pace weakened	10
20Feb99-6GP	fst	1 1/16	:233	:472	1:123	1:453	FntnOYth-G1	95	1	32	41½	41¼	3½	31	Desormeaux K J	L117 f	7.10	78-29	*Vicar*114nk Cat Thief119¾ Certain1172¼	Bumped late, willingly	10
1Feb99-9GP	sly	1 1/16	:234	:474	1:133	1:462	Alw 44000NC	89	5	45½	48½	41½	11½	13¼	Sellers S J	L119	3.10	75-29	Certin1193¼ Cryptodiplomcy1171¼ ThGroomIsRd1194½	Strong wide move	6
12Dec98-10Crc	fst	1 1/16	:234	:48	1:122	1:47	WhtAPlsr-G3	94	1	32	43	44	21	13¼	Castellano J J	L115	2.80	81-24	*Certin*1153¼ Throwthebooktem115nk LuckyAppel1152¼	Drew clear, driving	8
23Nov98-10Crc	fst	1 1/16	:24	:481	1:134	1:482	Alw 23500N1X	76	3	32	32½	1hd	1½	11½	Castellano J J	L120	*1.30	74-23	*Certain*1201½ Silver Honors120nk Miners Gamble120½	Steady urging	7
6Nov98-11Crc	fst	1	:24	:48	1:134	1:40	Md Sp Wt 22k	85	2	1½	1½	13	14	15	Castellano J J	L118	*.50	87-18	*Certain*1185 *Private Leon*1187 Ruc1184½	Drew off, ridden out	8
17Oct98-6Crc	fst	6f	:214	:454	:582	1:121	Md Sp Wt 25k	78	8	1	84½	72½	24	2¾	Castellano J J	118	6.50	85-11	*San Gennaro*118¾ *Certain*1184½ Dan's Report118¾	Bmpd str, closed well	11
19Sep98-9Crc	sly	6f	:222	:46	:593	1:131	Md Sp Wt 27k	64	2	6	63½	53½	31	21	Castellano J J	117	9.70	80-18	Lucky Appeal1121 Certain117nk Francisco1173	Closed well,gained 2nd	9

CHIEF THREE SOX (Chief Honcho—Ramona Kay, by Our Native). Texas. A sprinter/miler by a stakes-winning son of Chief's Crown (Danzig), his Texas-bred foals should have fair speed at 2, and be better as they mature. His runners could also provide value on grass. (HT^2)

Chief Three Sox
Own: Richey and Strode Stables LLC

Ch. h. 9 (Mar)
Sire: Chief Honcho (Chief's Crown)
Dam: Ramona Kay (Our Native)
Br: Don M. Clark (Tex)
Tr: Hodges Jodie(0 0 0 0 .00) 2004:(2 0 .00)

Life	44	8	4	14	$353,620	104	D.Fst	39	7	4	14	$293,620 104
2001	8	0	0	1	$9,380	96	Wet(384)	1	1	0	0	$60,000 92
2000	11	2	0	3	$106,680	92	Turf(239)	4	0	0	0	$0 76
	0	0	0	0	$0	-	Dst(0)	0	0	0	0	$0 -

6Oct01-8Ret	fm	1 1/16	Ⓣ	:234 :474 1:11 1:404	3↑ [S]TexHallFam100k	38	9	2½	32½	811	817	826½	Melancon L J	L114	36.00	74 -	[D]ChuffeAuRoug1153 GoldNuggt115nk TinSmithn113½	Through after half	9
Placed 7th through disqualification																			
21Sep01-9Ret	fm	7½f	Ⓣ	:233 :464 1:112 1:294	3↑ Alw 18000N1Y	62	3	1	22½	21½	67	611½	Garner C J	L119 b	4.80	82-10	*Dynaboy*1191¼ Two Way Streak1191 In a Run1164¼	Stalked3wd, tired	7
18Aug01-6Ret	fst	1		:243 :49 1:133 1:39	3↑ Alw 22000NC	96	5	53	51¾	2hd	2hd	32½	Chapa R	L119 b	5.40	90-17	*Avsllstr*1191 *LghtsOnBrodwy*1231½ ChfThrSox1193¼	Steadied 1st,bid4w,hng	6
30Jun01-8LS	fst	1 1/16		:222 :452 1:093 1:421	3↑ [S]Assault150k	76	3	2½	2hd	21	65¼	610¼	Dupuy A C	L114 b	7.20	83-09	LghtsOnBrdwy117nk DsrtDrby1141½ *CptnCntdn*1201¼	Speed, dropped back	7
3Jun01-9LS	fst	1		:232 :46 1:101 1:362	3↑ Alw 38000N1Y	93	2	11	1½	1½	1hd	43¼	Dupuy A C	L119 b	15.70	90-22	*Unrullah Bull*1192½ T. B. Track Star119hd Snuck In119¾	Close throughout	5
13May01-9LS	fst	1		:231 :454 1:10 1:361	4↑ Alw 39000N$Y	87	8	3½	3½	2hd	43½	46¼	Dupuy A C	L116 b	20.00	88-17	L. A. Spider Legs1163¼ T.B.TrackStar1161½ Custer1161½	Speed, evenly late	8
21Apr01-9LS	fst	6f		:213 :434 :554 1:082	4↑ Alw 39000N$Y	90	8	5	55	53½	45¼	44¾	Dupuy A C	L116 fb	22.00	94-09	DixieDoodle116nk VinniesBoy1161¾ LeaveaLegcy1192¾	Mild bid, no factor	8
5Apr01-1LS	fst	1		:23 :461 1:102 1:372	3↑ [S]Premiere50k	82	7	65	63¼	44½	55½	67¾	Dupuy A C	L117 b	12.40	80-22	CptinCountdown1233 DesrtAir117nk DsrtDmon1172½	In middle, no threat	9
2Dec00-8Hou	fst	1 1/16		:23 :464 1:12 1:44	3↑ [S]StarOfTex100k	61	4	21	31½	54½	713	719¼	Dupuy A C	L122 b	6.00	74-09	*LghtsOnBrodwy*1163¾ *CptnCntdwn*116½ HzFstTb1162¼	Weakened gradually	8
28Oct00-9Ret	fm	7½f	Ⓣ	:224 :46 1:104 1:303	3↑ NoLeHaceS25k	76	8	10	810	87¼	88¾	77	Dupuy A C	L123 b	3.80	83-07	Dickey Rickey114no PawnsandKings114no *Gratteau*1142¾	Failed to menace	11
7Oct00-8Ret	sly	1 1/16	⊗	:232 :474 1:134 1:474	3↑ [S]TexHallFam100k	92	3	22	1½	13	12½	17	Dupuy A C	L115 b	2.80	77-20	ChiefThreSox1157 GoldNuggt1235½ *DsrtDrby*1094½	Bore out 2nd trn,drvng	8
16Sep00-8Ret	fst	1		:24 :471 1:13 1:393	3↑ CLangJrMmH35k	92	4	2½	11	11½	11½	17¾	Dupuy A C	L116 b	*.60	90-10	*ChiefThreeSox*1167¾ BusttheRcord114no CinSs1125½	3w-1st trn,ridden out	6
Previously trained by Thomas Bret																			
4Aug00-10LaD	fst	170		:233 :461 1:10 1:401	3↑ Alw 25000N$Y	90	2	44¼	45	45	43½	45½	Lambert C T	L114 b	5.40	92-12	Remington Rock1211 Our Town1173 Valadour1141½	Turned in even effort	6
29May00-6LS	fst	7f		:221 :441 1:084 1:212	3↑ [S]Assault50k	67	6	1	3½	3½	66¾	610¾	Ardoin R D	L114 b	7.30	89-02	LighteningBll1173 HezFstTb120nk DignitsDncr1141½	Broke out, retreated	6
28Apr00-8LS	fst	1 1/16		:233 :471 1:11 1:432	3↑ Alw 38000N1Y	84	9	51¾	4¾	42½	24	36¾	Ardoin R D	L116 b	5.20	80-14	Right Revved1166 Cleat116¾ Chief Three Sox116¾	Finished willingly	9
13Apr00-1LS	fst	1 1/16		:233 :47 1:111 1:441	3↑ [S]Premiere75k	88	1	11	11	1hd	21½	34¾	Ardoin R D	L116 b	4.60	78-17	Dividend M1193 *LighteningBall*1191¾ ChiefThreeSox1161¼	Speed, no finish	9
Previously trained by Richey Tony J																			
19Feb00-9Hou	fst	1		:234 :47 1:114 1:371	3↑ [S]JersyVllge25k	75	3	2½	2½	22	34	59	Murphy B G	L124 b	*2.00	89-18	*DividendM*1243½ HezaFastTab1182 WingsofJones1181¼	Stalked pace, tired	7
22Jan00-9Hou	fst	1⅛		:474 1:12 1:371 1:492	3↑ MaxmGldCpH100k	90	2	11½	1½	1hd	2hd	35	Meche L J	L117 b	6.30	91-12	*Allen's Oop*117nk Vilaxy1154¾ Chief Three Sox1174¼	Flattened out	10
1Jan00-9Hou	fst	7f		:222 :444 1:091 1:213	3↑ HouSprintH50k	79	1	7	116¾	119¾	97¼	78½	Beasley J A	L118 b	2.60	94-07	*AllensOop*1143 DividendM1171¾ Rhonsqurtrswish116no	Passed tiring rivals	11
10Dec99-6Hou	fst	1 1/16		:471 1:104 1:434	3↑ [S]StarofTex100k	86	3	21½	21	1hd	1hd	2nk	Meche D J	L124 b	3.70	99 -	LighteningBll117nk ChiefThrSox1242¾ HzFstTb1241¾	Failed to sustain bid	6
24Oct99-6LaD	fst	1 1/16		:233 :474 1:122 1:432	3↑ AllianceH30k	104	10	21½	31½	3½	13	12	Meche L J	L117 b	4.30	96-17	Chief Three Sox1172 *Vllaxy*1181 Deer Creek1142½	Came in start, clear	11
18Sep99-9Ret	fst	1		:242 :474 1:121 1:382	3↑ CLangJrMmH25k	89	5	31	21½	2½	2hd	21¾	Lambert C T	L119 b	*1.50	94-16	Heza Fast Tab1181¾ *Chief Three Sox*1195¼ Simud1151¾	Came up empty	6
21Aug99-8RP	fst	1⅛		:47 1:104 1:353 1:482	3↑ EdmondH125k	92	1	21	22	2½	31½	36	Doocy T T	LB111 b	4.60	92-10	Leave a Legacy1132 Baytown1184 ChiefThreeSox1116¼	Weakened stretch	7
24Jly99-6LaD	fst	1⅛		:462 1:103 1:35 1:48	3↑ ArkLaTxH-G3	95	2	43	53½	76¼	47½	37½	Simington D E	L110 b	18.40	98 -	*MochExpress*1182½ *LeveLegcy*1125 ChiefThrSox1103	Steadied early, 4-wide	7
9Jly99-8LS	fst	6f		:221 :443 :563 1:091	3↑ [S]CMcGregrJr50k	81	2	5	42	43	42½	54	Ardoin R D	L123 b	4.40	92-12	Best Dressed Truck120½ *Smiling Time*1162 Power Flame114¾	Even effort	7
5Jun99-8LS	fst	7f		:214 :433 1:084 1:22	3↑ [S]Assault50k	94	4	4	55	66	55	35	Ardoin R D	L123 b	5.10	93-12	*Desert Air*1232 Malted1203 Chief Three Sox123nk	Finished willingly	9
1May99-8LS	fst	6½f		:222 :442 1:091 1:153	3↑ Crescent78k	96	3	4	61¾	63	41	1nk	Ardoin R D	L117 b	15.10	92-08	Chief Three Sox117nk Spiritbound120¾ Chindi1202	Up late	8
15Apr99-1LS	fst	1 1/16		:223 :461 1:113 1:444	3↑ [S]Premiere75k	85	4	43	33	21	21½	22¾	Ardoin R D	L119 b	6.80	77-20	Desert Air1222¾ *Chief Three Sox*1192 Best Dressed Truck1142	No match	10
6Mar99-8OP	fst	1 1/16		:224 :462 1:114 1:441	4↑ Alw 27000N2X	96	7	31½	21½	1hd	14½	14	Lopez J	L116 b	23.60	83-18	Chief Three Sox1164 Dixie Road1222½ DaDevil1161¾	Stalked 3-wide, drivig	10
7Feb99-1OP	fst	1		:231 :461 1:11 1:37	4↑ Alw 30000N$Y	91	4	1hd	1hd	1hd	2hd	31¾	Court J K	L116 b	17.60	92-09	*Mr Ross*116¾ *Charley Gunn*1161 *Chief Three Sox*1161½	Dueled, grudgingly	7
26Dec98-9Hou	fst	1		:233 :473 1:123 1:373	[S]HouMile25k	71	2	710	911	96¾	711	511¼	Frazier R L	L120	4.90	83-11	DesertAir1146¼ *Putinagoodword*1161¼ *HezaFastTb*1201½	5 wide into stretch	10
5Dec98-6Hou	fst	1 1/16		:232 :463 1:104 1:441	3↑ [S]StarOfTex100k	68	6	67	55	56	66	510¾	Ardoin R D	L120	3.90	86-05	Heza Fast Tab120½ *Daggett's Crossing*1221 Snow Shower1194¾	No factor	8
21Nov98-9Hou	fst	7f		:223 :453 1:103 1:234	Conroe26k	74	6	9	109¼	109¼	85¼	32	Frazier R L	L116 b	3.50	85-13	*Heza Fast Tab*1202 Stowe Creek115no Chief Three Sox1161	7 wide rally	10
30Oct98-9LaD	fst	170		:232 :464 1:103 1:394	3↑ Alw 20000N4L	90	3	33½	34½	33	34½	34½	Perrodin E J	L114 b	6.40	95 -	OurTown1144½ HsGonContry113hd ChfThrSox1143	Stalked pace, bid,hung	7
9Oct98-9LaD	fst	6f		:223 :453 :57 1:101	3↑ OC 25k/N3X-N	85	7	4	3½	32	35	32	Perrodin E J	L114 b	2.30	91-17	My Boy Charlie1191½ *Our Town*116½ Chief Three Sox1143	Willingly late	8
24Sep98-9LaD	fst	1 1/16		:223 :484 1:121 1:432	3↑ Alw 20000C	84	4	54	52½	43½	45	34	Simington D E	L114 b	*1.20	89-14	No Native1141 *My Boy Charlie*1163 ChiefThreeSox1141	Broke in air, rallied	6
22Aug98-9LaD	fst	6f		:22 :442 :562 1:093	Airline30k	82	4	5	56	47	36	23½	Perrodin E J	L117 b	7.30	92-13	SmilingTime1223½ ChifThrSox117½ DiscrtionAdvisd1176	Up late for place	7
11Jly98-8LS	fst	7f		:224 :452 1:094 1:222	[S]AlBoganMem30k	76	1	4	31	23	24	25¼	Perrodin E J	L119 b	3.50	91-10	[D]Desert Air1225¼ Chief ThreeSox1198 ApianWay119	Driving, up for place	4
Placed first through disqualification																			
26Jun98-4LS	fm	1	Ⓣ	:242 :481 1:122 1:372	3↑ Alw 28000N2X	70	2	1hd	2hd	2hd	41½	76½	Perrodin E J	L114 b	2.20	73-22	HomeaWinner1191¼ WolfEmUp116¾ VirginiAccount1161¼	Used up, faded	8
10May98-7LS	fst	1 1/16		:231 :47 1:12 1:442	3↑ Alw 25440N2L	101	3	12	11	13	14	15¼	Perrodin E J	L114 b	4.70	82-26	ChiefThreeSox1145¼ *SummerSquir*1147½ Txstoothpick1145¾	Unchallenged	10
18Apr98-9LS	fst	6f		:221 :453 :582 1:112	[S]LonghrnSpr50k	84	2	7	76¾	64¼	35	34¾	Perrodin E J	L119 b	45.30	80-20	Zuper1193¾ Beverly Greedy1161 *Chief Three Sox*119½	Closed willingly	13
9Apr98-5LS	fst	6f		:223 :454 :581 1:112	3↑ [S]Md Sp Wt 26k	74	4	7	53½	55½	23½	11	Perrodin E J	L116 b	5.30	85-14	Chief Three Sox1161 *Royal Finder*1161½ *High Amigo*1168¼	Prevailed	14
27Feb98-10OP	fst	1		:231 :474 1:144 1:421	3↑ Md 20000	56	3	53½	65	41½	2½	33	Bourque K	L112 b	*1.50	67-33	*Rhonsqurtrswsh*1122½ *BrosSndncr*122½ *ChfThrSox*1126	Failed to sustain bid	12
8Feb98-2OP	fst	6f		:221 :462 :592 1:12	3↑ Md 25000(25-20)	55	11	8	82½	52¾	53½	46½	Bourque K	114 b	6.10	77-16	Mr Ross1144½ Weberrunnin1191 Raja's Strength1121	5 wide, bid,hung	11

CITY ZIP (Carson City—Baby Zip, by Relaunch). New York. The Empire State scored a major coup by landing City Zip. An extremely fast son of speed influence Carson City, he is out of a mare who also produced the talented Ghostzapper. There is uncommon speed from both sides of his pedigree and his runners should waste no time, winning early and often in statebred races at 2, and continue to be sprint specialists as they mature. (SP^2)

City Zip
Own: Thompson Charles R., Bowling, Carl, T

Ch. h. 6 (Feb)
Sire: Carson City (Mr. Prospector) $35,000
Dam: Baby Zip (Relaunch)
Br: Adena Springs (Ky)
Tr: Rice Linda(0 0 0 0 .00) 2004:(179 23 .13)

Life	23	9	5	4	$818,225	104	D.Fst	20	8	5	3	$765,640	104
2001	12	4	2	3	$401,920	104	Wet(439)	1	1	0	0	$25,085	94
2000	11	5	3	1	$416,305	95	Turf(283)	2	0	0	1	$27,500	102
	0	0	0	0	$0	-	Dst(0)	0	0	0	0	$0	-

27Oct01-5Bel fm 1	Ⓣ :223 :452 1:083 1:32 3↑	BCMile-G1	101	6 1½ 1hd 1½ 2½ 96	Chavez J F	L123 b	32.25	92 -	Val Royal126 1¾ Forbidden Apple126¾ Bach126 1½	Dueled outside, tired	12		
6Oct01-9Bel yl 1	Ⓣ :233 :481 1:132 1:363 3↑	KelsoH-G2	102	6 2½ 2½ 2hd 4nk 31	Chavez J F	L112 b	8.60	74-25	Forbidden Apple118½ Sarafan114½ City Zip112no	Game between rivals	9		
22Sep01-11TP fst 6f	:212 :443 :564 1:091	KyCpSpnt-G2	102	4 2 32½ 2½ 1½ 2nk	Ferrer J C	L122 b	*.60	95-14	Snow Ridge114nk City Zip1225¼ *Dream Run*1179½	4 wide bid	5		
3Sep01-3Med fst 6f	:212 :434 :554 1:083	BergenCo100k	100	2 2 41¼ 3½ 1hd 12¼	Ferrer J C	L122 b	*.40	96-08	City Zip1222¼ *San Nicolas*117¾ Sea of Green1196¾	4-deep turn,bid,drvg	5		
25Aug01-9Sar fst 7f	:22 :441 1:083 1:214	KngsBshp-G1	97	4 4 62¼ 32 23½ 34½	Chavez J F	L124 b	3.30	91-08	Squirtle Squirt1213½ Illusioned1191¼ *City Zip*1245	Steadied backstretch	8		
3Aug01-8Sar fst 6f	:213 :444 :572 1:11	Amstrdam-G2	100	2 5 2hd 2hd 1hd 11	Chavez J F	L123 b	*.50	89-15	City Zip1231 *Speightstown*1181 Smile MyLord1182¼	Bumped 1/4 pole, drive	6		
4Jly01-3Mth fst 6f	:213 :44 :562 1:09	JerShrBC-G3	102	4 1 21½ 31½ 11 14¼	Ferrer J C	L119 b	1.50	94-11	*CityZip*1194¼ *SeaofGreen*1171¼ Songandaprayer1222	Outside into lane,drvg	5		
12May01-9Pim fst 6f	:224 :452 :572 1:101	HrshJacobs75k	104	6 3 2½ 2½ 11½ 13	Chavez J F	L122 b	2.40	95-15	*City Zip*1223 Sea of Green1194 *Stake Runner*1172	Pressed 2wd,riddn out	7		
14Apr01-9Aqu fst 7f	:223 :454 1:094 1:222	BayShore-G3	77	3 5 52 62 47½ 48¾	Chavez J F	L123	*1.00	79-09	SkptothSton1201¾ MltplChoc1167 FrdysCmn120no	Between foes, no rally	8		
10Mar01-11GP fst 1⅛	:464 1:112 1:37 1:494	FlaDerby-G1	73	6 31½ 2½ 1hd 810 919¼	Nakatani C S	L122	9.60	69-13	Monarchos1224½ Outofthebox1222½ Invisible Ink122½	Check 1/4 pl, tired	13		
17Feb01-10GP fst 1 1/16	:234 :464 1:104 1:432	FntnOYth-G1	95	5 53½ 54¼ 33½ 34½ 33¼	Santos J A	L117	4.00	88-14	Songandpryer1172½ Outofthebox114¾ CityZip1174½	3 wide, some late gain	11		
27Jan01-10GP fst 7f	:221 :444 1:091 1:223	Hutchesn-G2	94	7 1 42 54 34 2½	Santos J A	L122	2.20	92-11	Yonaguska119½ City Zip1226½ Sparkling Sabre1122	Gaining quickly	11		
4Nov00-8CD fst 1 1/16	:232 :464 1:111 1:42	BCJuven-G1	92	8 31½ 41 51¾ 45½ 74	Santos J A	L122	32.80	96 -	Macho Uno122no *Point Given*1221½ *Street Cry*122½	Force pace,flatten out	14		
14Oct00-9Bel fst 1 1/16	:223 :45 1:092 1:412	Champagn-G1	72	5 62 72¼ 62¾ 68¾ 714¾	Santos J A	L122	5.30	75-09	A P Valentine1221¾ Point Given122¾ Yonaguska1221	5 wide, no response	10		
17Sep00-9Bel fst 1	:23 :461 1:113 1:374	Futurity-G1	90	7 2hd 3½ 1hd 12½ 1no	Santos J A	L122	*1.55	76-23	[D]CityZip122no BurningRoma1224¾ Scorpion122nk	Came out late, bumped	9		
Disqualified and placed second													
2Sep00-9Sar fst 7f	:223 :461 1:111 1:242	Hopeful-G1	86	9 2 3½ 71¾ 31½ 1nk	•Santos J A	L122	*1.40	83-14	[DH]Yonaguska122 [DH]City Zip122nk *Macho Uno*1227¼	Came 6 wide, driving	11		
16Aug00-9Sar fst 6½f	:22 :451 1:101 1:164	SarSpcl-G2	91	3 1 2½ 2hd 11½ 12¼	Santos J A	L122	*.75	90-12	*City Zip*1222¼ Scorpion1142¼ Standard Speed1172	When roused, driving	8		
27Jly00-9Sar fst 6f	:21 :451 :571 1:103	Sanford-G2	90	1 2 2½ 31½ 2½ 13½	Santos J A	L119	3.20	92-09	*City Zip*1193½ *Yonaguska*119½ Scorpion1143¼	Came wide, driving	7		
3Jly00-6Bel fst 5½f	:214 :452 :572 1:034	Tremont-G3	95	4 2 23 21½ 1½ 12¾	Santos J A	L116	6.90	93-13	*City Zip*1162¾ The Goo1163 Scorpion1163	Speed outside, driving	5		
9Jun00-7Bel fst 5f	:214 :444 :574	Flash82k	85	2 1 42½ 53¼ 46 33¾	Santos J A	L115	4.20	89-17	Yonaguska1152½ The Goo1151¼ *City Zip*115no	Good finish on rail	7		
Previously trained by Chapman James K													
29May00-9CD fst 5½f	:223 :46 :572 1:033	KyBC-G3	93	1 1 11 1½ 1hd 2½	Hebert T J	L115 f	3.60	99-10	*Gold Mover*113½ City Zip1156 Unbridled Time121no	Held on stubbornly	6		
13May00-3CD sly 5f	:223 :453 :574	Md Sp Wt 39k	94	8 2 2hd 2hd 11½ 16¾	Hebert T J	L119 f	*.80	99-07	City Zip1196¾ *Firststatedeposit*1193 Red's Honor119nk	Dueled, ridden out	9		
28Apr00-2Kee fst 4½f	:214 :453 :52	Md Sp Wt 50k	-	6 3 2½ 1hd 2hd	Martinez W	L118 f	9.10	97-11	Love's Connection118hd *City Zip*1185½ *Homem Ra*118½	Bumped 1/4 pole	11		

CIVILISATION (Gone West—Toussaud, by El Gran Senor). West Virginia. Famous for being the only foal out of stakes winner and Broodmare of the Year Toussaud not to win a race. A half-brother to Empire Maker, Chester House, Honest Lady, Decarchy, and Chiselling, he should sire runners who have speed and certainly have an affinity for grass. (HT^2)

Civilisation
Own: Juddmonte Farms Inc

Dk. b or b. h. 6 (Apr)
Sire: Gone West (Mr. Prospector) $150,000
Dam: Toussaud (El Gran Senor)
Br: Juddmonte Farms (Ky)
Tr: Frankel Robert J(0 0 0 0 .00) 2004:(288 83 .29)

Life	3	M	0	0	$980	74	D.Fst	0	0	0	0	$0	-
2001	3	M	0	0	$980	74	Wet(351)	0	0	0	0	$0	-
2000	0	M	0	0	$0	-	Turf(331)	3	0	0	0	$980	74
	0	0	0	0	$0	-	Dst(0)	0	0	0	0	$0	-

10Nov01-9Hol fm 1	Ⓣ :231 :463 1:103 1:352 3↑	Md Sp Wt 38k	-	9 1219 1220 - - -	Ramirez Marco A	LB120	13.50	- 17	DvlsBndt120½ ContlssMmnt120½ GrtWhtFthr120nk	Off slow,outrun,eased	12
26Aug01-1Dmr fm 1⅛	Ⓣ :491 1:14 1:381 1:50 3↑	Md Sp Wt 50k	55	8 51¾ 54½ 53½ 812 612¼	Ramirez Marco A	LB117	*1.40	71-11	Tyler Rex117hd Rafid1221½ Vixen Storm1172½	Bore out 1/4,weakened	8
13Aug01-3Dmr fm 1	Ⓣ :221 :46 1:10 1:351 3↑	Md Sp Wt 49k	74	3 811 914 811 66 53½	Ramirez Marco A	LB117	14.60	85-10	Brisote1172 On My Honour117½ Almuhathir1171	Off slow, strong run	10

CLOUD HOPPING (Mr. Prospector—Skimble, by Lyphard). Florida. Cloud Hopping only won a maiden race in three starts in England, but his pedigree warranted a stud career. His dam, a multiple Grade 2 winner, also produced two-time Pacific Classic winner Skimming, and the classy stakes-producing female family produced Contredance, Eltish, Forest Gazelle, and Wheelaway. His runners should have speed on all surfaces.

Cloud Hopping
Own: Mr K. Abdulla

Ch. h. 7 (Jan)
Sire: Mr. Prospector (Raise a Native)
Dam: Skimble (Lyphard)
Br: Juddmonte Farms (Ky)
Tr: Hra Cecil(0 0 0 0 .00) 2004:(0 0 .00)

Life	3	1	0	0	$6,562	-	D.Fst	0	0	0	0	$0 -
2000	3	1	0	0	$6,562	-	Wet(418)	0	0	0	0	$0 -
1999	0	M	0	0	$0	-	Turf(351)	3	1	0	0	$6,562 -
	0	0	0	0	$0	-	Dst(0)	0	0	0	0	$0 -

Previously trained by Henry Cecil

29Sep00♦Newmarket (GB) gd 1¼ Ⓣ Str 2:073 James Levett Handicap 1616 Quinn T 118 10.00 Shrivar108½ Barton Sands118nk *Bonaguil*1221 22
Timeform rating: 63 Hcp 20200 *Never a factor.Moon Solitaire (131) 11th,Cornelius (133) 12th*

26Jly00♦Sandown Park (GB) gd 1¼ Ⓣ RH 2:102 3↑ Traders Maiden Stakes 13 Quinn T 123 1.50 Cloud Hopping1233 Shadowblaster1233½ Queen of Fashion128no 4
Timeform rating: 79+ Maiden 10100 *Led throughout,drew clear over 1f out,ridden out*

13Jly00♦Newmarket (GB) yl 1¼ Ⓣ RH 2:072 Bedford Lodge Hotel Maiden Stk 68½ Quinn T 126 5.50 Inaaq1212 *Royal Tryst*126½ White House1212½ 9
Timeform rating: 72 Maiden 13100 *Rated towards rear,progress halfway,weakened 2f out*

Clure
Own: Eagle Oak Ranch LLC

Ch. h. 11 (Feb)
Sire: Theatrical*Ire (Nureyev) $75,000
Dam: Garimpeiro (Mr. Prospector)
Br: Allen E. Paulson (Ky)
Tr: Lynch Brian A(0 0 0 0 .00) 2004:(51 13 .25)

Life	50	7	12	6	$361,174	100	D.Fst	2	0	0	0	$3,000 88
2001	7	0	0	1	$9,680	93	Wet(368)	0	0	0	0	$0 -
2000	14	1	3	1	$66,810	95	Turf(366)	48	7	12	6	$358,174 100
	0	0	0	0	$0	-	Dst(0)	0	0	0	0	$0 -

1Jly01-3Hol fm 1 Ⓣ :233 :473 1:11 1:343 4↑ Clm 50000(50-45) 87 6 109 104¾ 65 64 52½ Smith M E LB118 f 12.10 88-12 LiterlProwlr118½ Cnltto118½ Qulitynotquntity118hd Hopped start,mild bid 11
20May01-8BM fm 1 1/16 Ⓣ :241 :481 1:113 1:421 3↑ FosterCtyH51k 92 5 55 55 43 53½ 52¼ Carr D LB115 17.20 99-04 Casino King120nk Rhapsodist1151 Shelter Cove115hd Rail trip, even 6
6May01-5Hol fm 1 1/16 Ⓣ :233 :471 1:104 1:404 4↑ Clm c-(50-45) 84 3 98¾ 105¾ 74¼ 83¼ 62¾ ♦Flores D R LB116 9.40 86-08 Foggy Day118hd DH *Bonotto*120 DH *Scattergun*114nk Split foes,mild bid 10
Claimed from Goldfarb Sanford J. for $45,000, Dutrow Richard E Jr Trainer 2001(as of 5/6): (157 41 21 30 0.26)
15Apr01-7SA fm 1 Ⓣ :23 :464 1:11 1:351 4↑ Clm 50000(50-45) 87 8 910 98¼ 87¼ 85¼ 53¼ Blanc B LB118 9.70 88-13 Marlwood118½ *LostinParadise*120½ ArmyofOne118¼ Squeezed,stdied strt 9
10Mar01-7SA gd 1 Ⓣ :232 :472 1:12 1:37 4↑ Clm 50000(50-45) 85 8 79½ 812 75¼ 73¼ 76 Blanc B LB118 7.70 76-20 Such Charisma1184 Zippersup118nk Royal Hill114½ Swung out,no bid 9
4Feb01-5SA fm 1½ Ⓣ :474 1:124 2:023 2:28 4↑ Clm c-(50-45) 86 10 86 1½ 1½ 21 53 Desormeaux K J LB119 5.00 83-14 Dad's Gun115nk Azure Ciel1192 Neotorque121hd 4wd bid,dueled,wkened 10
Claimed from Baker, Ivan C. and Curtis R. for $50,000, Pinfield Timothy Trainer 2000: (134 9 10 16 0.07)
19Jan01-4SA fm 1 Ⓣ :231 :47 1:104 1:352 4↑ Clm 50000(50-45) 93 2 52¼ 52 63½ 52¼ 32 Enriquez I D LB119 6.30 00-12 Bonotto119½ *Naninja*121½ Clure119hd Saved ground to 1/4 8
26Dec00-9SA fm 1 Ⓣ :242 :474 1:112 1:36 3↑ Clm 55000(62.5-55) 89 10 100¾ 1017 1012 108¼ 67¾ Blanc B LB116 25.50 76-22 *Such Charisma*119nk Prairieton1191 Prevalence119nk Swung out,late bid 10
18Nov00-5Hol fm 1⅛ Ⓣ :483 1:114 1:353 1:473+3↑ Clm 80000(80-70) 85 4 21½ 2½ 21½ 41½ 54½ Desormeaux K J LB119 13.50 86-08 ComeBckRonnie121hd *Quinlong*119½ FoggyDy1192½ 3wd into lane,wkened 8
29Oct00-6SA fm *1½ Ⓣ :502 1:16 2:051 2:274 3↑ CFBurkeH-G3 66 7 52¼ 31 88 811 819 Sorenson D LB110 71.00 - - Timboro1142½ DH Kerrygold116 DH ResJudict115¾ Stalked 3wd, weakened 9
1Oct00-3BM fst 1 1/16 :231 :47 1:11 1:413 3↑ SanCarlosH45k 88 5 42 41¾ 31 43 47 Warren R J Jr LB115 5.80 84-20 *CrownngMtng*1153½ *PrfndScrt*1161 GnStrmnnrmn1162½ Closed 3w, faltered 6
4Sep00-6Dmr gd 1⅜ Ⓣ :474 1:122 1:362 2:123 3↑ DelMarH-G2 89 2 74½ 75¼ 74¼ 54 67½ Sorenson D LB111 44.10 97 - NorthernQuest1161½ D AlvoCerto1151 Prssont1142½ Lacked late response 8
20Aug00-10Bmf fm 1 1/16 Ⓣ :241 :474 1:113 1:424 3↑ SanMateanH45k 95 4 53¼ 44 31 2hd 1hd Baze R A LB116 2.50 87-09 Clure116hd Hallo Bert1151½ HereComesBigC1162½ Swung out, dueld, drvg 7
12Jly00-7Hol fm 1¼ Ⓣ :511 1:152 1:384 2:024 3↑ OC 62k/N2X 92 4 53½ 41½ 52¼ 42 31¾ Blanc B LB118 12.50 80-15 CompanyApproval118nk *ChelseBrrcks*1181½ *Clure*118no Waited bit 3/8 & 1/8 6
10Jun00-6Hol fm 1 Ⓣ :24 :471 1:103 1:34 4↑ Clm c-(50-45) 91 1 129¾ 118¾ 96¼ 85¾ 24 Delahoussaye E LB116 *1.70 89-10 *Starmaniac*1124 Clure116nk *Teddy Boy*115½ 4wd into lane,late 2nd 12
Claimed from Popovich Douglas M. for $50,000, Cerin Vladimir Trainer 2000(as of 6/10): (-)
19May00-5Hol fm 1⅛ Ⓣ :474 1:113 1:352 1:48 +4↑ Clm 50000(50-45) 87 1 111 131 1012 99½ 74¼ 42 Nakatani C S LB119 *2.50 86-13 Take a Left112no *B. Mr. Lucky*116¾ Shanawi1121¼ Crowded 3/16 12
22Apr00-10SA fm 1 Ⓣ :224 :463 1:103 1:351 4↑ Clm 50000(50-45) 86 12 1117 1217 1110 77¾ 44½ Solis A LB118 6.00 78-20 StrConnection1182¾ *CheyenneGold*1181 Prevlence120¾ 6 wide into stretch 12
8Apr00-4SA fm 1 Ⓣ :232 :47 1:104 1:352 4↑ Clm 62500(62.5-55) 85 3 810 810 87¾ 86¼ 74½ Nakatani C S LB118 b 8.00 77-11 *ArmyofOne*118hd PrizeGiving118¾ GrciousPrize118hd Rail trip,imp position 10
11Mar00-9SA fm 1 Ⓣ :234 :48 1:113 1:354 4↑ Clm c-(50-45) 79 9 66 65 77½ 77¾ 76 Delahoussaye E LB118 *1.30 74-18 SidEnough116no *ArmyofOne*1181½ Fstsspednbulit1181½ 4 wide into stretch 10
Claimed from Cossey Ernest for $50,000, Carava Jack Trainer 1999: (-)
5Feb00-10SA fm 1 Ⓣ :234 :48 1:121 1:36 4↑ Clm 50000(50-45) 88 5 106 106¼ 86 73¾ 21½ Delahoussaye E LB118 *1.40 77-18 Porbandar1161½ Clure118½ Classic Renown118½ Waited,tight 2nd turn 11
14Jan00-4SA fm 1 Ⓣ :223 :454 1:10 1:334 4↑ Clm 62500(62.5-55) 93 1 79 77 64½ 43 21 Delahoussaye E LB118 4.10 89-14 ChmpgnePrince1181 Clure118½ GrciousPrize1181½ Came out,finished well 10
19Dec99-3Hol fm 1 1/16 Ⓣ :251 :484 1:121 1:414+3↑ Clm 62500(62.5-55) 75 7 21½ 21 21 34 69 Pincay L Jr LB118 *2.70 75-14 *Prize Giving*118no Rotar1152½ Kraal1182 Stalked pace, weakened 7
17Nov99-4Hol fm 1 1/16 Ⓣ :244 :49 1:123 1:422 3↑ Clm 80000(80-70) 90 6 42½ 44½ 42½ 32 53 Stevens G L LB118 *2.00 78-19 AlrttoG1182½ ThKyRnbw118nk *ChmpgnPrnc*118nk Chased btwn,outkicked 7
29Sep99-5SA fm 1 Ⓣ :234 :473 1:104 1:35 3↑ Clm c-(62.5-55) 95 1 65 64½ 43½ 41½ 2nk Stevens G L LB118 f *1.40 84-12 Fit for a King115nk Clure1181½ Zippersup118hd Bid,just missed,gamely 9
Claimed from Granja Mexico and Van Doren for $62,500, Palma Hector O Trainer 1999(as of 9/29): (-)
20Aug99-7Dmr fm 1 1/16 Ⓣ :241 :481 1:114 1:414 3↑ Ⓡ SolanBeach76k 68 4 66 65 75½ 99¾ 916½ Pedroza M A LB118 19.10 79-06 Poteen1203 Pavillon118½ Shellbacks118no Pulled,tight past 7/8 9
29Jly99-4Dmr fm 1 1/16 Ⓣ :252 :504 1:141 1:432+3↑ Clm 100000(100-85) 93 3 65 63¼ 63¼ 64 42 Delahoussaye E LB121 2.40 86-15 RollerSkte119½ *ChmpgnePrince*1191 Montjoy116½ Awkward start,mild bid 6
14Jly99-3Hol fm 1 1/16 Ⓣ :244 :481 1:113 1:412 3↑ OC 100k/N3X 98 5 12 11 1½ 3nk 1no Delahoussaye E LB119 *1.30 86-14 Clure119no Foggy Day116hd Blue Sky1172 Game btwn foes lane 5
20Jun99-3Hol fm 1 1/16 Ⓣ :24 :473 1:10 1:401 3↑ OC 80k/N3X 98 1 43½ 42 43½ 42 1no Delahoussaye E LB116 3.00 92-12 *Clure*116no *Takarian*1162 *Flying With Eagles*1172¼ Up final stride 6
6Jun99-4Hol fm 1⅛ Ⓣ :471 1:103 1:341 1:47 +3↑ OC 100k/N$MY 87 4 54 55 63¾ 34½ 56½ Flores D R LB117 f 5.10 86-12 Eternity Range1161¼ Kahal1175 Naninja116hd Saved ground 6
19May99-7Hol fm 1 Ⓣ :23 :451 1:084 1:334 3↑ OC 100k/N3X 100 2 711 614 68½ 65 31¼ Flores D R LB117 3.90 93-12 Mateo119hd Fabulous Guy1161¼ Clure117no Saved ground to lane 9
28Apr99-2Hol fm 1⅛ Ⓣ :473 1:104 1:341 1:462 3↑ OC 100k/N3X 97 5 35 37 35 22½ 22¼ Antley C W LB119 *1.90 93-05 Stanton Harcourt1172¼ Clure1193½ Tavildaran1166 Chased, second best 5
3Apr99-11SA fm 1 Ⓣ :231 :452 1:12 1:36 4↑ Clm c-(50-45) 97 6 87½ 86 53½ 31½ 13 Stevens G L LB118 *1.70 79-20 Clure1183 Flew the City1181½ Flight116¾ Boxed 2nd turn,handily 9
Claimed from Paulson Allen E. for $50,000, Baffert Bob Trainer 1999(as of 4/3): (-)
11Mar99-7SA fm 1 Ⓣ :241 :483 1:122 1:354 4↑ OC 80k/N$Y -N 93 7 64 64½ 64¼ 32 31¾ Stevens G L LB118 1.90 78-19 SuchCharisma120½ FlyingWithEgles1181¼ *Clure*118½ Pulled,bid,outkicked 7
Previously trained by Mott William I
22Nov98-7Aqu fm 1 Ⓣ :233 :471 1:113 1:363 3↑ Alw 52000c 96 6 43½ 53¼ 41¼ 31 62¼ Bailey J D L117 3.95 100-07 PrmirKrscht117no CurrncyArbtrg117no OptcNrv122nk Wide move, gamely 9
21Oct98-8Bel gd 1 Ⓣ :233 :47 1:11 1:344 3↑ Alw 45000N3X 92 3 52¾ 31½ 41¼ 31 33½ Bailey J D L119 *.70 82-16 Hardy's Halo1131½ *Premier Krischief*1172 Clure119½ Good finish inside 7
4Oct98-6Bel fst 1 :24 :471 1:11 1:36 3↑ Alw 54000c 67 6 41½ 42 53¾ 69 618¾ Bailey J D L119 2.85 65-24 *Mr. Sinatra*1152½ Fenton Lane119nk Liberty Gold1194 Wide trip, tired 6
30Aug98-7Dmr fm 1 1/16 Ⓣ :241 :473 1:113 1:412 3↑ OC 80k/N$Y -N 96 6 2hd 25 23 1½ 2nk McCarron C J LB117 *1.10 99-02 King Clef117nk Clure1171½ *Senor Senor*117½ Bid,led,just missed 8
1Aug98-10Dmr fm 1 1/16 Ⓣ :234 :471 1:111 1:413 3↑ Alw 50000N$Y 96 3 54¼ 46 41¼ 11 11 Stevens G L LB117 4.10 98-03 Clure1171 Silverani117nk Siouxrouge1174 Tight 3/8,waited 1/4 10
5Oct97-7Bel fm 1 Ⓣ :23 :452 1:09 1:332 3↑ Alw 41000N2X 95 3 31½ 21 1½ 1½ 2¾ Smith M E L117 *1.10 94-06 Premier Krischief115¾ *Clure*1171¼ Play Smart117¾ Wide move,gamely 9
31Aug97-5Dmr fm 1 Ⓣ :23 :48 1:121 1:361 3↑ Alw 50000N2X 95 3 32 42 52½ 42 4¾ Stevens G L LB117 2.20e 89-13 *Puissant*117hd Really Sovereign117nk Barricade117½ In tight str 9
14Aug97-7Dmr fm 1⅛ Ⓣ :494 1:134 1:382 1:503 3↑ Alw 50200N2X 89 5 42 31½ 31 2hd 41¼ Stevens G L LB117 *.70 81-18 Adorjinsky117no Zippersup1151 Andthelivinissy117hd Bid btwn horses 1/4 7
27Jly97-7Dmr fm 1 Ⓣ :233 :481 1:124 1:374 3↑ Alw 51200N2X 96 4 33 54½ 53½ 54 2½ Stevens G L LB117 *1.00 81-22 Mr Sunsation117½ Clure1171 Global Performance117½ Split hrses,rallied 8
28Jun97-8Bel fm 1 Ⓣ :221 :444 1:09 1:333 3↑ Alw 40000N3L 99 8 83¾ 72¾ 4¾ 11½ 2½ Bailey J D L121 *1.40 93-08 Winter Quarters119½ Clure1216½ Bomfim121¾ Clear stretch,gamely 10
7Jun97-1Bel fm 1 Ⓣ :222 :45 1:083 1:332 3↑ Alw 40000N2X 97 8 63¼ 43 3nk 11 1nk Bailey J D L119 *1.20 95-03 Clure119nk D Navillus1212 Hedge119½ 3w move,prevalled 12
17Nov96-4Aqu fm 1 1/16 Ⓣ :243 :491 1:134 1:44 3↑ Alw 37444N2X 89 5 32 33 31½ 1hd 2½ Bailey J D L112 *1.40 87-05 Notoriety113½ *Clure*1123½ Indian Wedding1151¼ Came wide 1/4p,gamely 12
Previously trained by John Hammond

28Jun96♦Chantilly (Fr) gd *1 Ⓣ RH 1:392 Prix du Portail 14 Asmussen C 126 3.30 Clure1204 *Alamo Bay*126? *Noro Zilzal*1265 7
Alw 34900 *Led throughout,broke alertly,quickly clear,unchallenged*

5Jun96♦Evry (Fr) gd *1¼ Ⓣ LH 2:02 Prix de Breme 21½ Asmussen C 126 *1.50 Steward1261½ *Clure*1262½ *Le Pirate*126¾ 10
Alw 34700 *Tracked in 4th,led briefly 1f out,second best*

1May96♦Saint-Cloud (Fr) gd *1 Ⓣ LH 1:43 Prix Bubbles 33 Asmussen C 126 2.50 Green Car1262½ *Cloud Forest*126½ Clure1261 5
Alw 34700 *Tracked in 3rd,lost duel for 2nd.Rising Colours 4th*

10Nov95♦Evry (Fr) gd *1 Ⓣ LH 1:423 Prix de Saint-Pierre Azif-EBF 2½ Asmussen C 126 - River Bay121½ Clure126½ *Cloud Forest*1261½ 10
Alw 34700 *Unhurried in 7th,bid 2f out,dueled 1f out,outgamed.Le Destin 4th*

20Oct95♦Maisons-Laffitte (Fr) yl *7½f Ⓣ Str 1:321 Prix Victrix-EBF 45 Asmussen C 121 - Dark Nile1211½ Alamo Bay1211½ Jirhan1262 8
Alw 34500 *Tracked in 4th,lacked rally*

CLURE (Theatrical—Garimpeiro, by Mr. Prospector). California. Not as talented as his full brother, Geri, he was an iron horse, making 50 starts from age 2 through 8, in France and North America. His only stakes victory came at age 7 in the minor San Matean Handicap at 1 1/16 miles on turf. His sire line and his own racing performance clearly suggest that his runners will be far superior on grass as mature runners. (T^2)

COASTAL STORM (Storm Cat—Pearl City, by Carson City). Pennsylvania. Unraced Coastal Storm is bred similarly to Hennessy, as he is out of Ballerina and Prioress Stakes winner Pearl City, a half-sister to both Hennessy and Shy Tom. His offspring should have good speed on all surfaces, but be particularly effective on grass, where they should initially offer fantastic value. (HT^2)

CONSCIENCE CLEAR (Relaunch—Gotta Wear Shades, by Kris S.). Florida. Stakes-placed at 3 on the turf, Conscience Clear is by a speed influence whose runners have been able to get middle distances if out of mares by a stamina influence, which is the case with Conscience Clear. His runners will be effective on all surfaces but should have a preference for grass. (T^2)

Conscience Clear
Own: Martin Stables Inc

B. h. 7 (Mar)
Sire: Relaunch (In Reality)
Dam: Gotta Wear Shades (Kris S.)
Br: Martin Stables Inc (Ky)
Tr: Byrne Patrick B(0 0 0 0 .00) 2004:(72 13 .18)

Life	14	3	5	2	$141,785	101	D.Fst	1	0	0	0	$2,700	77
2001	9	1	4	1	$79,140	101	Wet(411)	0	0	0	0	$0	-
2000	5	2	1	1	$62,645	89	Turf(337)	13	3	5	2	$139,085	101
	0	0	0	0	$0	-	Dst(0)	0	0	0	0	$0	-

8Nov01-6CD	fm	1⅛	Ⓣ :474 1:121 1:37 1:493	3↑ Alw 44200N$Y	85	3	31½	21	21	3nk	32¼	Melancon L	L116 b	*2.40	86- 10	DevilTime114nk LiketoTalk1182 ConscienceCler116nk	Pressed,led,weaken	10
10Oct01-9Kee	fm	1 1/16	Ⓣ :231 :472 1:112 1:422	3↑ Alw 58663N3X	86	6	2hd	1hd	11½	12	2¾	Melancon L	L119 b	5.70	88- 14	JustLikeJimmy119¾ ConsciencClr119no DominiqusCt119nk	Could not last	10
16Sep01-9KD	fm	1	Ⓣ :474 1:121 1:371	3↑ OC 50k/NC -N	86	5	2hd	2hd	2½	1hd	2½	Melancon L	L122 b	3.30	88- 17	BricksndIvy118½ ConscienceClr1221½ RosCrk122no	Pressed,led,outfinishd	7
9Aug01-9EIP	fm	1 1/16	Ⓣ :233 :472 1:12 1:43	3↑ Alw 24940N$Y	84	9	64½	31½	3nk	1½	24¼	Melancon L	L116 b	1.90	75- 24	AdvncedEdition1164¼ ConsciencClr116¾ Ctniro1131	Stalked,led,no match	10
26Jly01-7AP	fst	1	⊗ :233 :472 1:123 1:371	3↑ Alw 50580N3X	77	6	31	31	3½	31½	48	Douglas R R	L121 b	2.80	80- 15	Ask the Lord1211 Just LikeJimmy1194 BigDaddyLonglegs1213	Weakened	9
1Jly01-9CD	fm	1	Ⓣ :232 :461 1:101 1:352	3↑ Alw 44200N$Y	84	2	32	41¾	31	31	45	Melancon L	L120 b	*1.40	91- 08	CocktilsndLies1181½ RoseCreek1201 *ThKnightSky*1162½	4w bid,empty late	9
20Jun01-7CD	yl	1	Ⓣ :234 :471 1:122 1:363	3↑ Alw 46260N2X	101	4	22½	21½	1½	13	14	Melancon L	L118 b	4.50	90- 13	ConscienceClr1184 Griftr1131 *TwoPointTwoMill*118½	Pressed,3-4w,driving	10
2Jun01-6CD	fm	1 1/16	Ⓣ :241 :482 1:123 1:434	3↑ Alw 46800N2X	89	1	2½	2hd	11	11	2½	Melancon L	L120 b	3.20	86- 14	Drwmn116½ *ConscncClr*120no TwoPontTwoMll118¾	Inside,dueled,good try	10
29Apr01-7CD	fm	1	Ⓣ :23 :461 1:11 1:36	3↑ Alw 46800N2X	87	1	1½	1½	11	11½	41¼	Chavez J F	L120 b	*1.90	92- 05	RoseCreek116¾ BuffloBob116hd TwoPointTwoMill120½	Pace,weaken late	10
25Sep00-7KD	sf	1	Ⓣ :273 :51 1:184 1:461	3↑ Alw 30000N2X	57	1	42	31½	52¼	63¼	713	Court J K	L115 b	*1.00	31- 66	Red Mountain1132 *Talkmeister*1162½ Dawn Flies By1163½	Faded in drive	9
26Aug00-9Mth	fm	1⅛	Ⓣ :484 1:123 1:364 1:493	Choice50k	87	3	1hd	11	12	11½	3¾	Bravo J	L114 b	*.80	85- 16	JysCrown116no IvrsBigPeceful121¾ ConscincClr1141½	Rated, yielded late	6
Previously trained by Willey Kevin																		
22Jly00-5AP	fm	1⅛	Ⓣ :464 1:11 1:362 1:491	Alw 34000N1X	89	3	11	1½	1½	12½	14	Guidry M	L122 b	*.60	91- 10	Conscience Clear1224 Shuailaan Jennings1202 Black Hole1181	Driving	8
1Jly00-10CD	fm	1⅛	Ⓣ :464 1:111 1:362 1:493	3↑ Md Sp Wt 44k	83	2	11	11½	11½	13	12¼	Court J K	L113 b	2.60	88- 11	*ConsciencClr*1132¼ MgiclMist113hd GoodnightTril1133¾	Pace, hand urging	10
Previously trained by Byrne Patrick B																		
29May00-2CD	gd	1 1/16	Ⓣ :24 :491 1:134 1:444	3↑ Md Sp Wt 41k	68	5	44	64	52½	43	21¼	Court J K	L112 b	8.60	79- 14	ShuilnJennings1111¼ *ConscienceCler*112½ SlteCrek1231	6wide bid,2nd best	10

DELAWARE TOWNSHIP (Notebook—Sunny Mimosa, by Sunny North). Florida. A two-time Grade 1-winning sprinter, he was a durable and consistent racehorse, winning 11 of 21 starts from ages

2 through 5. Both his sire and damsire are noted sources of speed, and his runners should get off to a quick start as juveniles, and be good sprinter/milers throughout their careers. (SP^2)

Delaware Township
Own: New Farm

Ch. h. 8 (Feb)
Sire: Notebook (Well Decorated) $15,000
Dam: Sunny Mimosa (Sunny North)
Br: Mr. & Mrs. Harry Bono (Fla)
Tr: Perkins B W Jr(0 0 0 0 .00) 2004:(86 16 .19)

Life	21	11	4	1	$996,950	116	D.Fst	20	11	4	1	$989,450	116
2001	9	4	3	0	$635,840	116	Wet(382)	1	0	0	0	$7,500	67
2000	8	4	1	1	$287,010	116	Turf(252)	0	0	0	0	$0	-
	0	0	0	0	$0	-	Dst(0)	0	0	0	0	$0	-

17Nov01-9Lrl	fst	6f	:212 :441 :562 1:09	3↑ DeFrncsM-G1	116	3	6	79¾	67½	32	13	Bailey J D	L125	3.40	94-19	DelawareTownship1253 EarlyFlyer115¾ *XtrHet*117nk	5wd move,drove clear	7
27Oct01-6Bel	fst	6f	:222 :443 :561 1:082	3↑ PnskBCSp-G1	112	7	8	83¾	73¼	75½	62¾	Coa E M	L126	10.50	93-03	Squirtle Squirt124½ Xtra Heat121nk Caller One126nk	Good finish outside	14
7Oct01-9Bel	fst	6f	:23 :46 :572 1:092	3↑ FrstHlsH-G2	115	2	1	31	2½	12	13¼	Coa E M	L118	*1.45	91-21	DlwrTownshp1183¼ HookndLddr114nk *Yngsk*1131½	When asked, hand ride	5
1Sep01-9Sar	fst	6½f	:213 :44 1:084 1:152	3↑ ForegoH-G1	109	4	9	85¼	62¾	1½	11¼	Bailey J D	L116	*2.65	98-03	*Delaware Township*1161¼ *Left Bank*115¾ Alannan1172¼	5 wide move, driving	9
5Aug01-9Sar	fst	6f	:214 :443 :562 1:082	3↑ AGVndbtH-G2	107	2	5	73¾	61½	22½	21½	Bailey J D	L116	2.60	100-05	FiveStarDay1171½ *DelawreTownship*1162 Bonpw1172½	Game finish outside	7
28Apr01-7Del	fst	6f	:22 :451 :58 1:11	3↑ Damitrius72k	103	4	4	44	32	31	11½	Black A S	L116	*.40	88-18	DlwrTownshp1161½ BbbysBckr118no *InCCsHnr*1162¾	Bumped start, rallied	4
14Apr01-8Aqu	fst	6f	:214 :45 :564 1:083	3↑ BoldRlrH-G3	107	3	2	43	5¾	32½	21½	Wilson R	L117	*1.55	92-09	SyFlrdSndy1171½ *DlwrTwnshp*1172¼ *LkPntchrtrn*113¾	Bumped 1/4, steadied	7
19Feb01-9Lrl	fst	7f	:222 :443 1:092 1:22	3↑ GenGrgeH-G2	105	3	5	43¼	43¾	2½	23½	Bravo J	L120	2.20	93-16	*PeepingTom*1143½ DelwrTownship1202¾ *DiscoRico*1171¾	3-4w,rzd 3/8,willing	7
15Jan01-9GP	fst	6f	:213 :442 :564 1:093	3↑ MrProspH-G3	99	6	9	84	73¾	41¾	42¼	Day P	L116	*1.40	89-14	*Istintaj*1162 Miners Gamble115nk Smokin Pete115hd	Finished willingly	13
4Nov00-6CD	fst	6f	:204 :432 :551 1:073	3↑ BCSprnt-G1	94	14	9	109¼	119½	1110	107½	Sellers S J	L126	14.10	99 -	*Kona Gold*126½ Honest Lady123½ BetOnSunshine1262	Wide early,no factor	14
14Oct00-7Bel	fst	6f	:213 :442 :561 1:082	3↑ FrstHlsH-G2	110	1	2	32	1hd	11½	11½	Day P	L114	2.80	96-10	DelawareTownship1141½ Bevo1144 ValintHlory1132¾	3 wide move, driving	7
23Sep00-9Bel	fst	7f	:221 :443 1:083 1:213	3↑ Vosburgh-G1	103	6	10	42	31	22½	43¾	Bravo J	L126 b	10.30	91-13	Trippi123½ More Than Ready1232¼ *One WayLove*1261	Sluggish start, inside	10
27Aug00-8Mth	fst	6f	:212 :433 :553 1:074	3↑ Longfellow75k	116	2	7	2hd	1hd	14	17	Bravo J	L113 b	2.80	102-11	Delaware Township1137 [D]LoadedGun1192 *SayFloridaSandy*122¾	Hand ride	8
22Jly00-9Mth	fst	1	:24 :474 1:121 1:371	3↑ SalvtrMH-G3	104	2	11½	1½	1hd	1hd	21¼	Bravo J	L112 b	4.50	87-12	LvIttoBzr1201¼ *DlwrTownship*1125 PrimDirctv1141¾	Broke thru gate,game	5
30Jun00-9Mth	fst	6f	:221 :452 :573 1:102	3↑ OC 50k/N4X-N	102	4	1	1½	12	13½	15½	Bravo J	L120 b	*.20	89-24	DlwrTownshp1205½ PonrSprt1185 WlknrondMony1165½	Clear, ridden out	4
1Jun00-8Mth	fst	6f	:22 :442 :562 1:084	3↑ OC 50k/N4X-N	96	5	3	3½	42½	32	32	Velasquez C	L120	*1.40	95-12	McKendree1182 *ProudestBull*118no *DelawreTownship*1204¾	Outside, gaining	7
13May00-4Pim	fst	6f	:234 :462 :581 1:102	3↑ OC 35k/N3X-N	96	6	7	2hd	1hd	12½	12	Wilson R	L119	*1.20	94-10	DlwrTownship1192 TwlghtPrnc1192 FortyEghtHours115nk	Off slow, clear	7
Previously trained by Perkins Benjamin W																		
5Sep98-12Crc	sly	7f	:221 :454 1:123 1:261	[R]FSAffirmed125k	67	6	7	61¾	2½	31½	48¼	Toribio A R	118	*.60	70-18	Sly Rajab1183¾ Grade One1181 *TenPoundTest*1183½	Drew even,nothing left	9
2Aug98-8Mth	fst	5½f	:214 :45 :572 1:034	Tyro50k	87	4	3	44	55½	34	2hd	Toribio A R	118	*.60	101-10	[D]Heroofthegame116hd DelawareTownship1183 PersonlNote1163¼	Missed	6
Placed first through disqualification																		
19Jun98-6Bel	fst	5½f	:221 :46 :58 1:042	Alw 37000N2L	80	1	3	32	2½	13	16	Toribio A R	116	*.65	93-10	*DelawreTownship*1166 RobinGoodfellow1162¾ Wller1162¼	Wde mve,driving	5
20May98-1Del	fst	4½f	:23 :472 :532	Md Sp Wt 24k	73	6	3	1½		12	19½	Toribio A R	118	*.40	97-19	*DlwrTownship*1189½ LttlMornngDw1184½ GlttrngStr1183¼	Drifted, drew off	6

DISCO RICO (Citidancer—Round It Off, by Apalachee). Maryland. By a sire who had high speed and out of a mare by an established source of speed, Disco Rico was born to sprint and he won nine races from 17 starts, with seven stakes victories. His runners should also be good 2-year-olds, showing speed from the start. (SP^2)

Disco Rico
Own: Dirico Alfred

B. h. 7 (Apr)
Sire: Citidancer (Dixieland Band) $12,500
Dam: Round It Off (Apalachee)
Br: C. Oliver Goldsmith (Md)
Tr: Testerman Valora A(0 0 0 0 .00) 2004:(115 9 .08)

Life	17	9	5	1	$532,244	115	D.Fst	16	8	5	1	$493,400	115
2001	9	5	1	1	$349,644	115	Wet(387)	1	1	0	0	$38,844	107
2000	5	2	3	0	$139,100	110	Turf(261)	0	0	0	0	$0	-
	0	0	0	0	$0	-	Dst(0)	0	0	0	0	$0	-

27Oct01-10Lrl	fst	6f	:22 :444 :57 1:094	3↑ LiteThFuse75k	109	5	1	1hd	12½	13½	12	Vega H	L119 f	*1.10	90-28	Disco Rico1192 In CC'sHonor124no SassyHound124½	Early duel 2w,driving	5
7Oct01-9Bel	fst	6f	:23 :46 :572 1:092	3↑ FrstHlsH-G2	96	5	3	1½	1½	22	57¼	Vega H	L117 f	1.85	84-21	DelawareTownship1183¼ HookndLdder114nk *Yongusk*1131½	Set pace, tired	5
7Sep01-9Med	fst	6f	:213 :434 :56 1:09	3↑ PatersonH91k	96	2	1	1hd	12	12½	21½	Vega H	L123 f	*.70	92-10	SayFloridaSandy1231½ DiscoRico1231 LodedGun114	Pace,rail,outfinished	3
19May01-10Pim	fst	6f	:221 :45 :571 1:102	3↑ MdBCH-G3	106	6	3	1hd	1½	13½	12½	Vega H	L118 f	3.20	94-10	Disco Rico1182½ Flame Thrower1141 Istintaj1161	Duel 2wd in hand,drvng	6
7Apr01-10Pim	fst	6f	:222 :444 :563 1:093	3↑ FirePlug72k	108	2	1	1½	12	14	13½	Vega H	L124 f	*.30	98-14	*Disco Rico*1243½ In C C's Honor1191¼ Dr. Max1247¾	Dictated rail,hand rde	4
17Mar01-9Lrl	sly	6f	:22 :45 :563 1:093	4↑ EndlsSrprs58k	107	3	2	12	12	15	15½	Vega H	L122 f	*.40	91-18	*Disco Rico*1225½ In C C's Honor122no Dr. Max122	Brushd st,2w,handily	3
19Feb01-9Lrl	fst	7f	:222 :443 1:092 1:22	3↑ GenGrgeH-G2	99	6	1	1hd	1hd	1½	36¼	Vega H	L117 f	4.70	91-16	*PeepingTom*1143½ DelwrTownship1202¾ *DiscoRico*1171¾	Dueled 2wd, faded	7
3Feb01-10Lrl	fst	6f	:22 :451 :57 1:091	4↑ Hoover54k	115	1	5	11	11	13½	13	Vega H	L115 f	*1.70	93-19	Disco Rico1153 Dr. Max1171¼ Trounce1178¾	Towards rail, driving	5
13Jan01-9Lrl	fst	5½f	:22 :444 :57 1:032	4↑ NrthrnWolf55k	98	7	2	12	11½	11	42¾	Delgado A	L116 f	*1.50	94-18	Dr. Max115½ Trounce1191¾ In C C's Honor117½	Rail, pace, tired	7
4Aug00-8Sar	fst	6f	:214 :442 :563 1:091	Amstrdam-G3	98	5	1	1½	1½	1hd	23	Migliore R	L123 f	3.65	96-13	Personal First1203 Disco Rico1232¾ *Trippi*1231¼	Strong pace, gamely	6
15Jly00-10Lrl	fst	6f	:221 :443 :561 1:08	Montpelier85k	110	5	1	1½	11½	11	1nk	Migliore R	L119 f	1.50	102-10	[D]Disco Rico119nk *Max's Pal*1226¾ Stormin Oedy1191¾	Drifted out, driving	5
Disqualified and placed second																		
24Jun00-9Mth	fst	6f	:211 :432 :553 1:09	JerShrBC-G3	99	6	1	1hd	11	11½	1nk	Bravo J	L115 f	1.50	96-09	Disco Rico115nk *Max's Pal*1222¼ Stormin Oedy1175	Drew clear,rated,drvg	6
3Jun00-7Del	fst	6f	:213 :444 :572 1:101	LegalLight75k	101	5	1	11½	1½	1½	2¾	Delgado A	L117 f	2.40	91-14	Max's Pal122¾ *Disco Rico*117¾ Stormin Oedy1225¼	Dueled, hung,saved 2nd	8
12May00-9Pim	fst	5½f	:214 :452 :571 1:033	OC 50k/N2X-N	97	3	2	11	11	13	14½	Delgado A	L117 f	*1.00	98-15	DiscoRico1174½ ClssicRomo122nk IWillifYouWill1172¾	Rail,mild hand ride	8
28Aug99-9Tim	fst	*6½f	:23 :47 1:112 1:163	BobbyHale40k	79	2	2	11½	11½	13½	14½	Delgado A	115	*1.60	100-06	*DiscoRico*1154½ *LightningPaces*1174½ SrtogRpture1151½	Rail, pace, handily	7
12Aug99-3Lrl	fst	5½f	:224 :462 :582 1:05	Md Sp Wt 25k	77	8	7	12½	12	11½	11½	Pino M G	120	*1.00	89-21	*DiscoRico*1201½ SpectacularKim120nk *Bemhit*1202¾	Rushed to lead,driving	8
15Jly99-5Lrl	fst	5f	:214 :452 :574	Md Sp Wt 25k	73	4	4	1½	12	11½	2no	Santiago M A	120	10.00	102-10	LightningPaces120no *DiscoRico*1203½ *SrtogRpture*1202¼	Bolted 1/4, erratic	9

DIXIE DOT COM (Dixie Brass—Sky Meadows, by Conquistador Cielo). California. By far the best runner by speed influence Dixie Brass, Dixie Dot Com is poised to become an exciting sire based in California because of all the speed he brings to the table. A miler who was able to stretch his speed successfully throughout his career, he is from a classy female family that produced Carson City and General Meeting. (SP^2)

Dixie Dot Com

Own: Chaiken Carole and Don, and Heller, M

B. h. 9 (Mar)
Sire: Dixie Brass (Dixieland Band) $10,000
Dam: Sky Meadows (Conquistador Cielo)
Br: Martha Buckner (Ky)
Tr: Morey W J Jr(0 0 0 0 .00) 2004:(122 17 .14)

	Life	23	8	6	1 $1,332,775 116	D.Fst	16 7 4 1 $1,138,960 116
	2001	7	2	3	0 $679,000 115	Wet(386)	4 1 1 0 $93,815 110
	2000	4	1	0	1 $156,000 116	Turf(297)	3 0 1 0 $100,000 105
		0	0	0	0 $0 –	Dst①(369)	0 0 0 0 $0 –

Ecton Park

Own: Stanley Mark H

Ch. h. 8 (Feb)
Sire: Forty Niner (Mr. Prospector) $31,482
Dam: Daring Danzig (Danzig)
Br: E. A. Cox, Jr. (Ky)
Tr: Walden W. E(0 0 0 0 .00) 2004:(113 20 .18)

	Life	23	6	4	6 $1,503,825 117	D.Fst	18 4 2 5 $1,048,065 117
	2001	2	0	0	0 $5,340 103	Wet(391)	5 2 2 1 $455,760 112
	2000	8	1	1	4 $645,850 113	Turf(297)	0 0 0 0 $0 –
		0	0	0	0 $0 –		0 0 0 0 $0 –

ECTON PARK (Forty Niner—Daring Danzig, by Danzig). Kentucky. Forty Niner has turned into a very successful sire of sires (Distorted Humor, End Sweep, Gold Fever, Jules, Roar, Ide, Luhuk, Coronado's Quest, Tactical Advantage), and Ecton Park won the Super Derby, Jim Dandy, and Risen Star Stakes at 3. His offspring should have speed but be best at 3 at middle distances.

EL CORREDOR (Mr. Greeley—Silvery Swan, by Silver Deputy). Kentucky. El Corredor was a brilliant miler, and was at his best winning the Cigar Mile at age 3 over Peeping Tom, Affirmed Success, More Than Ready, and Left Bank. He has speed on top and bottom, and his runners should emulate his style and be best as sprinter/milers. Keep in mind that his sire is also a hidden turf sire. (SP^2 and HT)

El Corredor
Own: Earnhardt Hal J

Dk. b or b. h. 7 (Mar)
Sire: Mr. Greeley (Gone West) $50,000
Dam: Silvery Swan (Silver Deputy)
Br: Needham-Betz Thoroughbreds/Liberation (Ky)
Tr: Baffert Bob(0 0 0 0 .00) 2004:(371 70 .19)

Life	10	7	1	0	$727,920	119	D.Fst	10	7	1	0	$727,920	119
2001	3	2	0	0	$240,000	119	Wet(352)	0	0	0	0	$0	-
2000	5	4	1	0	$462,360	114	Turf(282)	0	0	0	0	$0	-
	0	0	0	0	$0	-	Dst(0)	0	0	0	0	$0	-

27Oct01-6Bel	fst	6f	:222 :443 :561 1:082	3↑ PnskBCSp-G1	85	10	4	73¼	83¼	1010	12123¾	Espinoza V	L126	4.40	83- 03	Squirtle Squirt124½ Xtra Heat121nk Caller One126nk	6 wide, no response	14
2Sep01-7Dmr	fst	1	:23 :461 1:101 1:351	3↑ DmrBCH-G2	114	3	31½	3½	2½	1hd	1hd	Espinoza V	LB121	*.20	99- 08	ElCorrdor121hd FiglioMo113nk PrformngMgc1163	Gamely btwn foes lane	6
12Aug01-8Dmr	fst	7f	:223 :443 1:081 1:202	3↑ POBrienH-G2	119	6	2	2½	2hd	11½	11½	Espinoza V	LB119	*1.50	103- 09	*El Corredor*1191½ SweptOverboard1171 *Ceeband*1144½	Dueled, clear, driving	7
25Nov00-8Aqu	fst	1	:23 :454 1:10 1:343	3↑ CigarMiH-G1	112	11	52¼	41	3½	11	11¾	Bailey J D	L116	*2.40	95- 17	*ElCorredor*1161¾ *PepingTom*111nk *AffirmdSuccss*1203½	4 wide move, driving	11
23Sep00-8Bel	fst	1	:223 :441 1:081 1:34	JeromeH-G2	114	3	4¾	42	41¼	3½	2¾	Bailey J D	L117	3.15	94- 05	FusichiPegsus124¾ *ElCorredor*1173¾ *AlbertthGrt*1208½	Game finish outside	6
3Sep00-9Dmr	fst	1	:223 :46 1:101 1:35	3↑ DmrBCH-G2	109	1	41½	41½	1hd	11½	12½	Espinoza V	LB111	*2.60	100- 08	El Corredor1112½ Cliquot1171 Literal Prowler1123	Rail trip, in hand late	8
7Aug00-7Dmr	fst	6f	:213 :442 :562 1:09	3↑ OC 62k/N2X-N	108	4	5	42¼	21	1hd	11	Espinoza V	LB113	*.80	95- 11	*El Corredor*1131 Riot1193½ Prenuptual Deal1171	Steady handling	7
15Jan00-5SA	fst	6½f	:22 :444 1:084 1:151	Alw 50000N1X	101	7	3	52¼	21	1hd	12	Flores D R	LB118	2.90	92- 09	*El Corredor*1182 Here's Zealous118nk Toqueville118½	3 wide move, handily	7
2Oct99-4SA	fst	6f	:22 :451 :572 1:092	Md Sp Wt 38k	89	6	1	1hd	11	13½	15½	Flores D R	LB120	*1.60	93- 09	*El Corredor*1205½ Hollywood Bull1206 Capote Sun1201	Drew off, easily	8
5Sep99-6Dmr	fst	5½f	:221 :453 :574 1:041	Md Sp Wt 46k	74	7	11	99	87¾	66	44½	Flores D R	LB118	12.60	87- 09	Orangeman118½ *HeresZealous*1182 UnderSurveillance1182	Slow into stride	11

EXCHANGE RATE (Danzig—Sterling Pound, by Seeking the Gold). Florida. Stakes-placed at 2, he won the Risen Star Stakes at 3 and the Tom Fool Handicap at 4. His runners should also have good speed, but he is another prime example of a hidden turf sire. His pedigree includes three powerful sources of grass breeding—Danzig, Spectacular Bid, and Nijinsky II. (HT^2)

Exchange Rate
Own: Padua Stables

Gr/ro. h. 7 (Apr)
Sire: Danzig (Northern Dancer) $200,000
Dam: Sterling Pound (Seeking the Gold)
Br: Philip Freedman (Ky)
Tr: Lukas D. W(0 0 0 0 .00) 2004:(359 40 .11)

Life	15	6	2	2	$479,803	111	D.Fst	8	3	2	1	$304,055	111
2001	6	2	0	2	$190,953	111	Wet(437)	3	1	0	0	$62,750	103
2000	6	3	0	0	$212,750	103	Turf(395)	4	2	0	1	$112,998	104
	0	0	0	0	$0	-	Dst(0)	0	0	0	0	$0	-

4Jly01-8Bel	fst	7f	:221 :443 1:083 1:211	3↑ TomFoolH-G2	110	4	1	2½	2hd	2½	1hd	Bailey J D	L114 b	6.50	97- 09	ExchngeRte114hd *SyFloridSndy*1172 HersZlous112¾	Game outside, driving	5
28May01-9Bel	my	1	:221 :45 1:102 1:37	3↑ MtropltH-G1	76	6	3nk	53	105½	99¾	1017¼	Chavez J F	L114 b	8.00	65- 20	Exciting Story116¾ Peeping Tom1192 Alannan1182¾	Finished after a half	10
5May01-3CD	fst	7f	:213 :433 1:074 1:202	4↑ LnEndCDH-G2	111	3	5	31½	31	3nk	31	Day P	L113 b	6.20	102 -	Alannan116½ *Bonapaw*116½ Exchange Rate1132¼	Grudgingly weakened	10
13Apr01-8Kee	fm	1	Ⓣ :232 :462 1:102 1:342	4↑ MakrsMrk-G2	103	2	79½	76¾	75½	74½	52	Espinoza V	L116 b	5.90	94- 03	NorthEstBond120nk Brhms1231¼ *StrtgcMsson*116no	Slow start, slight gain	8
3Mar01-7SA	gd	1	Ⓣ :231 :472 1:113 1:354	4↑ FKilroeH-G2	104	9	11	42	42	41½	31	♦Nakatani C S	LB115 b	3.80	87- 12	*Road to Slew*1171 *Val Royal*117hd DH HawksleyHill118	Speed, stalked, willing	10
31Jan01-7SA	fm	*6½f	Ⓣ :22 :441 1:071 1:131	4↑ Alw 67402N$Y	103	1	6	43	43¼	3½	1nk	Espinoza V	LB122 b	3.40	94- 08	Exchange Rate122nk Lord Smith1191 Jokerman1181	Led past 1/8, held	8
17Jun00-9CD	sly	7f	:221 :452 1:102 1:231	Hcp 100000	103	2	5	54½	31½	31	1¾	Borel C H	L119 b	2.80	89- 14	*ExchangeRate*119¾ *JimieSon*1132¾ *UltimteWrrior*1182¾	Brsh rail, no room, str	6
6May00-8CD	fst	1¼	:454 1:094 1:353 2:01	KyDerby-G1	78	16	74	84¾	125½	1210	1219¾	Borel C H	L126 b	59.20	85 -	FusichiPegsus1261½ Aptitude1264 Impechment126½	Wide, tired after 7/8s	19
15Apr00-9Aqu	wf	1⅛	:464 1:102 1:352 1:474	WoodMem-G2	84	7	33	51½	65¾	79¾	916¼	Chavez J F	L123 b	7.50	82- 10	*Fusaichi Pegasus*1234¼ *RedBullet*1231½ Aptitude123nk	Chased outside, tired	12
12Mar00-9FG	fst	1 1/16	:23 :461 1:11 1:431	LaDerby-G2	100	5	43	42½	32½	33	42½	Nakatani C S	L122 b	3.20	92- 13	Mighty1222 More Than Ready122½ Captain Steve122hd	Lacked late kick	10
20Feb00-9FG	fst	1 1/16	:24 :47 1:114 1:441	RisenStar125k	97	4	21	21½	2hd	1hd	11¼	Nakatani C S	L119 b	*1.60	90- 18	Exchange Rate1191¼ *Mighty*122no Ifitstobeitsuptome1142¾	Hit gate break	8
2Feb00-7SA	fm	*6½f	Ⓣ :221 :452 1:082 1:141	Alw 50000N1X	91	1	6	45½	42	1hd	11	Nakatani C S	LB119 b	*.60	87- 13	*ExchngRt*1191 NowVoygr1191 DsgndforLck117nk	Lackd room, bulled btwn	7
18Aug99-7Dmr	fst	6½f	:22 :443 1:094 1:162	BestPal-G3	96	5	2	31	31	1½	2½	Nakatani C S	LB117 b	4.70	88- 13	DixieUnion121½ *ExchangeRate*1175½ CaptainSteve1174½	Bid 3 wide, gamely	5
18Jly99-5Hol	fst	6f	:213 :443 :57 1:094	HolJuvCh-G3	85	3	4	31	2hd	1hd	21¼	Nakatani C S	LB117 b	1.80	87- 11	*DixieUnion*1171¼ ExchngeRte1173½ *HighYield*1156½	Lugged in 1/8, outkickd	5
27Jun99-10Hol	fst	5f	:214 :45 :57	Md Sp Wt 41k	91	4	6	11	12½	14	14½	Nakatani C S	LB118 b	3.20	98- 05	ExchngeRte1184½ ColdwterCnyon1183 SvntnCndls118½	Inside, ridden out	9

FANTASTIC LIGHT (Rahy—Jood, by Nijinsky II). England. He may be standing in Great Britain, but some of his offspring are sure to race in the U.S., especially as older runners. A racehorse of the highest quality, Fantastic Light was strictly a turf horse and his runners will also be grass horses who should improve with age and distance. If his juveniles do show up in late-season grass races, they must be respected, especially at distances over seven furlongs. (T^2)

Fantastic Light
Own: Godolphin Racing Inc

B. h. 8 (Feb)
Sire: Rahy (Blushing Groom*Fr) $80,000
Dam: Jood (Nijinsky II)
Br: Gainsborough Farm, Inc. (Ky)
Tr: bin Suroor Saeed(0 0 0 0 .00) 2004:(0 0 .00)

Life	25 12 5	3 $8,486,957	117
2001	6 4 2	0 $3,634,859	117
2000	9 3 2	1 $4,525,766	107
	0 0 0	0 $0	-

D.Fst	0 0 0 0	$0	-
Wet(347)	0 0 0 0	$0	-
Turf(366)	25 12 5	3 $8,486,957	117
Dst(0)	0 0 0 0	$0	-

27Oct01–9Bel fm 1½ ⊕:48 1:12¹ 2:01 2:24¹ 3↑ BCTurf-G1   117 2 42½ 41½ 2² 12½ 1¾ Dettori L   L126 *1.40 108 – Fantastic Light126¾ Milan1215¾ Timboroa126½   Well placed, driving 11
Previously trained by Suroor Saeed Bin

8Sep01♦Leopardstwn (Ire)   gd 1¼ ⊕ LH 2:01⁴ 3↑ Irish Champion Stakes-G1   1hd Dettori L   130 2.25   Fantastic Light130hd Galileo123⁶ Bach130⁴   7
Timeform rating: 133   Stk 949600   Unhurried in 3rd,led 1-1/2f out,dueled over 1f out,very game

28Jly01♦Ascot (GB)   gd 1½ ⊕ RH 2:27³ 3↑ King George VI & Queen Eliz St-G1   2² Dettori L   133 3.50   Galileo121² Fantastic Light133¹ Higtor1/133hd   12
Timeform rating: 130+   Stk 1069000   Rated in 9th,progress 2f out,strong bid 1f out,outfinished

20Jun01♦Ascot (GB)   gd 1¼ ⊕ RH 2:04² 4↑ Prince of Wales's Stakes-G1   12½ Dettori L   126 3.30   Fantastic Light126½ Kalanisi126¾ Hightori126½½   9
Previously trained by Suroor Saeed Bin   Stk 349500   Rated in 6th,angled out 2f out,led 1f out,driving.Observatory 4th

27May01♦Curragh (Ire)   yl 1⅜ ⊕ RH 2:13² 4↑ Tattersalls Gold Cup-G1   1nk Dettori L   126 *1.25   Fantastic Light126nk Golden Snake126³ Kalanisi126¹   6
Timeform rating: 128   Stk 218600   Tracked in 3rd,4th 3f out,led 1f out,driving.Bach 5th

24Mar01♦Nad Al Sheba (UAE)   fm *1½ ⊕ LH 2:28¹ 4↑ Dubai Sheema Classic-G2   2no Dettori L   123 –   Stay Gold123no Fantastic Light123² Silvano123¾½   16
Previously trained by Suroor Saeed Bin   Stk 2000000   Rated in 6th,led over 1f out,headed on line.Endless Hall 4th

17Dec00♦Sha Tin (HK)   gd *1¼ ⊕ RH 2:02¹ 3↑ Hong Kong Cup-G1   11¾ Dettori L   126 *1.90   Fantastic Light126¼½ Greek Dance126no Jim and Tonic126¼½   13
Timeform rating: 128   Stk 1794800   Trckd ldrs,2nd 3f out,led over 1f out,driving.Forbidden Apple 4th

26Nov00♦Tokyo (Jpn)   fm *1½ ⊕ LH 2:26 3↑ Japan Cup-G1   3nk Dettori L   126 7.90   T.M.Opera O126nk Meisho Doto126no Fantastic Light126¼⅜   16
Previously trained by Suroor Saeed Bin   Stk 4278300   Wide in 11th,bid 1f out,gaining late.Ela Athena4th,John's Call9th

4Nov00–9CD fm 1½ ⊕:50¹1:15¹ 2:03³2:26⁴ 3↑ BCTurf-G1   107 2 6⁴ 64½ 6³ 5³ 5² Dettori L   L126 11.90 107 – Kalanisi126½ Quiet Resolve126no John's Call126hd   Checked deep stretch 13

7Oct00–9Bel fm 1½ ⊕:50²1:15³ 2:03⁴2:28² 3↑ TfClscIv-G1   103 1 84½ 53½ 4⁴ 47½ 43½ Dettori L   L126 *1.40 83– 18 John's Call126⁵ Craigsteel125¹⅜ Ela Athena123¼½   Came wide, stayed on 12

9Sep00–9Bel fm 1⅜ ⊕:50¹1:16 1:41 2:17² 3↑ ManOWar-G1   106 1 7⁷ 73½ 6¹⅜ 2hd 11 Bailey J D   L126 *.65 68– 31 Fantastic Light126¹ Ela Athena123nk Drama Critic126²   3 wide move, clear 8

29Jly00♦Ascot (GB)   gd 1½ ⊕ RH 2:29⁴ 3↑ King George VI & Queen Eliz St-G1   21½ Reid J   133 12.00   Montjeu133¹⅜ Fantastic Light133³¼ Daliapour133¹   7
Timeform rating: Stk 1127600   Rated in 6th,2nd 200y out,no chance with winner.Beat All 4th

8Jly00♦Sandown Park (GB)   gd 1¼ ⊕ RH 2:05¹ 3↑ Eclipse Stakes-G1   5⁶ Reid J   133 5.00   Giant's Causeway122hd Kalanisi133¼½ Shiva130¼½   8
Timeform rating: 114   Stk 544800   Tracked in 4th,ridden without response 2f out.Sakhee 4th

9Jun00♦Epsom (GB)   yl 1½ ⊕ LH 2:41³ 4↑ Coronation Cup-G1   2¾ McCarron C   126 1.75   Daliapour126¾ Fantastic Light126¾ Border Arrow126⁷   4
Previously trained by Michael Stoute   Stk 377300   Trckd in 3rd,2nd hfwy,3rd 2-1/2f out,in tight,regained 2nd 1f out

25Mar00♦Nad Al Sheba (UAE)   gd *1½ ⊕ LH 2:27³ 4↑ Dubai Sheema Classic-G3   1³ Fallon K   121 –e   Fantastic Light121³ Caitano124² High-Rise124²   16
Rated twrd rear,rallied to lead over 1f out,drifted right, driving

30Oct99♦Longchamp (Fr)   hy *1½ ⊕ RH 2:38² 3↑ Prix de l'Arc de Triomphe-G1   11²⁹ Reid J A   123 33.40   Montjeu123¼ El Condor Pasa131⁶ Croco Rouge131⁵   14
Towards rear throughout.Tiger Hill 5th,Borgia 7th,Daylami 9th

19Sep99♦Newbury (GB)   yl 1⅜ ⊕ LH 2:21² 3↑ Arc Trial (Listed)   1¾ Fallon K   126 2.25   Fantastic Light126¾ High-Rise128⁹ Pegnitz126³¼   6
Timeform rating: 125   Trailed,ridden 4f out,dueled 1f out,drftd rght & lft,led 150y out

17Aug99♦York (GB)   gd 1½ ⊕ LH 2:29 4↑ Great Voltigeur Stakes-G2   11¼ Stevens G   121 4.00   Fantastic Light121¼½ Bienamado121½½ Glamis121¹   7
Timeform rating: 121   Stk 160400   Tracked in 4th,led over 3f out,ridden out.Mutafaweq 4th

3Jly99♦Sandown Park (GB)   gd 1¼ ⊕ RH 2:06² 3↑ Eclipse Stakes-G1   3¾ Stevens G   122 6.00   Compton Admiral122nk Xaar133½ Fantastic Light122¼½   8
Timeform rating: 121   Stk 465100   Tracked in 5th,bid 1f out,outfinished.Croco Rouge7th,LearSpear8th

15Jun99♦Ascot (GB)   gd 1¼ ⊕ RH 2:04¹ 3↑ Prince of Wales's Stakes-G2   2hd Stevens G   117 14.00   Lear Spear129hd Fantastic Light117²¼ Xaar129¹   8
Timeform rating: 120   Stk 239100   Settled in 8th,bid 1-1/1f out,dueled 1f out,gamely.Shiva 7th

8May99♦Lingfield (GB)   gd 1⅞ ⊕ LH 2:30¹ 4↑ Lingfield Derby Trial-G3   46¾ Tani K   122 3.00   Lucido119¹⅛ Daliapour121½ Royal Rebel119⁵   5
Timeform rating: 104   Stk 86900   4th early,ridden hfwy,drifted left & bumped 3f out,wknd 1f out

24Apr99♦Sandown Park (GB)   sf 1¼ ⊕ RH 2:15³ 3↑ Thresher Classic Trial-G3   1no Holland D   123 6.50   Fantastic Light123no Dehoush123¹½ Glamis123²   7
Timeform rating: 106+   Stk 108600   Tracked in 4th,led 1f out,rider misjudged finish,just lasted

11Sep98♦Goodwood (GB)   yl 1 ⊕ RH 1:44³ Stardom Stakes (Listed)   32¼ Cochrane R   123 2.25   Mutaahab123¾ Glamis123² Fantastic Light123   3
Timeform rating: 103   Stk 33500   Tracked pacesetting winner,outpaced final furlong

22Aug98♦Sandown Park (GB)   gd 1 ⊕ RH 1:44¹ Sun Conditions Stakes   1¾ Reid J   126 3.50   Fantastic Light126¾ Aesops123²½ Adnaan123²½   5
Timeform rating: 103+   Alw 11900   Prominent,2nd halfway,dueled 1f out,led 70y out

2Aug98♦Sandown Park (GB)   gd 7f ⊕ RH 1:33¹ Carshalton Novice Stakes   11¾ Reid J   124 8.00   Fantastic Light124¹¾ Sicnee130² Sampower Star132²   5
Timeform rating: 82+   Alw 10400   Dwelt,outpaced 3f out,raced greenly,led 75y out,going away

FLAME THROWER (Saint Ballado—Metromane, by Metrograd). Florida. Winner of the Del Mar Futurity, Norfolk, and Best Pal Stakes at 2, Flame Thrower should be another son of high-speed influence Saint Ballado to be a successful sire of 2-year-olds. His runners should continue to be good sprinters as they mature. (SP^2)

Flame Thrower
Own: Garber Gary M

Ch. h. 6 (May)
Sire: Saint Ballado (Halo) $125,000
Dam: Metromane (Metrogrand)
Br: Suzanne Collins (Fla)
Tr: Baffert Bob(0 0 0 0 .00) 2004:(434 80 .18)

Life	7	4	2	0	$458,200	105	D.Fst	7	4	2	0	$458,200	105
2001	2	0	2	0	$70,000	105	Wet(338)	0	0	0	0	$0	-
2000	5	4	0	0	$388,200	105	Turf(267)	0	0	0	0	$0	-
Aik Ⓣ	0	0	0	0	$0	-	DstⓉ(331)	0	0	0	0	$0	-

9Jun01-8Bel	fst	7f	:214	:442	1:082	1:213	RivaRidg-G2	105	5	4	21	21½	23	2nk	Bailey J D	L120	*1.35	95-05	Put ItBack120nk FlameThrower1202¾ *TouchTone*1231¼	Gamely, vanned off	6
19May01-10Pim	fst	6f	:221	:45	:571	1:102	3↑ MdBCH-G3	100	2	6	36	56½	46	22½	Bailey J D	L114	2.70	91-10	Disco Rico1182½ Flame Thrower1141 Istintaj1161	3wd 3/8,rallied btwn	6
4Nov00-8CD	fst	1 1/16	:232	:464	1:111	1:42	BCJuven-G1	87	12	21½	2½	2½	78½	86¾	Espinoza V	L122	5.40	93 -	Macho Uno122no *Point Given*1221½ *Street Cry*122½	Pressed pace,weakened	14
7Oct00-6SA	fst	1	:23	:463	1:101	1:344	Norfolk-G2	105	1	11	1½	1½	11	1nk	Espinoza V	LB118	*1.00	97-03	Flame Thrower118nk Street Cry1185½ Mr Freckles1183½	Very game on rail	8
13Sep00-8Dmr	fst	7f	:22	:441	1:09	1:22	DmrFut-G2	103	6	4	1hd	1½	1½	1hd	Bailey J D	LB119	*1.00	95-08	*Flame Thrower*119hd Street Cry1163½ *Arabian Light*1195	Game rail lane	8
23Aug00-7Dmr	fst	6½f	:214	:444	1:094	1:162	BestPal-G3	96	7	2	1½	11	12	12¾	Nakatani C S	LB117	4.30	91-13	*FlameThrower*1172¾ *Trailthefox*1215 LegendaryWeve1176	4wd early,driving	7
26Jly00-7Dmr	fst	6f	:221	:453	:574	1:101	Md Sp Wt 47k	95	4	4	1hd	11	11	1¾	Nakatani C S	LB118	*1.50	89-13	*Flame Thrower*118¾ High Tech Exec1188 Matta118½	Inside duel, gamely	10

FLAMING QUEST (Rainbow Quest—Nearctic Flame, by Sadler's Wells). Texas. Another stallion whose offspring would be better suited to European racing. Given that his pedigree is top-heavy with stamina and grass, his runners will have little impact on dirt, and will just start to run at 1⅛ miles on turf at 3 and older. (T^2)

Flaming Quest (GB)
Own: Hodges James E

B. h. 8 (Mar)
Sire: Rainbow Quest (Blushing Groom*Fr) $62,426
Dam: Nearctic Flame*Ire (Sadler's Wells)
Br: Cheveley Park Stud (GB)
Tr: Hodges Jodie(0 0 0 0 .00) 2004:(2 0 .00)

Life	9	2	3	0	$27,403	69	D.Fst	0	0	0	0	$0	-
2001	2	0	0	0	$0	50	Wet(455)	1	0	0	0	$0	50
2000	1	0	0	0	$0	69	Turf(369)	8	2	3	0	$27,403	69
Aik Ⓣ	0	0	0	0	$0	-	DstⓉ(341)	0	0	0	0	$0	-

13Apr01-8LS	fm	1	Ⓣ :233	:481	1:133	1:382	4↑ Alw 33000N3X	28	2	57½	78	85¼	818	827¼	Bourque C C	L116	10.70	49-23	CleverActor116½ DevilMCr1191 Fortunfivhundrd1165¼	In middle, stopped	8
Previously trained by Shulman Sanford																					
24Feb01-7SA	wf	1½	⊗ :474	1:134	2:053	2:31	4↑ Clm 40000(40-35)	50	5	44	43½	615	623	634¼	Jauregui L H	LB119 f	7.10	68 -	Clonmany117¾ Armstrong115hd Gracious Prize1198	Gave way outside	6
16Dec00-7Hol	fm	1⅛	Ⓣ :504	1:142	1:372	1:491	+3↑ Alw 47235N2X	69	5	42	32	42	85½	89	Sorenson D	LB117	16.40	73-15	Entorchado1171¼ Irish Nip120½ Rimsky Korsakov117hd	Off bit slow,pulled	8
Previously trained by Michael Stoute																					

17Aug99 York (GB)	gd	1½ Ⓣ LH 2:29	Great Voltigeur Stakes-G2	717¾	Fallon K	121	10.00	*Fantastic Light*1211¼ Bienamado1211¼ Glamis1211		7
Timeform rating: 90			Stk 160400					*Led to over 3f out,soon weakened.Mutafaweq 4th,Elmutabaki 5th*		
3Jly99 Haydock (GB)	yl	1½ Ⓣ LH 2:384	July Trophy (Listed)	23	Ryan W	122	3.00	Elmutabaki1223 Flaming Quest1223 Helvetius1223½		4
Timeform rating: 106			Stk 33700					*Tracked leader,wide into stretch 4f out,second best.Red Sea 4th*		
19Jun99 Ascot (GB)	fm	1½ Ⓣ RH 2:322	New Stakes (Listed)	23½	Stevens G	123	*.50	Zarfoot1233½ Flaming Quest123nk Helvetius1237		4
Timeform rating: 102			Stk 34300					*Rank on rail behind slow pace in 3rd,angled out to get up for 2nd*		
31May99 Chepstow (GB)	gd	1½ Ⓣ LH 2:373	St Arvans Novice Stakes	19	Sprake T	130	*.40	Flaming Quest1309 Stormy Skye12419 Mattan11915		5
Timeform rating: 106			Alw 8900					*Rated well in hand in 3rd,led over 3f out,easily*		
24May99 Leicester (GB)	gd	1½ Ⓣ RH 2:383	Levy Board Maiden Stakes	12½	Dettori L	126	*.25	*Flaming Quest*1262½ Ashgar126hd Precious Persian1211¼		6
Timeform rating: 84+			Maiden 9300					*Led after 1f,quickened over 3f out,,drew clear in hand*		
15May99 Newbury (GB)	sf	1¼ Ⓣ LH 2:093	Heatherten Maiden Stakes	21½	Weaver J	126	10.00	*Fairy Godmother*1211½ *Flaming Quest*1267 Anschluss1261½		14
Timeform rating: 106			Maiden 12100					*Rated at rear,progress 2-1/2f out,bid 1f out,raced greenly*		

FOREST CAMP (Deputy Minister—La Paz, by Hold Your Peace). Kentucky. Winner of the Del Mar Futurity, Forest Camp was bred strictly for speed and his runners should be excellent 2-year-olds and also have high speed as they mature. (SP^2)

Forest Camp
Own: Jones Aaron U. and Marie D

Dk. b or b. h. 7 (Feb)
Sire: Deputy Minister (Vice Regent) $100,000
Dam: La Paz (Hold Your Peace)
Br: Twin Creeks Farm (Ky)
Tr: Inda Eduardo(0 0 0 0 .00) 2004:(41 1 .02)

Life	11	4	2	0	$339,984	115	D.Fst	10	3	2	0	$312,384	115
2001	4	1	0	0	$43,449	105	Wet(364)	0	0	0	0	$0	-
2000	3	1	1	0	$78,935	115	Turf(256)	1	1	0	0	$27,600	97
Aik(T)	0	0	0	0	$0	-	Dst(T)(348)	0	0	0	0	$0	-

2Dec01-8Hol	fst	6f		:22	:441	:561	1:09	3↑ VOUndrwd-G3	97	3	4	31½	31½	42	52¼	McCarron C J	LB116	5.70	93- 12	Men's Exclusive120½ Tavasco114nk *Caller One*1241½	Pulled,inside,no bid	7
7Nov01-5Hol	fm	5½f	(T)	:213	:434	:561	1:022	3↑ Alw 46000N3x	97	4	2	2hd	2hd	11	2½	McCarron C J	LB118	*1.50	91- 08	[D]Tavasco118½ Forest Camp1181 Martel1182½	Dueled,worn down late	5
Placed first through disqualification																						
6Oct01-8SA	fst	6f		:211	:432	:553	1:073	3↑ AnTtlBCH-G1	105	4	4	21	22½	31½	46½	Smith M E	LB115	13.70	94- 12	SweptOverboard1162½ KonaGold1273 *ILoveSilver*1161	Stalked,outfinished	6
1Sep01-8Dmr	fst	6f		:212	:433	:553	1:084	3↑ [R]PirtsBntyH71k	90	3	5	33	36	35	55½	Flores D R	LB119	*1.60	90- 12	Freespool1213 Tavasco1151 Capo Di Capo115hd	Lacked late response	8
14Oct00-7Bel	fst	6f		:213	:442	:561	1:082	3↑ FrstHlsH-G2	88	6	5	2hd	3nk	33½	48¼	McCarron C J	L116	*1.05	88- 10	Delaware Township1141½ Bevo1144 Valiant Halory1132¾	Vied inside, tired	7
9Sep00-3Dmr	fst	6f		:22	:443	:562	1:083	3↑ [R]PirtsBntyH72k	115	2	3	2hd	13½	14	14	McCarron C J	LB118	*.50	97- 12	ForestCamp1184 TreasureHunt115nk ChampsStr11812	Inside,clear,easily	5
Previously trained by Baffert Bob																						
8Jan00-8SA	fst	6f		:22	:443	:562	1:084	SMiguel-G3	106	1	4	1hd	1½	1½	2no	McCarron C J	LB121	*.70	95- 13	*SweptOverbord*116no *ForestCmp*1212¾ JoopyDoopy1183	Inside, game effort	6
6Nov99-8GP	fst	1 1/16		:221	:46	1:101	1:421	BCJuven-G1	84	10	22	21	12	31½	610	Flores D R	L122	*2.70	86 -	Anees1222½ Chief Seattle122¾ High Yield1222¼	Drift in start,tired	14
10Oct99-7SA	fst	1		:221	:454	1:094	1:353	Norfolk-G2	103	1	11½	11	11½	11	2½	Flores D R	LB118	*.30	92- 15	Dixie Union118½ Forest Camp1184½ *Anees*1189½	Game inside in lane	6
8Sep99-8Dmr	fst	7f		:222	:444	1:09	1:213	DmrFut-G2	106	5	1	31	1½	13½	15½	Flores D R	LB116	2.10	95- 09	ForestCamp1165½ *DixieUnion*1212 *CaptinSteve*1151¼	Pulled,led 4wd,handily	5
7Aug99-5Dmr	fst	5f		:213	:453		:58	Md Sp Wt 46k	87	3	6	31½	32	2½	12	Flores D R	LB118	*1.50	94- 11	*ForestCamp*1182 CllMeAgin118nk SevenJillion118½	Stmbld strt,waited trn	9

FREUD (Storm Cat—Mariah's Storm, by Rahy). New York. Group-placed at 3 in England, and winner of only one race in 12 starts, Freud will never be confused with his illustrious full brother, Giant's Causeway. Nevertheless, because he is obscure to most players, his runners will offer tremendous value on all surfaces, and especially when they show up on turf in statebred races. (HT^2)

Freud
Own: Michael Tabor

B. h. 6 (Feb)
Sire: Storm Cat (Storm Bird) $500,000
Dam: Mariah's Storm (Rahy)
Br: Orpendale (Ky)
Tr: O'Brien Aidan P(0 0 0 0 .00) 2004:(0 0 .00)

Life	12	1	2	1	$44,016	-	D.Fst	0	0	0	0	$0	-
2001	9	1	1	1	$34,273	-	Wet(409)	0	0	0	0	$0	-
2000	3	M	1	0	$9,743	-	Turf(361)	12	1	2	1	$44,016	-
Aik(T)	0	0	0	0	$0	-	Dst(T)(414)	0	0	0	0	$0	-

7Oct01	Tipperary (Ire)	sf	7f	(T) LH 1:41	3↑ Concorde Stakes-G3 Stk 75800	1217¾	O'Donoghue C	124	12.00	Montecastillo1261½ Toroca121½ *Gaelic Queen*121hd	*Never a factor*	12
29Sep01	Ascot (GB)	sf	6f	(T) Str 1:173	3↑ Diadem Stakes-G2 Stk 147400	117¼	Spencer J P	124	16.00	Nice One Clare123nk Orientor124no Bahamian Pirate126no	*Behind, ridden over 2f out, never dangerous*	15
26Aug01	Deauville (Fr)	yl	*6f	(T) Str 1:092	3↑ Prix de Meautry-G3 Stk 58500	66¼	Kinane M J	123	9.60	Do The Honours1203 *Invincible Spirit*1271½ Hot Tin Roof123no	*Held up, switched left & headway 1 1/2f out, stayed on one pace*	9
12Aug01	Leopardstwn (Ire)	sf	6f	(T) Str 1:132	3↑ Phoenix Sprint Stakes-G3 Stk 62400	62	Kinane M J	124	*3.30	Bahamian Pirate128no One Won One1281 Munjiz128nk	*Tracked leader in 5th, ridden 2f out, kept on, no gain final f*	9
12Jly01	Newmarket (GB)	gd	6f	(T) Str 1:094	3↑ July Cup-G1 Stk 323700	108¾	Spencer J P	125	16.00	*Mozart*1253½ Cassandra Go1281 Misraah131no	*Held up, headway over 1f out, led that group in final f*	18
21Jun01	Ascot (GB)	gd	6f	(T) Str 1:132	3↑ Cork and Orrery Stakes-G2 Stk 169900	32½	Spencer J P	119	25.00	Harmonic Way1261 Three Points1261½ Freud119½	*In rear, progress over 1f out, ran on to take 3rd in final f*	21
26May01	Curragh (Ire)	yl	1	(T) Str 1:412	Irish 2000 Guineas-G1 Stk 245900	711¾	Spencer J P	126 b	9.00	*Black Minnaloushe*1262 *Mozart*126¾ Minardi1263½	*Progress 2f out, 7th & ridden 1 1/2f out, no gain*	12
7May01	Curragh (Ire)	yl	1	(T) RH 1:441	Second Empire Maiden Maiden 18100	11½	Kinane M J	128 b	*.40	Freud1281½ *Julie Jalouse*1231 Scottish Minstrel128no	*Slow into stride, tracked, going easily 3f out, drew clear late*	14
17Apr01	Leopardstwn (Ire)	sf	6f	(T) Str 1:231	Ballyboden Maiden Maiden 14000	2hd	Kinane M J	128	*1.10	Turtles Reprisal123hd *Freud*1281½ *Baron de Feypo*128nk	*Tracked ldrs, 6th 1 1/2f out, led in final f, ridden, headed late*	14
21Oct00	Doncaster (GB) Timeform rating: 97	sf	1	(T) LH 1:454	Racing Post Trophy-G1 Stk 253900	59	Kinane M J	126	*2.00	*Dilshaan*1262½ Tamburlaine126¾ Bonnard1265	*Rated in 6th,bumped slightly 1-1/2f out,never a factor.Darwin 4th*	10
14Oct00	Newmarket (GB) Timeform rating: 110	yl	7f	(T) Str 1:274	Dewhurst Stakes-G1 Stk 312100	52¼	Spencer J P	126	11.00	Tobougg1261¼ Noverre126hd Tempest126½	*Tracked in 4th,outpaced 2f out,mild late gain.Mozart 4th*	10
1Jly00	Curragh (Ire) Timeform rating: 91	yl	6f	(T) Str 1:173	EBF Maiden Maiden 12100	2½	Kinane M J	128	*.20	Blixen123½ Freud1281 John Dorans Melody1281½	*Tracked in 5th,ridden 1-1/2f out,2nd 100y out*	10

HOLLYCOMBE (Capote—Confirm, by Proudest Roman). Texas. Obviously due to physical problems, Hollycombe did not make his career debut until age 5, but went on to win the Del Mar Breeders' Cup Handicap. In a career defined by starts and stops, he returned at age 7 to finish second behind Kona Gold in the Portrero Grande Breeders' Cup Handicap. He is bred for speed top and bottom, and his runners will also be blessed with good speed. (SP^2)

Hollycombe
Own: Toffan John A

B. h. 10 (Apr)
Sire: Capote (Seattle Slew) $30,000
Dam: Confirm (Proudest Roman)
Br: Carolyn T. Groves (Ky)
Tr: Gonzalez J. P(0 0 0 0 .00) 2004:(39 2 .05)

Life	15	5	4	0	$356,453	111	D.Fst	11	5	3	0	$332,360 111
2001	6	0	3	0	$73,200	111	Wet(353)	1	0	0	0	$9,693 103
2000	3	1	0	0	$56,193	103	Turf(258)	3	0	1	0	$14,400 104
Aik Ⓣ	0	0	0	0	$0	-	DstⓉ(313)	0	0	0	0	$0 -

15Aug01- 3Dmr	fst	1		:23 :47 1:11 1:35^2	3↑ Alw 73780N$MY	99	5	1$1\frac{1}{2}$	1^1	1^2	1^2	2$\frac{1}{2}$	McCarron C J	LB117 b	*1.30	97- 06 Penamacor121$\frac{1}{2}$ Hollycombe117$2\frac{1}{2}$ Stormy Jack119^{hd}	Met bid turn, caught	5
22Jly01- 8Dmr	fst	6f		:22 :44^1 :55^{4}1:08^1	3↑ BCrsbBCH-G2	103	3	3	4^7	4$5\frac{1}{2}$	4$4\frac{1}{2}$	4$6\frac{1}{4}$	Stevens G L	LB116	9.80	93- 07 KonaGold126$\frac{3}{4}$ CallerOne124$\frac{1}{2}$ SweptOverbord115^5	Awkwrd,crowded start	4
28May01- 8Hol	fm	1	Ⓣ	:23^1 :45^3 1:09^{1}1:33^3	3↑ ShoeBCM-G1	96	1	1^1	1$\frac{1}{2}$	1$\frac{1}{2}$	3$1\frac{1}{2}$	7^5	Delahoussaye E	LB124	11.00	91- 11 *Irish Prize*124^{nk} TouchoftheBlues124^{nk} Brahms124$1\frac{1}{2}$	Speed,inside,wkened	9
1Apr01- 7SA	fst	6$\frac{1}{2}$f		:21^1 :44 1:08^{2}1:15	4↑ PtrGrBCH-G2	111	1	4	2$2\frac{1}{2}$	2$1\frac{1}{2}$	3$\frac{1}{2}$	2^{nk}	↓McCarron C J	LB114	8.00	93- 12 *Kona Gold*126^{nk} DH Hollycombe114 DH Explicit116^4	Bid btwn,gamely	4
3Mar01- 7SA	gd	1	Ⓣ	:23^1 :47^2 1:11^{3}1:35^4	4↑ FKilroeH-G2	94	2	2^1	1^{hd}	2^{hd}	2$\frac{1}{2}$	7$5\frac{1}{2}$	McCarron C J	LB116	8.90	82- 12 *Road to Slew*117^1 *Val Royal*117^{hd} DH Hawksley Hill118	Bid btwn,rail duel	10
9Feb01- 2SA	fm	1	Ⓣ	:24^1 :48^4 1:11^{3}1:34^4	4↑ Alw 72432N$MY	104	4	1$1\frac{1}{2}$	1^1	1$\frac{1}{2}$	1^1	2no	McCarron C J	LB117	3.20	93- 07 Hawksley Hill117^{no} Hollycombe117$1\frac{1}{2}$ Bing Bang117^2	Very game inside	5
29Mar00- 7GG	fst	1		:22^4 :46^1 1:10 1:35^3	3↑ BerkelyH-G3	96	2	3$2\frac{1}{2}$	3$1\frac{1}{2}$	3$2\frac{1}{2}$	4^5	4$6\frac{1}{4}$	McCarron C J	LB115	*1.00	88- 17 VoicofDstiny113$\frac{3}{4}$ MrDoubldown115^2 *TwilightAffir*115$3\frac{1}{2}$	Stlkd 2-3w, empty	8
4Mar00- 4SA	gd	7f		:23^2 :46^2 1:10 1:22	4↑ SnCrlosH-G2	103	3	5	4^2	5^2	3$1\frac{1}{2}$	4$2\frac{1}{2}$	McCarron C J	LB117	3.70	92- 10 SonofaPistol117^{no} *KonGold*122$2\frac{1}{2}$ OldTopper116^{no}	4wd into lane,outkickd	6
15Jan00- 3SA	fst	7f		:23 :45^3 1:09^{3}1:22^1	4↑ Alw 65000N$Y	99	2	5	3^2	3^1	2^{hd}	1^{hd}	McCarron C J	LB122	*.60	94- 09 Hollycombe122^{hd} YoungAtHrt116^2 *SonofPistol*120^1	Off bit slow,3wd,game	5
16Oct99- 8SA	fst	1⅛		:46^{3}1:10^2 1:35^{1}1:48^1	3↑ GdwdBCH-G2	99	4	1^{hd}	1$1\frac{1}{2}$	2^{hd}	6^6	6$11\frac{1}{4}$	Stevens G L	LB117	5.70	83- 17 Budroyle119^{nk} GenerlChllenge120^3 OldTrieste120^2	Inside duel,weakened	6
5Sep99- 8Dmr	fst	1		:22^2 :45^3 1:09^{2}1:35^2	3↑ DmrBCH-G2	106	1	1^1	1$\frac{1}{2}$	1^{hd}	1^{hd}	1^1	Stevens G L	LB116	9.40	95- 09 Hollycombe116^1 FlyingWithEgles115^{nk} OldTrist122^{no}	Inside duel,gamely	8
21Aug99- 4Dmr	fst	1		:22^2 :45^1 1:10 1:36^3	3↑ OC 62k/N$Y -N	92	3	1^1	1$\frac{1}{2}$	1^{hd}	1^1	1$2\frac{1}{2}$	McCarron C J	LB119	*1.80	89- 13 *Hollycombe*119$2\frac{1}{2}$ *SonsCoron*119$\frac{1}{2}$ DncingAflet119$5\frac{1}{2}$	Bmpd, met bid, gamely	7
24Jly99- 3Dmr	fst	1$\frac{1}{16}$		:23^2 :46^3 1:10^{4}1:42^4	3↑ Alw 58000N2X	91	4	1$1\frac{1}{2}$	1^1	1$\frac{1}{2}$	1$1\frac{1}{2}$	2^1	McCarron C J	LB119	*1.50	89- 13 *National Saint*117^1 *Hollycombe*119^5 Futural115$2\frac{3}{4}$	Inside, worn down	5
27Jun99- 4Hol	fst	7f		:21^3 :44^1 1:08^{3}1:22	3↑ Alw 48530N1X	92	7	4	1^{hd}	1^{hd}	1$\frac{1}{2}$	1^3	McCarron C J	LB119	*1.40	92- 05 Hollycombe119^3 *Aplomado*122$\frac{1}{2}$ *RoundboutRock*115$3\frac{1}{2}$	Dueled,clear,driving	9
19Mar99- 6SA	fst	6f		:21^4 :44^3 :56^{4}1:09^2	4↑ Md Sp Wt 45k	107	2	3	1^1	1^1	1$2\frac{1}{2}$	1^3	McCarron C J	LB122	2.00	93- 12 *Hollycomb*122^3 RojoWrrior117^4 BombrsMoon122^6	Inside,steady handling	7

HURRICANE CENTER (Storm Cat—Devil's Sister, by Alleged). Canada. A winner of just one race in eight starts, Hurricane Center is certainly bred to be a better stallion. His unraced dam produced two stakes winners, Hishi Natalie and Blacksburg, and more significantly, she was a half-sister to Ballade, the dam of Glorious Song, Devil's Bag, and Saint Ballado. Expect his runners to have more of an impact on grass. (HT^2)

Hurricane Center
Own: Overbrook Farm

Dk. b or b. h. 8 (Feb)
Sire: Storm Cat (Storm Bird) $500,000
Dam: Devil's Sister (Alleged)
Br: Overbrook Farm (Ky)
Tr: Lukas D. W(0 0 0 0 .00) 2004:(430 49 .11)

Life	8	1	1	2	$35,658	88	D.Fst	7	1	1	1	$31,158 88
2000	2	0	1	0	$2,688	66	Wet(374)	1	0	0	1	$4,500 67
1999	4	1	0	1	$27,080	88	Turf(359)	0	0	0	0	$0 -
	0	0	0	0	$0	-	DstⓉ(396)	0	0	0	0	$0 -

28Dec00- 7TP	fst	6f	:21^4 :44^3 :56^{4}1:09^4	3↑ Clm 30000(30-20)N2L	63	6	3	4^3	4^3	4^4	6$6\frac{1}{4}$	Peck B D	L116	*2.20	86- 10 Deputize Me111$1\frac{1}{2}$ Arrow Point115^3 Demon's Law112$\frac{1}{2}$	3 wide late turn	9
30Nov00- 7TP	fst	6$\frac{1}{2}$f	:22^4 :46^2 1:12^{3}1:19^2	3↑ Clm 30000(30-20)N2L	66	6	2	2$\frac{1}{2}$	2^{hd}	1$1\frac{1}{2}$	2$3\frac{3}{4}$	Peck B D	L116	3.40	74- 26 Gifted Flight114$3\frac{3}{4}$ Hurricane Center116$2\frac{1}{4}$ GardenCat120^{nk}	No match late	8
27Dec99- 8FG	fst	6f	:22 :45^4 :58^{1}1:11	3↑ Alw 30000N1X	30	8	7	8$5\frac{1}{4}$	7$4\frac{3}{4}$	9^{17}	9$20\frac{3}{4}$	Albarado R J	L117	4.90	68- 11 Encanto115$2\frac{1}{2}$ Markarian115$\frac{1}{2}$ Two Pair119$\frac{1}{2}$	No speed, no threat	9
23Nov99- 4CD	fst	6f	:21^2 :44^3 :56^{3}1:10	3↑ Alw 36720N1X	61	5	5	6$5\frac{1}{4}$	5$7\frac{1}{2}$	5^8	5$12\frac{1}{2}$	Day P	L119	2.00	80- 10 *Skeptic*116$\frac{3}{4}$ *Encanto*112$3\frac{1}{4}$ Cielo Rey112^1	No rally	7
31Oct99- 1CD	fst	6f	:21^4 :45^2 :58^{2}1:11	3↑ Md Sp Wt 34k	88	2	4	1^{hd}	1^{hd}	2^{hd}	1^3	Day P	L120	*2.00	88- 12 HurricnCntr120^3 CinnmonLd120$3\frac{1}{2}$ NorthrnNinr120^2	Dueled, hand urging	12
9Oct99- 2Kee	sly	6$\frac{1}{2}$f	:22^2 :46^2 1:11^{2}1:17^4	3↑ Md Sp Wt 44k	67	5	2	4^2	5$4\frac{1}{2}$	4$3\frac{1}{2}$	3^5	Day P	L119	*1.50	81- 17 *Hall Pass*119^2 Burning Marque119^3 *Hurricane Center*119^4	4 wide mid turn	9
14Nov98- 4CD	fst	7f	:22^2 :45^1 1:11 1:24^3	Md Sp Wt 37k	75	4	4	2$\frac{1}{2}$	2^{hd}	2^2	4^2	Day P	L120	4.00	83- 12 Mi Buddy120$\frac{1}{2}$ Etbauer120^{hd} *Call Me Tricky*120$1\frac{1}{2}$	Off inside, weakened	11
22Oct98- 3Kee	fst	6f	:22 :45^3 :58 1:10^2	Md Sp Wt 40k	58	8	2	4$1\frac{3}{4}$	5^4	4$6\frac{1}{2}$	3$9\frac{3}{4}$	Day P	L122	3.00	79- 14 Deep Gold122$\frac{3}{4}$ *Chief Howcome*122^9 HurricaneCenter122$1\frac{1}{4}$	Lacked late bid	12

JAZZ CLUB (Dixieland Band—Hidden Garden, by Mr. Prospector). Maryland. Jazz Club could be the next big stallion in Maryland. He is by the same sire as Citidancer, Dixie Brass, and Dixie Union (speed), and his dam is a half-sister to Up the Flagpole, the dam of seven major stakes winners. The 2003 Horse of the Year, Mineshaft, also comes from this high-class female line. Jazz Club's offspring should be precocious at 2, and have good speed at 3. With the Northern Dancer sire line on top and Herbager in his dam's pedigree, they should also be effective on grass. (SP^2 and HT)

Jazz Club
Own: Farish William S. and Jamail, Joseph

B. h. 9 (Feb)
Sire: Dixieland Band (Northern Dancer) $50,000
Dam: Hidden Garden (Mr. Prospector)
Br: William S. Farish & Joseph Jamail (Ky)
Tr: Howard Neil J(0 0 0 0 .00) 2004:(120 27 .22)

Life 22 8 2 2	$417,679	114	D.Fst	11 5 2 1	$356,185	114
2001 1 0 0 0	$0	54	Wet(404)	2 0 0 1	$7,740	73
2000 1 0 0 1	$5,940	73	Turf(328)	9 3 0 0	$53,754	89
Aik Ⓣ 0 0 0 0	$0	-	DstⓉ(395)	0 0 0 0	$0	-

24Jun01-9CD	fst	7f	:224 :453 1:10 1:223	3↑ Alw 55900N$Y	54	7	5	63½	67	716	719¾	Day P	L115	3.90	72-11	Better Road122no *On the Tee*1171¾ Coast of Mane115½	Faded	7
24Aug00-7Sar	gd	7f	:222 :453 1:10 1:232	4↑ Alw 49140N$Y	73	2	3	34½	35½	36½	312½	Day P	L120	2.20	75-12	Istintaj1163 Tejano Couture1239½ Jazz Club120	Inside trip, no rally	3
11Nov99-9Aqu	fst	1⅛	:471 1:114 1:364 1:493	3↑ StuyvntH-G3	94	3	31	33½	41½	54½	68¼	Day P	L120	*1.60	80-29	BestofLuck114½ WildImagintion1153 Durmiente1132¼	Chased pace, tired	9
15Oct99-8Med	fst	1⅛	:464 1:103 1:344 1:47	3↑ MedCupH-G2	110	4	2½	2hd	2hd	2hd	2hd	Day P	L118	3.80	95-12	Pleasant Breeze110hd JazzClub1181¼ VisionandVerse1125¼	Rated, gamely	8
24Sep99-9Med	fst	1 1/16	:23 :454 1:091 1:411	3↑ Alysheba58k	100	4	43½	43¾	22	1hd	14	Bravo J	L122	1.70	95-02	Jazz Club1224 Red Weasel115½ Key Lory1175¾	Driving	4
14Aug99-3Sar	my	1⅛	:48 1:113 1:364 1:501	4↑ Alw 60000c	–	5	42	53	513	521	-	Day P	L122	*.95	- 28	EarlyWarning1171¼ GoldStarDeputy1146¼ *Hanarsn*1171	Tired badly, eased	5
24Jly99-4Del	fst	1 1/16	:223 :453 1:101 1:423	3↑ RRMCarpMem100k	101	4	67	56½	31	11½	17¾	Day P	L122	*1.50	94-10	JazzClub1227¾ RealityRoad114½ FredBearClw1194¼	Rated, bid, ridden out	6
12Jun99-8Bel	fst	1⅛	:461 1:10 1:34 1:461	3↑ BroklynH-G2	92	4	22½	43½	74¼	69½	615¼	Migliore R	L115	11.90	85-08	Running Stag1177¼ Deputy Diamond1132¼ Sir Bear1193¼	Tired after 3/4s	8
16May99-8WO	fst	1 1/16	:23 :464 1:112 1:43	4↑ EclipseH-G3	96	4	32	22	23	25½	37½	Perret C	L119	*.75	81-23	SocialCharter1136½ VictorCooley1181 JazzClub119½	Lacked late response	10
23Apr99-8Kee	fst	1⅛	:481 1:113 1:36 1:48	4↑ BenAli-G3	104	6	21½	21	21	1½	12½	Day P	L115	*1.70	95-13	Jazz Club1152½ Smile Again115¾ Early Warning1151	Hand urging, clear	6
13Mar99-10GP	fst	1 1/16	:232 :464 1:11 1:423	3↑ CrmFrchH-G3	114	5	34½	34	33	1hd	12	Day P	L114	4.50	94-19	*Jazz Club*1142 Rock and Roll1132¾ Hanarsaan1136¼	Rallied, proved best	7
13Feb99-1GP	fst	1 1/16 ⊗	:234 :473 1:124 1:444	4↑ Alw 44000c	99	6	2hd	2hd	1hd	11½	2½	Day P	L122	*1.10	82-18	Behaviour122½ *Jazz Club*1226¾ Mi Narrow1222½	Vied, outfinished	6
17Jan99-4GP	fst	1 1/16 ⊗	:242 :48 1:123 1:44	4↑ Alw 44000c	104	7	11	11½	12	13	14¾	Sellers S J	L115	10.80	87-19	Jazz Club1154¾ PowerfulGoer1152¼ Dixie'sHome11515	Vigorous hand ride	7
15Nov98-8CD	fm	1 1/16 Ⓣ	:24 :482 1:131 1:444	3↑ Alw 52000c	76	4	21½	21	41¼	55	67½	Sellers S J	L118	*2.60	72-18	RojoDinero116¾ DixiesHome121nk Doublethebetwic1162	Speed to stretch	10
25Oct98-9Kee	fm	1 Ⓣ	:222 :454 1:11 1:353	3↑ Alw 46890N2x	89	5	58½	44½	32	11½	15½	Day P	L110	*1.10	90-12	Jazz Club1105½ Mr Festus1101 Associate114nk	Waited, bumped, steadd	9
16Sep98-7Del	fm	*1 1/16 Ⓣ	:241 :483 1:123 1:44	3↑ Alw 27500c	79	3	87¼	88¾	85¾	44	1½	Bartram B E	114	8.90	87-13	*Jazz Club*114½ Danzatame1162¼ Sushi Amazon114no	Wldn't load, bled	10

Previously trained by Paul Cole

5Jun98 Epsom (GB) Timeform rating: 68	gd	7f	Ⓣ LH 1:233	Vodafone Network Handicap Hcp 64700	129	Quinn T	124 b	33.00	Apache Red127hd Bodfari Pride112½ *Shalad'or*112nk	*Never a factor.Gift Of Gold (110) 4th,Sunley Seeker (118) 16th*	17
23May98 Haydock (GB)	yl	1	Ⓣ LH 1:472	Silver Bowl Handicap (Listed) Hcp 54800	1018½	Quinn T	126	20.00	French Connection107½ Lucayan Indian130hd Tom Dougal1231	*Chased leaders,weakened 2f out,not persevered with*	10
5May98 Chester (GB)	gd	7½f	Ⓣ LH 1:332	Earl of Chester Handicap Hcp 46800	97¼	Quinn T	133	14.00	Bodfari Pride109nk Gift of Gold108½ *Plan-B*123nk	*Rated kindly in mid-pack,weakened 2-1/2f out.Pelagos (123) 8th*	13
11Oct97 Ascot (GB)	hy	7f	Ⓣ Str 1:374	Hyperion Conditions Stakes Alw 20200	543	Quinn T R	125	3.50	*La-Faah*1233 Batswing1237 Chips1315	*Always outrun,tailed off*	5
19Aug97 York (GB)	gd	7f	Ⓣ LH 1:26	Acomb Conditions Stakes Alw 45000	612¾	Eddery P	128	7.00	Saratoga Springs1225 Chester House1261¾ Mutawwaj1221¾	*Led to over 2f out,weakened over 1f out.La-Faah 7th*	9
8Aug97 Haydock (GB)	gd	6f	Ⓣ Str 1:132	Cntrywde Frght Conditions Stks Alw 12900	11¾	Lynch F	120	8.00	Jazz Club1201¾ Hayil1288 Friar Tuck1281½	*Soon tracking leaders,led over 2f out,ridden out*	6

JIMRAN (Seattle Dancer—Kaikilani, by Wavering Monarch). Arkansas. His sire was a half-brother to Seattle Slew by Nijinsky II and was a stakes winner on turf. Jimran is bred exclusively for grass and so are his runners. (T^2)

Jimran
Own: Williams Jo and Bush

B. h. 9 (May)
Sire: Seattle Dancer (Nijinsky II) $10,035
Dam: Kaikilani (Wavering Monarch)
Br: Glencrest Farm (Ky)
Tr: Azpurua L J Jr(0 0 0 0 .00) 2004:(0 0 .00)

Life 3 M 1 0	$4,530	64	D.Fst	3 0 1 0	$4,530	64
1999 1 M 0 0	$130	4	Wet(264)	0 0 0 0	$0	-
1998 2 M 1 0	$4,400	64	Turf(279)	0 0 0 0	$0	-
0 0 0 0	$0	-	Dst(0)	0 0 0 0	$0	-

10Sep99-10Crc	fst	6f	:221 :461 :592 1:13	3↑ Md 32000(32-30)	4	8	2	86¾	97½	813	825	Rivera J A II	L122 f	8.80	58-17	Jolie's Intention119¾ *Island Force*1174¼ Fast Search119hd	Showed little	9
Previously trained by Young Troy																		
23May98-5LS	fst	6f	:221 :451 :574 1:103	3↑ Md Sp Wt 22k	45	12	13	119¾	1013	814	818½	Doocy T T	L116 f	*1.60	70-16	Vincent Vega1168½ Jon Jon1162½ *Dixie Doodle*1162¾	Lunged start, empty	14
25Apr98-3LS	fst	6f	:22 :454 :59 1:122	3↑ Md Sp Wt 22k	64	13	11	95¾	36½	25	22¾	Doocy T T	116	6.00	77-19	Lake Bruin1162¾ Jimran1161½ Wayne's Loan1161	Closed fast	14

KING CUGAT (Kingmambo—Tricky Game, by Majestic Light). Kentucky. Bred for turf top and bottom, King Cugat showed an immediate preference for grass at 2, winning the Prized Stakes and finishing second in both the Summer and Pilgrim Stakes. He was a multiple stakes winner on turf at 3 and 4, which indicates that his runners may not have the speed or develop quickly enough to be as good at 2 as they will be at 3. (T^2)

King Cugat
Own: Centennial Farms

B. h. 7 (Mar)
Sire: Kingmambo (Mr. Prospector) $225,000
Dam: Tricky Game (Majestic Light)
Br: Dinwiddie Farm (Ky)
Tr: Mott William I(0 0 0 0 .00) 2004:(480 93 .19)

Life	16	7	7	1	$1,293,782	114		D.Fst	0	0	0	0	$0	-
2001	6	1	4	1	$555,980	114		Wet(304)	0	0	0	0	$0	-
2000	6	4	1	0	$541,162	106		Turf(340)	16	7	7	1	$1,293,782	114
Aik Ⓣ	0	0	0	0	$0	-		DstⓉ(328)	0	0	0	0	$0	-

29Sep01-9Bel	gd	1½	Ⓣ	:504 1:162 2:051 2:292	3↑ TfClscIv-G1	104	4	63	31	2½	22½	23	Bailey J D	L126	*.65	79-18	Timboroa1263 King Cugat1261¼ Cetewayo1261¾	Wide move, game finish 6
11Aug01-9Sar	gd	1½	🅃	:474 1:124 2:021 2:262	3↑ SwrdDncH-G1	108	1	86½	73	65	43¼	2¾	Bailey J D	L120	*1.95	103-03	*With Anticipation*114¾ King Cugat1201¼ SlewValley114¾	Steadied, checked 9
7Jly01-8Bel	fm	1⅜	🅃	:472 1:104 1:342 2:103	3↑ BwlnGrnH-G2	114	2	77¼	62½	62½	1hd	1½	Bailey J D	L119	*.80	102-06	KingCugat119½ SlewValley1126 *ManFromWicklow*112no	Quick 5 wide move 7
9Jun01-9Bel	fm	1¼	🅃	:484 1:132 1:371 2:003	3↑ ManhttnH-G1	108	3	85¾	41	42	33½	2¾	Bailey J D	L120 b	*1.45	87-10	Forbidden Apple117¾ *King Cugat*120½ Tijiyr1152	Steadied second turn 10
5May01-7CD	fm	1⅛	Ⓣ	:474 1:113 1:361 1:483	3↑ TurfClsc-G1	107	5	86¼	86	85¾	51¾	2nk	Bailey J D	L120	*1.80	93-08	White Heart116nk King Cugat1201¼ Brahms123hd	Hopped start,7w bid 8
25Mar01-8FG	fm	*1⅛	Ⓣ	:484 1:131 1:38 1:503	4↑ ExploBdH-G2	106	3	66	67	64¼	65	3¾	Day P	L121	*1.60	90-12	Tijiyr110nk Northcote Road115½ King Cugat1211¾	Angled ot, closed late 13
4Nov00-5CD	fm	1	Ⓣ	:234 :474 1:112 1:343	3↑ BCMile-G1	97	7	148½	148½	127½	127¾	115	Bailey J D	L123	3.50	97 -	War Chant123nk North East Bound126no Dansili126no	Clipped heels, 7w 14
15Oct00-8Bel	fm	1⅛	🅃	:514 1:154 1:381 1:493	JamaicaH-G2	95	8	84½	51½	62¼	21½	1no	Bailey J D	L123	*.45	80-21	KingCugat123no MandarinMrsh1141½ PrdeLeder1152	Fast finish, got nod 8
19Aug00-11AP	yl	1¼	Ⓣ	:474 1:12 1:371 2:013	Secretar-G1	106	2	78	76	41¼	1½	21	Bailey J D	L123	*.60	98-04	*Ciro*1201 *King Cugat*1234½ Guillamou City1173	Circled, led, 2nd best 8
1Jly00-8AP	fm	1⅛	Ⓣ	:47 1:112 1:36 1:48	ArlClsc-G2	106	5	37	39	23	11½	12¾	Albarado R J	L123	*.05	97-07	King Cugat1232¾ Boyum1147¼ El Ballezano1142½	Ridden out 5
10Jun00-9CD	fm	1⅛	Ⓣ	:48 1:12 1:352 1:471	JeffrsnCup287k	106	2	53	33½	31½	13½	16¼	Albarado R J	L122	*.50	100 -	*King Cugat*1226¼ *Four On the Floor*122nk Field Cat1222¾	5wide, ridden out 10
5May00-8CD	fm	1 1/16	Ⓣ	:232 :464 1:11 1:411	AmerTurf-G3	99	10	94¾	83¼	41½	11½	12¾	Bailey J D	L123	*2.10	98-02	*King Cugat*1232¾ *Lendell Ray*1163¼ Go Lib Go1233¼	4wide trip,driving 11
5Nov99-4GP	gd	*1⅛	Ⓣ	:49 1:14 1:40 1:514	Prized200k	91	6	66¾	46	44¾	11½	11¾	Bailey J D	112	2.80	77-20	*King Cugat*1121¾ *Four On theFloor*1201¼ ThadyQuill1101½	4 wide trip,driving 8
24Oct99-9Bel	sf	1⅛	🅃	:504 1:16 1:413 1:543	Pilgrim-G3	75	2	72¼	72¾	4nk	1½	2¾	Bailey J D	113	*.90	54-43	Kachemak Bay117¾ *King Cugat*1133¼ Aldo1171	4 wide move, gamely 7
11Sep99-8WO	fm	1	Ⓣ	:231 :463 1:11 1:352	Summer-G2	83	1	64½	53½	42	31	21¾	Castillo H Jr	122	*1.00	85-13	*Four On the Floor*1221¾ King Cugat1222 *Precise End*1221¾	Closed willingly 7
20Aug99-2Sar	fm	1	🅃	:251 :501 1:142 1:374	Md Sp Wt 41k	72	2	41	41	41¼	11½	14	Bailey J D	116	3.05	82-11	King Cugat1164 Pisces1161¼ Trentino116½	Split rivals, driving 10

LAKE AUSTIN (Storm Cat—Lakeway, by Seattle Slew). Florida. A modest racehorse, he has a chance to do well in the Florida market. His dam was a multiple Grade 1 stakes winner; his second dam is a full sister to Saratoga Six; and his third dam is a full sister to Bold Forbes. (SP^2)

Lake Austin
Own: Stonerside Stable LLC and Rutherford

Dk. b or b. h. 7 (Mar)
Sire: Storm Cat (Storm Bird) $500,000
Dam: Lakeway (Seattle Slew)
Br: Mike G. Rutherford (Ky)
Tr: Stewart Dallas(0 0 0 0 .00) 2004:(198 35 .18)

Life	13	3	3	0	$124,373	96		D.Fst	8	2	3	0	$86,345	94
2001	3	0	0	0	$3,200	71		Wet(410)	0	0	0	0	$0	-
2000	10	3	3	0	$121,173	96		Turf(359)	5	1	0	0	$38,028	96
Aik Ⓣ	0	0	0	0	$0	-		DstⓉ(423)	0	0	0	0	$0	-

22Nov01-10CD	fm	1	Ⓣ	:234 :474 1:122 1:362	3↑ Alw 49000N$Y	66	6	816	811	87	810	815¼	Espinoza V	L116 fb	11.20	76-08	Strawberry Affair1121 Kick Boxer1166 Image1131½	Slow start,outrun 8
30Oct01-8CD	fst	6f		:212 :441 :56 1:091	3↑ Alw 50700N$Y	70	4	6	47	46½	714	713½	Day P	L116 b	6.00	78-13	*Accelernt*1153¼ MountinGenerl1182¼ HereComsRockt116hd	Tired after 1/2 8
10Oct01-7Kee	fst	6½f		:223 :452 1:093 1:16	3↑ Alw 64000N3X	71	1	6	67	510	49	415¾	Chavez J F	L119 fb	4.70	77-22	Slider1176½ C. Mo1143½ Here Comes Rocket1195¾	Bobble start,no threat 6
2Nov00-5CD	fm	1⅛	Ⓣ	:471 1:112 1:361 1:483	3↑ Alw 50800N$Y	82	8	31½	21½	21½	33	57¼	Day P	L118 b	7.80	86-07	GlfStorm1182½ HollywoodBldct1133 Kplngr114nk	Forced pace,4w,weaken 9
14Oct00-8Kee	fm	1	Ⓣ	:232 :463 1:101 1:341	SeattleSlw74k	72	4	44	33	34	47	814	Gomez G K	L118 b	4.60	87-05	*Brahms*1182 Final Row1182¼ *Gulf Storm*1182½	Sluggish start,faded 8
3Sep00-9Sar	gd	1 3/16	Ⓣ	:483 1:124 1:372 1:552	SaranacH-G3	96	8	31	3½	3½	1hd	41½	Smith M E	L116 b	19.30	79-24	RobsSprt120nk WhtBrnstrm1171 DwnfthCndr117nk	Vied 3 wide, stayed on 9
18Aug00-5Sar	gd	1 1/16	🅃	:242 :483 1:132 1:442	Alw 50000c	90	1	43	42	41¾	21	1hd	Day P	L117 b	3.55	80-21	LkeAustin117hd SintJoseph1191 AnOscrforBert1173	Bumped start, inside 6
15Jly00-10Tdn	fst	1⅛		:464 1:111 1:374 1:502	OhioDrby-G2	73	4	21	21	2hd	911	919¼	Castillo H Jr	L114 fb	21.20	70-17	MilwukeeBrew116hd BrvQust1132¼ KissNtiv116no	Drew even,flattend out 10
30Jun00-5CD	fst	1 1/16		:232 :471 1:12 1:44	Alw 48500N1X	91	1	1½	11	1hd	1hd	1no	Day P	L121 fb	1.60	90-15	LkeAustin121no MrBuster112hd ImHowlin11814¼	Bump repeatedly strtch 6
14Jun00-10CD	fst	1 1/16		:233 :48 1:13 1:451	3↑ Md Sp Wt 44k	94	3	23	22½	24	2hd	1hd	Day P	L112 b	*1.10	84-22	*Lake Austin*112hd Mahie Gold1123¼ *District*1136	Narrowly best 10
17May00-6CD	fst	6½f		:222 :45 1:092 1:154	3↑ Md Sp Wt 40k	92	9	2	31	3nk	1hd	2¾	Day P	L112	*.50	97-04	Decade112¾ *Lake Austin*1124½ *West Code*1121½	Dueled,led,outfinished 9
16Apr00-3Kee	fst	6½f		:214 :451 1:11 1:171	Md Sp Wt 50k	72	8	4	1hd	1hd	1hd	23	Day P	L121	*.50	85-12	Level Three1213 Lake Austin1211½ Maestro's Debut1214	Dueled, 2nd best 12
27Mar00-5FG	fst	6f		:22 :451 :571 1:094	Md Sp Wt 35k	86	8	7	66	45	45	2½	Day P	L119	1.90	94-09	*St. Martin's Cloak*119½ Lake Austin1191½ Corrian1191½	Bumped break 10

LIBERTY GOLD (Crafty Prospector—Restless Colony, by Pleasant Colony). Washington. A stakes winner at age 7, Liberty Gold's most important race was his third-place finish in the 1999 Metropolitan Handicap behind Sir Bear and Crafty Friend. A sprinter/miler who was able to win at 1 1/16 miles, he should sire runners who show good speed in statebred races at Emerald Downs and could also stretch out on occasion.

Liberty Gold
Own: Peace John H

Ch. h. 10 (Feb)
Sire: Crafty Prospector (Mr. Prospector) $20,000
Dam: Restless Colony (Pleasant Colony)
Br: M. Riordan & Foxfield Thoroughbreds, Inc. (Ky)
Tr: Arnold G R II(0 0 0 0 .00) 2004:(105 11 .10)

Life	44	10	5	9	$598,963	112	D.Fst	36	6	5	8	$449,320	112
2002	1	0	0	0	$0	88	Wet(412)	8	4	0	1	$149,643	108
2001	10	1	0	2	$117,673	106	Turf(264)	0	0	0	0	$0	-
	0	0	0	0	$0	-	Dst(0)	0	0	0	0	$0	-

21Feb02-8Aqu	fst	1	⊡	:243 :483 1:123 1:364	4↑ Alw 54000c	88	2	74	71¾	63¾	59½	67½	Samyn J L	L118 fb	13.70	86-26	Jarf118½ Runspastum1182½ John Little1182¾	Steadied stretch	8
29Dec01-7Aqu	fst	6f	⊡	:23 :454 :573 1:101	3↑ Alw 54000n$y	80	5	6	66	66½	47	57½	Samyn J L	L121 fb	12.30	86-12	[D]Trounce1164¼ Arromanches1212¼ RichRewrd121¾	Saved ground,no rally	6
24Nov01-10CD	sly	1 1/16		:234 :472 1:114 1:431	3↑ OC 100k/c-N	80	9	43½	53½	42	56½	714	Perret C	L114 fb	5.50	80-10	BetOnSunshine1137¼ PardeLeder1181 NobleRuler1161¾	Tired near stretch	9
13Nov01-8CD	fst	6f		:211 :441 :56 1:084	3↑ OC 80k/nc-N	87	7	6	78¼	77¼	76½	75¾	Perret C	L116 fb	6.00	88-11	Bet Me Best114hd He Be Irish1181¼ Valiant Style121nk	6w trip,no factor	7
28Oct01-9CD	fst	7½f		:223 :451 1:101 1:283	3↑ AckAckH-G3	90	1	11	108¾	109¼	66	68	Borel C H	L114 fb	13.90	93-13	Illusiond1183¾ StrwbrryAffir112nk FppsNotbook116½	6-7w, no late response	11
19Sep01-8Bel	fst	1		:23 :452 1:101 1:353	4↑ Alw 57000n$y	88	9	95½	93	71½	54	57¼	Samyn J L	L120 b	10.30	82-15	Honorifico116¾ Postponed118nk Durmiente1202	Steadied turn, wide	11
28Jun01-7Bel	fst	1 1/16		:24 :463 1:101 1:40	4↑ Alw 54000c	70	2	44½	35½	44	415	422½	Samyn J L	L123 b	2.00	74-03	Jarf1157¾ Grady1182¾ Country Be Gold11512	Inside trip, tired	5
26May01-8Del	sly	1		:243 :482 1:122 1:371	3↑ Brandywine75k	101	1	31½	42	42½	31½	32	McCarthy M J	L116 fb	*1.70	91-23	PineDnce116¾ QuickPunch1161¼ LibrtyGold1164¼	Circled,bid,not enough	7
5May01-3CD	fst	7f		:213 :433 1:074 1:202	4↑ LnEndCDH-G2	106	10	2	914	913	75	43¼	Nakatani C S	L114 b	15.30	100 -	Alannan116½ Bonapaw116½ Exchange Rate1132¼	7-8w stretch,mild gain	10
14Apr01-7Kee	fst	7f		:22 :443 1:092 1:221	3↑ CmwlthBC-G2	90	8	3	812	89½	54	34¾	Perret C	L118 fb	8.60	86-13	Alannan1184 Valiant Halory118¾ Liberty Gold1181¼	5w lane,no threat	8
20Jan01-8Aqu	sly	1 1/16	⊡	:223 :463 1:111 1:421	3↑ AquH-G3	104	2	44	41½	31	11	12½	Bravo J	L115 b	*2.50	95-12	LibertyGold1152¼ CoyoteLakes116nk TlksChep1161½	3 wide move, driving	7
23Dec00-8Aqu	fst	6f	⊡	:223 :454 :573 1:094	3↑ GravesdH-G3	99	8	9	106	84	22½	21¾	Samyn J L	L115 b	7.60	91-13	SyFlordSndy1161¾ LbrtyGold1151½ LkPntchrtrn1161¾	Pinched strt,stdy 1/4	11
17Nov00-9CD	fst	7½f		:223 :451 1:093 1:284	3↑ Alw 52675n$y	103	6	2	45	45	11	12½	Sellers S J	L116 b	*1.20	100-08	LibrtyGold1162½ FghtforMldy1141¼ WouldntWAll116hd	5w, mild hand ride	7
2Nov00-8Aqu	fst	1		:232 :463 1:11 1:361	3↑ Alw 54000n$y	99	2	41¾	31	2hd	21	43½	Santos J A	L120 b	*2.90	83-21	Lumberman1201¼ Boston Party123½ Pooska Hill1201¾	3 wide, tired	8
18Jun00-3Bel	fst	7f		:23 :454 1:103 1:24	4↑ Alw 54000c	87	3	3	2½	2hd	21½	45	Santos J A	L115 b	*1.45	78-23	FireKing1173¾ Momsmerceds115hd Punchr1221¼	Pressed pace, weakened	5
29May00-9Bel	fst	1		:23 :452 1:10 1:343	3↑ MtropltH-G1	98	5	64¼	64½	61¾	44	58¾	Santos J A	L114 b	13.40	83-19	Yankee Victor1174¾ Honest Lady112¾ Sir Bear117¾	Between rivals turn	8
28Apr00-7Kee	fst	1⅛		:462 1:102 1:354 1:49	4↑ BenAli-G3	101	4	33	42	22	2½	2no	Torres F C	L116 b	3.50	90-15	MdwyMgstrt116no LbrtyGold116hd ErlyWrnng1183	Hit gate start,bumped	7
9Apr00-7Kee	fst	7f		:223 :452 1:094 1:223	4↑ Alw 63538n$y	102	7	2	3½	2hd	2hd	21½	Torres F C	L123 b	*2.30	87-15	KimbrlitPip1161½ LibrtyGold1231¼ RockndRoll1231¼	Stalked,led, 2nd best	7
15Mar00-10GP	fst	7f		:224 :451 1:094 1:23	4↑ Alw 53000n$y	93	5	4	42	31	31½	3nk	Santos J A	L117 b	1.80	85-21	WcklwHghlnds115nk ExcllntLck115no LbrtyGld1171¾	Three wide bid turn	8
27Nov99-8Aqu	my	1		:222 :443 1:084 1:34	3↑ CigarMiH-G1	81	5	86¾	85¾	76½	510	614½	Santos J A	L114 b	8.90	83-11	Affirmed Success1185 Adonis115¾ Honorifico1131	Angled wide, flattened	9
24Oct99-6Bel	fst	1		:234 :464 1:104 1:35	3↑ Alw 60000n$y	103	1	2½	2hd	1hd	12½	13¼	Santos J A	L119 b	*1.05	89-23	LibertyGold1193¼ PhonetheKing1153¾ DicDncr1172½	Speed inside, driving	5
25Sep99-9Bel	fst	7f		:221 :443 1:083 1:213	3↑ Vosburgh-G1	93	6	2	67¾	66¾	66½	68¼	Santos J A	L126 b	11.90	86-09	Artax1263½ Stormin Fever126hd Mountain Top126½	Good inside run turn	6
6Sep99-9Sar	fst	7f		:221 :441 1:081 1:211	3↑ ForegoH-G2	92	9	5	94¾	98	66¾	610½	Santos J A	L114 b	13.00	88-12	CrftyFrind119nk AffirmdSuccss1191¼ SirBr1192¼	Angled out,no response	9
22Jly99-6Mth	sly	170		:23 :461 1:10 1:394	3↑ Alw 44000c	108	2	42½	43½	2hd	1½	13¾	Elliott S	L116 b	*.60	99-18	Liberty Gold1163¾ Red Weasel1166½ Tamarillo11911¼	Circled field turn	5
29May99-9Bel	fst	1		:222 :443 1:09 1:342	3↑ MtropltH-G1	109	7	75¾	77¼	51¾	42¼	32½	Santos J A	L114 b	10.10	89-22	Sir Bear1171¾ Crafty Friend114¾ Liberty Gold1142¼	Game finish outside	8
1May99-4CD	fst	7f		:223 :452 1:101 1:224	4↑ CDH-G2	104	2	6	67½	67½	33½	2½	Santos J A	L114 b	6.30	90-08	RockndRoll112½ LibrtyGold1141¼ RunJohnny1132	Broke awkward,closing	7
11Apr99-6Kee	fst	7f		:221 :442 1:084 1:213	4↑ Alw 58720n1s	112	3	4	45	43	11½	13	Santos J A	L118 b	6.50	94-09	Liberty Gold1183 Deputy Diamond115½ Burkhardt1153	4-wide, hand urging	6
7Nov98-5Aqu	fst	7f		:224 :451 1:091 1:212	3↑ SportPgH-G3	102	5	4	61¾	62¼	4¾	54½	Samyn J L	L114 b	15.70	92-09	Stormin Fever1202½ Olympic Cat1131¼ Adverse113nk	4 wide move turn	9
4Oct98-6Bel	fst	1		:24 :471 1:11 1:36	3↑ Alw 54000c	97	4	21	2½	1hd	1hd	32¾	Samyn J L	L119 b	2.80	81-24	Mr. Sinatra1152½ Fenton Lane119nk Liberty Gold1194	Speed, outfinished	6
18Sep98-8Bel	fst	1 1/16		:231 :462 1:104 1:423	3↑ Alw 56000c	104	4	3nk	3nk	2hd	2hd	1hd	Samyn J L	L118 b	7.00	86-25	Liberty Gold118hd Laredo1161¾ Gray Raider116no	3w, prolonged drive	6
6Aug98-6Sar	fst	6½f		:221 :45 1:093 1:154	4↑ Alw 43000n4x	98	3	1	52¼	53½	32½	37½	Coa E M	L119 b	7.40	87-10	AffirmedSuccess1197 GrayRider114½ LibertyGold119no	Broke through gate	5
8Jly98-8Bel	fst	1		:23 :46 1:101 1:353	3↑ Alw 42000n3x	104	5	3½	31	1½	15	14½	Coa E M	L123 fb	10.40	86-15	Liberty Gold1234½ Fire King1197 Teddy Boy1141	3w,drew away,driving	6
5Jun98-6Bel	fst	1 1/16		:233 :47 1:111 1:431	4↑ Alw 42000n3x	90	2	3½	31	2hd	2hd	46¾	Coa E M	L114 b	5.50	76-17	Pacificbounty116¾ Fire King1146 Dan's Promise114hd	In tight 1/2p	6
13May98-7Bel	fst	1⅛		:454 1:092 1:342 1:474	3↑ Alw 42000n3x	96	2	74¾	43	53¼	41¾	44¾	Coa E M	L118 b	5.00	86-16	Ordway116nk Las Vegas Ernie120½ Dan's Promise1164	Middle move,faded	8
10Apr98-9Kee	gd	1 1/16		:231 :462 1:104 1:422	4↑ Alw 48000n2x	98	4	21½	1½	1hd	12½	17	Coa E M	L112 b	4.10	96-04	Liberty Gold1127 Faux Art1131 Jack Flash113hd	Drew clear, handily	11
8Mar98-6GP	fst	7f		:224 :45 1:093 1:221	4↑ Alw 33000n3l	87	5	6	65¼	63¾	32½	32¾	Davis R G	L117 b	2.10	86-12	Don Gato1172¾ Colonel Bradley119hd Liberty Gold1174¾	Circled, fast pace	6
18Oct97-3Bel	fst	1		:232 :454 1:094 1:342	3↑ Alw 41000n2x	84	6	43½	52½	2hd	31	45	Smith M E	L115 b	3.25	87-04	BlackForest117½ Ordwy1134½ EsteemedFriend113hd	4w move,nothing left	8
21Sep97-3Bel	fst	7f		:22 :444 1:094 1:223	3↑ Alw 39000n2x	94	6	5	613	610	21½	2nk	Day P	L116 b	5.40	88-16	Star of Valor116nk Liberty Gold1164½ Falo1145	Wide move,game finish	6
30Aug97-5Sar	fst	7f		:223 :453 1:104 1:232	3↑ Alw 37000n1x	96	1	7	66¼	67¾	31½	11½	Day P	L114 b	9.10	88-12	Liberty Gold1141½ Black Tie Attire1165 Grim Reaper1161	4w move,clear late	7
4Aug97-4Sar	my	6f		:221 :46 :582 1:11	3↑ Alw 37000n1x	62	2	8	62¼	52½	69	614½	Day P	114 b	8.00	72-18	JimsMistake1143 JailRock116hd DncingOutlw1164½	Checked 1/2 mile pole	8
26Apr97-9Aqu	fst	7f		:223 :454 1:103 1:224	3↑ Alw 33000n1x	78	3	10	72½	62½	31	35	Alvarado F T	114 b	13.70	88-10	Steak Scam1113 Oro de Mexico1132 Liberty Gold1141¼	Steadied,4w move	10
29Mar97-6Aqu	fst	7f		:22 :45 1:092 1:222	Alw 33000n1x	80	6	6	53¼	42¾	44	34¼	Alvarado F T	115 b	25.75	91-10	BombyGold115nk GryRider1154 LibrtyGold1151¾	Rated betwn,good finsh	7
15Mar97-12GP	fst	7f		:231 :472 1:12 1:243	Alw 31000n1x	71	7	5	72¾	62¼	55¾	58¾	Davis R G	117	11.60	72-17	Banker'sGold120nk ThunderReef1201 CraftyOne1203	Lacked late response	7
7Dec96-2Aqu	sly	6f	⊡	:224 :461 :59 1:121	Md Sp Wt 31k	73	2	7	78¾	52¼	1½	1½	Alvarado F T	118	12.80	86-08	Liberty Gold118½ Stormscope1182 Nasello1186	Bumpd start,came wide	7

MANCINI (Mr. Prospector—Trolley Song, by Caro). Kentucky. Five years younger than his half-brother Unbridled's Song, Mancini was a disappointment as a racehorse, never winning in just four starts. But his offspring should have speed, and because he is relatively unknown, his runners could pop at a price in sprints.

Mancini
Own: Tabor Michael and Magnier, Mrs. John

Gr/ro. h. 6 (May)
Sire: Mr. Prospector (Raise a Native)
Dam: Trolley Song (Caro*Ire)
Br: Orpendale & Newbyth Stud (Ky)
Tr: Lukas D. W(0 0 0 0 .00) 2004:(427 48 .11)

Life	4	M	0	1	$7,140	70	D.Fst	4	0	0	1	$7,140	70
2001	2	M	0	1	$7,140	70	Wet(392)	0	0	0	0	$0	-
2000	2	M	0	0	$0	59	Turf(348)	0	0	0	0	$0	-
Aik Ⓣ	0	0	0	0	$0	-	DstⓉ(415)	0	0	0	0	$0	-

28Jan01-4Aqu	fst	1⅛	⊡	:48 1:122 1:383 1:513	Md Sp Wt 42k	70	6	12	11½	1½	2½	32¾	Bravo J	L120 b	5.40	76-16	Holiest Punch1201¼ FastModem1201½ Mancini1207¼	Stayed on well inside	9
1Jan01-6Aqu	fst	170	⊡	:232 :48 1:133 1:423	Md Sp Wt 42k	58	1	76½	96¾	97¼	814	412¾	Bravo J	L120 b	9.50	68-13	Balto Star12011 Romantic Bull1201¼ Devil's Dandy120½	Some interest late	10
14Oct00-3Bel	fst	6f		:221 :46 :58 1:103	Md Sp Wt 41k	59	4	2	22	31½	78	88¾	Gryder A T	118 b	7.50	76-10	BincoAppel1183 CobrCltic1181¾ Dtswtitslbout118nk	Between rivals, tired	10
23Sep00-5Bel	fst	7f		:224 :46 1:11 1:23	Md Sp Wt 41k	49	2	3	2hd	43½	510	620¼	Arroyo N Jr	118	16.40	68-13	A P Valentine1184¼ Pure Prize11812 Bopman118½	Between rivals, tired	9

MEDFORD (Meadowlake—Really Quick, by In Reality). West Virginia. Medford was built similarly to his speedy sire, and was able to finish second in the Federico Tesio Stakes at 1⅛ miles. His runners will also have good speed and be best from five furlongs to 1¹⁄₁₆ miles. (SP²)

Medford
Own: New Farm

Ch. h. 9 (Mar)
Sire: Meadowlake (Hold Your Peace) $20,000
Dam: Really Quick (In Reality)
Br: Foxfield (Ky)
Tr: Perkins B W Jr(0 0 0 0 .00) 2004:(114 22 .19)

Life	15	3	2	2	$128,370	95	D.Fst	12	3	2	2	$119,070	95
2000	1	0	0	1	$5,170	84	Wet(356)	2	0	0	0	$9,000	88
1999	2	1	0	0	$17,760	89	Turf(238)	1	0	0	0	$300	68
Aik Ⓣ	0	0	0	0	$0	-	DstⓉ(409)	0	0	0	0	$0	-

```
5Jan00-8Aqu fst 6f ⊡ :23 :46 :58 1:10 4↑ Alw 47000N3x   84 1 6 42 51 43 38  Luzzi M J  L115 b 7.10 84-18 Falkenburg122hd Greek Tycoon1178 Medford115¾  Came wide, no punch 7
9Nov99-8Med fst 6f :22 :443 :562 1:083 3↑ Alw 30000N3x   83 3 3 21 42¼ 42¼ 42  Diaz L F  L120 b *.70 94-09 Raysin Thunder118½ Hibbing1181 Wichita Lineman118½  Finished well 5
27Oct99-8Lrl fst 5½f :222 :46 :58 1:04 3↑ Alw 28000N2x   89 3 2 1½ 12 11 1¾  Diaz L F  L117 b 4.20 94-13 Medford1171¾ HrrimnsImge117¾ ArcdiStret114hd  Pace 2w,drftd out,drvg 7
  Previously trained by Perkins Benjamin W
30Jun98-7Del fm *11/16 Ⓣ :244 :484 1:13 1:441 3↑ Alw 28900N2x   68 1 86¼ 78 56 510 69¼  Toribio A R  L113 b 2.80 77-20 Matchless116hd Christian Crusade1221 Galloping Gael1223  No factor 8
14Jun98-7Del fst 1 1/16 :232 :464 1:102 1:422 LRichards150k   92 5 56½ 55½ 54½ 66 78¼  Toribio A R  L113 b 11.20 93-07 Scatmandu1142½ Hot Wells115¾ True Silver1131  4 wide 1/4 pole, tired 7
16May98-5Pim fst 1 1/16 :232 :474 1:121 1:43 SirBarton100k   95 3 55 64 74½ 64¼ 4¾  Prado E S  L115 b 5.90 88-13 ThomasJo122½ SilverLunch117nk SwerbyDixie115no  Rail,swung 6wd,rallied 7
18Apr98-10Pim fst 1⅛ :454 1:103 1:364 1:50 FdrcoTesio155k   94 5 69¼ 511 64¼ 35½ 22½  Prado E S  L115 b 3.50 87-17 ThomasJo1172½ Medford1152¾ MonksFalcon..1171½  Std'd 1/4,rallied btwn 9
21Mar98-8Aqu sly 1 :224 :454 1:11 1:362 Gotham-G3   88 6 97¾ 98¾ 95¾ 44½ 44¾  Chavez J F  L112 b 5.80 82-16 Wasatch1172¼ Dr J1191 Late Edition1141½  Bumped strt,gamely out 10
8Feb98-8GP fst 7f :223 :454 1:11 1:24 Alw 32000N2x   88 5 4 53 31½ 34 45½  Smith M E  L117 b 2.90 74-21 SouthernBostonion117½ Hitech1174¾ BrillintCod117nk  Middle move 5 wide 8
  Previously trained by Perkins Ben W Jr
11Jan98-3GP fst 6f :222 :45 :57 1:104 Alw 30000N2x   87 1 4 42 34 32½ 34½  Bailey J D  L117 b *1.40 83-18 Zippy Zeal1203¼ Hitech1171¼ Medford1172¾  Lacked late response 5
  Previously trained by Perkins Benjamin W
26Nov97-8Aqu fst 6f :213 :444 :571 1:10 Huntington56k   89 10 7 105¼ 95½ 43 22¼  Smith M E  L122 b 11.30 87-19 Risky Buy1152¼ Medford122no Not Tricky117½  Bumped strt,8w 1/4p 10
26Oct97-9Aqu gd 6½f :22 :444 1:081 1:141 Cowdin-G2   74 8 2 53¼ 43 78½ 712¾  Wilson R  L122 b 6.90 91-06 CoronadosQuest1225½ NotTricky122no Scatmandu1222  Chasd for a 1/2,tired 8
27Sep97-8Del fst 6f :22 :453 :59 1:12 Dover50k   85 3 6 1½ 11 12 15  Rocco J  113 b *.50 82-20 Medford1135 Noble Cat114¾ Carnivorous Habit114¾  Drew off 6
16Aug97-11Mth fst 6f :212 :442 :562 1:093 Sapling-G3   76 8 5 2½ 2½ 47 77¼  Gryder A T  122 b 3.00 87-10 Double Honor1222 Jigadee122¾ E Z Line1223  Pressed pace empty 8
2Aug97-6Mth fst 5½f :222 :454 :574 1:042 Md Sp Wt 22k   83 5 4 2½ 11½ 14 15¼  Gryder A T  118 b *.60 98-14 Medford1185¼ Pasha1185¼ Last Bet1184  Much the best stretch 9
```

MINARDI (Boundary—Yarn, by Mr. Prospector). Kentucky. Has the potential to be an explosive sire of sprinter/milers, and his juveniles should win early on dirt and grass. With high speed on top and bottom, Minardi was a champion 2-year-old in England and Ireland, and hc is a half-brother to the successful Tale of the Cat and Myth, the dam of 2-year-old champion Johannesburg. (SP²/T)

Minardi
Own: Mr M. Tabor & Mrs John Magnier

Dk. b or b. h. 6 (May)
Sire: Boundary (Danzig) $10,000
Dam: Yarn (Mr. Prospector)
Br: Indian Creek (Ky)
Tr: O'Brien Aidan P(0 0 0 0 .00) 2004:(0 0 .00)

Life	8	2	1	1	$291,017	-	D.Fst	0	0	0	0	$0	-
2001	5	0	0	1	$44,462	-	Wet(409)	0	0	0	0	$0	-
2000	3	2	1	0	$246,555	-	Turf(324)	8	2	1	1	$291,017	-
	0	0	0	0	$0	-	Dst(0)	0	0	0	0	$0	-

```
8Sep01♦Haydock (GB)  hy 6f Ⓣ Str 1:151 3↑ Haydock Park Sprint Cup-G1  917½ Duffield G  124  8.00  Nuclear Debate1263 Mount Abu126¾ Monkston Point126hd  12
                                         Stk 219200                    Switched left after 1 1/2f, ridden 3f out, weakened over 1f out
12Aug01♦Deauville (Fr)  sf *6½f Ⓣ 1:191 3↑ P Maurice de Gheest-G1  65¼ Sanchez F  123  *.80  King Charlemagne123nk Three Points1282 Kier Park1282  9
                                         Stk 119300                    Mid divison, 6th at half, never dangerous
19Jun01♦Ascot (GB)  gd 1 Ⓣ RH 1:411  St James's Palace Stakes-G1  84½ Kinane M J  126  5.00  Black Minnaloushe126nk Noverre126hd Olden Times126½  11
                                         Stk 378200                    Tracked leadr, driven to lead 2f out, headed near final f, beaten
26May01♦Curragh (Ire)  yl 1 Ⓣ Str 1:412  Irish 2000 Guineas-G1  32¾ Kinane M J  126  *2.00  Black Minnaloushe1262 Mozart126¾ Minardi1263½  12
                                         Stk 245900                    Tracked leaer in modest 4th, 2nd 2f out, ridden & no gain final f
5May01♦Newmarket (GB)  gd 1 Ⓣ Str 1:372  2000 Guineas Stakes-G1  44½ Kinane M J  126  5.00  Golan1261¼ Tamburlaine126nk Frenchmans Bay1263  18
                                         Stk 431000                    Headway and not clear run over 1f out, ran on, not reach leaders
28Sep00♦Newmarket (GB)  gd 6f Ⓣ Str 1:123  Middle Park Stakes-G1  11½ Kinane M J  123  *.00  Minardi1231½ Endless Summer123¾ Red Carpet1231½  10
  Timeform rating: 119p                  Stk 225300                    Dwelt,rated rear,rallied to lead ovr 1f out,drifted right,driving
13Aug00♦Leopardstwn (Ire)  gd 6f Ⓣ Str 1:121  Heinz 57 Phoenix Stakes-G1  15 Kinane M J  126  3.50  Minardi1265 Superstar Leo123¾ Dora Carrington123½  10
  Timeform rating: 115                   Stk 200600                    Tracked in 4th,led over 1-1/2f out,going away.La Vida Loca 5th
29Jly00♦Ascot (GB)  gd 6f Ⓣ Str 1:153  EBF Crocker Bulteel Maiden Stk  25 Kinane M J  123  *1.25  Rumpold1235 Minardi1232 Magnusson123nk  9
  Timeform rating: 89                    Maiden 15500                  Rated in mid-pack,2nd & drftd left over 1f out,no chance w/winner
```

MISBAH (Gilded Time—For Dixie, by Dixieland Band). Kentucky. A winner of four of 17 starts in England, Dubai, and North America, he is by a 2-year-old champion and his female family produced the very fast Full Pocket, another source of high speed. (SP2)

Misbah
Own: Shadwell Stable

B. h. 9 (Jan)
Sire: Gilded Time (Timeless Moment) $17,500
Dam: For Dixie (Dixieland Band)
Br: J. D. Squires (Ky)
Tr: McLaughlin Kiaran P(0 0 0 0 .00) 2004:(333 62 .19)

Life	17	4	5	2	$96,947	96	D.Fst	8	2	3	2	$66,674	96
1999	9	2	3	2	$69,674	96	Wet(377)	0	0	0	0	$0	-
1998	5	1	1	0	$19,239	-	Turf(280)	9	2	2	0	$30,273	90
Aik Ⓣ	0	0	0	0	$0	-	DstⓉ(369)	0	0	0	0	$0	-

24Sep99-7Bel	gd	1 1/16	Ⓣ :242 :48 1:114 1:43	3↑ Alw 50000N4x	90 1 21½ 2½ 32 33 44¼	Santos J A	L122	15.10	73-28 Draw Shot115½ *Scagnelli*1221 Nat's Big Party1222¾	With pace, no rally	7
23Aug99-6Sar	fst	1⅛	:474 1:114 1:37 1:50	3↑ Alw 47000N3x	96 2 11 1½ 1½ 12 14¾	Velazquez J R	L118	5.00	86-18 Misbah1184¾ Legal Street1143 Fourth and Six1185¼	Lost whip 3/16s pole	6
7Aug99-3Sar	fst	1⅛	:482 1:122 1:38 1:511	3↑ Alw 47000N3x	86 1 41 31 42½ 32½ 36½	Velazquez J R	L118	3.65	73-16 FireandRain1186¼ SaratogSunrise118nk *Misbh*1181½	Outfinished for place	6
23Jly99-6Bel	fst	1 1/16	:234 :471 1:112 1:424	3↑ Alw 47000N3x	91 4 4¾ 2hd 1hd 2½ 22½	Velazquez J R	L119	4.60	80-20 Crafty Man1212½ Misbah1191¾ Fourth and Six1211¾	Between foes, gamely	5
19Jun99-7Bel	fst	7f	:224 :45 1:091 1:214	3↑ Alw 46000N3x	91 5 4 43 26 37 37½	Migliore R	L119	6.10	85-13 Doneraile Court1163 Iron Will1194½ Misbah1191¼	Rated outside, no bid	8
26May99-6Bel	fst	1	:234 :474 1:123 1:373	3↑ Alw 47000N3x	90 1 11 1½ 1hd 1hd 42¼	Migliore R	L118	*1.45	74-35 FourthandSix1182 *WellNoted*118hd NotSoFast118hd	Vied between, gamely	6
14Mar99 Nad Al Sheba (UAE) Timeform rating: 106	ft	*7f	LH 1:234	4↑ Al Futtaim Trading Trophy Alw 19100	23	Hills R	122	-	*Ramp and Rave*1193 Misbah122½ Yalaietanee1193¼	*Tracked leader,led 3f out,headed 100y out.Susu 4th.No betting*	5
11Feb99 Nad Al Sheba (UAE) Timeform rating: 106	ft	*7½f	LH 1:291	4↑ Shadwell Farm Inc Handicap Hcp 15000	11¾	Hills R	131	-	Misbah1311¾ Ariant1221½ Bashaayeash1291¼	*Close up in 4th,led 1-1/2f out,driving.No betting*	8
17Jan99 Nad Al Sheba (UAE) Timeform rating: 104	ft	*7f	LH 1:251	4↑ Handicap Hcp 15000	21¼	Ahern E	132	-	Bashaayeash1281¼ *Misbah*1323 Mansab1262	*Rated in 6th,finished well.Ramp and Rave (129) 5th.No betting*	7
Previously trained by Ben Hanbury											
29Aug98 Goodwood (GB) Timeform rating: 93	gd	7f	Ⓣ RH 1:254	3↑ Pertemps Rated Handicap Hcp 28800	66	Hills R	128	12.00	Rock Falcon130¾ Swiss Law1331½ Risque Lady1202½	*Tracked in 4th,one-paced last quarter*	12
8Aug98 Ascot (GB) Timeform rating: 74	gd	7f	Ⓣ Str 1:274	3↑ Tote International Handicap Hcp 244400	1313¾	Dwyer M	112	14.00	Jo Mell1163½ Gaelic Storm120¾ Ramooz129½	*Chased leaders for a half,weakened.Decorated Hero (139) 6th*	25
7Jly98 Newmarket (GB) Timeform rating: 101	gd	6f	Ⓣ Str 1:103	Lincoln Mild Cigars Rated Hcp Hcp 25000	11¼	Hills R	128	*3.50	Misbah1281¼ Second Wind119½ Zizi112½	*Tracked leaders,led 2f out,ridden out.Pool Music (131) 8th*	15
16Jun98 Ascot (GB) Timeform rating: 99	yl	1	Ⓣ Str 1:422	Britannia Handicap Hcp 76000	93¼	Hills R	123	20.00	Plan-B119¾ *Pantar*117½ *Lucayan Indian*130nk	*Mid-pack,brief bid 1-1/2f out,one-paced late.The Editor(129)5th*	31
16May98 Thirsk (GB) Timeform rating: 99	gd	1	Ⓣ LH 1:402	Dishforth Conditions Stakes Alw 22000	21¼	Fortune J	127	1.75	Sharp Play1361¼ Misbah127hd *Tracking*13416	*Led to over 2f out,dueled to over 1f out,yielded grudgingly*	4
22Oct97 Yarmouth (GB)	gd	7f	Ⓣ Str 1:234	Wickhampton Maiden Stakes Maiden 8100	11½	Hills R	126	3.50	Misbah1261½ *Chattan*1264 Captain Tim1261¾	*Led throughout,quickened over 1f out,driving*	13
5Oct97 Leicester (GB)	gd	7f	Ⓣ Str 1:251	Playquest UK Mdn Stks (Div 2) Maiden 8000	21¼	Ryan W	126	*1.25	*Florazi*1261¼ *Misbah*1261¼ *Prospectress*1163½	*Rated in 5th,led over 1f out,headed 100y out*	11
18Sep97 Newbury (GB)	gd	7f	Ⓣ Str 1:274	Amerada Maiden Stakes Maiden 28200	44½	Drowne S	126	33.00	*Dr Fong*126½ *Distant Mirage*126½ Mubrik1263½	*Rated in mid-pack,mild bid 2f out,hung.Pelagos 6th*	17

MOJAVE MOON (Mr. Prospector—East of the Moon, by Private Account). Maryland. Securing young stallions like Mohave Moon, Maryland breeders are improving the quality of their stock. Stakes-placed Mohave Moon has a pedigree with unlimited potential. In addition to his sire, his dam was a 3-year-old champion in France and is a half-sister to Kingmambo and Miesque's Son. Mojave Moon's second dam is multiple champion and two-time Breeders' Cup Mile winner Miesque. While his runners will win on dirt, they should be especially good on turf. (HT)

Mojave Moon
Own: Flaxman Holdings Ltd

Ch. h. 8 (Apr)
Sire: Mr. Prospector (Raise a Native)
Dam: East of the Moon (Private Account)
Br: Flaxman Holdings, Ltd. (Ky)
Tr: Frankel Robert J(0 0 0 0 .00) 2004:(342 101 .30)

Life	8	2	1	1	$135,191	102	D.Fst	4	2	1	1	$132,360	102
2001	1	0	0	0	$0	90	Wet(430)	1	0	0	0	$0	90
2000	3	1	1	1	$103,560	102	Turf(333)	3	0	0	0	$2,831	–
Aik Ⓣ	0	0	0	0	$0	-	DstⓉ(422)	0	0	0	0	$0	–

3Mar01- 3SA	gd	1 1/16	:23 :462 1:11 1:424	4↑ⓇSeabiscuit90k	90	5	810	813	88¾	87¾	88½	Espinoza V	LB120 b	*2.20	81- 10	Lesters Boy1224 Dig for It1201 *Red Eye*1222	Off bit slow,outrun	8
7Oct00- 7Kee	fst	1 3/16	:47 1:102 1:354 1:544	3↑FayettBC-G3	97	1	57	58	56½	3nk	21½	Solis A	L118 b	4.10	93- 05	Jadada1181½ Mojave Moon118½ Get Away With It1182	Lean in bump 1/8 pl	5
11Jun00- 4Hol	fst	1⅛	:471 1:111 1:362 1:491	3↑Calfrnin-G2	89	1	57	59¾	58½	46½	39¼	Blanc B	LB116 b	3.20	74- 19	Big Ten116¾ *Early Pioneer*1188½ Mojave Moon1163	Along for third	5
12May00- 2Hol	fst	1 1/16	:232 :464 1:111 1:43	3↑Alw 51000N1x	102	1	614	610	54½	21	1¾	Blanc B	LB121 b	7.00	85- 15	Mojave Moon121¾ *No Armistice*1153½ *Brigade*1193	3wd move,stdy handling	6
21Aug99- 1Dmr	fst	1 1/16	:233 :481 1:123 1:44	3↑Md Sp Wt 48k	86	4	37	32½	31	4nk	1½	Blanc B	LB118 b	8.80	84- 13	*Mojave Moon*118½ Storm Dog122nk *Timber Baron*1181	4w bid, fnshd bst	6

Previously trained by Jonathan Pease

14Jly99 Deauville (Fr)	gd *1¼ Ⓣ RH 2:063	Prix de Martinvast Alw 28000	52¾	Asmussen C	126	6.00	Boulevard126hd Devon Deputy1261½ Bedawin1261	*Tracked leader,faded through stretch*	11
Timeform rating: 89									
27Jun99 Longchamp (Fr)	gd *1 Ⓣ RH 1:392	Prix du Louvre Alw 28600	54¾	Guillot S	126	7.00	Midnight Foxtrot126¾ Good Journey1262½ Tounant130no	*Never a factor*	6
Timeform rating: 87									
8Oct98 Longchamp (Fr)	hy *1⅛ Ⓣ RH 2:092	Prix de Sablonville-EBF Maiden 32900	67¾	Asmussen C	128	2.50	Royal Line1281½ Sendawar128nk *Le Rhone*1283	*Unruly pre-start,trailed,progress halfway,weakened 2f out*	7
Timeform rating: 82									

MONARCHOS (Maria's Mon—Regal Band, by Dixieland Band). Kentucky. Winner of the 2001 Kentucky Derby, Monarchos is getting every opportunity as a stallion to reproduce his talent by standing at Claiborne Farm with a high-quality book of broodmares. Since he is from a stellar Darby Dan female family that produced Dynaformer, Darby Creek Road, Memories of Silver, and Sunshine Forever, expect Monarchos's offspring to be better bred for the classics than for juvenile races. With Majestic Light on top and Northern Dancer on the bottom, do not be surprised if Monarchos also gets many grass runners. (HT^2)

Monarchos
Own: Oxley John C

Gr/ro. h. 6 (Feb)
Sire: Maria's Mon (Wavering Monarch) $35,000
Dam: Regal Band (Dixieland Band)
Br: J. D. Squires (Ky)
Tr: Ward J T Jr(0 0 0 0 .00) 2004:(58 7 .12)

Life	10	4	1	3	$1,720,830	116	D.Fst	10	4	1	3	$1,720,830	116
2002	1	0	0	1	$5,200	87	Wet(372)	0	0	0	0	$0	–
2001	7	4	1	1	$1,711,600	116	Turf(307)	0	0	0	0	$0	–
	0	0	0	0	$0	-	Dst(0)	0	0	0	0	$0	–

19Jan02- 6GP	fst	1 1/16	:24 :481 1:123 1:46	4↑OC 100k/N4x -N	87	3	48½	45½	54¾	45¼	38¾	Chavez J F	L120	*.50	69- 22	*Mongoose*1226¼ WtchYourPnnis1202½ Monrchos1203	Slow st, no response	5
9Jun01-10Bel	fst	1½	:48 1:113 2:003 2:262	Belmont-G1	98	5	75¼	66¾	35	38	313	Chavez J F	L126	5.00	94- 02	*Point Given*12612¼ A P Valentine126¾ Monarchos1261	Mild move, flattened	9
19May01-11Pim	fst	1 3/16	:471 1:114 1:362 1:552	Preaknes-G1	99	7	1115	1112	84¾	67½	67½	Chavez J F	L126	2.30	86- 11	*Point Given*1262¼ APValentine126nk *Congaree*1261¼	5-6w,mild mve,flattend	11
5May01- 8CD	fst	1¼	:444 1:091 1:35 1:594	KyDerby G1	116	16	1315	107½	62¼	2½	14¾	Chavez J F	L126	10.50	104 -	Monarchos1264¾ Invisible Ink126no Congaree1264	Bmp start,rally 6wide	17
14Apr01-10Aqu	fst	1⅛	:46 1:10 1:35 1:474	WoodMem-G2	103	2	57	57¼	55¼	25	22¾	Chavez J F	L123	*.90	94- 14	Congaree1232¾ *Monarchos*1237 *Richly Blended*1234	Inside run, gamely	6
10Mar01-11GP	fst	1⅛	:464 1:112 1:37 1:494	FlaDerby-G1	105	7	117¾	117¾	71½	12	14½	Chavez J F	L122	*1.40e	88- 13	Monrchos1224½ Outofthebox1222½ InvisibleInk122½	Strong six wide move	13
3Feb01-10GP	fst	1 1/16	:24 :474 1:122 1:431	Alw 35000N1x	103	3	32	22½	21½	1½	14¾	Chavez J F	L120	*2.00	92- 13	*Monarchos*1204¾ *Distilled*1203¾ Thunder Blitz1227	Drew away, driving	11
13Jan01- 8GP	fst	7f	:222 :452 1:101 1:221	Md Sp Wt 31k	95	3	8	32	11	13	16	Chavez J F	L122	5.50	95- 11	*Monarchos*1226 Tampa1223¼ Judge Silver122½	Inside, drew away	12
24Nov00- 7CD	fst	6½f	:214 :453 1:112 1:18	Md Sp Wt 40k	69	6	10	1113	1113	711	35¼	Martinez W	L120	13.50	82- 12	*Dream Run*120hd *Big Talkin Man*1205¼ *Monarchos*120½	No late threat	12
7Oct00- 4Kee	fst	7f	:22 :454 1:093 1:221	Md Sp Wt 50k	61	11	7	73½	64	109¼	812½	Cooksey P J	L120	9.80	78- 11	Devil's Domain1204 *Private Son*1201¼ Me and Thee120hd	Tired after 1/2	12

MONROAN (Maria's Mon—Share the Fun, by Deputy Minister). Indiana. By a 2-year-old champion, Monroan was unplaced in just one start at 3, but his second dam, Share the Fantasy, won the Spinaway Stakes. His runners should have speed and do well in state-bred races, on dirt and turf.

Monroan
Own: Full O Run Racing Team

Gr/ro. h. 6 (Apr)
Sire: Maria's Mon (Wavering Monarch) $35,000
Dam: Share the Fun (Deputy Minister)
Br: John R. Williams & Bennet B. Williams (Ky)
Tr: Greenhill Jeffrey L(0 0 0 0 .00) 2004:(93 14 .15)

Life	1	M	0	0	$0	-	D.Fst	1	0	0	0	$0	-
2001	1	M	0	0	$0	-	Wet(373)	0	0	0	0	$0	-
2000	0	M	0	0	$0	-	Turf(297)	0	0	0	0	$0	-
Aik Ⓣ	0	0	0	0	$0	-	DstⓉ(319)	0	0	0	0	$0	-

5Apr01-5TP fst 6½f :22² :45¹ 1:10¹ 1:16³ Md Sp Wt 26k – 7 7 3¹ - - - Prescott R L122 13.90 - 10 Ray's Treasure1224½ Flirt to Music1222¼ Time to Tell1221 Eased turn 12

NOT IMPOSSIBLE (Sadler's Wells—Ball Chairman, by Secretariat). Canada. Runners sired by the unraced Irish-bred Not Impossible should be ordinary on dirt but will come to life on grass at distances over seven furlongs. (T^2)

OLD KENTUCKY HOME (Kris S.—Shared Magic, by Devil's Bag). Kentucky. A winner of one of four starts in France at 3, Old Kentucky Home is by a stallion and sire line known for stamina. Many runners by the versatile Kris S. win on dirt and turf, but the combination of Kris S. (Roberto) and Devil's Bag suggests runners by this stallion will have more success on turf. (T^2)

Old Kentucky Home
Own: Nb Hunt

Dk. b or b. h. 6 (Apr)
Sire: Kris S. (Roberto) $150,000
Dam: Shared Magic (Devil's Bag)
Br: Andrea Singer Pollack Revocable Trust (Ky)
Tr: Rouget J. C(0 0 0 0 .00) 2004:(0 0 .00)

Life	4	1	0	0	$7,284	-	D.Fst	0	0	0	0	$0	-
2001	4	1	0	0	$7,284	-	Wet(377)	0	0	0	0	$0	-
2000	0	M	0	0	$0	-	Turf(336)	4	1	0	0	$7,284	-
	0	0	0	0	$0	-	Dst(0)	0	0	0	0	$0	-

Previously trained by Jean-Claude Rouget

9Jly01♦Clairefontaine (Fr)	sf *1⅜ Ⓣ RH 2:20³	Prix de Clerville Alw 14700	4²½ Jarnet T	128 b	3.50	Ken Scott123½ Actionnaire121½ Totally Majestic1281½ *Tracked leader,led 2f out,dueled 150y out,weakened late*	13
5Jun01♦Maisons-Laffitte (Fr) Timeform rating: 84	yl *1 9/16 Ⓣ RH 2:40²	Prix d'Ellon Alw 24000	6⁸¼ Dubosc J R	126	6.00	Roman Saddle126hd *Sharbayan*126³ Abajo126nk *Trailed to 3f out,never threatened*	9
30Apr01♦Salon (Fr)	gd *1¼ Ⓣ RH	Prix Robert Picardat Maiden 9500	1½ Dubosc J R	128	*.50	Old Kentucky Home128½ *Prince Solon*1282½ Sopran Tour128hd *Tracked leaders,bid 1f out,led near line. Time not taken*	13
6Apr01♦Le Bouscat (Fr)	hy *1 Ⓣ LH	Prix Rose de Mai Maiden 10700	4⁵¼ Coutreau N	118	-	Litaneo1281½ Solon's Girl125nk Archalous1283½ *Rated at rear,some late progress. Time not taken*	12

ONE WAY LOVE (Regal Classic—First Class Gal, by Geiger Counter). Canada. A Canadian stakes winner at 2, 3, 4 and 5; his runners should have good speed on all surfaces and be useful juveniles. (SP^2)

PERFORMING MAGIC (Gone West—Performing Arts, by The Minstrel). New York. Winner of three stakes, including the Illinois Derby, Performing Magic is a son of Gone West and should be a versatile statebred sire, getting winners on fast and wet tracks. They should also be price plays on grass. (HT^2)

One Way Love

Own: Schickedanz Bruno and Hillier, John

Dk. b or b. h. 9 (Apr)
Sire: Regal Classic (Vice Regent) $10,000
Dam: First Class Gal (Geiger Counter)
Br: James E. Day (Ont-C)
Tr: Katryan Abraham R(0 0 0 0 .00) 2004:(187 16 .09)

Life	41	15	6	6	$962,518	111	D.Fst	36	14	6	6	$948,208	111
2000	12	6	1	1	$516,464	111	Wet(353)	3	1	0	0	$13,695	74
1999	10	3	3	2	$214,882	106	Turf(281)	2	0	0	0	$615	55
Aik Ⓣ	0	0	0	0	$0	-	DstⓉ(327)	1	0	0	0	$615	55

5Nov00-8WO	fst	1 1/16	:242 :482 1:122 1:432	3↑ AutumnH-G3	**103**	3	1½	1hd	11½	1½	1hd	Husbands P	L126 fb	*.50	90-20	One Way Love126hd *A Fleets Dancer*1165½ Tiltam1146¼	All out	4
23Sep00-9Bel	fst	7f	:221 :443 1:083 1:213	3↑ Vosburgh-G1	**105**	7	2	62¼	62¾	44	32¾	Chavez J F	L126 fb	10.60	92-13	Trippi123½ More Than Ready1232¼ *One Way Love*1261	Good finish inside	10
30Aug00-9Sar	fst	6½f	:213 :441 1:082 1:15	3↑ ForegoH-G2	**109**	5	3	43	52	41	52	Husbands P	L116 fb	8.10	97-07	ShadowCaster1131 Intidb118no SuccessfulAppel119nk	Bid between, tired	10
20Aug00-8WO	fst	6½f	:22 :44 1:09 1:152	3↑ [S]Shepperton127k	**109**	2	2	2½	24	2hd	14½	Husbands P	L126 fb	*.80	96-14	One Way Love1264½ Great Defender1211 *Regal Sahib*115¾	Much the best	5
22Jly00-8WO	fst	6½f	:214 :441 1:093 1:161	3↑ BldVenturH107k	**103**	4	2	32	2hd	2½	1nk	Husbands P	L126 fb	*.85	92-17	*One Way Love*126nk Praise From Dixie1152¼ Regal Sahib115no	Driving	6
5Jly00-5WO	fst	7f	:221 :442 1:092 1:221	3↑ [S]Overskate104k	**111**	6	1	21½	3½	15	110½	Husbands P	L126 fb	*.70	95-15	*One Way Love*12610½ *Doug's Legacy*1171¼ Hopeful Moment1192½	Driving	7
31May00-8WO	fst	1 1/16	:23 :463 1:113 1:443	3↑ [S]StdyGrowth100k	**101**	4	1½	1hd	11	15	19¼	Husbands P	L115 fb	*.85	84-24	*One Way Love*1159¼ No Foul Play1161¾ Rowdy Ruckus1182½	Much the best	5
14May00-8WO	fst	1 1/16	:233 :463 1:112 1:453	4↑ EclipseH-G2	**93**	2	2hd	2hd	2hd	22	57½	Husbands P	L121 b	*1.65e	71-31	Black Cash1193 *The Fed*1123¼ Catahoula Parish115hd	Dueled, weakened	10
29Apr00-8WO	fst	7f	:22 :442 1:091 1:223	4↑ VigilH-G3	**109**	5	2	3½	1hd	13	13¾	Husbands P	L120 b	*2.05	93-19	OneWayLove1203¾ CatahoulaPrish1141½ SrtogPrince1171¼	Driving inside	9
14Apr00-7WO	fst	6f	:214 :442 :563 1:10	4↑ JcqCartier111k	**98**	7	3	62¼	74¼	42½	2hd	Husbands P	L119 b	4.25e	90-17	Randy Regent117hd *One Way Love*119nk Burger Day113¾	Just missed	9
Previously trained by Fehr Alec																		
13Feb00-8Aqu	fst	6f	⊡ :222 :443 :563 1:09	4↑ Alw 57000N$Y	**71**	5	5	64½	712	713	714½	Castillo H Jr	L114 b	7.60	82-11	UnrelMdnss1151½ *Blncthbudgt*1143 KingRuckus114hd	Wide trip, no factor	7
29Jan00-9Aqu	fst	6f	⊡ :23 :46 :574 1:094	3↑ PaumonokH81k	**86**	5	1	22	52¼	67	77¾	Velasquez C	L116 b	4.60	85-14	Falkenburg1151½ Brushed On113nk He's a Charm1133½	Speed inside, tired	7
Previously trained by Wright Michael Jr																		
27Nov99-8WO	fst	6f	:211 :424 :551 1:08	3↑ KennedyRd85k	**97**	12	1	63½	66	45½	33½	Olguin G L	L121 b	6.00	97-08	GretDefender1142 MrEpperson1151½ OnWyLov121no	Finished well 4 wide	12
17Oct99-3WO	fst	6f	:214 :44 :562 1:09	3↑ HilandrH-G2	**97**	3	4	71	31½	22½	22¼	Husbands P	L120 b	2.70	94-06	*Vice n' Friendly*1182¼ One Way Love1201½ Mr. Epperson1151½	Second best	9
Previously trained by Wright Michael W																		
18Sep99-8Med	fst	6f	:223 :451 :57 1:09	3↑ SkipTrial50k	**99**	1	7	3nk	1½	11	2½	Husbands P	L122 b	2.50	93-14	Diamond117½ One Way Love1224½ Siftaway115hd	Speed, gave way	7
Previously trained by Wright Michael Jr																		
21Aug99-8WO	fst	6½f	:22 :443 1:094 1:162	3↑ [S]Shepperton101k	**97**	4	1	31½	3½	3½	1hd	Husbands P	L124 b	*1.55	93-19	OneWayLove124hd AlasknSunburn1151¼ GrecinsRebel1153	Driving, inside	5
24Jly99-8WO	fst	6½f	:22 :443 1:10 1:163	3↑ BldVenturH81k	**106**	4	1	1hd	21	2hd	1½	Husbands P	L116 b	3.40	92-23	*One Way Love*116½ *Mr. Epperson*1104¼ *Hawk in Sight*1102¼	Driving	6
26Jun99-4WO	fst	6f	:22 :444 :564 1:091	3↑ Alw 41400N$Y	**88**	5	2	22	21	2hd	1¾	Husbands P	L122 b	4.65	95-07	*One Way Love*122¾ My Imperial Slew1191¾ Tailor's Thread1193½	Driving	6
2Jun99-8WO	sly	1 1/16	:224 :46 1:113 1:442	3↑ [S]StdyGrowth52k	**60**	5	2hd	1½	1hd	54½	516	Walls M K	L121 b	1.70	66-22	Silks Or Scarlet1154 David's Discovery1174 *Avalon Gold*1152	Faded	5
22May99-8WO	fst	6f	:22 :441 :562 1:092	3↑ [S]NwProvdnce100k	**82**	4	1	53¾	57½	58	47¼	Walls M K	L117 b	2.05	87-12	Deputy Inxs124nk Alaskan Sunburn1132½ Randy Regent1174½	No threat	5
1May99-8WO	fst	7f	:222 :451 1:102 1:232	4↑ VigilH-G3	**97**	1	8	61	31½	42½	21	Walls M K	L117 b	6.55	88-15	*Deputy Inxs*1221 One Way Love117nk Cache In1183½	Good effort	10
10Apr99-8WO	fst	6f	:214 :442 :563 1:10	4↑ JcqCartier81k	**90**	4	4	45½	57	47	34	Kabel T K	L119 b	5.55	87-12	Transferred1134 Cache In121no One Way Love1191	Best stride late	6
5Dec98-8WO	fst	6f	:22 :443 :562 1:091	3↑ KennedyRd64k	**96**	3	3	31½	43¼	26	25¼	Kabel T K	L117 b	5.25	90-18	Uncle Woger1145¼ One Way Love1174 Rushiscomingup119nk	Second best	6
21Nov98-8WO	fst	1 1/16	:234 :464 1:112 1:444	[S]SirBarton76k	**85**	3	2hd	1hd	2hd	2hd	1½	Clark D	L115 b	*.35	80-22	One Way Love115½ Rowdy Ruckus1185½ Ray Poosay1136	Driving	5
28Oct98-8WO	fst	7f	:222 :45 1:094 1:231	3↑ OC 62k/N4X-N	**95**	1	3	1hd	2hd	11½	14¼	Clark D	L115 b	*1.30	87-15	*One WayLove*1154¼ BartholomewBandy117no *MyImperialSlew*115nk	Driving	5
14Oct98-8WO	fst	7f	:22 :441 1:094 1:23	[R]DepMinistr38k	**87**	4	2	1hd	1hd	11½	1nk	Clark D	L117 b	*1.35	88-19	*One Way Love*117nk Starlight Gazer1181¼ Kinkennie1172½	Driving	9
19Sep98-8WO	fst	1⅛	:463 1:111 1:373 1:503	ClMcLghlnH66k	**92**	6	21	2hd	11	1hd	31	Montpellier C	L117 b	7.35	88-20	Ski Maker1151 *Fancy Touch*116no *One Way Love*1175¼	Gamely	8
16Aug98-8WO	fm	1½	Ⓣ :492 1:141 2:053 2:301	[R]Breeders300k	**46**	8	11	1hd	73¼	816	825½	Husbands P	L126 b	10.95	55-19	Pinafore Park1211¾ Patriot Love1263¼ Comet Kris1266	Faltered 2nd turn	9
19Jly98-8FE	fst	1 3/16	:454 1:10 1:361 1:551	[R]PrncOWales197k	**93**	3	1hd	1hd	2hd	32½	38	Ramirez M R	L126 b	29.30	91-17	ArchersBy1261¾ NiteDremer1266¼ OnWyLov1263¾	Fast pace,dueled,wknd	6
21Jun98-8WO	fst	1¼	:453 1:102 1:364 2:021	[R]QueensPlt500k	**86**	4	21	2hd	3nk	56	713¾	Clark D	L126 b	41.10	80-22	*Archers Bay*1264¾ Brite Adam1264¼ Kinkennie126no	Checked uppr str,tired	13
6Jun98-7WO	fst	1 1/16	:234 :473 1:124 1:454	3↑ Alw 30900N2X	**84**	2	1hd	11	11	16	16	Clark D	L113 b	*1.35	75-28	One Way Love1136 Pints ofBarley1181½ FrequentFlyGuy118no	Ridden out	5
17May98-8WO	fst	1 1/16	:234 :472 1:113 1:461	Marine82k	**76**	5	41½	41¾	52¼	54¼	45½	McKnight J	L119 b	13.60	67-32	*SilverTlk*113¾ RggdKingdom114hd ThundrBow1174¾	Lacked late response	7
19Apr98-9Hia	fst	7f	:224 :452 1:094 1:233	Bahamas50k	**81**	9	1	41½	2½	33	45	Elliott S	L119 b	5.90	83-18	GllptsAss1133¾ Ovrlord119hd MdnghtCoyot1121¼	Bumped,chase fast pace	9
22Mar98-9Tam	fst	1 1/16	:232 :471 1:122 1:441	TampaByDby150k	**77**	8	33	32½	31	63½	79¾	Davis R G	L120 b	7.20	88-08	ParadeGround118nk MiddlesexDrive1181 RockndRoll1161¾	Chased, faded	8
21Feb98-9GP	fst	7f	:22 :443 1:093 1:23	[R]GrtNavigtr52k	**82**	7	3	72¾	73¾	44½	45¾	Davis R G	L119 b	48.80	79-13	SouthernBostonion1152¾ *Voymericn*1153 Swig117no	Lost whip late stretch	8
6Dec97-5WO	fst	1 1/16	:232 :473 1:12 1:46	[S]Kingarvie79k	**77**	4	2½	2hd	2hd	1hd	1½	Clark D	L114 b	7.10	74-20	OneWayLove114½ IceWater1171¼ Itpaystobelte1138	Driving, well handled	7
Previously trained by Wright Michael W																		
15Nov97-7Haw	sly	1 1/16	:232 :472 1:132 1:464	HawJuv150k	**57**	8	55½	53¾	42¾	69½	619¼	Meier R	L113 b	20.80	60-21	WellNoted1149 RoguishPrince1151 GryVlvt1131½	Stumbled startwidetrip	8
1Nov97-1WO	sly	6f	:224 :462 :591 1:122	Md c-(50-45)	**74**	9	1	1hd	12½	14	12¾	Clark D	L115 b	2.75	81-22	One Way Love1152¾ Essa's Secret1163 Regal Sahib110¾	Driving	9
Claimed from Day By Day Farm for $50,000, Day James E Trainer 1997(as of 11/1): (-)																		
17Aug97-9WO	gd	6½f	Ⓣ :232 :481 1:142 1:21	Md Sp Wt 20k	**55**	2	4	62½	72¾	53½	56¼	Clark D	120	2.40	63-27	Star On Fire115no *Gudai Might*1153 Carlin1202½	Blocked mid stretch	12
26Jly97-8WO	fst	6f	:222 :452 :58 1:111	[S]BullPage80k	**65**	1	4	2hd	32½	33½	32½	Clark D	115 b	4.30e	84-16	Pino's Pride117½ *Lah Konoc*1152 One Way Love1154	In tight 3/8 pole	7
9Jly97-2AP	fst	5f	:232 :471 1:00	Md Sp Wt 19k	**55**	3	2	21	41¼	31	24	Sibille R	119 b	3.00	88-17	Dirty Mike1194 One WayLove119½ *Letthebigredroll*1192¾	Intightinside turn	7

Performing Magic

Own: The Thoroughbred Corporation

Ch. h. 7 (Apr)
Sire: Gone West (Mr. Prospector) $150,000
Dam: Performing Arts*Ire (The Minstrel)
Br: Swettenham Stud (Ky)
Tr: Shirreffs John A(0 0 0 0 .00) 2004:(139 12 .09)

Life	18	5	3	5	$723,170	113	D.Fst	9	3	1	2	$676,765	113
2001	3	0	0	1	$39,900	113	Wet(328)	1	0	1	0	$22,290	89
2000	7	3	2	1	$659,155	102	Turf(324)	8	2	1	3	$24,115	-
	0	0	0	0	$0	-	DstⓉ(372)	0	0	0	0	$0	-

22Sep01-12TP	fst	1⅛	:464 1:103 1:351 1:474	3↑ KyCpClH-G2	**95**	6	53½	43½	35½	48¼	510½	Espinoza V	L115	4.90	85-06	Guided Tour119nk Ballo Star1148¼ *A Fleets Dancer*115¾	3 wide, tired	6
2Sep01-7Dmr	fst	1	:23 :461 1:101 1:351	3↑ DmrBCH-G2	**113**	1	53½	42	3½	2hd	3nk	Stevens G L	LB116	11.80	99-08	ElCorrdor121hd FiglioMio113nk PrformingMgc1163	Rail bid,led late,game	6
9Aug01-7Dmr	fst	6f	:22 :441 :561 1:084	3↑ Alw 65390N$Y	**96**	2	1	57½	47½	45½	44	Stevens G L	LB123	3.90	92-13	BeaumesdeVenise1173 CapoDiCpo117hd Tvsco1171	Inside,mild bid at 3rd	5
7Oct00-9Hoo	fst	1 1/16	:224 :46 1:101 1:414	IndianaDby307k	**98**	5	5¾	42	2½	11	2½	Sellers S J	LB122 f	*.60	101-18	MistrDvill119½ PrformingMgic1226¾ OnCllClos1193¼	Outside bid, 2nd best	5
27Aug00-9RP	fst	1⅛	:472 1:112 1:37 1:501	RPDerby-G3	**96**	6	62¼	4nk	2hd	2½	1nk	Sellers S J	LB124	*.90	89-24	Performing Magic124nk *Mister Deville*1242¾ Del Mar Danny1241½	Just up	9
Previously trained by Hassinger Alex L Jr																		
1Jly00-8Hol	fst	1 1/16	:231 :46 1:101 1:421	AffirmdH-G3	**74**	6	52	52¾	53½	68¾	516¼	Sellers S J	LB121	2.40	73-18	Tiznow111nk *Dixie Union*1222 Millencolin1172	4wd early,gave way	6
13May00-8Spt	fst	1⅛	:483 1:12 1:372 1:504	IllDerby-G2	**101**	1	41¼	32	43½	21½	1hd	Sellers S J	L119	2.10	83-15	Performing Magic119hd Country Only1172½ Country Coast114nk	Just up	9
29Apr00-9CD	fst	1	:224 :454 1:104 1:354	DerbyTrl-G3	**102**	7	42½	53¼	3½	2hd	11¼	Day P	L114	4.50	91-19	*PerformingMagic*1141¼ SunCat1176¾ ValintHlory1141¼	3wide, steady drive	8
19Mar00-9Aqu	fst	1	:224 :453 1:093 1:341	Gotham-G3	**91**	8	41¾	61¼	42	4¾	34½	Gomez G K	L114	8.90	92-11	Red Bullet113½ Aptitude1134 *PerformingMagic*114¾	4 wide move, stayed on	9
27Feb00-7SA	wf	6½f	⊗ :21 :433 1:094 1:163	Baldwin-G3	**89**	1	6	55½	55	53	21½	Desormeaux K J	LB116	14.30	83-16	Fortifir1141½ PrformingMgc116hd JoopyDoopy117nk	Swung 4wd into lane	8
Previously trained by Henry Cecil																		

9Oct99 Ascot (GB) **Timeform rating: 58**	yl	1	Ⓣ RH 1:464	Autumn Stakes (Listed) Stk 37700	1119	Peslier O	123	11.00	French Fellow123nk One Step At A Time118½ Total Love1182	*Chased in 4th,weakened over 2f out*	11
4Sep99 Haydock (GB) **Timeform rating: 95**	gd	1	Ⓣ LH 1.424	Stanley Racing Conditions Stks Alw 20400	1¾	Ryan W	124	8.00	Performing Magic124¾ Michele Marieschi1242 Blue Gold124hd	*Rated in 4th,angled out for bid 2f out,led 1f out,drftd left late*	4
18Aug99 York (GB) **Timeform rating: 84**	gd	5f	Ⓣ Str 1:002	Roses Stakes (Listed) Stk 44100	63¼	Kinane M J	123	6.00	Buy Or Sell123hd Alfailak1231¼ Melon Place123½	*Trailed,ridden after 2f,never threatened*	7
4Aug99 Leicester (GB) **Timeform rating: 78**	gd	5f	Ⓣ Str 1:01	EBF Maiden Stakes Maiden 10500	1½	Ryan W	126	*1.50	Performing Magic126½ *Awake*1261 Poppy's Song1212	*Tracked in 3rd,led 170y out,drifted left near line*	7
9Jly99 Lingfield (GB) **Timeform rating: 77**	gd	6f	Ⓣ Str 1:114	Rydon Group Maiden Stakes Maiden 9300	33½	Fallon K	126 b	1.60	Shafaq121½ *Don't Surrender*1263 *Performing Magic*1263½	*Slowly away,pressing pace after 2f,faded final furlong*	6
24Jun99 Newcastle (GB) **Timeform rating: 74**	gd	7f	Ⓣ LH 1:294	Newcastle United FC Maiden Stk Maiden 8500	32¾	Fallon K	126	*.35	Aston Mara126¾ Bold Ewar1262 Performing Magic1263	*Tracked leaders,dueled 2f out,weakened and drifted left 1f out*	7
3Jun99 Yarmouth (GB) **Timeform rating: 80+**	gd	6f	Ⓣ Str 1:153	EBF Breckland Maiden Stakes Maiden 11200	2½	Fallon K	126	*.25	Barathea Guest126½ Performing Magic1261 *Miraki*1265	*Led to 100y out,gamely*	5
19May99 Goodwood (GB) **Timeform rating: 82+**	gd	6f	Ⓣ Str 1:13	EBF Plantation Maiden Stakes Maiden 10700	34	Fallon K	126	*.55	Perugia1213 *Night Style*1261 Performing Magic1261¼	*Twrds rear when carried wide by riderless horse after 1f,unlucky*	11

PERIGEE MOON (Hennessy—Lovlier Linda, by Vigors). Canada. A half-brother to the late Old Trieste, Perigee Moon won the Killavullan Stakes as a 2-year-old in Ireland. Hennessy is a very potent speed influence and strong hidden turf sire and likewise, Perigee Moon's runners should have high speed on grass. (HT^2)

Perigee Moon
Own: Mrs John Magnier

Ch. h. 6 (Mar)
Sire: Hennessy (Storm Cat) $35,000
Dam: Lovlier Linda (Vigors)
Br: John R. Gaines Thoroughbreds & Orpendale (Ky)
Tr: O'Brien Aidan P(0 0 0 0 .00) 2004:(0 0 .00)

Life	3	2	0	0	$42,149	-	D.Fst	0	0	0	0	$0	-
2001	1	0	0	0	$0	-	Wet(354)	0	0	0	0	$0	-
2000	2	2	0	0	$42,149	-	Turf(316)	3	2	0	0	$42,149	-
	0	0	0	0	$0	-	Dst(0)	0	0	0	0	$0	-

Previously trained by Aidan O'Brien

22Apr01♦Curragh (Ire)	hy 7f Ⓣ Str 1:38¹	3↑ Gladness Stakes-G3	68¼	Kinane M J	123	*1.00	Softly Tread118² Social Harmony136½ Rush Brook133³	7
Timeform rating: 100		Stk 63000					Dueled to 2f out,weakened 1-1/2f out	
30Oct00♦Leopardstwn (Ire)	hy 7f Ⓣ LH 1:38³	Killavullan Stakes-G3	1¹	Kinane M J	122	4.00	Perigee Moon122¹ *Dr. Brendler*1224½ Love Me True1191½	12
Timeform rating: 109p		Stk 48100					Twrds rear,wide bid to lead over 1f out,driving.Lethal Agenda 4th	
30Sep00♦Curragh (Ire)	sf 6f Ⓣ Str 1:20	Ballymany EBF Maiden	12½	O'Donoghue C	128	7.00	*Perigee Moon*1282½ America Calling1231½ Delude128¹	18
Timeform rating: 93		Maiden 16800					Close up,led 2f out,handily	

PIKEPASS (Forty Niner—Deanna's Special, by Storm Bird). Kentucky. A minor stakes winner at 4 by sire of sires Forty Niner, he is from the family that produced Broad Brush and the outstanding broodmare Too Bald, the dam of Capote, Exceller, Baldski, American Standard, and Vaguely Hidden. His offspring should have abundant speed. (SP^2)

Pikepass
Own: Jiles E. W

Dk. b or b. h. 8 (Apr)
Sire: Forty Niner (Mr. Prospector) $31,482
Dam: Deanna's Special (Storm Bird)
Br: E. W. Jiles (Ky)
Tr: Smith Kenny P(0 0 0 0 .00) 2004:(116 15 .13)

Life	5	3	2	0	$101,763	106	D.Fst	3	2	1	0	$48,323	98
2000	2	1	1	0	$60,000	106	Wet(337)	2	1	1	0	$53,440	106
1999	3	2	1	0	$41,763	91	Turf(261)	0	0	0	0	$0	-
AikⓉ	0	0	0	0	$0	-	DstⓉ(379)	0	0	0	0	$0	-

19Aug00-9ElP fst 1	:23¹ :46 1:10³ 1:36³	3↑ GovernorsH75k	**98**	7	1²	1½	1hd	1hd	21½	Court J K	L115 f	3.50	96-10	Jadada1131½ Pikepass1151¼ Midway Magistrate1193¼	Pace, 2nd best	8
23Jan00-9FG sly 1$\frac{1}{16}$	:24¹ :47³ 1:12¹ 1:44	4↑ DiplmtWayH75k	**106**	3	11½	1²	1²	11½	15½	Doocy T T	L111 f	8.00	91-18	Pikepass1115½ Phil the Grip113hd Desert Air117⁵	Drew away late	5
26Nov99-4CD sly 1$\frac{1}{16}$	:24² :48³ 1:13⁴ 1:45³	3↑ Alw 42200N2x	**89**	1	11½	1¹	1hd	1½	2¹	Albarado R J	L111 f	*1.30	81-21	Steelsilverblack113¹ *Pikepass*1112¾ Munnings1153½	Lean in brush 1/16 pl.	6
16Oct99-3Kee fst 6f	:21² :44³ :56⁴ 1:09¹	3↑ Alw 44222N2L	**89**	10	4	33½	2½	1¹	12½	Albarado R J	L116 f	*1.30	96-05	Pikepass1162½ *Saltworks*116½ Ballistic116nk	Stalked, hand urging	10
28Aug99-4RP fst 6f	:22² :44² 1:09⁴	Md Sp Wt 12k	**91**	3	3	2¹	2½	1¹	11¼	Doocy T T	LB122 f	*.80	92-16	*Pikepass*1221¼ *Homefieldhit*1225¼ Dark Fool122²	Ridden out	7

POINT GIVEN (Thunder Gulch—Turko's Turn, by Turkoman). Kentucky. One of the best 3-year-olds of the past 10 years, Point Given was not only 3-year-old champion but also Horse of the Year. He was a late-developing juvenile, and his classically bred 2-year-olds should begin to show talent in the second half of their season and blossom at 3 and 4. Bred for distance on dirt and turf.

Point Given
Own: The Thoroughbred Corporation

Ch. h. 6 (Mar)
Sire: Thunder Gulch (Gulch) $50,000
Dam: Turko's Turn (Turkoman)
Br: The Thoroughbred Corporation (Ky)
Tr: Baffert Bob(0 0 0 0 .00) 2004:(434 80 .18)

Life	13	9	3	0	$3,968,500	117	D.Fst	12	8	3	0	$3,518,500	117
2001	7	6	0	0	$3,350,000	117	Wet(315)	1	1	0	0	$450,000	110
2000	6	3	3	0	$618,500	101	Turf(273)	0	0	0	0	$0	-
Aik Ⓣ	0	0	0	0	$0	-	DstⓉ(291)	0	0	0	0	$0	-

25Aug01-10Sar	fst	1¼	:473 1:111 1:354 2:012	Travers-G1	117	7	31½	3½	2½	1hd	13½	Stevens G L	L126 br	*.65	98-02	Point Given1263½ E Dubai1261¼ *Dollar Bill*126¾	3 wide trip, driving	9
5Aug01-11Mth	fst	1⅛	:464 1:111 1:362 1:493	HsklInvH-G1	106	6	56¾	55½	31½	31	1½	Stevens G L	L124 br	*.30	88-10	*PointGiven*124½ TouchTone115no BurningRom119¾	Outside,lugged in,drvg	6
9Jun01-10Bel	fst	1½	:48 1:113 2:003 2:262	Belmont-G1	114	9	31	1hd	12	17	112¼	Stevens G L	L126 b	*1.35	107-02	*Point Given*12612¼ A PValentine126¾ Monarchos1261	5 wide, strong urging	9
19May01-11Pim	fst	1 3/16	:471 1:114 1:362 1:552	Preaknes-G1	111	11	910	67½	3nk	1½	12¼	Stevens G L	L126 b	*2.30	94-11	*Point Given*1262¼ A P Valentine126nk *Congaree*1261¼	Brk slw,5wd,lug in str	11
5May01-8CD	fst	1¼	:444 1:091 1:35 1:594	KyDerby-G1	99	17	76¼	73¾	21½	44½	511½	Stevens G L	L126 b	*1.80	92 -	Monarchos1264¾ Invisible Ink126no Congaree1264	Broke in bmp,flattened	17
7Apr01-5SA	wf	1⅛	:462 1:104 1:352 1:473	SADerby-G1	110	1	21	21	11	12½	15½	Stevens G L	LB122 b	*.70	97-08	Point Given1225½ CraftyC.T.1223 ILoveSilver1222½	Led in hand,ridden out	6
17Mar01-7SA	fst	1 1/16	:223 :461 1:102 1:414	SnFelipe-G2	105	8	55	54	1hd	12	12¼	Stevens G L	LB122 b	*.40	95-13	*PointGiven*1222¼ ILoveSilver1161½ JamicnRum1197	5wd move, led, cleared	8
16Dec00-4Hol	fst	1 1/16	:23 :464 1:104 1:421	HolFut-G1	101	4	45	3½	3½	2hd	11	Stevens G L	LB121 b	*.30	89-15	*PointGiven*1211 *MillnniumWind*1217 GoldnTickt1215	3wd,lugged in bit,best	4
4Nov00-8CD	fst	1 1/16	:232 :464 1:111 1:42	BCJuven-G1	99	1	106½	127	1410	67	2no	Stevens G L	L122 b	8.10	100 -	Macho Uno122no *Point Given*1221½ *Street Cry*122½	10w strtch,closed fast	14
14Oct00-9Bel	fst	1 1/16	:223 :45 1:092 1:412	Champagn-G1	95	2	41	1hd	3nk	2hd	21¾	Desormeaux K J	L122 b	4.60	88-09	A P Valentine1221¾ Point Given122¾ Yonaguska1221	Vied inside, gamely	10
16Sep00-12TP	fst	1 1/16	:221 :453 1:12 1:47	KyCupJuv-G3	81	7	89½	67½	53	13	13½	Sellers S J	L114 b	3.30	68-23	Point Given1143½ Holiday Thunder1144 *The Goo*116½	Broke a bit in air	11
26Aug00-7Dmr	fst	7f	:223 :452 1:102 1:232	Md Sp Wt 47k	93	1	6	4¾	1½	11	12	Espinoza V	LB118 b	*1.20	88-10	*PointGiven*1182 HighandLowVixen1184 Qwqeb1188	Inside duel,clear,dvng	7
12Aug00-6Dmr	fst	5½f	:221 :451 :572 1:04	Md Sp Wt 47k	74	9	6	109¾	99½	79¾	25½	Take Y	LB118 b	19.00	86-17	HighCascade1185½ *PointGiven*1182½ WestwrdAngel118no	4wd turn,late 2nd	11

PRIME TIMBER (Sultry Song—Wine Taster, by Nodouble). New York. Was considered to be a serious Kentucky Derby contender at one time, but various injuries compromised his talent. His statebred runners should be better at 3 than 2, and be effective from seven furlongs to 1⅛ miles.

Prime Timber
Own: Sez Who Racing

B. h. 8 (Feb)
Sire: Sultry Song (Cox's Ridge) $5,000
Dam: Wine Taster (Nodouble)
Br: John B. Penn (Fla)
Tr: Casse Mark E(0 0 0 0 .00) 2004:(167 24 .14)

Life	17	4	4	0	$621,238	106	D.Fst	15	3	4	0	$578,728	106
2001	2	0	0	0	$5,208	83	Wet(335)	0	0	0	0	$0	-
2000	4	0	1	0	$62,600	99	Turf(297)	2	1	0	0	$42,510	96
	0	0	0	0	$0	-	Dst(0)	0	0	0	0	$0	-

4Aug01-6WO	fst	1 1/16	:23 :462 1:112 1:442	3↑OC 80k/n1m-N	78	3	65	57	63½	68¼	58¼	Husbands P	L116	*2.05	76-24	Grand End Sweep1161 Hot Pepper Hill1161 Opus Won116nk	No threat	7
21Jly01-7WO	fst	6½f	:222 :444 1:093 1:16	3↑BldVenturH107k	83	1	5	54	55¼	56½	56½	Husbands P	L116	4.50	86-16	TemperedAppl1141¼ CthoulPrish1111¼ *MrEpprson*117no	Off slowly, trailed	5
Previously trained by Inda Eduardo																		
3Sep00-9Dmr	fst	1	:223 :46 1:101 1:35	3↑DmrBCH-G2	87	6	810	86¼	64¾	79	611½	McCarron C J	LB117	2.60	88-08	El Corredor1112½ Cliquot1171 Literal Prowler1123	4wd 2nd turn,no bid	8
6Aug00-8Dmr	fst	1 1/16	:223 :454 1:093 1:41	3↑SnDiegoH-G3	99	1	46	55	56	37	28	McCarron C J	LB116	11.40	90-02	*Skimming*1128 PrimeTimber1161½ NationalSaint1173½	Saved ground to 1/8	7
15Jly00-8Hol	fst	1 1/16	:233 :47 1:104 1:413	3↑BelAirH-G2	97	3	31½	41¼	65¾	54½	45¾	Delahoussaye E	LB118 b	7.10	86-08	Euchre1141¼ Sultry Substitute1142½ River Keen1222	Bit tight 7-1/2	7
4Jun00-4Hol	fst	7½f	:223 :451 1:091 1:273	3↑Alw 63000n$y	92	2	3	52½	53½	44¼	48	Delahoussaye E	LB116 b	2.60	85-12	National Saint116¾ Cliquot122nk Crows1167	Angled in, weakened	5
Previously trained by Baffert Bob																		
26Dec99-6SA	fst	7f	:221 :441 1:084 1:22	Malibu-G1	95	1	6	712	710	54½	53¼	Flores D R	LB119 b	7.70	92-08	LoveThatRed119nk StraightMan118hd CtThief123½	Bumped start,off slow	7
23Oct99-8SA	fm	1⅛ Ⓣ	:471 1:11 1:344 1:463	OakTrDby-G2	90	9	46	56½	57½	65	64½	Flores D R	LB120 b	*2.50	91-14	Mula Gula1181¼ Eagleton118nk *Super Quercus*118hd	Bobbld strt,5wd bid	9
1Oct99-7SA	fm	1 Ⓣ	:234 :473 1:11 1:344	ⓇInExcess74k	96	6	53	42	52¾	31	11½	Flores D R	LB116 b	*1.30	85-15	PrimeTimber1161½ FirstTitnium114no SpiceGuy114nk	Off bit slow, 3 wide	6
3Sep99-2Dmr	fst	1	:222 :454 1:104 1:353	3↑OC 80k/n3x-N	84	1	44	43	31	33½	410¼	Flores D R	LB116 b	*.50	84-09	Kona Wind119¾ Crows1195½ Storm Wreck1194	Inside,bid,weakened	5
1May99-8CD	fst	1¼	:474 1:122 1:372 2:031	KyDerby-G1	105	13	114¾	115	53½	44	42¼	Flores D R	L126 b	6.30	87-14	*Charismatic*126nk Menifee126¾ Cat Thief1261¼	Forced out 1/16 pole	19
3Apr99-5SA	fst	1⅛	:471 1:112 1:361 1:484	SADerby-G1	102	2	53	53½	53	27½	23½	Flores D R	LB120 b	*2.40	87-13	GenerlChllenge1203½ PrimTimbr1203½ DsrtHro1201¼	Angled out, 2nd best	8
13Mar99-7SA	fst	1 1/16	:23 :464 1:111 1:42	SnFelipe-G2	106	1	27	45	32	32½	12	Flores D R	LB116 b	2.80	93-17	Prime Timber1162 Exploit122½ High Wire Act1164½	3w into str,driving	7
28Feb99 7SA	fst	1	:222 :454 1:10 1:362	SnRafael-G2	95	7	75	62¾	4¾	1hd	2nk	Stevens G L	LB115	2.30	89-11	Desert Hero116nk *PrimeTimber*115hd Capsized115nk	Wide thru out, collard	9
12Dec98-8Hol	fst	1 1/16	:221 :45 1:092 1:423	HolFut-G1	92	1	33½	33	32½	2hd	2½	McCarron C J	LB121	2.30	86-13	*TcticlCt*121½ PrimeTimbr1214½ PrmirProprty1212	Led past 1/8,worn down	5
22Nov98-3Hol	fst	7½f	:223 :453 1:101 1:292	Alw 33792n$y	95	2	5	2hd	2½	2½	1nk	Stevens G L	LB120	1.70	84-17	PrimeTimber120nk NationalSint1205 TheChng1201¼	Hard drive,game rail	6
1Nov98-9SA	fst	6f	:214 :452 :574 1:101	Md Sp Wt 33k	84	6	6	64¼	42	1½	1¾	Stevens G L	LB120	*1.10	89-13	*PrimeTimbr*120¾ *BrightVlour*120nk SydnysOlympics1204	4 wide bid, gamely	9

PUT IT BACK (Honour and Glory—Miss Shoplifter, by Exuberant). Florida. Blessed with the high speed of his sire, Put It Back won the Riva Ridge and Best Turn Stakes and he is a great candidate to be a top sire of 2-year-olds—not only in Florida, but also around the country who will be top sprinters as they mature. (SP^2)

Put It Back
Own: Hobeau Farm

Dk. b or b. h. 6 (Feb)
Sire: Honour and Glory (Relaunch) $17,500
Dam: Miss Shoplifter (Exuberant)
Br: Hobeau Farm Ltd. (Fla)
Tr: Jerkens H. A(0 0 0 0 .00) 2004:(293 58 .20)

Life	7	5	1	1	$232,895	108	D.Fst	6	4	1	1	$202,895	108
2001	5	5	0	0	$220,185	108	Wet(352)	1	1	0	0	$30,000	104
2000	2	M	1	1	$12,710	76	Turf(264)	0	0	0	0	$0	-
Aik Ⓣ	0	0	0	0	$0	-	DstⓉ(349)	0	0	0	0	$0	-

9Jun01-8Bel	fst	7f	:214 :442 1:082 1:213	RivaRidg-G2	106	6	2	11	11½	13	1nk	Wynter N A	120	4.60	95-05	PutItBck120nk FlmeThrower1202¾ *TouchTon*1231¼	Dug in gamely, held on	6
23May01-4Bel	sly	7f	:221 :444 1:091 1:222	Alw 48500N$Y	104	1	4	11	1½	13½	15¼	Wynter N A	122	*.80	91-19	*Put It Back*1225¼ Windsor Castle1224¾ Fistfite1222¼	Set pace, driving	4
21Apr01-6Aqu	fst	7f	:223 :444 1:091 1:223	3↑ Alw 45000N2X	97	4	3	1½	1½	13½	11¼	Wynter N A	115	*.75	87-11	*Put It Back*1151¼ High Note1211½ Sir Ghost121nk	Set pace, driving	8
Previously trained by Jerkens James A																		
24Feb01-8Aqu	fst	6f	⊡ :221 :451 :564 1:09	BestTurn80k	108	1	4	11½	11½	15	15½	Wynter N A	116	*.80	100-11	*Put It Back*1165½ Stake Runner1164 *My NewLove*1161¾	Set pace, ridden out	6
3Feb01-4Aqu	fst	6f	⊡ :223 :46 :58 1:103	Md Sp Wt 41k	98	1	10	1½	11½	16	17¼	Wynter N A	120	*1.20	92-12	*PutItBck*1207¼ *DontQuitOnM*1202½ ToDiforAgin1202¼	Speed inside, driving	10
Previously trained by Jerkens H Allen																		
1Oct00-2Bel	fst	6f	:22 :443 :572 1:104	Md Sp Wt 41k	75	2	6	1hd	1hd	3½	34	Wynter N A	118 f	*1.25	80-17	SolitryVision118hd SwpthWorld1184 *PutItBck*1181¼	Crowded backstretch	8
10Aug00-6Sar	fst	5½f	:221 :454 :581 1:044	Md Sp Wt 41k	76	2	8	51¾	41½	2½	21	Wynter N A	118 f	17.20	92-09	Mr. John1181 Put It Back1184½ Rock Slide118¾	Tough trip, gamely	8

ROCK AND ROLL (Cure the Blues—Secret's Halo, by Halo). New York. A stakes winner at 3, 4 and 6, he was an accomplished sprinter/miler who stretched his speed 1⅛ miles to win the Pennsylvania Derby. His late sire was a leading New York-based stallion, and his statebred runners should also be off to a good start as 2-year-olds.

Rock and Roll
Own: Paulson Madeleine and Craig, Jenny

Ch. h. 9 (Feb)
Sire: Cure the Blues (Stop the Music)
Dam: Secret's Halo (Halo)
Br: Pin Oak Stud (Ky)
Tr: Mott William I(0 0 0 0 .00) 2004:(480 93 .19)

Life	38	10	10	7	$708,557	121	D.Fst	32	8	6	7	$635,882	110
2001	5	2	0	1	$73,545	102	Wet(351)	6	2	4	0	$72,675	121
2000	9	1	3	3	$88,885	100	Turf(259)	0	0	0	0	$0	-
Aik Ⓣ	0	0	0	0	$0	-	DstⓉ(379)	0	0	0	0	$0	-

5Aug01-5Mth	fst	1	:232 :463 1:11 1:363	3↑ SalvtrMH-G3	83	3	42¼	41½	42¼	63¼	79¼	Day P	L120 b	3.70	82-10	SeofTrnquility1151½ KnockAgin1121½ HlsHope1171½	In tight briefly start	7
25May01-9CD	fst	1 1/16	:232 :464 1:103 1:422	3↑ Alw 60960c	98	1	21½	2½	1hd	3½	34¼	Day P	L123 b	*.60	94-13	Connected1203¾ CstelliSecrts116½ RockndRoll123¾	Pressed,led,weakened	6
11Apr01-9OP	fst	1 1/16	:231 :463 1:102 1:43	3↑ 5thSnBC-G3	82	7	32½	21	3nk	79	711¼	Johnson J M	L119 b	*1.00	78-22	RemingtonRock114hd KombtKt1143½ DDevil114nk	3-w bid,gave way drive	7
28Feb01-9GP	fst	1 1/16	:232 :471 1:11 1:43	4↑ Cryptclrnc67k	102	4	11	11½	11½	13	13½	Bailey J D	L118 b	*.70	93-22	Rock and Roll1183½ Day Trade1161½ Reporter1161¾	Inside, drew clear	6
7Feb01-9GP	fst	1 1/16	:234 :472 1:112 1:422	4↑ Alw 47000N$MY	102	4	11½	12½	12	13	13¾	Bailey J D	L118 b	*1.20	96-19	*Rock and Roll*1183¾ Cat's At Home1201¾ Day Trade1163¾	Inside, driving	7
25Nov00-7CD	sly	1 1/16	:243 :482 1:132 1:454	3↑ Alw 56350c	100	1	11½	12½	2hd	22½	25½	St Julien M	L114 b	*.80	75-34	Gatewood1165½ *RockndRoll*1145 Unloosened1213¾	Bmp foe start,no match	5
14Nov00-8CD	fst	1 1/16	:241 :472 1:113 1:44	3↑ Alw 48720c	92	5	2hd	2½	2hd	1hd	2nk	Day P	L114 b	*.90	90-18	Fax a Freddy118nk Rock and Roll114hd Inkatha1141¾	Duel,led,2ndbest	6
19Aug00-9EIP	fst	1	:231 :46 1:103 1:363	3↑ GovernorsH75k	84	4	22	2½	3nk	55	69	Melancon L	L121 b	*1.40	89-10	Jadada1131½ Pikepass1151¼ MidwayMagistrte1193¼	Bid,flattened out bad	8
23Jly00-3Hpo	fst	1	:243 :474 1:123 1:371	3↑ OmahaH100k	100	4	23	21½	2½	1hd	2½	Compton P	LB121 b	*1.10	102-11	Hustler114½ RockndRoll1216 SureShotBiscuit1182	Bid outsd, outfinished	8
10Jun00-7CD	fst	1 1/16	:242 :482 1:122 1:431	3↑ Alw 51400c	100	4	21½	21	2hd	12½	14¾	St Julien M	L123 b	2.10	94-12	RockndRoll1234¾ KimbrlitPip118½ MrronGlc1162¾	Pressed,took over,drvg	6
4May00-8CD	fst	1	:223 :444 1:084 1:344	3↑ Alw 56240c	99	4	32	33	3½	3½	32½	Bailey J D	L120 b	*.80	93-13	DpGold113½ MstrOFoxhonds1162 *RockndRll*1206½	Bumpd start,empty late	7
9Apr00-7Kee	fst	7f	:223 :452 1:094 1:223	4↑ Alw 63538N$Y	99	1	4	51¾	42¼	31½	32¾	Bailey J D	L123 b	2.40	86-15	KimbrlitPip1161½ LbrtyGold1231¼ RockndRoll1231¼	Angled 4wide,no rally	7
5Feb00-10GP	fst	1⅛	:464 1:104 1:354 1:482	3↑ DonnH-G1	88	10	96¼	96	97	913	919½	Davis R G	L115 b	47.10	75-18	StephenGotEven115¾ GoldenMissil1144½ *Bhrns*1214	Wide early, no threat	10
8Jan00-8GP	fst	1 1/16	:232 :47 1:11 1:423	3↑ BrowardH-G3	100	1	2½	2hd	1½	21½	35½	Bailey J D	L120 b	*1.30	89-17	HorseChestnut1175½ Isypete116hd RockndRoll1203	On rail, led, weakened	6
5Nov99-3GP	fst	1 1/16	:24 :483 1:124 1:424	3↑ ⓇAPIndy75k	98	4	34½	31	3nk	1hd	1nk	Bailey J D	L119 b	1.50	93-13	RockandRoll119nk *DancingGuy*1174½ DancetheBalldo115½	3 wide, prevailed	6
11Sep99-3Bel	fst	1	⊗ :223 :444 1:093 1:352	3↑ Alw 57230c	94	4	1½	13	11½	2hd	21¾	Bailey J D	L122 b	*.60	85-15	Hanarsaan1171¾ *Rock and Roll*1222 Willing1151¾	Strong pace, gamely	4
28Aug99-9Mth	fst	1	:232 :454 1:094 1:35	3↑ SlvtrMIH-G3	99	6	31	3½	11	2½	22¾	Castillo H Jr	L119 b	*.90	96-08	Truluck1152¾ Rock and Roll1194 Siftaway1144½	Second best	6
6Aug99-3Sar	fst	7f	:222 :443 1:094 1:232	3↑ Alw 52000N$Y	97	3	1	2hd	2hd	1½	1½	Bailey J D	L123 b	1.70	88-15	RockndRoll123½ CryptcRscl1181½ ForthndSx1181½	Dueled outs, prevailed	5
4Jly99-8Bel	fst	7f	:223 :444 1:08 1:203	3↑ TomFoolH-G2	101	5	1	43½	42½	43	45¾	Bailey J D	L114 b	7.20	93-08	*Crafty Friend*116¾ Affirmed Success1195 Artax117hd	Close up, no response	5
29May99-9Bel	fst	1	:222 :443 1:09 1:342	3↑ MtropltH-G1	68	3	4¾	41½	72¼	810	824¼	Day P	L114 b	7.60	68-22	Sir Bear1171¾ *Crafty Friend*114¾ *Liberty Gold*1142¼	Speed inside, empty	8
1May99-4CD	fst	7f	:223 :452 1:101 1:224	4↑ CDH-G2	105	3	7	43½	44	22½	1½	Day P	L112 b	6.50	91-08	RockandRoll112½ LibertyGold1141¼ RunJohnny1132	Lunged start, driving	7
7Apr99-9OP	fst	1 1/16	:232 :47 1:111 1:421	3↑ 5thSnBC-G3	106	6	31	1½	11	2½	31	Judice J C	L114 b	*.70	92-23	Truluck114¾ SlidetotheLft114nk *RockndRoll*1143½	Last away,between foes	8
13Mar99-10GP	fst	1 1/16	:232 :464 1:11 1:423	3↑ CrmFrchH-G3	110	2	22½	21½	11½	2hd	22	Bailey J D	L113 b	*1.40	92-19	*Jazz Club*1142 Rock and Roll1132¾ Hanarsaan1136¼	Stalked, outfinished	7
11Nov98-9Aqu	wf	1⅛	:453 1:092 1:352 1:48	3↑ StuyvntH-G3	108	1	1hd	1½	13	2hd	2¾	Bailey J D	L114 b	*.00	95-11	Mr. Sinatra115¾ Rock andRoll1147 Accelerator1143¾	Dug in gamely on rail	5
25Sep98-8Med	fst	1⅛	:463 1:102 1:343 1:464	PegasusH-G2	89	3	11½	11	1hd	34½	412¼	Bailey J D	L117 b	3.40	87-09	Tomorrows Cat1133 Limit Out1151¾ Comic Strip1197½	Led, tired	6
7Sep98-11Pha	fst	1⅛	:47 1:103 1:35 1:473	PaDerby-G3	110	1	11	11	11½	1hd	11¼	Castillo H Jr	L114 b	5.50	102-08	RockandRoll1141¼ *TomorrowsCt*1141¼ BlckBlde1192¼	Rail,pace, stiff drive	11
9Aug98-8Sar	fst	1⅛	:464 1:112 1:363 1:50	JimDandy-G2	94	7	11½	11½	1½	2hd	55¼	Sellers S J	L114 b	21.10	81-22	FvoritTrick119no DputyDimond114nk RffsMjsty1141½	Set pace, weakened	7
12Jly98-8Bel	fst	1 1/16	:224 :452 1:093 1:422	Dwyer-G2	82	2	31	3½	2hd	35½	410¾	Bailey J D	L114 b	5.40	76-17	*Coronado's Quest*1245 Ian's Thunder112¾ Scatmandu1225	Crowded start	5
13Jun98-6Bel	sly	1 1/16	:231 :46 1:094 1:392	3↑ Alw 40000N2X	121	4	11½	12	11½	18	114	Bailey J D	L112 b	3.10	102-11	RockandRoll11214 IansThunder1143½ DocMrtin1111½	Set pace,ridden out	5
29May98-6Bel	fst	7f	:23 :461 1:102 1:23	3↑ Alw 39000N2X	88	3	1	2½	3½	35	411	Bailey J D	L112 fb	7.40	76-18	*Good and Tough*1146 Sahm1193 Silk Song1192	Chased inside,tired	6
2May98-8CD	fst	1¼	:453 1:103 1:353 2:021	KyDerby-G1	15	9	21	23½	1520	1441	1462	Torres F C	L126 b	50.60	32-02	*RealQuiet*126½ VictoryGallop1262¼ IndinChrlie126hd	Speed, stopped badly	15
Previously trained by Williams Charlie J																		
22Mar98-9Tam	fst	1 1/16	:232 :471 1:122 1:441	TampaByDby150k	92	7	21½	21½	2½	2hd	31¼	Houghton T D	L116 b	10.30	97-08	PrdeGround118nk MiddlsxDriv1181 RockndRoll1161¾	Dueled, good effort	8
28Feb98-9Tam	gd	1 1/16	:232 :48 1:132 1:461	SamFDavis28k	86	6	22½	2½	2hd	1hd	2hd	Houghton T D	L116 fb	*1.80	88-14	DbnyCrr113hd RockndRoll11610 MdnghtCoyot1161¾	Long drive, gd effort	10
31Jan98-9Tam	fst	7f	:23 :464 1:12 1:251	BudChalngr33k	76	5	4	3½	22½	2hd	2¾	Lopez R D	L116 b	10.00	86-15	SejmRun120¾ RockndRoll1162¼ RoguishPrinc1161¾	Stalked, led lte, hung	11
6Jan98-6Tam	fst	6f	:222 :46 :574 1:12	Alw 7200N2L	68	2	5	1hd	1½	1½	14¼	Lopez R D	L119 b	*.40	92-10	Rock and Roll1194¼ Fiddling Nero116¾ Acting Tips1165½	Ridden out	8
20Dec97-9Tam	fst	6f	:221 :454 :583 1:113	Inaugural27k	71	9	5	51¾	2hd	1hd	31½	Lopez R D	L114 b	6.50	91-09	Sejm Run1221½ Glow Over Pyrite113no *Rock and Roll*114½	Bid 4w, led, hung	9
22Nov97-10Det	wf	1	:242 :482 1:132 1:414	Troy27k	73	3	3nk	2hd	1½	1hd	2no	Doser M E	L114 b	2.80	68-34	*DimondGte*121no RockndRoll11419 ArizonMc1176	Duel,swrv,bump mid str	5
24Oct97-6Det	wf	5½f	:233 :471 :593 1:061	Md Sp Wt 11k	65	8	3	11	11½	14½	17¼	Doser M E	L118 b	*.50	86-20	RockndRoll1187¼ *ExplodngHnr*1182 AnjsDvd1181¼	Wider lead,kept roused	9

SANDPILE (Cure the Blues—Geraldine, by Deputy Minister). New York. Many stakes-winning sons of former leading New York sire Cure the Blues are now young stallions, such as Sandpile, who should carry on his sire's legacy of speed and class. Sandpile's second dam is a New York favorite, the multiple stakes winner Talc Shaker. Sandpile's runners should be quick, win-early types at 2, and because he is not widely known, his runners will offer good value.

Sandpile
Own: Edwards James F

B. h. 9 (Apr)
Sire: Cure the Blues (Stop the Music)
Dam: Geraldine (Deputy Minister)
Br: CBF Corporation (NY)
Tr: Bond H. J(0 0 0 0 .00) 2004:(125 25 .20)

Life	4	3	0	0	$104,580	92	D.Fst	3	2	0	0	$44,580 89
1998	4	3	0	0	$104,580	92	Wet(369)	1	1	0	0	$60,000 92
1997	0	M	0	0	$0	-	Turf(259)	0	0	0	0	$0 -
	0	0	0	0	$0	-	Dst(0)	0	0	0	0	$0 -

20Jun98-5Bel	fst	1	:233 :47 1:112 1:354	3↑	S Alw 40000N2x	89	7	1½	11	1hd	13½	15½	Bridgmohan S X5	L109 b	*.75	85-12	Sndpile1095½ CittionJet119nk *SophistictedMn*1143¾	Drew away,kept to drv	8
19Apr98-8Aqu	gd	1	:23 :461 1:104 1:361		R NYStlTmSqr100k	92	2	2½	1hd	2hd	1hd	11	Chavez J F	L115 b	5.20	88-19	*Sandpile*1151 Mellow Roll122¾ Diplomatic Corps1155	Pace on rail,driving	7
25Mar98-5Aqu	fst	1	:221 :461 1:112 1:374		S Alw 33000N1x	65	5	43	52¼	52¼	52¾	42¼	Chavez J F	L121	*.85	78-16	*MissionaryMonk*116nk ProKaine116¾ PltosLove1161¼	Bobbled strt,wde trp	7
11Mar98-6Aqu	fst	1⅛	:482 1:141 1:41 1:541		S Md Sp Wt 31k	72	1	2hd	1hd	1hd	1½	13½	Chavez J F	L119	*.95	65-30	Sandpile1193½ PrivteDecision1191 *SprtnMission*1142	Drew clear,kept busy	7

SMOKIN MEL (Phone Order—She's Smokin, by Husar). New York. Winner of the Gotham and third in the Wood Memorial Stakes behind Captain Bodgit and Accelerator, Smokin Mel was bred to be fast. His obscure sire has a recognizable pedigree. Phone Order is by Fappiano and is a half-brother to Toussaud, the dam of five high-quality stakes winners, including Empire Maker. Being inbred to Dr. Fager and with Mr. Prospector in his pedigree, Smokin Mel's offspring should be fast and ready to win at 2. (SP^2)

Smokin Mel
Own: Port Sidney L

Gr/ro. h. 10 (Mar)
Sire: Phone Order (Fappiano)
Dam: She's Smokin (Husar*Mex)
Br: Annabelle Stute (Wash)
Tr: De Stefano J M Jr(0 0 0 0 .00) 2004:(94 13 .14)

Life	17	5	3	2	$318,719	108	D.Fst	12	4	3	1	$238,399 108
1998	3	1	1	0	$34,360	108	Wet(342)	2	1	0	1	$77,800 100
1997	11	2	2	2	$252,184	101	Turf(231*)	3	0	0	0	$2,520 92
Aik (T)	0	0	0	0	$0	-	Dst(T)(400)	1	0	0	0	$2,520 92

18Jly98-6Bel	fst	6½f	:221 :45 1:09 1:151	3↑	Alw 41000N3x	108	1	1	22½	2hd	1hd	1½	Bailey J D	L119 b	1.90	96-13	Smokin Mel119½ *Dice Dancer*11410 Oro Bandito1211	Dug in gamely	6
20Jun98-6Bel	fst	6½f	:214 :442 1:09 1:152	3↑	Hcp 52000	98	6	6	31	3½	2½	52	Bridgmohan S X	L113 b	9.20	93-11	KngRollr117nk DH *JohnnyLgt*117 DH BondlssMmnt120nk	Spd 3w,weakened	6
30May98-7Bel	fst	6f	:222 :452 :564 1:084	4↑	Alw 41000N3x	86	5	1	42½	3½	23	28	Bridgmohan S X5	L109 b	3.65	89-11	AffrmdSccss1148 SmoknMl1091¾ LdngthChrg1172½	Wide,rallyd for place	6
5Oct97-4Bel	fm	1 1/16 (T)	:251 :483 1:111 1:41		Alw 50000NC	45	4	21½	21½	41¼	712	725¾	Davis R G	L117	7.20	66-15	*Subordination*1238¾ A Little Luck1202¼ Erv114hd	Tired after 3/4's	7
20Sep97-7Bel	fst	1	:23 :462 1:11 1:354		JeromeH-G2	77	3	1hd	2hd	2½	38	318¼	Velazquez J R	L115	11.70	67-15	Richter Scale1181¼ Trafalger11717 Smokin Mel115nk	Contested pce,tired	8
27Aug97-9Sar	sf	1⅛ (T)	:492 1:141 1:401 1:524		Saranac-G3	71	8	11½	11	1½	46	716	Velazquez J R	L114	7.30	50-18	*River Squall*1144 Daylight Savings1143 Inkatha1141	Set pace, tired	10
1Aug97-8Sar	fst	6f	:213 :444 :572 1:102		ScreenKing82k	93	2	7	43	31½	32	54	Velazquez J R	L122	5.40	85-19	Oro de Mexico117½ Trafalger1221 *Kelly Kip*1221½	Bumpd strt,rail move	7
5Jly97-9Bel	fst	1 1/16	:232 :454 1:10 1:421		Dwyer-G2	73	3	2hd	1hd	2hd	47	517½	Velazquez J R	L122	4.80	70-11	Behrens1171¼ Glitman1147 Banker's Gold1223½	Contested pace,tired	6
22Jun97-8Bel	sly	6f	:214 :443 :57 1:101	3↑	Alw 38000N2x	90	2	4	1½	1hd	1½	1½	Velazquez J R	L111	*.80	90-08	Smokin Mel111½ *Oro de Mexico*1126 Roll Again114½	Set pace,long drive	5
12Apr97-8Aqu	sly	1⅛	:472 1:112 1:354 1:481		WoodMem-G2	100	7	11	1½	1½	1hd	33	Luzzi M J	L123	6.80	92-06	Captain Bodgit1232 Accelerator1231 *Smokin Mel*1233½	Set pace,gamely	10
29Mar97-8Aqu	fst	1	:212 :433 1:09 1:341		Gotham-G2	101	9	49½	410	1hd	1hd	1½	Velazquez J R	L112	15.60	99-06	Smokin Mel112½ Ordway122nk Wild Wonder1197	3w move,prevailed	11
Previously trained by Stute Melvin F																			
15Feb97-4SA	fm	*6½f (T)	:21 :43 1:081 1:121		Alw 50400N1x	92	8	3	42½	43	51¼	4½	Garcia M S	B115	3.00	96-04	Rarecard115hd *Flaming West*117hd Klinsman117nk	Finished well	12
31Jan97-2SA	fst	6½f	:214 :443 1:091 1:16		Alw 42000N1x	91	1	1	3nk	2hd	2½	2¾	Garcia M S	B115	*1.10	89-16	HigherWithFire117¾ SmokinMl1152½ ZroHnry1155	Fast pace, outfinished	6
18Jan97-8SA	fst	6f	:213 :44 :56 1:082		SanMiguel104k	98	6	2	2½	2hd	2hd	23	Garcia M S	B114	9.60	93-10	*Thisnerlywsmine*1183 SmokinMel1143½ Rntri1161¾	Rapid pace,second best	6
31Dec96-1SA	fst	6f	:213 :444 :57 1:10		Clm 50000(50-45)	92	2	3	1½	1hd	1½	11	Garcia M S	B118	3.70	88-14	SmokinMel1181 *OneStarFlg*118hd PrinceIrish1184	Bumpd start,held gamly	6
27Jun96-4Hol	fst	5f	:221 :444 :584		Md 32000(32-28)	63	7	5	41½	3nk	11	1hd	Douglas R R	B118	2.20	91-11	*SmokinMel*118hd *PlesursllMin*1181¾ SnstionlBrz1182	Step slow,strong rally	7
21Mar96-2SA	fst	2f	:212		Md Sp Wt 37k	–	9	9			932	933¼	Douglas R R	B118	5.40	- -	GoldenBronze118hd *TheTexsTunnel*1181 Reforce118½	Veered sharply start	9

SNUCK IN (Montbrook—Love Child, by Mugassas). Florida. A three-time stakes winner at 2, Snuck In won the Rebel Stakes and was second in the Arkansas Derby at 3. Montbrook is a speed influence and Snuck In's runners should also have speed and be best from five furlongs to 1 1/16 miles.

Snuck In
Own: Ackerley Brothers Farm

B. h. 7 (Apr)
Sire: Montbrook (Buckaroo) $20,000
Dam: Love Child (Mugassas)
Br: Barbara Licwinko (Fla)
Tr: Asmussen Steven M(0 0 0 0 .00) 2004:(1524 372 .24)

Life	18	5	4	2	$563,230	108	D.Fst	14	4	4	2	$499,370	108
2001	6	0	1	1	$31,410	108	Wet(323)	3	1	0	0	$62,720	101
2000	5	1	1	0	$172,000	101	Turf(245)	1	0	0	0	$1,140	82
Aik ⓣ	0	0	0	0	$0	-	Dstⓣ(322)	0	0	0	0	$0	-

17Nov01-3Hoo	fst	1	:224	:462	1:103	1:352	3↑ SchaeferMl103k	108	6	54½	41½	31½	2½	21	Meche D J	LB115	13.20	91-33	Freon Flier1181 Snuck In1152½ Tiltam1152	Inside bid1/8,no match	7
24Oct01-6Kee	sly	6f	:221	:454	:574	1:102	3↑ Alw 55360N1Y	85	2	3	2hd	2hd	32½	46½	Meche D J	L118	6.90	80-21	SmolderinHert120¾ *VlintStyle*1235 ProvenCure123¾	Between foes,weaken	6
24Jun01-7LS	fm	1 1/16 ⓣ	:233	:48	1:114	1:431	3↑ Alw 38000N1Y	82	2	52¼	52	52½	63½	53¾	Lanerie C J	L119	*2.70	80-16	ColonilPower121nk BestofKC121nk Pirnhurst1211¾	In middle, never close	8
3Jun01-9LS	fst	1	:232	:46	1:101	1:362	3↑ Alw 38000N1Y	94	5	32	31	3½	2hd	32½	Lanerie C J	L119	*.90	90-22	*Unrullah Bull*1192½ T. B.TrackStar119hd SnuckIn119¾	Outfinished for place	5
5May01-3CD	fst	7f	:213	:433	1:074	1:202	4↑ LnEndCDH-G2	80	8	4	62¾	64	89	914¾	Meche D J	L114	20.10	88 -	Alannan116½ *Bonapaw*116½ Exchange Rate1132¼	4w, tired stretch	10
23Mar01-9FG	fst	6f	:214	:444	:563	1:09	4↑ Alw 43500N$Y	95	9	2	53½	44½	45	44	Meche D J	L117	3.30	95-09	My Halo1172½ Fantastic Finish117½ Zarb's Luck1161	Wide trip	9
15Jly00-10Tdn	fst	1⅛	:464	1:111	1:374	1:502	OhioDrby-G2	91	10	63½	66	84¼	75¼	78¼	Asmussen C B	L117	3.80	81-17	MilwaukeeBrew116hd BraveQuest1132¼ KissNtive116no	Failed to respond	10
18Jun00-7Del	fst	1 1/16	:233	:464	1:112	1:44	LRichards200k	91	6	2½	1hd	2hd	1hd	43	Asmussen C B	L117	*.70	84-17	*Grundlefoot*1131¾ Perfect Cat114nk Mercaldo1141	Came in early, wknd	8
20May00-10Pim	gd	1 3/16	:463	1:111	1:37	1:56	Preaknss-G1	98	2	42½	42	41½	52	57¼	Asmussen C B	L126	19.60	78-11	RedBullet1263¾ *FusichiPegsus*126hd Impechmnt126nk	Steadied along early	8
15Apr00-9OP	fst	1⅛	:464	1:113	1:363	1:49	ArkDerby-G2	98	9	63½	64½	63	33½	23¾	Asmussen C B	L122	*2.10	89-16	Graeme Hall1183¾ SnuckIn122hd Impeachment1181¼	4-w 1/4, just held 2nd	14
25Mar00-10OP	gd	1 1/16	:232	:47	1:112	1:424	Rebel-G3	101	3	32	33	32½	1hd	1nk	Asmussen C B	L119	*1.10	90-16	SnuckIn119nk BigNumbers1144¼ FantheFlame1133½	Restraind,all out late	12
10Dec99-7Hou	fst	1 1/16		:47	1:114	1:431	GalFurnJuv200k	92	1	11	11	11	1hd	14	Asmussen C B	L118	1.60	102 -	*Snuck In*1184 *Ifitstobeitsuptome*1143 *Connected*114½	Led throughout	7
23Oct99-11Crc	fst	1 1/16	:224	:464	1:113	1:442	Ⓡ FSNReality400k	92	2	41¼	41	41	21½	25	Albarado R J	L120	1.60	89-15	Kiss a Native1205 *Snuck In*1202½ Megacles1201½	Stdy,checked 1st turn	8
4Sep99-12Crc	fst	7f	:224	:461	1:112	1:241	Ⓡ FSAffirmed125k	83	8	3	3nk	3½	11	14¼	Albarado R J	L116	*.30	88-16	Snuck In1164¼ B L's Appeal116½ Bold Meridian116½	Strong hand ride	8
7Aug99-12Crc	fst	6f	:212	:444	:573	1:11	Ⓡ FSDrFager75k	88	8	2	31½	2½	13½	13¾	Albarado R J	L116	*1.30	93-12	*Snuck In*1163¾ American Bullet1161¼ Megacles116hd	Drew clear, driving	10
26Jun99-10CD	fst	6f	:212	:45	:57	1:101	BshfdMnr-G2	72	4	6	41¼	53	47	37¾	Borel C H	115	8.40	84-09	Dance Master1153 SkyDweller1154¾ *SnuckIn*115hd	Broke awkwardly, tired	8
6Jun99-4CD	fst	5½f	:22	:453	:574	1:041	Md Sp Wt 33k	81	6	2	2hd	1½	11½	12¾	Albarado R J	L118	*2.00	97-07	Snuck In1182¾ Frazee's Folly118no *Mighty*1185¾	Pace, driving	12
16May99-1CD	fst	5f	:221	:451		:573	Md Sp Wt 37k	74	8	9	63¾	53¼	54	34	Albarado R J	118	21.60	96-07	Sky Dweller1181 Ⓓ *Dance Master*1183 *Snuck In*1182	6-wide stretch,no gain	9

Placed second through disqualification

SONGANDAPRAYER (Unbridled's Song—Alizea, by Premiership). Florida. Songandaprayer had blazing speed and was able to get 1 1/16 miles, winning the Fountain of Youth Stakes. He also finished second in the 1 1/8-mile Blue Grass Stakes. But Songandaprayer's offspring will be best sprinting, and his runners are bred to be quick, win-early 2-year-olds. (SP^2)

Songandaprayer
Own: Hurley Leslie and R. and D. J. Stable

B. h. 6 (Mar)
Sire: Unbridled's Song (Unbridled) $125,000
Dam: Alizea (Premiership)
Br: Donna M. Wormser (Ky)
Tr: Dowd John F(0 0 0 0 .00) 2004:(82 11 .13)

Life	8	3	1	1	$380,480	105	D.Fst	5	1	1	1	$311,000	105
2001	6	1	1	1	$314,000	105	Wet(359)	3	2	0	0	$69,480	94
2000	2	2	0	0	$66,480	94	Turf(288)	0	0	0	0	$0	-
	0	0	0	0	$0	-	Dst(0)	0	0	0	0	$0	-

4Jly01-3Mth	fst	6f	:213	:44	:562	1:09	JerShrBC-G3	88	5	2	31½	1½	21	35½	Bravo J	L122 f	*.80	88-11	*City Zip*1194¼ *Sea of Green*1171¼ Songandaprayer1222	3-deep bid,led,tired	5
5May01-8CD	fst	1¼	:444	1:091	1:35	1:594	KyDerby-G1	75	1	11½	11½	41¾	1212	1327	Gryder A T	L126 f	35.90	77 -	Monarchos1264¾ Invisible Ink126no Congaree1264	Hustled inside,faded	17
14Apr01-9Kee	fst	1⅛	:462	1:102	1:352	1:481	BlueGras-G1	105	6	21½	21	2hd	21½	25¼	Prado E S	L123 f	6.50	89-14	MllnnmWnd1235¼ Songndpryr1231¾ DollrBll1231½	Pressed, no match late	7
10Mar01-11GP	fst	1⅛	:464	1:112	1:37	1:494	FlaDerby-G1	88	9	52	3½	3nk	32	510¼	Prado E S	L122 f	4.80	78-13	Monarchos1224½ Outofthebox1222½ InvisibleInk122½	Wide trip, weakened	13
17Feb01-10GP	fst	1 1/16	:234	:464	1:104	1:432	FntnOYth-G1	101	3	11½	14	12½	13	12½	Prado E S	L117 f	18.00	91-14	Songandaprayer1172½ Outofthebox114¾ City Zip1174½	Inside, driving	11
20Jan01-10GP	gd	1 1/16	:222	:454	1:121	1:46	HolyBull-G3	81	4	2½	11½	2hd	41¾	55	Day P	L117 f	3.10	73-23	Radical Riley119hd Buckle Down Ben119½ Cee Dee1174	Off rail, tired	8
26Nov00-8Aqu	sly	6f	:214	:443	:572	1:102	Huntington84k	94	5					1nk	Gryder A T	L116 f	10.80	85-22	Songandaprayer116nk Native Heir1182½ *Voodoo*1161	Dense fog, driving	10
15Jun00-5Mth	gd	5f	:213	:442		:573	Md Sp Wt 26k	78	1	6	12	14	15	1½	Bravo J	118 f	*.20	92-09	*Songandpryer*118½ *Strbury*11810¾ UndercoverCper118½	Clear,widened,held	7

STRATEGIC MISSION (Mr. Prospector—Sultry Sun, by Buckfinder). New York. A stakes-winning son of Mr. Prospector, Strategic Mission is a half-brother to stakes winners Sultry Song and Solar Splendor, and he is one of the best-bred stallions standing in New York. His runners should have high speed on all surfaces and be excellent 2-year-olds. (SP^2)

Strategic Mission
Own: Live Oak Plantation

Dk. b or b. h. 9 (May)
Sire: Mr. Prospector (Raise a Native)
Dam: Sultry Sun (Buckfinder)
Br: Live Oak Stud (Ky)
Tr: Mott William I(0 0 0 0 .00) 2004:(414 83 .20)

Life	24	7	5	4	$414,320	108	D.Fst	1	0	0	0	$0	49
2001	9	3	1	3	$191,620	108	Wet(399)	1	0	0	0	$0	-
2000	8	2	3	0	$161,040	105	Turf(305)	22	7	5	4	$414,320	108
	0	0	0	0	$0	-	Dst(0)	0	0	0	0	$0	-

11Nov01-8CD	fm	1⅛	Ⓣ	:474 1:114 1:36 1:474	3↑RivrCtyH-G3	100	8	12	11	11½	1hd	32¼	Chavez J F	L115 b	3.70	95-03	Dr. Kashnikow1161½ Tijiyr117¾ Strategic Mission115½	Pace,weakened late	8
19Oct01-7Med	fm	1	Ⓣ	:23 :461 1:10 1:334	3↑JohnHenry100k	100	8	1½	1hd	1hd	12	21	Bailey J D	L117 b	*1.90	101-09	BeckonthKing1131 StrtgicMission1172½ BuyingRin115no	Outfinished late	12
22Sep01-8Med	gd	1 1/16	Ⓣ	:233 :473 1:113 1:43	3↑ClfHngrH-G3	97	4	21½	21	11½	12½	63	Bailey J D	L118 b	2.20e	82-21	CrashCourse1141¾ SolitryDncer114no UnionOne114½	Clear turn,tired late	10
8Aug01-8Sar	fm	1	[T]	:233 :471 1:11 1:341	4↑Alw 57000c	106	2	12½	11½	13	16	12¼	Bailey J D	L120 b	*1.15	97-04	StrtegicMission1202¼ CityWest118½ *SejmsMdnss*1201¾	Soon clear, driving	6
4Jly01-10CD	gd	1	Ⓣ	:23 :461 1:102 1:343	3↑FrckrBCH-G2	90	1	11	2hd	52¾	43½	67¾	Guidry M	L116 b	6.70	92 -	Irish Prize122no [D]Where's Taylor1141¼ Aly's Alley1174½	Inside, faded	7
5May01-8Aqu	fm	1 1/16	Ⓣ	:24 :484 1:122 1:413	3↑FtMarcyH-G3	106	4	1½	1½	12½	13½	11	Migliore R	L118 b	*.85	96-04	StrategicMission1181 *PineDance*1162 LegalJousting114¾	Set pace, driving	9
13Apr01-8Kee	fm	1	Ⓣ	:232 :462 1:102 1:342	4↑MakrsMrk-G2	105	5	11½	11½	1½	2hd	31½	Bailey J D	L116 b	6.50	94-03	NorthEstBound120nk Brhms1231¼ *StrtgicMisson*116no	Pace,weakened late	8
3Mar01-9GP	fm	*1 1/16	Ⓣ	:233 :471 1:102 1:404	+4↑OC 100k/N4X-N	108	3	1½	12	13	13½	13½	Bailey J D	L118 b	*2.00	98-14	StrategicMission1183½ SpecialCoch1182 LouisinAllen1171	Inside, driving	10
24Jan01-8GP	fm	*1 1/16	Ⓣ	:234 :492 1:14 1:454	4↑OC 100k/N4X-N	95	5	2hd	1½	11	11½	33½	Bailey J D	L118	*.70	69-30	IvrsBigPcful1181¾ KingsCrown1181¾ *StrtgicMission*1184¼	Inside, gave way	10
28Oct00-8Haw	gd	1	Ⓣ	:231 :471 1:113 1:361	3↑CareyMmH-G3	91	2	22	3½	42	43½	55½	Guidry M	L119	*1.30	80-14	Where's Taylor1171½ Dernier Croise1133 *Associate*115nk	Weakened	11
7Oct00-8Kee	fm	1	Ⓣ	:231 :461 1:094 1:333	3↑KeeTurfM-G2	105	2	41	43	31½	1½	2nk	Lopez J	L126	29.40	104-04	Altibr126nk StrtegicMission1262 QuietResolve126hd	4wide,bid,outfinished	9
16Aug00-8Sar	sf	1⅛	Ⓣ	:501 1:144 1:394 1:523	4↑Alw 50000N4x	98	5	2½	1hd	1hd	1hd	2nk	Bailey J D	L116	*2.35	66-34	Icantheryou116nk StrtegicMission1162 Hlcyon118nk	Argued pace, gamely	8
23Jly00-7Bel	fm	7f	Ⓣ	:231 :451 1:08 1:194	4↑Alw 49000N4x	98	2	3	11½	12	1hd	21½	Bailey J D	L117 b	*.85	99 -	*Officilprmission*1121½ StrtgicMission117¾ Wthrbird1171¾	Set pace, gamely	8
4Jly00-8Bel	gd	1	Ⓣ	:232 :462 1:093 1:34	3↑PokerH-G3	97	8	14½	12½	1½	21½	64¾	Castillo H Jr	L114 b	6.20	83-12	*Affirmed Success*1171¾ Rabi114½ Weatherbird1131¾	Set pace, gave way	10
29May00-9Mth	fm	1	Ⓣ	:232 :463 1:10 1:344	3↑RedBankH-G3	101	5	21½	2hd	11½	11½	51¾	Smith M E	L114 b	*1.50	93-09	Mi Narrow1141¼ Deep Gold114no Inkatha117no	Drew clear, weakened	9
5Feb00-7GP	fm	1 1/16	Ⓣ	:233 :472 1:104 1:40	+4↑Alw 36000N3x	100	7	11½	12½	12½	13½	11¾	Bailey J D	L122 b	*.40	96-10	StrategicMission1221¾ TheKnightSky1171¼ Sibercrsher1174½	In hand late	10
17Jan00-7GP	fm	1	Ⓣ	:23 :461 1:093 1:331	4↑Alw 34000N2x	101	6	11½	11½	14	16	16¼	Bailey J D	122 b	*.70	102-03	*Strategic Mission*1226¼ Awol Honey119hd Le Sabre114¾	Ridden out	12
13Nov99-5Aqu	fm	1⅛	Ⓣ	:47 1:111 1:36 1:48	3↑Alw 44000N1x	102	5	1hd	11½	11½	18	19	Bailey J D	118 b	3.05	103 -	*StrtegicMission*1189 DdsGun118½ *DncingRomeo*1151½	Bumped start, driving	9
Previously trained by Kelly Patrick J																			
30Aug98-9Sar	fm	1⅛	Ⓣ	:461 1:094 1:34 1:461	3↑Alw 38000N1x	79	11	62¼	42¾	31	34	310	Davis R G	117 b	4.40	89-09	DstntMrg1145 MoonlghtMl1145 *StrtgcMssn*1172¼	Caught wide both turns	11
14Aug98-7Sar	fm	1⅛	Ⓣ	:464 1:103 1:35 1:472	3↑Alw 38000N1x	88	3	22	21½	2½	1½	22¼	Davis R G	116 b	2.65	91-12	HeavensEst1202¼ [D]StrtegicMission1161 WildBrin1161½	Came in deep str	8
Disqualified and placed 4th																			
26Jly98-9Bel	fm	1⅛	[T]	:483 1:12 1:36 1:472	3↑Md Sp Wt 36k	89	2	1½	11½	12½	15½	14	Davis R G	115 b	*.90	91-16	StrtegicMission1154 *Wterville*1223 LightBggg1086	Cruisd along,riddn out	7
10Jly98-6Bel	fm	1	Ⓣ	:224 :454 1:10 1:341	3↑Md Sp Wt 36k	88	2	22½	22	1hd	2hd	2nk	Davis R G	115 b	13.50e	89-12	Wild Brain115nk *Strategic Mission*1158 Dr. Bart115no	Gamely,inside	11
21Jun98-4Bel	fst	7f		:222 :454 1:104 1:232	3↑Md Sp Wt 35k	49	7	6	31	3½	86½	815½	Bailey J D	120 b	4.40	69-16	CraftyMn120½ *PurringPnther*120½ Momsmercedes1205½	Bumpd strt,3 wide	9
16Apr98-4Kee	my	6f		:214 :46 :583 1:121	Md Sp Wt 37k	-0	9	8	88½	816	817	931¾	Bailey J D	L122	2.80	48-14	A Man of Class1223 Rare Money122½ *Devil Rum*1223½	No speed, outrun	9

TALK IS MONEY (Deputy Minister—Isle Go West, by Gone West). Kentucky. This is one stallion who is worth much more than his meager $5,000 stud fee. A $1.8 million sales yearling, he showed exciting promise early in his career, winning the Miracle Wood Stakes before fizzling in the Kentucky Derby. Had high speed, and his dam is a half-sister to Hennessy. His runners should have great speed at 2, should be best between five furlongs and 1 1/16 miles, and have a high potential on grass. (SP^2/HT^2)

Talk Is Money
Own: Borislow Daniel M

Ch. h. 6 (Feb)
Sire: Deputy Minister (Vice Regent) $100,000
Dam: Isle Go West (Gone West)
Br: Dr. George S Stefanis & Linda Phillips (Ky)
Tr: Scanlan John F(0 0 0 0 .00) 2004:(54 6 .11)

Life	7	2	1	1	$104,110	101	D.Fst	6	1	1	1	$89,290	101
2001	6	1	1	1	$89,290	101	Wet(385)	1	1	0	0	$14,820	86
2000	1	1	0	0	$14,820	86	Turf(297)	0	0	0	0	$0	-
	0	0	0	0	$0	-	Dst(0)	0	0	0	0	$0	-

5May01-8CD	fst	1¼	:44^{4} 1:09^{1} 1:35 1:59^{4}	KyDerby-G1	**–**	11	8$^{6\frac{1}{4}}$	17^{16}	-	-	-	Bailey J D	**L**126 fb	47.10	- -	Monarchos126$^{4\frac{3}{4}}$ Invisible Ink126^{no} Congaree126^{4}	Bmp,distanced eased	17
21Apr01-9Pim	fst	1⅛	:48 1:11^{2} 1:36 1:49	FdrcoTesio145k	**101**	1	1$^{3\frac{1}{2}}$	1$^{1\frac{1}{2}}$	1^{2}	1^{hd}	2$^{1\frac{1}{4}}$	Verge M E	**L**119 fb	4.00	93- 11	Marciano119$^{1\frac{1}{4}}$ TlkIsMoney119$^{1\frac{3}{4}}$ *BurningRom*122$^{2\frac{1}{4}}$	Rail,brushd winner 1/8	4
7Apr01-11Hia	fst	1⅛	:47^{1} 1:11 1:35^{3} 1:48^{1}	Flamingo-G3	**82**	2	2$^{1\frac{1}{2}}$	2$^{1\frac{1}{2}}$	3^{1}	3^{5}	3$^{10\frac{1}{2}}$	Velasquez C	**L**122 fb	8.60	85- 16	ThunderBlitz118$^{6\frac{3}{4}}$ TouroftheCat118$^{3\frac{3}{4}}$ TalkIsMoney122$^{\frac{3}{4}}$	4 wide, gave way	9
10Mar01-11GP	fst	1⅛	:46^{4} 1:11^{2} 1:37 1:49^{4}	FlaDerby-G1	**73**	10	9$^{5\frac{1}{4}}$	9$^{4\frac{1}{4}}$	9$^{3\frac{1}{2}}$	10^{11}	8$^{19\frac{1}{4}}$	McCarthy M J	**L**122 fb	23.90	69- 13	Monrchos122$^{4\frac{1}{2}}$ Outofthebox122$^{2\frac{1}{2}}$ InvisiblInk122$^{\frac{1}{2}}$	Bobbled brk, wide trip	13
17Feb01-10GP	fst	$1\frac{1}{16}$	:23^{4} :46^{4} 1:10^{4} 1:43^{2}	FntnOYth-G1	**72**	1	10$^{8\frac{3}{4}}$	11^{11}	11^{11}	9^{10}	10$^{16\frac{1}{2}}$	Verge M E	**L**117 f	11.60	74- 14	Songandaprayer117$^{2\frac{1}{2}}$ Outofthebox114$^{\frac{3}{4}}$ City Zip117$^{4\frac{1}{2}}$	Dwelt start	11
27Jan01-8Lrl	fst	$1\frac{1}{16}$	:24 :47^{3} 1:12 1:45^{4}	MiraclWood57k	**92**	8	3^{1}	2^{hd}	2^{hd}	1^{hd}	1$^{\frac{3}{4}}$	Verge M E	**L**115 f	*1.50	80- 24	Talk Is Money115$^{\frac{3}{4}}$ *Marciano*117$^{3\frac{1}{4}}$ Bay Eagle115$^{3\frac{1}{4}}$	4wd to far turn,drivng	8
16Dec00-5Lrl	my	6f	:22^{3} :46^{3} :59^{2} 1:12^{1}	Md Sp Wt 26k	**86**	3	5	3^{2}	1^{hd}	1$^{4\frac{1}{2}}$	1$^{9\frac{3}{4}}$	Verge M E	**L**120 f	1.80	81- 22	*Talk Is Money*120$^{9\frac{3}{4}}$ Forever Gold120^{nk} Winkaway120$^{\frac{1}{2}}$	3wd turn, ridden out	9

TIZNOW (Cee's Tizzy—Cee's Song, by Seattle Song). Kentucky. What do you make of a horse who was bred to be a nice California-bred sprinter but ended up winning the Breeders' Cup Classic two years in a row, was a champion and Horse of the Year at 3, and champion older male at 4? Tiznow is one of three full siblings who became prominent stakes winners (along with Budroyale and Tizdubai), and his offspring should have good speed. Because of his achievements, he was bred to mares of high quality and his runners should be able to get middle distances.

Tiznow
Own: Cees Stable LLC

B. h. 7 (Mar)
Sire: Cee's Tizzy (Relaunch) $15,000
Dam: Cee's Song (Seattle Song)
Br: Cecilia Straub Rubens (Cal)
Tr: Robbins Jay M(0 0 0 0 .00) 2004:(49 5 .10)

Life	15	8	4	2	$6,427,830	119	D.Fst	15	8	4	2	$6,427,830	119
2001	6	3	1	2	$2,981,880	117	Wet(413)	0	0	0	0	$0	-
2000	9	5	3	0	$3,445,950	119	Turf(220)	0	0	0	0	$0	-
	0	0	0	0	$0	-	Dst(0)	0	0	0	0	$0	-

27Oct01-10Bel	fst	1¼	:47 1:11^{1} 1:35^{4} 2:00^{3}	3↑ BCClasic-G1	**117**	10	3$^{1\frac{1}{2}}$	3$^{1\frac{1}{2}}$	2^{1}	3$^{\frac{1}{2}}$	1no	McCarron C J	**L**126	6.90	91- 12	Tiznow126^{no} *Sakhee*126$^{1\frac{3}{4}}$ Albert the Great126$^{2\frac{3}{4}}$	Prevailed, gamely	13
7Oct01-8SA	fst	1⅛	:45^{2} 1:09^{2} 1:35^{2} 1:48^{4}	3↑ GdwdBCH-G2	**106**	5	3$^{2\frac{1}{2}}$	3$^{1\frac{1}{2}}$	3^{1}	3$^{2\frac{1}{2}}$	3$^{1\frac{1}{2}}$	McCarron C J	**LB**124	*1.10	89- 09	Freedom Crest116^{1} Skimming123$^{\frac{1}{2}}$ *Tiznow*124^{4}	Bid 3wd,slow gain late	6
8Sep01-9Bel	fst	1⅛	:46^{3} 1:10^{1} 1:34^{3} 1:47^{2}	3↑ Woodward-G1	**110**	2	2$^{\frac{1}{2}}$	2$^{\frac{1}{2}}$	2$^{\frac{1}{2}}$	3$^{\frac{1}{2}}$	3$^{1\frac{1}{2}}$	McCarron C J	**L**126	2.40	91- 14	Lido Palace126^{1} Albert the Great126$^{\frac{1}{2}}$ Tiznow126$^{8\frac{1}{4}}$	Speed inside, gamely	5
3Mar01-9SA	fst	1¼	:46^{2} 1:10^{3} 1:35^{4} 2:01^{2}	4↑ SAH-G1	**117**	5	2$^{\frac{1}{2}}$	2^{hd}	1^{hd}	1$^{2\frac{1}{2}}$	1^{5}	McCarron C J	**LB**122	*1.00	96- 10	Tiznow122^{5} Wooden Phone117$^{1\frac{1}{2}}$ Tribunal116^{2}	Dueled, drew clear	12
3Feb01-8SA	fst	1⅛	:47^{1} 1:10^{2} 1:35^{2} 1:48^{2}	Strub-G2	**105**	6	3^{1}	3^{nk}	4$^{\frac{3}{4}}$	2$^{2\frac{1}{2}}$	2^{2}	McCarron C J	**LB**123	*.30	91- 12	Wooden Phone117^{2} *Tiznow*123$^{3\frac{1}{2}}$ Jimmy Z117$^{\frac{3}{4}}$	Vied 3wd,4wd,2nd best	6
13Jan01-8SA	fst	$1\frac{1}{16}$	:23^{1} :46^{3} 1:10^{4} 1:42	SnFndoBC-G2	**108**	6	2$^{\frac{1}{2}}$	2^{hd}	2$^{\frac{1}{2}}$	2^{1}	1$^{1\frac{1}{4}}$	McCarron C J	**LB**122	*.30	94- 12	Tiznow122$^{1\frac{1}{4}}$ Wlkslikeduck120$^{\frac{3}{4}}$ *WoodenPhone*116^{2}	3wd bid,brushd,gamely	6
4Nov00-10CD	fst	1¼	:47^{2} 1:12 1:36 2:00^{3}	3↑ BCClasic-G1	**116**	12	1^{hd}	2^{hd}	1^{hd}	1^{hd}	1^{nk}	McCarron C J	**L**122	9.20	107 -	*Tiznow*122^{nk} GiantsCusewy122$^{3\frac{1}{4}}$ *CptinSteve*122^{hd}	Duel,headed,gamely,drv	13
15Oct00-7SA	fst	1⅛	:47 1:10^{4} 1:35 1:47^{1}	3↑ GdwdBCH-G2	**119**	7	1$^{1\frac{1}{2}}$	1^{1}	1$^{\frac{1}{2}}$	1^{hd}	1$^{\frac{1}{2}}$	McCarron C J	**LB**116	*1.20	99- 13	*Tiznow*116$^{\frac{1}{2}}$ Captain Steve117$^{1\frac{1}{2}}$ Euchre115^{4}	Rated, repulsed rival	7
30Sep00-6LaD	fst	1¼	:47^{1} 1:10^{2} 1:35^{1} 1:59^{4}	SpDbyXXI-G1	**114**	4	1$^{\frac{1}{2}}$	1^{hd}	1^{1}	1^{3}	1^{6}	McCarron C J	**L**124	*.80	103- 05	*Tiznow*124^{6} Commendable124^{1} Mass Market124^{9}	Restrained, ridden out	6
26Aug00-8Dmr	fst	1¼	:45^{2} 1:09^{4} 1:35 2:01^{1}	3↑ PacifcCl-G1	**115**	4	3$^{3\frac{1}{2}}$	2^{1}	2$^{1\frac{1}{2}}$	2$^{2\frac{1}{2}}$	2^{2}	McCarron C J	**LB**117	4.00	93- 14	Skimming124^{2} *Tiznow*117$^{1\frac{1}{4}}$ Ecton Park124$^{\frac{1}{2}}$	Chased,bid, 2nd best	7
23Jly00-6Hol	fst	1⅛	:46^{4} 1:10^{3} 1:35^{2} 1:48	Swaps-G1	**107**	1	4$^{1\frac{1}{2}}$	4^{2}	4^{1}	2$^{1\frac{1}{2}}$	2$^{2\frac{1}{2}}$	Espinoza V	**LB**118 b	2.90	86- 11	Captain Steve120$^{2\frac{1}{2}}$ Tiznow118^{1} Spacelink118^{2}	Pulld,trapped rail 3/8	6
1Jly00-8Hol	fst	$1\frac{1}{16}$	:23^{1} :46 1:10^{1} 1:42^{1}	AffirmdH-G3	**103**	3	4^{2}	3^{1}	3$^{\frac{1}{2}}$	2^{hd}	1^{nk}	Espinoza V	**LB**111 b	10.80	89- 18	Tiznow111^{nk} *Dixie Union*122^{2} Millencolin117^{2}	Tight rail 7-1/2 & 3/8	6
31May00-4Hol	fst	$1\frac{1}{16}$	:23^{3} :46^{2} 1:10^{4} 1:42^{4}	3↑ Md Sp Wt 52k	**95**	5	2$^{\frac{1}{2}}$	2^{hd}	1^{2}	1$^{4\frac{1}{2}}$	1$^{8\frac{1}{2}}$	Solis A	**LB**115 b	*1.30	86- 21	*Tiznow*115$^{8\frac{1}{2}}$ *ColdwterCnyon*116$^{3\frac{1}{2}}$ FctulEvidenc115^{hd}	Drew off, ridden out	9
11May00-6Hol	fst	$1\frac{1}{16}$	:23^{2} :47 1:12 1:43^{1}	3↑ Md Sp Wt 47k	**99**	3	7$^{3\frac{1}{4}}$	4$^{1\frac{1}{4}}$	4^{2}	2^{1}	2^{nk}	Solis A	**LB**115 b	*2.20	84- 15	*SpicyStuff*115^{nk} *Tiznow*115^{4} ColdwaterCanyon116$^{\frac{1}{2}}$	Crowded strt,waitd 1/4	9
22Apr00-7SA	fst	6f	:21^{2} :44^{1} :56^{3} 1:10	Md Sp Wt 47k	**82**	8	5	6$^{3\frac{3}{4}}$	8^{10}	7$^{8\frac{1}{4}}$	6^{3}	Solis A	**B**122 b	13.80	86- 13	MrWondrful122$^{2\frac{1}{2}}$ *ProgrmmdAppl*122no *CocontWlly*122^{hd}	Steadied near 3/8	10

TRAJECTORY (Gone West—Dream Launch, by Relaunch). Canada. A multiple stakes winner, Trajectory has speed top and bottom, and his runners are bred for speed on dirt and turf. (SP^2/HT^2)

Trajectory
Own: Pin Oak Stable LLC

Dk. b or b. h. 7 (Feb)
Sire: Gone West (Mr. Prospector) $150,000
Dam: Dream Launch (Relaunch)
Br: Jayeff B Stables (Ky)
Tr: Motion H. G(0 0 0 0 .00) 2004:(247 49 .20)

Life 10 6 3 0 $279,784 108 | D.Fst 7 4 3 0 $208,984 108
2001 2 1 1 0 $91,855 101 | Wet(387) 3 2 0 0 $70,800 100
2000 8 5 2 0 $187,929 108 | Turf(319) 0 0 0 0 $0 -
0 0 0 0 $0 - | Dst(0) 0 0 0 0 $0 -

5Aug01- 8WO fst 1 1/16 :241 :482 1:131 1:434 3↑ SeagramCup133k 101 3 5 2½ 3 3½ 3 2½ 2 1 1nk Dominguez R A L113 f 2.55 87- 22 Trajectory113nk Exciting Story1214 Catch theRing1141 Up in final strides 5
3Jly01- 8Del fst 1 1/16 :242 :482 1:12 1:44 3↑ ShkyGreenH58k 95 4 3 1½ 2 1 2hd 2 3½ 2 3¾ Dominguez R A L117 f *1.10 83- 13 *B Flat Major*115 3¾ *Trajectory*1172 Judge'sCase1194 Fractious gate,no matc 6
25Oct00- 8Kee fst 1 1/16 :232 :47 1:104 1:412 Ⓡ McCnlSprng77k 108 4 5 4 4 2 4 2 2 2 1 2½ Dominguez R A L118 1.80 98- 15 Trajectory118 2½ Bare Outline1184 Sun Cat118hd Ck 3/4 pl,split 3w,drv 5
4Sep00-11Pha sly 1⅛ :454 1:11 1:362 1:49 PaDerby-G3 98 8 7 6½ 5 6½ 4 ¾ 3 2½ 4 4 Dominguez R A L119 2.80 89- 07 Pine Dance1223 Mass Market122½ Cherokeeinthehills114½ Wide, faded 10
19Aug00- 9Pha fst 1 :231 :464 1:121 1:371 Warminster53k 103 4 7 6 5 3 4 2 1hd 1 4 Dominguez R A L117 *.80 93- 13 Trajectory1174 Icarian122 7¾ *Lord Sanford*117 1¼ Drew off, drvg 10
Previously trained by Mott William I
15Jly00- 7Bel sly 7f :233 :471 1:11 1:232 3↑ Alw 45000N2X 100 2 4 3 2 3½ 2½ 1½ Bailey J D L114 *1.20 86- 21 *Trjectory*114½ *VlintHlory*114 5¼ CherokeeProspct111 4¼ 3 wide move, in time 6
10Jun00- 1Bel fst 7f :212 :453 1:102 1:23 3↑ Alw 45000N2X 89 7 9 4 4 5 2½ 3 2 2 4½ Bailey J D L117 2.65 84- 13 *Left Bank*115 4¼ *Trajectory*117nk Valiant Halory117 2½ Game finish inside 9
19May00- 6Bel my 7f :223 :454 1:113 1:243 Alw 43000N2L 90 5 5 5 1¼ 4 ¾ 1 2 1 4¼ Bailey J D L116 3.00 80- 26 Trajectory116 4¼ Famous Again116½ *Canfield*1167 4 wide move, driving 6
11Mar00- 4GP fst 7f :222 :454 1:111 1:25 Md Sp Wt 35k 78 7 11 4 2½ 4 ¾ 2hd 1¾ Bailey J D L122 *.60 75- 21 *Trajectory*122¾ Prince Judge122hd Jo Jo Pace122¾ In tight st, prevailed 12
12Feb00- 7GP fst 7f :221 :452 1:104 1:234 Md Sp Wt 30k 80 9 10 8 5 6 3¼ 3 1½ 2no Bailey J D 122 6.80 81- 15 *Fajardo*122no *Trajectory*122 1¼ Albert the Great1221 Poor st, just failed 11

TRIPPI (End Sweep—Jealous Appeal, by Valid Appeal). Florida. A sprinter/miler by a source of high speed, Trippi was able to win the Flamingo Stakes at 1⅛ miles, but his runners are bred to be pure sprinters and should make excellent 2-year-olds. (SP^2)

Trippi
Own: Dogwood Stable

B. h. 7 (Mar)
Sire: End Sweep (Forty Niner) $34,980
Dam: Jealous Appeal (Valid Appeal)
Br: Harry T. Mangurian, Jr. (Fla)
Tr: Pletcher Todd A(0 0 0 0 .00) 2004:(570 146 .26)

Life 14 7 1 2 $666,220 111 | D.Fst 13 7 1 2 $666,220 111
2001 4 0 1 1 $45,720 108 | Wet(373) 1 0 0 0 $0 95
2000 10 7 0 1 $620,500 111 | Turf(278) 0 0 0 0 $0 -
0 0 0 0 $0 - | Dst(0) 0 0 0 0 $0 -

11Aug01- 3Sar fst 6f :221 :452 :571 1:094 4↑ Alw 52000N1Y 100 5 2 2½ 1hd 2hd 3½ Bailey J D L122 *.35 94- 08 Big E E116nk Bet Me Best116nk Trippi1223 Game finish outside 5
28May01- 9Bel my 1 :221 :45 1:102 1:37 3↑ MtropltH-G1 95 9 2hd 2½ 1hd 2½ 6 7¼ Bailey J D L118 6.50 75- 26 Exciting Story115¾ Peeping Tom1192 Alannan118 2¾ Vied outside, tired 10
5May01- 3CD fst 7f :213 :433 1:074 1:202 4↑ LnEndCDH-G2 96 1 6 1hd 2hd 4 2¾ 7 7¾ Bailey J D L120 *1.30 95 - Alannan116½ *Bonapaw*116½ Exchange Rate113 2¼ Bmp foe start,tired 10
9Mar01- 9GP fst 7f :22 :434 1:082 1:214 3↑ GPBCSprH-G2 108 5 4 2hd 2 1½ 2 1 2½ Bailey J D L120 *.90 96- 14 HookandLadder115½ Trippi120½ RollinWithNoln116¾ Stumbled st, gamely 6
4Nov00- 6CD fst 6f :204 :432 :551 1:073 3↑ BCSprnt-G1 96 2 2 2½ 3 2 3 4 9 6¾ Bailey J D L124 8.90 100 - *Kona Gold*126½ Honest Lady123½ Bet On Sunshine1262 Ck 1/2 pl,tired lane 14
23Sep00- 9Bel fst 7f :221 :443 1:083 1:213 3↑ Vosburgh-G1 111 1 8 1½ 1 1 1 2½ 1½ Bailey J D L123 3.60 95- 13 Trippi123½ More Than Ready123 2¼ *One Way Love*1261 Set pace, driving 10
4Aug00- 8Sar fst 6f :214 :442 :563 1:091 Amstrdam-G3 91 4 3 2½ 2½ 3 1½ 3 5¾ Bailey J D L123 *.50 93- 13 Personal First1203 Disco Rico123 2¾ *Trippi*123 1¼ Speed 3 wide, tired 6
2Jly00- 8Bel fst 7f :22 :442 1:084 1:213 3↑ TomFoolH-G2 106 2 3 1½ 1 1½ 1 5½ 1 4½ Bailey J D L112 *.95 95- 13 Trippi112 4½ Cornish Snow1131 Sailor's Warning111 2¼ Pace, clear, driving 6
10Jun00- 6Bel fst 7f :22 :451 1:102 1:233 RivaRidg-G2 101 2 6 2hd 1½ 1 5½ 1 9 Bailey J D L123 2.10 85- 13 *Trippi*1239 Bevo120no Sun Cat116 1¼ When roused, driving 6
6May00- 8CD fst 1¼ :454 1:094 1:353 2:01 KyDerby-G1 80 5 21 2½ 2hd 9 6 11 18¾ Chavez J F L126 6.20e 86 - FusichiPegsus126 1½ Aptitude1264 Impechment126½ Dueled, tired stretch 19
8Apr00-11GP fst 1⅛ :462 1:111 1:364 1:50 Flamingo-G3 100 1 11 1½ 1 3 1 2½ 1 1 Coa E M L119 *.80 87- 12 Trippi1191 Kombat Kat119 8½ Skip a Grade119 1¼ Off rail, prevailed 11
11Mar00- 5GP fst 7f :22 :442 1:092 1:232 Swale-G3 98 5 4 2 1½ 2 1 2 2 1 1¾ Bailey J D 113 *.80 83- 21 *Trippi*113 1¾ UltimateWarrior117 2¼ HarlanTraveler114¾ 3 wide, edged away 8
19Feb00- 8GP fst 7f :214 :442 1:09 1:221 Alw 34000N1X 91 1 7 1hd 1½ 1 6 1 9¼ Bailey J D 122 *.40 89- 12 *Trippi*122 9¼ Rich Stars119 2½ *Stormin Oedy*119 2½ Drew off, handily 10
29Jan00- 3GP fst 6f :214 :444 :572 1:101 Md Sp Wt 30k 87 1 8 1hd 1½ 1 3 1 4¾ Bailey J D 122 2.10 88- 13 *Trippi*122 4¾ Family Hero122 3¾ Lead the Charge122 2¾ Slow st, ridden out 8

UNBRIDLED MAN (Unbridled—Honoria, by Danzig). Indiana. Based on his pedigree, he was a disappointment as a racehorse, winning just once in four starts. By a stamina influence, his female family is all class, having produced grass champion Manila. His offspring should mature slowly and be better at 3.

Unbridled Man
Own: Bogue Mike

B. h. 6 (Mar)
Sire: Unbridled (Fappiano) $200,000
Dam: Honoria (Danzig)
Br: Calumet Farm (Ky)
Tr: Bogue Mike(0 0 0 0 .00) 2004:(2 0 .00)

Life 4 1 0 0 $7,100 65 | D.Fst 4 1 0 0 $7,100 65
2001 4 1 0 0 $7,100 65 | Wet(434) 0 0 0 0 $0 -
2000 0 M 0 0 $0 - | Turf(334) 0 0 0 0 $0
0 0 0 0 $0 - | Dst(0) 0 0 0 0 $0 -

6Nov01- 3CD fst 6½f :23 :461 1:112 1:18 3↑ Clm c-(10-9) 63 9 6 2½ 2hd 3½ 6 4¼ Meche D J L115 b 13.10 81- 15 CinnmonLd1161 *AmricnUpThr*116hd Slwmgoo116no Duel,between,faltered 11
Claimed from Horton Stable, Inc. for $10,000, Lukas D Wayne Trainer 2001(as of 11/6): (588 86 79 81 0.15)
28Oct01- 1CD fst 6½f :223 :46 1:11 1:174 3↑ Clm 13500(13.5-11.5) 58 9 2 1hd 3nk 4 6 4 9½ Meche D J L114 b 12.20 76- 13 *Echo Canyon*114 2½ Natural Ridge116 2¾ *Schooling*116 4¼ 4abreast,weakened 9
30Sep01- 2TP fst 6f :222 :461 :584 1:121 3↑ Md 15000(15-10) 65 6 3 1hd 1hd 1hd 1¾ Lopez J L119 b 3.60 80- 21 UnbridledMan119¾ *Whtshppnenbro*119½ OldWestPoint1192 Inside, driving 8
14Apr01- 1Kee fst 6½f :22 :46 1:11 1:171 Md Sp Wt 44k 23 8 10 10 10 11 15 10 18 10 29¼ Pincay L Jr L121 b 7.90 58- 13 SeekingtheShow121 8½ HereComesTurner121 1¼ Icntmember121 2¾ Outrun 11

UNCLE ABBIE (Kingmambo—Lassie Connection, by Seattle Slew). Texas. Considering his royal lineage, Uncle Abbie was a major disappointment on the track, but could surprise as a stallion. His dam is a full sister to Charming Lassie, the dam of Lemon Drop Kid, and is also a half-sister to Weekend Surprise, the dam of A.P. Indy, Summer Squall, and Honor Grades. His runners will show their best on turf, from seven furlongs to 1¼ miles. (HT)

Uncle Abbie
Own: Kilroy Mrs. William S

B. h. 7 (Apr)
Sire: Kingmambo (Mr. Prospector) $225,000
Dam: Lassie Connection (Seattle Slew)
Br: W. S. Kilroy (Ky)
Tr: Howard Neil J(0 0 0 0 .00) 2004:(105 25 .24)

Life	18	3	4	1	$137,795	99		D.Fst	15	3	3	1	$126,495	99
2001	2	0	0	0	$2,400	77		Wet(342)	1	0	1	0	$9,700	93
2000	10	2	3	1	$93,545	99		Turf(340)	2	0	0	0	$1,600	75
	0	0	0	0	$0	-		Dst(0)	0	0	0	0	$0	-

2Jun01-7CD	fst	1 1/16		:241	:471	1:11	1:42	3↑ Alw 48400N$Y	76	5	4¾	52¼	65½	512	518	Day P	L118 fb	4.00	82 -	StormDy1204¼ *CoolNCollectiv*120½ GnrousRosi1169	Broke slow,lunged,tire	6
19May01-8CD	fst	1		:24	:473	1:121	1:362	3↑ Alw 52000N$Y	77	1	1hd	1½	52¼	57	510¼	Meche D J	L120 fb	4.40	75- 19	Wedlock1151¾ Miner's Prize1181¼ Coast of Mane1163¼	Weakened on turn	6
25Oct00-8Kee	fst	1 1/16		:232	:47	1:104	1:412	[R]McCnlSprng77k	–	1	44	56½	-	-	-	Day P	L118 b	*1.20	- 15	Trajectory1182½ Bare Outline1184 Sun Cat118hd	Inside, pulled up	5
22Sep00-7Bel	fst	1 1/16		:231	:461	1:102	1:422	3↑ Alw 48000N3X	98	2	55	55½	43	21½	2no	Day P	L119 b	2.60	85- 15	Top Official121no Uncle Abbie1195 Corroborator1198	Game finish inside	7
4Sep00-3Sar	fst	1⅛		:473	1:12	1:371	1:494	3↑ Alw 48000N3X	99	3	45½	41½	32½	22½	23	Day P	L119 b	2.40	89- 12	Ground Storm1233 Uncle Abbie1197½ Malagot1154	Game finish outside	6
10Aug00-9Sar	fst	1⅛		:483	1:124	1:372	1:494	3↑ Alw 46000N2X	99	1	52½	52½	54½	4¾	12¼	Day P	L118 b	1.95	92- 09	Uncle Abbie1182¼ Strike Three118nk Senor Fizz1212½	Wide move, driving	8
27Jly00-3Sar	fst	1⅛		:491	1:13	1:374	1:501	3↑ Alw 46000N2X	93	5	54	65	66	34½	33¾	Day P	L118 b	3.50	86- 12	*Cat's AtHome*1143 CountryCoast114¾ *UncleAbbie*1187¼	Good finish outside	6
7Jly00-8CD	fst	1 1/16		:223	:454	1:113	1:433	3↑ Alw 48500N1X	93	11	711	57¼	21½	11½	13	Day P	L108 b	*1.70	92- 14	UncleAbbie1083 TwoPointTwoMill1121¾ Marisin1093½	4wide,hand urging	11
18Jun00-10CD	sly	1		:224	:46	1:112	1:381	Alw 48500N1X	93	5	54¼	65¼	48	24½	21	Day P	L121 b	9.70	78- 26	OneCllClos1181 *UnclAbbi*1212¼ TwoPointTwoMill1185½	Closed well, 6wide	10
18May00-8CD	fst	6f		:204	:442	:563	1:091	Alw 43200N1X	81	11	2	1111	107¼	78	68½	Albarado R J	L121 b	13.20	90- 06	Mansleeter1181¼ *Twilight Road*1181½ *Level Three*1214¾	Not a threat	12
26Jan00-7GP	gd	*1⅛	Ⓣ	:501	1:143	1:391	1:504	Alw 32000N1X	58	8	97½	88½	95¼	910	913	Day P	119	3.90	69- 18	Powerful Appeal1191 CardinalVerse1222¼ PrinceofTheater122½	No factor	10
9Jan00-7GP	fm	1 1/16	Ⓣ	:24	:482	1:124	1:421	+ Alw 32000N1X	75	11	88	89	86½	63½	44½	Sellers S J	119	2.60	80- 11	Tubrok119nk *Spring Street*1192½ Lambeau Leap1191¾	Passed tired rivals	12
10Nov99-6CD	fst	1 1/16		:233	:472	1:123	1:451	Alw 38740N1X	65	7	85¼	72¾	74¼	84¾	710¼	Day P	121	*1.30	74- 13	HtofDixi1152¼ BlushingIrish1212 HousBurnr1212½	Bumpd foe start,no bid	9
29Oct99-7Kee	fst	1 1/16		:224	:464	1:114	1:434	Alw 51000N2L	80	7	64½	65½	65	46½	43¾	Day P	116	*1.30	85- 17	Ubiquity1192½ *Land*118¾ Connected117½	Mild rail gain	9
19Sep99-6Bel	fst	1		:232	:454	1:103	1:36	Futurity-G1	84	8	75¼	66	51¼	53¾	58¼	Gryder A T	122	27.25	76- 22	*Bevo*122nk *GreenwoodLake*122nk MoreThanRedy122¾	Good inside run turn	8
1Sep99-3Sar	fst	6½f		:222	:46	1:103	1:171	Alw 42000N1X	82	4	5	44	32	33½	2¾	Day P	118	5.50	87- 13	Entepreneur116¾ UncleAbbie1182¼ GrnwoodLk1181¾	Game finish outside	7
31Jly99-4Sar	fst	6f		:22	:46	:583	1:112	Md Sp Wt 40k	75	8	2	1½	1hd	1½	11	Day P	116	*1.65	84- 10	Uncle Abbie1161 *Windrush*1162 McIlheny1161¾	Set pace, driving	9
11Jly99-4Bel	fst	5½f		:223	:453	:573	1:04	Md Sp Wt 40k	66	8	10	97¾	75¼	56	45¾	Day P	116	3.15	89- 09	TroubleCity1163¾ MandarinMrsh116no Impressor1162	Pinched back start	10

UNLOOSENED (Unbridled—Flying Loose, by Giboulee). Illinois. Stakes-placed twice in 28 starts, Unloosened is out of a half-sister to 2-year-old champion Fly So Free. His offspring should be better at 3 and appreciate distances over seven furlongs.

Unloosened

Own: Hebel Carol W. and Loren

B. h. 9 (Mar)
Sire: Unbridled (Fappiano) $200,000
Dam: Flying Loose (Giboulee)
Br: Ms. Loren Hebel & Carol W. Hebel (Ky)
Tr: Penrod Steven C(0 0 0 0 .00) 2004:(26 2 .08)

	Life	28	6	3	7	$256,016	98	D.Fst	19	4	3	5	$190,166	98
	2001	2	0	0	0	$134	86	Wet(353)	7	2	0	2	$65,510	97
	2000	9	2	2	1	$112,608	98	Turf(257)	2	0	0	0	$340	75
		0	0	0	0	$0	—	Dst(0)	0	0	0	0	$0	—

VISION AND VERSE (Storm Cat—Bunting, by Private Account). Kentucky. Vision and Verse was an aberration—a late-blooming son of Storm Cat who was most effective at $1\frac{1}{8}$ and $1\frac{1}{4}$ miles. From a strong Greentree Stud female family, his second dam is a half-sister to Stop the Music and Hatchet Man. His runners should be most effective at 3 and 4, from seven furlongs to $1\frac{1}{4}$ miles.

Vision and Verse

Own: Lunsford Bruce and Ito, Y

B. h. 8 (Mar)
Sire: Storm Cat (Storm Bird) $500,000
Dam: Bunting (Private Account)
Br: Bruce Lunsford (Ky)
Tr: Mott William I(0 0 0 0 .00) 2004:(414 83 .20)

	Life	21	4	3	5	$1,030,330	112	D.Fst	17	3	3	4	$1,005,500	112
	2001	3	0	1	1	$37,330	108	Wet(423)	4	1	0	1	$24,830	100
	2000	6	1	0	1	$172,860	112	Turf(343)	0	0	0	0	$0	—
		0	0	0	0	$0	—	Dst(0)	0	0	0	0	$0	—

4

THE HIDDEN TURF
FACTOR

PEDIGREE HANDICAPPING ENCOMPASSES a wide array of betting angles, but the most lucrative—by far—is what I call the hidden turf factor.

Stallions who had success on turf themselves, such as Round Table, Cozzene, Herbager, Roberto, and all the Northern Dancer-line stallions who were champions in Europe, were *expected* to be good grass sires. However, stallions who never raced on turf but were bred to love the surface are labeled hidden turf sires, and their offspring thus have the hidden turf factor. Because the turf ability is "hidden," the offspring of these sires are usually ignored at inflated prices when they appear on turf for the first time. While runners by known grass influences Caro, Diesis, Dynaformer, Irish River, and Theatrical are all usually well-bet, runners by hidden turf sires are almost always tasty overlays.

In the United States, unlike the rest of the world, dirt racing reigns supreme. With some notable exceptions (such as Christophe

Clement, Michael Dickinson, Bobby Frankel, and Bill Mott), most trainers of horses who have strong grass pedigrees usually start those horses' careers on dirt. Sometimes this is not the fault of the trainer, as many racetracks do not offer turf racing for 2-year-olds, and other tracks, such as Emerald Downs and Oaklawn, do not even have a turf course. It is not unusual to see half a dozen starts or more on dirt *before* a horse with a turf pedigree finally gets his preferred surface.

Separating those stallions who are expected to be good turf sires (such as Cozzene, Dynaformer, Lear Fan, Red Ransom, Sadler's Wells, Silver Hawk, and Theatrical) from those who are hidden turf sires (such as Deputy Commander, Forestry, Grand Slam, Hennessy, Holy Bull, Langfuhr, Louis Quatorze, Maria's Mon, Menifee, Pulpit, Rodeo, Stormy Atlantic, Tale of the Cat, Tomorrows Cat, and Touch Gold) is the key to some big paydays.

Below are examples of some stallions I have labeled hidden turf sires whose success on dirt precluded them from being grass stars. Runners from these sires have won at boxcar prices on the turf. Stallions' ages are current as of 2004.

Go for Gin
Own: W J Condren & J M Cornacchia

B. h. 13 (Apr)
Sire: Cormorant (His Majesty)
Dam: Never Knock (Stage Door Johnny)
Br: Pamela Darmstadt duPont (Ky)
Tr: Zito Nicholas P(0 0 0 0 .00) 2004:(281 45 .16)

Life 19 5 7 2 $1,380,866 112
1995 3 0 2 1 $27,730 103
1994 11 2 4 1 $1,178,596 112
0 0 0 0 $0 –

D.Fst 13 2 4 2 $547,526 111
Wet(316) 6 3 3 0 $833,340 112
Turf(320) 0 0 0 0 $0 –
Dst(0) 0 0 0 0 $0 –

(past performance race lines)

Go for Gin

When horses perform well on dirt there is little reason to change surfaces, since the majority of prestigious stakes in the U.S. are run on dirt. When Go for Gin won the Remsen Stakes at 2, his fate was sealed. Trainer Nick Zito immediately put him on the Triple Crown trail and was rewarded with a Kentucky Derby victory when the track came up sloppy, a surface for which Go for Gin clearly had an affinity. Obviously, the decision to keep the colt on dirt paid off. Although he never won another race, Go for Gin will forever be remembered as a Kentucky Derby winner. But as a stallion, there was something else to consider.

Go for Gin actually had a sterling pedigree for grass. He is by Cormorant, a stakes winner who had speed on dirt but also had a great grass pedigree. Cormorant was by the strong turf influence His Majesty (Ribot), a stakes-winning full brother to the more brilliant Graustark. Cormorant also got more turf breeding (and a ton of speed) from his damsire, Tudor Minstrel, a horse of stunning ability on the grass in Europe.

And that only covers Go for Gin's turf influences from his sire's family. Go for Gin's dam is Never Knock, a daughter of renowned grass (and stamina) influence Stage Door Johnny. Go for Gin had an exquisite grass pedigree but never had the chance to show it—but his offspring had every right to perform well on turf. Because he has a double dose of turf influences up close in his pedigree (from his sire and damsire), I designated Go for Gin as having an HT^2 pedigree.

While Go for Gin was certainly capable of getting winners on dirt (his most successful dirt runner is Albert the Great), he had all the genetic tools to be a good sire of turf runners, and the difference was that his grass runners were going to be big prices, ignored by horseplayers because Go for Gin was not associated with grass.

This is the definition of the hidden turf sire, and offspring by such sires are considered to have the hidden turf factor.

Now, if a mare who was bred to Go for Gin was also by a turf influence (such as Silver Hawk, Danzig, etc.), the resulting horse would be even more likely to be better on turf and would be considered an HT^2, like Go for Gin himself.

Go for Gin has had five full crops, and the majority of runners have raced on dirt, showing speed like their sire and sire's sire. But when his runners showed up on grass, they proved to be different animals and it started paying dividends immediately.

Hallucinogin, from Go for Gin's first crop, showed nothing on dirt but woke up dramatically when he first raced on turf. Hallucinogin showed speed for the first time and nearly stole a 1 1/16-mile maiden race at 46-1 before tiring right before the wire over a soft grass course. Away seven months after that effort, Hallucinogin returned on grass to win a 1 1/8-mile maiden race at 7-1.

Hallucinogin
Own: Centennial Farms
PRADO E S (85 20 15 12 .24) 2000:(697 119 .17)

B. c. 3 (May) KEESEP98 $95,000
Sire: Go for Gin (Cormorant) $7,500
Dam: Impetuous Image (Mr. Prospector)
Br: Cox E A Jr (Ky)
Tr: Schulhofer Flint S(13 6 0 2 .46) 2000:(68 17 .25)

116

Life	4	1	0	0	$27,720	D.Fst	2	0	0	0	$0 33
2000	1	1	0	0	$25,200	Wet	0	0	0	0	$0 -
1999	3	M	0	0	$2,520	Turf	2	1	0	0	$27,720 83
Bel Ⓣ	2	1	0	0	$27,720	DistⓉ	0	0	0	0	$0 -

10May00-5Bel fm	1⅛ Ⓣ	:512 1:16 1:40 1:52	3↑ Md Sp Wt 42k	83	9	2	2½	2hd	1hd	11	Prado E S	115	7.20	68-27	Hallucinogin1151 A. P. Delta115nk Maestro Brott1082¼	With pace, driving	11
15Oct99-6Bel sf	1 1/16 Ⓣ	:243 :492 1:143 1:48	Md Sp Wt 42k	60	2	1	1hd	1½	2hd	42	Bridgmohan S X	118	46.25	50-44	DelMrShow118nk SintJoseph1181½ RedGmbler118nk	Bumped soundly start	1
1Oct99-5Bel fst	1 1/16 ⊗	:23 :462 1:121 1:461	Md Sp Wt 42k	29	9	9	1114	1013	1018	1027¾	Davis R G	118	2.85e	38-32	MandarinMarsh1183¾ TwigN'Berries1184 SaturdyPlyer118hd	No response	14
21Aug99-4Sar fst	6½f	:223 :463 1:12 1:184	Md Sp Wt 40k	33	7	10	107	118½	1012	1019	Luzzi M J	117	18.60e	61-18	GroupLeader1173¼ KendallPoint1171¼ ScoutingReport117½	Lacked a rally	12

WORKS: May30 Bel 4f fst :51 B 18/21 May18 Bel 4f fst :501 B 20/31 May5 Bel 4f fst :493 B 12/31 Apr30 Bel 4f fst :491 B 17/27 Apr25 Bel 4f fst :491 B 25/72 Apr20 Bel 4f fst :492 B 28/72

Gasperillo Daze (Go for Gin—La Cucina, by Last Tycoon) was also strongly bred for grass from both sides of his pedigree. His dam-sire, Last Tycoon, won the 1986 Breeders' Cup Mile and was from the Northern Dancer sire line. But when Gasperillo Daze appeared on grass, bettors ignored him because they did not associate Go for Gin with grass, and once again, the hidden turf factor paid off handsomely. Gasperillo Daze returned $47.

Hennessy
Own: Robert B. & Beverly J. Lewis

Ch. h. 11 (Mar)
Sire: Storm Cat (Storm Bird) $500,000
Dam: Island Kitty (Hawaii)
Br: Overbrook Farm (Ky)
Tr: Lukas D. W(0 0 0 0 .00) 2004:(359 40 .11)

Life	9	4	3	0	$580,400	103	D.Fst	8	4	2	0	$380,400	102
1995	9	4	3	0	$580,400	103	Wet(378)	1	0	1	0	$200,000	103
1994	0	M	0	0	$0	-	Turf(344)	0	0	0	0	$0	-
	0	0	0	0	$0	-	Dst(0)	0	0	0	0	$0	-

17Dec95-5Hol fst	1 1/16	:231 :463 1:101 1:413	HolFut-G1	86	1	55½	42	53	25	410	Stevens G L	LB121	*.30	- -	Matty G1217 Odyle1211 Ayrton S1212	Steadd early,blockd3/8
19Nov95-9Hol fst	7f	:221 :444 1:084 1:211	HolPrvBC-G3	102	3	4	31	3½	2hd	2½	Stevens G L	LB121	*.60	- -	*Cobra King*121½ Hennessy1212¾ Exetera1167	Outfinished,long drive
28Oct95-6Bel my	1 1/16	:222 :452 1:102 1:413	BCJuven-G1	103	11	31	31	1hd	1hd	2nk	Barton D M	122	7.60	- -	UnbrdldsSong122nk Hnnssy1224 EdtorsNot122hd	Took over 5w turn,game
7Oct95-9Bel fst	1 1/16	:223 :451 1:102 1:421	MoetChmp-G1	95	5	45	26	2hd	42½	65½	Stevens G L	122	*1.05	- -	Maria'sMon1223¾ Diligence122¾ *DevilsHonor*122¾	Good ins move trn,wknd
27Aug95-8Sar fst	7f	:222 :453 1:102 1:232	Hopeful-G1	100	6	2	51¾	4¾	11	13¼	Stevens G L	122	*.80	- -	Hennessy1223¼ Louis Quatorze1223¼ *Maria's Mon*1229	4w move,drew clear
12Aug95-10Mth fst	6f	:214 :454 :581 1:104	Sapling-G2	77	5	6	21½	11½	14½	19¾	Barton D M	122	*.40e	- -	*Hennessy*1229¾ Built forPleasure1221½ CashierCoyote1221¼	Much the best
24Jly95-8Hol fst	6f	:212 :442 :563 1:094	HolJuvCh-G2	91	7	5	52	11	13	15½	Stevens G L	B117	*.50	- -	*Hennessy*1175½ Reef Reef117nk Desert Native1174	Drew off, much best
2Jly95-4Hol fst	5f	:22 :45 :57	Md Sp Wt 34k	91	7	2	2½	1hd	12	16½	Stevens G L	B118	*.40	- -	*Hennssy*1186½ DubiousConnction1183½ Brzori118nk	Drew clear, ridden out
3Jun95-3Hol fst	5f	:214 :444 :57	Md Sp Wt 34k	88	5	2	2hd	1hd	2½	2hd	Stevens G L	B118	*1.50	- -	Andthelivinisesy118hd *Hennssy*1185½ RgntAct1184½	Outfinished,long drive

Hennessy

Hennessy only raced at 2, when he won four of nine starts, including the Hopeful, Sapling, and Hollywood Juvenile Championship Stakes. A colt with high speed, Hennessy came up a neck shy of a probable juvenile championship when he was narrowly defeated by Unbridled's Song in the Breeders' Cup Juvenile. Unbridled's Song had not done quite enough as a juvenile to be named champion and that honor went to Maria's Mon, who had racked up victories in the Champagne, Futurity, and Sanford Stakes, but had to sit out the Breeders' Cup due to an injury.

If any horse had a pedigree for turf, it was Hennessy. In addition to his sire line, which is synonymous with grass (Storm Cat-Storm Bird-Northern Dancer), Hennessy is out of a mare by Hawaii, a champion in his native South Africa before he was named grass champion in the U.S. in 1969. Thus, Hennessy is the perfect example of an HT^2 (hidden turf x 2) sire. The likelihood of his offspring having an affinity on turf is magnified by so many grass influences in Hennessy's pedigree. Of course, if Hennessy is bred to a mare by yet another source of turf (such as a mare by any Roberto- or In Reality-line stallion), this only further accentuates the likelihood that this runner should love turf.

Because of the relatively recent practice of shuttling some stallions to the Southern Hemisphere for stud duty after the North American breeding season is over, Hennessy's early crops featured a barrage of winners on grass in Australia, including Group 1 winners Grand Armee and Half Hennessy; Group 2 winner Courvoisier; and Group 3 winners Living Spirit, Diamond Dash, Perigee Moon, and Perfect Storm (a 2-year-old champion in Turkey).

Storm Cat's sons are known for transmitting high speed (Forest Wildcat, Tale of the Cat, Forestry, Harlan, Storm Boot, Storm Creek, Scatmandu, Stormin Fever, Stormy Atlantic, Sea of Secrets, Tactical Cat, Tomorrows Cat), and such runners as Madcap Escapade and Harmony Lodge have made Hennessy a superior source of speed on dirt.

On April 10, 2004, at Keeneland, Scripture, a 3-year-old colt by Hennessy making his career debut, wired a field of 11 to win a six-furlong maiden race by four lengths at 4-1. What made Scripture so attractive to astute pedigree handicappers was the fact that he is a full brother to stakes winner Wiseman's Ferry. Their unraced dam,

Emmaus (by speed influence Silver Deputy), is a half-sister to stakes winners Country Cat, Bernstein, Caress (the dam of Sky Mesa), and Della Francesca. Scripture's fourth dam, Finance, is a half-sister to the legendary Buckpasser, thus the speed of Hennessy combined with such an imposing female family warranted a confident win bet in his debut. Scripture returned $10.80.

RACE 6 Kee–10Apr04 6 Furlongs (1.07³), 3 yo Md Sp Wt
Value of Race: $47,300. 1st $31,270 ; 2nd $8,200 ; 3rd $4,100 ; 4th $2,500 ; 5th $1,230 . Mutuel Pools: $543,169 Ex $372,192, Tri $295,534, Super $88,848, Pick–3 $76,681 Quin $16,815

Last Raced	Horse	M/Eq	A	Wt	PP	St	¼	½	Str	Fin	Odds$1
	Scripture	L b	3	120	2	2	1³	11½	11½	14	4.40
5Mar04 7FG²	Ocotillo	L	3	120	9	1	2¹	22½	22½	2½	2.90
	Honest Chance	L	3	120	7	3	5½	7½	61½	3no	53.70
19Sep03 NOT⁴	Kaseh	L	3	120	1	10	8hd	6³	3½	4¾	2.30
20Mar04 4TP⁷	Warped	L b	3	120	4	6	4²	4²	4²	52¾	63.70
21Feb04 4GP⁴	Haiaccept	L	3	120	8	5	7²	5½	51½	64½	8.20
6Mar04 12GP⁶	Looming	L b	3	120	10	4	3hd	3½	7³	7¾	5.10
14Mar04 3SA⁷	Major Contender	L b	3	120	11	7	9¹⁰	9⁸	8³	8²	28.00
	J. Brookfield	L	3	120	3	9	103½	101½	9³	97½	72.10
	Number One Trick	L b	3	120	5	11	11	11	11	102¼	63.30
	Soos Maheer	L	3	115	6	8	6½	8²	10²	11	10.80

OFF 3:46 Start Good For All But J. BROOKFIELD. Won driving. Track fast.
TIME :21⁴, :46, :58³, 1:11⁴ (:21.85, :46.11, :58.72, 1:11.99)

2 – SCRIPTURE		10.80	5.20	4.40
9 – OCOTILLO			3.80	3.00
7 – HONEST CHANCE				13.20

$2 Ex (2-9) 41.60 $2 Tri (2-9-7) 1,085.60 $2 Super (2-9-7-1) 4,963.20
$2 Pick-3 (6-4-2) 78.60 $2 Quin (2-9) 16.40

Ch. c, (Mar), by Hennessy – Emmaus , by Silver Deputy . Trainer Flint Bernard S. Bred by Nursery Place & Robert T. Manfuso (Ky).

SCRIPTURE moved clear near the inside early, remained near the inside the remainder and was going under strong handling in the drive. OCOTILLO chased the winner from the outset while four or five wide and couldn't match strides in the drive while fully extended to maintain second position. HONEST CHANCE, well placed early, lost a bit of position around the turn while between foes, angled in to follow the winner from the rail in the final furlong and finished willingly. KASEH, off a bit slow, was outsprinted early; came out between rivals five or six wide when straightened for the drive, loomed threat for the last eighth but came up empty. WARPED, within easy striking distance near the inside into the stretch, flattened out. HAIACCEPT lunged a bit at the start, raced in contention five wide into the final furlong and failed to rally. LOOMING drifted out at the start, quickly recovered to track the leaders five wide into the stretch and weakened while drifting out a bit. MAJOR CONTENDER also drifted out at the break and failed to menace. J. BROOKFIELD broke in the air and was outrun. NUMBER ONE TRICK, reluctant to load into the gate, hopped while breaking slowly and never was close. SOOS MAHEER tired early on the turn.

Jockeys– 1, Bejarano R; 2, Sellers S J; 3, Guidry M; 4, Migliore R; 5, Diego I; 6, Albarado R J; 7, Santos J A; 8, Flores D R; 9, Lumpkins J; 10, Martinez J R Jr; 11, Graham J

Trainers– 1, Flint Bernard S; 2, Asmussen Steven M; 3, Hyland Angel; 4, McLaughlin Kiaran P; 5, Mauk Fletcher; 6, Romans Dale; 7, Terranova John P II; 8, Lukas D Wayne; 9, Schlansky Desra; 10, Jackson James R; 11, Kassen David C

Owners– 1, Conway-Hillerich Racing LTB Inc and Childers Miles; 2, Winchell Thoroughbreds LLC; 3, Noriega Justo Jr; 4, Shadwell Stable Hamdan Al Maktoum; 5, Davis III Kathi and Horace N; 6, Jones Frank L Jr; 7, Sovereign Stable and Gatsas Stables; 8, Overbrook Farm; 9, Desra Schlansky; 10, N J Samford Trust; 11, Slavin Larry

Scratched– Dash of Fame (28Mar04 5Beu³)

On July 17, 2004, Primary Suspect, a first-time starter by Hennessy, romped to a 10 ¾-length victory in a six-furlong maiden race at Monmouth Park over Unleashedthedragon, who was favored off two second-place finishes in his only starts. While Unleashedthedragon certainly had an SP^2 pedigree (Belong to Me/Valid Appeal cross), Primary Suspect had a pedigree with even better speed, and also had a very classy female family. His stakes-winning dam, Deb's Honor, is out of stakes winner Hear the Bells, and Primary Suspect's fourth dam, Special Account, is a full sister to champion Numbered Account.

9 Primary Suspect
Own: Lee Lewis
Teal, Blue Diamond Belt, Teal Bars On
VELEZ J A JR (138 22 21 18 .16) 2004: (218 27 .12)

Ch. c. 3 (May)
Sire: Hennessy (Storm Cat) $35,000
Dam: Deb's Honor (Affirmed)
Br: Lee Lewis (Ky)
Tr: Hennig Mark (30 6 6 3 .20) 2004:(277 39 .14)

118

	Life	0 M 0 0	$0	–	D.Fst	0 0 0 0	$0	–
	2004	0 M 0 0	$0	–	Wet(336)	0 0 0 0	$0	–
	2003	0 M 0 0	$0	–	Turf(329)	0 0 0 0	$0	–
	Mth	0 0 0 0	$0	–	Dst(326)	0 0 0 0	$0	–

WORKS: ● Jly11 Mth 4f fst :473 Hg 4/36 Jly4 Mth 4f fst :482 Bg 3/34 Jun28 Mth 5f fst 1:03 B 4/9 Jun22 Mth 5f fst 1:023 B 5/14 Jun15 Sar tr.t 5f fst 1:033 B 1/3 Jun8 Sar tr.t 5f fst 1:05 B 3/4
Jun1 Sar tr.t 4f fst :504 B 2/5 May26 Sar tr.t 4f fst :523 B 40/46 May17 Sar tr.t 4f fst :502 B 8/21 May10 Sar tr.t 3f fst :382 B 2/8
TRAINER: 1stStart(90 .11 $2.32) 1stLasix(55 .18 $1.43) Dirt(648 .16 $1.83) Sprint(304 .14 $2.02) MdnSpWt(302 .14 $2.25)

SIXTH RACE
Monmouth
JULY 17, 2004

6 FURLONGS. (1.074) MAIDEN SPECIAL WEIGHT . Purse $37,000 FOR MAIDENS, THREE YEAR OLDS AND UPWARD. Three Year Olds, 118 lbs.; Older, 122 lbs.

Value of Race: $37,000 Winner $22,200; second $7,030; third $3,700; fourth $1,480; fifth $370; sixth $370; seventh $370; eighth $370; ninth $370; tenth $370; eleventh $370. Mutuel Pool $194,638.00 Exacta Pool $187,740.00 Trifecta Pool $168,604.00

Last Raced	Horse	M/Eqt.	A.	Wt	PP	St	¼	½	Str	Fin	Jockey	Odds $1
	Primary Suspect	L	3	118	10	2	2¹	23½	1³	110¾	Velez J A Jr	3.50
23Jun04 4Mth²	Unleashedthedrgon	L	3	118	2	5	1½	1hd	2⁵	22¾	Bravo J	a- 0.70
	D. G. Dusty	L bf	3	118	9	1	4½	31	32½	31	Trujillo E	21.10
6Jly04 9Del⁶	Subtle Glitz	L b	4	122	8	6	10³	72	5hd	42½	Baze M C	42.00
	Chateau Haut Brion	L f	3	118	11	3	3hd	4½	41	5¾	Decarlo C P	25.60
3Jly04 2Mth⁶	Outskier		3	118	3	7	11	101½	8hd	6¾	King E L Jr	43.00
	Slippery Slick	L f	3	118	1	9	7½	6hd	61½	71	Suckie M C	a- 0.70
	Skippy's Flite	L b	3	118	4	11	8¹	9½	7hd	85½	Clemente A V	13.40
27Sep03 6Mth⁶	Sorvel	L f	3	118	7	4	9hd	11	10hd	91	Elliott S	56.80
	Silver Leap	L	3	118	5	8	6⁵	8hd	11	105½	Lopez C C	4.60
23Jun04 4Mth¹⁰	Nile Pyramids	L b	3	118	6	10	5½	5⁵	9³	11	Maysonett F	95.20

a–Coupled: Unleashedthedragon and Slippery Slick.

OFF AT 3:23 Start Good For All But SILVER LEAP. Won ridden out. Track fast.
TIME :22, :443, :563, 1:092 (:22.03, :44.71, :56.76, 1:09.45)

$2 Mutuel Prices:
9 – PRIMARY SUSPECT	9.00	3.00	3.20
1A– UNLEASHEDTHEDRGON(a–entry)		2.20	2.20
8 – D. G. DUSTY			4.00

$2 EXACTA 9–1 PAID $21.20 $2 TRIFECTA 9–1–8 PAID $162.40

Ch. c, (May), by Hennessy – Deb's Honor , by Affirmed . Trainer Hennig Mark. Bred by Lee Lewis (Ky).
PRIMARY SUSPECT rated in good position about the three path, raced alongside the pacesetter from mid turn, drew clear into the stretch, was flagged approaching the furlong pole and drew off from there, ridden out. UNLEASHEDTHEDRAGON rated a short lead off the rail, was challenged approaching the quarter pole, proved no match for the winner but remained clear for place. D. G. DUSTY gave chase toward mid track and proved empty in the stretch. SUBTLE GLITZ showed no speed outside then passed some tiring rivals while drifting widest. CHATEAU HAUT BRION gave chase from the outside, dropped back widest on the turn then finished empty off the rail. OUTSKIER dropped back early and never factored. SLIPPERY SLICK showed no speed and had no rally. SKIPPY'S FLITE was a step slow to break, saved ground on the turn and never threatened. SORVEL never factored. SILVER LEAP brushed the gate, gave early chase then faded on the turn. NILE PYRAMIDS broke a step slow, kept off the early pace off the rail then gave way.
Owners– 1, Lewis Lee; 2, Drazin Dennis A; 3, Ljoka Daniel J; 4, Hardacre Farm LLC; 5, Tracey Reichey & Savage Stable; 6, Stoney Lawrence; 7, Drazin Dennis A; 8, Generazio Patricia A; 9, Thompson Gilbert M and Velsor Jim; 10, Wertheimer and Frere; 11, Castle Raymond
Trainers– 1, Hennig Mark; 2, Servis Jason; 3, Kelly Timothy J; 4, Tarrant Amy; 5, McMullin Stacy; 6, Sherwood Colin; 7, Servis Jason; 8, Generazio Frank Jr; 9, Forbes John H; 10, Pletcher Todd A; 11, Tammaro John J III

A runner by Hennessy will always be dangerous sprinting on dirt, but playing Hennessy runners on the grass continues to offer even better value.

Hennessy hit a home run in his second crop with Johannesburg, who displayed a devastating turn of foot while winning all seven of his starts at 2. His juvenile campaign included six stakes victories, and four of his Grade or Group 1 wins were achieved in four

RACE 9 GP–9Apr04 @1¹⁄₁₆ Miles Ⓣ (1.40²), 3 yo Md 50000

Value of Race: $19,000. 1st $11,400 ; 2nd $3,420 ; 3rd $2,090 ; 4th $950 ; 5th $190 ; 6th $190 ; 7th $190 ; 8th $190 ; 9th $190 ; 10th $190 . Mutuel Pools: $250,707 Ex $186,096, Tri $171,272, Super $63,570, DD $57,628, Pick–3 $42,642, Pick–4 $45,122 Pick–6 $13,652 Carryover Pool $14,596

Last Raced	Horse	M/Eq	A	Wt	PP	St	¼	½	¾	Str	Fin	Odds$1
	Our Remy	L	3	120	8	7	11½	1hd	1hd	13	1nk	4.00
11Mar04 4GP9	El Segundo Joe	L b	3	122	4	4	5½	51	7½	31	2½	4.50
	Scabbard	L	3	122	7	6	21½	31½	4hd	2hd	33½	8.20
15Jan04 5GP6	Amsterdam Ave.	L	3	122	10	8	41	4hd	52	41	4¾	18.10
16Feb04 4GP9	Charmer Jim	L b	3	122	6	9	6hd	61	3hd	6hd	5nk	16.20
27Mar04 8GP3	Stars of Silver	L bf	3	122	3	1	94	94½	81½	95	6½	6.50
28Mar04 5GP5	Fairly True	L b	3	122	1	2	71	71	61	5hd	7½	2.70
	Good Tip	L b	3	122	2	3	81	81	91	81½	8nk	21.60
26Mar04 5GP8	Best Call	L	3	122	5	5	31	21½	21½	7hd	98½	42.80
	Suppertime	L	3	122	9	10	10	10	10	10	10	7.70

OFF 6:36 Start Good . Won driving. Course firm.

TIME :23⁴, :48⁴, 1:13⁴, 1:38¹, 1:44² (:23.93, :48.94, 1:13.87, 1:38.35, 1:44.52)

8 – OUR REMY	10.00	5.20	4.40
4 – EL SEGUNDO JOE		4.20	3.00
7 – SCABBARD			5.00

$1 Ex (8-4) 38.70 $1 Tri (8-4-7) 167.90 $1 Super (8-4-7-10) 2,167.10
$2 DD (4-8) 81.80 $1 Pick-3 (1-4-8) 516.80 $1 Pick-4 (6-1-4-8) 2,578.40
$2 Pick-6 (4-4-6-1-4-8) 4 Correct 227.40

B. c, (Jan), by Hennessy – Garvin's Gal , by Seattle Slew . Trainer Pletcher Todd A. Bred by David Garvin (Ky).

OUR REMY set the pace under pressure along the rail, drew clear in early stretch, then ducked in at the eighth pole and was fully extended to last over EL SEGUNDO JOE. The latter, reserved racing along the rail, steadied along leaving the backstretch, got hooked up along the rail around the turn, eased outside OUR REMY in the stretch and rallied to just miss. SCABBARD stalked the pace along the inside, angled out for the drive, was outmoved by the winner in early stretch, then was gaining on that rival at the wire. AMSTERDAM AVE. tracked the leaders into the stretch and weakened. CHARMER JIM rated off the pace, made a run three wide on the far turn to loom a threat, then tired in the drive. STARS OF SILVER unhurried early, raced three wide on the far turn and failed to menace. FAIRLY TRUE reserved in striking position off the pace, faltered in the drive. GOOD TIP allowed to settle, steadied in behind EL SEGUNDO JOE leaving the backstretch and was not a factor. BEST CALL moved up leaving the first turn to press the pace outside OUR REMY into the far turn, then gave way. SUPPERTIME off slowly, jumped a couple of spots in the early going and trailed.

Claiming prices– 1, 45000; 2, 50000; 3, 50000; 4, 50000; 5, 50000; 6, 50000; 7, 50000; 8, 50000; 9, 50000; 10, 50000

Jockeys– 1, Coa E M; 2, Homeister R B Jr; 3, Douglas R R; 4, Castro E; 5, Peck B D; 6, Toribio A Jr; 7, Bravo J; 8, Trujillo E; 9, King E L Jr; 10, Boulanger G

Trainers– 1, Pletcher Todd A; 2, Alonso Enrique; 3, Clement Christophe; 4, Bracken James E; 5, Margolis Stephen R; 6, Mikhalides George; 7, White William P; 8, Baker James E; 9, Perry William W; 10, Hills Timothy A

Owners– 1, Scatuorchio James T; 2, Dwyer Denis A and Reynolds John; 3, Schaedle Robert G III; 4, Rales Norman; 5, J T Hines; 6, Buckram Oak Farm; 7, Jayaraman Kalarikkal K and Vilasini D; 8, Knight Cynthia; 9, Hidden Point Farm Inc; 10, Welsh Pat

Scratched– Global Arena (11Feb04 9GP 4) , Carson Unleashed (11Mar04 4GP 7) , Elusive Glory (03Mar04 9GP 3) , Brickell (03Mar04 9GP 3)

Gulfstream Park Attendance: 4,463 Mutuel Pool: $475,105.00 ITW Mutuel Pool: $248,828.00 ISW Mutuel Pool: $4,398,133.00

different countries (England, France, Ireland, and the United States), an unprecedented feat. His only dirt victory came in the Breeders' Cup Juvenile, but he was probably best on grass.

As his pedigree suggests, Hennessy is a versatile sire, getting winners on fast and wet tracks, but while his runners are expected to show high speed sprinting on dirt, they are still largely ignored on turf in this country despite the heroics of Johannesburg, and stakes winners Orchard Park and Silver Tree.

There are many more examples of Hennessy's prowess as a hidden turf sire. On April 9, 2004, Our Remy, a 3-year-old colt making his first start in a maiden race at about 1¹/₁₆ miles on the turf, went wire-to-wire to defeat nine other colts and paid $10 (see chart, opposite).

In a maiden special weight race on grass on July 2, 2004, Good Job, a son of Hennessy out of a mare by grass influence Al Hattab (and thus, a T^2 pedigree), made his second career start and his first on turf. He had trouble in his dirt debut, finishing eighth of nine runners at one mile in a race originally carded for grass. Sent off as the 5-1 fourth choice in a field of 10, Good Job showed the speed Hennessy runners are famous for, and wired the field, paying $13.60.

Likewise, Hennessy's young sons (such as Wiseman's Ferry, Orchard Park, and Heckle) should also be versatile as stallions, getting winners on turf as well as dirt. Johannesburg, in particular, should be an explosive freshman sire when his first crop of babies reaches the races in 2006, and of course, they should be bet with confidence on grass.

Holy Bull
Own: W. A. Croll Jr

Gr. h. 13 (Jan)
Sire: Great Above (Minnesota Mac)
Dam: Sharon Brown (Al Hattab)
Br: Pelican Stable (Fla)
Tr: Croll W A Jr(0 0 0 0 .00) 2004:(0 0 .00)

Life	16	13	0	0	$2,481,760	122	D.Fst	13	12	0	0	$2,412,400	122
1995	2	1	0	0	$51,000	117	Wet(333)	3	1	0	0	$69,360	103
1994	10	8	0	0	$2,095,000	122	Turf(317)	0	0	0	0	$0	–
	0	0	0	0	$0	–	Dst(0)	0	0	0	0	$0	–

11Feb95- 9GP	fst	1⅛	:462	1:103	1:363	1:493	3↑ DonnH-G1	–	9	21	22	-	922	-	Smith M E	127	*.30	-	-	*Cigar*1155½ Primitive Hall1122 Bonus Money1123½	Pulled up in distress	9
22Jan95- 9GP	fst	7f	:223	:451	1:093	1:22	3↑ OlympicH100k	117	5	3	2½	2½	1hd	12½	Smith M E	126	*.40	-	-	Holy Bull1262½ Birdonthewire1192¾ Patton115¾	Fast pace, handily	6
17Sep94- 8Bel	fst	1⅛	:462	1:102	1:343	1:464	3↑ Woodward-G1	116	5	21	21	1½	12½	15	Smith M E	121	*.90	-	-	*Holy Bull*1215 Devil His Due1261½ *Colonial Affair*1263½	Drew off, ridden out	8
20Aug94- 7Sar	fst	1¼	:461	1:102	1:354	2:02	Travers-G1	115	1	2hd	13	14	11	1nk	Smith M E	126	*.80	-	-	*Holy Bull*126nk Concern12617 *Tabasco Cat*1261	Dueled gamely, drvng	5
31Jly94-10Mth	fst	1⅛	:472	1:112	1:354	1:481	HsklInvH-G1	115	3	11	12	12	11½	11¾	Smith M E	126	*.20	-	-	*Holy Bull*1261¾ *Meadow Flight*1181¾ Concern1181	Repell foe,confidently	6
3Jly94- 8Bel	fst	1 1/16	:222	:451	1:092	1:41	Dwyer-G2	119	1	11	11	11½	13	16¾	Smith M E	124	*.30	-	-	*Holy Bull*1246¾ Twining1225 Bay Street Star1199	Pace, ridden out	4
30May94- 8Bel	fst	1	:224	:45	1:092	1:334	3↑ MtropltH-G1	122	6	11	11	1½	12	15½	Smith M E	112	*1.00	-	-	*Holy Bull*1125½ Cherokee Run118no *Devil His Due*1222	Drew off, driving	10
7May94- 8CD	sly	1¼	:471	1:114	1:373	2:033	KyDerby-G1	85	4	53½	63¼	99	1019	1218¼	Smith M E	126	*2.20	-	-	Go for Gin1262 Strodes Creek1262½ Blumin Affair126¾	Off slow, gave way	14
16Apr94- 9Kee	fst	1⅛	:474	1:123	1:374	1:50	BlueGras-G2	113	1	12	12½	12½	12	13½	Smith M E	121	*.60	-	-	HolyBull1213½ ValiantNature1215 MahoganyHll1212¼	Drew off, hand ride	7
12Mar94-10GP	fst	1⅛	:46	1:10	1:344	1:473	FlaDerby-G1	115	6	12	12	12½	13	15¾	Smith M E	122	2.70	-	-	*Holy Bull*1225¾ Ride the Rails122no Halo's Image1221	Led, handily	14
19Feb94- 9GP	gd	1 1/16	:224	:453	1:102	1:443	FntnOYth-G2	57	4	1hd	1hd	2½	66¾	624¼	Smith M E	119	*1.30	-	-	Dehere119¾ Go for Gin1191¼ Ride the Rails1173¾	Vied for lead, tired	6
30Jan94- 9GP	fst	7f	:213	:44	1:081	1:211	Hutchesn-G2	108	1	3	11½	11	2hd	1¾	Smith M E	122	*.50	-	-	Holy Bull122¾ *Patton*1133 You and I1193	Came again,impressive	5
23Oct93-11Crc	fst	1 1/16	:23	:462	1:113	1:461	[R]InReality400k	93	9	11½	11½	12	14	17½	Smith M E	120	*.50	-	-	*Holy Bull*1207½ Rustic Light1201 ForwardtoLead1201½	Handily, convincing	12
18Sep93- 6Bel	sly	7f	:222	:453	1:101	1:231	Futurity-G1	103	2	1	11	1½	13	1½	Smith M E	122	3.10	-	-	*Holy Bull*122½ *Dehere*1225 Prenup1228	Set pace, driving	6
2Sep93- 7Bel	fst	6½f	:22	:441	1:094	1:17	Alw 28000N1x	91	3	1	1½	1hd	13½	17	Smith M E	119	*.90	-	-	*Holy Bull*1197 Goodbye Doeny1173 End Sweep119½	Set pace, handily	6
14Aug93- 7Mth	fst	5½f	:213	:444	:571	1:034	Md Sp Wt 16k	101	1	3	11	11½	11½	12½	Rivera L Jr	118	*1.10	-	-	*Holy Bull*1182½ Palance1187½ *Hold My Tongue*1189	Super speed,green,drvg	9

Holy Bull

Holy Bull is another horse who was so successful on dirt that a career on grass was never in the stars. As good as he was on dirt, however, it is downright scary to think what he could have accomplished on turf. Holy Bull is by Great Above, a stakes-winning sprinter by outstanding grass star Minnesota Mac out of champion sprinter Ta Wee. Bred similarly to the great Dr. Fager (from the Rough'n Tumble sire line out of the Aspidistra female family), Great Above had blazing speed on dirt but was also bred to succeed on grass because of his sire, Minnesota Mac.

Holy Bull's female family had an equal number of grass influences. His dam, Sharon Brown, is by Al Hattab (by the very strong grass influence The Axe II, who was a major stakes winner on grass), and her damsire was Grey Dawn II, a champion at 2 in France, by the influential and popular turf sire Herbager.

From his very first crop, Holy Bull's offspring showed their sire's speed on dirt and also demonstrated ability on turf. Confessional, a member of Holy Bull's first crop, won the Frizette Stakes and later turned into a stakes-winning machine sprinting on grass. His best dirt runner has been Macho Uno, a champion at 2. As with Holy Bull, however, beware of Macho Uno's runners on grass (his first crop will be 2-year-olds of 2007). While they should win on dirt, they will be dismissed on grass and will provide great value. Not only is Macho Uno by Holy Bull, but he is also out of a mare by Blushing

Groom, a champion miler in Europe and a powerful turf influence. Macho Uno will be a strong hidden turf (HT^2) sire and I expect his offspring to post some double-digit upsets on grass.

Holy Bull's runners were largely ignored when they first appeared on grass because, once again, his name was not particularly synonymous with turf.

Keep It Holy (Holy Bull—Sweet Willa, by Assert) had raced three times on dirt, showing absolutely nothing, but sprang to life in his first turf appearance, wiring a maiden special weight field going $1\frac{1}{16}$ miles at 26-1. Not only was Keep It Holy by a hidden turf sire, he also had a T^2 pedigree because his damsire, Assert, was a major group winner on turf in Europe by Be My Guest (a son of Northern Dancer). In fact, Keep It Holy's victory was the key to Steve Terelak winning the NYRA Handicapping Tournament in June 2000 (see Chapter 7, "Playing the Handicapping Tournaments by Pedigree").

Bianconi
Own: Mme John Magnier/M. Tabor

Dk. b or b. h. 9 (Apr)
Sire: Danzig (Northern Dancer) $200,000
Dam: Fall Aspen (Pretense)
Br: Katom Ltd, Ashford Stud & Hullin N. V. (Ky)
Tr: O'Brien Aidan P(0 0 0 0 .00) 2004:(0 0 .00)

Life	12	3	2	0	$134,520	–	D.Fst	0	0	0	0	$0	–
1999	4	0	0	0	$1,713	–	Wet(377)	0	0	0	0	$0	–
1998	7	3	1	0	$131,224	–	Turf(403)	12	3	2	0	$134,520	–
	0	0	0	0	$0	–	Dst(0)	0	0	0	0	$0	–

Previously trained by Aidan O'Brien

3Aug99♦Deauville (Fr) Timeform rating: 103	sf *6½f Ⓣ Str 1:18¹ 3↑	Prix Maurice de Gheest-G1 Stk 139400	$8^{8\frac{1}{2}}$	Sanchez F	128 b	6.00	*Diktat*128¹ Gold Away128½ Bertolini123²	10	Close up in 5th,weakened 1-1/2f out.Tomba 5th,Keos 6th
3Jly99♦Newmarket (GB) Timeform rating: 113	gd 6f Ⓣ Str 1:09² 3↑	July Cup-G1 Stk 257300	9^{7}	Murtagh J	131	25.00	*Stravinsky*125⁴ Bold Edge131nk Bertolini125½	17	Pressed pace,wknd over 1f out.Wannabe Grand 7th,Dyhim Diamond16th
17Jun99♦Ascot (GB) Timeform rating: 107	gd 6f Ⓣ Str 1:13⁴ 3↑	Cork and Orrery Stakes-G2 Stk 175300	11^{7}	Kinane M J	130	6.00	Bold Edge126 1¼ *Russian Revival*126½ Vision of Night119½	19	Pressed pace,outpaced 2 out,weakened 1f out.Bold Fact 17th
22May99♦Curragh (Ire) Timeform rating: 113	gd 6f Ⓣ Str 1:12¹ 3↑	Greenlands Stakes-G3 Stk 57100	$4^{2\frac{1}{4}}$	Kinane M J	137	*1.10	Eastern Purple130no Gaelic Storm130¾ One Won One130 1½	10	Tracked in 3rd,2nd halfway,4th 1f out,one-paced to line
4Oct98♦Longchamp (Fr) Timeform rating: 100	sf *5f Ⓣ Str :58⁴ 2↑	Prix de l'Abbaye de Longchamp-G1 Stk 153900	12	Kinane M J	137	2.30	My Best Valentine137⁷ Averti137½ Sainte Marine133¹	14	Chased in 6th,weakened 2-1/2f out.Lochangel 6th
26Sep98♦Ascot (GB) Timeform rating: 123	gd 6f Ⓣ Str 1:13⁴ 3↑	Diadem Stakes-G2 Stk 169600	$1^{2\frac{1}{2}}$	Murtagh J	124	7.00	Bianconi124 2½ Russian Revival126 1¼ Averti126 2½	9	Tracked in 3rd,led 2f out,drew clear
Aug98♦Leopardstwn (Ire) Timeform rating: 110	gd 6f Ⓣ Str 1:10¹ 3↑	Phoenix Sprint Stakes-G3 Stk 42500	2^{nk}	C Roche	124	*2.25	March Star125nk *Bianconi*124² Monaassib132½	8	Led,dueled after 1-1/2f,led over 1f out,caught near line
8Jly98♦Leopardstwn (Ire) Timeform rating: 106+	gd 6f Ⓣ Str 1:13¹ 3↑	Cantrell & Crowley Co-Op Race Alw 10600	$1^{4\frac{1}{2}}$	C Roche	131	*.50	Bianconi131 4½ Remarkable Style129 2½ Symboli Kildare132⁵	6	Tracked leader,dueled 2f out,led over 1f out,quickly clear
Jun98♦Ascot (GB) Timeform rating: 99+	gd 7f Ⓣ Str 1:28²	Jersey Stakes-G3 Stk 108500	5^{7}	Kinane M J	122	6.00	Diktat122² Bold Edge122¾ *Lovers Knot*120 3½	16	Tracked leaders,weakened final furlong
May98♦Curragh (Ire) Timeform rating: 99+	gd 1 Ⓣ Str 1:35⁴	Irish 2000 Guineas-G1 Stk 28600	4^{9}	Swinburn W R	126	5.50	Desert Prince126³ Fa-Eq126¹ Second Empire126⁵	7	Tracked in 4th,no rally
5Apr98♦Navan (Ire) Timeform rating: 110	hy 5f Ⓣ Str 1:19¹	Dunleek Maiden Maiden 8500	1^{13}	C Roche	128	*1.25	Bianconi128¹³ *Crystal Wind*128½ Magical Peace123½	23	Tracked leaders,led 2-/12f out,clear over 1f out,easily
Oct97♦Curragh (Ire)	yl 6f Ⓣ Str 1:15¹	PG Duffy & Sons EBF Maiden Maiden 10200	2^{nk}	Roche C	126	*1.75	*Strike Hard*123nk *Bianconi*126³ Taispeain123¹	18	Tracked leaders,2nd halfway,led 170y out,headed near line

Bianconi

Bianconi does not really fit the profile of a hidden turf sire because he was successful on grass in Europe, but he is included here because, by and large, American horseplayers have no clue who he is, and his runners have won at huge prices on turf. By world-class sire Danzig (Northern Dancer), Bianconi was certainly bred for turf, and was a champion at 3 in Ireland. He is one of nine stakes winners out of his remarkable dam, Fall Aspen. His first crop of juveniles raced in 2003, and most of his starters ran on dirt in the U.S. While his runners showed speed and won on dirt, they are infinitely better suited for grass.

Cinematic is a case in point. A gelding by Bianconi out of the Raise a Native (brilliant speed influence) mare Raise a Sweetheart, Cinematic showed nothing in his debut in a March 6 maiden race on dirt at Santa Anita, finishing 12th, but it was a totally different story on April 10 at Santa Anita, when he wired 11 other 3-year-olds to win a maiden turf race at about 6½ furlongs. Thus far, not many runners by Bianconi have shown up on the grass and I was salivating at the fact that Cinematic was 40-1 in his turf debut. The surface switch resulted in a dramatic turnaround, and Cinematic paid $83 and caused a carryover in that day's pick six.

In fact, the two largest payoffs that day at Santa Anita were generated by Cinematic and Toasted, a 3-year-old son of Hennessy who returned to grass in the La Puente Stakes (see page 143). Toasted, who had finished third in a listed stakes in France at age 2, did not show the same spark on dirt in his previous race at Santa Anita on March 14, but woke up on turf at 25-1. Toasted, who gets a double dose of turf from his damsire, Seattle Song (and thus, a designation of T^2), rallied strongly from last in the nine-horse field to win going away by 1¼ lengths and returned $53.20. As noted previously in this chapter, you would think that with all these grass winners by Hennessy, his turf runners would get more respect. Toasted subsequently won the Arlington Classic on the turf.

RACE 10 SA–10Apr04 @6½ Furlongs Ⓣ (1.11), 3 yo Md Sp Wt

Value of Race: $44,000. 1st $26,400 ; 2nd $8,800 ; 3rd $5,280 ; 4th $2,640 ; 5th $880 . Mutuel Pools: $453,364 Ex $280,826, Quin $27,599, Tri $318,261, Super $172,006, DD $139,429, Pick–3 $145,705, Pick–6 $775,014 Carryover Pool $578,231;, Place Pick All $32,773 Pick–4 $353,465

Last Raced	Horse	M/Eq	A	Wt	PP	St	¼	½	Str	Fin	Odds$1
6Mar04 11SA12	Cinematic	LB	3	115	8	4	11½	11	22½	11½	40.50
11Mar04 4SA2	El Cordoves	LB	3	120	10	3	2hd	3hd	1hd	22	10.30
6Mar04 2SA5	Tapio-Ire	LB b	3	120	2	11	92	91½	61½	31	3.20
14Feb04 4SA11	Under the Sun	LB b	3	120	1	10	82½	82½	51	41	68.80
21Mar04 6SA3	Cherokee Benge	LB	3	120	12	2	7hd	71	71	51	7.70
6Mar04 11SA9	Photon Torpedo	LB	3	120	4	9	11½	111	92	6½	21.10
17Jly03 3Hol8	Sandyford	LB	3	120	9	8	12	12	113	7no	60.60
6Mar04 2SA2	Lucky Leo	LB	3	120	3	7	3hd	2½	31	8½	2.10
	Crimson Caper	LB	3	120	7	6	101	102½	8hd	9nk	16.30
25Jan04 4SA2	Pvt. Lynch	LB	3	120	6	5	5hd	52	4hd	103	8.30
	Multiplication	LB b	3	120	11	1	61½	4hd	10hd	1181½	13.70
9Nov03 6SA9	Yes	LB	3	113	5	12	4hd	6hd	12	12	9.70

OFF 5:16 Start Good . Won driving. Course firm.
TIME :214, :44, 1:07, 1:131 (:21.94, :44.06, 1:07.16, 1:13.29)

	83.00	49.00	16.00
9 – CINEMATIC		10.20	7.20
11 – EL CORDOVES			3.80
3 – TAPIO–IRE			

$1 Ex (9-11) 398.10 $2 Quin (9-11) 458.80 $1 Tri (9-11-3) 3,908.20
$1 Super (9-11-3-All) 15,255.00 $2 DD (6-9) 749.40 $1 Pick-3 (6-6-9) 8,946.20
$1 Place Pick All (9-OF-10) 594.60
$1 Pick-4 (5/8-6-6-9) 21,702.70
$2 Pick-6 (4-4-5/8-6-6-9) 5 Correct 6,873.40

Ch. g, (Mar), by Bianconi – Raise a Sweetheart , by Raise a Native . Trainer Shirreffs John. Bred by Coal Creek Farm (Ky).

CINEMATIC sped to the early lead, set the pace off the rail, angled in entering the stretch, responded when headed and gamely came back on to prove best. EL CORDOVES stalked the pace five wide on the hill, took a short lead three deep into the stretch, continued outside the winner and was outgamed. TAPIO (IRE) unhurried a bit off the rail, went around a rival into the stretch and again in upper stretch, angled in past midstretch and gained the show. UNDER THE SUN settled inside, came off the rail on the hill and three deep into the stretch and was outfinished for third. CHEROKEE BENGE cut the corner at the right hand curve then chased outside, came five wide into the stretch, had the rider lose the whip in midstretch and lacked the needed rally. PHOTON TORPEDO between horses early, angled in and saved ground off the pace and improved position inside. SANDYFORD broke inward, settled off the rail, came three deep into the stretch and was not a threat. LUCKY LEO saved ground stalking the pace to the stretch and weakened. CRIMSON CAPER dropped back between horses early, chased off the rail then outside on the hill and a bit wide into the stretch and did not rally. PVT. LYNCH well placed stalking the pace between horses down the hill, weakened in the stretch. MULTIPLICATION was in a good position stalking the leader four wide on the hill, came five wide into the stretch and also weakened. YES off a bit slowly, pulled his way between horses chasing the pace, angled in leaving the hill, dropped back, had the rider lose the whip in midstretch and gave way. Rail on hill at zero.

Jockeys– 1, Ruis M; 2, Jauregui L H; 3, Nakatani C S; 4, Puglisi I; 5, Valdivia J Jr; 6, Nuesch D; 7, Garcia M S; 8, Desormeaux K J; 9, Baze T C; 10, Almeida G F; 11, Steiner J J; 12, Bisono A

Trainers– 1, Shirreffs John; 2, Mullins Jeff; 3, Shirreffs John; 4, Greely C Beau; 5, Ellis Ronald W; 6, Sahadi Jenine; 7, Jackson Declan A; 8, Machowsky Michael; 9, Mullins Jeff; 10, Veiga Frank D; 11, Baffert Bob; 12, Gonzalez J Paco

Owners– 1, Krikorian George; 2, Cornejo Racing Inc; 3, Moss Mr and Mrs Jerome S; 4, Columbine Stable; 5, Hughes B Wayne; 6, Chaiken Family Trust and Green Lantern Stables LLC; 7, Jackson Declan Kirby Robert and Schow Howard B; 8, Monarch Stables Inc; 9, Desperado Stables Inc; 10, Amity and Bench; 11, McIngvale James; 12, Toffan John A

Scratched– Geniusatwork (06Mar04 2SA3) , Coronado's Pride (21Mar04 6SA8)

Santa Anita Park Attendance: 10,759 Mutuel Pool: $3,179,199.00 ITW Mutuel Pool: $5,016,340.00 ISW Mutuel Pool: $6,328,123.00

RACE 8 SA–10Apr04 1 Mile ⊤ (1.31⁴), 3 yo LaPuente

Value of Race: $110,500. 1st $66,300 ; 2nd $22,100 ; 3rd $13,260 ; 4th $6,630 ; 5th $2,210 .
Mutuel Pools: $618,678 Ex $366,561, Quin $33,864, Tri $381,373, Super $142,285, DD $38,939
Pick–3 $126,689

Last Raced	Horse	M/Eq	A	Wt	PP	St	¼	½	¾	Str	Fin	Odds$1
14Mar04 5SA8	Toasted	LB	3	115	6	8	9	9	8³	4½	1¹½	25.60
17Mar04 7SA2	Erewhon	LB	3	116	5	6	6¹	6¹½	7¹	5²½	2½	2.20
13Mar04 7GG2	Seattle Borders	LB	3	116	7	5	4ʰᵈ	4ʰᵈ	2ʰᵈ	2¹½	3¹	4.20
29Nov03 5Hol4	Terroplane-FR	LB b	3	116	9	9	7ʰᵈ	7½	6ʰᵈ	3ʰᵈ	4²	2.10
31Mar04 2SA1	Tricky Flash Flood	LB b	3	118	3	1	1¹½	1¹½	1¹½	1ʰᵈ	5²	60.90
17Mar04 7SA3	Four Song Limit	LB	3	114	8	4	3²	3²½	4¹½	6ʰᵈ	6²	4.90
17Mar04 7SA5	Gwaihir-Ire	LB b	3	117	2	3	5¹	5½	5¹½	7¹½	7³	12.70
28Feb04 8SA8	Trois Villes	LB b	3	114	1	2	2ʰᵈ	2²½	3¹	8³	8²	50.80
28Feb04 8SA7	MoulindMougins-Ire	LB	3	114	4	7	8¹½	8¹	9	9	9	18.10

OFF 4:15 Start Good . Won-driving. Course firm.

TIME :22³, :45³, 1:09⁴, 1:22, 1:34 (:22.64, :45.70, 1:09.87, 1:22.14, 1:34.18)

6 – TOASTED	53.20	15.00	7.20
5 – EREWHON		3.60	2.80
7 – SEATTLE BORDERS			3.40

$1 Ex (6-5) 113.80 $2 Quin (5-6) 101.60 $1 Tri (6-5-7) 452.90
$1 Super (6-5-7-9) 1,336.10 $2 DD (8-6) 177.60 $1 Pick-3 (4-5/8-6) 577.80

Dk. b or br. c, (Apr), by Hennessy – Burrows , by Seattle Song . Trainer De Seroux Laura. Bred by James D Haley (Ky).

TOASTED settled a bit off the rail, went outside a rival on the second turn, waited a bit then bid three deep into the stretch, split rivals in midstretch then rallied between foes under some late urging to prove best. EREWHON chased outside a rival then three deep on the backstretch and second turn, came five wide into the stretch and finished well late for second. SEATTLE BORDERS between horses early, stalked outside a rival then a bit off the rail, moved up toward the inside on the second turn, came out into the stretch, gained a short lead outside a foe past the eighth pole and was outfinished late. TERROPLANE (FR) off a bit slowly, angled in and saved ground off the pace, came out on the second turn and into the stretch, split rivals in midstretch and also was outfinished. TRICKY FLASH FLOOD sped to the early lead, set the pace inside, fought back inside a rival in upper and midstretch but weakened in the final furlong. FOUR SONG LIMIT pulled early, stalked outside a rival then off the rail, came four wide into the stretch and weakened. GWAIHIR (IRE) pulled his way along early, angled in on the first turn and saved ground chasing the pace but lacked the needed response. TROIS VILLES also pulled early, stalked inside then a bit off the rail, went three deep into the stretch and weakened. MOULIN DE MOUGINS (IRE) allowed to settle outside, went three deep into the second turn, continued off the rail and had no response in the stretch.

Jockeys– 1, Almeida G F; 2, Valdivia J Jr; 3, Garcia M S; 4, Desormeaux K J; 5, Saint-Martin E; 6, Santana J Z; 7, Nakatani C S; 8, Ruis M; 9, Sorenson D

Trainers– 1, De Seroux Laura; 2, Dollase Wallace; 3, Frankel Robert; 4, Drysdale Neil; 5, Sides Robert C; 6, Mullins Jeff; 7, Lewis Craig A; 8, Polanco Marcelo; 9, Cassidy James

Owners– 1, Port Sidney L and Trust 720270; 2, Flaxman Holdings Ltd; 3, Gann Edmund A; 4, Bienstock Papiano & Winner; 5, Sides Clay R; 6, Englander Richard A; 7, Kirkwood Al and Saundra S; 8, Everest Stables Inc; 9, Jim Ford Inc Pearson Daron and Sweesy Jack

Tomorrows Cat
Own: Zuckerman Donald S. and Roberta Mary

Dk. b or b. h. 9 (May)
Sire: Storm Cat (Storm Bird) $500,000
Dam: Tomorrow's Child (Al Nasr*Fr)
Br: Donald S. & Roberta Mary Zuckerman, as Tenants by the (Ky)
Tr: Baffert Bob(0 0 0 0 .00) 2004:(440 83 .19)

Life	15	4	4	2	$516,090	110	D.Fst	14	4	4	1	$511,370	110
1998	11	3	3	2	$482,890	110	Wet(384)	1	0	0	1	$4,720	89
1997	4	1	1	0	$33,200	91	Turf(328)	0	0	0	0	$0	-
	0	0	0	0	$0	-	Dst(T)(376)	0	0	0	0	$0	-

26Dec98-8SA	fst	7f	:23	:452	1:09	1:212		Malibu-G1	96	8	2	72¾	3½	53	74¾	Stevens G L	LB121 b	14.70	93-08	Run Man Run1151½ Artax1192 Event of the Year121nk	5 wide move 3/8	10
25Nov98-7CD	fst	1 1/16	:25	:49	1:131	1:444	3↑	Alw 50400N$Y	100	3	2hd	2½	1½	1hd	1hd	Sellers S J	L118 b	*.40	87-17	Tomorrows Cat118hd Winter Time1153¼ Whist1182¼	Lost whip 1/8 pole	6
Previously trained by Hennig Mark																						
16Oct98-8Med	fst	1⅛	:444	1:081	1:324	1:46	3↑	MedCupH-G1	40	3	43½	44½	814	829	839¼	Bravo J	L111 fb	4.60	64 -	K. J.'s Appeal1121¼ *Hal's Pal*116nk *Sir Bear*119½	Eased in distress	8
25Sep98-8Med	fst	1⅛	:463	1:102	1:343	1:464		PegasusH-G2	110	2	21½	21	2hd	12½	13	Bravo J	L113 fb	8.50	99-09	TomorrowsCt1133 LimitOut1151¾ ComicStrip1197½	Pressed pace, driving	6
7Sep98-11Pha	fst	1⅛	:47	1:103	1:35	1:473		PaDerby-G3	108	6	21	21	21½	2hd	21¼	Bravo J	L114 b	10.30	101-08	RockandRoll1141¼ *TomorrowsCat*1141¼ BlckBlde1192¼	Close, bid, held 2nd	11
9Aug98-11Mth	fst	1⅛	:47	1:104	1:353	1:483		BckHskIH-G1	86	6	44	46	56	514	514½	Turner T G	L114 b	30.00	80-13	*Coronado's Quest*1241¼ Victory Gallop125½ Grand Slam1188¼	No factor	6
19Jly98-9Mth	fst	1 1/16	:232	:47	1:11	1:43		LngBrnchBC100k	101	1	2hd	2hd	2hd	2hd	2hd	Turner T G	L113 b	8.80	86-14	*FvoritTrck*116hd TomorrowsCt1133½ ArctcSwp1142¼	Long drive just failed	6
19Jun98-6CD	fst	1 1/16	:233	:464	1:114	1:442	3↑	Alw 51600N1x	92	2	2hd	2½	1½	12	12	Borel C H	L113 b	*1.00	89-06	TomorrowsCt1132 CostofMne1162 *EglCounty*1161¼	Inside, dueled,driving	8
21May98-3CD	fst	1 1/16	:233	:48	1:13	1:44		Alw 47970N1x	93	4	11	1½	1hd	1hd	2½	Albarado R J	L118 b	1.70	90-16	Da Devil121½ *Tomorrows Cat*1182½ Battle Royale1187¼	Led, outfinished	8
8May98-8CD	sly	6½f	:223	:453	1:102	1:17	3↑	Alw 47200N1x	89	1	8	53½	56½	610	39	Day P	L107	*.90	83-18	LghtnnGlch1133¼ *MyFrndPrkr*1195¾ TomorrwsCt1072½	Passed tiring rivals	9
4Apr98-5Kee	fst	7f	:22	:441	1:092	1:22		Alw 43495N1x	77	8	5	75¾	68	35½	310½	Santos J A	L119	4.00	84-06	Arch1224½ Wild Jazz1176 Tomorrows Cat1193½	Void early speed	8
21Sep97-9Bel	fst	1	:222	:453	1:102	1:353		Futurity-G1	58	7	74¼	83¾	98	812	621½	Day P	L122	34.75	64-12	*Grand Slam*1226½ K. O. Punch1222¼ Devil's Pride1224½	Betwn foes,no bid	10
30Aug97-8Sar	fst	7f	:214	:45	1:103	1:234		Hopeful-G1	51	5	5	65½	54½	68	518½	Bailey J D	L122	10.30	67-12	*Favorite Trick*1221½ K. O. Punch1225 Jess M1227½	Steadied,ins mve trn	7
10Aug97-4Sar	fst	6f	:22	:452	:58	1:111		Md Sp Wt 34k	91	4	2	22	2½	1hd	14½	Bailey J D	L119	*.35	85-15	Tomorrows Cat1194½ Baquero1198 Meggett1194	Speed in hand,driving	9
23Jly97-2Sar	fst	5½f	:22	:454	:581	1:043		Md Sp Wt 34k	86	7	2	34½	34	22½	2¾	Bailey J D	L119	2.55	95-13	Hitech119¾ *Tomorrows Cat*1195½ *Slievenamon*119½	Inside trip,game fin	9

Tomorrows Cat

More often than not, the hidden turf factor will uncover legitimate plays at juicy odds, but sometimes the trainer's reputation may drastically reduce the odds. Such was the case on June 16, 2004, at Belmont when Tomorrows Champ, making his turf debut in a 1⅛-mile maiden race after three dirt efforts, was sent off as the 2-1 second choice—thanks to the popularity of his trainer, Todd Pletcher.

To be fair, it was obvious that Pletcher had wanted to get Tomorrows Champ on grass long before this race. His last two races were taken off the turf, so the intent was clearly there. That, plus a smart five-furlong bullet breeze (1:00) on the Saratoga turf training track showed Tomorrows Champ liked the surface.

Most importantly, Pletcher realized that Tomorrows Champ had a ton of turf in his pedigree. Tomorrows Champ is by yet another hidden turf sire, Tomorrows Cat. While Tomorrows Cat (a son of Storm Cat) won the Pegasus Handicap and finished second in the Pennsylvania Derby, he was strongly bred for turf. Not only is he by Storm Cat, his dam is by Al Nasr, a son of Lyphard. Thus, Tomorrows Cat is inbred to Northern Dancer, a pedigree pattern that is usually a powerful indicator for grass.

In addition to Tomorrows Cat on the top half of his pedigree, Tomorrows Champ is out of a Lear Fan mare (and thus, a T^2 pedigree). Lear Fan was a group winner by one of the world's great turf and stamina influences, Roberto, and he is a powerful turf presence in a pedigree.

Tomorrows Champ was always within striking position of the early leaders and rallied from sixth to win drawing away by 4½ lengths, paying $6.80.

The 9-5 favorite, Ross to Dublin, finished a nonthreatening sixth, seven lengths behind Tomorrows Champ. Ross to Dublin had trouble in his only other start, a maiden race on turf, but he is not particularly bred for turf. His sire, Event of the Year (Seattle Slew), is capable of getting winners on turf, but is a better sire of dirt horses. Ross to Dublin gets much more grass from his damsire, Assert, but it is an iffy pedigree for grass, and he was certainly an underlay at 9-5.

But a curious longshot who could have been used in the exotics was Red Haze, a first-time starter by the good sire Smart Strike, whose Canadian-bred offspring win at a high clip on both dirt and grass in that country. Adding to his appeal was his damsire, the very obscure Kefaah. A little homework uncovered a crucial piece of information. Kefaah, by Blushing Groom out of a Vaguely Noble mare (who happened to be a sibling to Lyphard and Nobiliary), had about as strong a grass pedigree as you will ever see. The fact that trainer Gary Contessa reached out to top rider Edgar Prado was the icing on the cake.

Red Haze finished a game second at 17-1 and the $2 exacta came back $94.50.

Fiddlers Cat, another son of Tomorrows Cat (and out of a mare by another hidden turf sire, Belong to Me), won his first start on turf at Belmont Park on July 9, 2004, in a one-mile grass race, returning $6.

Langfuhr
Own: Schickedanz Gustav

B. h. 12 (Feb)
Sire: Danzig (Northern Dancer) $200,000
Dam: Sweet Briar Too (Briartic)
Br: Gustav Schickedanz (Ont-C)
Tr: Keogh Michael(0 0 0 0 .00) 2004:(45 8 .18)

Life	23	9	7	1	$698,574	113		D.Fst	15	8	4	0	$570,780	113
1997	3	2	1	0	$343,020	112		Wet(390)	3	1	1	0	$97,493	106
1996	9	4	2	0	$271,205	113		Turf(379)	5	0	2	1	$30,301	93
	0	0	0	0	$0	-		Dst(0)	0	0	0	0	$0	-

26May97-9Bel	fst	1		:221	:442	1:074	1:33	3↑MtropltH-G1	112	3	95¾	62¾	52½	31	1nk	Chavez J F	L122	4.90	99-	15	Lngfuhr122nk WesternWintr115¾ NorthrnAflt117nk	Quick move,prevailed	10
4May97-8Aqu	gd	7f		:221	:45	1:093	1:224	3↑CarterH-G1	106	8	4	84¼	56¼	24½	1nk	Chavez J F	L122	3.65	93-	07	*Lngfuhr*122nk StlwrtMember1133 WestrnWintr1121½	Along in final strides	9
20Apr97-8WO	fst	7f		:223	:443	1:09	1:214	4↑VigilH65k	102	5	2	51¼	31	22	21¼	Ramsammy E	L124	1.90e	93-	13	Kiridashi1241¼ *Langfuhr*1245 Mindy Gayle109½	Closed willingly	5
26Oct96-5WO	fst	6f		:213	:44	:561	1:083	3↑BCSprint-G1	101	11	11	128¾	98½	108½	85	Chavez J F	L126	6.80	-	-	LitdeJustice1261¼ *PyingDues*126nk HonourndGlory1231¼	Lost ground turn	13
21Sep96-9Bel	fst	7f		:23	:454	1:084	1:211	3↑Vosburgh-G1	113	7	5	73	2hd	11½	11¼	Chavez J F	L126	14.30	-	-	Lngfuhr1261¼ HonourndGlory122¾ LitethFus1262½	4w sweep turn,drew clr	8
2Sep96-9Sar	fst	7f		:22	:442	1:091	1:214	3↑ForegoH-G2	109	6	1	67	58½	3½	1nk	Chavez J F	L110	19.00	-	-	*Langfuhr*110nk Top Account1154 Lite the Fuse121nk	Up in final strides	7
4Aug96-9WO	fst	7f		:222	:451	1:093	1:22	3↑OC 80k/N$Y-N	102	4	3	44	44	13	12½	McAleney J S	L116	2.40	-	-	*Langfuhr*1162½ *Basqueian*1163 Carey the Belle1141½	Driving	5
4Jly96-8Bel	gd	1	Ⓣ	:23	:453	1:091	1:333	3↑PokerH-G3	88	2	42	85¾	104¾	105½	910½	Penna D	L113	59.75	-	-	Smooth Runner1131¼ Mighty Forum1162 *Da Hoss*1191½	In tight,stdied 1/2p	10
16Jun96-9WO	fm	1⅛	Ⓣ	:453	1:091	1:332	1:46	3↑KngEdBCH-G3	83	3	512	512	48	55	46¼	Ramsammy E	L111	23.90	-	-	Kiridashi1171½ *Desert Waves*1153¼ Jet Freighter1191½	Best stride late	6
2Jun96-4WO	fm	6½f	Ⓣ	:224	:452	1:083	1:144	3↑OC 62k/N4x-N	89	3	1	1hd	1hd	2hd	21½	Kabel T K	L121	*1.70	-	-	Always a Rainbow1181½ Langfuhr1211 Quiet Victory1212¼	Second best	5
18May96-8WO	fm	7f	Ⓣ	:222	:444	1:084	1:211	3↑Alw 29600N$Y	93	8	1	62¼	53¾	2½	2no	Kabel T K	L115	*2.45	-	-	Roche Rock117no Langfuhr1152¾ Astlle Lonnie1151¼	Outfinished	13
19Apr96-8WO	fst	6½f		:231	:453	1:104	1:173	4↑OC 62k/N4x-N	89	3	4	3½	2hd	12½	14	McAleney J S	L118	1.25	-	-	Langfuhr1184 Dangerous Current1185½ Ocala Flame114½	Ridden out	5
3Dec95-7WO	my	6f		:214	:44	:564	1:094	3↑KenRdBCH76k	85	1	6	68	66¼	65¾	54¼	Dos Ramos R A	L112 b	2.00e	-	-	Blitzer1172½ Premier Explosion115hd Le Magister1201½	No threat	6
12Oct95-8WO	fst	7f		:223	:444	1:092	1:222	3↑Alw 24900N2x	98	2	5	1hd	12½	12½	1nk	McAleney J S	L114 b	*.50	-	-	Langfuhr114nk Counter Combo11513 Almighty Buck1181½	All out	5
17Sep95-6WO	fst	6f		:222	:452	:574	1:11	3↑OC 50k/N3x-N	89	5	1	32½	2½	22	2nk	McAleney J S	L114 b	*1.45	-	-	Tuxedo Landing121nk *Langfuhr*1144½ T. P.'s Way121½	Second best	8
4Sep95-10Pha	fst	1⅛		:452	1:091	1:35	1:48	PaDerby-G2	77	12	2½	2½	1hd	46½	918¾	Platts R	L114 b	9.70	-	-	PineingPatty1221¾ RoyalHaven1176¼ TenantsHrbor1171¾	Dueled, used up	12
7Aug95-3WO	fst	7f		:223	:453	1:104	1:241	Alw 23300N2L	86	2	6	41¼	1hd	1hd	11½	McAleney J S	L114 b	*.80	-	-	Langfuhr1141½ Panarus119¾ Stanley Silver1134½	Driving	8
29Jly95-6WO	yl	1	Ⓣ	:232	:454	1:093	1:35	Alw 25600N2L	83	6	73¼	65	52½	4¾	3nk	McAleney J S	L114	*.70	-	-	*It's I.*113hd *For Pete's Sake*113hd *Langfuhr*1141¼	Closed willingly	10
9Jly95-9WO	fst	1¼		:454	1:103	1:37	2:034	ⓇQueensPlt436k	88	8	1hd	2hd	2hd	55	67½	Stevens G L	126	2.15	-	-	Regal Discovery1261¼ FreedomFleet1264½ Mt.Sassafras126¾	Dueled, tired	14
25Jun95-8WO	fst	1⅛		:47	1:11	1:364	1:503	ⓇPlateTrial109k	96	2	1½	1½	2hd	1hd	2no	McAleney J S	126	*1.35	-	-	All Firmed Up126no Langfuhr1261 Mt. Sassafras1266	Outfinished, gamely	7
28May95-6WO	sly	1 1/16		:231	:464	1:123	1:444	Alw 25600N2L	98	1	2hd	1½	2hd	21	2½	McAleney J S	114	*.60	-	-	Freedom Fleet114½ Langfuhr11414½ For Pete's Sake1131	Came again	6
14May95-5WO	fst	1 1/16		:232	:473	1:124	1:433	Alw 24400N2L	93	7	54½	21	2hd	2hd	21¼	McAleney J S	114	*1.55	-	-	*Smart Strike*1141¼ Langfuhr1142 Mt. Sassafras11316	Weakened	8
22Apr95-10WO	fst	7f		:224	:451	1:103	1:233	3↑Md Sp Wt 21k	79	5	9	51¼	42½	3½	12½	McAleney J S	114	2.60	-	-	Langfuhr1142½ Kidnap the Wife116hd Card Trick114½	Prevailed, driving	9

Langfuhr

Langfuhr is finally beginning to get the recognition he deserves, but despite his success as a stallion, his runners—especially on turf—are still providing pedigree handicappers with some tremendous overlays because he is an exceptional hidden turf sire.

A late-blooming sprinter who did not become a stakes winner until age 4, when he captured the Vosburgh Stakes and Forego Handicap, he was also named champion Canadian sprinter. He returned at 5 to post his most important victory in the Metropolitan Handicap and also added a win in the Carter Handicap.

Langfuhr's first crop yielded 55 winners from 67 starters, with four stakes winners, topped by the high-class filly Imperial Gesture, who finished second in the Breeders' Cup Juvenile Fillies. She then scored important victories in the Beldame Stakes and Gazelle Handicap, and also finished third in the Breeders' Cup Distaff at age 3.

Langfuhr's second crop included 3-year-old Canadian champion Wando and his shadow, the stakes winner Mobil.

Langfuhr's third crop included Imperialism, who finished a troubled third behind Smarty Jones and Lion Heart in the 2004 Kentucky Derby. Imperialism had shown good form on turf earlier in his career, and will probably prove best on the green as he has a T^2

pedigree, with strong turf influences from his dam's sire line (Pass the Tab-Al Hattab-The Axe II).

A top stakes-winning sprinter/miler on dirt, Langfuhr was an ideal candidate to be labeled a hidden turf sire when he first went to stud because of his pedigree. Not only is Langfuhr by the powerful turf influence Danzig, he is inbred to Nearctic (the sire of Northern Dancer).

On June 23, 2004, E. Ticket, a 3-year-old filly by Langfuhr out of the He's Bad mare Special Date, made her turf debut at Belmont Park in a one-mile allowance for New York-breds. E. Ticket had won her career debut over statebreds on May 22 in a six-furlong race, but showed nothing in her second start on the dirt at seven furlongs on June 13.

After being steadied at the start and dropping to last in the 12-horse field, E. Ticket rallied five-wide on the far turn to take the lead powerfully in the stretch, winning by 2¾ lengths. Because players have still not grasped the fact that Langfuhr is a superior sire of turf runners, E. Ticket was dismissed at 19-1 and returned $40.80.

Recent grass performers by Langfuhr include the 1-2 finishers of a six-furlong allowance race on turf on July 9, 2004. Langfleur, a 4-year-old colt, won the turf sprint as the 4-5 favorite over Langburg, a 3-year-old gelding, who was 18-1. The $2 exacta came back a respectable $51.60.

That same day, Langfuhr had another impressive grass winner when Lanlicia, a 3-year-old filly out of a mare by yet another strong turf influence, Majesty's Prince (His Majesty), won her grass debut at about $1\frac{1}{16}$ miles at Arlington Park, paying $8.40.

All sons of Danzig have license to be superior grass sires, and Langfuhr has proven no different. While it seems incredible now, there were serious doubts about sons of Danzig as stallions when they first went to stud. As soon as runners by these Danzig sons started racing on turf, however, it was very clear: Danzig was going to have a great impact as a sire of sires, predominantly on turf.

Chief's Crown, a member of Danzig's first crop and a champion at 2 on dirt, was among the first sons of Danzig to enter stud, and his success as a stallion correlated with the brilliance of his runners in Europe on grass, beginning with juvenile champion Grand Lodge.

Group and graded stakes winners on turf by Danzig who are turf influences are led by the incomparable Danehill and also include Anabaa, Bertolini, Bianconi, Dayjur, Dove Hunt, Dumaani, Elnadim, Foxhound, Golden Snake, Green Desert, Lech, Lost Soldier, Lure, Mujahid, Masterful, Mull of Kintyre, Polish Patriot, Polish Precedent, Snaadee, and Zieten. Undoubtedly, the highly regarded 2004 freshman sire War Chant, winner of the Breeders' Cup Mile, and stakes winner Brahms will join this group in the near future.

Since these sons of Danzig were stakes winner on turf, they were expected to also be grass sires, but other sons of Danzig who found success on dirt are the ones who qualify as strong hidden turf sires. This list includes Adjudicating, Belong to Me, Boundary, Chief's Crown, Danzig Connection, Eagle Eyed, Exchange Rate, Langfuhr, Partner's Hero, Pine Bluff, Polish Navy, Slavic, and Strolling Along.

HIDDEN TURF SIRES

STALLION	SIRE/DAMSIRE CROSS	
Abaginone	(Devil's Bag/Spectacular Bid)	HT^2
Adcat	(Storm Cat/Riverman)	HT^2
Affirmed	(Exclusive Native/Crafty Admiral)	HT^2
Afternoon Deelites	(Private Terms/Medaille d'Or)	HT^2
Albert the Great	(Go for Gin/Fappiano)	
Alphabet Soup	(Cozzene/Arts and Letters)	HT^2
American Chance	(Cure the Blues/Seattle Slew)	
American Standard	(In Reality/Bald Eagle)	
Appealing Skier	(Baldski/Valid Appeal)	HT^2
Aptitude	(A.P. Indy/Northern Dancer)	
Arch	(Kris S./Danzig)	HT^2
Awesome Again	(Deputy Minister/Blushing Groom)	HT^2
Bartok	(Fairy King/Shirley Heights)	HT^2
Behrens	(Pleasant Colony/Mari's Book)	HT^2
Belong to Me	(Danzig/Exclusive Native)	HT^2
Bernstein	(Storm Cat/Affirmed)	HT^2
Bertrando	(Skywalker/Buffalo Lark)	HT^2
Best of Luck	(Broad Brush/Chief's Crown)	HT^2
Bianconi	(Danzig/Pretense)	HT^2
Black Tie Affair	(Miswaki/Al Hattab)	HT^2
Boston Harbor	(Capote/Vice Regent)	
Boundary	(Danzig/Damascus)	
Brahms	(Danzig/Mr. Prospector)	
Buddha	(Unbridled's Song/Storm Cat)	
Came Home	(Gone West/Clever Trick)	
Capote	(Seattle Slew/Bald Eagle)	
Cat Thief	(Storm Cat/Alydar)	
Catienus	(Storm Cat/Mr. Prospector)	
Century City	(Danzig/Alysheba)	HT^2
Changeintheweather	(Gone West/Pleasant Colony)	HT^2
Charismatic	(Summer Squall/Drone)	HT^2
Cherokee Run	(Runaway Groom/Silver Saber)	

STALLION	SIRE/DAMSIRE CROSS	
Chief's Crown	(Danzig/Secretariat)	HT^2
Chief Honcho	(Chief's Crown/Riva Ridge)	
Citidancer	(Dixieland Band/Tentam)	HT^2
Civilisation	(Gone West/El Gran Senor)	HT^2
Cloud Cover	(Storm Cat/Naskra)	
Cobra King	(Farma Way/Fabled Monarch)	HT^2
Commendable	(Gone West/In Reality)	HT^2
Concern	(Broad Brush/Tunerup)	HT^2
Concerto	(Chief's Crown/In Reality)	HT^2
Congaree	(Arazi/Mari's Book)	HT^2
Constant Demand	(Summer Squall/Drone)	HT^2
Crown Ambassador	(Storm Cat/Key to the Mint)	HT^2
Cryptoclearance	(Fappiano/Hoist the Flag)	
Crypto Star	(Cryptoclearance/Sir Ivor)	
Cure the Blues	(Stop the Music/Dr. Fager)	
Dance Master	(Gone West/Nijinsky II)	HT^2
David	(Mt. Livermore/Turkoman)	HT^2
Decarchy	(Distant View/El Gran Senor)	HT^2
Defrere	(Deputy Minister/Secretariat)	HT^2
Dehere	(Deputy Minister/Secretariat)	HT^2
Demidoff	(Mr. Prospector/Secretariat)	
Deputy Commander	(Deputy Minister/Malinowski)	HT^2
Devil His Due	(Devil's Bag/Raise a Cup)	
Devil's Bag	(Halo/Herbager)	HT^2
Devon Lane	(Storm Cat/Relaunch)	
Disco Rico	(Citidancer/Apalachee)	HT^2
Distant View	(Mr. Prospector/Irish River)	
Dixie Union	(Dixieland Band/Capote)	
Dollar Bill	(Peaks and Valleys/Saratoga Six)	
Double Honor	(Gone West/Storm Bird)	HT^2
Dr. Adagio	(Cure the Blues/Silly Season)	HT^2
Dream Run	(Cherokee Run/Naevus)	
Easyfromthegitgo	(Dehere/Easy Goer)	

STALLION	SIRE/DAMSIRE CROSS	
Editor's Note	(Forty Niner/Caveat)	HT^2
E Dubai	(Mr. Prospector/Lord at War)	
El Corredor	(Mr. Greeley/Silver Deputy)	
Elusive Quality	(Gone West/Hero's Honor)	HT^2
Empire Maker	(Unbridled/El Gran Senor)	
Entepreneur	(Cure the Blues/Miswaki)	
Essence of Dubai	(Pulpit/Summing)	
Exchange Rate	(Danzig/Seeking the Gold)	
Exclusive Native	(Raise a Native/Shut Out)	
Exploit	(Storm Cat/My Dad George)	
Fabulous Frolic	(Green Dancer/Cherokee Fellow)	
Flame Thrower	(Saint Ballado/Metrogrand)	
Flying Continental	(Flying Paster/Transworld)	HT^2
Forestry	(Storm Cat/Pleasant Colony)	HT^2
Forest Camp	(Deputy Minister/Hold Your Peace)	
Forest Wildcat	(Storm Cat/Bold Native)	
French Deputy	(Deputy Minister/Hold Your Peace)	HT^2
French Envoy	(Deputy Minister/Seattle Slew)	
Freud	(Storm Cat/Rahy)	
Fusaichi Pegasus	(Mr. Prospector/Danzig)	
Fusaichi Zenon	(Sunday Silence/Northern Taste)	HT^2
Game Plan	(Danzig/Alydar)	
Gen Stormin'norman	(Storm Cat/Restless Native)	
Gentlemen	(Robin des Bois/Loose Cannon)	HT^2
Glitterman	(Dewan/In Reality)	
Globalize	(Summer Squall/Fit to Fight)	
Go for Gin	(Cormorant/Stage Door Johnny)	HT^2
Gone for Real	(Gone West/Drone)	HT^2
Gone West	(Mr. Prospector/Secretariat)	HT^2
Graeme Hall	(Dehere/Crafty Prospector)	
Grand Slam	(Gone West/El Gran Senor)	HT^2
Greenwood Lake	(Meadowlake/Dancing Champ)	HT^2
Grindstone	(Unbridled/Drone)	

STALLION	SIRE/DAMSIRE CROSS	
Gulch	(Mr. Prospector/Rambunctious)	
Halory Hunter	(Jade Hunter/Halo)	
Halos and Horns	(Saint Ballado/Flip Sal)	
Halo's Image	(Halo/Valid Appeal)	
Hansel	(Woodman/Dancing Count)	
Harlan	(Storm Cat/Halo)	
Harlan's Holiday	(Harlan/Affirmed)	HT^2
Helmsman	(El Gran Senor/King's Bishop)	HT^2
Hennessy	(Storm Cat/Hawaii)	HT^2
High Demand	(Danzig/Forli)	HT^2
High Yield	(Storm Cat/Forty Niner)	
Hold for Gold	(Red Ransom/Mr. Prospector)	
Holy Bull	(Great Above/Al Hattab)	HT^2
Holzmeister	(Woodman/Danzig)	HT^2
Honour and Glory	(Relaunch/Al Nasr)	
Horse Chestnut	(Fort Wood/Col Pickering)	HT^2
Housebuster	(Mt. Livermore/Great Above)	HT^2
Huddle Up	(Sir Ivor/Never Bend)	
Humble Eleven	(Lac Ouimet/Alleged)	HT^2
Impeachment	(Deputy Minister/Criminal Type)	
Incurable Optimist	(Cure the Blues/Seattle Slew)	
Invisible Ink	(Thunder Gulch/Conquistador Cielo)	
Jade Hunter	(Mr. Prospector/Pharly)	
Jambalaya Jazz	(Dixieland Band/Graustark)	HT^2
Jazz Club	(Dixieland Band/Mr. Prospector)	
Johannesburg	(Hennessy/Ogygian)	
Judge TC	(Judge Smells/Secretariat)	HT^2
Just a Cat	(Storm Cat/Alydar)	
Katwain	(Cherokee Run/Moment of Hope)	
Kelly Kip	(Kipper Kelly/John's Gold)	HT^2
Key of Luck	(Chief's Crown/Gay Mecene)	HT^2
Kipper Kelly	(Valid Appeal/Tentam)	HT^2
Kissin Kris	(Kris S./Your Alibhai)	

STALLION	SIRE/DAMSIRE CROSS	
Langfuhr	(Danzig/Briartic)	HT^2
Lemon Drop Kid	(Kingmambo/Seattle Slew)	
Leo Castelli	(Sovereign Dancer/Raise a Native)	
Light of Morn	(Alleged/Olden Times)	
Lil's Lad	(Pine Bluff/Vanlandingham)	
Limit Out	(Northern Flagship/Miswaki)	
Lion Cavern	(Mr. Prospector/Secretariat)	
Lion Hearted	(Storm Cat/Alydar)	
Littleexpectations	(Valid Appeal/Iron Constitution)	
Lord Avie	(Lord Gaylord/Gallant Man)	
Lost Soldier	(Danzig/Secretariat)	HT^2
Louis Quatorze	(Sovereign Dancer/On to Glory)	
Lucky Lionel	(Mt. Livermore/Crafty Prospector)	
Lucky North	(Northern Dancer/Olden Times)	
Lucky Roberto	(Belong to Me/Roberto)	HT^2
Macho Uno	(Holy Bull/Blushing Groom)	HT^2
Magic Cat	(Storm Cat/Fappiano)	
Mahogany Hall	(Woodman/Majestic Light)	
Malabar Gold	(Unbridled/Tsunami Slew)	
Malagra	(Majestic Light/Viceregal)	HT^2
Malibu Wesley	(Storm Cat/Capote)	
Mancini	(Mr. Prospector/Caro)	
Marfa	(Foolish Pleasure/Stratmat)	HT
Maria's Mon	(Wavering Monarch/Caro)	HT^2
Mazel Trick	(Phone Trick/Ramahorn)	
Meadowlake	(Hold Your Peace/Raise a Native)	
Meadow Monster	(Meadowlake/Vice Regent)	
Menifee	(Harlan/Never Bend)	
Mighty	(Lord at War/Mr. Prospector)	
Mighty Magee	(Cormorant/Halo)	
Millennium Wind	(Cryptoclearance/Drone)	
Millions	(Dehere/Native Charger)	
Milwaukee Brew	(Wild Again/Wolf Power)	

STALLION	SIRE/DAMSIRE CROSS	
Minardi	(Boundary/Mr. Prospector)	
Miswaki	(Mr. Prospector/Buckpasser)	
Mizzen Mast	(Cozzene/Graustark)	HT^2
Mongoose	(Broad Brush/Cox's Ridge)	
More Than Ready	(Southern Halo/Woodman)	
Moscow Ballet	(Nijinsky II/Cornish Prince)	
Mr. Greeley	(Gone West/Reviewer)	
Mt. Livermore	(Blushing Groom/Crimson Satan)	
Mud Route	(Strawberry Road/Sunny's Halo)	
Muqtarib	(Gone West/The Minstrel)	HT^2
No Armistice	(Unbridled/Hold Your Peace)	
Old Trieste	(A.P. Indy/Vigors)	
Open Forum	(Deputy Minister/Graustark)	
Ordway	(Salt Lake/Vaguely Noble)	HT^2
Orientate	(Mt. Livermore/Cox's Ridge)	
Outflanker	(Danzig/Alydar)	
Out of Place	(Cox's Ridge/Damascus)	
Partner's Hero	(Danzig/Winning Hit)	
Patton	(Lord at War/Seattle Slew)	
Peaks and Valleys	(Mt. Livermore/Green Dancer)	HT^2
Pembroke	(Gone West/Boldnesian)	HT^2
Perfect Mandate	(Gone West/The Minstrel)	HT^2
Perfect Vision	(Storm Cat/Sharpen Up)	HT^2
Performing Magic	(Gone West/The Minstrel)	HT^2
Perigee Moon	(Hennessy/Vigors)	HT^2
Pine Bluff	(Danzig/Halo)	
Point Given	(Thunder Gulch/Turkoman)	HT^2
Polish Navy	(Danzig/Tatan)	
Precocity	(Aford/Super Concorde)	
Prime Timber	(Sultry Song/Nodouble)	
Proud Citizen	(Gone West/Green Forest)	HT^2
Proud Irish	(Irish River/Delta Judge)	
Pulpit	(A.P. Indy/Mr. Prospector)	HT^2

STALLION	SIRE/DAMSIRE CROSS	
Pure Prize	(Storm Cat/Seeking the Gold)	
Put It Back	(Honour and Glory/Exuberant)	HT^2
Pyramid Peak	(Mt. Livermore/Stalwart)	
Raffie's Majesty	(Cormorant/Surumu)	
Rail	(Majestic Light/Believe It)	HT^2
Red Bullet	(Unbridled/Caro)	
Repent	(Louis Quatorze/Cipayo)	
Richter Scale	(Habitony/Bel Bolide)	HT^2
Ride the Rails	(Cryptoclearance/Herbager)	
Rock and Roll	(Cure the Blues/Halo)	
Rodeo	(Gone West/Damascus)	
Rubiano	(Fappiano/Nijinsky II)	
Runaway Groom	(Blushing Groom/Call the Witness)	
Running Stag	(Cozzene/Orsini)	HT^2
Run Softly	(Deputy Minister/Riverman)	HT^2
Sahm	(Mr. Prospector/Sadler's Wells)	
Salt Lake	(Deputy Minister/Queen City Lad)	
Sandpile	(Cure the Blues/Deputy Minister)	
Scatmandu	(Storm Cat/Alydar)	
Score Early	(Northern Score/Life Cycle)	
Score Quick	(Northern Score/Quack)	
Sea of Secrets	(Storm Cat/Mr. Prospector)	
Sea Salute	(Danzig/Seattle Slew)	
Service Stripe	(Deputy Minister/Blushing Groom)	HT^2
Shotiche	(Northern Dancer/Cyane)	
Siphon	(Itajara/Kublai Khan)	
Sir Cat	(Storm Cat/Private Account)	
Sky Mesa	(Pulpit/Storm Cat)	HT^2
Slew Gin Fizz	(Relaunch/Seattle Slew)	
Snow Ridge	(Tabasco Cat/Woodman)	
Songandaprayer	(Unbridled's Song/Premiership)	
Southern Halo	(Halo/Northern Dancer)	
Spectacular Bid	(Bold Bidder/Promised Land)	HT^2

STALLION	SIRE/DAMSIRE CROSS	
Stack	(Nijinsky II/Tom Rolfe)	HT^2
Storm Boot	(Storm Cat/Mr. Prospector)	
Storm Broker	(Storm Cat/Affirmed)	HT^2
Storm Creek	(Storm Cat/Mr. Prospector)	
Storm Day	(Storm Cat/Graustark)	HT^2
Stormin Fever	(Storm Cat/Seattle Slew)	
Stormy Atlantic	(Storm Cat/Seattle Slew)	
Straight Man	(Saint Ballado/Cornish Prince)	
Strategic Mission	(Mr. Prospector/Buckfinder)	
Street Cry	(Machiavellian/Troy)	HT^2
Struggler	(Night Shift/Known Fact)	HT^2
Successful Appeal	(Valid Appeal/Fortunate Prospect)	HT^2
Sultry Song	(Cox's Ridge/Buckfinder)	
Summer Squall	(Storm Bird/Secretariat)	HT^2
Supremo	(Gone West/Danzig)	HT^2
Sweetsouthernsaint	(Saint Ballado/Tri Jet)	
Syncline	(Danzig/Nebbiolo)	HT^2
Tabasco Cat	(Storm Cat/Sauce Boat)	HT^2
Tactical Cat	(Storm Cat/Caro)	HT^2
Take Me Out	(Cure the Blues/Tom Rolfe)	
Tale of the Cat	(Storm Cat/Mr. Prospector)	HT^2
Talk Is Money	(Deputy Minister/Gone West)	HT^2
Tamayaz	(Gone West/The Minstrel)	HT^2
Tejano Run	(Tejano/Wavering Monarch)	HT^2
Tethra	(Cure the Blues/New Prospect)	
Three Wonders	(Storm Cat/Woodman)	HT^2
Thunder Gulch	(Gulch/Storm Bird)	HT^2
Tiger Ridge	(Storm Cat/Secretariat)	HT^2
Tomorrows Cat	(Storm Cat/Al Nasr)	HT^2
Touch Gold	(Deputy Minister/Buckpasser)	
Trajectory	(Gone West/Relaunch)	HT^2
Tribal Rule	(Storm Cat/Grenfall)	HT^2
Tribunal	(Deputy Minister/Secretariat)	HT^2

STALLION	SIRE/DAMSIRE CROSS	
Truckee	(Danzig/Seattle Slew)	
Twilight Agenda	(Devil's Bag/Grenfall)	HT^2
Unbridled's Song	(Unbridled/Caro)	
Unbridled Time	(Unbridled's Song/Halo)	
Uncle Abbie	(Kingmambo/Seattle Slew)	
Unusual Heat	(Nureyev/Glacial)	HT^2
Valid Expectations	(Valid Appeal/Iron Constitution)	
Valid Wager	(Valid Appeal/Bold Bidder)	
Vicar	(Wild Again/El Gran Senor)	
Victory Gallop	(Cryptoclearance/Vice Regent)	
Vision and Verse	(Storm Cat/Private Account)	
Volponi	(Cryptoclearance/Sir Harry Lewis)	HT^2
Wavering Monarch	(Majestic Light/Buckpasser)	
Way West	(Gone West/Targowice)	HT^2
Wekiva Springs	(Runaway Groom/Tri Jet)	
Western Borders	(Gone West/J.O. Tobin)	HT^2
Western Expression	(Gone West/Majestic Light)	HT^2
Western Fame	(Gone West/Topsider)	HT^2
Whiskey Wisdom	(Wild Again/Lord at War)	HT^2
Whywhywhy	(Mr. Greeley/Quiet American)	
Wild Event	(Wild Again/Northfields)	
Wild Rush	(Wild Again/Plugged Nickle)	
Wild Wonder	(Wild Again/Pass the Tab)	
Wild Zone	(Wild Again/The Minstrel)	
Wised Up	(Dixieland Band/Smarten)	
Wiseman's Ferry	(Hennessy/Silver Deputy)	
Woodman	(Mr. Prospector/Buckpasser)	
World Stage	(Sadler's Wells/Secretariat)	HT^2
Yankee Victor	(Saint Ballado/Caro)	
Yarrow Brae	(Deputy Minister/Miswaki)	HT^2
Yonaguska	(Cherokee Run/Silver Ghost)	
You and I	(Kris S./Ups)	
Zamindar	(Gone West/The Minstrel)	HT^2

5

HANDICAPPING THE KENTUCKY DERBY BY PEDIGREE

ASIDE FROM MAIDEN races, perhaps the greatest interest in pedigrees is focused on the 3-year-olds and America's most famous race, the Kentucky Derby—and there is a simple explanation why.

The Kentucky Derby is unique because it is the first time that 3-year-olds are asked to run 1¼ miles in this country. (Canonero II, however, ran and won twice at that distance in Venezuela before upsetting the 1971 Kentucky Derby.) The winners of the Derby usually have to have a combination of early maturity along with the bloodlines to be effective at 1¼ miles. But there are always exceptions, and lately, exceptions have been the rule. War Emblem (2002), Funny Cide (2003), and Smarty Jones (2004) did not have the kind of pedigrees that screamed "distance," but they peaked at the right time, matured faster than their contemporaries, and pulled off the upsets. These latest results may signal a significant change in how we view the Triple Crown races.

For the past 30 years, American breeders have altered the development of the Thoroughbred by breeding for speed, with little or no regard to stamina. This is largely a response to the changing economics of the game, which is now dominated by commercial breeders catering to buyers who want to reap a quick return on their purchases of young horses. The result has been the proliferation of runners who are bred to be precocious, win-early types, and the long-term effect of these actions is now reflected in the stakes programs in this country. Important, historical dirt races that were run at 1½ miles have all but vanished from the American racing scene. Aside from the sanctified Belmont Stakes, horses are never asked to run that far in this country, except on turf, and I believe that this has diminished a once-great sport. The Jockey Club Gold Cup was a fixture on the racing calendar and was run at two miles from 1921 through 1975. It was reduced to 1½ miles in 1976 and remained at that distance through 1989, and then it was again shortened to its current distance of 1¼ miles.

The loss of classic influences Pleasant Colony and Kris S. in 2002, and Unbridled in 2001, were tremendous blows to racing and leave only a small sample of sires—such as A.P. Indy, Cryptoclearance, Deputy Commander, Dynaformer, El Prado, Gulch, Kingmambo, and Thunder Gulch—as the only proven stamina influences for dirt in the U.S. today. Young stallions such as Aptitude, Empire Maker, Lemon Drop Kid, Monarchos, Mineshaft, Point Given, Touch Gold, and Victory Gallop have the potential of boosting the gene pool with their staying influence.

A very small percentage of turf sires have consistent success with dirt runners, but two stallions who have shown tremendous versatility with their offspring are Dynaformer and El Prado. There are other stallions who are sources of stamina, but they are generally turf sires, and their offspring may be able to go long but are at a disadvantage on dirt. A perfect example of this was provided in 2004 by Castledale. He won the Santa Anita Derby, and it was difficult to fault his connections for wanting to try the Kentucky Derby, since they knew that distance would never be the problem. Although he did win the Santa Anita Derby, he was always better bred for turf (from the second crop of the very impressive Prix de l'Arc de Triomphe winner Peintre Celebre), and when Churchill Downs came up a quagmire on Derby Day, Castledale's fate was sealed, much like the track.

Runners by Theatrical, Royal Academy, Alphabet Soup, Red Ransom, With Approval, Sky Classic, Sadler's Wells, and Silver Hawk inherit plenty of stamina but their dirt form has never been as good as their grass form. In addition, offspring by these staying influences usually mature late and rarely run in the Triple Crown.

Thus, the past three years have seen winners by stallions that are considered speed influences, and until an exhaustive overhaul of the breeding industry is implemented, it is likely that there will be more winners of the Kentucky Derby by improbable sires. Every horse can race 1¼ miles, but the key is, will he run the distance in 2:00, or in 2:04? If future Kentucky Derbies feature horses by such stallions as Elusive Quality, Tale of the Cat, Distorted Humor, Our Emblem, Hennessy, Grand Slam, and Silver Deputy, it will come down to which sprinter/miler can last the 10 furlongs better than the rest.

Pedigree handicapping has often spotlighted the contenders and pretenders in past Kentucky Derbies—although it was easier when there were actually horses with mile-and-a-quarter pedigrees trying the distance for the first time.

Here is a look back at the Kentucky Derby since 1990:

1990: Unbridled, Summer Squall, and Pleasant Tap finished 1-2-3 and all were well qualified to win at 1¼ miles. Unbridled's sire, Fappiano, was atypical of most sons of Mr. Prospector, and was a strong source of stamina. His other notable sons include Crypto-clearance, Quiet American, and Signal Tap. But runners who were at a disadvantage going 1¼ miles that year and who could have been eliminated from consideration were the highly touted Mister Frisky (by Marsayas), who finished eighth, Real Cash (Tank's Prospect,

11th), Dr. Bobby A. (Dr. Carter, 12th), Pendleton Ridge (Cox's Ridge, 13th), Burnt Hills (Conquistador Cielo, 14th), and Fighting Fantasy (Fighting Fit, 15th).

Unbridled — **b. c. 1987, by Fappiano (Mr. Prospector)–Gana Facil, by Le Fabuleux** — **Lifetime record: 24 8 6 6 $4,489,475**

Own.– Frances A. Genter Stable Inc
Br.– Tartan Farms Corp (Fla)
Tr.– Carl A. Nafzger

2Nov91- 8CD	fst 1¼	:482 1:123 1:38 2:024 3↑	BC Classic-G1	7 11 1016 85¾ 45½ 33¾	Perret C	LB 126	4.30	92-09	Black Tie Affair1261¼Twilight Agenda1262½Unbridled126nk	Mild rally	11
6Oct91- 8Kee	fst 1⅛	:472 1:112 1:36 1:484 3↑	Fayette H-G2	1 5 56½ 43½ 31½ 23	Perret C	LB 122	1.90	88-17	SummrSquall1223Unbridled1222½SecrtHllo1151¾	Veered out	5
10Aug91- 3Dmr	fst 1¼	:454 1:094 1:341 1:594 3↑	Pacific Classic 1000k	8 7 79 56 44½ 33¾	Perret C	LB 124	6.20	- -	Best Pal1161Twilight Agenda1242¾Unbridled1241¼	Came on	8
3Aug91- 5AP	fst 7f	:223 :444 1:084 1:21 3↑	Alw 25500	2 6 610 610 25 16½	Day P	L 122	*.40e	98-12	Unbridled1226½SpnshDrummr1191¾Prfcton1174	Strong finish	7
11May91- 9Pim	fst 1 3/16	:464 1:10 1:341 1:522 4↑	Pim Spl H-G1	4 5 510 57½ 610 610	Perret C	L 122	2.40	93-13	FarmaWay1193SmmrSqll1202½Jol'sHlo119nk	Weakened,bled	7
13Apr91- 8OP	sly 1⅛	:463 1:104 1:354 1:48 4↑	Oaklawn H-G1	5 8 815 815 75¾ 56	Day P	L 124	2.00	89-03	Festin115¾Primal1153¼Jolie's Halo1201	Belated rally	8
16Mar91- 6GP	fst 7f	:22 :442 1:091 1:214 3↑	Deputy Minister H 50k	4 9 814 814 34 13	Day P	L 119	3.10	97-07	Unbridled1193Housebuster122noShuttleman1145	Ridden out	9
27Oct90- 9Bel	fst 1¼	:454 1:094 1:353 2:021 3↑	BC Classic-G1	14 13 1311 96¾ 32½ 11	Day P	121	6.60e	86-15	Unbridled1211IbnBey1261ThirtySixRed121no	Strong drive	14
23Sep90-10LaD	fst 1¼	:462 1:111 1:361 2:02	Super Derby-G1	9 9 94¾ 32 43½ 23½	Velez JA Jr	L 126	*.90	102-00	HomeatLast1263½Unbridled126nkCee'sTzzy1261	Six wide ⅜	9
3Sep90- 8AP	fm 1¼Ⓣ	:491 1:131 1:372 2:013	Secretariat-G1	4 7 75½ 63¼ 3nk 2¾	Fires E	L 126	*.50e	103-03	SuperAbound114¾Unbridld1261½SuperFan117¾	Brushed start	8
18Aug90- 9AP	fst 1	:224 :451 1:092 1:342 3↑	Alw 23500	1 4 42 21 13 111½	Fires E	L 112	*.30	99-12	Unbridled11211Lampkin Cache116½Remington's Pride1194	Much the best	8
9Jun90- 8Bel	gd 1½	:48 1:121 2:014 2:271	Belmont-G1	5 6 42½ 44½ 46 412¾	Perret C	126	*1.10	81-13	GoandGo1268¼ThirtySixRd1262BrondVux1262½	Bid wide,tired	9
19May90-10Pim	fst 1 3/16	:47 1:104 1:353 1:533	Preakness-G1	6 9 87¼ 54 2hd 22¼	Perret C	126	*1.70	96-12	SmmerSqull1262¼Unbrdld1269MstrFrsky126½	Best of others	9
5May90- 8CD	gd 1¼	:46 1:11 1:373 2:02	Ky Derby-G1	8 11 1214 2½ 11 13½	Perret C	126	10.80	101-00	Unbrdld1263½SummrSqull1266PlsntTp1263	Tight st.,driving	15
14Apr90- 8Kee	my 1⅛	:474 1:121 1:351 1:483	Blue Grass-G2	4 5 52 41¾ 31½ 33¾	Perret C	121	4.10	87-10	SmmerSquall1211¾LandRush1212Unbridld1213	Flattened out	5
17Mar90-10GP	fst 1⅛	:482 1:123 1:39 1:52	Florida Derby-G1	4 5 42 41¾ 31 14	Day P	122	2.50	77-22	Unbridled1224Slavic122nkRunTurn1221	Brushed str,driving	9
3Mar90-10GP	fst 1 1/16	:232 :473 1:122 1:443	Fountain of Youth-G2	5 10 127 99¼ 51¾ 3½	Day P	117	7.60e	87-24	Shot Gun Scott122½Smelly119noUnbridled117¾	Lacked room	13
14Jan90-10Crc	fst 1⅛	:483 1:131 1:384 1:522	Trop Park Derby-G3	4 3 32 32½ 43½ 55¾	Perret C	119	*1.30	91-11	Run Turn1174¼Country Day112hdShot Gun Scott119½	Tired	8
24Dec89-10Crc	fst 1 1/16	:233 :481 1:131 1:451	What a Pleasure 56k	9 8 85½ 74¼ 2hd 15	Velez JA Jr	112	*1.50	96-11	Unbridled1125Fiery Best1172½Always Running115nk	Bumped,drew clear	10
22Oct89-10Crc	fst 1 1/16	:25 :494 1:143 1:473	Ⓡ In Reality (FSS) 450k	4 10 85¼ 54¼ 32 22¾	Velez JA Jr	120	5.20	81-19	Shot Gun Scott1202¾Unbridled120¾Swedaus1203½	Rallied	14
24Sep89- 9Cby	fst 1	:231 :461 1:11 1:371	Cby Juvenile 150k	1 4 74½ 42½ 2½ 2½	Smith ME	120	5.20e	89-15	Appealing Breeze120½Unbridled1204½Table Limit1203½	Hung	7
13Sep89- 8AP	sly 7f	:223 :461 1:112 1:24	Arch Ward 37k	1 5 54½ 54 312 319¾	Smith ME	115	3.30	62-31	Karen'sTom1122¾SecretHello12217Unbridld1157½	No threat	5
23Aug89- 8AP	fst 6½f	:221 :45 1:104 1:171	Waukegan BC 55k	7 7 79½ 613 38½ 37	Smith ME	116	*1.10	82-21	SecretHello1165Karen'sTom1132Unbridld1161¼	Broke inside	8
2Aug89- 4AP	fst 6f	:223 :461 1:113	Md Sp Wt	10 11 64¾ 11½ 17 110½	Smith ME	122	*3.10	82-20	Unbrdld12210½SoundofCannons122½HomeatLast122nk	Easily	1

1991: Strike the Gold's victory exposed the fatal flaw of the modern theory of Dosage and the Kentucky Derby. While the original theory of Dosage is a very real and viable method of determining a horse's aptitude at a distance (short or long), the crack in the modern version of Dosage's armor regarding its influence on the Kentucky Derby is due to two major factors. 1) As Dosage figures are assigned by a single person (and not a committee), they are too arbitrary, and 2) the awarding of Chefs-de-Race (select stallions who have had an influence on the breed) status is flawed because young stallions cannot be designated Chefs-de-Race until they have proven themselves—which, in the case of many sires of Derby winners, is after the fact.

The case of Strike the Gold was simply common sense. His sire, Alydar, was an established sire by the time Strike the Gold was 3, but inexplicably, as everyone now knows, Alydar was not given Chef-de-Race status until *after* the Derby. As a result, Strike the

Gold's Dosage was way over the 4.00 maximum, which was terribly misleading. Devout Dosage followers stayed away from Strike the Gold, despite the fact that his pedigree screamed stamina. He was by Alydar out of a mare by Hatchet Man (by strong stamina influence The Axe II), and pedigree handicappers never needed a number to tell them Strike the Gold would be at the top of his game at 1¼ miles and beyond. And his style of running bore this out. In the Florida Derby, he lost by a length to the more brilliant Fly So Free, but it was clear that Strike the Gold was improving with each race at age 3. He turned the tables on Fly So Free when he defeated the 2-year-old champion by three lengths in the Blue Grass Stakes immediately preceding his Derby score. Blindly dismissing his chances in the Derby due to his false high Dosage spelled the beginning of the end for Dosage.

Fly So Free was an example of a very talented horse who just was not meant to be at his best at 1¼ miles. A champion at 2 when he won four of six starts, including his last two juvenile races, the Champagne Stakes and Breeders' Cup Juvenile, Fly So Free was

Strike the Gold
Own: William J. Condren

Ch. h. 5 (Mar)
Sire: Alydar (Raise a Native)
Dam: Majestic Gold (Hatchet Man)
Br: Calumet Farm (Ky)
Tr: Zito Nicholas P(0 0 0 0 .00) 2004c:(281 45 .16)

Life 31 6 8 5 $3,457,026 112
1993 3 1 0 1 $75,600 110
1992 13 2 5 1 $1,920,176 112

D.Fst 24 3 7 5 $2,662,106 112
Wet(377) 4 2 1 0 $777,520 111
Turf(278) 0 0 0 0 $0 –
Dst(0) 0 0 0 0 $0 –

[race past performance chart rows]

─── **163** ───

essentially a miler who was able to stretch his speed an extra fur-long because of his high class. Fly So Free was by Time for a Change (a half-brother to Adjudicating and Dispute, by Damascus), a horse of considerable speed who captured Hialeah's two glamour races for 3-year-olds, the Everglades and Flamingo Stakes in 1984, when those races had national prominence. But Time for a Change, who died young, was a speed influence, siring such runners as Technology, Time Bandit, Term Limits, Iron Gavel, and Why Change. Fly So Free was easily the best runner sired by Time for a Change, but he was always questionable at $1\frac{1}{4}$ miles.

1992: By the rather obscure stallion At the Threshold (who finished third in the 1984 Kentucky Derby), Lil E. Tee did not have the most fashionable pedigree, but with Buckpasser as his paternal grandsire, he certainly had staying power, and his races leading up to the Derby (second behind Pine Bluff in the Arkansas Derby and win-ner of the Jim Beam Stakes) suggested he was capable of compet-ing at the highest level at the distance. With pre-race favorite A.P. Indy scratched on the morning of the Derby, favoritism went to Arazi due to the memory of his stunning performance winning the Breeders' Cup Juvenile over the Churchill strip only six months ear-lier. But that was a different Arazi, the one before surgery, who was possibly the best example of a special animal who was mishandled just to get into the Derby. His light European campaign at age 3 left him ill-suited for a try in the Derby, and Arazi finished a game but tired eighth out of 18 runners.

Runners who could have been dismissed that year included Technology (10th), by Time for a Change; West By West (11th), essentially a miler, by Gone West; Thyer (13th), a colt by Nijinsky II who was better suited to grass; Ecstatic Ride (14th), by another turf sire, I'm Glad; Sir Pinder (15th), by Baldski, purely a sire of speed; and Pistols and Roses (16th), who had nothing but speed top and bottom (Darn That Alarm out of a mare by Princely Pleasure).

Lil E. Tee
Own: W. Cal Partee

B. c. 4 (Mar)
Sire: At the Threshold (Norcliffe) $1,500
Dam: Eileen's Moment (For The Moment)
Br: Larry Littman (Pa)
Tr: Whiting Lynn S(0 0 0 0 .00) 2004:(94 16 .17)

Life	13	7	4	1	$1,437,506	116	D.Fst	10	5	3	1	$1,043,594 109
1993	3	2	1	0	$260,400	116	Wet(277)	3	2	1	0	$393,912 116
1992	6	3	1	1	$1,148,000	107	Turf(270)	0	0	0	0	$0 –
	0	0	0	0	$0	-	Dst(0)	0	0	0	0	$0 –

10Apr93-8OP	fst	1⅛	:464 1:102 1:353 1:483	4↑ OaklawnH-G1	109	7	21½	21½	1hd	13	21¼	Day P	L123 f	*1.10	- -	Jovial1171¼ Lil E. Tee1231¼ Best Pal1231¼	Rallied, outfinished	10
20Mar93-10OP	my	1 1/16	:223 :46 1:102 1:412	4↑ RazrbakH-G2	116	3	47	43¾	1½	11	11¼	Day P	L123 f	*.40	- -	Lil E. Tee1231¼ Zeeruler1157 Senor Tomas114nk	Gamely	7
20Feb93-8OP	fst	6f	:214 :45 1:082	4↑ Alw 34000N$Y	108	3	3	43	32	21	11¼	Day P	L115 f	*1.10	- -	*Lil E. Tee*1151¼ *Darrell Darrell*1214 *Guns of Cielo*1152	Blocked, late rally	8
16May92-10Pim	fst	1 3/16	:461 1:104 1:36 1:553	Preaknes-G1	96	9	118¼	914	87¼	57	55	Day P	126	4.20	- -	Pine Bluff126¾ *Alydeed*1261½ Casual Lies126¾	Swung wide,closed well	14
2May92-8CD	fst	1¼	:474 1:121 1:373 2:03	KyDerby-G1	107	10	105½	105¼	55	2½	11	Day P	B126	16.80	- -	Lil E. Tee1261 Casual Lies1263¼ Dance Floor1262	Circled field,driving	18
18Apr92-9OP	fst	1⅛	:473 1:113 1:37 1:492	ArkDerby-G2	107	6	42	21	2hd	2hd	2nk	Day P	122 f	2.10	- -	Pine Bluff122nk *Lil E. Tee*1227 Desert Force1222½	Dueled,second best	6
28Mar92-10TP	gd	1⅛	:463 1:12 1:393 1:532	JimBeam-G2	95	3	65¾	55	51¾	11	11	Day P	B121 f	4.50	- -	Lil E. Tee1211 Vying Victor121nk *Treekster*121no	Well placed,driving	11
7Mar92-10OP	fst	1	:23 :463 1:11 1:363	Southwest100k	106	4	52	41¼	43	33	32½	Day P	115 f	2.10	- -	Big Sur1192½ *Pine Bluff*122hd *Lil E. Tee*1158	Late rally	6
9Feb92-8OP	fst	6f	:214 :454 1:101	Alw 22000NC	92	6	5	53¾	52	11	14½	Day P	116 f	*.70	- -	Lil E. Tee1164½ Rockford1142½ Mr. Shocker1163	Handily	8
12Nov91-4CD	fst	1	:223 :46 1:122 1:39	Alw 22395NC	–	7	43½	2hd	12	12	13	Day P	LB115	*.60	- -	*Lil E. Tee*1153 Correntino1183 In My Footsteps121nk	Driving	8
1Nov91-4CD	sly	1 1/16	:241 :49 1:15 1:484	Alw 26040NC	–	2	12½	12½	11½	2hd	2nk	Day P	LB112	*.70	- -	Choctaw Ridge118nk *Lil E. Tee*1127 Seaside Dancer121¾	Outfinished	6
Previously trained by Trivigno Michael																		
6Oct91-4Crc	fst	7f	:224 :46 1:111 1:242	Md Sp Wt 16k	–	7	1	4nk	2hd	15	111½	St Leon G	118	*.70	- -	LilETee11811½ KindergrtnChmp1183 LtItBsunny1182	Drew off, ridden out	9
28Sep91-4Crc	fst	6f	:213 :451 1:112	Md Sp Wt 18k	–	2	5	43½	43	23	24½	St Leon G	117	3.70	- -	*ImaBigLeaguer*1174½ *LilE.Tee*1173½ *Bruce'sFolly*1173	No match, second best	10

1993: While the track was listed as fast, the racing gods smiled on Sea Hero (Polish Navy) when the surface really had plenty of moisture in it. Like the majority of runners from the Danzig sire line, Sea Hero had already shown an affinity for off tracks when he won the Champagne Stakes over a wet surface. Although he finished a nonthreatening fourth in the Blue Grass Stakes, he remains a great example of a horse who blossomed big-time in the weeks leading up to the Derby.

Runners who were unlikely to be at their best at 1¼ miles and who finished up the track that year were Mi Cielo (14th), by speed influence Conquistador Cielo; and Storm Tower (16th), winner of a very weak Wood Memorial Stakes that year and by speed sire Irish Tower.

Sea Hero
Own: Rokeby Stable (Paul Mellon)

B. c. 4 (Mar)
Sire: Polish Navy (Danzig) $5,000
Dam: Glowing Tribute (Graustark)
Br: Paul Mellon (Va)
Tr: Miller MacKenzie L(0 0 0 0 .00) 2004:(0 0 .00)

Life	24	6	3	4	$2,929,869	109	D.Fst	13	2	1	2	$1,519,899 109
1994	8	1	2	2	$105,959	106	Wet(296)	3	2	0	0	$1,324,000 105
1993	9	2	0	2	$2,484,190	109	Turf(238)	8	2	2	2	$85,970 106
	0	0	0	0	$0	-	Dst(0)	0	0	0	0	$0 –

15Oct94-8Kee	fst	1⅛	:473 1:12 1:372 1:50	3↑ Fayette-G2	100	7	713	47½	37	56½	56¾	Bailey J D	L114 b	*.90e	- -	SnnySnrs1201¼ KyContndr1172 PowrflPnch117no	Middle move, slow pace	7
3Sep94-8Bel	fm	1 1/16 Ⓣ	:241 :471 1:102 1:40	3↑ BelBdBCH-G3	101	10	41½	52	43½	62¼	52½	Bailey J D	117 b	*2.00e	- -	AnSocology1162 FourstrsAllstr119nk HomofthFr114no	Angled out str, bid	10
20Aug94-8Sar	sf	1⅛ [T]	:482 1:121 1:37 1:494	3↑ Hcp 50000	105	6	64	63½	73¼	42½	31½	Bailey J D	121	3.50	- -	DominantProspect1171½ *RoylMountinInn*120hd SeHero121nk	Split foes, bid	7
30Jly94-9Sar	gd	1½ [T]	:462 1:114 2:283	3↑ SwdDncrH-G1	77	6	712	49	43½	78	717¼	Bailey J D	117	3.30	- -	Alex the Great118¾ Kiri's Clown1122 L'Hermine112hd	Midpack, no bid	10
2Jly94-7Bel	fm	1⅜ [T]	:50 1:14 1:37 2:131	3↑ BwlnGrnH-G2	104	1	31½	31½	43	22½	22¾	Luzzi M J	117	2.20	- -	Turk Passer1102¾ Sea Hero117nk Fraise124nk	Came again, got 2nd	6
18Jun94-8Bel	fst	1⅛	:46 1:092 1:342 1:463	3↑ BroklynH-G2	100	4	34	35½	35½	34	39½	Bailey J D	119	2.10	- -	*Devil His Due*1208¼ Wallenda1181¼ Sea Hero1194	Tired	7
30May94-7Bel	fm	1 1/16 Ⓣ	:23 :46 1:10 1:394	3↑ Alw 44000N$MY	106	2	22	31½	21	11	2nk	Bailey J D	119	*.70	- -	Fourstars Allstar119nk Sea Hero1195 Roman Envoy1195½	Outfinished	6
17May94-8Bel	my	7f	:231 :461 1:102 1:223	3↑ Alw 40000C	105	4	1	32½	21	11½	11¼	Bailey J D	119	*1.70	- -	SeHero1191¼ RockingJosh1152½ DominntProspect1151	4 wide, ridden out	5
19Sep93-8WO	fst	1⅛	:474 1:112 1:362 1:491	MlsonMil-G2	102	3	62¼	53½	54½	68½	35¼	Bailey J D	L126	2.05	- -	Peteski1214½ Cheery Knight117¾ *Sea Hero*1262½	Best stride late	6
21Aug93-7Sar	fst	1¼	:47 1:113 1:37 2:014	Travers-G1	109	7	86¾	83¼	3½	2hd	12	Bailey J D	126	6.70	- -	Sea Hero1262 Kissin Kris1261 Miner's Mark126hd	Circled 4w, driving	11
1Aug93-8Sar	fst	1⅛	:472 1:114 1:362 1:49	JimDandy-G2	93	4	56½	66	52¼	43	47½	Bailey J D	126	5.50	- -	Miner's Mark117nk Virginia Rapids1214½ Colonial Affair1262¾	No late bid	6
5Jun93-9Bel	gd	1½	:484 1:134 2:294	Belmont-G1	86	10	53¾	65	89¾	710	715	Bailey J D	126	3.20	- -	Colonial Affair1262¼ *Kissin Kris*126¾ Wild Gale1262	No rally	13
15May93-10Pim	fst	1 3/16	:464 1:111 1:37 1:563	Preaknes-G1	85	9	98¾	108¼	74¼	75¼	58½	Bailey J D	126	4.30	- -	Prairie Bayou126½ Cherokee Run1267 El Bakan126nk	Wide 2nd turn,no bid	12
1May93-8CD	fst	1¼	:463 1:111 1:364 2:022	KyDerby-G1	105	6	128¼	114½	87¾	12	12½	Bailey J D	L126	12.90	- -	Sea Hero1262½ *Prairie Bayou*126hd Wild Gale126nk	Angled inside driving	19
10Apr93-8Kee	fst	1⅛	:481 1:121 1:37 1:490	BlueGras-G2	91	1	54½	55½	41¾	4¾	42¾	Bailey J D	L121 b	7.70	- -	Prairie Bayou1212 Wallenda121no Dixieland Heat121¾	Even effort	9
Previously trained by Schulhofer Flint S																		
25Feb93-5GP	fm	*1 1/16 Ⓣ	1:463	Alw 33000NC	91	2	21	21½	2½	31½	31½	Bailey J D	120 b	*1.20	- -	*Icy Warning*110¾ Departing Cloud120¾ Sea Hero1205	Stalked pace, hung	5
7Feb93-10GP	fst	1 1/16	:231 :472 1:123 1:462	PalmBch-G3	66	9	49½	45½	53¾	98¼	912½	Bailey J D	117 b	*1.00	- -	Kissin Kris112¾ Pride Prevails1122½ Awad119¾	Well placed, tired	10
Previously trained by Miller Mackenzie																		
31Oct92-8GP	fst	1 1/16	:223 :46 1:102 1:432	BCJuven-G1	72	6	67	63½	62½	75¼	78¾	Bailey J D	122 b	2.40	- -	GildedTime122¾ It'salilknownfact122½ *RiverSpecial*1225	Mid pack, no rally	13
10Oct92-7Bel	gd	1	:22 :443 1:09 1:344	Champagn-G1	99	1	73	31½	2hd	11	15¾	Bailey J D	122 b	8.80	- -	Sea Hero1225¾ Secret Odds1225¾ *Press Card*1222½	Drew off, driving	10
21Sep92-7Bel	fm	1 Ⓣ	:23 :463 1:093 1:343	Alw 29000NC	86	7	43½	42½	3nk	11	13¾	Bailey J D	122 b	*.70	- -	*Sea Hero*1223¾ Similar Star117¾ Compadre1171¼	Ridden out	7
7Sep92-5Bel	fm	1 Ⓣ	:23 :462 1:102 1:352	Md Sp Wt 26k	83	1	53	3½	3nk	1½	12¼	Bailey J D	118	*.90	- -	*Sea Hero*1182¼ *Halissee*1182½ Awad1181½	Drew clear, driving	11
21Aug92-6Sar	fst	7f	:23 :46 1:11 1:24	Md Sp Wt 24k	69	4	8	72¾	63¾	31½	21¼	Madrid A Jr	118	3.00	- -	Thriller Chiller1181¼ *Sea Hero*118nk All Gone1183¼	Bore in start, rallied	10
2Aug92-4Sar	fst	6f	:222 :454 :58 1:102	Md Sp Wt 24k	63	5	3	61¾	63¼	74¼	57¼	Madrid A Jr	118	6.80	- -	Wallenda1182 All Gone1184 D'Orazio118no	Steadied	12
3Jly92-5Bel	fst	5½f	:221 :452 :571 1:03	Md Sp Wt 24k	56	5	6	67	68½	58	413¼	Bailey J D	118	*1.30	- -	StrollngAlong1182½ DvlshlyYors1188½ *DrAlfos*1182¼	Lacked late response	10

1994: Go for Gin (Cormorant) certainly had ability, but a sloppy track moved him up considerably when he won over the more talented but delicate Strodes Creek (Halo). Runners who were total throwouts in 1994 were Powis Castle (eighth), a colt by sprint sire Rare Brick; Smilin Singin Sam (10th), by sprint champion Smile, a pronounced speed influence by In Reality; and Meadow Flight (11th); by strong speed influence Meadowlake.

Go for Gin
Own: W J Condren & J M Cornacchia

B. c. 4 (Apr)
Sire: Cormorant (His Majesty)
Dam: Never Knock (Stage Door Johnny)
Br: Pamela Darmstadt duPont (Ky)
Tr: Zito Nicholas P(0 0 0 0 .00) 2004:(281 45 .16)

Life	19	5	7	2	$1,380,866	112	D.Fst	13	2	4	2	$547,526	111
1995	3	0	2	1	$27,730	103	Wet(316)	6	3	3	0	$833,340	112
1994	11	2	4	1	$1,178,596	112	Turf(320)	0	0	0	0	$0	-
	0	0	0	0	$0	-	Dst(0)	0	0	0	0	$0	-

6May95-5CD	fst	7f	:223	:451	1:092	1:213	4↑CDH-G3	98	7	9	87¼	78	68	32¾	Antley C W	115	3.80	- -	Goldseeker Bud1092 *Level Sands*112¾ Go for Gin115¾	Angled out 6 wide	11
7Apr95-7Kee	fst	*7f	:224	:45	1:094	1:26	4↑Alw 36800N$Y	101	1	2	2½	1hd	21	21½	Antley C W	114	*.70	- -	Prenup1151½ Go for Gin114hd Bonus Money121½	Dueled, gave way	8
4Mar95-10GP	fst	6½f	:222	:452	1:101	1:164	4↑Alw 44000N$Y	103	2	4	36	33	44	2nk	Bailey J D	115	*1.30	- -	*Ponche*119nk Go for Gin115no Lynn's Notebook1153¼	Off slow, rallied	5
5Nov94-10CD	fst	1¼	:463	1:111	1:363	2:022	3↑BCClasic-G1	101	3	43	73¼	74¼	79½	89¼	Pincay L Jr	122	13.20	- -	*Concern*122nk TabascoCat1221½ DrmticGold1221½	Pressed pace, gave way	14
8Oct94-9Bel	fst	1¼	:46	1:10	1:354	2:02	3↑JkyClbGC-G1	91	3	2½	21½	73½	79½	814¾	McCarron C J	121	5.70	- -	Colonial Affair1262 Devil His Due126¾ Flag Down126½	Dueled, flattened	8
17Sep94-8Bel	fst	1⅛	:462	1:102	1:343	1:464	3↑Woodward-G1	99	3	32	32	31½	45	410	McCarron C J	121	7.00	- -	*Holy Bull*1215 Devil His Due1261½ *Colonial Affair*1263½	No late bid	8
24Aug94-9Sar	fst	7f	:244	:473	1:11	1:223	3↑ForegoH-G2	104	6	5	41½	41½	31½	31¾	McCarron C J	117	1.80	- -	American Chance1131 Evil Bear114¾ Go for Gin1173	Rallied inside	7
11Jun94-9Bel	fst	1½	:472	1:111		2:264	Belmont-G1	104	1	11	12	11½	21	22	McCarron C J	126	1.50	- -	Tabasco Cat1262 Go for Gin126½ *Strodes Creek*1263½	Set pace, 2nd best	6
21May94-10Pim	fst	1 3/16	:472	1:114	1:37	1:562	Preaknes-G1	111	2	2½	2hd	1hd	1hd	2¾	McCarron C J	126	*2.80	- -	*Tabasco Cat*126¾ Go for Gin1266 Concern126½	Pace 2-wide, gamely	10
7May94-8CD	sly	1¼	:471	1:114	1:373	2:033	KyDerby-G1	112	8	1½	11½	11	14½	12	McCarron C J	126	9.10	- -	Go for Gin1262 Strodes Creek1262½ Blumin Affair126¾	Drew off, drifted	14
16Apr94-9Aqu	gd	1⅛	:472	1:112	1:362	1:49	WoodMem-G1	107	7	42	31	2hd	21	21½	Bailey J D	123	*.90e	- -	Irgun1231½ *Go for Gin*1238¾ Shiprock1236½	Rallied, 2nd best	9
12Mar94-10GP	fst	1⅛	:46	1:10	1:344	1:473	FlaDerby-G1	104	13	62¾	53½	43½	45	46¾	Bailey J D	122	*2.40e	- -	*Holy Bull*1225¾ Ride the Rails122no Halo's Image1221	Well placed, evenly	14
19Feb94-9GP	gd	1 1/16	:224	:453	1:102	1:443	FntnOYth-G2	98	3	43½	44½	32½	3nk	2¾	Bailey J D	119	1.60	- -	Dehere119¾ Go for Gin1191½ Ride the Rails1173¾	Rallied, gamely	6
22Jan94-9GP	fst	1 1/16	:233	:472	1:112	1:413	Preview75k	100	3	41¼	3½	2hd	1½	13½	Bailey J D	119	*.70	- -	Go forGin1193½ Halo'sImage1141 SenorConquistador1125½	Rated, handily	6
27Nov93-6Aqu	fst	1⅛	:502	1:152	1:394	1:523	Remsen-G2	95	1	11½	11	11	14	18½	Bailey J D	117	*.40e	- -	*Go for Gin*1178½ Arrovente1133½ Linkatariat113hd	Drew off, driving	7
6Nov93-1Aqu	sly	1	:231	:46	1:104	1:37	ChiefsCrwn54k	90	2	1½	11	14	15	19¾	Samyn J L	117	*.40	- -	*Go for Gin*1179¾ Linkatariat11712½ River Arly11712	Drew off, ridden out	4
21Oct93-5Aqu	sly	1	:223	:453	1:101	1:352	Md Sp Wt 27k	90	3	31½	21	21	15	110½	Bailey J D	118	*.90	- -	*Go for Gin*11810½ Retrospection1181¾ *A Track Attack*1183	Ridden out	7
3Oct93-2Bel	my	1	:224	:462	1:114	1:372	Md Sp Wt 27k	79	2	21½	2½	1½	12	21¾	Bailey J D	118	1.90	- -	Arrovente1181¾ *Go for Gin*11812 King of Kolchis1183	Outfinished	5
13Sep93-5Bel	fst	6f	:221	:454	:582	1:11	Md Sp Wt 25k	70	6	11	86½	75½	66½	59¼	Chavez J F	118	22.90	- -	*You and I*1181½ Palance1181¼ *Hussonet*1182¾	Mild rally	11

1995: Thunder Gulch was a late-blooming 2-year-old who was dismissed in the Derby because of a poor effort in the Blue Grass, and he proved once and for all that his champion sprinter/miler sire, Gulch, could get more than just milers. Two years before Thunder Gulch won the Derby, Gulch's son Wallenda captured the Super Derby when it was still run at 1¼ miles. Finishing behind Thunder Gulch were two horses, Tejano Run and Timber Country, who were very playable. Tejano Run was by Tejano, a stakes winner by Caro (sire of 1988 Derby winner Winning Colors) from an especially prolific female family of quality stakes runners. Champion 2-year-old Timber Country was by Woodman, who had sired 3-year-old champion Hansel, winner of the Preakness and Belmont Stakes; in addition, Timber Country's dam, Fall Aspen (1994 Broodmare of the Year), was one of the great broodmares of the last 30 years.

Timber County was coupled in the wagering with fellow D. Wayne Lukas trainee Serena's Song, who, on her own, would have been the worst play in the 1995 Derby. A champion who was one of the most accomplished fillies of the decade, Serena's Song won five straight stakes (including a victory over Tejano Run in the Jim Beam Stakes) leading into the Derby. Her forte was her high cruising speed, and many no doubt saw similarities to Lukas's 1988 champion 3-year-old filly, Winning Colors, who wired her field in the Derby. Unlike Winning Colors, however, Serena's Song was not bred to be at her best against her own sex at 1¼ miles, let alone high-class males. She finished a badly beaten 16th, and Lukas tried her twice more at the distance without success.

Other runners who were at a disadvantage going 1¼ miles in the 1995 Derby were the brilliant Afternoon Deelites (by Private Terms, who finished ninth as the lukewarm 3-1 favorite in the 1988 Kentucky Derby), who finished eighth; and Suave Prospect, who was second in the Fountain of Youth, Florida Derby, and Blue Grass, but was not bred to handle 1¼ miles (by speed influence Fortunate Prospect) and finished 11th. Talkin Man, who had shown speed and class, was by grass star With Approval and was better suited to turf; he finished 12th. Dazzling Falls, by high speed influence Taylor's Falls (In Reality), was 13th; Ski Captain (who was by grass influence Storm Bird out of a mare by Royal Ski, a source of speed) finished 14th.

Thunder Gulch
Own: Michael Tabor

Ch. c. 3 (May)
Sire: Gulch (Mr. Prospector) $50,000
Dam: Line of Thunder (Storm Bird)
Br: Peter M. Brant (Ky)
Tr: Lukas D. W(0 0 0 0 .00) 2004:(359 40 .11)

Life	16	9	2	2	$2,915,086	110	D.Fst	15	9	1	2	$2,890,798	110
1995	10	7	0	1	$2,644,080	110	Wet(340)	1	0	1	0	$24,288	79
1994	6	2	2	1	$271,006	99	Turf(292)	0	0	0	0	$0	-
	0	0	0	0	$0	-	Dst(0)	0	0	0	0	$0	-

7Oct95-10Bel	fst	1¼	:48	1:112	1:36	2:011	3↑JkyClbGC-G1	90	4	21	31	45	49½	514	Stevens G L	121 b	3.05	-	-	*Cigar*1261 UnaccountedFor1269¾ StarStandard1212	Hard ridden turn,tired	7
23Sep95-10TP	fst	1⅛	:473	1:114	1:364	1:492	3↑KyCpClsscH396k	108	5	52¾	43	2½	2hd	11	Stevens G L	121 b	*.20	-	-	Thunder Gulch1211 *JudgeTC*1121½ BoundbyHonor1138	Raced 4 wide, clear	6
19Aug95-8Sar	fst	1¼	:471	1:112	1:371	2:033	Travers-G1	110	5	41½	42	1½	1½	14½	Stevens G L	126 b	*.75	-	-	*Thunder Gulch*1264½ Pyramid Peak1262 Malthus1262½	Quick outs move	7
23Jly95-8Hol	fst	1⅛	:462	1:101	1:353	1:49	Swaps-G2	101	4	21	2½	21	1hd	12	Stevens G L	B126 b	*.90	-	-	*Thunder Gulch*1262 *Da Hoss*118¾ *Petionville*120¾	Drew clear, driving	7
10Jun95-9Bel	fst	1½	:501	1:151		2:32	Belmont-G1	101	10	31	2½	2hd	1hd	12	Stevens G L	126 b	*1.50	-	-	*ThunderGulch*1262 StarStandard1263½ Citdeed1261½	Prominent, prevailed	11
20May95-10Pim	fst	1 3/16	:471	1:104	1:352	1:542	Preaknes-G1	105	11	54½	55	54½	4¾	3¾	Stevens G L	126 b	3.80	-	-	TmbrCountry126½ OlvrsTwst126nk *ThundrGlch*1264	3w advance,outfnshed	11
6May95-8CD	fst	1¼	:454	1:101	1:353	2:011	KyDerby-G1	108	16	53½	42	21	12	12¼	Stevens G L	126 b	24.50	-	-	ThundrGulch1262¼ TjnoRun126hd *TimbrCountry*126¾	Drew clear ridden out	19
15Apr95-7Kee	fst	1⅛	:49	1:131	1:372	1:491	BlueGras-G2	101	4	31½	31	3½	42¼	44½	Day P	121 b	*1.30	-	-	WildSyn1212½ SuveProspect121hd TejnoRun1212	Pressed pace, gave way	6
11Mar95-10GP	fst	1⅛	:471	1:113	1:362	1:493	FlaDerby-G1	101	7	32½	31½	2½	21½	1no	Smith M E	122 b	2.00	-	-	Thunder Gulch122no Suave Prospect1225 Mecke1222	All out, just up	10
18Feb95-9GP	fst	1 1/16	:231	:464	1:11	1:431	FntnOYth-G2	105	9	72	62	3nk	1hd	1nk	Smith M E	119 b	4.70	-	-	*ThunderGulch*119nk SuaveProspect1174 JamblyJzz1193½	Dueled, prevailed	12
18Dec94-8Hol	fst	1 1/16	:224	:46	1:093	1:403	HolFut-G1	99	1	47	47½	47	25	26½	Nakatani C S	B121 b	3.80	-	-	*Afternoon Deelites*1216½ *Thunder Gulch*12110 A. J. Jett121½	Best of rest	5
26Nov94-7Aqu	fst	1⅛	:481	1:14	1:402	1:534	Remsen-G2	89	9	75	73¾	41¼	21	1nk	Stevens G L	115	5.60	-	-	ThunderGulch115nk WestrnEcho1193 MightyMg114¾	Lugged in str, drvng	10
Previously trained by Kimmel John C																						
11Nov94-8Aqu	fst	1	:23	:461	1:111	1:372	Nashua-G3	79	6	42½	42½	41½	42½	44¾	Bailey J D	112	*1.35	-	-	Devious Course1142 Mighty Magee1122¾ Old Tascosa122no	No threat	7
23Oct94-8Aqu	my	7f	:222	:454	1:111	1:243	Cowdin-G2	79	4	7	65	74	35	22½	Velazquez J R	122	4.40	-	-	Old Tascosa1222½ Thunder Gulch1221½ Adams Trail1222¼	Rallied inside	8
4Oct94-3Bel	fst	6f	:224	:463	:583	1:11	Md Sp Wt 28k	82	4	3	73¼	31	31	1no	Velazquez J R	118	*1.00	-	-	Thunder Gulch118no Porphyry118½ Last Effort1181½	Driving	9
16Sep94-3Bel	fst	6f	:224	:463	:584	1:111	Md Sp Wt 28k	69	2	3	41¼	51¼	31	3nk	Velazquez J R	118	6.50	-	-	Crusader's Story118no Porphyry118nk *Thunder Gulch*1181½	Rough trip	8

1996: Unbridled, winner of the 1990 Kentucky Derby and Breeders' Cup Classic, established himself as a budding superstar stallion when he sired a Derby winner (Grindstone) in his first crop, as well as the immensely talented, but equally unsound, Unbridled's Song. This was a year where many of the starters had the pedigree to be effective at 1¼ miles, including the runner-up, Cavonnier, who was dismissed by many because of his obscure sire (Batonnier).

Cavonnier won the Santa Anita Derby, and while his sire did not have the appeal of a Danzig or a Mr. Prospector, he was certainly bred for stamina. Batonnier was a stakes winner by the very successful sire His Majesty (Ribot) out of Mira Femme, one of the best 2-year-old fillies of her generation and a prominent member of Verne Winchell's broodmare band. Cavonnier not only inherited stamina from his sire line, but also from his damsire, Caveat (winner of the 1983 Belmont Stakes), a very strong source of stamina as well. The piece de resistance, however, was Cavonnier's female family, cultivated by John Nerud and Tartan Farms. His fourth dam was the legendary Aspidistra, the dam of Horse of the Year Dr. Fager (Rough'n Tumble), champion sprinter Ta Wee (Intentionally), and the unraced Magic (Buckpasser), who was not only Cavonnier's third dam, but also the third dam of Unbridled.

Finishing a close third to Grindstone and Cavonnier was Prince of Thieves (Hansel), a three-quarter brother to Timber Country, and a definite contender.

But some highly regarded Derby runners that year who had little chance at 1¼ miles were Diligence (Miswaki, ninth); Victory Speech (Deputy Minister, 10th); Zarb's Magic (Zarbyev, 13th); Semoran (Phone Trick, 14th); In Contention (Devil's Bag, 15th); Matty G. (Capote, 17th); Honour and Glory (Relaunch, 18th); and Built for Pleasure (Homebuilder, 19th).

Grindstone
Own: Overbrook Farm

Dk. b or b. h. 11 (Jan)
Sire: Unbridled (Fappiano) $200,000
Dam: Buzz My Bell (Drone)
Br: Overbrook Farm (Ky)
Tr: Lukas D. W(0 0 0 0 .00) 2004:(454 53 .12)

Life	6	3	2	0	$1,224,510	112	D.Fst	6	3	2	0	$1,224,510	112
1996	4	2	2	0	$1,201,000	112	Wet(381)	0	0	0	0	$0	-
1995	2	1	0	0	$23,510	90	Turf(275)	0	0	0	0	$0	-
	0	0	0	0	$0	-	Dst(T)(336)	0	0	0	0	$0	-

4May96-8CD	fst	1¼	:46	1:10	1:35	2:01	KyDerby-G1	**112**	15	1512	137¾	89	43½	1no	Bailey J D	126	5.90e	-	-	Grindstone126no Cvonnier1263½ PrincofThivs126nk	Angld out just up late	19
13Apr96-9OP	fst	1⅛	:45	1:094	1:361	1:491	ArkDerby-G2	**100**	12	89¾	813	65½	21	2nk	Bailey J D	122	*1.60	-	-	Zarb's Magic122nk *Grindstone*1222¾ Halo Sunshine122no	Gaining 4 wide	12
17Mar96-9FG	fst	1 1/16	:231	:462	1:112	1:423	LaDerby-G3	**102**	4	43	33	41¾	1hd	13½	Bailey J D	118	2.40	-	-	Grindstone1183½ *ZarbsMgic*1224 CommndersPlce1182	Well placed, driving	8
16Feb96-3SA	fst	1	:224	:47	1:112	1:36	Alw 46000N1x	**92**	6	74¼	52½	41	22½	23	Stevens G L	B115	*1.60	-	-	Budroyale1163 *Grindstone*115¾ Tibet117nk	Wide trip, held 2nd	7
1Jly95-9CD	fst	6f	:211	:452		1:112	BshfdMnr-G3	**84**	6	7	54	74¾	711	41¼	Barton D M	115	*.90	-	-	*AVEight*1151 AggieSouthpw115nk SkrsRwrd115no	Bumpd hard altrd cours	8
11Jun95-2Bel	fst	5f	:222	:463		:59	Md Sp Wt 30k	**90**	2	5	56¼	42	11½	15	Santos J A	116	3.05	-	-	Grindstone1165 Sierra Grande1168 Fig Fest1161	Quick 5 wide move	5

1997: This was a year in which pedigree did not play a role. There was nothing in Silver Charm's pedigree to suggest he would become a stakes winner (nor, for that matter, in the pedigree of either Captain Bodgit or Free House, who finished second and third), let alone a dual classic winner. While his sire, Silver Buck, was a solid if not dazzling stakes winner and had a super pedigree (by Buckpasser out of a high-quality C.V. Whitney female family), his female family was—to put it bluntly—abysmal. But Silver Charm, Captain Bodgit, and Free House had proven long before the Derby that they were a formidable trio—pedigree or no pedigree.

Captain Bodgit was from the first crop of Saint Ballado (a stakes-winning full brother to champions Devil's Bag and Glorious Song), and to date, he is one of the few runners by Saint Ballado (a pronounced speed influence) who was effective at 1¼ miles.

Free House also had humble beginnings. His modest pedigree (by Smokester out of a Vigors mare) belied true talent and grit and he epitomized the phrase "outrunning his pedigree."

Horses that were questionable at the Derby distance, however, were Phantom on Tour (by speed influence Tour d'Or), who finished sixth, and Hello (by grass sire Lycius), eighth.

Silver Charm
Own: Lewis Robert B. and Beverly J

Gr/ro. h. 5 (Feb)
Sire: Silver Buck (Buckpasser) $7,500
Dam: Bonnie's Poker (Poker)
Br: Mary Lou Wootton (Fla)
Tr: Baffert Bob(0 0 0 0 .00) 2004:(371 70 .19)

Life	**24**	**12**	**7**	**2**	**$6,944,369**	**123**	**D.Fst**	**23**	**11**	**7**	**2**	**$6,644,369**
1999	5	1	0	2	$431,363	118	Wet(309)	1	1	0	0	$300,000
1998	9	6	2	0	$4,696,506	123	Turf(235)	0	0	0	0	$0
	0	0	0	0	$0	-	Dst(0)	0	0	0	0	$0

12Jun99-9CD	fst	1⅛	:464 1:11 1:352 1:471	3↑ SFosterH-G2	**104**	3	42½	44½	42½	44	48½	Antley C W	L123	1.40	98-03	*VictoryGllop*1205 *NiteDremr*110¾ Littlbitlivly1152¾ Hopped start,weakened
Previously trained by Baffert Bob																
28Mar99♦Nad Al Sheba (UAE)	ft	*1¼	LH 2:003	4↑ Dubai World Cup-G1 Stk 5000000							614¼	Stevens G	126	-		Almutawakel126¾ Malek126¾ *Victory Gallop*1261½
Timeform rating: 101																*Tracked in 5th,weakened over 2f out.Daylami 5th,Running Stag*
Previously trained by Baffert Bob																
6Mar99-5SA	fst	1¼	:472 1:112 1:352 2:003	4↑ SAH-G1	**118**	1	31½	41¼	42¼	41½	31	Stevens G L	LB124	*1.00	97-11	FreeHouse123½ EventoftheYer119½ SilvrChrm1243 Came back on outsid
30Jan99-10GP	fst	1⅛	:463 1:102 1:353 1:481	3↑ DonnH-G1	**106**	12	99½	99¼	76¾	63½	35¼	Stevens G L	L126	*.80	91-14	Puerto Madero1202¾ *Behrens*1132½ Silver Charm126nk Mild wide ral
10Jan99-8SA	fst	1¹⁄₁₆	:242 :472 1:104 1:413	4↑ SnPsqalH-G2	**109**	3	33	38½	36	31	11¼	Stevens G L	LB125	*.30	95-10	Silver Charm1251¼ Malek1193½ Crafty Friend1182 Rallied,good handlir
27Nov98-11CD	fst	1⅛	:472 1:112 1:361 1:49	3↑ ClarkH-G2	**113**	2	1hd	1hd	2hd	2½	1hd	Stevens G L	L124	*.30	99-14	*SilverChrm*124hd Littlebitlively1131 WildRush117½ Dueled, headed, game
7Nov98-10CD	fst	1¼	:473 1:12 1:371 2:02	3↑ BCClasic-G1	**115**	8	52¼	41	2½	1hd	2¾	Stevens G L	L126	2.50	94-07	Awesome Again126¾ *Silver Charm*126nk Swain126no Led, drifted la
17Oct98-8SA	fst	1⅛	:464 1:101 1:343 1:471	3↑ GdwdBCH-G2	**111**	5	34½	31½	3½	1hd	12½	Stevens G L	LB124	*.50	100-07	Silver Charm1242½ *Free House*1242½ Score Quick1156 Bid 3 wide, drivir
26Sep98-10TP	fst	1⅛	:462 1:10 1:343 1:472	3↑ KyCpClH-G3	**123**	1	32	31	2hd	2hd	117	♦Stevens G L	L123	*.50	100-14	DH *SilverCharm*123 DH WildRush11717 Acceptable1175 Long drive, brushe
25Jly98-8Dmr	fst	1¹⁄₁₆	:23 :464 1:102 1:41	3↑ SnDiegoH-G3	**63**	4	21½	21	31	510	527	Stevens G L	LB125	*.30	72-09	Mud Route1176 Hal's Pal1135½ Benchmark1175½ Stalked,gave wa
13Jun98-9CD	fst	1⅛	:464 1:11 1:36 1:483	3↑ SFosterH-G2	**116**	1	35	44	31	1½	21	Stevens G L	L127	*.40	100-07	*AwesomeAgain*1131 SilverCharm1275¼ Semoran1142¼ Drifted, bumped 1/
Previously trained by Baffert Bob																
28Mar98♦Nad Al Sheba (UAE)	ft	*1¼	LH 2:041	4↑ Dubai World Cup-G1 Stk 4000000							1no	Stevens G	126	-		Silver Charm126no Swain1262½ Loup Sauvage126no
Timeform rating: 129+																*Tracked in 3rd,led over 2f out,repelled challenges,a*
Previously trained by Baffert Bob																
7Feb98-8SA	wf	1⅛	:472 1:11 1:344 1:471	Strub-G2	**113**	3	21	32	3½	12	14	Stevens G L	LB123	*.30	100-07	*Silver Charm*1234 *Mud Route*1172 Bagshot1177 4 wide 2nd tu
17Jan98-8SA	fst	1¹⁄₁₆	:241 :482 1:121 1:414	SnFndoBC-G2	**112**	1	21½	21½	2½	1hd	11	Stevens G L	LB122	*.20	94-13	*Silver Charm*1221 Mud Route1163 *Lord Grillo*12010 Left handed urgi
26Dec97-8SA	fst	7f	:222 :45 1:092 1:212	Malibu-G1	**109**	6	5	51¾	41½	31	2½	Stevens G L	LB123	*.30e	96-13	Lord Grillo119½ *SilverCharm*1233 SwissYodeler1152 Blocked upper stret
7Jun97-9Bel	fst	1½	:491 1:134 2:284	Belmont-G1	**109**	2	31	2hd	1hd	1hd	2¾	Stevens G L	L126	*1.05	89-14	*Touch Gold*126¾ Silver Charm1261 *FreeHouse*12614 Speed outside,led,ga
17May97-10Pim	fst	1³⁄₁₆	:464 1:102 1:352 1:544	Preaknes-G1	**118**	7	44½	31½	21	21	1hd	Stevens G L	L126	3.10	93-15	SilverChrm126hd FreeHouse126hd CptinBodgit1261¼ Stalk 3w,all out bt
3May97-8CD	fst	1¼	:472 1:121 1:371 2:022	KyDerby-G1	**115**	5	42½	41¼	3½	1hd	1hd	Stevens G L	L126	4.00	93-05	*SilverChrm*126hd CptinBodgit1263½ FreeHouse1263 Steadied, brushd las
5Apr97-6SA	fst	1⅛	:45 1:09 1:342 1:473	SADerby-G1	**110**	3	2½	2½	2hd	1hd	2hd	Stevens G L	LB120	2.10	95-10	Free House120hd *Silver Charm*1202 Hello120no Fast pace,just mis
16Mar97-7SA	fst	1¹⁄₁₆	:223 :46 1:101 1:422	SnFelipe-G2	**102**	6	51¾	54	53¾	32	2¾	McCarron C J	LB122	*1.10e	90-12	*FreeHouse*119¾ SilverCharm1221 KingCrimson116¾ Angled out,finshd w
8Feb97-6SA	fst	7f	:222 :444 1:084 1:21	SnVicnte-G3	**110**	5	5	31	42½	1½	11¾	McCarron C J	LB120	2.60e	99-13	Silver Charm1201¾ *Free House*1202 *Funontherun*114½ Perfect trip, driv
11Sep96-8Dmr	fst	7f	:223 :451 1:093 1:224	DmrFut-G2	**97**	7	3	21	31½	2hd	1hd	Flores D R	LB116	1.60e	86-15	*SilvrChrm*116hd GoldTribut1153½ SwissYodlr1212¾ Wore down entry m
24Aug96-6Dmr	fst	5½f	:214 :444 :57 1:031	Md Sp Wt 37k	**95**	2	2	1hd	1½	11½	11¼	Flores D R	LB118	*.40e	97-09	*Silver Charm*1181¼ Gold Tribute1188 So Easy1185 Fast pace, driv
10Aug96-3Dmr	fst	6f	:214 :444 :572 1:10	Md Sp Wt 37k	**77**	2	4	1hd	1hd	1½	24	Flores D R	B118 b	2.80e	85-08	DeedsNotWords1184 *SilverChrm*1181 *ConstntDemnd*118¾ Rushed,fast p

1998: Real Quiet was from the third crop of NYRA Mile winner Quiet American, who also finished second in the Charles H. Strub Stakes (at 1¼ miles) and the Woodward (at 1⅛ miles). Real Quiet's dam was by the talented Believe It (In Reality), who had the misfortune of being in the same crop as superstars Affirmed and Alydar. Real Quiet's true allure was his female family—his second dam was a full sister to 1969 Derby and Preakness winner Majestic Prince and English 2-year-old champion Crowned Prince. This extraordinary female line produced five-time Horse of the Year Kelso, as well as Graustark and His Majesty.

Derby runner-up Victory Gallop had a pedigree for a mile and a quarter—and beyond. He was by Cryptoclearance, a son of Fappiano (also the sire of Quiet American and Unbridled), and his running style also suggested he would be effective at the Derby distance.

Santa Anita Derby winner Indian Charlie, who was undefeated entering the Derby, was always suspect at 1¼ miles because of his sire, In Excess, but his class allowed him to finish third in what was, sadly, his last race.

The big toss in the 1998 Derby was champion 2-year-old and Horse of the Year Favorite Trick. A colt of unquestionable ability, he was by sprint sire Phone Trick and was always doubtful to get 1¼ miles. The handwriting was on the wall when he finished third in the Arkansas Derby behind Victory Gallop after leading all the way. Favorite Trick was no factor in the Kentucky Derby and finished a tired eighth, 12½ lengths behind Real Quiet.

Artax, who showed speed at 2 finishing second behind Real Quiet in the Hollywood Futurity, was exposed as a sprinter/miler in the Santa Anita Derby, where he finished a poor third, beaten 9¼ lengths. Despite this showing, Artax got some support in the Kentucky Derby at 11-1, but finished 13th out of 15 starters. By Marquetry (a speed influence by Conquistador Cielo), Artax got more speed and little stamina from his damsire, the very quick Apalachee, a champion 2-year-old in Europe.

Real Quiet
Own: Pegram Michael E

B. c. 4 (Mar)
Sire: Quiet American (Fappiano) $35,000
Dam: Really Blue (Believe It)
Br: Little Hill Farm (Ky)
Tr: Baffert Bob(0 0 0 0 .00) 2004:(371 70 .19)

Life	20	6	5	6	$3,271,802	115	D.Fst	18	6	5	5	$3,268,462 115
1999	5	2	2	1	$1,101,880	115	Wet(360)	2	0	0	1	$3,340 74
1998	6	2	3	0	$1,788,800	111	Turf(256)	0	0	0	0	$0 -
	0	0	0	0	$0	-	Dst(0)	0	0	0	0	$0 -

Previously trained by Baffert Bob

27Jun99-5Hol	fst	1¼	:47 1:102 1:342 1:593	3↑HolGldCp-G1	115	2	42	41½	41½	31½	1½	Bailey J D	LB124 b	*.90	97-03	Real Quiet124½ Budroyale124nk *Malek*1247	Trapped rail 2nd turn	4
29May99-13Suf	fst	1⅛	:472 1:11 1:36 1:49	3↑MassH-G2	112	2	2½	21	3½	32	33¼	Stevens G L	LB121 b	*.80	88-16	*Behrens*118½ *Running Stag*1132¾ *Real Quiet*1214½	3p, bid 2nd, weakened	6
8May99-6Pim	fst	1 3/16	:47 1:111 1:36 1:541	3↑PimSpclH-G1	113	5	34	32½	33	2hd	1nk	Stevens G L	L120 b	1.90	94-19	RealQuiet120nk FreeHouse1245 FredBearClw1132	Aim 3w,dueled,long drv	5
18Apr99-7LS	fst	1	:24 :471 1:111 1:353	3↑TexsMile-G3	110	5	43½	34½	1½	2½	2nk	Stevens G L	L116 b	*.50	94-15	Littlebitlively116nk *Real Quiet*1161¾ Allen's Oop1134¾	Outfinished	8
7Mar99-8FG	fst	1⅛	:483 1:124 1:364 1:49	4↑NwOrlnsH-G3	102	6	31½	21½	21	2½	2½	Desormeaux K J	L122 b	*.50	94-13	Precocity118½ Real Quiet122nk Allen's Oop108¾	3w, 4w, bid, no match	6
6Jun98-9Bel	fst	1½	:483 1:132 2:29	Belmont-G1	110	7	64	31	1½	14	2no	Desormeaux K J	L126 b	*.80	99-09	Victory Gallop126no Real Quiet1266 *Thomas Jo*1261¼	Clear, bumpd missed	11
16May98-10Pim	fst	1 3/16	:462 1:11 1:354 1:543	Preaknss-G1	111	10	85½	69	51¾	1½	12¼	Desormeaux K J	L126 b	2.50	92-13	Real Quiet1262¼ *Victory Gallop*126¾ Classic Cat1263¾	4-6wd trip,lug in,drvg	10
2May98-8CD	fst	1¼	:453 1:103 1:353 2:021	KyDerby-G1	107	3	68	65¾	11	11½	1½	Desormeaux K J	L126 b	8.40	94-02	*Real Quiet*126½ Victory Gallop1262¼ Indian Charlie126hd	Led mile, lasted	15
4Apr98-5SA	fst	1⅛	:46 1:094 1:342 1:47	SADerby-G1	107	7	66	56½	45	23	22¼	Desormeaux K J	LB120 b	3.00	99-05	Indian Charlie1202¼ *Real Quiet*1207 Artax1206	Slowly gaining	7
14Mar98-8SA	fst	1 1/16	:224 :464 1:104 1:413	SnFelipe-G2	108	5	32½	33	2½	21	2hd	Desormeaux K J	LB119 b	4.10	95-11	Artax122hd Real Quiet1197 Prosperous Bid1166	Gaining late stretch	5
18Jan98-7GG	sly	1 1/16	:222 :461 1:104 1:431	GGDerby200k	59	7	76½	55½	65¾	812	822½	Desormeaux K J	LB120 b	*1.10	63-19	CloverHunter1206½ MantlesStar1201½ AllensOop1204	Gave way btwn foes	8
14Dec97-7Hol	fst	1 1/16	:223 :454 1:101 1:411	HolFut-G1	102	2	42½	41¾	21½	1hd	11	Desormeaux K J	LB121 b	*1.50e	95-11	Real Quiet1211 Artax1211¾ Nationalore1211	Fully extended	11
29Nov97-11CD	fst	1 1/16	:232 :47 1:12 1:434	B&WKyJC-G3	93	6	106½	86¾	62¾	55½	31¾	Flores D R	L116 b	12.40	90-09	*Cape Town*113½ *Time Limit*1191¼ *Real Quiet*1161½	Late bid finished well	11
18Oct97-3SA	fst	1 1/16	:232 :472 1:122 1:441	Md Sp Wt 35k	87	7	63	51½	42	2½	13	Desormeaux K J	LB120 b	1.60	82-19	Real Quiet1203 Opine1207 Sydney Harbour1205	Wide early,strng finsh	7
5Sep97-6Dmr	fst	1	:221 :454 1:104 1:363	Md Sp Wt 39k	78	7	66	78½	55	33½	48	Stevens S A	LB118 f	2.20e	79-13	Old Trieste1182½ *Johnbill*1185½ Just Ruler118no	Mild rally	9
24Aug97-8Sfe	fst	7f	:221 :444 1:10 1:234	IndnNtFtCp571k	68	2	8	95	65¼	34	32¾	Stevens S A	L120 f	4.60	86-12	Grady120nk *General Gem*1202½ Real Quiet1202½	Gaining	12
8Aug97-8Sfe	fst	7f	:22 :442 1:10 1:234	[R]Alw 10000NC	54	1	9	2hd	2hd	25	37½	Stevens S A	L120 f	2.10	81-15	General Gem1207 Thatsaknife120½ Real Quiet1205	Empty	10
19Jly97-7Hol	fst	5½f	:221 :443 :562 1:023	Md Sp Wt 34k	75	4	4	3nk	32	34	36½	Flores D R	LB118	2.30	93-08	MeadowPrayer1184½ KonaWind1132 RelQuiet11813	Lacked late response	6
29Jun97-1CD	my	6f	:212 :451 :572 1:10	Md Sp Wt 41k	74	1	5	34	44½	37	38½	Steiner J J	L118 f	10.70	84-09	*PolishedBrass*1181½ *TropicLightning*1187 RelQuiet1185	Chased pace evenly	10
15Jun97-1CD	fst	5f	:22 :451 :574	Md Sp Wt 36k	57	1	3	45½	48	612	710	Steiner J J	L119 f	5.00	89-12	Dice Dancer1191 *Polished Brass*1195 Da Devil1192½	Close up, faded inside	11

1999: Summer Squall finished second in the 1990 Derby and then won the Preakness over Unbridled. Aside from champion 2-year-old filly Storm Song, Summer Squall had not sired a Grade 1 stakes winner of any significance until Charismatic (31-1) won the 1999 Kentucky Derby and Preakness. Unlike his sire, Charismatic was a late-blooming colt who began to improve quickly for trainer D.

Wayne Lukas in a year when all the 3-year-olds had serious question marks. This was a wide-open Derby ripe for a bomb.

Leading up to the Derby, Menifee appeared to have more talent than his stakes-winning sprinter sire, Harlan. But Menifee was out of the blue hen producer Anne Campbell (1999 Broodmare of the Year), who previously foaled Desert Wine (Damascus), second in the 1983 Kentucky Derby and Preakness. The enigmatic Cat Thief took the lead entering the stretch but could not hold off Charismatic and Menifee.

Tosses that year included the classy Worldly Manner (Riverman, 7th), whose pedigree strongly suggested he would be more effective on turf; General Challenge (11th), who was ill-suited to 1¼ miles; and the good filly Three Ring (Notebook, 19th and last), who was not bred to get the Derby distance against fillies, let alone colts.

Charismatic
Own: Lewis Robert B. and Beverly J

Ch. c. 3 (Mar)
Sire: Summer Squall (Storm Bird) $50,000
Dam: Bali Babe (Drone)
Br: Parrish Hill Farm & W. S. Farish (Ky)
Tr: Lukas D. W(0 0 0 0 .00) 2004:(359 40 .11)

Life	17	5	2	4	$2,038,064	108	**D.Fst**	15	5	2	4	$2,035,934	108
1999	10	4	2	1	$2,007,404	108	**Wet(319)**	1	0	0	0	$2,130	71
1998	7	1	0	3	$30,660	85	**Turf(276)**	1	0	0	0	$0	24
	0	0	0	0	$0	-	**Dst(0)**	0	0	0	0	$0	-

5Jun99-9Bel	fst	1½	$:47^{3}$	1:12	$2:01^{4}$	$2:27^{4}$	Belmont-G1	**107**	4	2^{hd}	2½	1^{hd}	2½	$3^{1\frac{1}{2}}$	Antley C W	L126	*1.60	103-06	LmonDropKid126^{hd} VisionndVrs126$^{1\frac{1}{2}}$ Chrismtic126$^{4\frac{3}{4}}$	Drifted, vanned off	12
15May99-10Pim	fst	$1\frac{3}{16}$	$:45^{1}$	$1:10^{1}$	$1:35^{1}$	$1:55^{1}$	Preaknss-G1	**107**	6	10^{6}	$10^{7\frac{3}{4}}$	$8^{3\frac{3}{4}}$	1^{3}	$1^{1\frac{1}{2}}$	Antley C W	L126	8.40	89-09	Charismatic126$^{1\frac{1}{2}}$ Menifee126^{hd} *Badge*126$^{2\frac{1}{2}}$	5wd mv,drftd 3/16,drvg	13
1May99-8CD	fst	1¼	$:47^{4}$	$1:12^{2}$	$1:37^{2}$	$2:03^{1}$	KyDerby-G1	**108**	16	$7^{3\frac{1}{2}}$	$7^{2\frac{3}{4}}$	$3^{1\frac{1}{2}}$	2½	1^{nk}	Antley C W	L126	31.30	89-14	*Charismatic*126^{nk} Menifee126¾ Cat Thief126$^{1\frac{1}{4}}$	5-wide trip,driving	19
18Apr99-8Kee	fst	$1\frac{1}{16}$	$:23^{1}$	$:46^{4}$	$1:10^{3}$	1:41	Lexingtn-G2	**108**	5	6^{5}	$4^{2\frac{1}{2}}$	$3^{1\frac{1}{2}}$	2^{hd}	$1^{2\frac{1}{2}}$	Bailey J D	L115	12.10	103-07	*Charismatic*115$^{2\frac{1}{2}}$ YnkeeVictor115¾ FindersGold115^{2}	3 wide 2nd turn,drvng	12
3Apr99-5SA	fst	1⅛	$:47^{1}$	$1:11^{2}$	$1:36^{1}$	$1:48^{4}$	SADerby-G1	**94**	8	$6^{3\frac{1}{2}}$	$6^{3\frac{3}{4}}$	6^{4}	5^{7}	$4^{8\frac{1}{4}}$	Pincay L Jr	LB120	44.30	83-13	GenrlChllng120$^{3\frac{1}{2}}$ PrimTimbr120$^{3\frac{1}{2}}$ DsrtHro120$^{1\frac{1}{4}}$	Improved position some	8
6Mar99-7BM	fst	$1\frac{1}{16}$	$:22^{4}$	:46	1:10	$1:43^{1}$	ElCamRlD-G3	**95**	2	$6^{7\frac{1}{2}}$	$6^{7\frac{1}{2}}$	$6^{4\frac{3}{4}}$	$3^{3\frac{1}{2}}$	2^{hd}	Warren R J Jr	LB115	10.60	83-24	Cliquot115^{hd} Charismatic115$^{3\frac{1}{2}}$ No Cal Bread117¾	Angled out, rallied	7
19Feb99-6SA	fst	7f	$:21^{4}$	$:43^{4}$	$1:08^{1}$	$1:21^{2}$	Alw 50000N$Y	**94**	2	4	$5^{9\frac{1}{2}}$	5^{9}	$3^{6\frac{1}{2}}$	2^{5}	Pincay L Jr	LB117	17.20	93-08	Apremont119^{5} Charismatic117^{2} *Forestry*119^{7}	Finished willingly	5
11Feb99-6SA	fst	6½f	$:21^{4}$	$:44^{2}$	$1:10^{2}$	$1:17^{1}$	Clm 62500(62.5-55)	**80**	8	7	$8^{6\frac{1}{4}}$	6^{5}	5^{4}	2^{nk}	McCarron C J	LB117	2.70	82-17	[D]What Say You110^{nk} Charismatic117^{nk} ValleyDon117^{1}	Bothered near 1/8	9
Placed first through disqualification																					
31Jan99-8SA	gd	$1\frac{1}{16}$	$:23^{4}$	$:47^{3}$	1:12	$1:42^{4}$	StCtlina-G2	**71**	2	$5^{2\frac{1}{2}}$	$5^{4\frac{1}{4}}$	5^{5}	$5^{7\frac{1}{2}}$	$5^{13\frac{1}{2}}$	Pincay L Jr	LB117	30.10	75-15	GeneralChallenge117^{3} BuckTrout120^{1} Brillintly115$^{3\frac{1}{2}}$	Bit tight 7/8,wkened	5
16Jan99-5SA	fst	$1\frac{1}{16}$	$:23^{3}$	$:47^{2}$	$1:11^{4}$	1:44	Alw 54000N$Y	**78**	8	$7^{3\frac{1}{4}}$	$7^{5\frac{3}{4}}$	$7^{3\frac{1}{2}}$	$7^{3\frac{1}{4}}$	5^{4}	Pincay L Jr	LB117	17.90	79-16	Mr. Broad Blade116^{hd} Brilliantly116^{1} Outstanding Hero116^{2}	Bit tight 3/4	10
27Dec98-1SA	fst	6½f	$:21^{3}$	$:44^{1}$	1:09	$1:15^{2}$	Alw 50000N$Y	**85**	5	7	$7^{8\frac{1}{4}}$	$7^{6\frac{3}{4}}$	$8^{5\frac{1}{4}}$	$3^{4\frac{1}{2}}$	Pincay L Jr	LB117	23.10	87-06	*BrightValour*116^{4} OutstndingHero116½ Chrismtic117^{nk}	Outside,late for 3rd	8
21Nov98-1Hol	fst	6½f	$:22^{2}$	$:45^{3}$	$1:10^{4}$	$1:17^{1}$	Md 62500(62.5-55)	**83**	3	5	4^{2}	$4^{1\frac{1}{2}}$	1^{2}	1^{5}	Pincay L Jr	LB119	*1.30	80-20	Charismatic119^{5} Wandering119^{2} Pick Up Stixs119^{6}	Rail trip,clearly best	6
17Oct98-4SA	fm	1	Ⓣ$:23^{2}$	$:47^{2}$	1:13	$1:38^{1}$	Md Sp Wt 35k	**24**	4	$1^{1\frac{1}{2}}$	1^{1}	$7^{3\frac{3}{4}}$	8^{12}	$9^{25\frac{3}{4}}$	McCarron C J	LB120 b	3.40	42-28	LxingtonBch120^{no} DncngMjsty120$^{1\frac{1}{4}}$ *CompnyApprovl*120$^{3\frac{1}{2}}$	Speed, stopped	9
1Oct98-1SA	fst	1	$:22^{1}$	$:45^{2}$	$1:10^{4}$	1:37	Md Sp Wt 35k	**60**	2	1^{3}	$1^{3\frac{1}{2}}$	1^{1}	2^{2}	$3^{10\frac{1}{4}}$	Pincay L Jr	LB120 b	2.10	76-15	CrownngStorm120^{10} NrthrnAvn120^{nk} Chrsmtc120^{4}	Inside, edged for 2nd	7
23Aug98-2Dmr	fst	5½f	$:22^{3}$	:46	$:58^{3}$	1:05	Md Sp Wt 36k	**57**	2	3	3½	3^{nk}	$4^{2\frac{1}{2}}$	4^{5}	McCarron C J	LB118 b	*.70	83-11	Out in Front118^{2} Round Four118^{hd} Kona Coast118^{3}	3 wide, weakened	4
25Jly98-4Dmr	fst	6f	$:22^{2}$	$:45^{4}$	$:58^{2}$	$1:11^{2}$	Md Sp Wt 37k	**66**	2	6	1^{1}	1^{2}	2½	$3^{1\frac{1}{2}}$	Nakatani C S	LB118 b	*2.00	80-12	Prized Demon118½ Seayabyebye118^{1} Charismatic118^{6}	Inside, outfinished	8
20Jun98-3Hol	fst	5f	$:22^{2}$	$:45^{3}$		$:57^{4}$	Md Sp Wt 37k	**48**	3	4	$4^{4\frac{3}{4}}$	3^{5}	$6^{8\frac{1}{2}}$	$6^{13\frac{1}{4}}$	Flores D R	B118	12.20	81-15	O'Rey Fantasma118$^{2\frac{1}{2}}$ *Aristotle*118^{2} Buck Trout118$^{3\frac{1}{2}}$	Inside, weakened	6

2000: This was a banner year for pedigree handicapping and the Kentucky Derby. I was convinced that Fusaichi Pegasus had no limits despite the fact that his sire, Mr. Prospector, had yet to sire a Derby winner. In fact, it was the one race that had eluded one of history's greatest stallions. But Forty Niner's loss by a neck to Winning Colors in 1988, along with victories in other Triple Crown races by Tank's Prospect (1985 Preakness) and Conquistador Cielo (1982 Belmont) suggested that a Mr. Prospector could certainly win the Derby. Fusaichi Pegasus also had enormous class from his female family. His dam, Angel Fever, was a full sister to 1992 Preakness winner Pine Bluff (Danzig) and was also a half-sister to multiple stakes winner Demons Begone (Elocutionist), who bled profusely as the favorite in the 1987 Kentucky Derby.

The exacta was completed by 11-1 Aptitude (A.P. Indy), who was out of Dokki (Northern Dancer), an unraced half-sister to Belmont Stakes winner Coastal (Majestic Prince) and dual champion Slew o' Gold (Seattle Slew). With A.P. Indy on top and a high-quality stakes-producing female family, Aptitude was bred to love 1¼ miles. His fine performances in the Gotham and Wood Memorial Stakes only enhanced his status for the Derby.

The cold $2 exacta returned $66, but there was more. Impeachment, who had a spectacular pedigree (by Deputy Minister out of a half-sister to sprint champion Gold Beauty—the dam of English Horse of the Year Dayjur and Maplejinsky), had shown ability rallying to finish second in the Tampa Bay Derby (to Wheelaway) and third in the Arkansas Derby (to Graeme Hall and Snuck In). Unfortunately, Impeachment was coupled in the betting with the well-regarded High Yield (Storm Cat, 15th); Trippi (End Sweep, 11th); and Commendable (Gone West, 17th), and was a huge underlay at 6-1. Had he not been part of that entry, Impeachment's odds could have been as high as 30-1, and the $2 trifecta would have been considerably higher than $435.

Tosses that year were China Visit (Red Ransom, 6th), who was turf-bred; Curule (Go for Gin, 7th), who was by a better sire of grass runners and at least needed a wet track to move him up; Captain Steve (Fly So Free, 8th), who was not able to get 1¼ miles yet; Trippi (End Sweep, 11th), a very good sprinter who had no business running 1¼ miles; The Deputy (by turf sire Petardia, 14th); High Yield (Storm Cat, 15th), whose wire-to-wire victory in the Blue Grass did not translate well over an entirely different Churchill surface; Hal's Hope (Jolie's Halo, 16th), who was just a pace factor and not bred to be at his best at 1¼ miles; and finally, Graeme Hall (Dehere, 19th and last), whose high speed was tailor-made for Oaklawn Park when he easily won the Arkansas Derby, but who was also only a pace factor at Churchill Downs at 1¼ miles.

Fusaichi Pegasus
Own: Sekiguchi Fusao, Haruya, Katsumi, Har

B. c. 3 (Apr)
Sire: Mr. Prospector (Raise a Native)
Dam: Angel Fever (Danzig)
Br: Arthur B. Hancock III & Stonerside Ltd. (Ky)
Tr: Drysdale Neil D(0 0 0 0 .00) 2004:(99 20 .20)

Life	9	6	2	0	$1,994,400	115	D.Fst	7	5	1	0	$1,344,400	115
2000	8	6	1	0	$1,987,800	115	Wet(445)	2	1	1	0	$650,000	111
1999	1	M	1	0	$6,600	95	Turf(383)	0	0	0	0	$0	-
Aik Ⓣ	0	0	0	0	$0	-	DstⓉ(447)	0	0	0	0	$0	-

4Nov00-10CD	fst	1¼	:472	1:12	1:36	2:003	3↑BCClasic-G1	105	8	72¾	83	86¼	66	67½	Desormeaux K J	L122	*1.20	99	-	*Tiznow*122nk GiantsCauseway1223¼ *CaptinSteve*122hd	7-8 wide trip,no rally	13
23Sep00-8Bel	fst	1	:223	:441	1:081	1:34	JeromeH-G2	115	1	52¾	52½	3nk	1hd	1¾	Desormeaux K J	L124f	*1.20	95-	05	FusichiPegsus124¾ *ElCorredor*1173¾ *AlberttheGrt*1208½	Vigorous hand ride	6
20May00-10Pim	gd	1³⁄₁₆	:463	1:111	1:37	1:56	Preaknss-G1	103	7	65	55	52	31½	23¾	Desormeaux K J	L126f	*.30	81-	11	RedBullt1263¾ *FusichiPgsus*126hd Impchmnt126nk	Pinched break,5wd trip	8
6May00-8CD	fst	1¼	:454	1:094	1:353	2:01	KyDerby-G1	108	15	138¾	116½	62¼	1hd	11½	Desormeaux K J	L126f	*2.30	105	-	FusichiPegsus1261½ Aptitude1264 Impchmnt126½	Angle 7wide,hand urged	19
15Apr00-9Aqu	wf	1⅛	:464	1:102	1:352	1:474	WoodMem-G2	111	5	53½	3½	32	1½	14¼	Desormeaux K J	L123f	*.90	98-	10	*Fusaichi Pegasus*1234¼ *Red Bullet*1231½ Aptitude123nk	Vigorous hand ride	12
19Mar00-7SA	fst	1¹⁄₁₆	:23	:454	1:101	1:423	SnFelipe-G2	106	5	21	22	22	11	1¾	Desormeaux K J	LB116f	*1.30	90-	14	*Fusaichi Pegasus*116¾ *The Deputy*1223 Anees119hd	Stalked, led, held	7
19Feb00-3SA	fst	1¹⁄₁₆	:231	:46	1:103	1:423	Alw 54000N1x	103	3	21	32	2½	12	13½	Desormeaux K J	LB117f	*1.20	90-	20	*Fusaichi Pegasus*1173½ Tribunal1193 Toqueville1174	Bid,clear,ridden out	7
2Jan00-1SA	fst	6f	:22	:454	:58	1:104	Md Sp Wt 45k	95	6	2	21½	3½	1hd	12	Desormeaux K J	B120f	*.20	85-	18	*FschPgss*1202 SpcyStff12011 LghtofthWoods1205½	3wd bid,mild hand ride	6
11Dec99-6Hol	fst	6½f	:224	:452	1:101	1:163	Md Sp Wt 33k	95	1	8	52½	2hd	1hd	2nk	Espinoza V	B120f	3.30	88-	20	DvidCopprfild120nk *FusichiPgsus*1205 Forboding1201	Inside,led,outgamed	10

2001: Point Given (Thunder Gulch) was universally regarded as a potential Triple Crown winner, but was uncharacteristically close to a suicidal pace, which many blamed for his defeat. Unleashing an overwhelming run was Monarchos (Maria's Mon), who proved that his stretch-running Florida Derby win was no fluke and drove yet another nail into the coffin for Dosage and the Kentucky Derby. Monarchos was from the first crop of 2-year-old champion Maria's Mon, and since Maria's Mon was not a Chef, Monarchos's Dosage rocketed over 4.00, the cut-off number for Dosage qualifiers. In the meantime, pedigree handicappers ran to the windows to collect on the generous 10-1 that Monarchos paid in the Derby. While Maria's Mon did little after his juvenile year due to injuries suffered at 2, he was a stallion who was qualified to get runners with stamina. Maria's Mon is by the late Wavering Monarch (Majestic Light) and is out of a mare by Caro (sire of Winning Colors).

But Monarchos was bred even better than his sire, as he is from a stellar Darby Dan female family that has produced Dynaformer, Offlee Wild, Darby Creek Road, Memories of Silver, Ryafan, and Sunshine Forever. Monarchos had a wonderful pedigree for 1¼ miles, full of class and stamina.

If you liked Thunder Gulch's son Point Given, then a case could have been made for Thunder Gulch's other son, Invisible Ink (although I surely did not use him), who finished a game second at 55-1. While obviously not in the same league as Point Given, he was one of a half-dozen runners who were playable in the minor spots for trifectas and superfectas despite having finished a weakening fourth in the Blue Grass Stakes. The classy Congaree (Arazi) ran a huge race to finish third despite posting blazing fractions over an unusually fast surface.

Horses that year who were pretenders included the talented miler Express Tour (by speed influence Tour d'Or, 8th); Startac (by Theatrical, strictly a top turf sire, 10th); Songandaprayer (by speed sire Saint Ballado out of a mare by Premiership, 13th); Balto Star (by speed sire Glitterman, 14th); and Keats (by speed and hidden turf sire Hennessy, 16th). Balto Star was eventually able to carry his speed over a distance of ground, but only as an older horse—and on grass.

Monarchos
Own: Oxley John C

Gr/ro. c. 3 (Feb)
Sire: Maria's Mon (Wavering Monarch) $35,000
Dam: Regal Band (Dixieland Band)
Br: J. D. Squires (Ky)
Tr: Ward J T Jr(0 0 0 0 .00) 2004:(58 7 .12)

Life	10	4	1	3	$1,720,830	116	D.Fst	10	4	1	3	$1,720,830	116
2002	1	0	0	1	$5,200	87	Wet(372)	0	0	0	0	$0	-
2001	7	4	1	1	$1,711,600	116	Turf(307)	0	0	0	0	$0	-
	0	0	0	0	$0	-	Dst(0)	0	0	0	0	$0	-

19Jan02-6GP	fst	1 1/16	:24	:481	1:123	1:46	4↑OC 100k/N4X-N	87	3	48½	45½	54¾	45¼	38¾	Chavez J F	L120	*.50	69-22	*Mongoose*1226¼ WtchYourPnnis1202½ Monrchos1203	Slow st, no response	5
9Jun01-10Bel	fst	1½	:48	1:113	2:003	2:262	Belmont-G1	98	5	75¼	66¾	35	38	313	Chavez J F	L126	5.00	94-02	*Point Given*12612¼ A PValentine126¾ Monarchos1261	Mild move, flattened	9
19May01-11Pim	fst	1 3/16	:471	1:114	1:362	1:552	Preaknes-G1	99	7	1115	1112	84¾	67½	67½	Chavez J F	L126	2.30	86-11	*Point Given*1262¼ APValentine126nk *Congaree*1261¼	5-6w,mild mve,flattend	11
5May01-8CD	fst	1¼	:444	1:091	1:35	1:594	KyDerby-G1	116	16	1315	107½	62¼	2½	14¾	Chavez J F	L126	10.50	104 -	Monarchos1264¾ Invisible Ink126no Congaree1264	Bmp start,rally 6wide	17
14Apr01-10Aqu	fst	1⅛	:46	1:10	1:35	1:474	WoodMem-G2	103	2	57	57¼	55¼	25	22¾	Chavez J F	L123	*.90	94-14	Congaree1232¾ *Monarchos*1237 *Richly Blended*1234	Inside run, gamely	6
10Mar01-11GP	fst	1⅛	:464	1:112	1:37	1:494	FlaDerby-G1	106	7	117¼	117¾	71½	12	14½	Chavez J F	L122	*1.40e	88-13	Monrchos1224½ Outofthebox1222½ InvisibleInk122½	Strong six wide move	13
3Feb01-10GP	fst	1 1/16	:24	:474	1:122	1:431	Alw 35000N1X	103	3	32	22½	21½	1½	14¾	Chavez J F	L120	*2.00	92-13	*Monarchos*1204¾ *Distilled*1203¾ Thunder Blitz1227	Drew away, driving	11
13Jan01-8GP	fst	7f	:222	:452	1:101	1:221	Md Sp Wt 31k	95	3	8	32	11	13	16	Chavez J F	L122	5.50	95-11	*Monarchos*1226 Tampa1223¼ Judge Silver122½	Inside, drew away	12
24Nov00-7CD	fst	6½f	:214	:453	1:112	1:18	Md Sp Wt 40k	69	6	10	1113	1113	711	35¼	Martinez W	L120	13.50	82-12	*Dream Run*120hd *Big Talkin Man*1205¼ *Monarchos*120½	No late threat	12
7Oct00-4Kee	fst	7f	:22	:454	1:093	1:221	Md Sp Wt 50k	61	11	7	73½	64	109¼	812½	Cooksey P J	L120	9.80	78-11	Devil's Domain1204 *Private Son*1201¼ Me and Thee120hd	Tired after 1/2	12

2002: War Emblem (Our Emblem) developed quickly in the spring of 2002 and was purchased by Bob Baffert for The Thoroughbred Corporation after a wire-to-wire victory in the Illinois Derby. Despite his lofty speed figures at 1⅛ miles, it was a real stretch to think that War Emblem was a true 1¼-mile horse. While War Emblem inherited some stamina points from his illustrious damsire, Lord at War, he was a son of Our Emblem (Mr. Prospector), who had not produced anything of note up to that point and was himself a stakes-placed sprinter. Pedigree-wise, there was very little to recommend War Emblem. The top three finishers ran 1-2-3 the entire distance and Medaglia d'Oro (El Prado), who closed to be fourth, was the only colt in the field of 18 to rally.

Despite owning the most impressive pedigree in that Derby, runner-up Proud Citizen was also very tough to come up with. By Gone West out of a mare by European high-weighted sprinter Green Forest (Shecky Greene), his female family produced Northern Dancer, Machiavellian, and Danehill, but the most prominent male names in his pedigree were all about speed and very little stamina. In fact, Proud Citizen displayed uncommon speed in winning a 5½-furlong maiden race at Belmont at age 2, and it was surprising to see him run a strong race at 1¼ miles. Proud Citizen underscored his high class, however, by running third in the Preakness.

Perfect Drift, who developed into a formidable if erratic handicap horse at 4, finished third and is one of many runners by Dynaformer who have performed well on dirt at the highest level of racing. Primarily known as a strong sire of turf runners (Riskaverse, Vergennes, Film Maker, Baptize, Blazing Fury, Majestic Dy), Dynaformer has been a breeder's dream because of the versatility of his offspring. In addition to Perfect Drift, his quality runners on dirt include Dynever, Critical Eye, Starrer, and Blumin Affair.

Horses who were questionable to be at their best at 1¼ miles on dirt included Johannesburg (Hennessy, 8th); Castle Gondolfo (Gone West, 12th); Private Emblem (Our Emblem, 14th); It'sallinthechase (Take Me Out, 16th); Ocean Sound (Mujadi, 17th); and Wild Horses (Saint Ballado, 18th).

Johannesburg was arguably the most impressive 2-year-old seen in decades. He was undefeated in seven starts at 2, and no Thoroughbred in history accomplished what he did as a juvenile, winning the most prestigious Group or Grade 1 stakes in four different countries (England, Ireland, France, and the U.S.). His Breeders' Cup Juvenile victory—his first start on dirt—was achieved with complete authority. As a son of Hennessy, however, Johannesburg was ill-equipped to be as brilliant at 1¼ miles.

War Emblem
Own: The Thoroughbred Corporation

Dk. b or b. c. 3 (Feb)
Sire: Our Emblem (Mr. Prospector) $15,000
Dam: Sweetest Lady (Lord At War*Arg)
Br: Charles Nuckols Jr. & Sons (Ky)
Tr: Baffert Bob(0 0 0 0 .00) 2004:(371 70 .19)

Life	13	7	0	0	$3,491,000	114	D.Fst	12	7	0	0	$3,491,000	114
2002	10	5	0	0	$3,455,000	114	Wet(336)	0	0	0	0	$0	-
2001	3	2	0	0	$36,000	83	Turf(267)	1	0	0	0	$0	44
	0	0	0	0	$0	-	Dst(0)	0	0	0	0	$0	-

26Oct02-10AP	fst	1¼	:463 1:101 1:352 2:011	3↑ BCClasic-G1	89	3	2 1½	2 1	3½	5 7½	8 18¼	Espinoza V	L121	4.00	79 -	Volponi126 6½ *Medaglia d'Oro*121nk Milwaukee Brew126 3	Bid turn, faltered	12
25Aug02-5Dmr	fst	1¼	:452 1:094 1:352 2:012	3↑ PacifcCl-G1	110	6	3 1½	3 2	2hd	2hd	6 4¼	Espinoza V	LB117	*1.20	88- 13	CameHome117¾ Momentum124 1½ MilwaukeeBrew124½	3wd bid,weakened	14
4Aug02-11Mth	fst	1⅛	:471 1:103 1:352 1:481	HskIInvH-G1	112	4	1½	1½	1 1½	1 4½	1 3½	Espinoza V	L124	*.30	99- 01	WarEmblem124 3½ MagicWeisner118¾ LikeHero117 3¾	Bit fractious in gate	5
8Jun02-10Bel	fst	1½	:48 1:121 2:032 2:293	Belmont-G1	82	9	4 1½	2hd	5 2¼	7 12	8 19½	Espinoza V	L126	*1.25	64- 12	Sarava126½ *Medaglia d'Oro*126 9½ Sunday Break126 1	Stumb brk,rank,tired	11
18May02-12Pim	fst	1 3/16	:46 1:103 1:361 1:561	Preaknes-G1	109	8	2hd	2hd	2hd	1 1½	1¾	Espinoza V	L126	*2.80	90- 14	WrEmblem126¾ MgicWeisnr126¾ ProudCitizn126 1½	Rated 3wd, stiff drive	13
4May02-9CD	fst	1¼	:47 1:113 1:363 2:01	KyDerby-G1	114	5	1 1½	1 1½	1 1½	1 1½	1 4	Espinoza V	L126	20.50	94- 05	*WrEmblem*126 4 ProudCitizen126¾ PerfectDrift126 3¼	Pace, 3w,hand urging	18
Previously trained by Springer Frank R																		
6Apr02-8Spt	fst	1⅛	:481 1:13 1:373 1:494	IllDerby-G2	112	4	1 1½	1 1½	1 2½	1 5	1 6¼	Sterling L J Jr	L114	6.30	92- 17	*War Emblem*114 6¼ Repent124 4½ Fonz's117 6½	Ridden out	9
17Mar02-8Spt	fst	1	:233 :47 1:122 1:391	Alw 48600NC	98	1	1 1	1 1½	1 1½	1 3	1 10¾	Juarez A J Jr	L118	*.80	87- 20	*War Emblem*118 10¾ *Colorful Tour*121 3 Boston Common115 8	Driving	6
17Feb02-9FG	fst	1 1/16	:23 :46 1:111 1:43	RisenStr-G3	85	3	3 1	4 2	4 1¾	7 6	6 9¾	Theriot H J II	L117	38.80	85- 08	*Repent*122 2¼ BobsImage115 3 Esyfromthegitgo122 2¼	Ranged up 3w, faded	9
26Jan02-9FG	fst	1	:24 :472 1:12 1:374	LeComte100k	86	3	2hd	1½	1½	2½	5 2¼	Theriot H J II	L117	12.40	93- 07	Esyfromthgitgo114no SkyTrrc119¾ Itsllinthchs122 1¼	Faltered final 1/16th	11
23Nov01-8FG	fst	1	:231 :471 1:122 1:39	Alw 32000N1X	83	6	5 3¼	3nk	1 1	1 3	1 4½	Theriot H J II	L119	2.00	84- 19	War Emblem119 4½ No Trouble119 6 Ski Hero119 1	Kept to task	6
20Oct01-8AP	gd	1	Ⓣ :233 :474 1:123 1:393	Manila75k	44	10	2 1	1hd	2hd	7 5¾	7 17½	Juarez A J Jr	116	8.00	65- 20	Rylstone116 3 U S S Tinosa120 1½ Jaha116 4	Tired, bled	12
4Oct01-5AP	fst	1	:23 :454 1:111 1:391	Md Sp Wt 28k	69	1	1hd	1 1	1½	1 4	1 1¾	Juarez A J Jr	121	16.40	78- 23	War Emblem121 1¾ Castner121 2 Thrym121 1½	Driving	9

2003: Like Grindstone and Monarchos, 2003 Derby winner Funny Cide was from his sire's first crop. Funny Cide is by Distorted Humor, a stakes-winning miler who was stakes-placed at middle distances, like many runners from the Forty Niner (Mr. Prospector) sire line. Although foaled in New York, Funny Cide is by a Kentucky sire, and actually descends from the exact same female family as the royally bred Empire Maker (Unbridled). Empire Maker had taken the measure of Funny Cide in the Wood Memorial at 1⅛ miles, and based on their sires and their running styles, it was logical to assume that the Derby's additional furlong would favor Empire Maker.

While Funny Cide won the Derby, is there any doubt who was the better horse? A sore foot curtailed Empire Maker's training schedule leading up to the Derby, and he was hardly at his best the day of the race, running second on class alone. His emphatic victory over Ten Most Wanted and Funny Cide in the Belmont Stakes clearly showed who was better suited to races longer than 1⅛ miles. And make no mistake about it, the sloppy track on Belmont Day had nothing to do with the result, as runners from Funny Cide's sire line move up a dozen lengths on wet tracks.

Peace Rules (Jules) finished a gutsy third in the Derby, just holding off a fast-closing Atswhatimtalknbout (A.P. Indy) by a head at a distance that was a furlong beyond his best. Peace Rules's late sire was a late-developing 2-year-old who won the Nashua Stakes and finished second in the Remsen and Cowdin Stakes. Jules was the best-bred of all of Forty Niner's stallions, but his career at stud was a lesson in mismanagement. His second dam, Raise the Standard, was a half-sister to Northern Dancer, and she was also the dam of one of Europe's most productive broodmares—Coup de Folie. Sent to South America, Jules was brought back to the U.S. and sired Peace Rules. Unfortunately, Jules's untimely death in 2003 at the relatively young age of 9 robbed racing of a promising stallion.

Horses who did not figure in the Derby based on their pedigrees—either because of the distance or the surface—were Buddy Gil (Eastern Echo, 6th); Ten Cents a Shine (Devil His Due, 8th); Domestic Dispute (Unbridled's Song, 10th); Supah Blitz (Mecke, 13th); Indian Express (Indian Charlie, 14th); and Lone Star Sky (Conquistador Cielo, 15th).

Funny Cide
Own: Sackatoga Stable

Ch. g. 4 (Apr) SARAUG01 $22,000
Sire: Distorted Humor (Forty Niner) $50,000
Dam: Belle's Good Cide (Slewacide)
Br: Win Star Farm, LLC (NY)
Tr: Tagg Barclay(0 0 0 0 .00) 2004:(187 27 .14)

Life	20	8	4	5	$3,174,485	114	D.Fst	16	6	3	4	$2,144,485	112
2004	9	3	2	3	$1,075,100	112	Wet(422)	4	2	1	1	$1,030,000	114
2003	8	2	2	2	$1,963,200	114	Turf(339)	0	0	0	0	$0	-
	0	0	0	0	$0	-	Dst(T)(367)	0	0	0	0	$0	-

2Oct04-10Bel	fst	1¼	:473 1:113 1:362 2:022	3↑ JkyClbGC-G1	112	7	2½	3nk	32	2½	1¾	Santos J A	L126	*2.80	85-13	FunnyCid126¾ Nwfoundlnd1261 ThCliffsEdg1223¾	Gamely between rivals	7
22Aug04-9Sar	fst	1¼	:462 1:104 1:36 2:004	3↑ SarBCH-G2	107	5	31½	41½	2½	2½	25	Prado E S	L118	*1.00	98-11	EveningAttire1155 *FunnyCide*1183¾ BowmnsBnd1161¼	3 wide trip, gamely	7
3Jly04-7Bel	fst	1¼	:461 1:091 1:334 1:592	3↑ SuburbnH-G1	111	1	31	2½	2hd	1½	3nk	Santos J A	L117	4.10	100 -	PeceRules120nk Newfoundlnd114no FunnyCide117¾	Speed on rail, gamely	8
19Jun04-10Suf	fst	1⅛	:483 1:122 1:363 1:49	3↑ MassH-G2	110	7	21	2½	2hd	3nk	2hd	Santos J A	LB117	*2.10	98-10	OfflWild113hd FunnyCid117hd ThLdysGroom1161½	2wd thru-out,game fin	9
31May04-9Bel	fst	1	:232 :46 1:10 1:352	3↑ MtropltH-G1	106	9	42½	51¾	41	52¼	55¼	Santos J A	L118	4.20	79-34	PicoCentrl119¾ BowmnsBnd1142¼ StrongHope1191½	Between foes, 3 wide	9
3Apr04-8Aqu	my	1⅛	:48 1:12 1:364 1:492	3↑ ExlsrBCH-G3	109	3	21½	2½	2hd	12	1½	Santos J A	L120	*1.30	92-08	Funny Cide120½ Evening Attire1198 Host114nk	Dug in gamely inside	5
29Feb04-9FG	fst	1⅛	:47 1:102 1:352 1:483	4↑ NwOrlnsH-G2	108	2	32½	33	32	43¼	32¾	Santos J A	L118	5.40	98-05	*Peace Rules*119hd Saint Liam1142¾ *Funny Cide*1181¼	Bumped, game for 3rd	8
7Feb04-10GP	fst	1⅛	:471 1:11 1:353 1:473	3↑ DonnH-G1	103	5	33	31	31½	34	38½	Santos J A	L119	3.00	92-09	Medaglia d'Oro1224¾ Seattle Fitz1133¾ Funny Cide1194	3 wide, tired	8
10Jan04-10GP	fst	7f	:223 :453 1:101 1:224	4↑ OC 100k/N$Y-N	102	2	3	4nk	11½	13	15	Santos J A	L118	*.40	88-20	FunnyCide1185 AmericnStyle1167½ WckyforLov1223	Drew off, ridden out	5
25Oct03-9SA	fst	1¼	:461 1:101 1:341 1:594	3↑ BCClasic-G1	97	4	52¼	65¼	78	1011	914¾	Krone J A	LB121	8.70	91-07	*PleasantlyPerfect*1261½ *Medagliad'Oro*126¾ *Dynever*121nk	Drifted wide, tired	10
3Aug03-11Mth	fst	1⅛	:47 1:104 1:36 1:491	HsklInvH-G1	94	5	52½	54½	55	47½	39	Santos J A	L123	*1.00	86-08	Peace Rules1211¾ Sky Mesa1187¼ Funny Cide1231	Outside 1/4,mild bid	7
7Jun03-11Bel	sly	1½	:483 1:132 2:023 2:281	Belmont-G1	104	4	11	1hd	21	33	35	Santos J A	L126	*1.00	86-14	EmpireMker126¾ TenMostWnted1264¼ FunnyCid1265¼	Set pace 3w, tired	6
17May03-12Pim	gd	1 3/16	:47 1:113 1:362 1:553	Preaknes-G1	114	9	32	21	2½	15	19¾	Santos J A	L126	*1.90	95-12	FunnyCide1269¾ MidwayRod126¾ Scrimshw126no	Bmpd brk,ratd 3w,clear	10
3May03-10CD	fst	1¼	:461 1:102 1:353 2:01	KyDerby-G1	109	5	32	31½	2½	1hd	11¾	Santos J A	L126	12.80	94-06	*Funny Cide*1261¾ *EmpireMaker*126hd PeaceRules126hd	Bmp start,stiff drive	16
12Apr03-8Aqu	my	1⅛	:471 1:11 1:354 1:483	WoodMem-G1	110	4	21½	21½	21	2hd	2½	Santos J A	L123	5.20	92-12	Empire Maker123½ *Funny Cide*1237½ Kissin Saint1231	Bumped after start	8
9Mar03-9FG	fst	1 1/16	:232 :463 1:103 1:423	LaDerby-G2	99	2	11	11½	1½	43½	33¼	Santos J A	L122	6.10	94-17	*Peace Rules*1222¼ [D]Kafwain1221 Funny Cide122½	Came again rail	10
Awarded second purse money																		
18Jan03-10GP	fst	1 1/16	:232 :471 1:112 1:43	HolyBull-G3	87	13	72¼	41½	44	44	56½	Santos J A	L122	5.30	87-10	Offlee Wild116hd Powerful Touch1163 Bham1182½	Hit gate, wide, tired	13
19Oct02-5Bel	fst	1	:232 :462 1:114 1:363	[S]SleepyHllo100k	89	2	3½	31	1hd	1½	1nk	Santos J A	L122	*.20	86-16	FunnyCid122nk *SpitthDvil*1153 GoRockinRobn1158½	Bumped start, driving	6
29Sep02-8Bel	fst	7f	:223 :454 1:102 1:224	[S]BFBongard83k	103	5	4	1hd	1½	18	19	Santos J A	L117	2.95	89-18	*FunnyCide*1179 SpitethDvil1172 InfinitJustic122nk	When asked, ridden out	10
8Sep02-6Bel	fst	6f	:223 :462 :584 1:111	[S]Md Sp Wt 43k	96	12	6	3½	11½	110	114¾	Santos J A	L119	*2.25	82-18	*FunnyCid*11914¾ HighPricd1191¾ PolishPosh1194½	When asked, ridden out	12

WORKS: Sep30 Bel 4f fst :47 B *2/27* ●Sep23 Bel 6f fst 1:113 B *1/6* ●Sep17 Bel 6f fst 1:123 B *1/4* Sep11 Bel 5f fst :594 B *8/83* ●Sep2 Sar 4f fst :464 B *1/40* Aug18 Sar 5f fst :591 B *4/50*

2004: Pedigree handicappers had to be scratching their heads after the 2004 Derby. How did a son of Elusive Quality out of a mare by Smile win America's most famous horse race, at the demanding distance of 1¼ miles?

The answer lies primarily in the track condition, which was classified as sloppy but more accurately could have been called miserable. While Smarty Jones might well have won over any kind of surface, there is no question that he relished the off going, while most of his competition was at a distinct disadvantage. The well-regarded The Cliff's Edge, for example, lost both front shoes during the race. Aside from Smarty Jones, the only horses to benefit were the second- and fourth-place finishers, Lion Heart and Limehouse, who also outran their pedigrees, and once again underscored the direction of breeding in America.

Up until Smarty Jones came along, no runner by Elusive Quality had won at 1¼ miles, and most were at their best up to 1¹⁄₁₆ miles. The enormous amount of class from his female line (which traces directly to racing's greatest broodmare, La Troienne) certainly explains Smarty Jones's high quality, but that is not the reason he was able to stay beyond 1⅛ miles.

As for Lion Heart, his sire, Tale of the Cat, had speed and was able to stretch that speed to middle distances (he finished second to Awesome Again in the 1⅛-mile Whitney Handicap). With two full crops to race, Tale of the Cat's runners have proven to be sprinter/milers who are especially effective on turf and over wet surfaces.

Limehouse is by Grand Slam (Gone West), who had top-class speed. Grand Slam won the Champagne and the Futurity Stakes at 2, won the Peter Pan Stakes at 1⅛ miles around one turn at Belmont, and finished second in the Breeders' Cup Sprint at age 3. Some of his runners have won at 1⅛ miles, such as Strong Hope and Grand Hombre, but his trademark is speed, and 2003 Breeders' Cup Sprint winner Cajun Beat, Riva Ridge Stakes winner Fire Slam, and Very Subtle Handicap winner Stellar are representative of the kind of brilliance Grand Slam is known to sire. In addition to being by Grand Slam, Limehouse descends from Blue Jean Baby and her dam, Jones Time Machine, two fillies who had blazing speed. The fact that Limehouse finished fourth at 1¼ miles was either a function of the sloppy surface, a poor reflection on the horses who finished behind him, or a combination of the two.

Thus, the results of the 2004 Triple Crown do not change the fact that Elusive Quality, Tale of the Cat, and Grand Slam are still brilliant (speed) influences. Most importantly, the victory by Smarty Jones at 1¼ miles does not mean that all of a sudden Elusive Quality is now a source of stamina.

Smarty Jones
Own: Someday Farm

Ch. c. 3 (Feb)
Sire: Elusive Quality (Gone West) $50,000
Dam: I'll Get Along (Smile)
Br: Someday Farm (Pa)
Tr: Servis John C(0 0 0 0 .00) 2004:(168 39 .23)

Life	9	8	1	0	$7,613,155	118	D.Fst	7	6	1	0	$1,128,355	118
2004	7	6	1	0	$7,563,535	118	Wet(329)	2	2	0	0	$6,484,800	107
2003	2	2	0	0	$49,620	105	Turf(282)	0	0	0	0	$0	-
	0	0	0	0	$0	-	Dst(0)	0	0	0	0	$0	-

5Jun04-11Bel	fst	1½	:483 1:113 2:002 2:272	Belmont-G1	100	9	31	1½	13½	11½	21	Elliott S	L126 f	*.35	94- 10	Birdstone1261 Smarty Jones1268 Royal Assault1263	Vied, clear, gamely	9
15May04-12Pim	fst	1 3/16	:471 1:112 1:362 1:552	Preaknes-G1	118	6	21½	22½	21	15	111½	Elliott S	L126 f	*.70	100- 13	SmrtyJons12611½ RockHrdTn1262 Eddington126hd	3-4w,angled in,driving	10
1May04-10CD	sly	1¼	:463 1:114 1:371 2:04	KyDerby-G1	107	13	42½	21½	2hd	1hd	12¾	Elliott S	L126 f	*4.10	79- 21	*Smarty Jones*1262¾ Lion Heart1263¼ Imperialism1262	Stalked,bid,clear	18
10Apr04-9OP	my	1⅛	:464 1:113 1:364 1:492	ArkDerby-G2	107	11	2½	2½	1hd	13	11½	Elliott S	122 f	*1.00	91- 17	*Smarty Jones*1221½ Borrego1181½ Pro Prado1223½	Cleared at will,drivng	11
20Mar04-10OP	fst	1 1/16	:232 :473 1:12 1:42	Rebel200k	108	7	21	21	2½	11	13¼	Elliott S	122 f	3.50	100- 16	*Smarty Jones*1223¼ Purge1173¾ Pro Prado1173¾	Kicked strongly clear	9
28Feb04-9OP	fst	1	:224 :454 1:111 1:372	Southwest100k	95	6	21½	22½	2hd	12	1¾	Elliott S	122 f	*.50	97- 18	*SmrtyJons*122¾ *TwoDownAtomtc*112½ ProPrd1177¼	Chased,took over,drvng	9
3Jan04-8Aqu	fst	170 ⊡	:231 :47 1:113 1:412	CountFleet81k	97	7	31	31	2hd	1½	15	Elliott S	116 f	*.40	91- 21	*Smarty Jones*1165 Risky Trick1166 Mr. Spock116½	Stumbled start, 3 wide	7
22Nov03-9Pha	fst	7f	:214 :441 1:083 1:214	[S]PennaNurse56k	105	1	10	12	12½	18	115	Elliott S	117 f	*.70	98- 17	*SmartyJones*11715 SaltyPunch1172¼ IsleofMirth1171½	Off slow, dominated	11
9Nov03-6Pha	fst	6f	:221 :451 :574 1:11	Md Sp Wt 23k	84	8	4	2hd	15	16	17¾	Elliott S	118 f	*1.10	84- 22	*Smarty Jones*1187¾ *Deputy Rummy*1132¾ Speedwell Beau1186	Handy score	10

6

HANDICAPPING THE BREEDERS' CUP BY PEDIGREE

AS NOTED IN Chapter 2, "Betting the 2-Year-Olds," the first half of the year is filled with baby sprints from three to 5½ furlongs. Juveniles with win-early, high-speed pedigrees are bred to be best from April to August, but things start changing in late August and certainly in the fall, when these 2-year-olds begin stretching out beyond one mile.

The Breeders' Cup Juvenile, usually run at 1¹⁄₁₆ miles, presents potential bonanzas for pedigree handicappers because the public, without fail, gravitates toward those 2-year-olds that have already had success in races at six and seven furlongs. Year after year, these flashy, early-developing types fail to be as effective at the longer, two-turn distance.

THE JUVENILE AND JUVENILE FILLIES

Three of the first four runnings of the Breeders' Cup Juvenile and the Juvenile Fillies were held at the distance of one mile. Since 1988 they have been run at 1$\frac{1}{16}$ miles, with the exception of 2002, when the distance was changed to 1$\frac{1}{8}$ miles because Arlington Park's track configuration did not allow for races at 1$\frac{1}{16}$ miles.

In 1989, Stella Madrid (Alydar) was the slight 2-1 choice over an emerging star, Go for Wand (Deputy Minister), who was 5-2. Stella Madrid had won three major races for juvenile fillies—the Spin-away, Matron, and Frizette Stakes—and defeated Go for Wand by a diminishing half-length in the Frizette. But the lightly raced Go for Wand was making her stakes debut in the Frizette after two easy wins in maiden and allowance company.

Go for Wand clearly had more upside than Stella Madrid, and the extra half-furlong of the Juvenile Fillies tipped the scales in her favor. Go for Wand showed her superiority, winning the Juvenile Fillies and paying $7, while Stella Madrid tired in the last eighth of a mile to finish third, beaten a half-length by Sweet Roberta (9-2, a filly by stamina influence Roberto out of a half-sister to Cure the Blues).

The 1991 Juvenile Fillies provided a great payday for followers of pedigree. Pleasant Stage, a late-maturing runner by the stamina influence Pleasant Colony, made her career debut on August 18 at Del Mar, finishing third in a six-furlong maiden race. She followed that with a second-place finish in a one-mile maiden race on September 6 at Del Mar, and won Santa Anita's Oak Leaf Stakes as a maiden in her third start on October 14, defeating Soviet Sojourn (who later produced Indian Charlie) and the royally bred La Spia.

In the Juvenile Fillies, Pleasant Stage rallied from 11th in the field of 14 to win in a dramatic finish over La Spia, with the under-rated Cadillac Women third. If any filly was bred to get better with maturity and distance, it was Pleasant Stage, who was from a spectacular Buckland Farm female family, and whose damsire was the legendary stamina influence Stage Door Johnny. Considering that

Pleasant Stage was already a winner at the Juvenile Fillies distance, getting stronger at the finish of the Oak Leaf Stakes, 5-1 was a generous price.

La Spia, a daughter of the 1986 Breeders' Cup Juvenile winner, Capote, showed that her third-place finish in the Oak Leaf was no fluke. She took the lead entering the stretch and looked like a winner at 29-1 until she was headed by Pleasant Stage right at the wire. La Spia was from a female family that produced juvenile champions. Her third dam, stakes-placed In the Clouds, was a full sister to stakes winner Sunrise Flight, and a half-sister to 1964 2-year-old champion Bold Lad and his full brother, 1966 2-year-old champion Successor. The $2 exacta returned $386.20.

Cadillac Women, who finished third in the Juvenile Fillies at 28-1, was by Carr de Naskra, who was doing well as a young stallion, and from a classy female family that produced Shy Dawn. It wasn't that far a reach to include her in minor spots in the exotics. Cadillac Women had finished second to the well-regarded Speed Dialer (Phone Trick) in the Arlington-Washington Lassie, but turned the tables in the Juvenile Fillies as Speed Dialer, the 7-2 second choice, closed to finish fourth. The big disappointment in the race was 2-1 favorite Preach (future dam of Pulpit), who tired to finish seventh.

The 1994 Juvenile was a memorable day for pedigree handicappers. While Timber Country (Woodman) was a solid favorite, the value in the race belonged solely to Eltish, a colt who had run well against the best of his division in England on the grass. But Eltish was by Cox's Ridge, a notoriously poor sire of grass runners. Eltish had performed admirably on turf despite not being bred particularly well for that surface, and I expected an even better effort when he tried dirt, his preferred surface.

Eltish was dismissed at nearly 17-1 and almost stole the race in the upper stretch until Timber Country flew up the rail to defeat him by two lengths. The $2 exacta with favored Timber Country on top returned a very healthy $132.60. It was not impossible to have Tejano Run, who finished third at 9-2, in the trifecta box.

Tejano Run, ridden by Jerry Bailey, was coming off a victory in the Breeders' Futurity at Keeneland. The $2 trifecta paid $658.40.

BANNER BREEDERS' CUP FOR PEDIGREE PLAYERS

The 1999 Breeders' Cup will forever be remembered as a pedigree handicapper's dream.

It started off with a bang with the first Breeders' Cup race of the day, the Juvenile Fillies. Chilukki was all the rage in 1999, reeling off six straight wins for trainer Bob Baffert. But according to pedigree handicapping, the speed-crazed filly by sprinter/miler Cherokee Run was going to be a vulnerable short-priced favorite going two turns in the Juvenile Fillies, and I was salivating over the prospect of beating her.

With a pronounced speed bias at Gulfstream for that day's Breeders' Cup, Chilukki certainly had to be used. But the front-running winner was Cash Run, who repelled Chilukki and won by 1¼ lengths, lighting up the board at $67.

I was extremely high on Cash Run after her devastating debut victory on June 6, 1999, and she was the subject of my weekly column in *Daily Racing Form* on June 19:

Cash Run only won a maiden race last Sunday, but the manner in which she humbled her rivals suggests she is stakes-bound. A half-sister to the promising stakes winner Forestry (a million-dollar yearling by Storm Cat), Cash Run is out of Shared Interest, a stakes-winning half-sister to Sewickley by Pleasant Colony. A $1.2 million yearling from the Keeneland July Select Sale, Cash Run is bred for the classics and should only get better at 3 as the distances increase.

The most interesting element of her pedigree is that she is the latest example of a quality individual that is inbred to an influential broodmare within five generations (the Rasmussen Factor). Cash Run is inbred 4 x 4 to the outstanding broodmare Sequence, dam of stakes winner Gold Digger (dam of Mr. Prospector), and Bold Sequence (granddam of Sewickley and Shared Interest).

It's early, but could we be looking at another champion filly by Seeking the Gold?

Cash Run had nagging physical problems after that race and did not make her second start until August 30, when she tired badly to finish fourth in a six-furlong allowance at Saratoga. She won a $6\frac{1}{2}$-furlong allowance race over a muddy Turfway Park surface by seven lengths, and then finished third in Keeneland's Alcibiades Stakes at $1\frac{1}{16}$ miles, her final prep for the Juvenile Fillies. While she seemed enigmatic, her 32-1 odds made it easy for me to use her in the exacta and trifecta. With Chilukki second at 3-2 and the exciting Surfside, who had a horrific trip going wide the entire way, finishing third at 5-2, the exacta came back $225.60 and the trifecta was $563.60.

But my best bet of the day came later on the Breeders' Cup card. While Cash Run was always going to be included in my gimmicks, I did not have nearly the confidence in her at that time that I did in Anees, whom I loved and knew would be a big price in the Juvenile.

Anees			B. c. 3 (Feb)	Life	7	2	0	2	$699,200	102	D.Fst	7	2	0	2	$699,200	102
Own: The Thoroughbred Corporation			Sire: Unbridled (Fappiano) $200,000	2000	3	0	0	1	$90,000	99	Wet(414)	0	0	0	0	$0	-
			Dam: Ivory Idol (Alydar)	1999	4	2	0	1	$609,200	102	Turf(286)	0	0	0	0	$0	-
			Br: Farfellow Farms, Ltd. (Ky)		0	0	0	0	$0	-	Dst(0)	0	0	0	0	$0	-
			Tr: Hassinger A L Jr(0 0 0 0 .00) 2004:(0 0 .00)														

6May00-8CD	fst	1¼	$:45^{4}$	$1:09^{4}$	$1:35^{3}$	2:01	KyDerby-G1	**77**	1	16^{11}	15^{8}	$11^{5½}$	11^{9}	$13^{20½}$	Nakatani C S	L126 b	17.10	84 -	FusichiPegsus$126^{1½}$ Aptitude126^{4} Impechmnt$126^{½}$	Awkward,swerve start	19
8Apr00-5SA	fst	1⅛	$:47^{1}$	$1:11^{2}$	$1:36^{2}$	1:49	SADerby-G1	**99**	3	6^{8}	$6^{9½}$	6^{8}	5^{4}	4^{6}	Nakatani C S	LB120 b	4.20	84-16	The Deputy120^{1} War Chant120^{2} Captain Steve120^{3}	Improved position	6
19Mar00-7SA	fst	$1\frac{1}{16}$	:23	$:45^{4}$	$1:10^{1}$	$1:42^{3}$	SnFelipe-G2	**99**	1	$6^{5½}$	5^{7}	$4^{4½}$	$4^{3½}$	$3^{3¾}$	Bailey J D	LB119 b	3.90	86-14	*Fusaichi Pegasus*$116^{¾}$ *The Deputy*122^{3} Anees119^{hd}	Saved grd, up for show	7
6Nov99-8GP	fst	$1\frac{1}{16}$	$:22^{1}$	:46	$1:10^{1}$	$1:42^{1}$	BCJuven-G1	**102**	9	14^{11}	14^{8}	$8^{7¾}$	$4^{1¾}$	$1^{2½}$	Stevens G L	L122 b	30.30	96 -	Anees$122^{2½}$ Chief Seattle$122^{¾}$ High Yield$122^{2¼}$	Bumped start,drifted	14
10Oct99-7SA	fst	1	$:22^{1}$	$:45^{4}$	$1:09^{4}$	$1:35^{3}$	Norfolk-G2	**95**	2	$6^{7½}$	$6^{8½}$	$3^{9½}$	3^{5}	3^{5}	Stevens G L	LB118 b	9.50	88-15	Dixie Union$118^{½}$ Forest Camp$118^{4½}$ *Anees*$118^{9½}$	Inside move,bested rst	6
3Sep99-3Dmr	fst	1	$:22^{4}$	:47	1:12	$1:37^{3}$	Md Sp Wt 48k	**82**	5	4^{5}	4^{4}	$4^{1¾}$	1^{hd}	1^{2}	Stevens G L	LB118 b	4.90	84-09	Anees118^{2} Silver Axe$118^{2½}$ Gilty Moment$118^{1½}$	4 wide bid, driving	8
21Aug99-5Dmr	fst	5½f	:22	$:45^{2}$	$:57^{4}$	$1:04^{2}$	Md Sp Wt 46k	**48**	9	6	9^{18}	9^{19}	8^{14}	6^{13}	Desormeaux K J	LB118	7.70	78-14	*Tavasco*$118^{3½}$ Brave Slew118^{nk} *Valiant Vision*$118^{¾}$	Lugged out start	9

In my column on November 11, 1999, in *Daily Racing Form*, I wrote about Anees's victory in the Juvenile and why I had selected him as my longshot of the day:

> One look at his pedigree and you knew that Anees (by Unbridled out of Ivory Idol, by Alydar) would love distances of more than one mile. Despite a good third to Dixie Union and Forest Camp in the Norfolk Stakes in only his third start, Anees was dismissed by the betting public and handicappers and returned $62.60 in an authoritative 2½-length victory in the Breeders' Cup Juvenile.
>
> Analyzing the Breeders' Cup races in last Thursday's column, I selected Anees in the Juvenile because the race set up for him. He was the colt I thought would benefit the most by the two-turn distance and the abundance of speed. Forest Camp (by Deputy Minister out of a Hold Your Peace mare) and Dixie Union (by Dixieland Band out of a Capote mare) were highly regarded because of their exploits in California, but their pedigrees were heavily slanted toward speed. The presence of other quality speed in the race (Chief Seattle, Personal First, and Captain Steve) combined with their poor post positions (Forest Camp had post 10; Dixie Union had 12) made others more enticing at far better odds.

The $2 exacta with Chief Seattle returned $406.40, while the $2 trifecta came back $2,484.80. Unfortunately, I did not have Mull of Kintyre, who finished fourth at 29-1, for a truly super $2 superfecta of $50,233.20!

THE 2000 JUVENILE

The 2000 Juvenile provided another great betting opportunity. You could have tossed three well-regarded 2-year-olds who figured to be at a disadvantage going 1 1/16 miles—City Zip (Carson City), Flame Thrower (Saint Ballado), and Yonaguska (Cherokee Run).

My choice that year was A P Valentine, a son of A.P. Indy who had won the Champagne Stakes in only his third career start as the tepid 3-1 choice over Point Given. But A P Valentine showed absolutely nothing in the Juvenile, finishing last as the 2-1 favorite.

Nevertheless, three colts who had a little legitimate chance at 1 1/16 miles, based on their pedigrees, were Macho Uno, Point Given, and Street Cry.

Macho Uno
Own: Stronach Stables

Gr/ro. c. 4 (Apr)
Sire: Holy Bull (Great Above) $15,000
Dam: Primal Force (Blushing Groom*Fr)
Br: Adena Springs (Ky)
Tr: Orseno Joseph F(0 0 0 0 .00) 2004:(210 24 .11)

Life	14	6	1	3	$1,851,803	116	D.Fst	14	6	1	3	$1,851,803	116
2002	6	2	0	1	$519,600	116	Wet(421)	0	0	0	0	$0	-
2001	4	1	1	1	$563,400	110	Turf(279)	0	0	0	0	$0	-
	0	0	0	0	$0	-	Dst(0)	0	0	0	0	$0	-

26Oct02-10AP	fst	1¼	:463	1:101	1:352	2:011	3↑	BCClasic-G1	101	6	75¾	75	63¼	46½	510¼	Stevens G L	L126 b	19.80	87	-	Volponi1266½ *Medagliad'Oro*121nk MilwaukeeBrew1263	Angled 5 wide turn	12
29Sep02-7AP	fst	1 3/16	:472	1:114	1:353	1:55	3↑	WashPkH-G2	97	2	33	32	31½	45¼	57¼	Stevens G L	L119 fb	*.70	-	-	*Tenpins*116nk Generous Rosi1151¼ *Bonus Pack*1154	No response	5
3Aug02-9Sar	fst	1⅛	:454	1:091	1:34	1:47	3↑	WhitneyH-G1	116	5	612	611	510	43½	42¾	Day P	L118 b	4.60	101	07	Left Bank1181¼ Street Cry123no *Lido Palace*1191½	Good finish inside	6
6Jly02-10Bel	fst	1¼	:483	1:124	1:37	2:004	3↑	SuburbnH-G2	111	5	53¼	42½	31	33	31¾	Stevens G L	L119 b	*1.10	88	10	E Dubai116¾ Lido Palace1191 Macho Uno1193¾	Game finish outside	7
1Jun02-13Suf	fst	1⅛	:462	1:103	1:37	1:502	3↑	MassH-G2	110	2	43½	53	51¾	41½	11¾	Stevens G L	LB117 b	2.10	91	13	Macho Uno1171¾ Evening Attire114nk Include1201¼	Altrd crs 1/8, in hand	9
23Mar02-9GP	fst	170	:23	:461	1:11	1:41	4↑	Alw 46000c	111	4	64	73¾	52¾	33	1½	Douglas R R	L120 b	*.70	96	17	*Macho Uno*120½ *Hail The Chief*1204¼ Proper Man1168¾	Up final strides	8
27Oct01-10Bel	fst	1¼	:47	1:111	1:354	2:003	3↑	BCClasic-G1	110	7	94¾	93¾	63¾	43	44½	Stevens G L	L122 fb	19.50	86	12	Tiznow126no *Sakhee*1261¾ Albert the Great1262¾	Even finish	13
29Sep01-11Tdn	fst	1⅛	:471	1:104	1:353	1:483		OhioDrby-G2	104	4	52¾	54½	43½	21½	3¾	Stevens G L	L119 fb	*.20	102	11	*WesternPride*119½ Woodmoon113nk MchoUno1194	Brushed,bid,outfinishd	6
3Sep01-11Pha	fst	1⅛	:483	1:123	1:371	1:493		PaDerby-G3	104	5	42½	43½	42½	3nk	11½	Stevens G L	L116 fb	*.90	90	17	Macho Uno1161½ Unbridled Elaine119½ Touch Tone1226¾	Outside, easily	6
25Jly01-8Sar	fst	7f	:222	:442	1:083	1:214	3↑	Alw 47000N3x	94	1	6	32½	32½	1hd	2no	Bailey J D	L116	*.95	96	05	Wicked Will116no *Macho Uno*1162 Country Only120½	Erratic deep stretch	7
4Nov00-8CD	fst	1 1/16	:232	:464	1:111	1:42		BCJuven-G1	99	4	42	51¼	41½	21	1no	Bailey J D	L122	6.30	100	-	Macho Uno122no *Point Given*1221½ *Street Cry*122½	Shied, ducked out wire	14
9Oct00-8WO	fst	1 1/16	:242	:48	1:13	1:44		GreyBC-G1	94	2	22	22	2½	12½	17	Bailey J D	L115	*.40	87	21	*Macho Uno*1157 *Indygo Shiner*1115¼ Stage Classic1136	Much the best	4
2Sep00-9Sar	fst	7f	:223	:461	1:111	1:242		Hopeful-G1	85	7	6	71½	61¼	21½	3nk	Prado E S	122	9.10	83	14	DH Yonaguska122 DH City Zip122nk *Macho Uno*1227¼	5 wide move, gamely	11
26Jly00-6Sar	fst	5½f	:224	:462	:58	1:042		Md Sp Wt 41k	84	7	4	2½	2½	1½	12¾	Prado E S	117	*.75	95	10	MchoUno1172¾ DevilsDomin1178¼ Mercenry1174½	Wrapped up under wire	7

Macho Uno, a son of speed sire Holy Bull, was a half-brother to Awesome Again, who won the 1998 Breeders' Cup Classic over Silver Charm and Swain. Macho Uno won his maiden debut at Saratoga by 2 3/4 lengths, and then, in only his second start, he finished third in the Hopeful Stakes, beaten only a neck by both Yonaguska and City Zip, who dead-heated for the win. Macho Uno next won the 1 1/16-mile Grey Breeders' Cup Stakes at Woodbine in his final prep for the Juvenile. On Breeders' Cup Day he stalked the pace, took the lead in midstretch, and just hung on to beat Point Given by a nose at 6-1. In doing so, he earned an Eclipse Award as best 2-year-old colt.

Point Given, a Thunder Gulch colt who had won the Kentucky Cup Juvenile and then finished second in the Champagne Stakes, was certainly bred to relish distances over one mile, and was clearly an overlay at 8-1.

Point Given
Own: The Thoroughbred Corporation

Ch. c. 3 (Mar)
Sire: Thunder Gulch (Gulch) $50,000
Dam: Turko's Turn (Turkoman)
Br: The Thoroughbred Corporation (Ky)
Tr: Baffert Bob(0 0 0 0 .00) 2004:(434 80 .18)

Life	13	9	3	0	$3,968,500	117	D.Fst	12	8	3	0	$3,518,500 117
2001	7	6	0	0	$3,350,000	117	Wet(315)	1	1	0	0	$450,000 110
2000	6	3	3	0	$618,500	101	Turf(273)	0	0	0	0	$0 -
Aik Ⓣ	0	0	0	0	$0	-	DstⓉ(291)	0	0	0	0	$0 -

25Aug01-10Sar	fst	1¼	:473 1:111 1:354 2:012	Travers-G1	117	7	31½	3½	2½	1hd	13½	Stevens G L	L126 br	*.65	98-02	Point Given1263½ E Dubai1261¼ *Dollar Bill*126¾	3 wide trip, driving	9
5Aug01-11Mth	fst	1⅛	:464 1:111 1:362 1:493	HsklInvH-G1	106	6	56¾	55½	31½	31	1½	Stevens G L	L124 br	*.30	88-10	*PointGiven*124½ TouchTone115no BurningRom119¾	Outside,lugged in,drvg	6
9Jun01-10Bel	fst	1½	:48 1:113 2:003 2:262	Belmont-G1	114	9	31	1hd	12	17	112¼	Stevens G L	L126 b	*1.35	107-02	*Point Given*12612¼ A PValentine126¾ Monarchos1261	5 wide, strong urging	9
19May01-11Pim	fst	1 3/16	:471 1:114 1:362 1:552	Preaknes-G1	111	11	910	67½	3nk	1½	12¼	Stevens G L	L126 b	*2.30	94-11	*Point Given*1262¼ A P Valentine126nk *Congaree*1261¼	Brk slw,5wd,lug in str	11
5May01-8CD	fst	1¼	:444 1:091 1:35 1:594	KyDerby-G1	99	17	76¼	73¾	21½	44½	511½	Stevens G L	L126 b	*1.80	92 -	Monarchos1264¾ Invisible Ink126no Congaree1264	Broke in bmp,flattened	17
7Apr01-5SA	wf	1⅛	:462 1:104 1:352 1:473	SADerby-G1	110	1	21	21	11	12½	15½	Stevens G L	LB122 b	*.70	97-08	Point Given1225½ CraftyC.T.1223 ILoveSilver1222½	Led in hand,ridden out	6
17Mar01-7SA	fst	1 1/16	:223 :461 1:102 1:414	SnFelipe-G2	105	8	55	54	1hd	12	12¼	Stevens G L	LB122 b	*.40	95-13	*PointGiven*1222¼ ILoveSilver1161½ JamicnRum1197	5wd move, led, cleared	8
16Dec00-4Hol	fst	1 1/16	:23 :464 1:104 1:421	HolFut-G1	101	4	45	3½	3½	2hd	11	Stevens G L	LB121 b	*.30	89-15	*PointGiven*1211 *MillnniumWind*1217 GoldnTickt1215	3wd,lugged in bit,best	4
4Nov00-8CD	fst	1 1/16	:232 :464 1:111 1:42	BCJuven-G1	99	1	106½	127	1410	67	2no	Stevens G L	L122 b	8.10	100 -	Macho Uno122no *Point Given*1221½ *Street Cry*122½	10w strtch,closed fast	14
14Oct00-9Bel	fst	1 1/16	:223 :45 1:092 1:412	Champagn-G1	95	2	41	1hd	3nk	2hd	21¾	Desormeaux K J	L122 b	4.60	88-09	A P Valentine1221¾ Point Given122¾ Yonaguska1221	Vied inside, gamely	10
16Sep00-12TP	fst	1 1/16	:221 :453 1:12 1:47	KyCupJuv-G3	81	7	89½	67½	53	13	13½	Sellers S J	L114 b	3.30	68-23	Point Given1143½ Holiday Thunder1144 *The Goo*116½	Broke a bit in air	11
26Aug00-7Dmr	fst	7f	:223 :452 1:102 1:232	Md Sp Wt 47k	93	1	6	4¾	1½	11	12	Espinoza V	LB118 b	*1.20	88-10	*PointGiven*1182 HighandLowVixen1184 Qwqeb1188	Inside duel,clear,dvng	7
12Aug00-6Dmr	fst	5½f	:221 :451 :572 1:04	Md Sp Wt 47k	74	9	6	109¾	99½	79¾	25½	Take Y	LB118 b	19.00	86-17	HighCascade1185½ *PointGiven*1182½ WestwrdAngel118no	4wd turn,late 2nd	11

Street Cry, who was by Machiavellian, a champion 2-year-old in France and a world-class sire, had finished second to Flame Thrower in both the Del Mar Futurity and Norfolk Stakes, and finished third in the Juvenile at 5-1.

The Macho Uno-Point Given $2 exacta paid $124.20 while the $2 trifecta with Street Cry returned $944.60.

Johannesburg
Own: Mr M. Tabor & Mrs John Magnier

B. c. 3 (Feb)
Sire: Hennessy (Storm Cat) $35,000
Dam: Myth (Ogygian)
Br: W. G. Lyster III & Jayeff B Stables (Ky)
Tr: O'Brien Aidan P(0 0 0 0 .00) 2004:(0 0 .00)

Life	10	7	1	0	$1,014,585	99	D.Fst	2	1	0	0	$520,000 9
2002	3	0	1	0	$11,691	95	Wet(333)	0	0	0	0	$0 -
2001	7	7	0	0	$1,002,894	99	Turf(289)	8	6	1	0	$494,585 -
	0	0	0	0	$0	-	Dst(0)	0	0	0	0	$0 -

22Jun02♦Ascot (GB)	gf	6f	Ⓣ Str 1:141	3↑ Golden Jubilee S.-G1							910	Kinane M J	123	*3.00		Malhub1301½ Danehurst127½ Three Points1301¾	1
Timeform rating: 90				Stk 404100												*Trckd ldrs,drifted right over 2f out,soon weakened.Continent 5t*	
4May02-9CD	fst	1¼	:47 1:113 1:363 2:01	KyDerby-G1	95	1	106½	105¼	98¼	88	813	Stevens G L	L126	8.10	81-05	*War Emblem*1264 Proud Citizen126¾ Perfect Drift1263¼	Inside trip,no rally 1
Previously trained by O'Brien Aidan P																	
7Apr02♦Curragh (Ire)	yl	7f	Ⓣ Str 1:313	3↑ Gladness Stakes-G3							2no	Kinane M J	125	*.30		*Rebelline*136no Johannesburg1251 Shoal Creek133¾	
Timeform rating: 114				Stk 61500												*Rank early tracking in 3rd,led 1f out,headed on lin*	
Previously trained by O'Brien Aidan P																	
27Oct01-8Bel	fst	1 1/16	:233 :464 1:11 1:421	BesTBCJv-G1	99	3	51¾	51¾	51¼	4nk	11¼	Kinane M J	L122	7.20	86-12	Johannesburg1221¼ *Repent*1221¼ *Siphonic*122¾	Split rivals, driving
Previously trained by O'Brien Aidan P																	
4Oct01♦Newmarket (GB)	yl	6f	Ⓣ Str 1:113	Middle Park Stakes-G1							13	Kinane M J	123	*.30		*Johannesburg*1233 Zipping1233 Doc Holiday123¾	
Timeform rating: 121+				Stk 221500												*Tracked in 4th,quickened to lead 1-1/2f out,soon cle*	
26Aug01♦Deauville (Fr)	yl	*6f	Ⓣ Str 1:102	Prix Morny-G1							11½	Kinane M J	126	*.60e		*Johannesburg*1261½ Zipping1261½ Meshaheer1261½	
Timeform rating: 120+				Stk 194900												*Tracked in 5th,rallied to lead 170y out,handily.Firebreak 4*	
12Aug01♦Leopardstwn (Ire)	sf	6f	Ⓣ Str 1:131	Phoenix Stakes-G1							15	Kinane M J	126	*.40		*Johannesburg*1265 Miss Beabea1231½ Agnetha123nk	
Timeform rating: 119+				Stk 255300												*Tracked in 5th,led over 1f out,quickly clear.Wiseman's Ferry 4*	
14Jly01♦Curragh (Ire)	yl	6f	Ⓣ Str 1:164	Anglesey Stakes (6f,63y)-G3							14	Kinane M J	127	*.80		*Johannesburg*1274 Wiseman's Ferry124nk High Society1213	
Timeform rating: 114+				Stk 65100												*Tracked in 3rd,angled right 1-1/2f out,led 1f out,quickly cle*	
21Jun01♦Ascot (GB)	gd	5f	Ⓣ Str 1:02	Norfolk Stakes-G3							11¼	Kinane M J	124	*1.35		*Johannesburg*1241¼ Waterside124no Lord Merlin1241½	
Timeform rating: 100+				Stk 77900												*Slowly away,soon tracking leaders,drifted right 2f out,led 1f c*	
30May01♦Fairyhouse (Ire)	fm	6f	Ⓣ RH 1:144	Ratoath EBF Maiden							13½	Kinane M J	128	*.30		*Johannesburg*1283½ Minaun Heights1235 Leinster Mills1234	
Timeform rating: 84+				Maiden 15200												*Well placed in 4th,led 1-1/2f out,drew clear in ha*	

The Incomparable Johannesburg

There have been many outstanding 2-year-old colts, but none of them has ever matched the accomplishments of Johannesburg, who was undefeated in seven starts in 2001, winning Grade or Group 1 stakes in four different countries—the United States, England, Ireland, and France.

Officer had ruled the juvenile ranks in this country that year, but his pedigree was highly questionable beyond one mile. While he did win the Champagne Stakes at $1\frac{1}{16}$ miles, that race was run around one turn at Belmont Park. With much more speed signed on in the Juvenile, I had little faith that he would be finishing strongly. By a speed sire, Bertrando, Officer had a pedigree top-heavy with brilliant (speed) influences, such as Septieme Ciel, Raise a Man, and Ack Ack. Undefeated in five starts and trained by Bob Baffert, Officer was 4-5 in the Juvenile, but after showing his customary speed, he hit the wall and tired to finish fifth. The highly regarded Came Home also was suspect at the distance and tired to finish seventh after chasing Officer.

Johannesburg rated beautifully behind the early pacesetters, burst through an opening in midstretch, and accelerated quickly to win by $1\frac{1}{4}$ lengths at 7-1. By speed influence Hennessy, who was beaten just a neck by Unbridled's Song in the 1995 Breeders' Cup Juvenile, Johannesburg is from an exceptional female family that has produced such runners as Round Table, Tale of the Cat, Pulpit, Preach, Announce, and Region.

But the big play was using Repent, a major overlay at 42-1. Repent, from the first crop of Preakness winner Louis Quatorze, was coming off a victory in the Kentucky Cup Juvenile at the Breeders' Cup Juvenile distance. While many in the field were suspect at $1\frac{1}{16}$ miles, Repent was perfectly suited to this race. The pedigree-handicapping exacta of Johannesburg and Repent returned $530.

Repent
Own: Select Stable

Dk. b or b. c. 3 (Feb)
Sire: Louis Quatorze (Sovereign Dancer) $6,000
Dam: Baby Grace*Arg (Cipayo*Arg)
Br: Taylor Made Farm Inc. (Ky)
Tr: McPeek Kenneth G(0 0 0 0 .00) 2004:(233 40 .17)

			Life	10	5	3	1	$1,255,660	112	D.Fst	7	4	2	1	$921,120	102
			2002	5	2	2	0	$840,000	112	Wet(327)	3	1	1	0	$334,540	112
			2001	5	3	1	1	$415,660	97	Turf(241)	0	0	0	0	$0	–
								$0	–	Dst(0)	0	0	0	0	$0	–

28Sep02–9Bel	gd	$1\frac{1}{4}$	:48	1:111	1:351	1:592	34 JkyClbGC-G1	98	6	$2\frac{1}{2}$	$87\frac{1}{2}$	8^6	8^{10}	$710\frac{1}{4}$	Prado E S	L122 b	*1.70	87–03	Evening Attire$126^{2\frac{3}{4}}$ Lido Palace$126\frac{3}{4}$ Harlan's Holiday122^{no}	Inside, tired	8
24Aug02–10Sar	sly	$1\frac{1}{4}$	:464	1:112	1:37	2:022	Travers-G1	112	4	6^{11}	$65\frac{1}{4}$	3^2	2^1	$2\frac{1}{2}$	Prado E S	L126 b	3.85	92–18	Medaglia d'Oro$126\frac{1}{2}$ Repent$126^{2\frac{1}{4}}$ Nothing Flat$126\frac{3}{4}$	Game finish outside	9
6Apr02–8Spt	fst	$1\frac{1}{8}$	:481	1:13	1:373	1:494	IllDerby-G2	102	9	$98\frac{1}{2}$	$97\frac{1}{4}$	5^4	2^5	$26\frac{1}{4}$	Bailey J D	L124 b	*.50	86–17	War Emblem$1146\frac{1}{4}$ Repent$1244\frac{1}{2}$ Fonz's$1176\frac{1}{4}$	No match, drifted late	9
10Mar02–9FG	fst	$1\frac{1}{8}$	:241	:481	1:13	1:434	LaDerby-G2	95	4	$53\frac{1}{2}$	$52\frac{1}{2}$	4^3	1^{hd}	1no	Bailey J D	L122 b	*.40	91–07	Repent122^{no} Easyfromthegitgo$122\frac{3}{4}$ Itsllinthchs$122\frac{1}{4}$	Drifted in&out drive	7
7Feb02–9FG	fst	$1\frac{1}{16}$	:23	:46	1:111	1:43	RisenStr-G3	102	7	$86\frac{1}{4}$	$87\frac{1}{4}$	8^6	$21\frac{1}{2}$	$12\frac{1}{4}$	D'Amico A J	L122 b	*.70	95–06	Repent$122^{2\frac{1}{4}}$ BobsImage115^3 Easyfromthegitgo$122^{2\frac{1}{2}}$	Swung out 8w, clear	9
4Nov01–11CD	sly	$1\frac{1}{16}$	:24	:474	1:122	1:442	KyJC-G2	92	4	6^5	$52\frac{1}{2}$	5^3	3^{nk}	$11\frac{1}{2}$	D'Amico A J	L122 b	*.80	88–10	Repent$122^{1\frac{1}{2}}$ Request for Parole117^{nk} High Star115^1	Steady 1/2p,rail,drvg	6
9Oct01–8Bel	fst	$1\frac{1}{16}$	:233	:464	1:11	1:421	BesTBCJv-G1	97	10	$94\frac{1}{2}$	8^7	$76\frac{1}{2}$	$62\frac{1}{2}$	$21\frac{1}{2}$	D'Amico A J	L122 b	42.25	85–12	Johannesburg$122^{1\frac{1}{4}}$ Repent$122^{1\frac{1}{4}}$ Siphonic$122\frac{3}{4}$	Game finish outside	12
2Sep01–9TP	fst	$1\frac{1}{16}$	:23	:463	1:11	1:433	KyCupJuv-G3	90	7	$64\frac{1}{4}$	$63\frac{1}{2}$	3^2	1^{hd}	$11\frac{1}{2}$	D'Amico A J	L114 b	6.50	93–06	Repent$1141\frac{1}{2}$ French Assault118^8 Gold Dollar114^3	4 wide trip, driving	7
7Sep01–1TP	fst	1	:232	:47	1:123	1:393	Md Sp Wt 24k	77	6	$54\frac{1}{2}$	$36\frac{1}{2}$	3^2	2^{hd}	1no	D'Amico A J	L120	*.70	77–28	Repent120^{no} Bay Monster$120^5\frac{1}{4}$ Patrol$1154\frac{1}{2}$	Bumped start, driving	6
3Aug01–2EIP	fst	6f	:224	:462	:584	1:113	Md Sp Wt 19k	72	3	11	91^1	6^9	$46\frac{1}{2}$	$32\frac{3}{4}$	D'Amico A J	L120	13.90	87–13	Halo Spirit120^{nk} World Champion$120^{2\frac{1}{4}}$ Repent$120^{2\frac{3}{4}}$	Inside, mild gain	12

The 2003 Juvenile was especially rewarding for pedigree players. All the winners of the major 2-year-old stakes skipped the Juvenile, either because of injury or by design. What was left was a watered-down field of juveniles, and the colts who had shown the most in earlier races, such as Cuvee and Chapel Royal, were very questionable at 1$\frac{1}{16}$ miles.

This is precisely where pedigree played a huge role. The following was my *Daily Racing Form* column in the days preceding the Breeders' Cup:

PEDIGREE HANDICAPPING
Juvenile: This Is When Distance Breeding Should Shine
By Lauren Stich

Perhaps more than any other year, championship honors are up for grabs in the Breeders' Cup Juvenile. Silver Wagon (Hopeful Stakes), Birdstone (Champagne Stakes), Eurosilver (Lane's End Futurity), and Ruler's Court (Norfolk Stakes) each won one major stakes, and by skipping the most important race for 2-year-olds, they leave the door wide open to crown the winner of the BC Juvenile as champion.

As their pedigrees indicated, Cuvee (Carson City) and Chapel Royal (Montbrook) showed brilliance early at 2, and a victory in the Juvenile would cement an Eclipse Award for either colt, especially since the winners of the division's major events are absent.

Cuvee and Chapel Royal are both classy individuals, but there is a big question regarding their ability to be as brilliant at 1$\frac{1}{16}$ miles, especially around two turns. Chapel Royal was a $1.2 million purchase last February at Ocala, Fla., where he dazzled onlookers with his blazing workouts. After reeling off three straight victories to begin his career, including easy romps in the Flash and

Sanford Stakes, he finished second to Silver Wagon in the Hopeful Stakes, and finished a game second over a tiring track to Birdstone in the $1\frac{1}{16}$-mile Champagne Stakes. By Montbrook out of a Cutlass mare, Chapel Royal gets a double dose of high speed, and his second dam is a half-sister to champion Fanfreluche. Chapel Royal will have plenty of speed to contend with early, most notably from Cuvee, Race for Glory, Capitano, and Siphonizer.

Aside from a rough start in the Bashford Manor Stakes, where he finished third, Cuvee has been perfect, winning his other four starts, including three stakes, all by lengthy margins. A flashy chestnut like so many runners by Carson City, Cuvee had his most significant victory in the Futurity Stakes, where he easily negotiated one mile around one turn at Belmont. But the Breeders' Cup Juvenile is around two turns, and he faces a stronger pace threat. Carson City was one of Mr. Prospector's fastest sons, and from the very start, his runners have proven to be best sprinting. Under ideal circumstances, they have occasionally managed to win at $1\frac{1}{16}$ miles. Cuvee's female family, which has been nothing short of sensational, was cultivated by the late Verne Winchell. Cuvee's dam, Christmas Star, is a half-sister to stakes winners Olympio, Call Now, and Your Call, as well as stakes-placed Carol's Wonder, the dam of stakes winners Wild Wonder and Acrylic. Bien Nicole, a starter in this year's Filly and Mare Turf, and stakes winner Early Flyer also come from this prolific family.

With an expected hot pace, the Juvenile sets up for a colt bred to appreciate distance, much like in 1999, when Anees (by Unbridled) won despite a pronounced Gulfstream Park speed bias to sweep by horses whose brilliance diminished beyond seven furlongs.

Three colts who should benefit from the strong pace and two-turn distance are Tiger Hunt, Minister Eric, and Action This Day.

Tiger Hunt and Action This Day are by the late Kris S., whose runners have had remarkable success in Breeders' Cup races, including Hollywood Wildcat (Distaff), Soaring Softly (Filly and Mare Turf), Prized (Turf), and Brocco (Juvenile).

Despite several bumping incidents in his July debut at Churchill Downs, Tiger Hunt rallied to win a six-furlong maiden race at 24-1. Off a two-month layoff, he won the Cradle Stakes at River Downs at $1\frac{1}{16}$ miles, and in his third and last start, he finished second to Eurosilver in the Lane's End Breeders' Futurity, rallying from nearly 10 lengths off the lead over Keeneland's speed-favoring surface and encountering traffic on the second turn.

Tiger Hunt is from the female family of Shy Dancer, whose descendants include champion 2-year-old filly Heavenly Cause, Two Punch, Shy Dawn, Purple Mountain, Petite Rouge, and Jacques Who.

Minister Eric and Action This Day are both trained by Richard Mandella, who also has Siphonizer, who will help set the table for his uncoupled stablemates. Minister Eric is by freshman sire Old Trieste, who died earlier this year. Having tactical speed, Minister Eric will be stalking the early leaders and will get first jump on the late runners. Minister Eric's third dam is Aladancer (Northern Dancer), a stakes-winning half-sister to the dam of Cryptoclearance. Distinguished runners from this family include Run Softly, Latin American, and Pico Teneriffe.

Action This Day has only had two starts, but in this watered-down Juvenile, he is the kind of fast-developing colt who could spring an upset. Action This Day will ultimately be most effective at distances longer than $1\frac{1}{8}$ miles on turf, but runners by the versatile Kris S. are reliable on dirt. Action This Day is out of a mare by Prix de l'Arc de Triomphe winner Trempolino, his second dam is by Forli, and his third dam is by the renowned European miler Habitat. As unlikely as it may seem, Action This Day could get a minor award, if not the victory itself.

Action This Day
Own: Hughes B. W

B. c. 3 (Feb) KEEJUL02 $150,000
Sire: Kris S. (Roberto) $150,000
Dam: Najecam (Trempolino)
Br: Jaime S. Carrion, Trustee (Ky)
Tr: Mandella Richard E(0 0 0 0 .00) 2004:(94 13 .14)

Life	7	2	1	0	$822,084	98	D.Fst	6	2	1	0	$822,084	98
2004	4	0	0	0	$4,884	98	Wet(353)	1	0	0	0	$0	87
2003	3	2	1	0	$817,200	92	Turf(338)	0	0	0	0	$0	-
	0	0	0	0	$0	-	Dst(0)	0	0	0	0	$0	-

1May04-10CD	sly	1¼	$:46^{3}$	$1{:}11^{4}$	$1{:}37^{1}$	2:04	KyDerby-G1	**87**	4	18^{13}	$18^{9\frac{3}{4}}$	14^{12}	12^{10}	$6^{13\frac{3}{4}}$	Flores D R	L126	43.40	65-21	*Smarty Jones*$126^{2\frac{3}{4}}$ Lion Heart$126^{3\frac{1}{4}}$ Imperialism126^{2}	Steadied 3/8,mild bid	18
10Apr04-9Kee	fst	1⅛	$:46^{3}$	1:11	$1{:}36^{4}$	$1{:}49^{2}$	BlueGras-G1	**89**	1	$5^{8\frac{1}{4}}$	6^{11}	$7^{7\frac{1}{2}}$	$6^{7\frac{1}{2}}$	$6^{13\frac{1}{2}}$	Flores D R	L123	10.30	80-20	The Cliff's Edge$123^{\frac{1}{2}}$ Lion Heart123^{6} Limehouse$123^{3\frac{3}{4}}$	No factor	8
14Mar04-5SA	fst	1 1/16	$:23^{1}$	$:46^{4}$	1:11	$1{:}42^{4}$	SnFelipe-G2	**84**	3	$4^{3\frac{1}{2}}$	$5^{5\frac{1}{2}}$	$6^{4\frac{1}{2}}$	$7^{6\frac{1}{2}}$	$7^{9\frac{1}{2}}$	Flores D R	LB119	2.60	81-09	Prechintthebr116^{no} StAveril$122^{4\frac{1}{2}}$ HrvrdAvenu116^{1}	Pulled,inside,wkened	9
8Feb04-8SA	fst	1⅛	:47	1:11	$1{:}36^{2}$	$1{:}49^{1}$	Sham81k	**98**	7	$6^{7\frac{1}{2}}$	$6^{7\frac{3}{4}}$	6^{6}	$4^{3\frac{1}{2}}$	$4^{1\frac{1}{4}}$	Flores D R	LB123	1.90	87-13	MasterDavid116^{1} Borrego120^{hd} *Preachinatthebr*116^{hd}	5wd into lane,rallied	7
25Oct03-7SA	fst	1 1/16	$:22^{1}$	:45	$1{:}09^{4}$	$1{:}43^{3}$	BCJuvnle-G1	**92**	2	12^{13}	12^{13}	$10^{6\frac{1}{4}}$	$3^{1\frac{1}{2}}$	$1^{2\frac{1}{4}}$	Flores D R	LB122	26.80	86-07	ActionThisDay$122^{2\frac{1}{4}}$ MinisterEric122^{5} ChpelRoyl122^{no}	4 wide, going away	12
28Sep03-1SA	fst	1 1/16	$:23^{2}$	$:47^{3}$	1:12	$1{:}45^{3}$	Md Sp Wt 45k	**79**	5	$7^{7\frac{3}{4}}$	7^{12}	$6^{9\frac{1}{2}}$	$5^{2\frac{1}{4}}$	1no	Solis A	LB117	*1.00	76-16	*ActionThisDy*117no NtiveApprovl$117^{\frac{1}{2}}$ CourgeousAct117^{4}	Bid btwn,gamely	7
5Sep03-2Dmr	fst	1	$:22^{4}$	$:46^{3}$	$1{:}10^{4}$	1:37	Md Sp Wt 51k	**74**	5	6^{6}	$6^{6\frac{3}{4}}$	$5^{7\frac{1}{2}}$	4^{6}	2^{7}	Solis A	LB120	4.10	82-10	Coldntight120^{7} *ActionThisDay*120^{nk} ThtsnOutrge120^{3}	Bit tight 1/16,late 2d	6

The late-developing Action This Day did appreciate the distance, whereas Cuvee found it too much to overcome. Cuvee's chances were further complicated by his outside post, 12, but that did not bother Halfbridled, who had no such distance limitations and won the Juvenile Fillies despite her even wider post (14). Clearly, this was a case where the favorite was extremely vulnerable.

Action This Day paid $55.60 to win, and the $2 exacta with his stablemate Minister Eric returned $376.80. I'm still cursing Chapel Royal, who just held on to defeat Tiger Hunt, who missed third and a gigantic trifecta, by a nose. Nevertheless, the $2 trifecta paid $4,490.80. The $1 superfecta with Action This Day-Minister Eric-Chapel Royal-Tiger Hunt was $9,123.40.

Pedigree handicapping has often played a significant role in the Breeders' Cup Juvenile and Juvenile Fillies, exposing many false favorites and uncovering live longshots. Again, this is due mostly to the vulnerability of 2-year-olds like Officer and Cuvee, who were so flashy at shorter distances before facing more speed and going 1 1/16 miles, as well as meeting late-maturing runners who were bred to get better as the distances increased.

7

PLAYING THE
HANDICAPPING
TOURNAMENTS
BY PEDIGREE

APPLYING KNOWLEDGE OF pedigrees to the lucrative handicapping tournaments is taking pedigree handicapping to the ultimate level. If you think breeding angles are only for pedigree geeks like me, just ask major handicapping tournament winners Ralph Siraco, Steve Terclak, and Judy Wagner, each of whom won a contest in the last race of the tournament with a play based strictly on pedigree handicapping. Using pedigrees, I was also fortunate to win first prize of $30,000 in the Bally's Summer Stakes in Las Vegas in 2000.

ORLEANS HANDICAPPING TOURNAMENT, OCTOBER 1998

In October 1998, Ralph Siraco, who is the host of the daily radio show "Race Day Las Vegas" and contributes a regular column in *Daily Racing Form*, was in the running for a major prize in the Orleans

Handicapping Contest going into the final day of the grueling three-day event, and was soliciting help from his national correspondents on his radio show, looking for live longshots.

I had been a regular guest on "Raceday Las Vegas" since 1997 and Ralph asked if I had a horse that could help him in the contest. While not a participant in that tournament, I was happy to suggest to Ralph a colt I thought had real value: Secret Advice R.N., who was running in a maiden special weight race on turf at Santa Anita. Secret Advice R.N. was a perfect fit for my favorite angle of pedigree handicapping, the hidden turf factor.

Secret Advice R. N
Own: Dedomenico Mark P

B. m. 9 (Feb)
Sire: Hansel (Woodman) $10,946
Dam: Secret Advice (Secreto)
Br: Jaime S. Carrion, Trustee (Ky)
Tr: Hofmans David E (0 0 0 0 .00) 2004:(66 11 .17)

Life	8 3 0 1	$62,970	90	**D.Fst**	5 1 0 1	$21,030	87
1999	1 0 0 0	$0	71	Wet(324)	1 1 0 0	$19,740	90
1998	7 3 0 1	$62,970	90	Turf(302)	2 1 0 0	$22,200	89
	0 0 0 0	$0	–	Dst(0)	0 0 0 0	$0	–

3Dec99-7Hol fm 5½f ⊤ :21⁴ :43⁴ :55⁴1:01⁴ 3↑⑤Alw 47025ɴ3x 71 6 2 68½ 6¹⁰ 68½ 6¹⁰ Delahoussaye E LB118 b 10.00 85– 05 *Hookedonthefeelin116³ Aviate116¹½ Sheza Valentine118³* Off rail, outrun 6
Previously trained by Hollendorfer Jerry
7Nov98-9BM sly 1½ ⊗ :46¹1:10³ 1:36²1:49³ ⑤PaloAlto37k 90 10 74½ 5⁴ 52½ 2ʰᵈ 1¾ Warren R J Jr LB115 b 6.90 83– 19 Secret Advice R. N115¾ Feverish116¹ ExcessLoot1195½ 4w 2nd turn, drvng 12
Previously trained by Dollase Craig
17Oct98-9SA fm *6½f ⊤ :21¹ :44¹ 1:08²1:14⁴ 3↑⑥Alw 37148ɴ$y 89 7 5 5⁸ 5¹¹ 4² 1½ Solis A LB117 b 9.00 83– 17 *Secret Advice R. N117¼ Beguiled117² Trapshut117¾* Rallied, up late 12
2Sep98-6Dmr fst 6f :21⁴ :45 :57²1:10² 3↑⑥Alw 43008ɴ$y 81 5 8 7⁴ 72½ 62¾ 42½ Nakatani C S LB115 b 2.80 85– 15 Lady Cadet117¹½ Beguiled116ⁿᵏ Sheza Valentine122¾ Widest into stretch 8
Previously trained by Hollendorfer Jerry
3Jly98-10Pln fst 6f :22³ :45² :57³1:11 ⑥Alw 33800ɴ$y 79 6 6 62¾ 42 32½ 31½ Castro J M LB117 6.70 86– 14 BoldCrscnt117ʰᵈ HrdAcktoFollow117¹½ ScrtLdvcRN117¹ 3w trn, bid,hung 10
17Apr98-7GG fst 6f :22 :44⁴ :57²1:10² ⑥Alw 32480ɴ$y 55 1 7 6⁵ 78½ 67½ 6¹⁰ Baze R A LB118 *.90 78– 15 Ourburiedtresur118¹ MdowVist118⁷ FirstTimAffir118ʰᵈ Svd grnd, no rally 10
29Mar98-1BM fst 6f :22² :45¹ :57³1:10¹ ⑥Md Sp Wt 25k 87 3 2 31½ 22½ 1¹ 11½ Baze R A LB117 *.80 88– 18 SecretAdviceRN117¹½ Strotyp117³ PrttyTimly117¹⁰ Angled out 1/4p, drvng 5
Previously trained by Baffert Bob
14Mar98-4SA fst 6½f :21³ :44² 1:09³1:16¹ ⑥Md Sp Wt 38k 67 11 3 4¾ 41½ 3⁵ 58½ Pedroza M A LB117 3.30 80– 09 DaLeprechun117⁴ CrypticMystery117¹½ LoveUFrn1172½ 4 wide, weakened 11

Lightly raced, Secret Advice R.N. had run on dirt with modest results but was trying grass for the first time. His sire, Preakness and Belmont Stakes winner Hansel, who was a champion at 3, had been a disappointment as a sire, but his runners were much better on turf. Like so many hidden turf sires who achieved success on dirt, Hansel was also bred to be good on grass. His sire, Woodman (Mr. Prospector), was a champion at 2 in Ireland, and in addition to Hansel, had sired 2-year-old champion Timber Country, now a successful stallion in Japan (where most of his runners race on grass). While Woodman's runners have excelled on all surfaces, they are unquestionably best on turf.

Woodman's notable offspring who have flourished on turf are Hishi Akebono, a champion sprinter/miler in Japan; Hawk Wing, a champion 3-year-old colt in England and Ireland; and the full siblings Hector Protector and Bosra Sham. Hector Protector was a champion 2-year-old in France, while Bosra Sham was a champion 3-year-old filly and older mare in England. Woodman's other European champions include Woodcarver, Dr Johnson, Way of Light, and Mujtahid.

Despite the considerable success of Woodman's horses on grass, most American horseplayers only know of him through his two best dirt runners—Timber Country and Hansel, and possibly stakes winners Mahogany Hall, Bound by Honor, and Patience Game. For this reason, his offspring, and especially his sons' offspring, are usually overlays on turf.

Mr. Prospector is the sire of hundreds of young stallions, and because of his initial success, Mr. Prospector was bred to a veritable Who's Who of broodmares.

Woodman is among the best-bred of all the Mr. Prospectors, and his female family has had enviable success over the past six decades.

His dam, Playmate, who was not much of a runner, was one of four full sisters (including Numbered Account, Special Account, and The Cuddler) to produce stakes winners. Numbered Account was head and shoulders the best of them, a champion 2-year-old filly who was as special as any broodmare bred and raced by Ogden Phipps. Numbered Account's most important foal was Private Account, who went on to sire Personal Ensign. Numbered Account also produced stakes winner Dance Number and stakes-placed Polish Numbers, who became a prominent speed influence standing in Maryland who died in 2002. Dance Number produced champion 2-year-old colt Rhythm, stakes winner Get Lucky (the dam of Accelerator), and Not for Love, a leading Maryland-based sprint sire. Dance Number is also the second dam of Mutakddim, the sire of Lady Tak and Hattiesburg. Special Account produced stakes winners Gallant Special and Gallant Sister, and the latter is the dam of Lyphard Gal, who produced $2 million-plus earner Heritage of Gold. The Cuddler produced stakes winner Verification.

But Secret Advice R.N. had much more going for him than the hidden turf influence of Hansel.

While I would have liked him on grass off Hansel alone, Secret Advice R.N. was also out of a mare by Secreto, a son of Northern Dancer who was a Group 1 winner in Europe. Thus, Secret Advice R.N. had a very strong T^2 pedigree, and I felt confident giving him out to Siraco, hoping the horse would be in the 10-1 range.

Looking at the results later that night, I was excited to see that Secret Advice R.N. had won, paying $20, but had no idea how Siraco fared or who won the tournament. The next morning I headed over to the Orleans, and heard the dramatic details. Dave ("the Maven") Gutfreund, who has won several major handicapping tournaments, was also in a position to win it all with two entries going into the last race of the three-day contest. But when Gutfreund saw me, he came running over and read me the riot act, half in jest and half in truth. He had heard the radio show that morning and cursed me for giving out Secret Advice R.N.

It seemed that Gutfreund had selected Secret Advice R.N. for his last "bullet" of the day and was jumping out of his skin, thinking he finished first *and* second in the contest with his two tournament entries. But his excitement turned into disbelief when he realized Siraco, sitting at a table across the ballroom, also had Secret Advice R.N.

Siraco won $96,000 for first place, while Gutfreund finished an admirable second and fourth with his two entries, collecting a total of nearly $70,000.

BELMONT SUMMER STAKES, JULY 2000

Steve Terelak, advertising director for *Horseplayer Magazine*, was looking for a price in the last race of the Belmont 2000 Summer Stakes contest in July 2000, a maiden special weight on the grass. A fellow player, Carolyn Hale, was not in position to garner a prize, but she mentioned to Terelak that she had bought the tapes of Daily Racing

Form's Horseplayers Expo 2000, which she had attended in Las Vegas that past February.

Driving to Belmont Park from her home in western Massachusetts, Hale had listened over and over to different sessions from that Expo, including my presentation on pedigree handicapping, which included the hidden turf factor. She remembered that I said that runners by Holy Bull were going to offer great value on grass because Holy Bull was not associated with that surface, although he was extremely well bred for it.

Keep It Holy
Own: Cassidy Brendan

Gr/ro. g. 7 (Apr)
Sire: Holy Bull (Great Above) $15,000
Dam: Sweet Willa (Assert*Ire)
Br: Lavin Bloodstock (Ky)
Tr: Jeannont Dianne M(0 0 0 0 .00) 2004:(52 5 .10)

Life	27	4	1	2	$98,503	89	D.Fst	5	0	0	0	$378	59
2004	2	0	0	0	$870	70	Wet(365)	0	0	0	0	$0	-
2003	4	0	0	0	$858	73	Turf(259)	22	4	1	2	$98,125	89
	0	0	0	0	$0	-	Dst(0)	0	0	0	0	$0	-

27Jun04-7Cnl	gd	1⅛	Ⓣ	:494 1:142 1:40 1:532	3↑ Alw 8500s	70	6	65	66	65½	78½	54¾	Rosado R J	L119 f	8.40	65 30	*Smart Agenda*1241½ Say No JustIn124nk Kemerton1191	Wide, no response	8
11Jun04-2Cnl	fm	1	[T]	:233 :48 1:132 1:393	3↑ Clm 6000(6.5-6)B	54	6	75½	85½	74½	35½	42	Rodriguez E D	L115 f	7.30	79-14	BrotherBlise109½ *RougeSenstion*119½ *ShdesCrek*1191	Wide, drifted out late	12
11Oct03-7Pha	fm	1 1/16	Ⓣ	:224 :473 1:132 1:464	3↑ Clm 16000(20-16)	50	12	85½	66	77	812	816½	Prado A J	L116 f	20.50	57-30	Captain Holloway1182¼ ReasontoSquall1141¼ PipeBomb120½	Not a threat	12
22Jly03-6Pha	fst	7f		:214 :44 1:094 1:242	3↑ Clm 7500N2Y	57	9	5	76¼	98¼	811	67½	DeAlba C5	L113 f	9.50	77-17	*Jazz Parade*113¾ *Humberto*118½ Hootend120¾	No factor	9
Previously trained by Dickey Keith																			
17Feb03-4FG	fst	140		:241 :49 1:142 1:423	4↑ Clm 12500	59	4	54	73½	77	79	59	Espinosa L E	L120 f	6.70	72-16	Clarksdale122no Chris's Turn1202¼ Straight Street1182¾	Rail, outrun	7
26Jan03-9FG	fm	*1 1/16	Ⓣ	:241 :501 1:161 1:502	4↑ Clm 17500	73	5	22	21	1hd	1½	52½	Meche D J	L120	5.50	58-35	Torioso118no Devil's Bandit118¾ *Ebee's*118½	Edge, weakened late	9
27Dec02-2FG	fm	*1	Ⓣ	:25 :50 1:151 1:392	3↑ Clm 17500	85	9	11½	11½	1½	12	1nk	Meche D J	L118	14.30	88-13	KeepItHoly118nk *NoJcketRequired*1181 *JustFourAustin*1161	Rated, held on	11
12Dec02-6FG	gd	*1 1/16	Ⓣ	:241 :483 1:132 1:444	3↑ Clm 17500	77	5	65¼	64½	51¾	44	44¼	Lanerie C J	L118	11.70	85-11	Image118½ Power and Panache1192½ Danzaman1181¼	Little impact	10
31Oct02-7Med	yl	1 1/16	Ⓣ	:224 :471 1:121 1:451	3↑ [R]Hcp 25000s	68	6	97¼	119½	107¼	910	910¾	Cruz C	L118	22.80	67-22	Platinum Setting120¾ He Flies1201 Homecooking Ruby1192½	No factor	11
5Oct02-5Med	gd	1⅜	Ⓣ	:50 1:152 1:404 2:182	3↑ Clm 20000(20-18)	79	4	72½	62½	74½	53	32½	Martin E M Jr	L116	6.30	75-20	TruckingBaron1141 CyberCht1171½ KeepItHoly116nk	Between, mild rally	10
13Sep02-4Med	fm	1⅜	Ⓣ	:482 1:134 1:381 2:143	3↑ Clm 25000(25-20)	56	4	62½	63¼	41½	87¾	1013¼	Toribio A R	L116	*1.30	84-01	RoyalRapids114¾ CllMeCsnov115nk MoorishPrince1162¼	Close 3wd,faded	11
4Aug02-10Sar	yl	1⅜	[T]	:49 1:15 1:392 2:154	4↑ Clm 40000(40-35)	49	10	31	31	95¾	1026	1026	Meche D J	L120	15.70	59-16	Castle Comer1225½ Zafonic'sSong120½ Frolicus1202¼	Chased 3 wide, tired	10
21Jly02-7Mth	fm	1⅛	Ⓣ	:471 1:111 1:352 1:473	3↑ Alw 35000N2X	81	9	97¾	96¾	98¼	75¼	64½	King E L Jr	L120	7.20	87-08	NobodysLstnng1221¼ CryptcCod1142 *SymblcCt*122nk	Broke bit awkwardly	9
23Jun02-7Mth	fm	1⅛	Ⓣ	:472 1:11 1:351 1:472	3↑ Alw 35000N2X	82	9	64	53½	41½	43	54	Toribio A R	L120	5.30	89-09	He Flies120nk Ettrick1201½ Pan de Vida120no	4-wide,no stretch bid	9
Previously trained by Clement Christophe																			
11May02-9Bel	fm	1⅜	[T]	:494 1:144 1:383 2:144	4↑ Clm 35000	87	7	52½	62½	52½	2hd	11	Santos J A	L120	3.05	79-13	KeepItHoly1201 AppIturnovrMik117no OnthFn1171¼	3 wide move, driving	11
10Mar02-6GP	fm	*1⅛	Ⓣ	:512 1:153 1:404 1:522	4↑ Alw 36000N2X	87	7	21½	31½	22½	2hd	33	Santos J A	L118	7.70	73-22	Dr. Brendler1221¾ *Fast City*1201¼ *Keep It Holy*118hd	Bid midstr, weakened	10
25Nov01-7Aqu	fm	1⅛	Ⓣ	:484 1:141 1:391 1:511	4↑ Clm 45000(45-35)	84	4	49	511	31½	42	53	Bridgmohan S X	L118	*2.45	79-18	*Sovereign Kit*1152¼ River Usk114no Exaltado114nk	Awkward start, inside	12
6Nov01-6Aqu	fm	1	Ⓣ	:233 :48 1:121 1:37	4↑ Clm 40000(40-35)	88	5	810	86¼	68	52¾	22½	Bridgmohan S X	L118	7.50	90-14	*Bodyguard*1142½ Keep It Holy118nk Tomlin's Flag113nk	Rallied outside	10
Previously trained by Johnson Philip G																			
22Nov00-4Aqu	fm	1⅛	Ⓣ	:493 1:14 1:391 1:512	3↑ Alw 46000N2X	85	8	41½	52½	52	33½	63½	Rojas R I	L117 b	10.80	78-18	Slowhnd1201¾ MnFromWicklow120no CochRiley1231	Came wide, no rally	10
14Oct00-4Bel	fm	1	Ⓣ	:23 :453 1:094 1:341	3↑ Alw 46000N2X	81	8	86½	710	64¼	66	65½	Samyn J L	L117	8.90e	81-12	Schumaker120no Tiger Lion1203¾ Blending Swords120¾	Had no rally	10
30Sep00-6Bel	gd	1⅛	[T]	:482 1:124 1:38 1:502	3↑ Alw 46000N2X	76	2	2hd	2½	2hd	83½	89	Bridgmohan S X	L116	4.30	67-25	MandarinMarsh1161½ DddysDrem122hd Trditionlly1161½	Vied inside, tired	9
30Aug00-8Sar	fm	1 1/16	Ⓣ	:233 :464 1:11 1:403	3↑ Alw 48000N3X	84	2	2hd	2hd	2½	74¼	77½	Davis R G	L115	5.10	85-13	Gulf Storm1171 WaitfortheSword121¾ DoctorCat119nk	Bobbled brk, tired	8
29Jly00-5Sar	fm	1 3/16	Ⓣ	:48 1:121 1:364 1:543	3↑ Alw 44000N1X	89	5	2hd	2½	1hd	11½	12¼	Bridgmohan S X	L118	18.30	85-15	Keep It Holy1182¼ Ask the Lord116hd Kassar121½	Pace, clear, driving	10
24Jun00-9Bel	fm	1 1/16	Ⓣ	:24 :474 1:121 1:414	3↑ Md Sp Wt 42k	80	4	2hd	1hd	2½	1½	1nk	Bridgmohan S X	L116	26.00	83-15	*KeepItHoly*116nk *PolishTims*1162¼ HighstMountin116no	Vied inside, driving	10
16Jun00-4Bel	fst	6f		:22 :46 :584 1:114	3↑ Md Sp Wt 41k	58	3	1	98	96¾	99¼	89	Davis R G	L116	19.30e	70-19	Renoir1162 Kris B1113¾ Starshooter116½	Steadied on rail turn	13
1Jun00-1Bel	fst	6f		:233 :472 :593 1:121	3↑ Md Sp Wt 41k	46	1	5	2½	42½	66	611	Davis R G	116	12.90	66-23	Chief Executive116½ Starshooter1161½ Kris B1164½	Bumped backstretch	8
Previously trained by Motion H Graham																			
9Dec99-7Lrl	fst	6f		:222 :46 :582 1:11	Md Sp Wt 25k	34	6	9	912	913	914	914¾	Delgado A	120	8.90e	72-11	Rajya Sabha1202 Stitched Up1201¼ Father of All Wins120no	Slow start	10

While looking at the field for Belmont's ninth race, Hale's eyes widened as she spotted Keep It Holy, a colt by Holy Bull who was making his first start on grass after unsuccessful dirt tries. At 26-1, and with the tape fresh in her mind, she figured it was worth mentioning to Terelak.

Thus, Terelak used Keep It Holy, praying for a bomb, and when he won, Terelak took the first prize of $25,000 and also earned a berth to the Daily Racing Form/NTRA National Handicapping Championship.

RIVER DOWNS HANDICAPPING TOURNAMENT, JULY 2004

Going into the 2001 Daily Racing Form/NTRA National Handicapping Championship, Judy Wagner was a relative unknown and just one of 203 handicappers, but parlayed a victory by $33 winner Hoovergetthekeys to win the $100,000 first prize.

Wagner had been introduced to handicapping by her husband, Bryan, only five years earlier and she now incorporates a variety of handicapping tools, including pedigree.

Wagner entered the River Downs handicapping contest that was held July 17-18, 2004, but nearing the end of the second day, she was far back of the leaders and needed a bomb for her last selection. Noting that the last event of the contest was a maiden race on the turf for Illinois-bred 3-year-old fillies, and realizing that it was the kind of race that usually offers the greatest value, she saved her last bullet for that race.

Wagner had circled first-time starter Ayla, a daughter of Sandpit, because she was making her career debut and had a super turf pedigree. At 35-1, Ayla was just the kind of filly Wagner needed. Four years ago, Wagner read my series, "How to Bet the 2001 Freshman Sires," and remembered that I labeled Sandpit strictly as a turf sire whose offspring would be most effective at middle distances.

Showing tactical speed in the one-mile race, Ayla rallied in the stretch to win by 1¾ lengths and catapulted Wagner into the winner's circle. She won the $25,000 first-place prize, the $4,000 second-day bonus, and earned her way into another Daily Racing Form/NTRA National Handicapping Championship in January 2005.

Ayla
Own: Wiseman Candice and John

B. f. 3 (Apr)
Sire: Sandpit*Brz (Baynoun*Ire) $3,500
Dam: Bangler Lynx (Bucksplasher)
Br: John Wiseman DVM & Candy Wiseman (Ill)
Tr: Scherer Richard R(0 0 0 0 .00) 2004:(181 27 .15)

	Life	2	1	0	0	$15,600	67	D.Fst	0 0 0 0	$0
	2004	2	1	0	0	$15,600	67	Wet(320)	0 0 0 0	$0
	2003	0	M	0	0	$0	–	Turf(301)	2 1 0 0	$15,600
			0	0	0	$0	–	Dst⊕(326)	2 1 0 0	$15,600

13Aug04-10AP fm *1 ⑦ :23² :47¹ 1:11⁴ 1:36² 3↑ⒻⓈAlw 33000N1x   45 9 2² 3² 33½ 108¾ 1012¼ Emigh C A   L120 fb 6.40 85 – Hug Me Hug Me118no Relicon119¹ Desirabledancer114¾   Bumped 1/4 pole
18Jly04- 9AP fm 1 ⑦ :233 :49⁴ 1:14³ 1:39² 3↑ⒻⓈMd Sp Wt 26k   67 12 4³ 3² 2¼ 2hd 11¾ Emigh C A   L120 b 35.80 78– 12 Ayla120¹¾ Killing M Softly120³ Jazz Bouquet1202¼   Driving
WORKS: Jly12 AP 5f fst 1:04² Bg 21/29 Jly3 AP 5f fst 1:02⁴ B 26/45

A little more than a month earlier, another runner by Sandpit had lit up a different tote board. On May 5, Marnie's Heirloom, a New York-bred 3-year-old filly by Sandpit out of a Lyphard's Wish mare (a T^2 pedigree) who had been beaten double-digit lengths in three dirt starts, made her turf debut in a 1⅛-mile maiden special weight on the grass. Marnie's Heirloom woke up on the new surface and wired the field, just lasting to win by a neck at 66-1. Players were still suspicious of the dramatic turnaround and sent her off at 12-1 in her next race, which was an allowance for nonwinners of one other than, also at 1⅛ miles on the turf. Five-wide the entire trip, she rallied this time to finish third, beaten only 1½ lengths.

2003 *DAILY RACING FORM/NTRA* HANDICAPPER OF THE YEAR

Not surprisingly, Steve Wolfson Jr., a grandson of Louis E. Wolfson of Harbor View Farm, who bred and raced 1978 Triple Crown winner Affirmed, also incorporates pedigree handicapping into his calculations. Wolfson's appreciation of bloodlines paid dividends when he used Offlee Wild ($56.80) to put himself into a position to win the 2003 Daily Racing Form/NTRA National Handicapping Championship.

Offlee Wild, who had won one of his three starts at 2, was making his 3-year-old and stakes debut in the Grade 3 Holy Bull Stakes at Gulfstream Park. Despite his high odds, he was by a successful sire (1984 Breeders' Cup Classic winner Wild Again) from a high-quality Darby Dan female family.

From a pedigree-handicapping angle (stamina and class), Offlee Wild was a huge overlay and a delicious play for Wolfson at 27-1.

Horseplayers have never had as many handicapping tools as they do today. Speed figures, trainer statistics, and more extensive data on foreign horses have fashioned a more sophisticated player better equipped to find winners and value. Pedigrees have always played a role in handicapping, but were usually relegated to a small and esoteric population of bettors. By incorporating pedigrees into their handicapping (as illustrated by the dozens of examples provided in these pages), players will ultimately raise their game to a much higher level.

About the Author

*L*AUREN STICH writes the "Pedigree Handicapping" column in both *Daily Racing Form* and *DRF Simulcast Weekly*. She has played professionally in Las Vegas since 1997 and won first prize in the inaugural Bally's Summer Stakes Handicapping Tournament in 2000. Stich is also the pedigree analyst for the "Race Day Las Vegas" radio show, and is a frequent speaker at seminars around the country.

Involved in the Sport of Kings since 1964, Stich is a racing historian and a Thoroughbred breeder, bloodstock agent, and consultant at sales auctions, and her horses are under the care of trainer Michael Dickinson.

Stich has written variously for *The Morning Telegraph*, *The Racing Times*, and *American Turf Monthly* and she was a contributing author of *Bet with the Best*, writing the chapter "Stich on Pedigree."